From Ideas to Assets

From Ideas to Assets

Investing Wisely in Intellectual Property

Edited by
Bruce Berman

John Wiley & Sons, Inc.

ISBN 0-471-40068-8

Printed in the United States of America.

10 9 8 7 6 5 4 3 2 1

About the Editor

Bruce Berman, editor, is president of Brody Berman Associates, Inc. in New York, the leading marketing and communications firm for intellectual property owners and investors. He conceived and edited *Hidden Value: Profiting from the Intellectual Property Economy* (Euromoney-Institutional Investor), a critically acclaimed anthology that was published in 1999. Mr. Berman is a member of the editorial advisory board of *Patent Strategy & Management*, and works closely with technology and life sciences companies, consulting organizations, law firms, and financial institutions.

Acknowledgments

A unified vision of intellectual assets lends itself to diverse perspectives. In addition to each and every author who devoted significant time and care, and without whom this book would be impossible, I am indebted to a number of people, several of whom should be singled out. Their thoughtful comments, counsel, and encouragement made a great deal of difference in the final product. They include Sam Adler of American Lawyer Media, Christopher Fine of Goldman Sachs, Stephen Fox of Hewlett-Packard, Thom Goodman of Corporate Legal Times, James Gould of Morgan & Finnegan, Dooyong Lee of LPS, Russell Parr of Intellectual Property Research Associates, Alexander Poltorak of General Patent Corporation, Kevin Rivette of Aurigin Systems, Dan Scotto of Banc Paribas, and Darlene Slaughter of IFI CLAIMS.

Producing *From Ideas to Assets* required almost two years of research and hundreds of telephone conversations, e-mails, voice messages, faxes, arguments, and revisions. One person deserves special mention: Dr. James Woods of Deloitte & Touche was a constant source of information and sober analysis. I am indebted to him and his crisp perspective for helping to keep objectives and audiences in clear sight, even when they appeared distant. Another source of eternal light was Samson Vermont of Hunton & Williams' IP practice, editor of *Patent Strategy & Management*. Not only did Sam write a significant chapter, his patient comments on various aspects of the book helped to make it stronger in many ways.

Jennifer Liu provided exhaustive research and organizational support on the Data Bank section of the book; Mary Sexton, the cover concept; and Maya Smith, editorial oversight. Not to be forgotten are Susan McDermott, my editor at John Wiley & Sons, and Associate Managing Editor Sujin Hong, whose editorial and organizational skills are in evidence throughout. Both bore the slings and arrows of my candid memoranda.

Finally, hugs for my wife, Sharon, and daughter, Jennifer, who in the course of compiling this book have come to recognize and, thankfully, tolerate the vicissitudes of lofty goals and untimely deadlines. They are my most tangible assets.

For Sandler, O'Neil & Partners, and
the victims and heroes of September 11, 2001

Contents

Part Four: **Intellectual Property Transactions and Finance**

Chapter 23   **The Relevance of IP Analysis in Technology-
Driven M&A Transactions**   **497**
R. Russ O'Haver

Chapter 24   **Patents on Wall Street**   **511**
Christopher R. Fine and Donald C. Palmer

Foreword

The publication of *From Ideas to Assets: Investing Wisely in Intellectual Property* by Bruce Berman comes at an opportune time. Businesses that rely on innovation, such as those in information technology and science, are at a crossroads. Following the longest continuous economic boom in U.S. history, the nation is caught in its worst economic downturn in decades.

Many companies that previously looked promising will soon fail. Others will survive, but gain little or any competitive positioning. A few will emerge better situated than when the recession began. A company's ability to innovate, protect, and maximize innovation faster and more effectively than its competitors will play a key role in its ability to prosper. Proprietary rights, such as patents, copyrights, trademark, trade secrets, and intellectual property-related licenses, already integral to the performance of public companies, are taking on new meaning. *From Ideas to Assets* is the first multidiscipline guide for practitioners, investors, and managers designed to help them stay on top of their own business as well as others'.

Companies have become increasingly competitive and dependent on market forces. Competitive industry characteristics, including capital requirements, industry profitability, and market growth rates, have changed the way Wall Street looks at companies. These characteristics are impacted by broader forces, including intra-industry rivalries and the threat of substitute or improved products, sometimes referred to as "disruptive technologies." Intellectual property helps to strengthen new products and sustain differentiation, which enable market growth and premium pricing, two fundamentals for achieving high rates of return. Understanding and evaluating a company's ability to innovate in a strategic and quantifiable manner is now the concern of securities analysts as well as patent attorneys.

Recently, I spent time with senior management of over 250 leading information technology companies. While they acknowledge the ominous economic climate, almost universally they expressed optimism that internal research and development initiatives would yield new or enhanced products which would strengthen their competitive position. While companies such as Compaq, Hewlett Packard, and Sun Microsystems have recently scaled back sharply on planned capacity and have cut staffs by 5 to 10 percent, R&D has remained largely untouched.

Some equity analysts are starting to attempt to monitor intellectual property productivity. Their goal is to go beyond a mere tallying of patent numbers and to look at how patents and other IP rights are actually being used by companies. IBM appears to be among the most effective in this regard. Not only has it amassed enormous numbers of patents, and in some cases, used them in conjunction with trademarks, it has done so with unprecedented success.

Of the 2,883 U.S. patents IBM was granted in 2000, nearly 1,000 were awarded for software. One third of calendar 2000's patented technologies were in the marketplace less than a year later. More important, IBM's patent and IP royalty licensing (including copyrights and trademarks) from all of its IP rights, and separate from product sales, generated $1.6 billion in revenues.

I see encouraging signs that companies like Hewlett Packard and Sun Microsystems, as well as those in other sectors, are increasing their external communication of patent productivity metrics. While these companies may not report IBM-like numbers for some time, patents and other IP are playing an increasingly crucial role in their success. H-P and Sun each spend 5 to 10 percent of annual sales on research and development.

Over the long haul businesses must continuously innovate to sustain product leadership. However, many are still practicing or analyzing innovation in an undisciplined or irrelevant manner. I believe that Bruce Berman's perceptive *From Ideas to Assets* offers investors, managers, and others involved in business decisions the greatest breadth and depth of any resource on intellectual property available today. The book's four structural segments, as well as its imaginative Data Bank, Glossary, and annotated web links make IP more compelling and easier to understand. They take readers from the lab through competitive advantage, economic return, quantitative analysis, and, finally, to consideration of how best to monetize intellectual property. For serious investors, and who among us is not in some manner an investor, *From Ideas to Assets* provides the background and context necessary to put today's innovation into tomorrow's financial perspective.

John B. Jones, Jr.
Managing Director,
Salomon Smith Barney

John B. Jones, Jr. has been following computer hardware, servers, and other technology sectors as a stock analyst since 1985. *Institutional Investor*, Greenwich Associates, Reuters, and *The Wall Street Journal* have consistently ranked him at or near the top in research, earnings forecasting, and stock selection.

Introduction
New Foundations, New Frontiers

Most investors agree that technology and innovation not only have changed how business is conducted, they have replaced the foundation on which it is based.

Suddenly, understanding the rights that protect various types of innovation, better known as intellectual property, and how to deploy them, have become a focal point foPr investors and executives concerned about superior performance and return. Fueled by the digitalization of information, really no one can afford to ignore the importance of certain patents, trademarks, and copyrights. The fact is, they still do.

IP AFFECTS MANY

Intellectual property (IP) affects a much broader range of owners and investors than it may at first appear to. Those with an important stake in IP include senior executives, especially CFOs and CEOs, investment bankers, inventors, marketing strategists, financial analysts, venture capitalists, employees, board members, research and development (R&D) directors, and money managers.

Patents, in particular, are abstract and seemingly impossible to understand without specialized training. 174,911 utility and design patents were granted in 2000 to U.S. and non-U.S. companies by the United States Patent and Trademark Office (USPTO). Based on current applications, more than 245,000 patents are projected for 2001. However, only a small percentage of all active patents appear to be "productive." (Fewer than 3 percent generate royalty income.) Despite their importance, patents and other IP remain more of a mystery than ever. The top business schools have yet to make IP a part of their curricula. Attorneys still remain the primary resource for facilitating IP business and investment decisions, not company executives and money managers. Moreover, investors are starting to hold those responsible for the care and nurturing of companies accountable for IP. Not only do intellectual assets represent a significant investment in R&D dollars, they represent much of the equity on which market value is based. Yes, IP rights and the inventions they protect are complex, but they are well within the reach of reasonably intelligent, motivated persons without specialized training.

From Ideas to Assets: Investing Wisely in Intellectual Property is intended to provide anyone affected by IP—especially those in the business and the financial communities—with grounding in the meaning and use of IP rights. What patents are and are not, and the critical role they play in creating value, is far too important to ignore. *From Ideas to Assets* is not a textbook or an instruction manual about picking stocks. It is, however, an overview of information and strategies designed to help demystify IP rights and the innovation they protect for those affected by them. It is best thought of as a beginning step, not an end, in understanding the inner workings of IP. *From Ideas to Assets* attempts to answer the question: "What and how much do I need to know about IP to be effective?"

From Ideas to Assets is organized into four general sections: Identifying and Understanding IP, Exploiting IP, Measuring IP Performance, and IP Transactions and Finance. These sections are intended not only to provide readers with a useful background, but also as a perspective on recent IP trends and developments. The authors have been encouraged to render their contributions timely and accessible. For this reason, there are more original graphs, charts, diagrams, and IP data in this book than in any previous IP work of its kind.

Contributors are derived from more than 25 of the top investment bankers, venture capitalists, licensing executives, financial analysts, in-house and outside patent attorneys, and valuation experts. Some of the chapters offer provocative perspectives on IP; others are more generally informative. All are thoroughly researched and highly relevant to persons either working in or interested in finance and business. The predominant focus of *From Ideas to Assets* is on patents, because of the unique challenges these proprietary rights present and the limitations of time and space in this book. This book required more than two years to research, organize, write, and edit, and is intended to be interesting to read as well as purposeful. As in a compendium of this nature, some topics may have been left out or only partially explored, and some inevitable overlap may occur. Still, you will find the compendium format well suited for exploring IP. The expression of similar points of view in different ways provides the reader with depth, as well as the opportunity to form his or her own perspective.

GETTING THE MOST OUT OF THIS BOOK

To derive maximum value from this book about understanding value, it can be read consecutively, as a linear narrative. However, readers should feel comfortable jumping directly into contributions that interest them or that affect them in the course of their business activities. Some will gravitate to timely topics like IP finance and securitization, or measuring IP performance. Others will find the charts and graphs in the "Data Bank" useful and provocative, and the sections on "Further Reading" and "IP Web Sites and Links" worthy of repeat visits.

Identifying and exploiting of IP assets has become less focused on technology and more market-driven. Companies can be found assembling teams of diverse professionals, including engineers, demographers, scientists, financial analysts, inventors, product mangers, and legal strategists, to identify and nurture inventions. In this evolved context, investors and other stakeholders not only need to know more, they need to get more involved. Their questions and concerns about IP make a difference, and encourage companies to better understand, monitor, and exploit IP assets. Managements that believe IP is too complex to present to Wall Street and other key audiences may be underestimating the motivation and needs of investors, and the potential for IP to move industries as well as individual companies.

Some people still feel that aggressive enforcement of patent rights for financial gain is an abuse of the patent system, particularly if the rights are asserted by a third party. This has particularly inflamed opponents of companies that are patenting the human genome. These roadblocks, or more accurately, toll roads, have been likened to "patentmail." Similar arguments were made against nineteenth century land speculators who acquired real estate (known legally as "real" property) where train lines were anticipated, profiting from strategic acquisitions. Rarely did these investors impede growth, and a good argument could be made that their astute financial vision may have even hastened it. People, especially business people, often find inspiration in obstacles.

Identifying how innovative technology in conjunction with legal rights and market demand shapes business assets is a vital part of financial and political evolution. The limited exclusivity that the government grants in the form of patents is fundamental to competition and the growth of our economy and the maintenance of our basic freedoms. While the system is not without its flaws, it has endured remarkably well for more than two centuries, and still gives companies of all sizes, worldwide, as well as independent inventors, ample opportunity to compete.

WHAT DO I NEED TO KNOW?

Understanding how market forces and proprietary rights can turn innovation into business assets is well within the grasp of most investors, managers, and dealmakers. The prospect of better returns is fueling the need for more and better IP information and performance measures. Most companies are capable of doing a better job of articulating their IP position, but will do so only if investors hold them accountable. The prospect of self-regulation is less onerous than required disclosures. Less than 50 years ago, underwriters thought SEC filings, such as S-1 registrations for initial public offerings, were too difficult for even serious investors to comprehend. Measures such as market capitalization and Price Earnings Ratios were also thought to be the exclusive province of financial professionals. When I edited *Hidden Value: Profiting from the Intellectual Property Economy* for Euromoney-Institutional Investor in 1999, contributors were still trying to prove to those who run businesses and advise on transactions that the information economy had taken

IP rights out of the file cabinet and onto the business page. Today, with that notion more widely accepted, we have moved on to the next question: "What information do I need to know about IP to compete?"

Bruce Berman
New York City
September 2001

If a man can write a better book, preach a better sermon, or make a better mousetrap than his neighbor, though he builds his house in the woods, the world will make a beaten path to his door.

—Ralph Waldo Emerson

A mind once stretched by a new idea never regains its original dimension.

—Oliver Wendell Holmes

Part One

Identifying and Understanding Intellectual Property

CHAPTER ONE

Intellectual Property "101"
What Executives and Investors Need to Know About Patent Rights and Strategy

by H. Jackson Knight

PERSPECTIVES

Whatever it is called—the "information economy," the "digital economy," or the "New Economy"—the result is largely the same for intellectual property: more innovation, greater value, and frequent disputes. What do non-IP professionals, such as business executives, investors, and dealmakers need to know about patents in order to function in this environment?

Having as much knowledge about intellectual property (IP) rights as a patent attorney is not likely to make a CEO more effective. However, knowing what patent rights are and how they function will. Over the past few years, smart bankers, executives, and technology and science investors have begun equipping themselves to understand patent basics. As a result, they are in a better position to understand the relative strengths of patents, red flags, and opportunities as they relate to a given industry. While it is unnecessary for an executive to be able to compare complex patent claims, the very essence of what imbues a patent with value (there are patent lawyers for that), it *is* necessary that he or she realize that the right claims are essential for a strong patent position. The right claims language, for example, can profoundly affect business decisions. For many affected by patents and other IP, knowing what one doesn't know is half the battle. Unfortunately, many CEOs and CFOs of some of the world's largest companies, including those businesses that focus on technology and science, do not have a clue when it comes to understanding and deploying IP rights.

Patent Strategy for Researchers & Research Managers by H. Jackson Knight was originally published in 1996 by John Wiley & Sons and updated in 2001. Barely 150 pages in length, it is the single most informative and well-written book about how patents function as business assets. It should be required reading at every business school and MBA program. (Lawyers, too, can learn from its clean writing and plain-language explanations of patent strategy, as well as the discussion of business objectives.) While intended for researchers and research directors, *Patent Strategy* provides the kind of basic information about patent "fences" and "swords" that makes inventors more productive, senior executives better managers, and investors more consistent.

The following chapter, Intellectual Property '101,' is a distillation of information found in *Patent Strategy*. Mr. Knight provides many of the IP business basics necessary for those who lack the desire to master all of the details. "Patent and trademark strategies that were previously delegated down the management ladder and addressed late in the development of a product are now addressed much sooner because of the major impact those strategies can have on business performance and value. We are in a new world of intellectual property," says Knight. "Understanding the basics of patent law and strategy puts business executives and investment professionals in a better position to comprehend and discuss innovation, as well as assess and capture its value."

KEYS TO BUSINESS SUCCESS

While always important to the overall health of a business, the cultivation of valuable intellectual property is now widely recognized as a key to business success. Patent and trademark strategies that were previously delegated down the management ladder and addressed late in the development of a product are now developed much sooner because of the major impact those strategies can have on business performance and value. Further, rapid and extensive changes in the patent laws have allowed new types of inventions to be patented and have opened the door for the more creative use of intellectual property. The perception of intellectual property has finally risen in stature to demand attention throughout the organization.

This chapter will help explain intellectual property concepts that may be unfamiliar to business executives and professional inventors; it is divided into three sections. The first, "Understanding Intellectual Property," discusses the protection intellectual property provides and some of the recent changes in the patent field. This section also contains a brief primer on the various types of intellectual property. The second section, "Understanding the Value of a Company's Intellectual Property," discusses how one assesses the value of individual patents and patent portfolios and why it is important to understand the degree of exclusivity they provide. This section also contains information on different types of patent strategy and how a company's intellectual property strategy, or lack thereof, is revealed by the inspection of the patent applications it files. The final section, "Using Intellectual Property Advisors Effectively," discusses how intellectual property professionals help an organization develop patent strategies, avoid infringement, enforce patents, and license technology.

UNDERSTANDING INTELLECTUAL PROPERTY—WHY BOTHER?

Intellectual property is a term used to describe many types of innovation, mental activity, and creative or artistic effort. Intellectual property can be in an intangible form, such as the knowledge and know-how one develops from research and experience, or it can be in a tangible form, including such things as inventions and patents. While patents are widely known as intellectual property, many other things, such as trade secrets, copyrights, trademarks, and service marks, are also intellectual property. Intellectual property is something either owned or possessed, something over which there is some measure of control. In considering the value of this control, the type of intellectual property must be understood along with the effective breadth of that intellectual property. To have real value, intellectual property must be commercially useful and must provide adequate exclusivity to give a business a competitive edge. A very common method of protecting the intellectual property developed for new products and services has been through the use of patents.

Patent systems are set up by governments to encourage innovation by protecting the interests of inventors. In general, patent systems help to secure an inventor's exclusive right to an invention for some period of time in return for disclosing the invention to the public. If patent systems were not in place, much technology would be kept in secret and hidden from public view. Therefore, patent systems also help disseminate information about new technology, which helps to promote innovation.

Patents enable the creation of economic wealth by providing exclusivity to inventors. The country issuing the patent actually grants a legal monopoly to the patent owner for a limited amount of time. This allows the patent owner to prevent others from making, using, or selling the patented invention in the country where the patent was issued. The patent does not, however, give the patent owner the right to practice the invention claimed in the patent. This is a confusing situation that arises frequently. One obtains a patent, so one could assume incorrectly to have the right to practice that invention. The truth of the matter is that patent owners have only the right to exclude others from their patented inventions. A patent owner may only legally use, make, or sell the patented invention if no other patents are infringed by doing so. For example, if Sally patents a widget, and John patents an improved widget, John may not be able to make his improved widgets if in making them he has to practice the invention claimed in Sally's patent.

A Brief History of Patents

Patents originated in the late fourteenth or early fifteenth century in the Italian city-states, where merchants who introduced new trades could obtain limited-term monopolies. The custom spread to parts of Europe, most notably England, where it became a part of law in the 1623 Statute of Monopolies as an exemption to the general ban on monopolies. With this basis in English law, many of the English colonies in America provided for patents, and this right was so strongly accepted that when the Constitution of the United States was written, it specifically provided for the granting of patents by the new centralized government (see Exhibit 1-1).

Later, with the passage of the Patent Act of 1790, the first patent law having a requirement for examination came into being. That is, the patent claim would have to be examined to determine whether or not the invention covered by the claim was sufficiently useful and important to be granted a patent. Unfortunately, the Patent Act required the involvement of the major heads of the new government, including the secretary of state, the secretary of war, and the attorney general. The involvement of officials with so many other governmental responsibilities slowed down the examination and issuance of patents; therefore, this system was replaced by a simple registration system in 1793, which lasted until 1836 in the United States. This registration system allowed one to register any invention and obtain a patent; patent validity was determined in the courts. Since there was no examination of the patent application, there were no official checks on the granting of official-looking but worthless patents. The proliferation of these worthless and sometimes fraudulent patents finally brought an end to the registration system, and a new, more workable examination system was put in place by the Patent Act of 1836. The

---

The Congress shall have Power....

**To promote the Progress of Science and useful Arts,
by securing for limited Times to Authors and Inventors
the exclusive Right to their respective Writings and
Discoveries.**

Exhibit 1-1   Article I, Section 8 of the United States Constitution specifically provides for patents.

matically in force in all OAPI member countries. Work continues on the development of a European Community Patent, which would function as do OAPI patents and be automatically in force in all European Union countries upon issuance; however, this is not yet a reality.

In general, each country decides what is patentable and also decides how patents will be enforced. Recently, international pressure has been put on countries through various new treaties to make patenting provisions and enforcement coverage much more uniform. For example, countries that previously did not allow patents on pharmaceuticals have been encouraged to include such protection in their intellectual property laws. The United States has adopted several provisions of typical foreign patent laws, such as the 20-year patent term from the filing date of the application and the publication of patent applications, in an effort to cooperate with this harmonization.

In the United States, there have traditionally been five types of inventions that were statutory subject matter for patents. These five invention classes included:

1. New compositions of matter, such as new chemical compounds
2. New processes or methods for making things
3. New machines
4. New manufactures, which can be thought of as manufactured parts or machines with no moving parts
5. Improvements over any of the previous four types of inventions

For many years, it was commonly accepted that a procedure for solving a mathematical problem, also known as a mathematical algorithm, could not be patented by itself. One could patent a process that had a mathematical algorithm as one of its steps, if the process met the statutory requirement without the algorithm. That is, if there were several steps in the process, and not simply an algorithm, then the process usually met the test for patentable subject matter. This changed recently with the important decision in *State Street Bank* v. *Signature Financial Group, Inc.*, where the Federal Circuit Court of Appeals ruled that the application of a mathematical algorithm to make a tangible result was patentable in the United States. It did not matter if the algorithm was simply involved with the abstract transformation of data. This decision has encouraged a whole new class of patent applications on what are now called business methods and has given a boost to software and Internet patents in general.

Biotechnology and genetic engineering have also been in the news and have sparked controversy over the ability of companies to obtain patents on genetic modification of naturally occurring forms. The exact item found in nature cannot be patented, but versions of those natural things that were actually never found in nature but made in a laboratory tend to be patentable, and patent offices are working on a tremendous number of patent applications concerning these inventions. One issue has been the ability to show that these genetically modified forms have utility, and patent offices around the world have come together to issue guidelines requiring that these genetic inventions must have a real-world use. That is, the genetic material has to have some real practical application, not just as a laboratory curiosity. Since the genetic field is so wide open, the hurdle that has been raised is the utility hurdle, requiring inventors not to simply change bits of genetic material, but to change it for some purpose. Still, the volume of patents should continue to increase, as this is an embryonic industry. Already, both business method and biotech patents are being challenged in court, and in the future, additional guidelines will determine which types of patents are valid and which are not. Still, a small company with a strong set of patents in these areas can wield significant leverage, whether or not it is for defensive or licensing purposes.

Protection Through Exclusivity: Creating an Asset

Patents provide exclusivity because they reserve the exploitation of the claimed invention for the patent owner. The patent owner can prevent others from making, using, or selling the claimed invention, and can prevent importation of the claimed invention into the country in which the patent is granted. In some countries, such as the United States, a patent on a process for making an item can be used to stop importation of a good made by that process, even if the process is actually practiced in another country where no patent has been granted. Therefore, patents give the patent owners the exclusive use (or nonuse) of the invention claimed and therefore can be powerful protectors of one's technology and commercial operations.

The exclusivity provided by a patent is impacted by the granted claims, the actions taken by the inventor to protect the invention, and the research decisions made by the inventor during the development of the invention. The claims in a patent can be broad or narrow, and thus the exclusivity can be broad or narrow. For example, the patent could claim a method for making snowmen, which would be very specific. The claim might instead claim a method for making ice crystals, which would have a much broader scope. Both claims would be exclusive; the degree of exclusivity would be different.

The features of the new invention that are already known dictate the degree of exclusivity obtained. For example, one cannot now claim a lock that can be opened by a key because such locks have been known for ages. One may be able to claim a special lock or key and obtain some exclusivity to that specific invention, but one cannot now get an exclusive right to all keyed locks.

The degree of exclusivity is also dictated by the function the invention performs and whether or not this function can be accomplished in a different manner. If a process is invented for making a product, and a patent is obtained on that process, then that patent will be very exclusive if the only way to make that product is to practice that invented process. If the product can be made using an alternate process that does not use the patented process, then the patent is not very exclusive.

The inventor can impact the exclusivity provided by a patent by actions taken before a patent application is filed. Clearly, if patent rights have not been preserved, then very little exclusivity will be obtained. For example, if the inventor publicly discloses the invention before the filing of a patent application, he or she will forfeit the ability to get a valid patent in many countries, such as the countries that are member states of the EPO, which require absolute novelty or no public disclosure of the claimed invention prior to the filing of the patent application. The United States is not an absolute-novelty country and instead gives an inventor a year's grace period on public disclosures before a patent application must be filed.

However, the United States has an additional provision that can impact the exclusivity and validity of a patent. Assuming the inventor wants to obtain a patent on an invention, he or she has one year after the first offer for sale in the United States, regardless if such action is public or private, to file his patent application in the United States. Therefore, if the inventor starts to secretly commercially use an invention in the United States, he has a year to file the patent application or he is barred from obtaining a valid United States patent. The situation is different in most other countries, where one's secret use of an invention does not prohibit one from later obtaining a patent on that invention. This illustrates there is no substitute for knowledge of the basic patent laws to prevent inadvertent disclosure and forfeiture of patent rights.

Finally, the exclusivity is also impacted by the decisions made during the research or development of the invention. Once an inventive concept is recognized, the inventor can either proceed to a commercial use or can delay such use and instead proceed to find all the possible practical versions of an invention. If a broader range of work is done during the research phase, then more support may be generated for potentially broader claims. However, if only specific work is done on one commercial product, it will be difficult to extend the patent claims to things not tested or researched. This is especially true in countries that require broad patent claims to be broadly exemplified; that is, the patent application must disclose several examples of the invention illustrating the breadth of the invention claimed. Many countries do not allow broad patent claims on a broad range of conditions when only a narrow range of conditions is shown in the examples in the patent application. Patent applicants can be very surprised when they are required to restrict the claims to only the ranges specifically disclosed in the examples in the application. The practical result is a weaker patent with coverage for only a very specific commercial version of an invention, leaving the door open for others to practice other potentially commercial versions of the invention.

The speed at which one desires to get the patent application in the patent office and commercialize the invention indirectly impacts exclusivity. This timing will impact how much research can be done and how many avenues can be investigated before the patent application is filed. In some cases, one can file a patent application on a very specific invention and continue work to try to broaden that invention; however, the information in the first patent application and any subsequent public disclosures of the invention can become prior art in some countries against any later broadening applications that are filed. Therefore, the inventor can risk losing a fair amount of exclusivity in the rush to capitalize on a marketplace opportunity.

Other Forms of Innovation Rights: Trademarks, Copyrights, Trade Secrets, and Know-How

In addition to patents, there are other types of intellectual property. The most common of these are trademarks, copyrights, trade secrets, and a broad collection of knowledge and experience called know-how. Most companies have a variety of these types of intellectual property, and when valuating a company, all of these can come into play. It is important to understand how they differ.

A *trademark* is a very important type of intellectual property. A company can obtain protection for its "mark" on a product to show that that product is uniquely theirs. By doing so, the trademark itself can develop a reputation, either for high quality, low cost, special taste, performance, or some other trait that can be associated with that product and the company that produced that product. The basic concept is to avoid confusion in the marketplace by differentiating one company's products from another company's products, even if they are essentially the same products. Close cousins to trademarks are service marks. Trademarks are commonly associated with goods while service marks are associated with services.

Trademarks do not have to be descriptive of the product. Almost any symbol or word that meets government guidelines and does not conflict with previous trademarks can be registered. Like patents, trademarks are generally registered in individual countries and are kept active by paying fees, although the fees are substantially less than patents. Unlike patents, if one continues to pay the fees, the trademark can be renewed essentially forever.

Trademarks are tremendously valuable to companies. If a company has a successful product with a strong trademark, it can launch new products more easily using the trademark as a method of achieving immediate trust for those new products with consumers. Trademarks can also form part of an intellectual property strategy and can help compensate for weak patents. For example, a company may introduce a new product that is trademarked and patented and is very successful. Even if the patents expire or are somehow found not to prevent another company from making a competing product, the continued commercial success of this product could rely on its well-known trademark. Many trademarked products have become widely known and desired over almost identical products that have unknown trademarks. In the minds of consumers, unknown trademarks can mean unknown origin.

When a trademark becomes widely recognizable, it then has licensing value, so one issue to consider when valuating a company is which trademarks are owned by that company and how well those trademarks are recognized and positioned. The trademark owner can decide how the trademark will be used and can concentrate on those situations that will be positive for the company and can avoid situations that pose a risk to the reputation of the trademark or the company. In fact, if a company does not do a good job of policing a trademark and the trademark falls into what is called generic use, the company runs the risk of losing the trademark. Businesses should therefore take care of their trademarks if they want them to be strong competitive weapons in the marketplace.

Copyrights are used to protect expressive works that have been authored, such as literature, drama, music, computer software, and such things as choreographic, pictorial, and architectural works. While patent claims can apply to and cover future inventions not fully contemplated by the inventor, copyrights protect the expression of ideas by preventing strict copying of the expressive work. Copyrights normally have much longer terms than patents, and like patents, copyright law has evolved over time and copyright protection can vary depending on the country. The length of term can also be dependent on whether or not the copyrighted work was made for hire or has an anonymous or pseudonymous author. For example, currently an author may obtain a copyright in the United States for a work and the copyright will last for the life of the author plus 70 years. If that same work was made for hire, or was anonymously or pseudonymously authored, the copyright term will last for 95 years from the date of publication, or 120 years from the date the work was created, whichever is the shorter time period. In many other countries, the copyright term can be different. It is quite common for the copyright term to be the life of the author plus 50 years.

Patents reveal secrets in return for a monopoly for a limited amount of time; however, if a business chooses to not patent an invention, it can take steps to keep and use that invention in secret. In addition, there are always details of production and other issues in a business that the business would like to maintain secret because they provide competitive advantages. These secreted inventions and details are known as *trade secrets* and can be very critical to the success of a business. Even though there is a complex field of laws to protect trade secrets, fundamentally, a business must take precautions to maintain the secrecy of its trade secrets. Once publicly disclosed, the value of those trade secrets can plummet.

Know-how is the information known by a company's employees that provides that company with a competitive advantage. Know-how is normally very practical experience and knowledge that allows the successful operation of a process or production of a product. In many cases, when a patent is licensed, the licensee will want the licensor's personnel to provide know-how concerning the licensed invention in addition to the license itself. Many times, the revealed know-how is more valuable than the patent license.

UNDERSTANDING THE VALUE OF A COMPANY'S INTELLECTUAL PROPERTY

Companies have a vision for their products, and if that vision is to be achieved via proprietary technology, it is normally protected by trade secrets and patents. This vision requires procedures to identify the intellectual property the company deems to be important to the long-term health of the business and to establish the necessary controls to make sure it is protected. To achieve a powerful exclusive position requires dedicated effort first to understand what exclusivity is possible and then to take actions to make that exclusively a reality. Companies that take concerted efforts to develop consistent intellectual property strategies have patent portfolios that reflect that planning. Their patents work together to provide protection for the product line.

Types of IP Strategies

Many people want to establish an intellectual property or patent strategy for their company, or analyze another company's intellectual property strategy, without giving much thought as to what is meant by the word "strategy." Some complicated definitions can be given and debated, but in a basic sense a strategy is a set of guidelines or a plan for achieving an end. The most important issue to understand when considering strategy, however, is the conceptual level on which the strategy is based.

For example, one conceptual level concerns developing a strategy for protecting a new invention (see Exhibit 1-4). This strategy might involve obtaining one or more patents or maintaining certain aspects of the invention as trade secrets. The

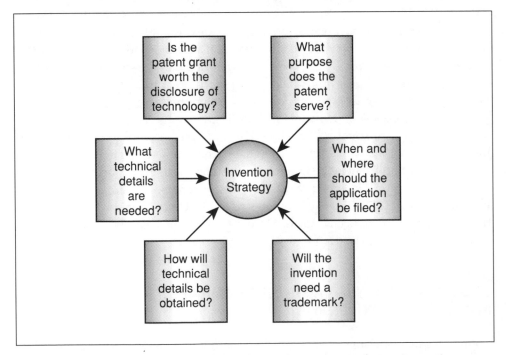

Exhibit 1-4   Developing an intellectual property strategy for an invention.

strategy might include establishing a trademark for the invention or products made from the invention. Typically, a patent strategy for an invention includes deciding what will be achieved by obtaining a patent and considering such practical details as what technical information will be needed for the patent, how this information will be obtained, and when the patent application must be filed. The strategy will also consider how broadly the invention can be claimed and whether the required disclosure is worth the potential claims. Finally, such a strategy will identify the countries where it makes business sense to obtain a patent on the invention. By developing this type of intellectual property strategy, one not only protects the invention with a positive impact on the company, but also actually develops the potential to greatly capitalize on the invention so that it has a major positive impact.

Another conceptual level deals with a series of related inventions or a general technology area. Normally this type of strategy deals with a technology that will have a major business impact and the possibility for a number of patents that will fit together like a jigsaw puzzle, protecting the technology from attack from many angles. Also, because this technology will have major impact, there will be a need for a strategy that involves the filing of successive patents to maintain some type of continuity of the monopoly grant to attempt to reserve the exclusivity of the technology for many years to come. In addition to the strategic issues consid-

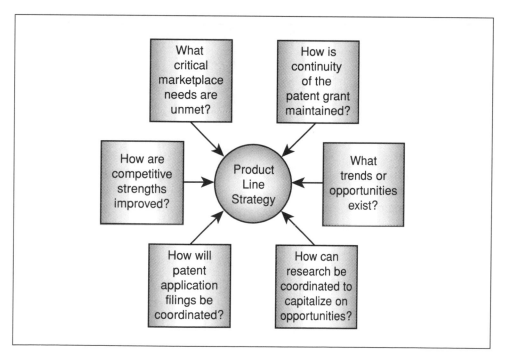

Exhibit 1-5   Developing an intellectual property strategy for a product line or series of inventions.

ered for a single invention, a patent strategy for a series of related inventions may include how the business will improve on its competitive strengths and address critical needs in the marketplace that a determined competitor could meet. The strategy could also include what kinds of opportunities exist and how the research work and the patent filings will be coordinated to capitalize on these opportunities (see Exhibit 1-5).

Finally, another conceptual level concerns an intellectual property strategy for an entire business or company (see Exhibit 1-6). This is a strategy that identifies the company's technology focus and its objective in obtaining intellectual property and establishes principles and procedures for developing, managing, and protecting intellectual property. This can be a very high-level strategy that provides the business with the framework that other more specific strategies work within. In addition, this type of a strategy addresses such things as how the business will protect unpatented technology, how strategic decisions will be made, and how the business will respond to competitive patents.

Good companies will have all of these strategies, and the strategies will work together for competitive advantage. Companies that are very successful spend a lot of time making sure that the patent strategy for an invention really contains all the possible things that can help make that invention commercially successful. It is very easy for the strategy simply to be obtaining a patent for the invention. It is much more difficult to consider what is needed to improve the protection of the

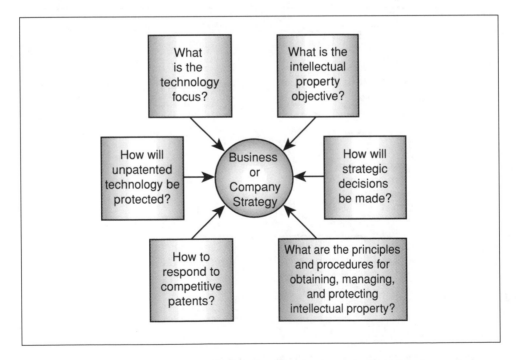

Exhibit 1-6 Developing an intellectual property strategy for a business or company.

technology or to generate additional intellectual property to make the total technology package more valuable. For example, one might be able to get claims for a new invention and the claims might look very broad. However, if no one considers how others might use alternate materials or designs to make something that achieves the same result as the invention, the potential claims might not be broad enough to provide practical exclusivity. Further, despite admirable efforts, the patent protection one obtains might be severely limited by close prior art, and therefore the combination of the invention and a trademark may be the route to future commercial success.

The most successful companies develop strategies for a series of inventions. This is the most difficult strategy to develop but also has the most value to a company. These companies know that having several good patents can be potentially stronger than one strong patent; with planning, a series of patented inventions can discourage probable infringers. This type of strategy involves year-to-year continuity with new inventions consciously developed to improve previously developed inventions and to extend the monopoly privilege while coordinating this development with established trademarks (see Exhibit 1-7).

Assessing the Value of Patents

When evaluating the patents in a company's patent portfolio, it is important to understand that simply having a patent does not necessarily mean that the company has a proprietary position. Everyone wants to have patents with broad claims, that is, patents that have claims that cover not only the commercial or well-known version of the invention, but also many practical alternative versions. In other words, the claims provide a competitive advantage in that they provide the exclusive position needed by the company. However, when there are already a num-

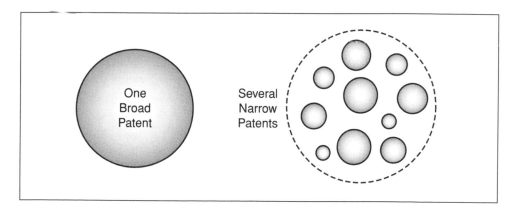

Exhibit 1-7   Several narrowly claimed patents in a technology field can provide more exclusivity than one broadly claimed patent.

ber of inventions in a technological area, it can be difficult to obtain broad claims. When this happens, new patents may still be issued, but the claims in those patents may be more narrowly worded. This means that these claims may not provide the exclusivity desired. The key to value depends on whether or not the claims prevent another from making, using, or selling a similar product or operating a similar process that would have a similar result. Narrow claims can be very beneficial if the claimed invention is the lowest cost or has some great competitive advantage over other versions of the invention that are not covered by the claims. It all depends on the practical value of the claims and on whether or not the claimed invention is truly a commercial and technical advance over the prior art.

When thinking about patents, it is helpful to think about inventions as products, processes or methods, and machines. From a strategic viewpoint, a product would be something a company produces, so it could be a molded part, a chemical, or anything one could go out and buy. A process or method would be the actions or procedures performed to make a product. Finally, a machine would be defined as something used to make a product. Note that if a company makes machines for sale, then from a strategic viewpoint, a patent on a machine is actually a product patent. A patent may have product claims, process claims, machine claims, or some combination of these.

Patents that have product claims are much easier to enforce because the product can usually be found easily in the marketplace. If the product is on sale and was not produced by the patent owner, he or she can trace the product back to the maker and initiate action against the maker. Patents that have solely process claims are more difficult to enforce unless the process leaves some imprint on the product that allows one to conclude that the product was made using the patented process. Still, even process patents that do not leave an imprint can be valuable. Most companies do not simply ignore patents, so process patents can provide a deterrent even though infringement can be difficult to detect. Patents on machines used in a process can have the same detection problems as process patents. In addition, unless one has a truly unique machine, many times a competitor can construct an alternative machine that will avoid the patent claims but will function the same in the process. Therefore, product patents typically have the most value, followed by process and machine patents.

Assessing the value of patent claims normally requires a person who has both knowledge of the technical area and patent matters. Armed with a prior art search of the state of the art in the technology area, such a technical expert can read a patent and quickly determine the significance of the claimed invention. This expert looks at the content of the patent, particularly the information contained in the examples if they are present, for keys to such things as the cost, practicality, and workability of the invention. If the patent is an improvement invention, the expert will look for the significance of the improvement. Using his or her experience, he or she can then estimate the value of the new technology.

The analysis cannot stop there, however. The expert must also have experience with patent claims to understand the restrictions in the claims; that is, whether the invention is broadly or narrowly claimed or what space in the technology area has been reserved for the patent holder. (In some cases, the expert may also need the help of an attorney to review the examination correspondence or file history for the patent, which can be obtained from the patent office, for clarification of the restrictions in the claims.) Finally, given the value of the technology and the breadth of the patent claims, the technical expert can form an opinion of the exclusivity the patent provides. For example, the patent may have very narrow claims, but those narrow claims may be for superior technology or the optimum product and therefore the best technology available. On the other hand, the patent may have narrow claims and the expert may see very obvious methods to engineer a solution around the patent and easily avoid those claims. Thus, the technical expert becomes a vital part of determining whether or not the claimed invention is truly substantial or simply an idle curiosity.

Evaluating a Patent Portfolio

Patents and patent portfolios can be used for offensive or defensive purposes. Patents can be used in an offensive manner as swords, to keep others from practicing certain technologies that the business utilizes for a profit, or to license patents to others for a profit (see Exhibit 1-8). Alternatively, patents can be used in a

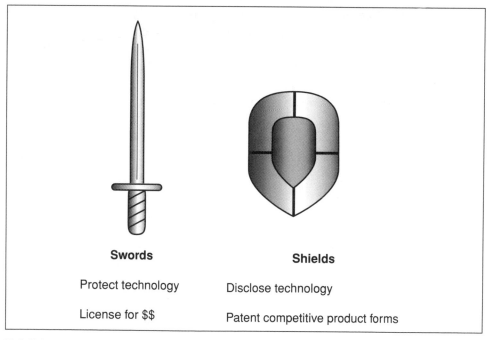

Exhibit 1-8 Patents can be used as offensive weapons as swords or as defensive weapons as shields.

defensive manner as shields. A particular patent can have a wealth of disclosures with only narrow claims with the primary aim of the patent being to disclose information in the public domain, via the publication of the patent application, and thus reduce the chance that others will obtain patents on the information disclosed. The other way a patent or a patent portfolio can be used in a defensive manner is by patenting inventions that a business does not intend to use, but which compete with a business's primary inventions. Therefore, these patents prevent others from providing products in the marketplace that would compete with a company's primary products. For example, if a company makes bookends out of marble, it might patent bookends made out of plastic, if bookends out of plastic might take away market share from the marble bookend market. The company retains maximum flexibility, because it can also license the plastic bookend technology to select markets if it so chooses. Therefore, some patents that are not used in commercial production can be just as valuable as those patents that represent a business's commercial products and processes.

Strategically developed patent portfolios have the markings of coordination. One particular indicator is the depth and breadth of the patent portfolio itself. A patent portfolio can have value to a company because a number of patents in a technology area can provide, collectively, a more effective deterrent than a single patent alone. This is particularly the case when a new invention is developed and, together with other patents the company also owns, represents the state of the art. This new patent thereby extends the monopoly privilege. By examining a company's patent portfolio, it becomes clear whether the company has patented a number of inventions that effectively cover the technology, making it difficult for others to simply jump in and start producing competitive products.

When evaluating a company's patent portfolio, it is revealing to study who is making the inventions. Does the company have 10 patents in a technology area with different inventors on each patent, indicating a major overall effort to develop the technology area? Or is there one primary prolific inventor on all 10 patents who

Exhibit 1-9   A company with many patents can have one prolific inventor or a strong core of several inventors.

is the driving force and the true knowledge behind the work? (See Exhibit 1-9.) Understanding how broadly the invention knowledge is spread throughout a company can be important when considering the acquisition of a company.

Another indicator of the value of patents is an analysis of how many patents are actually used to protect the production of the products of a company from competitive attack. As stated before, some of the patented inventions in a patent portfolio will be actually in use; however, there may be some that are purely defensive patents, reserving patented technology for the business. A well-maintained patent portfolio contains only patents that make sense for the business and have a reason to exist. All other patents are abandoned to eliminate those costs from the business. But more importantly, a strategically developed patent portfolio has patent applications that follow a theme and work together, whereas a haphazard portfolio has very little rhyme or reason.

When evaluating a patent portfolio, a careful eye should be given to the global reach of the patents. This is another possible indicator of the strength of a patent portfolio and reveals if the company's patent filings match the company's business strategy. Some companies decide to file patents only in the United States, while others file broadly in many countries throughout the world, and still others file in only a few select countries worldwide. For example, if a company only has business in the United States, then patenting only in the United States may be appropriate. However, a problem arises when a company that has been focused on one country decides to branch out into other new countries; if the company has not obtained patents in those countries, the company's products are vulnerable to competitive attack. The company's patent portfolio provides no protection because patents were never obtained in those new countries. We live in a global economy with global competitors, and no longer can a company that desires to be global have patents in only one or two countries. Patents are long-term instruments, and a company's strategy can change over a number of years. Filing patents globally can help the business expand, if the company is willing to pay for that insurance. Now it is not necessary to have patents in all countries where products are sold, but it is important to have a worldwide presence if for no other reason than for providing a business with intellectual property for future negotiations with potential partners.

When patents are filed globally, companies with good patent portfolios have patents in the countries where the patents will most impact competitors. For example, patents on new processes for making products or patents on new machines used in those manufacturing processes should be filed in countries where competitors would actually use the processes or the machines. Patents on new products should be obtained not only in the countries where competitive companies manufacture, but also in the countries where there are major markets for those products. A quick check of a company's global patent portfolio, if compared with the locations of a company's primary competitors, should reveal whether the company is using good judgment in the filing of its global patent applications.

HOW TO USE IP ADVISORS EFFECTIVELY

At one time, intellectual property professionals were support personnel who were brought in after a major technology development to take care of the patents a business needed. In today's world, however, one could develop a major product and then find out that there is a patent infringement issue after a significant amount of time and money has been spent. Intellectual property advisors—patent attorneys, intellectual property managers, and prior art searchers—should play a major part in a business and should be involved early in the research process and during all the product development. In addition to obtaining intellectual property, these advisors help with developing strategies, avoiding infringement, and assisting in the licensing of intellectual property.

One key to using IP advisors effectively is simply staffing adequately to provide proactive service. For example, developing strategies requires concentrated time and effort from an organization, and a business's IP advisors do a tremendous amount of background work to review the patent art and to devise and propose potential routes to success. It is difficult to take such proactive actions if the advisors are overloaded with shorter-term crisis work. In developing strategy, a business would be better off not scrimping on the mental resources, especially since most businesses need not only good advice, but they need that good advice delivered quickly.

Developing Patent Strategies: Orchestrating Exclusivity

When IP strategies are considered concurrently with the development of new products, IP advisors can provide information on previous patents and publications that can help shorten the development time by not reinventing inventions that have already been disclosed. This input can help improve the reach and direction of the research, and even optimize the amount of resources devoted to the development. For example, if the area is wide open for exploitation, the intellectual property strategy may show the potential for numerous patentable inventions that in turn will require a team of researchers. On the other hand, if there is limited opportunity for proprietary development, then perhaps very few or no technical resources should be devoted to that product, or those resources should be geared to buying or licensing the technology.

Avoiding Infringement

One service intellectual property advisors provide is advice on whether or not new products and processes have any freedom-to-operate issues. With each passing year more and more patents are granted, making the collection of possibly infringed patents grow at a fantastic rate. Intellectual property advisors can search the patent art to see if any existing patents may be infringed if a new product is introduced or a new process or machine is operated. If there is an issue with an existing patent, intellectual property advisors are well suited to help develop a strategy for handling the patent, either through licensing or some other route.

This freedom to operate, or clearance process, is very valuable to a business. When intellectual property advisors are brought into the clearance process early in a development, a company can avoid spending a large amount of money and time developing a product or process that might never be commercially operated because of patent problems. There is one difficulty in this approach, however. It is fairly easy for an intellectual property advisor to determine whether there are any concerns with a *specific* new product or process or machine. After an invention is completed, most of the characteristics of the invention are known and the properties or the arrangement of whatever is critical to the invention are specified. It is much more difficult for the advisor to determine whether a general invention concept would have any freedom-to-operate problems before the invention is made. Concepts are not inventions, so it is difficult to know how broadly or narrowly to search the prior art. Given a concept early in development, the intellectual property advisor will put some limits on the invention and identify the patents that might have an impact based on these limits. This information by itself can be highly valuable to a researcher; however, everyone involved with the project must remember that additional searches will be necessary as the invention is developed or reduced to practice. When intellectual property advisors are brought in early, they can only give answers as good as the development of the invention at the time. This classic chicken-and-egg syndrome means that continual involvement of intellectual property advisors will be needed throughout the development of the invention.

Opposing and Enforcing Patents

When granted, patents in Europe and Japan can be opposed via opposition procedures if someone believes that the granted patent claims should be narrowed or revoked because the patentee was given more than he or she was entitled to. The United States has a reexamination procedure for somewhat the same purpose. Many times it is easier and more cost-effective to oppose a patent at this stage rather than initiating something in the courts of individual countries. Patent advisors play a major role in reviewing new patents in critical technologies and preparing and implementing strategies to oppose these patents. These advisors will gather previous publications that will show that the claimed invention was previously known, is an obvious extension, or is not a technical advance over previous inventions. These same patent advisors will also help to generate strategies to answer opponents when others oppose a company's patents.

Every problem, every issue that detracts from the possible validity of a patent in court, limits a patent owner's options when an attempt is made to enforce the patent. The possibility that a patent may have to be enforced in court is the reason that when a business obtains patents, they should be of high quality. Intellectual property advisors help a business obtain the best possible patents and then analyze competitive activity to make sure competitors are honoring the company's patents. If infringement is detected, these same advisors can help generate a strategy that will meet the business's need to protect its intellectual property.

Licensing

Finally, intellectual property advisors help with the licensing of patents. When a company is facing possible litigation due to potential infringement of another's patent, that company is also facing a potentially very expensive resolution process. Patent disputes are complex and are often costly to resolve. The seemingly simple act of discovery by both parties during litigation can involve the substantial cost of producing and reviewing millions of pages of documents, consuming both technical and business resources, before actual legal fees are added into the mix. In many cases, licensing may be a low-cost option, even though the amount of money that may have to be paid for the license might be significant. In any case, licensing allows intellectual property advisors to negotiate potentially creative deals that are beneficial to both parties, and therefore, licensing has become a major part of most companies' intellectual property strategy.

In addition, intellectual property advisors can help the company fully utilize the value of its intellectual property by licensing that property to others. If a company owns patents on inventions that are commercially useful but are not critical to the business, these patents may have value to others in the marketplace and additional revenue can be obtained by allowing others to use those inventions. Even with close competitors, with the creative negotiations of the intellectual property advisors, the potential exists for a company to obtain licenses and cross-licenses that might provide for additional revenue and the freedom to operate new inventions.

A FINAL THOUGHT

The world of intellectual property is constantly changing. In the recent past, many patent laws and regulations have changed, and the courts have generated new interpretations of intellectual property law that will impact the value of granted patents and pending applications. This trend should continue for the foreseeable future because the value of intellectual property increases every year and more and more things are patented that were previously not considered patentable. The only way to keep up with these changes will be through intellectual property advisors who can interpret these developments and translate them into useful strategies for a business.

More importantly, however, we are in a new world of intellectual property. Understanding the basics of patent law and strategy puts business executives and investment professionals in a better position to comprehend and discuss innovation as well as assess and capture its value. Companies will need to cultivate a new attitude to have the opportunity to proactively affect the bottom line of their businesses with their intellectual property. It takes more than a simple expectation that intellectual property will generate or enhance revenue. It takes more than simply trying to sell or license patents. It requires looking at intellectual property as a business itself and developing, coordinating, and taking advantage of a company's patents, trademarks, and other intellectual property. It also requires more than managers who are simply conversant in patents and licensing. It requires people experienced in the many facets of intellectual property who can think strategically, and enough of those people to have a critical mass to act proactively. The companies that provide adequate resources to take proactive action will be better able to capitalize on the opportunities this new world of intellectual property provides.

ABOUT THE AUTHOR

H. Jackson Knight is Senior Patent Specialist for E. I. Du Pont De Nemours & Co. He manages intellectual property for Dupont's Advanced Fiber Systems businesses with responsibility for DuPont's Kevlar® fiber, Nomex® fiber, and Teflon® fiber. For over 12 years, he has been involved in all phases of patenting and business development activity and is registered to practice before the United States Patent & Trademark Office. Prior to his involvement with intellectual property, Mr. Knight had a variety of assignments in all phases of technology development, including methanol process design engineering, research and development for DuPont's Sontara® spunlaced nonwoven products, and process engineering and product applications research for DuPont's Tyvek® spunbonded polyolefin products. He holds a Masters of Engineering in Chemical Engineering from the University of Virginia and a Bachelor of Science in Chemical Engineering from Auburn University.

Mr. Knight is the author of *Patent Strategy for Researchers and Research Managers* (John Wiley & Sons), a book which bridges the gap between the legal system and scientific research and encourages researchers, business managers, and investors to regard the practical aspects of intellectual property. A revised second edition of *Patent Strategy* was published in June 2001. Mr. Knight is on the Board of Editors for *Patent Strategy & Management*, published by Law Journal Newsletters. Mr. Knight's ideas on patent strategy were also featured in the European Patent Office's 1995 Annual Report.

CHAPTER TWO

How to "Read" a Patent
Understanding the Language of Proprietary Rights

by Walter G. Hanchuk

PERSPECTIVES

Patents are a mystery to almost everyone they affect. For most managers and investors, they appear to be hieroglyphics-encoded tomes, elusive to all but those with specialized training and green eyeshades. Does anyone other than patent attorneys actually know what patents say? Does anyone actually read them? Indeed, it is difficult to care about patents if we do not know what they say. Most patent attorneys are not business executives, nor are they investors, entrepreneurs, inventors, or investment bankers, nor should they be.

There is hope. Not that long ago, 10K's and S-1 registrations associated with initial public offerings, and even consolidated financial statements found in company annual reports were considered too onerous for those untrained in accounting and finance to understand. Intellectual property stakeholders—owners, managers, inventors, and shareholders—have begun to make necessity the mother of invention (no pun intended). They are learning how to wrap their arms and minds around patents, and are discovering how to be smarter about deploying them in businesses. More important, they are refusing to let these complex documents intimidate them. They have discovered that a grounding in the language and iconography of patents can be a valuable business tool.

"While a little knowledge can at times be dangerous," says patent attorney Walter G. Hanchuk, "patent owners, managers, and investors who 'know what they don't know' may be in a better position to identify strengths and weaknesses, opportunities and threats, and how to discuss them with counsel."

In the following chapter, Mr. Hanchuk takes the reader step-by-step from the file number on the cover page to the assignees. His overview of the types of information provided in a patent also suggests what to do with this information. He explains what to look for, including what lawyers mean by "claims comparison," the essence of a patent. Mr. Hanchuk dissects the anatomy of a patent, attempting to understand the criteria for interpreting claims and what they cover as patent attorneys and the courts use them. His sample claims chart is a first in a book intended for a broad business and investor audience. Lawyers will benefit from Mr. Hanchuk's discourse if only to equip themselves to better discuss pertinent information with their clients. Investors will read the chapter and no doubt return to it as a handy reference. The following are a few of Hanchuk's possible patent red flags and green lights—a useful guide for the uninitiated.

Possible signs of patent strengths:
- Use of different independent claims formats of varying scope (from broad to narrow)
- Use of many nested dependent claims
- Discussion of many embodiments in the body of an application
- Old filing date
- Detailed and lengthy prior art section
- Lengthy search classification
- Series of patents clustered around a particular technology/product

Possible signs of patent weakness
- Very few claims
- Contains only long independent claims
- Contains only short independent claims
- Very brief detailed description
- Relatively recent filing date

INTRODUCTION

Everyone seems to have an opinion about patents, yet almost no one seems to actually read them. Perhaps it is because patents appear to be too cryptic for many people whom they affect. Perhaps it is because people believe that it will take them too long to sit down and scrutinize one. When confronted with a patent, most business executives, investors, and even inventors will simply demand that "someone find a patent lawyer." Examining patents first hand can be surprisingly rewarding for those serious about the business of innovation, even if it is just to get a basic sense of what patents cover.

If you or your company are threatened with a patent infringement suit, you absolutely must retain a patent lawyer to represent you. However, if your need is business development, licensing, or corporate finance, obtaining an immediate and better understanding of a single patent's or a group of patents' scope and content can be useful. This chapter is intended to help those who are not patent attorneys to "read" and understand patents.

Various other tips in this chapter will allow you to do a more meaningful five-minute review of the patent. These tips will provide insight about the nature and value of the protection that the patent might afford. Also, while a little knowledge can at times be dangerous, patent owners, managers, and investors who "know what they don't know" may be in a better position to identify strengths and weaknesses, opportunities and threats, and how to discuss them with counsel.

THE ANATOMY OF A PATENT

The now-famous Amazon one-click patent—the legend of many *Doonesbury* jokes—is the topic of discussion of many *New York Times* and *Wall Street Journal* articles. To provide a better sense of how to read a patent, a page-by-page review of the Amazon patent may prove rather enlightening.

The Patent Cover Page

The front cover of a patent provides some particularly useful information. The front cover of the Amazon one-click patent is reproduced in Exhibit 2-1.

While the title may give you a 50,000-foot view of the patent's subject matter, the reader should not assume that a patent is limited to features or general subject matter spelled out in the title (see Exhibit 2-2) or anywhere on the cover page. As discussed in greater detail later in this chapter, the legal scope of a patent is defined by the patent claims, which are enumerated in numbered paragraphs at the very end of a patent document. As the reader will soon see, patents claims are truly the heart and soul of the patent.

The patent number 5,960,411 is a number assigned (chronologically) to all patents. There are now well over 6 million U.S. patents, with over 100,000 issuing every year (see Exhibit 2-3).

The patent abstract is often the *last* thing most individuals (particularly non-patent attorneys) read in a patent (see Exhibit 2-4). While the abstract is often a very helpful and insightful single paragraph, it too is often not descriptive of the actual patent right the patent document confers. Much of this stems from the fact that patent abstracts are also written at a relatively high-level view (perhaps 10,000 feet, as compared with the title's 50,000-foot view).

To better understand why a patent abstract often does not describe the patent right a patent confers, it is worth explaining a little about the process of obtaining

United States Patent [19]

Hartman et al.

[11] **Patent Number:** **5,960,411**

[45] **Date of Patent:** **Sep. 28, 1999**

[54] **METHOD AND SYSTEM FOR PLACING A PURCHASE ORDER VIA A COMMUNICATIONS NETWORK**

[75] Inventors: **Peri Hartman; Jeffrey P. Bezos; Shel Kaphan; Joel Spiegel**, all of Seattle, Wash.

[73] Assignee: **Amazon.com, Inc.**, Seattle, Wash.

[21] Appl. No.: **08/928,951**

[22] Filed: **Sep. 12, 1997**

[51] Int. Cl.[6] G06F 17/60

[52] U.S. Cl. 705/26; 705/27; 345/962

[58] Field of Search 705/26, 27; 380/24; 380/25; 235/2, 375, 378, 381; 395/188.01; 345/962

[56] **References Cited**

U.S. PATENT DOCUMENTS

4,937,863	6/1990	Robert et al. 380/4
5,204,897	4/1993	Wyman 380/4
5,260,999	11/1993	Wyman 384/4
5,627,940	5/1997	Rohra et al. 395/12
5,640,501	6/1997	Turpin 395/768
5,640,577	6/1997	Scharmer 395/768
5,664,111	9/1997	Nahan et al. 705/27
5,715,314	2/1998	Payne et al. 380/24
5,715,399	2/1998	Bezos 705/27
5,727,163	3/1998	Bezos 705/27
5,745,681	4/1998	Levine et al. 395/200.3
5,758,126	5/1998	Daniels et al. 395/500

FOREIGN PATENT DOCUMENTS

0855659 A1	1/1998	European Pat. Off.	.... G06F 17/30
0855687 A2	1/1998	European Pat. Off.	.... G07F 19/00
0845747A2	6/1998	European Pat. Off.	.... G06F 17/60
0883076A2	12/1998	European Pat. Off.	.... G06F 17/60
WO 95/30961	11/1995	WIPO	.... G06F 17/60
WO 96/38799	12/1996	WIPO	.... G06F 17/60
WO 98/21679	5/1998	WIPO	.... G06F 17/60

OTHER PUBLICATIONS

Jones, Chris. "Java Shopping Cart and Java Wallet; Oracles plans to join e–commerce initiative." Mar. 31, 1997, Info-World Media Group.

"Pacific Coast Software Software creates virtual shopping cart." Sep. 6, 1996. M2 Communications Ltd 1996.

"Software Creates Virtual Shopping Cart." Sep. 5, 1996. Business Wire, Inc.

Terdoslavich, William. "Java Electronic Commerce Frame-work." Computer Reseller News, Sep. 23, 1996, CMP Media, Inc., 1996, pp. 126, http://www.elibrary.com/id/101/101/getdoc . . . rydocid=902269@library_d&dtype= 0–0&dinst=. [Accessed Nov. 19, 1998].

"Internet Access: Disc Distributing Announces Interactive World Wide." Cambridge Work–Group Computing Report, Cambridge Publishing, Inc., 1995, http://www.elibrary.com/id/101/101/getdoc . . . docid=1007497@library_a&dtype= 0–0&dinst=0. [Accessed Nov. 19, 1998].

(List continued on next page.)

Primary Examiner—James P. Trammell
Assistant Examiner—Demetra R. Smith
Attorney, Agent, or Firm—Perkins Coie LLP

[57] **ABSTRACT**

A method and system for placing an order to purchase an item via the Internet. The order is placed by a purchaser at a client system and received by a server system. The server system receives purchaser information including identifica-tion of the purchaser, payment information, and shipment information from the client system. The server system then assigns a client identifier to the client system and associates the assigned client identifier with the received purchaser information. The server system sends to the client system the assigned client identifier and an HTML document identify-ing the item and including an order button. The client system receives and stores the assigned client identifier and receives and displays the HTML document. In response to the selection of the order button, the client system sends to the server system a request to purchase the identified item. The server system receives the request and combines the pur-chaser information associated with the client identifier of the client system to generate an order to purchase the item in accordance with the billing and shipment information whereby the purchaser effects the ordering of the product by selection of the order button.

26 Claims, 11 Drawing Sheets

Exhibit 2-1 Amazon "one-click" patent front cover.

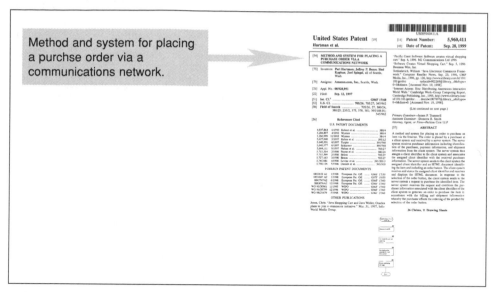

Exhibit 2-2   The title of the Amazon one-click patent.

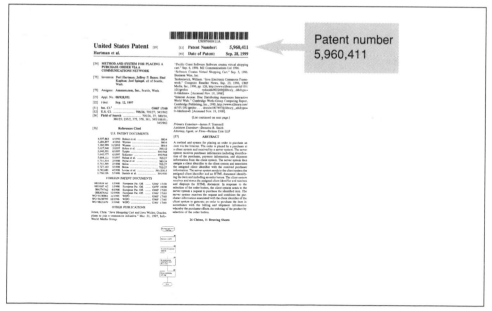

Exhibit 2-3   The patent number of the Amazon one-click patent.

patents. Most originally filed patent claims are often first rejected by a U.S. Patent & Trade Office (USPTO) examiner. In response to the rejections, patent attorneys frequently amend the claims in what is called patent prosecution before the USPTO. Yet, few patent attorneys actually amend the patent abstract to reflect the amended patent claims. As such, patent abstracts and patent claims are often somewhat divorced during the patenting process.

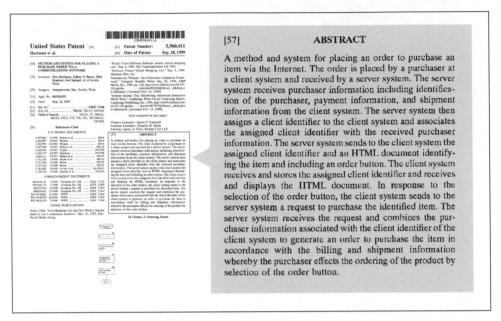

Exhibit 2-4   Abstract of the Amazon one-click patent.

Why all this talk of patent claims? If claims are so important, why do patent readers not simply read patent claims without reading the rest of the patent document? The entire patent document actually can affect the interpretation of patent claims, and therefore can greatly impact the scope and content of a patent. In addition, a quick review of a patent cover can often tell you *volumes* about the scope and *quality* of a patent. A few additional basics regarding the body of the patent document can also help the reader conduct these quick reviews of the patent before analyzing the patent claims.

The cover of every patent lists references which the patent examiner considered before issuing the patent. These references were either found by the examiner during the search, or provided by the patent applicant during the prosecution of the patent. In fact, every patent applicant (and his or her attorneys and anyone else substantively involved in the prosecution of the patent) has an obligation to submit information which would be material to the patentability of the patent application. Although there is no duty for patent applicants to do their own search, many patent applicants do conduct searches. Once search results are obtained, this duty to disclose material information applies. Failure to submit such known material information could result in a court finding the patent unenforceable in a future case.

If many references are listed on the face of the patent, either the patent examiner uncovered many references and/or the patent applicant submitted them to the examiner. Either way, a lengthy "References Cited" section may suggest that a patent was well searched. A short (or nonexistent) "References Cited" section may, on the other hand, suggest that the patent was not well searched either by the patent examiner or the applicant. It may also suggest simply that no one could find any material prior art information.

Additional information regarding the examiner's search can also be obtained from the "Field of Search" section (see Exhibit 2-5). The USPTO has classified all of its search materials (patents, publications, etc.) into a series of classes and sub-classes to assist patent examiners and others (like a patent applicant) to search for material "prior art" information. Skilled searchers and patent lawyers will often review the scope of the examiner's search to determine whether the examiner conducted a proper and thorough search.

The inventors of a patent include those individuals who conceived of the claimed invention and (perhaps) reduced the invention to practice (see Exhibit 2-6). Inventorship is an extremely important topic in U.S. patent law. Intentionally leaving off an inventor is grounds for finding a patent invalid, regardless of whether the invention is otherwise patentable.

The assignee listed on the face of a patent is the owner of the patent at the time that the issue fee was paid for the patent (several months before the patent issued). If no assignee is listed, either the patent is owned by the inventors, or perhaps the patent actually is assigned, but this information was not listed on the face of the patent. In addition, it is important to note that if the patent owner changes (after the issue fee was paid and/or after the patent issued), the USPTO will *not* issue a revised patent cover page. As such, the assignee information on the cover of a patent is often not current. There are, however, several commercial on-line services which can obtain such information relatively inexpensively.

The application number (often called the serial number) is exactly that—a number assigned to the patent application (see Exhibit 2-7). All correspondence to and from the USPTO during the pendency of the patent application references this number.

The classification section indicates in which classes and subclasses the patent examiner has decided to issue the patent (see Exhibit 2-8). In so doing, copies of the newly issued patent will be classified in those areas to assist future examiners and searchers in their search for information. Incidentally, further information regarding the USPTO's classification system can also be obtained (for free) at the USPTO's website (*www.uspto.gov*).

Several dates are listed on the face of the patent (see Exhibit 2-9). The issue date (September 28, 1999) is listed just below the patent number. A patent becomes enforceable in the United States as of this date. The filing date (September 12, 1997) of the patent application provides important information as to the term of the patent and as to what other references could be used to invalidate the patent. All patent applications filed in the United States after June 8, 1995 have a term of 20 years from their original U.S. filing date. As such, the Amazon patent will expire on September 12, 2017 (assuming that USPTO maintenance fees are paid 4, 8, and 12 years after the issuance of the patent). If the application had been filed prior to

US005960411A

United States Patent [19]

Hartman et al.

[11] Patent Number: 5,960,411

[45] Date of Patent: Sep. 28, 1999

[54] METHOD AND SYSTEM FOR PLACING A PURCHASE ORDER VIA A COMMUNICATIONS NETWORK

[75] Inventors: Peri Hartman; Jeffrey P. Bezos; Shel Kaphan; Joel Spiegel, all of Seattle, Wash.

[73] Assignee: Amazon.com, Inc., Seattle, Wash.

[21] Appl. No.: 08/928,951

[22] Filed: Sep. 12, 1997

[51] Int. Cl.⁶ G06F 17/60
[52] U.S. Cl. 705/26; 705/27, 345/962
[58] Field of Search 705/26, 27, 380/24, 380/25, 235/2, 375, 378, 381; 395/188.01; 345/962

[56]   References Cited

U.S. PATENT DOCUMENTS

4,937,863	6/1990	Robert et al.	3804
5,204,897	4/1993	Wyman	3804
5,260,999	11/1993	Wyman	3844
5,627,940	5/1997	Rohra et al.	395/12
5,640,501	6/1997	Turpin	395/768
5,640,577	6/1997	Scharmer	395/768
5,664,111	9/1997	Nahan et al.	705/27
5,715,314	2/1998	Payne et al.	380/24
5,715,399	2/1998	Bezos	705/27
5,727,163	3/1998	Bezos	705/27
5,745,681	4/1998	Levinc et al.	395/200.3
5,758,126	5/1998	Daniels et al.	395/500

FOREIGN PATENT DOCUMENTS

0855659 A1	1/1998	European Pat. Off.	G06F 17/30
0855687 A2	1/1998	European Pat. Off.	G07F 19/00
0845747A2	6/1998	European Pat. Off.	G06F 17/60
0883076A2	12/1998	European Pat. Off.	G06F 17/60
WO 95/30961	11/1995	WIPO	G06F 17/60
WO 96/38799	12/1996	WIPO	G06F 17/60
WO 98/21679	5/1998	WIPO	G06F 17/60

OTHER PUBLICATIONS

Jones, Chris. "Java Shopping Cart and Java Wallet; Oracles plans to join e-commerce initiative." Mar. 31, 1997, Info-World Media Group.

"Pacific Coast Software Software creates virtual shopping cart." Sep. 6, 1996. M2 Communications Ltd 1996.
"Software Creates Virtual Shopping Cart." Sep. 5, 1996. Business Wire, Inc.
Terdoslavich, William. "Java Electronic Commerce Framework." Computer Reseller News, Sep. 23, 1996, CMP Media, Inc., 1996, pp. 126, http://www.elibrary.com/id/101/101/getdoc . . . rydocid=902269@library_a&dtype= 0-0&dinst=. [Accessed Nov. 19, 1998].
"Internet Access: Disc Distributing Announces Interactive World Wide." Cambridge Work–Group Computing Report, Cambridge Publishing, Inc., 1995, http://www.elibrary.com/id/101/101/getdoc . . . docid=1007497@library_a&dtype= 0-0&dinst=0. [Accessed Nov. 19, 1998].

(List continued on next page.)

Primary Examiner—James P. Trammell
Assistant Examiner—Demetra R. Smith
Attorney, Agent, or Firm—Perkins Coie LLP

[57]   ABSTRACT

A method and system for placing an order to purchase an item via the Internet. The order is placed by a purchaser at a client system and received by a server system. The server system receives purchaser information including identification of the purchaser, payment information, and shipment information from the client system. The server system then assigns a client identifier to the client system and associates the assigned client identifier with the received purchaser information. The server system sends to the client system the assigned client identifier and an HTML document identifying the item and including an order button. The client system receives and stores the assigned client identifier and receives and displays the HTML document. In response to the selection of the order button, the client system sends to the server system a request to purchase the identified item. The server system receives the request and combines the purchaser information associated with the client identifier of the client system to generate an order to purchase the item in accordance with the billing and shipment information whereby the purchaser effects the ordering of the product by selection of the order button.

26 Claims, 11 Drawing Sheets

Field of search

Exhibit 2-5   Prior art section and field of search of the Amazon one-click patent.

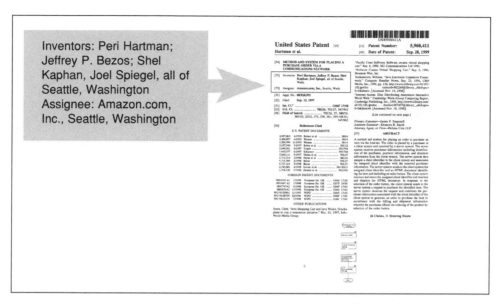

Exhibit 2-6 Inventors and assignee of the Amazon one-click patent.

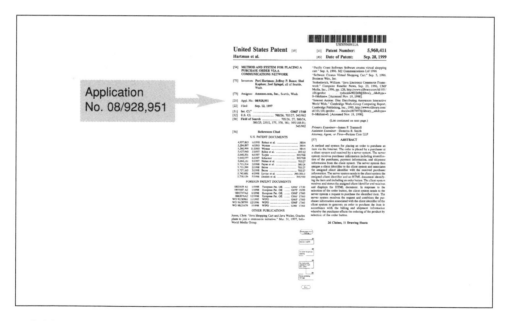

Exhibit 2-7 Application number of the Amazon one-click patent.

Exhibit 2-8 Classification of the Amazon one-click patent.

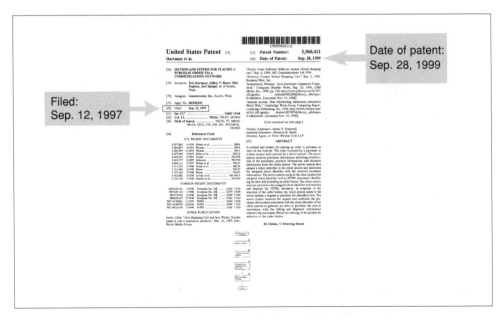

Exhibit 2-9 Dates (issue, filing, priority) of the Amazon one-click patent.

June 8, 1995, the term of the patent would have been 17 years from issuance or 20 years from filing, whichever is longer.

With regard to maintenance fees, it is important to note that if a patent is over four years old, it is quite possible that the patent owner may not have paid the appropriate maintenance fees, thereby allowing the patent to go abandoned. Maintenance fee records can be obtained directly from the USPTO, or through several commercial services.

Although the following does not apply to the Amazon patent, many U.S. patent applications have so-called parent U.S. patent applications and/or parent foreign applications. For reasons that will be discussed later in this chapter, many U.S. applications are divided into multiple U.S. applications and/or refiled (so-called Continuation and Divisional applications). Such applications are treated as if they were filed on the date of the original application. This is called "priority" data on the face of U.S. patent applications. The 20-year term of the patent runs from the filing date of the original application filed in the United States (not the original foreign application).

Body (Specification)

Beyond the cover of a patent lies what many refer to as the patent specification. In reality, all of the subject matter of a patent document (cover page, claims, etc.) make up the patent specification. However, many simply refer to the subject matter between the cover page and the claims as the patent specification.

In a nutshell, the patent specification must fulfill the following legal criteria: (1) it must contain a sufficient "written description" to enable "one of ordinary skill" in the art to re-create the claimed invention without undue experimentation; and (2) it must set forth the "best mode" for carrying out the invention, as of the filing date of the patent application.

The reader may ask why this is important for a proper understanding of the patent document. Many believe that patent documents are far too cryptic—primarily because of the pages and pages of drawings and description. It is important for a patent document to contain such a description so as to fulfill the two legal criteria noted above. Otherwise, the patent application, and/or any patent which issues from it, may be found deficient and therefore unpatentable or invalid.

Most patent specifications contain several sections, although many of them are not required under the law. Typical sections include the following: technical field, background of the invention, objects of the invention, summary of the invention, brief description of the drawings, detailed description, claims, and drawings. Depending on how the application is drafted, one or more of these sections may be limiting on the scope of the actual patent. However, one or more sections may simply be exemplary in nature, and therefore not limiting on the actual patent. A brief review of each of these sections should prove helpful to the patent reader.

The technical field section is typically very brief (see Exhibit 2-10). It often simply sets forth the general area of the subject matter of the patent.

The background of the invention section typically describes what others have done in the past (see Exhibit 2-11). It may also describe some of the deficiencies of those prior activities and set forth the need which the patented subject matter satifies.

The patent applicant may also set forth a number of "objects" of the invention in the background or a separate section. For example, it may say, "It is an object of the present invention to alleviate each of the problems set forth in the background section."

The summary of the invention should, in theory, describe that which is patented (see Exhibit 2-12). This section is typically more detailed than the abstract, and often looks very much like the language used in the patent claims. As such, many readers are surprised by how unreadable this section may be. To better understand why this may be the case, it may help to understand how many patent attorneys draft this section. Typically, this section is drafted by the patent attorney by simply rewording the claim language, presumably into something that better resembles English. The reader should also know that although the patent attorney often amends the claims of a patent application in response to USPTO rejections, many patent attorneys do not similarly amend the summary section to reflect the changes in the claims. As such, the summary section is often divorced from the claim language through the patent application amendment process. In fact, it is not uncommon for the summary section to be completely nondescriptive of the actual claimed subject matter. As such, although the summary section often can be very useful in understanding a patent, it may often not tell you the real story with regard to the actual scope of the patent.

The brief description of the drawings is just that—a one-sentence description of each drawing (see Exhibit 2-13). This section can often be very helpful in understanding how certain drawings interrelate. For example, one drawing in a mechanical patent may depict a cross-section of another. The brief description section can give you a quick and accurate helping hand in determining how such cross-sectional drawings interrelate.

The detailed description section is ordinarily the longest (and meatiest) section of the entire patent document. It sets out a step-by-step walk through the drawings, and often describes various alternative embodiments. In a first high-level review of a patent (a one-minute review), a review of this section is often not necessary. However, in a more detailed review of the patent (a five-minute review), a review of this section may be very necessary. Depending on how this section and the claims are drafted, the detailed description section can severely limit or greatly expand the scope of patent protection. To better understand how this section may limit the patent's scope, it will be most helpful to first gain an understanding of the many different types of patent claim formats and how they are to be interpreted in light of the patent specification.

1

METHOD AND SYSTEM FOR PLACING A PURCHASE ORDER VIA A COMMUNICATIONS NETWORK

TECHNICAL FIELD

The present invention relates to a computer method and system for placing an order and, more particularly, to a method and system for ordering items over the Internet.

BACKGROUND OF THE INVENTION

The Internet comprises a vast number of computers and computer networks that are interconnected through communication links. The interconnected computers exchange information using various services, such as electronic mail, Gopher, and the World Wide Web ("WWW"). The WWW service allows a server computer system (i.e., Web server or Web site) to send graphical Web pages of information to a remote client computer system. The remote client computer system can then display the Web pages. Each resource (e.g., computer or Web page) of the WWW is uniquely identifiable by a Uniform Resource Locator ("URL"). To view a specific Web page, a client computer system specifies the URL for that Web page in a request (e.g., a HyperText Transfer Protocol ("HTTP") request). The request is forwarded to the Web server that supports that Web page. When that Web server receives the request, it sends that Web page to the client computer system. When the client computer system receives that Web page, it typically displays the Web page using a browser. A browser is a special-purpose application program that effects the requesting of Web pages and the displaying of Web pages.

Currently, Web pages are typically defined using Hyper-Text Markup Language ("HTML"). HTML provides a standard set of tags that define how a Web page is to be displayed. When a user indicates to the browser to display a Web page, the browser sends a request to the server computer system to transfer to the client computer system an HTML document that defines the Web page. When the requested HTML document is received by the client computer system, the browser displays the Web page as defined by the HTML document. The HTML document contains various tags that control the displaying of text, graphics, controls, and other features. The HTML document may contain URLs of other Web pages available on that server computer system or other server computer systems.

The World Wide Web is especially conducive to conducting electronic commerce. Many Web servers have been developed through which vendors can advertise and sell product. The products can include items (e.g., music) that are delivered electronically to the purchaser over the Internet and items (e.g., books) that are delivered through conventional distribution channels (e.g., a common carrier). A server computer system may provide an electronic version of a catalog that lists the items that are available. A user, who is a potential purchaser, may browse through the catalog using a browser and select various items that are to be purchased. When the user has completed selecting the items to be purchased, the server computer system then prompts the user for information to complete the ordering of the items. This purchaser-specific order information may include the purchaser's name, the purchaser's credit card number, and a shipping address for the order. The server computer system then typically confirms the order by sending a confirming Web page to the client computer system and schedules shipment of the items.

Since the purchaser-specific order information contains sensitive information (e.g., a credit card number), both

2

vendors and purchasers want to ensure the security of such information. Security is a concern because information transmitted over the Internet may pass through various intermediate computer systems on its way to its final destination. The information could be intercepted by an unscrupulous person at an intermediate system. To help ensure the security of the sensitive information, various encryption techniques are used when transmitting such information between a client computer system and a server computer system. Even though such encrypted information can be intercepted, because the information is encrypted, it is generally useless to the interceptor. Nevertheless, there is always a possibility that such sensitive information may be successfully decrypted by the interceptor. Therefore, it would be desirable to minimize the sensitive information transmitted when placing an order.

The selection of the various items from the electronic catalogs is generally based on the "shopping cart" model. When the purchaser selects an item from the electronic catalog, the server computer system metaphorically adds that item to a shopping cart. When the purchaser is done selecting items, then all the items in the shopping cart are "checked out" (i.e., ordered) when the purchaser provides billing and shipment information. In some models, when a purchaser selects any one item, then that item is "checked out" by automatically prompting the user for the billing and shipment information. Although the shopping cart model is very flexible and intuitive, it has a downside in that it requires many interactions by the purchaser. For example, the purchaser selects the various items from the electronic catalog, and then indicates that the selection is complete. The purchaser is then presented with an order Web page that prompts the purchaser for the purchaser-specific order information to complete the order. That Web page may be prefilled with information that was provided by the purchaser when placing another order. The information is then validated by the server computer system, and the order is completed. Such an ordering model can be problematic for a couple of reasons. If a purchaser is ordering only one item, then the overhead of confirming the various steps of the ordering process and waiting for, viewing, and updating the purchaser-specific order information can be much more than the overhead of selecting the item itself. This overhead makes the purchase of a single item cumbersome. Also, with such an ordering model, each time an order is placed sensitive information is transmitted over the Internet. Each time the sensitive information is transmitted over the Internet, it is susceptible to being intercepted and decrypted.

SUMMARY OF THE INVENTION

An embodiment of the present invention provides a method and system for ordering an item from a client system. The client system is provided with an identifier that identifies a customer. The client system displays information that identifies the item and displays an indication of an action (e.g., a single action such as clicking a mouse button) that a purchaser is to perform to order the identified item. In response to the indicated action being performed, the client system sends to a server system the provided identifier and a request to order the identified item. The server system uses the identifier to identify additional information needed to generate an order for the item and then generates the order.

The server system receives and stores the additional information for customers using various computer systems so that the server system can generate such orders. The server system stores the received additional information in association with an identifier of the customer and provides

---

The present invention relates to a computer method and system for placing an order and, more particularly, to a method and system for ordering items over the Internet.

Exhibit 2-10   The technical field of the Amazon one-click patent.

1

METHOD AND SYSTEM FOR PLACING A
PURCHASE ORDER VIA A
COMMUNICATIONS NETWORK

TECHNICAL FIELD

The present invention relates to a computer method and system for placing an order and, more particularly, to a method and system for ordering items over the Internet.

BACKGROUND OF THE INVENTION

The Internet comprises a vast number of computers and computer networks that are interconnected through communication links. The interconnected computers exchange information using various services, such as electronic mail, Gopher, and the World Wide Web ("WWW"). The WWW service allows a server computer system (i.e., Web server or Web site) to send graphical Web pages of information to a remote client computer system. The remote client computer system can then display the Web pages. Each resource (e.g., computer or Web page) of the WWW is uniquely identifiable by a Uniform Resource Locator ("URL"). To view a specific Web page, a client computer system specifies the URL for that Web page in a request (e.g., a HyperText Transfer Protocol ("HTTP") request). The request is forwarded to the Web server that supports that Web page. When that Web server receives the request, it sends that Web page to the client computer system. When the client computer system receives that Web page, it typically displays the Web page using a browser. A browser is a special-purpose application program that effects the requesting of Web pages and the displaying of Web pages.

Currently, Web pages are typically defined using Hyper-Text Markup Language ("HTML"). HTML provides a standard set of tags that define how a Web page is to be displayed. When a user indicates to the browser to display a Web page, the browser sends a request to the server computer system to transfer to the client computer system an HTML document that defines the Web page. When the requested HTML document is received by the client computer system, the browser displays the Web page as defined by the HTML document. The HTML document contains various tags that control the displaying of text, graphics, controls, and other features. The HTML document may contain URLs of other Web pages available on that server computer system or other server computer systems.

The World Wide Web is especially conducive to conducting electronic commerce. Many Web servers have been developed through which vendors can advertise and sell product. The products can include items (e.g., music) that are delivered electronically to the purchaser over the Internet and items (e.g., books) that are delivered through conventional distribution channels (e.g., a common carrier). A server computer system may provide an electronic version of a catalog that lists the items that are available. A user, who is a potential purchaser, may browse through the catalog using a browser and select various items that are to be purchased. When the user has completed selecting the items to be purchased, the server computer system then prompts the user for information to complete the ordering of the items. This purchaser-specific order information may include the purchaser's name, the purchaser's credit card number, and a shipping address for the order. The server computer system typically confirms the order by sending a confirming Web page to the client computer system and schedules shipment of the items.

Since the purchaser-specific order information contains sensitive information (e.g., a credit card number), both

2

vendors and purchasers want to ensure the security of such information. Security is a concern because information transmitted over the Internet may pass through various intermediate computer systems on its way to its final destination. The information could be intercepted by an unscrupulous person at an intermediate system. To help ensure the security of the sensitive information, various encryption techniques are used when transmitting such information between a client computer system and a server computer system. Even though such encrypted information can be intercepted, because the information is encrypted, it is generally useless to the interceptor. Nevertheless, there is always a possibility that such sensitive information may be successfully decrypted by the interceptor. Therefore, it would be desirable to minimize the sensitive information transmitted when placing an order.

The selection of the various items from the electronic catalogs is generally based on the "shopping cart" model. When the purchaser selects an item from the electronic catalog, the server computer system metaphorically adds that item to a shopping cart. When the purchaser is done selecting items, then all the items in the shopping cart are "checked out" (i.e., ordered) when the purchaser provides billing and shipment information. In some models, when a purchaser selects any one item, then that item is "checked out" by automatically prompting the user for the billing and shipment information. Although the shopping cart model is very flexible and intuitive, it has a downside in that it requires many interactions by the purchaser. For example, the purchaser selects the various items from the electronic catalog, and then indicates that the selection is complete. The purchaser is then presented with an order Web page that prompts the purchaser for the purchaser-specific order information to complete the order. That Web page may be prefilled with information that was provided by the purchaser when placing another order. The information is then validated by the server computer system, and the order is completed. Such an ordering model can be problematic for a couple of reasons. If a purchaser is ordering only one item, then the overhead of confirming the various steps of the ordering process and waiting for, viewing, and updating the purchaser-specific order information can be much more than the overhead of selecting the item itself. This overhead makes the purchase of a single item cumbersome. Also, with such an ordering model, each time an order is placed sensitive information is transmitted over the Internet. Each time the sensitive information is transmitted over the Internet, it is susceptible to being intercepted and decrypted.

SUMMARY OF THE INVENTION

An embodiment of the present invention provides a method and system for ordering an item from a client system. The client system is provided with an identifier that identifies a customer. The client system displays information that identifies the item and displays an indication of an action (e.g., a single action such as clicking a mouse button) that a purchaser is to perform to order the identified item. In response to the indicated action being performed, the client system sends to a server system the provided identifier and a request to order the identified item. The server system uses the identifier to identify additional information needed to generate an order for the item and then generates the order.

The server system receives and stores the additional information for customers using various computer systems so that the server system can generate such orders. The server system stores the received additional information in association with an identifier of the customer and provides

Background of the invention

Exhibit 2-11   Background of invention of the Amazon one-click patent.

1

METHOD AND SYSTEM FOR PLACING A PURCHASE ORDER VIA A COMMUNICATIONS NETWORK

TECHNICAL FIELD

The present invention relates to a computer method and system for placing an order and, more particularly, to a method and system for ordering items over the Internet.

BACKGROUND OF THE INVENTION

The Internet comprises a vast number of computers and computer networks that are interconnected through communication links. The interconnected computers exchange information using various services, such as electronic mail, Gopher, and the World Wide Web ("WWW"). The WWW service allows a server computer system (i.e., Web server or Web site) to send graphical Web pages of information to a remote client computer system. The remote client computer system can then display the Web pages. Each resource (e.g., computer or Web page) of the WWW is uniquely identifiable by a Uniform Resource Locator ("URL"). To view a specific Web page, a client computer system specifies the URL for that Web page in a request (e.g., a HyperText Transfer Protocol ("HTTP") request). The request is forwarded to the Web server that supports that Web page. When that Web server receives the request, it sends that Web page to the client computer system. When the client computer system receives that Web page, it typically displays the Web page using a browser. A browser is a special-purpose application program that effects the requesting of Web pages and the displaying of Web pages.

Currently, Web pages are typically defined using Hyper-Text Markup Language ("HTML"). HTML provides a standard set of tags that define how a Web page is to be displayed. When a user indicates to the browser to display a Web page, the browser sends a request to the server computer system to transfer to the client computer system an HTML document that defines the Web page. When the requested HTML document is received by the client computer system, the browser displays the Web page as defined by the HTML document. The HTML document contains various tags that control the displaying of text, graphics, controls, and other features. The HTML document may contain URLs of other Web pages available on that server computer system or other server computer systems.

The World Wide Web is especially conducive to conducting electronic commerce. Many Web servers have been developed through which vendors can advertise and sell product. The products can include items (e.g., music) that are delivered electronically to the purchaser over the Internet and items (e.g., books) that are delivered through conventional distribution channels (e.g., a common carrier). A server computer system may provide an electronic version of a catalog that lists the items that are available. A user, who is a potential purchaser, may browse through the catalog using a browser and select various items that are to be purchased. When the user has completed selecting the items to be purchased, the server computer system then prompts the user for information to complete the ordering of the items. This purchaser-specific order information may include the purchaser's name, the purchaser's credit card number, and a shipping address for the order. The server computer system typically confirms the order by sending a confirming Web page to the client computer system and schedules shipment of the items.

Since the purchaser-specific order information contains sensitive information (e.g., a credit card number), both

2

vendors and purchasers want to ensure the security of such information. Security is a concern because information transmitted over the Internet may pass through various intermediate computer systems on its way to its final destination. The information could be intercepted by an unscrupulous person at an intermediate system. To help ensure the security of the sensitive information, various encryption techniques are used when transmitting such information between a client computer system and a server computer system. Even though such encrypted information can be intercepted, because the information is encrypted, it is generally useless to the interceptor. Nevertheless, there is always a possibility that such sensitive information may be successfully decrypted by the interceptor. Therefore, it would be desirable to minimize the sensitive information transmitted when placing an order.

The selection of the various items from the electronic catalogs is generally based on the "shopping cart" model. When the purchaser selects an item from the electronic catalog, the server computer system metaphorically adds that item to a shopping cart. When the purchaser is done selecting items, then all the items in the shopping cart are "checked out" (i.e., ordered) when the purchaser provides billing and shipment information. In some models, when a purchaser selects any one item, then that item is "checked out" by automatically prompting the user for the billing and shipment information. Although the shopping cart model is very flexible and intuitive, it has a downside in that it requires many interactions by the purchaser. For example, the purchaser selects the various items from the electronic catalog, and then indicates that the selection is complete. The purchaser is then presented with an order Web page that prompts the purchaser for the purchaser-specific order information to complete the order. That Web page may be prefilled with information that was provided by the purchaser when placing another order. The information is then validated by the server computer system, and the order is completed. Such an ordering model can be problematic for a couple of reasons. If a purchaser is ordering only one item, then the overhead of confirming the various steps of the ordering process and waiting for, viewing, and updating the purchaser-specific order information can be much more than the overhead of selecting the item itself. This overhead makes the purchase of a single item cumbersome. Also, with such an ordering model, each time an order is placed sensitive information is transmitted over the Internet. Each time the sensitive information is transmitted over the Internet, it is susceptible to being intercepted and decrypted.

SUMMARY OF THE INVENTION

An embodiment of the present invention provides a method and system for ordering an item from a client system. The client system is provided with an identifier that identifies a customer. The client system displays information that identifies the item and displays an indication of an action (e.g., a single action such as clicking a mouse button) that a purchaser is to perform to order the identified item. In response to the indicated action being performed, the client system sends to a server system the provided identifier and a request to order the identified item. The server system uses the identifier to identify additional information needed to generate an order for the item and then generates the order.

The server system receives and stores the additional information for customers using various computer systems so that the server system can generate such orders. The server system stores the received additional information in association with an identifier of the customer and provides

Summary of the invention

Exhibit 2-12 Summary of the invention of the Amazon one-click patent.

Exhibit 2-13   Brief and detailed descriptions of the Amazon one-click patent.

Claims

At the end of every patent specification are a series of numbered paragraphs called patent claims. Claims set forth the actual patented subject matter. It is this claimed subject matter which defines what others are prevented from making, using, or selling in the United States because of the patent. As such, many patent specifications may describe a process A through Z, but the claims may be limited to elements D, E, and F, requiring the infringer to make, use, or sell elements D, E, and F to infringe the patent. The public is free to use all of the other elements described in the patent specification.

A closer look at a patent claim will often help the reader understand the true scope of a patent (see Exhibit 2-14). As such, independent claim 1 of the Amazon patent requires, among other things, that in response to a "single action," the following occurs: a request is received, information regarding the purchaser is re-

9

Although the algorithm has been described as having two stages, it could be implemented in an incremental fashion where the assessment of the first and second stages are redone after each order is scheduled. One skilled in the art would recognize that there are other possible combinations of these stages which still express the same essential algorithm.

FIGS. 8A–8C illustrate a hierarchical data entry mechanism in one embodiment. When collecting information from a user, a Web page typically consists of a long series of data entry fields that may not all fit onto the display at the same time. Thus, a user needs to scroll through the Web page to enter the information. When the data entry fields do not fit onto the display at the same time, it is difficult for the user to get an overall understanding of the type and organization of the data to be entered. The hierarchical data entry mechanism allows a user to understand the overall organization of the data to be entered even though the all data entry fields would not fit onto the display at the same time. FIG. 8A illustrates an outline format of a sample form to be filled in. The sample form contains various sections identified by letters A, B, C, and D. When the user selects the start button, then section A expands to include the data entry fields for the customer name and address. FIG. 8B illustrates the expansion of section A. Since only section A has been expanded, the user can view the data entry fields of section A and summary information of the other sections at the same time. The user then enters data in the various data entry fields that are displayed. Upon completion, the user selects either the next or previous buttons. The next button causes section A to be collapsed and section B to be expanded so that financial information may be entered. FIG. 8C illustrates the expansion of section B. If the previous button is selected, then section A would collapse and be displayed as shown in FIG. 8A. This collapsing and expanding is repeated for each section. At any time during the data entry, if an error is detected, then a Web page is generated with the error message in close proximity (e.g., on the line below) to the data entry field that contains the error. This Web page is then displayed by the client system to inform the user of the error. In addition, each of the data "entry" fields may not be editable until the user clicks on the data entry field or selects an edit button associated with the data entry field. In this way, the user is prevented from inadvertently changing the contents of an edit field. When the user clicks on a data entry field, a new Web page is presented to the user that allows for the editing of the data associated with the field. When editing is complete, the edited data is displayed in the data "entry" field. Because the fields of the form are thus not directly editable, neither "named-submit" buttons nor Java are needed. Also, the form is more compact because the various data entry options (e.g., radio button) are displayed only on the new Web page when the field is to be edited.

Although the present invention has been described in terms of various embodiments, it is not intended that the invention be limited to these embodiments. Modification within the spirit of the invention will be apparent to those skilled in the art. For example, the server system can map a client identifier to multiple customers who have recently used the client system. The server system can then allow the user to identify themselves by selecting one of the mappings based preferably on a display of partial purchaser-specific order information. Also, various different single actions can be used to effect the placement of an order. For example, a voice command may be spoken by the purchaser, a key may be depressed by the purchaser, a button on a television remote control device may be depressed by the purchaser, or

10

selection using any pointing device may be effected by the purchaser. Although a single action may be preceded by multiple physical movements of the purchaser (e.g., moving a mouse so that a mouse pointer is over a button), the single action generally refers to a single event received by a client system that indicates to place the order. Finally, the purchaser can be alternately identified by a unique customer identifier that is provided by the customer when the customer initiates access to the server system and sent to the server system with each message. This customer identifier could be also stored persistently on the client system so that the purchaser does not need to re-enter their customer identifier each time access is initiated. The scope of the present invention is defined by the claims that follow.

We claim:

1. A method of placing an order for an item comprising:
   under control of a client system,
      displaying information identifying the item; and
      in response to only a single action being performed, sending a request to order the item along with an identifier of a purchaser of the item to a server system;
   under control of a single-action ordering component of the server system,
      receiving the request;
      retrieving additional information previously stored for the purchaser identified by the identifier in the received request; and
   generating an order to purchase the requested item for the purchaser identified by the identifier in the received request using the retrieved additional information; and
   fulfilling the generated order to complete purchase of the item
   whereby the item is ordered without using a shopping cart ordering model.

2. The method of claim 1 wherein the displaying of information includes displaying information indicating the single action.

3. The method of claim 1 wherein the single action is clicking a button.

4. The method of claim 1 wherein the single action is speaking of a sound.

5. The method of claim 1 wherein a user of the client system does not need to explicitly identify themselves when placing an order.

6. A client system for ordering an item comprising:
   an identifier that identifies a customer;
   a display component for displaying information identifying the item;
   a single-action ordering component that in response to performance of only a single action, sends a request to a server system to order the identified item, the request including the identifier so that the server system can locate additional information needed to complete the order and so that the server system can fulfill the generated order to complete purchase of the item; and
   a shopping cart ordering component that in response to performance of an add-to-shopping-cart action, sends a request to the server system to add the item to a shopping cart.

7. The client system of claim 6 wherein the display component is a browser.

8. The client system of claim 6 wherein the predefined action is the clicking of a mouse button.

9. A server system for generating an order comprising:
   a shopping cart ordering component; and

Claims

Exhibit 2-14 Claims of the Amazon one-click patent.

trieved, an order is generated, and the order is fulfilled. Claim 1 further requires that the item be ordered "under control of a single-action ordering component of [a] server system" and "without using a shopping cart model." As such, if someone were to implement a system which used two actions ("two clicks") to performed these steps and/or used a shopping cart model, they would not infringe this patent claim.

To further understand these and other patent claims, a brief review of the different types of patent claims should prove helpful to the reader.

Independent versus Dependent

In general, a claim which does not refer to another patent claim is an independent claim, while a claim which specifically recites another claim is a dependent claim. With reference to the Amazon patent, claim 1 is an independent claim and claim 2 is a dependent claim. Most patents will typically include several claims of both types. In order to infringe a patent, a third party need only infringe *one* independent claim. This is an extremely important point to remember.

In a five-minute review of a patent, it is important to review every independent claim to determine the scope of the patent. A thorough review of the patent (by patent counsel or others), however, would most certainly focus on *every* claim in the patent.

A dependent claim is to be read as if it contained every limitation recited in the independent claim upon which it relies. As such, claim 2 of the Amazon patent includes all of the limitations of claim 1, plus the additional limitation recited in claim 2. It is often unnecessary to initially review every dependent claim in such a five-minute review, simply because of the following: If one does not infringe any independent claim in a patent, one cannot infringe any of the dependent claims either.[1] Remember: a dependent claim must include all of the limitations of the claim from which it depends. As such, if an alleged infringer does not make, use, or sell all of the elements of an independent claim, the alleged infringer could not be making, using, or selling each of the elements of a dependent claim.

Bear in mind that dependent claims can be written so that they depend on other dependent claims, which in turn depend from an independent claim.

The reader may be wondering why patents even need to contain dependent claims, if infringement of only one independent claim is necessary to assert a patent infringement case. There are several reasons for having dependent claims. It is possible that an independent claim may be found invalid in litigation. For a patent to be found completely invalid, one must prove that each patent claim is invalid. Therefore, it is quite possible for the independent claims of a patent to be found invalid, while many dependent claims are found valid.

In addition, there is a doctrine called *claim differentiation* which can often be used to actually broaden the interpretation of independent claims, through the use of a sophisticated dependent claim structure. As previously noted, a dependent claim must include each of the limitations of the claims from which it depends. As such, a dependent claim is narrower than its independent claim. The independent claim actually does not specifically require the limitation found in the dependent claim, and therefore must be interpreted to be broader in scope than the dependent claim.

A specific example of how claim differentiation impacts the interpretation of a claim may be helpful to the reader. Independent claim 1 of the Amazon patent recites the use of a single action to make a purchase. Dependent claim 3 further defines this single action as "the clicking of a button." Because dependent claim 3 lists a specific type of single action, the independent claim could actually encompass other types of single actions which could be found to infringe independent claim 1. For example, if an entity were to perform each of the actions recited in independent claim 1, including the "speaking of a sound" as a single action to make a purchase, such an action would likely infringe claim 1, but it would not infringe dependent claim 3. A defendant would find it quite difficult to argue that claim 1 is limited to "the clicking of a button" as the single action, since this specific action is listed in dependent claim 3 and is specifically not recited in independent claim 1. To make matters worse for this theoretical defendant, the single action of "speaking a sound" is also specifically recited in dependent claim 4. As such, this theoretical defendant would infringe independent claim 1 and dependent claim 4.

Type (Product, Process)

There are several different types of general claim formats, which can be generally broken down into two categories: product claims and process claims. Claim 1 of the Amazon patent is an example of a process claim. Claim 6 is an example of a product claim. As their respective titles suggest, a process claim is directed to a unique process, while a product claim is directed to a unique product. In many cases, the product claim is directed to a product which is made by the unique process claimed in the process claim. These are often called product-by-process claims. In other cases, the product claim is directed to a generic product which is specifically configured to perform a unique process.

Why are such claim formats important to the patent reader? It is not uncommon for a potential patent infringer to infringe more than one type of independent claim in a patent. It is therefore important for the patent reader to understand that such different claim formats exist, and must be considered when reviewing a third party's patent.

For example, a patent reader may note that they simply do not make, use, or sell a claimed product (as recited in a product claim), but nevertheless perform all of the functions of a claimed process in the patent. Remember: a third party need only infringe *one* independent claim of a patent to be liable for patent infringement.

Interpretation of Claims

In addition to the aforementioned claim interpretation issues, it is important to gain some additional understanding as to how specific claim language is interpreted under U.S. law. Patent applicants may create their own words and terms, and use these new words/terms in claim language. Many patent lawyers will repeat U.S.

law in this regard by noting, "A patentee can be their own lexicographer." If a patentee uses a special term in a claim, reference may be made to the patent specification to understand the scope and meaning of the special term. As such, limitations from the patent specification may be used to limit the scope of a special term in a claim. If, however, a patentee uses a term in a claim which has a plain and ordinary meaning, it is unnecessary to refer to the specification to determine the definition of the term. In such an instance, the specification would *not* limit the interpretation of the plain and ordinary term.

Why is this important? Many patent readers will read a claim and immediately begin interpreting various claim elements in view of the entire patent specification. This is often an incorrect way to interpret a patent claim. Many patent claim elements have ordinary meanings. As such, one cannot interpret that claim element to include extraneous limitations from the patent specification. For example, claim 1 of the Amazon patent refers to the purchase of an "item." Assume for the purposes of this discussion that the Amazon patent specification only described the purchase of books. Would the purchase of an "item" be limited to books? The claim does not specify the purchase of books. Also, an "item" has a plain and ordinary meaning. As such, independent claim 1 would therefore not be limited to the purchase of books.

Claim interpretations issues are often greatly contested in patent litigation. As such, these issues are often not particularly clear. Nevertheless, it is important for the patent reader to understand that the claims often cannot be limited by other portions of the patent, such as the title, abstract, and detailed description. A patent reader should not assume that the patent is limited to certain features in the specification, unless each of the independent claims recites that feature.

A Sample Claim Chart

Now that certain features of the Amazon patent have been reviewed, it may be helpful to the reader to review the following claim chart, which compares the claims of the Amazon patent to the activities of BarnesandNoble.com (see Exhibit 2-15). As the reader may know, the Amazon patent was asserted against BarnesandNoble.com. Although the matter is still in litigation at the time that this chapter is being prepared, the following claim analysis (regarding claims 1 to 5 and 11 to 22) was generally set forth by the U.S. Court of Appeals for the Federal Circuit in a decision dated February 14, 2001, and an earlier Federal District Court decision. Although the Appeals Court found that BarnesandNoble.com likely infringed the Amazon patent, the court required further litigation on the matter because of a number of questions[2] involving the validity of the Amazon patent. Whether the validity of the Amazon patent will be upheld remains to be seen.

As is evident from the claim chart, various claims of a patent may be infringed, while other claims are not infringed. One need only infringe one claim of a patent, however, to be liable for patent infringement.

Claims of Amazon's One-Click Patent (USP #5,960,411)	BarnesandNoble.Com's (BN) Original Express Lane System
1. A method of placing an order for an item comprising:	BN offered an Express Lane system which allowed customers who had registered for the Express Lane option to perform each of the claimed features.
under control of a client system,	
displaying information identifying the item; and	As noted by the Federal Appeals Court:
in response to only a single action being performed, sending a request to order the item along with an identifier of a purchaser of the item to a server system;	The BN system allowed users "to purchase items simply by 'clicking' on the 'Express Lane' button provided on the 'detail page' or 'product page' describing and identifying the book or other item to be purchased. The text beneath the Express Lane button invited users to 'Buy it now with just one click!'
under control of a single-action ordering component of the server system,	
receiving the request;	BN's allegedly infringing web site thus may be characterized as having 'page 1' (the 'menu' page), which displays a catalog listing several items but which does not contain an 'order' icon, and "page 2" (the 'product' or 'detail' page), which includes information on one item and also shows an order icon. Someone shopping at this web site would look at the catalog on page 1 and perform a first click to go to page 2. Once at page 2, a second click on the ordering icon would cause the order request to be sent. Under the claim construction set forth herein, BN likely infringes claim 1 because on page 2, the item is there displayed (meeting step 1 of the claim) and only a single action thereafter causes the order request to be transmitted (meeting step 2). The method implemented on page 1 of the BN web site does not infringe, but the method on page 2 does."
retrieving additional information previously stored for the purchaser identified by the identifier in the received request; and	
generating an order to purchase the requested item for the purchaser identified by the identifier in the received request using the retrieved additional information; and	
fulfilling the generated order to complete purchase of the item;	
whereby the item is ordered without using a shopping-cart ordering model.	
	Amazon.com, Inc. v. *BarnesandNoble.com, Inc,* Slip.Op. 00-1109, (Fed. Cir. February 14, 2001).

Exhibit 2-15 Claim chart example.

Claims of Amazon's One-Click Patent (USP #5,960,411)	BarnesandNoble.Com's (BN) Original Express Lane System
2. The method of claim 1, wherein the displaying of information includes displaying information indicating the single action.	BN site also performed the displaying of information indicating the single action.
3. The method of claim 1, wherein the single action is clicking a button.	The single action was the clicking of a button.
4. The method of claim 1, wherein the single action is speaking of a sound.	No such action performed (claim not infringed).
5. The method of claim 1, wherein a user of the client system does not need to explicitly identify themselves when placing an order.	BN site apparently allowed a user to not explicitly identify themselves.
11. A method for ordering an item using a client system, the method comprising: displaying information identifying the item and displaying an indication of a single action that is to be performed to order the identified item; and in response to only the indicated single action being performed, sending to a server system a request to order the identified item; whereby the item is ordered independently of a shopping cart model and the order is fulfilled to complete a purchase of the item.	As noted with respect to claim 1, BN operated a site which allowed the ordering of an item using a client system, whereby: information was displayed to identify the item and display an indication of a single action (Express Lane checkout) to order the identified item; in response to the selection of a single action (Express Lane checkout), a request was sent to BN's server system to order the identified item; whereby the item was ordered independently of a shopping cart model and the order was fulfilled to complete the purchase of the item.
12. The method of claim 11, wherein the server system uses an identifier sent along with the request to identify additional information needed to generate an order for the item.	BN's system used an identifier sent along with the request to identify various information needed to generate the order.
13. The method of claim 12, wherein the identifier identifies the client system and the server system provides the identifier to the client system.	Not found in the BN system (claim not infringed).

Exhibit 2-15 *(continued)*

Claims of Amazon's One-Click Patent (USP #5,960,411)	BarnesandNoble.Com's (BN) Original Express Lane System
14. The method of claim 11, wherein the client system and server system communicate via the Internet.	BN used the Internet to facilitate communication between the client system and the server system.
15. The method of claim 11, wherein the displaying includes displaying an HTML document provided by the server system.	BN used an HTML document in the displaying process.
16. The method of claim 11, including sending from the server system to the client system a confirmation that the order was generated.	BN sent a confirmation to the client system to confirm the order was delivered.
17. The method of claim 11, wherein the single action is clicking a mouse button when a cursor is positioned over a predefined area of the displayed information.	BN used such a system where the single action was the clicking of a mouse button when a cursor is positioned over displayed information.
18. The method of claim 11, wherein the single action is a sound generated by a user.	BN's system did not include such an action (claim not infringed).
19. The method of claim 11, wherein the single action is selection using a television remote control.	BN's system did not include such an action (claim not infringed).
20. The method of claim 11, wherein the single action is depressing of a key on a key pad.	BN's system did not include such an action (claim not infringed).
21. The method of claim 11, wherein the single action is selecting using a pointing device.	BN's system involved the use of a cursor/ mouse as a pointing device.
22. The method of claim 11, wherein the single action is selection of a displayed indication.	BN's system involved the selection of a displayed indication of the Express Lane checkout option.

Exhibit 2-15 (*continued*)

Now that certain features of the Amazon patent have been reviewed, it may prove helpful to review several additional issues to assist the reader in understanding how to read (and interpret) other patents.

Another Sample Patent

Although the Amazon patent is an excellent example of an e-commerce patent, or a so-called business process patent, there are many other types of patentable subject matter which are directed to different technologies. For example, patents directed to mechanical inventions can often have highly complex mechanical components. Electrical patents often claim and depict sophisticated electronic circuitry. Biotech patents often contain lengthy sequence listings. While the general criteria for issuing patents in any technology does not differ (an invention must be novel and nonobvious to qualify for patent protection in any technology), the presentation and interpretation of such different patents may differ greatly.

Although it is somewhat beyond the scope of the present chapter to present and discuss examples of patents in each of these technologies, the sample mechanical patent in Exhibit 2-16 should give the reader a flavor of some of the differences among such patents.

As the reader will note, mechanical patent claims can often be significantly more complex than process patent claims (such as those found in the Amazon patent). However, a step-by-step review of this claim should reveal to the reader that even a highly complex patent claim can be read by the nonpatent lawyer. To really understand the scope and content of such a claim (particularly if one is ever threatened with a patent infringement situation), one must consult with patent counsel.[3]

The File History

The file history is made up of a series of documents including those documents the patent applicant filed, and those documents the USPTO forwarded to the patent applicant (or his or her representative). Documents filed by the applicant include the patent application, any amendments, fee transmittal documents, and the like. Documents the USPTO forwards include official filing receipts, official actions (rejections of the application), notices of allowance, and the like.

Although the file history is not currently available on-line, it can be obtained from the USPTO once the patent is issued. As of March 2001, U.S. patent applications which are also filed in a foreign country will be published in the United States 18 months from filing. Such published patent applications will have their file history also made available to the public.

United States Patent [19]

Lindgren et al.

[11] E Patent Number: Re. 34,056

[45] Reissued Date of Patent: Sep. 8, 1992

US00RE34056E

[54] **TISSUE SAMPLING DEVICE**

[75] Inventors: **Per G. Lindgren; Dan Akerfeldt,** both of Upsala, Sweden

[73] Assignee: **C.R. Bard, Inc.,** Murray Hill, N.J.

[21] Appl. No.: **695,451**

[22] Filed: . **May 3, 1991**

Related U.S. Patent Documents

Reissue of:
[64] Patent No.: **4,699,154**
Issued: **Oct. 13, 1987**
Appl. No.: **890,543**
Filed: **Jul. 30, 1986**

U.S. Applications:
[63] Continuation of Ser. No. 387,864, Jul. 31, 1989, abandoned.

[51] Int. Cl.⁵ **A61B 10/00**
[52] U.S. Cl. **128/754**
[58] Field of Search 128/749, 751–754

[56] **References Cited**

U.S. PATENT DOCUMENTS

4,476,864	10/1984	Tezel	128/755
4,570,632	2/1986	Woods	128/751
4,600,014	7/1986	Beraha	128/754

FOREIGN PATENT DOCUMENTS

0010321	4/1980	European Pat. Off.	128/754
0141108	4/1980	Fed. Rep. of Germany	128/754
SE83/00112	3/1983	PCT Int'l Appl. .	
175611	3/1966	U.S.S.R.	128/754

Primary Examiner—Max Hindenburg
Attorney, Agent, or Firm—Jones, Askew & Lunsford

[57] **ABSTRACT**

A device for tissue sampling by thick needle punctuation including a needle assembly including a hollow first needle and second needle extending through the hollow first needle. The needle assembly is contained in a housing having an opening through which the needles extend. Compressed springs in the housing are caused to expand to urge the needles away from the housing during the sampling of tissue. A rod is provided extending from the housing to simultaneously place the springs in a compressed condition.

23 Claims, 2 Drawing Sheets

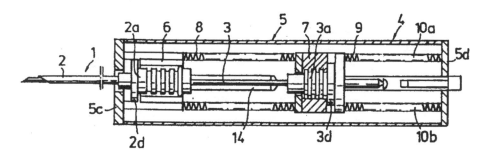

Exhibit 2-16 Sample mechanical patent.

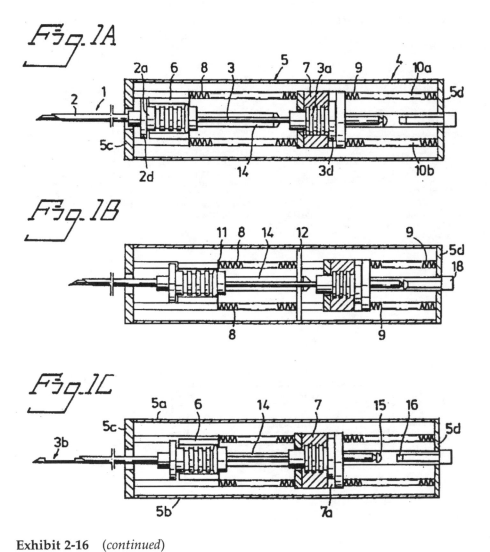

Fig. 1A

Fig. 1B

Fig. 1C

Exhibit 2-16 (*continued*)

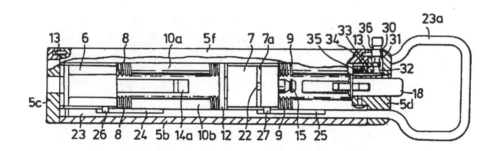

Fig. 2

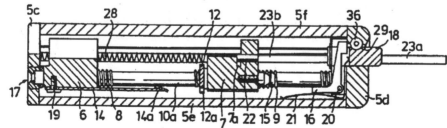

Fig. 3

Exhibit 2-16   *(continued)*

Sample claim from US Patent No. Re. 34 056

1. A tissue sampling device comprising:

a housing having a longitudinal axis extending from a first housing end to a second housing end, said first housing end having a first opening and said second housing end having a second opening;

a hollow first needle positioned within said housing and extendable from said first opening, said hollow first needle being moveable along said axis;

a second needle extending through said hollow first needle and moveable along said axis, said second needle having a pointed end which is extendable from said hollow first needle and said first opening, and including a tissue sample receiving recess;

a first slide coupled to said hollow first needle and positioned within said housing for movement along said axis to thereby move said hollow first needle along said axis;

a second slide coupled to said second needle and positioned within said housing for movement along said axis to thereby move said second needle along said axis;

first power means positioned within said housing in contact with said second slide for storing energy in a compressed mode and releasing energy in an expanded mode, said first power means being expandable to urge said second slide along said axis towards said first opening causing said pointed end to be extended from said hollow first needle so that a tissue sample can be captured within said recess;

second power means positioned within said housing in contact with said first slide for storing energy in a compressed mode and releasing energy in a expanded mode, said second power means being expandable to urge said first slide along said axis towards said first opening causing said hollow first needle to be extended from said first opening so that said recess of said second needle is enclosed by said hollow first needle;

a first latch means positioned within said housing and extending out of said second opening for releasably holding said first power means in said compressed mode;

a second latch means positioned within said housing for releasably holding said second power means in said compressed mode and being releasable in response to and subsequent to release of said first power means; and,

energizing means extending through said second housing end into said housing and being operably coupled to said first slide and said second slide and moveable along said axis for moving said first slide and said second slide along said axis towards said second housing end for simultaneously causing said first latch means to hold said first power means in said compressed mode and said second latch means to hold said second power means in said compressed mode.

Exhibit 2-16   (*continued*)

When is it necessary to review the file history? Once an initial review of a patent reveals a potential interest in the patented subject matter, patent attorneys will routinely order a copy of the file history (a process that could take several days or several weeks) to further study the scope and content of the patent. The patent applicant's arguments and the USPTO rejections can have a profound impact on the scope of a patent. Under a doctrine called "File Wrapper Estoppel," or "Prosecution History Estoppel," a patent cannot encompass subject matter which was specifically given away in arguments before the USPTO. For example, if a patent applicant argued that the invention was directed to X and *not* Y, the patent cannot be later interpreted to include Y.

If a patent reader believes that they may be interested in certain subject matter (perhaps because they may infringe the patent or because they may be interested in licensing the patent), the reader should then consult with patent counsel to undertake a full review of the patent and its file history.

TYPES OF PATENTS

Utility, Design, Plant

In general, there are three types of patents: utility, design, and plant patents. Utility patents are generally directed to inventions with new and nonobvious structural or functional features. Design patents are directed to the ornamental appearance of an original design. Plant patents are directed to distinct and new varieties of plants which are asexually reproduced.

The vast majority of issued U.S. patents are utility patents. To date, over 6 million U.S. utility patents have been issued. As such, a utility patent can easily be recognized by the seven-digit U.S. patent number, such as Amazon's U.S. patent number 5,960,411.

A design patent is easily recognizable by its patent number, which always begins with the letters "Des." An example of a design patent is provided in Exhibit 2-17.

A plant patent is easily recognizable by the leading letters "PP" in its patent number. A sample plant patent is provided in Exhibit 2-18.

Reissue, Reexam

After the issuance of a U.S. patent, the patent applicant may seek to have the USPTO reissue or reexamine the patent to cure possible defects in the patent. For example, a patent applicant may seek to amend the claims of an issued patent to clear up vague and indefinite language in the patent claims. In addition, the patent applicant may have learned of additional information regarding the patented in-

United States Patent [19]

Akerfeldt

[11] Patent Number: **Des. 306,070**

[45] Date of Patent: ∗∗ **Feb. 13, 1990**

[54] **NEEDLE HEAD FOR BIOPSY CANNULA**

[75] Inventor: **Dan Åkerfeldt,** Uppsala, Sweden

[73] Assignee: **C. R. Bard, Inc.,** Murray Hill, N.J.

[∗∗] Term: **14 Years**

[21] Appl. No.: **28,322**

[22] Filed: **Mar. 20, 1987**

[52] U.S. Cl. **D24/25**

[58] Field of Search D24/24, 25; 128/754, 128/751

[56]   **References Cited**

U.S. PATENT DOCUMENTS

1,867,624	7/1932	Hoffman	128/754
3,175,554	3/1965	Stewart	128/754
3,995,619	12/1976	Glatzer .	
4,178,810	12/1979	Takahashi .	
4,476,864	10/1984	Tezel	128/755
4,570,632	2/1986	Woods	128/751
4,600,014	7/1986	Beraha	128/754
4,609,370	9/1986	Morrison	128/754 X
4,685,904	8/1987	Krebs	128/754 X
4,702,261	10/1987	Cornell et al. .	
4,735,215	4/1988	Goto et al. .	
4,766,907	8/1988	de Groot et al. .	
4,776,346	10/1988	Beraha et al. .	

FOREIGN PATENT DOCUMENTS

0010321	4/1980	European Pat. Off.	128/754
0141108	4/1980	Fed. Rep. of Germany	128/754
175611	3/1966	U.S.S.R.	128/754

Primary Examiner—A. Hugo Word
Assistant Examiner—Stella M. Reid
Attorney, Agent, or Firm—Jones, Askew & Lunsford

[57]   **CLAIM**

The ornamental design for a needle head for biopsy cannula, as shown and described.

DESCRIPTION

FIG. 1 is a top perspective view of a needle head for biopsy cannula, showing my new design;
FIG. 2 is a bottom perspective view thereof; and
FIG. 3 is an elevational view of the end opposite that shown in FIGS. 1 and 2.
The broken line showing of the cannula in FIGS. 1 and 2 is for illustrative purposes only and forms no part of the claimed design.

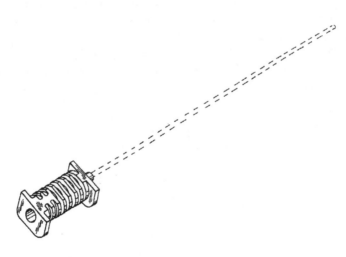

Exhibit 2-17   Sample design patent.

US00PP11807P2

(12) **United States Plant Patent**

Lyrene

(10) **Patent No.:** **US PP11,807 P2**
(45) **Date of Patent:** **Mar. 13, 2001**

(54) BLUEBERRY PLANT NAMED 'JEWEL'

(76) Inventor: **Paul M. Lyrene**, 2211 NW. 58 Ter., Gainesville, FL (US) 32605

(*) Notice: Subject to any disclaimer, the term of this patent is extended or adjusted under 35 U.S.C. 154(b) by 0 days.

(21) Appl. No.: **09/175,101**

(22) Filed: **Oct. 19, 1998**

(51) Int. Cl.[7] A01H 5/00
(52) U.S. Cl. Plt./157
(58) Field of Search Plt./157

(56) **References Cited**

U.S. PATENT DOCUMENTS

P.P. 11,033 * 8/1999 Lyrene Plt./157

* cited by examiner

Primary Examiner—Bruce R. Campell
Assistant Examiner—Wendy Anne Baker

(57) **ABSTRACT**

A new and distinct low-chill tetraploid highbush blueberry (Vacinnium) variety of complex ancestry, based largely on *V.* *corymbosum* L with some genes from *V. darrowi* Camp. Its novelty consists of the following unique combination of features:

1. Produces a bush that is upright, but somewhat spreading.
2. Has a medium level of resistance to cane canker (*Botryosphaeria corticis*), stem blight (*Botryosphaeria dothidia*), and root rot (*Phytophthora cinnamomi*).
3. Flowers very early in north central Florida (Gainesville). Date of full bloom in Gainesville averages about February 10, seven days before 'Sharpblue' (an unpatented variety that is widely grown in Florida).
4. Produces numerous flower buds and flowers heavily and synchronously in areas that receive 250 hours or more of temperatures below 45° F. per winter.
5. Ripens 5–7 days earlier than 'Sharpblue'. First commercial harvest averages April 15 in Gainesville, Fla., and peak harvest is about April 25.
6. Produces fruit that are large, firm, have a good picking scar, with tart to sweet flavor and good texture.
7. Can be propagated asexually by softwood cuttings.

3 Drawing Sheets

1

ORIGIN OF THE VARIETY

'Jewel' was selected as a seedling from a cross made in Gainesville in 1988. The parents were advanced-generation selections from a recurrent selection program in which the large fruit size, high fruit quality, and short flowering-to-ripening interval of northern highbush cultivars from Michigan and New Jersey were being combined with the low chill requirement, summer heat tolerance, and other southern adaptation features of the native Florida species, *Vaccinium darrowi*. 'Jewel' was selected as a seedling in a high-density nursery in May 1990 and as a spaced plant in the second-evaluation plots in May 1992. The principal selection criteria were large fruit, high fruit quality, early ripening, and strong, leafy bush. Cuttings were taken in the summer of 1992 to establish an 8-plant plot at the University of Florida Horticultural Unit in Gainesville. These ramets were planted in the field in January 1994 and were observed annually during the flowering and fruiting seasons from 1995 through 1998. A 20-plant plot of 'Jewel' was established at Windsor in north-central Florida in January 1997 and was observed during the fruiting seasons of 1997 and 1998. Twenty plants of 'Jewel' were grown in pots of peat in a greenhouse in Gainesville and assessed for the ability to set fruit with self-pollination. 'Jewel' was selected after comparison with many other test selections because of its low chilling requirement, heavy flowering, and high fruit quality.

ASEXUAL PROPAGATION OF THE VARIETY

'Jewel' has been propagated by softwood cuttings on numerous occasions in Gainesville, Fla. (Alachua County).

2

In every case, all resulting plants have displayed the characteristics of the variety.

BRIEF DESCRIPTION OF THE FIGURES OF THE DRAWING

The first drawing shows a 4-year-old plant of 'Jewel' revealing the upper and lower surfaces of the leaves and the clusters of ripening fruit.

The second drawing shows, in larger scale, clusters of opened and unopened flowers of 'Jewel' indicating the color of the calyx and corolla, the shape of the corolla tubes, and the clustering habit of the flowers in the inflorescence.

The third drawing shows, in large scale, the ripe fruit of 'Jewel', indicating the color and shape of the berry and the shape of the calyx lobes.

DESCRIPTION OF THE VARIETY

The following is a detailed botanical description of 'Jewel', its flowers, fruit and foliage, based on observation of specimens grown in the field in Gainesville, Fla. Color descriptions, except those given in common terms, use terminology from "The Pantone Book of Color" by Leatrice Eiseman and Lawrence Herbert; Harry N. Abrams, Inc. Publishers, New York. While the coloration shown in the photographic illustrations provided is as close as is reasonably possible to attain in an illustration of this character, the color designations provided in the specification should be considered to be the closest possible representation of the coloration of the instant plant.

Exhibit 2-18 Sample plant patent.

3

Bush: Bush size of 4-year old plants grown in medium quality blueberry soil, with irrigation, pine-bark mulch, and annual summer pruning:

Plant height.—100 cm.

Canopy diameter.—105 cm.

Vigor.—Medium.

Growth habit.—Semi-upright, somewhat spreading.

Flower bud density (number per unit length of stem).—Very high.

Cold hardiness.—Except for the flower and the fruit, some of which have been killed in some years in Gainesville, by freezes in February and March, 'Jewel' has not suffered freeze damage to the bush in Gainesville. Dormant plants have withstood temperatures of 18° F. without damage.

Chilling requirement.—Based on the time and completeness of vegetative and flower bud break in Sebring, Fla., 'Jewel' appears to have a chilling requirement of about 250 hours below 45° F. after the plants have become winter dormant.

Productivity.—Four-year-old plants on medium-good soil in Gainesville have averaged 3 to 4 pounds of fruit per plant per year.

Suckering tendency.—After 4 years in the field, plants have 6 to 10 major trunks.

Color of 2-year-old wood.—"Pelican", Pantone 14-6305.

Color of trunks 4 years old and older.—"Champagne Beige" Pantone 14-012.

Twigs:

Color of previous summer twigs observed January 30.—"Moth" Pantone 13-0611.

Internode length.—1.2 cm on strong upright shoots.

Leaves:

Leaf length excluding petiole.—60 mm.

Leaf width.—35 mm.

Shape.—Obovate.

Margin.—Entire.

Color of upper surface.—"Four leaf clover" Pantone 18-0420.

Color of lower surface.—"Sage" Pantone 16-0421.

Pubescence, upper surface.—Numerous short, white hairs on midribs and main veins.

Pubescence, lower surface.—Essentially glabrous.

Pubescence, leaf margins.—Essentially glabrous.

Synchrony of leafing and flowering.—New leaves begin to form at the time of or shortly after flowering.

Flowers:

Length, pedicel attachment point to the corolla tip.—11.0 mm.

Diameter of corolla tube at widest point.—8.0 mm.

Corolla aperture diameter.—3.2 mm.

Corolla color at anthesis.—"Pearl" Pantone 12-1304.

Flower fragrance.—None.

Pollen abundance.—High.

Pollen staining with acetocarmine dye.—Excellent, near 100%. This indicates that nearly all of the pollen

grains are well developed and starch filled. Aborted pollen grains will not stain with the procedure used. Because southern highbush blueberries are derived from interspecific hybrids, many clones have reduced pollen fertility. This reduced fertility is indicated by lower percentage of stainable pollen grains. The percentage of stainable pollen varies widely from clone to clone, but is relatively constant within clones. This makes it a useful cultivar descriptor.

Flowering period.—Full bloom averages February 10 in Gainesville.

Flower cluster.—Medium to open.

Average number of flowers per cluster.—5–6. Stamens and pistil are typical for highbush blueberry.

Self-compatibility.—Partially self-compatible but must be cross-pollinated for full fruit size and number.

Berry:

Weight.—First berries to ripen average 1.7 to 2.5 g.

Calyx lobes.—Irregular and not well developed.

Berry height.—14 mm.

Berry width.—15 mm.

Diameter of calyx aperture on mature berry.—6 mm.

Exterior berry color.—"Dapple gray" Pantone 16-3907.

Exterior berry color with surface wax removed.—"Slate Black", Pantone 19-0814.

Interior berry flesh color.—"Frozen Dew" Pantone 13-0513, which is a whitish-green.

Color of washed, dried seeds.—"Almond", Pantone 16-1432, a shade of brown.

Surface wax.—Medium persistent.

Pedicel scar.—Small and dry.

Berry firmness.—Medium to high.

Berry flavor.—Sweet to tart.

Berry fragrance.—None.

Berry texture.—Good: thin skins, small seeds, inconspicuous scleroids.

Resistance to rain cracking.—Moderately resistant but will crack if wet for over 24 hours.

Intended market class.—Fresh fruit.

Maturity date.—First pick averages April 15 in Gainesville. Peak harvest about April 25.

Diseases, insects, and mites:

Cane canker.—Partially resistant.

Dieback due to stem blight and root rot.—Moderately resistant.

Leaf spots.—Medium resistant.

Bud mites.—Resistant.

Ease of propagation: Roots readily from softwood cuttings.

We claim:

1. A new and distinct southern highbush blueberry variety as illustrated and described, characterized by a low chilling requirement and early season ripening, which produces large fruit of high fresh-market quality.

* * * * *

Exhibit 2-18 *(continued)*

vention (such as the existence of additional prior art) which may warrant consideration by the USPTO. A third party may also ask the USPTO to reexamine a patent based on previously unconsidered prior art information.

   In response to such requests for the reissance or reexamination of a U.S. patent, the USPTO may grant a Reissued U.S. patent or a Reexamination certificate. A reissue patent is easily recognizable by the leading letters "Re" in the patent number or the "Reissue" designation before the issue date. A reexamination certificate is aptly titled "Reexamination Certificate."

Divisional, Continuation, and Continuation-in-Part Applications

An original application may often contain several distinct inventions. If so, the USPTO may require the patent applicant to separate the distinct inventions into several cases. Such cases are called divisional applications. Divisional applications are often simple photocopies of the original application, with an amendment to cancel all claims not directed to the invention which the applicant elected to maintain in that application. No new disclosure materials (new inventions, new components or features of an invention, etc.) can be added to a divisional application. Divisional applications are given the same effective filing date as the original application.

   A continuation application also typically takes the form of a photocopy of the original application, and is given the same effective filing date as the original application. A continuation application also cannot contain any new disclosure materials. As its names implies, a continuation application is often filed to continue the patent prosecution process. For example, a continuation application is typically filed after an indication of allowability of one or more claims in the original application, and the patent applicant wishes to pursue allowance of certain patent claims in a separate application. For example, a patent examiner may reject certain claims in an original application, and indicate that other claims are allowable. The patent applicant may elect to limit the original application to the allowed claims (thereby obtaining a first patent), and pursue allowance of the rejected claims in a continuation application.

   A continuation-in-part (CIP) application is similar to a continuation application. A very important distinction is that the CIP application may contain new disclosure materials or "new matter." Any patent claim in the CIP which contains such new matter is entitled only to the actual filing date of the CIP. Any claim in the CIP which is supported by the disclosure of the original application is entitled to the original application's filing date.

The cover page of the application will contain information regarding whether a particular application is entitled to any filing dates of a possible parent application.

Provisional and Nonprovisional Patent Applications

Within the subset of utility applications, two additional types of applications are permitted. A nonprovisional application is an application which contains each of the aforementioned sections of field of the invention, background, summary, detailed description, claims, and drawings. Effective in 1995, the USPTO began accepting so-called provisional applications, which require no patent claims and can be filed for a substantially discounted fee. Within one year of the filing of a provisional application, a nonprovisional application containing patent claims directed to the subject matter of the provisional must be filed. If filed within the one-year period, the claims of the nonprovisional application will be given an effective filing date equal to the filing date of the provisional application (if supported by provisional).

Provisional patent applications are never published by the USPTO, and will go abandoned one year after filing unless converted into a nonprovisional application by the one-year deadline. Also, provisional applications cannot be amended to contain additional subject matter. It is possible, however, to file several provisional applications within one year and file a nonprovisional application (within one year of the first provisional application) directed to the subject matter of all the provisional applications.

If a patent claims priority to such a provisional application, such information will also be printed on the face of the patent. In order to obtain a copy of the provisional application, a patent reader would need to obtain a copy of the file history of the issued patent. To determine whether an issued patent claim is entitled to the filing date of a provisional application, it would be necessary to obtain such a copy of the file history. If a patent relies upon an insufficient, defective, or improperly filed provisional application, that patent may be invalid. Unfortunately, the patent reader cannot make an assessment regarding the substantiality of the provisional patent application from a simple reading of the patent. If there is an interest in determining the scope of a provisional application, this is a strong signal for the reader to contact patent counsel to further investigate the validity of the patent.

HOW TO EVALUATE STRENGTHS AND WEAKNESSES OF A PATENT

Now that one has a better understanding of the different parts and types of a patent, let us turn to various signs of strength and weakness that a relatively quick review of a patent can reveal. While it is often difficult to generalize about patent documents, the following checklist of possible strengths and weaknesses of a patent may prove helpful to the patent reader who is not a patent lawyer. A further explanation follows the lists.

PATENT CHECKLIST

Possible Signs of Strength

- Use of different independent claims formats of varying scope (from broad to narrow)
- Use of many nested dependent claims
- Discussion of many embodiments in the body of an application
- Old filing date
- Detailed and lengthy prior art section
- Lengthy search classification
- Series of patents clustered around a particular technology/product

Possible Signs of Weakness

- Very few claims
- Contains only long independent claims
- Contains only short independent claims
- Very brief detailed description
- Relatively recent filing date

With regard to possible strengths of a patent, many of the aforementioned bullet points are directed to the number and scope of the patent claims. A large number of independent and dependent claims may point to a careful process of drafting and obtaining the patent document. The large number of patent claims may also support various claim differentiation arguments, which could assist the patent owner in maintaining a relatively expansive and powerful patent position.

The discussion of many different embodiments of an invention within the body of the patent may also provide support for a broad interpretation of the patent. It may also point to a careful and thorough patent drafting process.

With regard to filing date, it is generally more difficult to invalidate an older patent than a younger patent. In order to invalidate a patent, a party seeking to invalidate the patent must locate prior art information prior to the filing date of the patent.

With regard to the list of prior art information and search classification listed on the face of the patent, in general, a lengthier prior art section and a lengthy search classification would indicate that the patent examiner considered significant prior art information prior to granting the patent. If no (or little) prior art information is listed on the face of the patent, an entity seeking to invalidate the patent may be more likely to uncover prior art information which the patent examiner never considered, prior to issuing the patent. This additional information may be sufficiently persuasive (to a court or the patent office) so as to render the patent invalid.

A patent applicant wishing to protect certain technology or a certain product may file one or more patent applications directed to various features of the invention. In addition, such a patent applicant may file several continuation, divisional, and/or CIP applications so as to obtain maximum patent protection on the invention(s). The existence of a cluster of such patents would generally be a significant indication of strength of the patent portfolio.

With regard to potential weaknesses, the existence of a few claims may indicate that the patent applicant was not particularly careful or aggressive in seeking patent protection. In addition, lengthy independent claims may also be signs of weakness, simply because lengthy claims will typically contain limitations which a third party can easily design around (or avoid). Many short patent claims with few limitations may also be a sign of weakness, as such claims are more likely to be found invalid. Properly drafted patent applications will typically have a series of short (broad) independent claims and lengthy (narrow) independent claims so as to provide a good mix of claim coverage and scope.

A very brief detailed description may also be a sign of weakness for a number of reasons. First, a brief detailed description will typically have little discussion regarding alternative embodiments, and therefore may not support a broad claim interpretation. In addition, a brief detailed description may also highlight deficiencies in the patent applicant's ability to prove that he or she satisfied the requirements of the patent law in preparing the patent application. For a patent to be properly granted, the patent applicant must provide, among other things, a sufficient written description to enable one of ordinary skill in the art to recreate the invention without undue experimentation, and must set forth the best mode for carrying out the invention on the original patent application filing date. An entity seeking to invalidate a patent may be able to convince a court that these criteria were not satisfied, particularly if the patent applicant filed a weak and short detailed description.

CONCLUSION

Although patents may often be rather cryptic or esoteric, they should not be particularly intimidating to the nonpatent lawyer, such as an investor, banker, or manager. The next time you see a patent discussed in the press or in some business transaction, take a look at the patent (free on the USPTO's web site *www.uspto.gov*). You may be surprised how readable the patent may be, particularly in view of a few of the tips discussed in this chapter. If you suspect you or your company may be infringing a patent, it is very important for you to contact patent counsel. If you suspect that someone may be infringing your patent (or your company's patent), it is also very important for you to contact patent counsel for a thorough review of the situation. If, however, you are simply trying to get a sense of what a particular patent is directed to, a quick one-minute review of a patent may be all that you need. In the final analysis, patents may not be so mysterious after all.[4]

NOTES

1. There is a rare exception to this rule, under what patent attorneys refer to as the *Wilson Sporting Goods* case. Although a full discussion of this exception is beyond the scope of this chapter, the reader is strongly encouraged to consult with patent counsel in the event that the reader becomes aware of a patent which may be infringed by the reader or the reader's company.
2. Should Amazon's patent be found invalid by the courts, BarnesandNoble.com cannot be found liable for infringement. One cannot legally infringe an invalid patent. In addition, please note that BarnesandNoble.com's web site no longer performs in the manner discussed in the flowchart shown in Exhibit 2-15.
3. In fact, Patent Re. 34,056 was ultimately found invalid by the courts. A reader would not know that such a patent was held invalid unless (1) the reader consulted with patent counsel and/or (2) the reader conducted his or her own search regarding the litigation history of the patent.
4. Walter G. Hanchuk is a partner in the New York office of Morgan & Finnegan, LLP. The views expressed herein are solely those of the author, and are not to be attributed to Morgan & Finnegan, LLP. The author notes that the instant chapter is not intended to displace the use of patent counsel when evaluating a patent. In fact, the reader is strongly advised to consult with patent counsel to determine the scope and content of patents brought to the reader's attention.

ABOUT THE AUTHOR

Walter Hanchuk is a partner in the New York office of Morgan & Finnegan, LLP, one of the leading law firms working exclusively in intellectual property. Mr. Hanchuk's practice is focused on the procurement and enforcement of intellectual property rights for matters involving electronic commerce, computer software, and financial services. His clients have included priceline.com, Walker Digital Corporation, Jupiter Media Metrix, CyberSettle.com, Screamingmedia.com, Opencola, Inc., and other software and Internet companies. Mr. Hanchuk is a frequent lecturer on the topics of the patentability of inventions in computer software, e-commerce, and financial services. He currently serves as a member of the board of advisors of *The E-commerce Law Journal* and of the *Alley Way* (a publication of American Lawyer Media). Prior to joining Morgan & Finnegan, Mr. Hanchuk was an examiner at the U.S. Patent & Trademark Office. He received his law degree from the George Washington University Law School and his engineering degree from Cooper Union.

Morgan & Finnegan is one of the largest and most experienced law firms specializing in securing, protecting, and litigating intellectual property rights. For more than a century, the firm has represented a wide variety of clients in all aspects of intellectual property law including patents, trademarks, copyrights, trade secrets, unfair competition, and antitrust matters. Morgan & Finnegan has compiled a distinguished record in patent and other complex intellectual property litigation. Several of the patent cases litigated by the firm have achieved landmark status. The firm has more than 100 partners, associates, and PhD level scientific advisors, all of whom are devoted entirely to intellectual property matters.

CHAPTER THREE

Capturing Innovation
Turning Intellectual Assets into Business Assets

by Jeffrey L. Brandt

PERSPECTIVES

Idea creation, while important, is not the primary goal of building a commercially successful business. What companies of almost every type and size really need is a better process for turning innovation into monetizable business assets. Individual inventors and businesses that fail to understand the implications of the expanded range of available methods of doing business are courting danger. "The clueless entity will become a free development laboratory for its competitors," says Jeffrey L. Brandt, an intellectual property strategist and patent attorney.

Inventing is little more than a futures game, says Mr. Brandt, familiar to managers of commodities, securities, and other risk portfolios. Patents and other intellectual assets represent "call" options—purchased, highly leveraged future rights of ownership on innovation. (For more on patents as options, see Chapter 5 by Alexander K. Arrow, "Managing IP Financial Assets: Principles from the Securities Markets.") A patent is a bet on performance, whose risk can be mitigated by purchasing a prudent hedging device. A patent is effectively a futures contract. Market-driven inventing is a way of increasing the chances for success. In many instances, brilliant technologists must yield to— or at least learn to team with—marketers, legal strategists, and senior executives to reach meaningful objectives. Large companies need to perform a kind of early patent triage, devoting their attention and R&D dollars to those areas with the greatest likelihood of success. This requires a more interactive invention model, with focus and teamwork at the core, and market demand driving innovation, not core technology. Companies of most sizes and types can benefit from this approach. Those who have already adopted it include many large and traditional innovators.

TURNING INTELLECTUAL ASSETS INTO VALUABLE BUSINESS ASSETS

Do We Really Need More Good Ideas?

The world today is flooded with good ideas. Some come from large, mature, well-organized companies. Some come from basement start-ups. Many are innovative. Some are brilliant. Most die a lonely death, never seeing the light of commercial success.

Do we really need more good ideas? While important, idea creation should not be the only, or even the main, goal in the building of commercially successful businesses. What most organizations, large or small, mature or nascent, really need is a better organized process for turning innovation into real, monetizable business assets.

The lifeblood of essentially all companies today is their intellectual assets. In every company, those assets include the intellectual output of their employees. In traditional manufacturing environments, the assets may be heavily focused around technological developments and know-how. In service-oriented companies such assets may include innovative and often proprietary processes and procedures. For content-oriented companies, the intellectual assets are typically the output of the creative process and may include art, text, music, and other creative materials. Woe to the company that fails to recognize and protect its assets. At best, its competitors will legally "steal" its innovations. At worst, its competitors will obtain patents and other intellectual property protections that will bite strongly into the company's revenue or even put it out of business.

Given the current state of the law, intellectual assets, from mechanical devices to entirely new methods of doing business, can be owned by the savvy inventor. What does this mean as a practical matter? It means that the smartest entities, whether a sole inventor or a large corporation, can effectively own the conceptual developments of their organizations. The clueless entity will become a free development laboratory for its competitors.

INNOVATION AND INVENTION

Let us look first at the fundamental question that all companies struggle with in allocating limited resources to mine business opportunities from limitless research and development (R&D) efforts. While it has been phrased in a multitude of different ways by many different askers, it remains basically the same across all organizations: How can I spend my money and resources so that I *only* invest in valuable stuff? The equivalent patent dilemma is: How do I limit my patent application filings to *only* the commercially valuable inventions?

The short and simple answer is: You cannot! Inventions, by definition, are new and nonobvious. Patents and other intellectual assets represent call options: purchased, highly leveraged future rights of ownership in innovation. If you could see the future, you would only purchase options on inventions that would increase in value. Since none of us can see the future, we cannot bet only certain bets. We can, however, use methods that hedge success. To the extent that any of these methods can be considered to be secret, we will take the opportunity to look at them together.

While the information proposed by this chapter applies to all intellectual assets, copyrights, trademarks, patents, and trade secrets, patents represent far and away the most expensive and often the most valuable of assets for technology-based companies. Accordingly, much of the rest of this chapter will focus on patent-centric issues.

Stimulating and Protecting Pure Research

In typical industrial environments, innovation is driven by the day-to-day work of the companies; that is, the ongoing research, development, and manufacturing of the organization provide the sole sources of innovative ideas and inventions. This is not bad. It is simply the way things work.

In most mature organizations, the majority of inventive concepts arise from the research laboratories, the corporate arm tasked with developing the technologies and processes of the future. Such R&D facilities typically provide focus in two overlapping areas: basic research and development in areas of interest to the corporation, and structured research and development pursued specifically to enhance the current product set. It certainly is important to protect the core product technologies and processes of an organization. It is also important to protect some percentage of basic research, in which significant resources may be invested.

Since, as described above, inventing is in large part a futures game, it stands to reason that the earlier in the process one identifies and protects innovation, the greater the uncertainty of the outcome and the value of that innovation and protection. However, a good hit may have a very high commercial value. Said another way, the earlier in the inventive process one begins identifying and protecting inventions: (1) the greater the number of wrong guesses will be, and (2) the more value a winning invention and patent will have. Notice the built-in tension; early protection of basic research results in more failed inventions, failure being defined as the lack of commercial value. But at the same time, early innovations typically encompass more fundamental innovations, which, if competitors subsequently adopt them, can yield significant commercial value.

With reference to Exhibit 3-1, a graphical illustration of intellectual asset development against research and product development, it is readily seen that early and forward-looking innovation, of the type typical of a research laboratory, is very much divorced from actual products, services, or commercialization. The secret to success in this environment? First, hire good researchers! Create an environment in which they can "play" within the boundaries of their skills and interests.

During the 1980s, certain world-class research and development laboratories morphed, mercilessly, from a pure R&D environment to a highly controlled, profit-driven development environment. The result was carnage. World-class scientists became lost in a world they did not know, or understand, or even like. Frantic efforts were made to monetize technologies either completely unfit or unready to see the commercial light of day. Great research was forever shut down and the commercial efforts never did succeed. Eventually, these laboratories drifted back

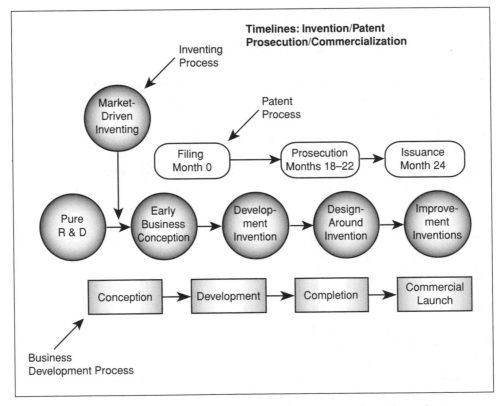

Exhibit 3-1   Intellectual asset development versus research and product development.

toward their original research direction, but with a loss of talent and infrastructure from which they may take years to recover. This is a graphic lesson in hiring the right people to do the right job.

Subsequent to developing appropriate staffing and infrastructure, protecting basic research and development is a lesson in risk modeling with a statistical likelihood of success. Thus, innovations should be protected on a mathematical basis. The higher the level of protection, typically measured in number of patents per million dollars of R&D investment, the greater the likelihood of obtaining success on a protected, commercially valuable invention.

Stimulating and Protecting Commercial Development

At the other end of the spectrum, the farther along the development path that an innovative concept is identified, the more likely it is to be used commercially. However, it will also be apparent that inventions identified in the late stages of development tend to be narrow, more focused, and possessed of diminished commercial value. Wary competitors can often design around them.

How to play to win here? As above, hire development personalities, then build a structured, controlled development environment. Just as pure research personalities do not prosper in a development environment, development people do not prosper in a research environment. They need the boundaries, controls, and structure that they are comfortable with.

Since the process is much closer to commercialization, in addition to statistics, intellect and careful selection can identify the inventions most likely to recognize commercial success. Such selection is often the charge of an invention disclosure evaluation team, some of whom are discussed in more detail below. The important thing to remember here is that the closer the proximity to actual commercial use, the easier it becomes to judge the commercial value of innovation. Thus, monies and resources spent on making smart decisions do amount in fact to more than just buying a crystal ball. Good invention review and analysis can help identify the best inventions in a later stage, commercial environment. Just remember that while the likelihood of success (identifing valuable inventions to protect) becomes more predictable, the ultimate value of those inventions concomitantly decreases. End-stage inventions, while of some importance, typically do not carry the value of a highly speculative early hit.

A New Type of R&D: Market Pull Versus Research Push

The obvious question is: Can the difference be split? Is there any way to identify and capture a higher percentage of commercially valuable innovations earlier in the research and development process?

There is at least one method of hedging to improve the success of the patent process. When simply stated, the advice sounds trite. If truly understood and practiced, however, the results can significantly improve the value of the patent process. Invent to solve the right problem!

The right problem to solve is not necessarily how to make the next generation of research laboratory technology; nor the next quantum improvement in speed, size, or performance. Researchers often focus fixedly on just these types of problems, problems which may be fixedly divorced from the commercial needs of the marketplace.

Neither is the right problem how to screw together the final product. Development and manufacturing may consider this important to a product launch, but competitors can often perform the same functions in many different manners. More particularly, your competitors will find ways to do final development in ways that are commercially competitive but avoid infringement of your intellectual property.

The right problem is the forward-thinking problem customers and marketers in your field of interest anticipate! The concept is simple. Your marketers and customers are by definition the holy grail of commercial value. They recognize what the market lacks and what it will pay value to have. They often identify these needs early in the business cycle, though perhaps not quite so early as may occur by random chance in a pure research environment.

In practice, this means that at least some percentage of inventive resource should be pulled from the organization by marketers and customers. This may be accomplished, for example, by inventing sessions driven by marketers and entrepreneurs.

The general concept is illustrated in Exhibit 3-2. In the "technology push" series of concentric circles on the left, technology enablers or researchers drive innovations outward through the organization and eventually into products. In the "marketing pull" series of concentric circles on the right, marketers or others closely tied to the commercial market pull innovation out through the organization and into the marketplace. Because the marketers' inventing is smart, the likelihood of success in terms of significant hits increases. This means that commercially valuable inventions are easier to identify and protect at earlier stages in the research-development-product launch cycle.

During the middle 1990s, several small, market-driven development laboratories were in operation. Bright, commercially knowledgeable people were tasked with inventing the future. Not a random future, but a future in which the problems that plagued their various industries were squarely addressed and solved. Extraordinary, valuable solutions were developed on an almost daily basis. Because the staffs were knowledgeable in their various industries, many of the innovations were successfully patented. The aura was intoxicating. For various reasons that cannot be identified here, the ultimate success of these businesses is still a matter to be determined. However, the research and intellectual asset protection processes were both successful and replicable by bright, motivated people.

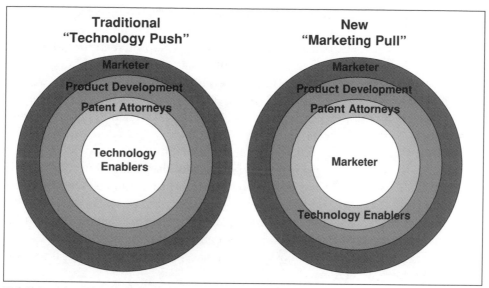

Exhibit 3-2   The invention process.

Don't Forget to Design Around: Head 'Em Off at the Pass!

In addition to the various R&D efforts and protection strategies discussed above, it pays to devote some resources to your competitive environment; more specifically, to determining how your competitors might design around your own protected ideas and how you might file patents or obtain other protections on these design-arounds. While a somewhat speculative process, patent protection on both your own products and your competitor's alternate paths can be a devastatingly powerful position.

Design-around is typically a task associated with late-stage development or even a commercially available product or service. Time is spent determining how your competition might solve the same problem and provide the same products or services, without infringing on your intellectual property. Then, to the extent that the solution can be protected, you do so.

Again, this process is somewhat speculative and requires a commitment of resources that is somewhat based in faith, a faith that not only can your company develop one commercially competitive product, but that it can also anticipate and obtain ownership rights in alternate paths that your competitors might pursue.

Hits in these areas can be extraordinarily valuable as well as devastating to competitors. Remember, what is being proposed here is not a methodology for improvements to existing products but a preemptive strike against similar, but not identical, competitive products. It involves conceptualizing and protecting, or owning, those products before your competitor does.

The Ideal Intellectual Asset Development Environment

What then constitutes the ideal intellectual asset development environment? For a large, diverse entity, the ideal environment constitutes the correct mix of all of the above. Such a mix is shown in Exhibit 3-1. Early, pure research and development is critical to the health and well-being of any prospering entity, and appropriate protections and patent filings should be based on statistical coverage sufficient to hedge all future bets.

Market pull research and development is ideally focused in core product areas where the company has both the expertise and vision to perform the process successfully. Inventions here may be less numerous but are more easily quantifiable as to value.

Development areas should have regular processes for collecting, evaluating, and protecting the most significant of development innovations. Wise review will identify inventions having the most potential and resources can be appropriately invested in their protection.

Finally, the really savvy entity will devote a small, parallel effort to design-around patents concomitant with all product developments and launches.

Stimulating and Rewarding Invention

How do the best-of-breed companies operate to stimulate and reward invention? In best-of-breed companies, including both large and small manufacturing and service institutions, the documenting and development of innovations is inherent in the company culture. Invention activity is expected as part of the normal job process. Inventors are rewarded both financially and with institutional recognition. Inventions are processed, evaluated, and developed in accordance with timely, fair, user-friendly, and repeatable processes.

In best-of-breed companies, employees know from the very first day that documented innovation is a core part of their job. Time is allowed for it. Rewards and recognition are paid for it. Inventions are timely and fairly evaluated in a process designed to protect and develop those that have value to the company. Inventors not only meet their employment expectations through participation in a good invention process, but they feel a sense of dignity, recognition, and self-worth as a result of participating in such a process.

What happens in a company with a second-rate invention process? In those companies, no time is allotted for the documentation and submission of innovation. There is no significant recognition of inventions and, in fact, inventive activity is often perceived as detracting from the core mission of the company. Innovators feel they are swimming upstream in their effort to help the company benefit from their inventions. They face a process that is frustrating, demoralizing, and which discourages future participation.

What is the practical outcome of good and bad invention processes? Because, by definition, inventions and patents are a futures game, a good outcome, as described above, is to some extent statistically dependent on the number of patents obtained. That is not to say that good people and ideas are not important; the old saw of garbage in/garbage out still applies. However, just as every unique carbon deposit does not develop into a perfect diamond, neither does every good invention develop into a monetizable asset. Thus, in a bad environment, not only will morale suffer due to lack of recognition and identified achievement, but the company will recognize less documented innovation, receive fewer patents, and ultimately be less successful in the commercial market.

GETTING GOOD PATENTS

Processing Invention Disclosures

When a company inculcates inventive activity into its culture, the end result is that everyone works to invent. As a practical matter, this means that not all inventions can be nurtured. It becomes necessary to develop a process for identifying invention disclosures that the company will invest in. As with all parts of the patent process, different methods of processing invention disclosures provide different results. Some are good, some not so good, and some plain bad.

Inventions are in some respects like children. While latchkey kids can grow into wonderful adults, parental attention and involvement provide a higher likelihood of success. Similarly with inventions, the greater the degree of inventor involvement at all stages of the process, the higher the likelihood of a good outcome.

The more inventor-friendly the invention disclosure process is, the higher the likelihood that inventors will participate. Don't let the invention evaluation process become too political!

Another common problem that yields poor results is to make the invention evaluation process too unwieldy or lengthy. If these processes become too unwieldy, participation in the invention process becomes discouraging and active inventorship drops off.

Consistent with the discussion above on identifying and protecting innovation at different stages in the business cycle, the best invention evaluation processes are tailored to the different stages of the process. In a pure research environment, the process should be geared toward statistically significant coverage of a broad cross-section of technology. Inventors should feel fairly treated and appropriately rewarded for their contributions. In a development environment, the invention evaluation process should be directed to intelligently identifying and pursuing the more easily recognizable, commercially valuable innovations. Inventors should feel that they were fairly heard and, again, fairly rewarded for their participation in the process.

In the best-of-breed process, the inventors are recognized and encouraged to participate. The evaluation process requires minimal documentation and bureaucracy. The evaluation itself is fast, expertly done, and is perceived to provide fair and consistent results.

Preparing Patent Applications

Up to this point in the process, the astute observer will recognize that, so long as an invention made its way through the system, little irreparable harm could have been done. Any invention that made it through the disclosure and evaluation process has likely achieved the attention of the organization. Resources have been committed to its development into a patent. It is like a small bud, pushed through the earth and ripe with the potential for health and growth. It can be nurtured and developed or, like a neglected child, malnourished and poorly tended. Good genetics can be squelched by poor nurturing.

The drafting of the patent application creates the first legally documented characterization of the nature of the invention. It results in a paper record affecting the interpretation and value of the invention that will survive, literally, forever. It is the first legal step in determining the ultimate value of any issued patent.

Start with the right patent attorney. All patent attorneys possess both a technical and legal background, and most have some modicum of intelligence. Select one who has some passing knowledge of the relevant technology and business, or is willing to expend some time and energy to learn. Most important, select a patent attorney who is motivated to make your patent commercially successful. Motivate your attorney to keep a focus on long-term success as well as short-term tasks. In-house attorneys are often around for the long haul and can be motivated through appropriate compensation packages to think of large, long-term success. If one is working with outside counsel, it makes sense to think of creative compensation programs that develop the same motivations.

Prior Art Searching

Another fundamental element of creating a patent of value: Search the invention in the prior art. Searching may be performed at the outset of the invention evaluation process or it may be performed at some later time prior to preparing the application. The important thing is to do a good, thorough prior art search.

Without a thorough prior art search by the applicant, the likelihood of developing a commercially valuable patent diminishes. Why? First, while the U.S. Patent & Trademark Office (USPTO) performs a patentability search as part of the examination process, their resources, like everyone else's resources, are limited. Further, like the rest of us, they are fallible. The completion of a prior art search by the applicant dramatically increases the likelihood that the most relevant art will be found and considered during the preparation and examination of the patent application. Budget 10 percent of your preparation and filing costs to do good searches. Even if it means filing a few less applications, it will be money well spent.

Involving the Inventor

As was discussed above, no one knows, loves, or appreciates the success of the invention more than the inventor. The wise organization involves the inventor in drafting the patent application. It develops a process that encourages, or even requires, the inventor to work with the attorney during the drafting of the patent application.

Don't accept the position that drafting the application is the legal department's responsibility. The invention is filed in the name of the inventor. The attorney is merely his or her representative.

Do not accept the excuse that the inventor cannot understand the application or that it is too full of legalese. In reality, the attorney may have gotten the invention wrong!

Prosecuting the Patent Application

Once a patent application is filed with the USPTO, it goes into the proverbial black hole of the patent examination queue. Barring any extraordinary process intervention by the applicant, a first response from the USPTO takes on average about eighteen months. That is a long time. Enthusiasm can wane. Institutional knowledge can be lost. Even after the application is picked up for examination within the USPTO, go-arounds between the applicant and the USPTO can average three to six months each, or more. The average patent application takes about 24 months to come to a resolution—allowed or rejected. It may subsequently take another six months to issue after an allowance.

Are there steps one can take to motivate a good result? Absolutely!

Whenever possible, involve the inventor in the prosecution of the patent application with the USPTO. The inventor is the single person best positioned to understand the potential value of the invention.

Work with an attorney having the skills and motivation to take the time and expend the energy necessary to extract the maximum commercial value from the invention. The record established during the prosecution of the patent is vitally important to the eventual interpretation and hence valuation of the issued patent.

Take the time and expend the energy to understand the value of the application to your business. Remember, when you filed the patent application, by definition you were at the forefront of that innovation in your industry. To some extent, the value of the basic invention was unknowable and speculative. At the time of prosecution you, the applicant, have gained a significant advantage: ap-

proximately 18 months of additional knowledge regarding the value and positioning of the invention in the industry. At the least, estimates and judgments can be
refined. In some instances, there is actual implementation of the invention within
the industry. If your company has started to use the invention, you can much better
estimate its value in the industry.

If your competitors have started to use the invention, you are in the extraordinary position of actually being able to prosecute the patent application in light
of your knowledge of competitive practices within the industry. In such an instance, it should be possible to tailor the direction of the application prosecution
to extract maximum value from any subsequently issued patent.

Much of the routine communication between the applicant's attorney and the
USPTO is handled by mail or other impersonal communication channels (i.e., fac-
simile, e-mail). The best results from patent prosecution are obtained, however,
through interpersonal communications with the patent examiner actually handling
your patent application.

Opinions and rumors abound about interacting with the USPTO to prosecute
a patent application. Much advice will indicate that it is best to keep a low profile,
to offer as little input as possible, and to avoid at all costs drawing attention to
oneself as an individual. This is wrong! There are no guarantees. However, the development of a human relationship with the expectation that intelligent people can
work together to the right result is the best path to patent prosecution success.

A Few Words on Quantity Versus Quality

As discussed above, inventions are by nature cutting-edge and speculative. It is
impossible to predict the future. Therefore, both emotions and rigorous mathematical analysis indicate that in speculative situations, such as gambling, a higher
quantity of plays is more likely to result in a winning result. There is substantial
and constant debate in the patent community about the trade-offs between quantity and quality.

The quality of a patent is always measured in hindsight. It is subject to absolutely uncontrollable variables (e.g., the skills of the examiner assigned by the
USPTO or an undiscoverable prior art reference that surfaces only after the issuance of the patent) and is typically evaluated in a high-pressure situation (e.g., with
the entire resources of a competitive law firm set loose to attempt to defame your
reputation and invalidate your patent). By definition, it is absolutely impossible to
prepare, prosecute, and issue a bulletproof patent. Using a 60/40 rule, 60 percent
of the possible effort and resources will result in a patent that is completely acceptable in quality, while an additional 40 percent may be expended in a vain attempt
to reach perfection. It is, in a word, ludicrous, to spend that last investment of
resources to improve one application when in fact it can be used to obtain a good
portion of a second, completely acceptable issued patent.

Managing the Issuance of the Patent

The patent, when it issues, will essentially constitute a compendium of all of the work that was put into obtaining it. The initial filing, the prosecution history, the cited search results, all these and more will form a part of the total mosaic that represents the ownership rights of the inventor in the issued patent. It is important to remember that the job is not yet done.

A prudent practitioner will take the time and energy to perform a careful and thorough review of the file to ensure that it stands in as good a position as possible. He or she will develop and implement a strategy for any ongoing continuation or divisional cases necessary to protect the invention appropriately. He or she will review the scope of the allowed claims against the list of inventors to determine if the inventorship remains accurate.

A rare but periodically occurring event is the destruction of a patent's value through its inappropriate management within the industry. While a patent can be lost at any time in its life—for example, through an unfavorable outcome in litigation—it is sad and inappropriate to see a patent die stillborn or prematurely through inappropriate handling within the industry.

An issued patent constitutes a valuable property right for the owner. It could be considered analogous to a precious jewel or a valuable antique. And like anything of substance and value, it needs loving and tender care to insure its ongoing worth and value. An untimely, rash act can nullify all of those efforts in the legal equivalent of a heartbeat.

TIMING: THE INTERRELATIONSHIP BETWEEN INNOVATION AND COMMERCIALIZATION

Timing Is Everything

As discussed above, fundamental invention may lead commercial innovation by many years. Market-driven, improvement, and design-around inventions are typically linked more closely, time-wise, to commercial development. Below is a discussion of the timing relating invention protection to commercial development with reference again to Exhibit 3-1.

While basic R&D may lag behind commercialization by a lengthy period of time, in many instances, an entrepreneur makes a fundamental invention concomitant with the early development of a business model or plan. In such instances, life becomes quite interesting because the typical time from filing to issuance of a patent application is about 24 months. (This figure varies among technology areas and is generally increasing from year to year.) Twenty-four months is a long time in the development of a business. Synchronizing the two processes, patent procurement and business development, in a manner that best utilizes the intellectual property to the ends of the business can be quite challenging.

While licensing is not the subject of this discourse, there are two fundamental concepts that should be kept in mind by anyone trying to coordinate the development of a business with an early patent filing. The first is that a patent is not legally enforceable until the day it issues. The second is that a pending patent application can in fact be licensed, on a voluntary basis between the parties, and thus has value to the business.

It is also to be noted that both patents and pending applications are capable of valuation. Using traditional methods, patent valuation is a factor of market size, claim scope, and many somewhat subjective determinations such as the quality of the file history. Discounted cash-flow analysis is often used to determine the value of a pending patent application or issued patent. One alternate valuation methodology to be noted is that of TRRU™ Metrics, a formula-based methodology proprietary to The Patent & License Exchange, Inc. (*www.pl-x.com*), that uses the Black-Scholes option pricing algorithm with modified inputs to value a license, assignment of a pending application, or issued patent.

Exhibit 3-1 graphically illustrates the timeline relationships between three interrelated processes: invention activity, patent procurement, and business development. The core timeline selected for purposes of this discussion is 24 months. Twenty-four months is, as we know, the average time a patent application pends in the USPTO before issuance. It is also not a bad estimate of a period for conception to initial launch of a fast-moving, entrepreneurial business. Individuals can make adjustments as their own experience dictates.

It is apparent that pure research and development can lead the adoption of innovation into commerce by various and lengthy periods of time. It is not at all unusual for patented inventions to lag market adoption (where they are adopted) by three to five years from conception to commercial utilization. Of course, this period varies wildly between technologies. There are many well-known instances of commercially valuable patents issuing on inventions filed as early as 20 or 30 years before market development. (Though, of course, this cannot happen under the current patent laws where a patent expires 20 years after the filing date.) The important concept to note is that typical pure R&D significantly lags even the conception of a commercial development and, as described above, is best protected using statistical processes for patenting as many inventions as affordable.

In contrast, while market-driven inventing can lag commercial conception, there is typically less time between conception and commercial use. Also, as noted above, a higher percentage of market-driven innovations will recognize commercial value. It stands to reason that if bright people recognize the market need, with solution sets being limited by definition, sooner rather than later, the first inventor or another party will implement the solution in the market. Thus, people involved in patents should think smart and use intelligent evaluation as a large part of the invention protection decision process.

Examining the relationship between the business development process and the related patent process, one can begin to see the value of timely action to protect entrepreneurial innovation. If an early business concept is filed prematurely, it may be incomplete or even so far off track as to significantly reduce the value of an issued patent to the actual business. If an early business concept is filed too late in the business development process, it is of less value at the launch of the business. What does this mean as a practical matter?

Value is lost in several areas when a patent application on a fundamental, commercialized business concept lags the launch of the business by any significant time. The initial investors' valuation of the business is discounted due to the risk that a patent may not issue. This is true both in the private market during early-round investing and as the company enters the public market. The value associated with the proprietary position a strong patent affords is diminished by the tenuous pendency of an application. During both private and public financing, forward-looking statements regarding the likelihood of patent issuance must be avoided so as to not to incur legal liability or the wrath of the SEC.

The deterrent value associated with an issued patent is, of course, either non-existent or dramatically diminished during the pendency of an application. Potential competitors do not face the increased barrier to entry an issued patent affords and are thus more likely to enter the market in hot pursuit of the owner of the application. While a subsequent issuance of a patent will afford the benefits of ownership, the patent owner will face some diminished value and increased difficulty necessary to overcome the inertia that may have developed during the pendency of the application.

There is, of course, no complete answer to the built-in tension between achieving an early filing date and delaying filing to gain the benefit of increased knowledge regarding a business or product. The best strategy is to actively manage the prosecution of the patent application, tailoring it to the development of the business. Voluntary amendments may be filed to put the best claims at the forefront of the application. Voluntary divisional applications can be filed to simultaneously prosecute multiple inventions of commercial value. Continuations-in-part may be filed to add new matter as necessary.

Timing and Utilization of Improvement Patents

Protecting improvements is, of course, easier from both a timing and a knowledge standpoint. Because improvement patent applications are typically directed to a functioning process or system, they are readily coordinated with the progress of the business. By definition, they cannot be identified and filed before their time. As mentioned above, the challenge with improvement patents is to identify the ones that are likely to yield the highest value and generate the most difficulty in designing around.

While the issuance of improvement patents may lag the progress of competitors' developments, a strong, core patent position arising from the earliest filings increases the value of pending improvement applications. More specifically, the ownership of core, basic patents gives one the opportunity to knock on competitors' doors. Once there, there are many straightforward negotiating strategies that involve the disclosure and use of pending improvement applications in a licensing negotiation. In essence, having one or more issued patents increases the immediate value of related, pending applications.

SUMMARY

In summary, innovation has always been and continues to be important to the success of business. Just as important, and perhaps even more so given both recent court decisions and today's fast-moving, global economy, is the ability to turn innovation into protected, monetizable business assets.

If you, as a business manager, don't work to own your company's innovations, they will at best be copied by your competitors and at worst be owned by others with better and more aggressive processes that will use those assets to your detriment.

To identify, develop, protect, and utilize intellectual assets requires a long-term perspective and the development of processes carefully tuned to the different phases of your business. "One size fits all" type processes will not work in a complex business environment. Instead, careful attention must be paid to the vastly different needs of research, product development, product improvement, and the foreseeable frequent, complex, and often contentious interaction with your competitors.

Companies that prudently develop the right processes and procedures for meeting the needs of their businesses will be situated to turn their intellectual assets into valuable business assets. They will be well positioned in the global marketplace. Companies that don't, if they survive, will eventually become free research and development facilities for their competition.

ABOUT THE AUTHOR

Jeffrey L. Brandt began his career in intellectual property as part of the prestigious General Electric intellectual property training program in Washington, D.C. In addition to his position as a patent attorney at the General Electric Research & Development facility in Schenectady, New York, Mr. Brandt served as Patent Attorney for the Eastman Kodak Corporation and as Patent Attorney, Location Patent Counsel, and Division Licensing Counsel for IBM. As founding attorney at Walker Digital Corporation, Mr. Brandt developed a comprehensive intellectual property function for supporting the development and protection of business process-related inventions. During his tenure at Walker Digital Corporation, Mr. Brandt acted in an "executive-on-loan" capacity as Senior Vice President, Intellectual Property &

Licensing, to priceline.com. Mr. Brandt developed and managed the intellectual property program for one of the leading electronic commerce businesses in operation and was responsible for the issuance of the famous "Priceline patent." Most recently, he has founded JLB Consulting, Inc., which provides strategic IP portfolio consulting to innovative businesses and investors.

In his position at JLB Consulting, Mr. Brandt serves as a director or advisor to many of his clients including the Patent & Licensing Exchange for which he is senior technical advisor and consultant. Mr. Brandt received his BS in Electrical Engineering from Lafayette College and his JD from the University of Baltimore School of Law.

JLB provides strategic intellectual property services to innovative companies and investors of all sizes, and assists in the identification, development, protection, and utilization of intellectual assets. For companies with established portfolios and programs, JLB assists with the revamping of legacy programs and the development of new programs. The firm has particular expertise in developing intellectual property programs tailored to different phases of the business/product life cycle, such as strategic alliances and initial public offering (IPO) and merger and acquisition (M&A) activities. JLB works with investors to evaluate the intellectual assets of potential investments, and works directly with those seeking funds to develop, organize, and improve their intellectual asset position.

CHAPTER FOUR

Clarifying Intellectual Property Rights for the New Economy

by Margaret M. Blair, Gary M. Hoffman, and
Salvatore P. Tamburo

PERSPECTIVES

A task force commissioned by the Brookings Institution in Washington, D.C., completed a two-year study in October 2000 to consider the implications of the growing importance of intangible assets for the U.S. economy. The task force co-chairs, a prominent economist and a former commissioner of the Securities and Exchange Commission (SEC), were joined by more than 40 key task force members, among them experts in finance, accounting, law, business, and analytics.

In a 75-page summary, *Unseen Wealth: Report of the Brookings Task Force on Intangibles,* the researchers concluded that despite a rapidly increasing reliance on intangible assets, United States companies have a decidedly poor handle on what they are and how to deploy them. This is especially true of patents and other intellectual property rights. The report's findings indicate that for a variety of reasons, from antiquated generally accepted accounting principles (GAAP) accounting to a lack of common vocabulary, intangibles are difficult to identify and value. As a result, investors are getting an incomplete picture of the status and potential of many U.S. companies.

In the following chapter, "Clarifying Intellectual Property Rights for the New Economy," three of the Brooking Report's key contributors consider how a lack of intellectual property identification and reporting might affect business and investment. "Today," assert authors Blair, Hoffman, and Tamburo, "new wealth and competitive advantage largely come from nonphysical assets, or 'intangibles,' including ideas, human capital, corporate competencies, and, importantly for this chapter, intellectual property rights."

Unlike hard assets, intangibles are difficult to measure, to manage, and even to define. They cannot be seen, touched, or weighed, and they generally do not show up on the balance sheets of corporations that create, develop, or use them. For the most part, they also are not recorded in the national accounts as part of national wealth. Since they are not measured, there are obvious problems in trying to estimate how important they are in the overall economy. Yet, say the authors of this chapter, there are at least three kinds of evidence that suggest that intangible inputs into wealth creation have become at least as important—and more important in many cases—as tangible inputs.

The Brookings task force concluded that the primary reasons why information about intangibles in the economy is so scarce and of such poor quality have to do with conceptual problems of deciding which financial assets to measure and how to measure them.

"The increased reliance by businesses, in general, upon the value generated by intellectual property highlights the need for better defined [property rights] rules . . . [that apply when] such assets are acquired, owned, and transferred . . . These reforms would help adjust the institutional and legal environment in the United States and internationally so that they will continue to support the kinds of investments needed in the economy of the third millennium."

INTRODUCTION

The so-called *new economy* is still something of a puzzle to most economists. But to people in the business world who are negotiating their way through it and attempting to capitalize on its new technology and exploit the new market niches being created, one feature of the new economy stands out: Physical assets—land, natural resources, office space, factories, machines—are rapidly becoming basic commodities. Anyone can buy or lease them, so there is no competitive advantage available to the company that controls them. Today, new wealth and competitive advantage largely come from nonphysical assets, or "intangibles," including ideas, human capital, corporate competencies, and, importantly for this chapter, intellectual property rights.

The authors of this chapter recently helped to lead a special task force, organized under the auspices of the Brookings Institution, to consider the policy implications of the growing importance of intangibles in the U.S. economy.[1] In this chapter, we draw heavily on, and discuss, the findings of that task force as they relate to the task force's proposals for reform of the intellectual property rights laws and institutions in the United States and in the international community.

In "The Growing Role of 'Unseen' Wealth," we review the evidence for the proposition that intangibles are rapidly eclipsing tangible assets in their importance in the U.S. economy and in other developed countries. We focus especially on intellectual property, though we recognize that organizational and human capital are also critical inputs into wealth creation, and probably complements to IP. In "The Measurement Problem," we note that one of the critical problems that the transformation of the economy is creating is the problem of performance measurement. How do we measure output, productivity, and economic growth in an economy dominated by the development and use of intangibles? How do managers in individual firms measure the effectiveness and profitability of investments in intangibles? We also discuss a framework for addressing the measurement problems the task force developed. In "The Role of the Government in Determining Property Rights over Intangibles," we briefly examine the historic role of the government in creating and enforcing property rights in intangible assets. In "The Brookings Proposals for Improving Intellectual Property Rights Protection," we present and discuss a specific set of proposals for reforming intellectual property rights laws put forth by the task force. In the final part, we draw conclusions and discuss some lessons we learned from the task force project.

THE GROWING ROLE OF "UNSEEN" WEALTH

Physical assets, such as buildings and machines, can be weighed, measured, and sold by one owner to another. We can measure what it cost to create them and what they are worth relatively easily. Financial assets likewise represent clear, legally enforceable claims on wealth or streams of income, and so, while they may not have a very impressive physical form, they can be readily valued. Thus, we can estimate with reasonable accuracy the value of physical and financial assets owned by a firm, or utilized in an economy.

Intangibles, by contrast, are hard to measure, manage, and even define. They cannot be seen, touched, or weighed, and they generally do not show up on the balance sheets of corporations that create, or develop, or use them.[2] For the most part, they also are not recorded in the national accounts as part of national wealth.[3] Since they are not measured, there are obvious problems in trying to estimate how important they are in the overall economy. Yet there are at least three kinds of evidence that suggest that intangible inputs into wealth creation have become at least as important—and more important in many cases—than tangible inputs.

Market-to-Book Ratios

In the past 20 years, there has been a very rapid expansion in the total market value of outstanding corporate securities—debt plus equity. The net value of financial securities issued by the nonfarm, nonfinancial corporate sector grew by 10.2 percent per year, from $1.016 trillion in 1973 to $10.496 trillion in 1997.[4]

But this growth in market value of financial claims cannot be explained by corporate investment in physical property, plant and equipment, which grew at an aggregate rate of only 6.8 percent during a similar period (1970–1997).[5] By the last half of the 1990s, an unprecedented gap had emerged between the market value of publicly traded corporations, and their book value (see Exhibit 4-1).

Professor Baruch Lev, of New York University's Stern School of Business, has estimated that, as of 2000, the ratio of the market value of equity of the firms that make up the Standard & Poor's (S&P) 500 index to the book value of those firms' assets exceeded six.[6] Using a conceptually similar but methodologically different way of measuring the gap, Professor Robert Hall of Stanford University estimated that as of 1999, the ratio of the market value of debt plus equity to the replacement cost of tangible assets in corporations had grown to 2.4.[7]

The only explanation for this discrepancy that is consistent with notions of rationality in financial markets, Professor Hall claims, is the possibility that corporations "own substantial amounts of intangible capital not recorded in the sector's books or anywhere in government statistics."[8]

Of course, the stock market could be wrong in its estimates of corporate value, and, indeed, by early 2001, stock prices had fallen somewhat from their lofty heights of early 2000. But equity prices would have to fall by two thirds or more from their peaks, across the board, for the significant discrepancy between market value and book value to disappear.[9] The fact that financial markets are volatile, and the possibility that they overshot the mark in the last year of the last century, does not mean that intangibles are not important and that we should ignore large and

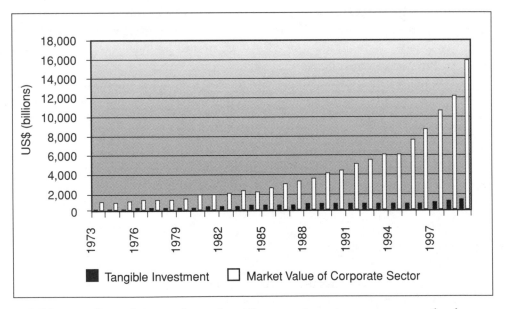

Exhibit 4-1   Growth in market value of corporate sector versus growth of tangible investment.

persistent discrepancies in financial markets. In fact, it was the opinion of members of the task force with whom we worked on the Brookings project that the growing importance of difficult-to-measure factors in corporate wealth is part of what has been making financial markets more volatile in recent years.

The Role of Services and Information Technology

The delivery of many kinds of services involves the use of intangible assets, ranging from the specialized skills of professionals, to reputational capital, to mailing lists and carefully cultivated customer relationships, to specialized software. Services have grown from about 22 percent of gross domestic product (GDP) in 1950 to 39 percent in 1999.[10]

Similarly, advances in information technology require not just new and more hardware, but new software programs and new ways to electronically link computers to each other to exchange information. There is also evidence that information technology in firms requires complementary investments in organizational changes that decentralize decision-making, higher levels of skill and good judgment, and more teamwork on the part of employees.[11] Professor Hall estimates that for every dollar a firm invests in computers, that firm needs about $9 worth of "intangible" investments,[12] such as investments in intellectual, organizational, and human capital. The rapid growth in services and in information technology, therefore, also suggests that intangibles are growing in importance in the economy.

What Corporate Executives Say (and What Business Consultants Do)

Numerous surveys of corporate executives in recent years suggest that they have become acutely aware of the importance of various kinds of intangibles in their businesses and are scrambling to do a better job of investing in and managing them. A series of Conference Board studies, for example, have indicated substantial corporate interest in such things as knowledge management, the development of intellectual capital, improving customer satisfaction and retention, and workplace practices.[13] One survey of chief financial officers, for example, found that CFOs expected creating and implementing new measures of performance to be their most important activity over the three years following the survey.[14]

Consulting firms and accounting firms have also been scrambling to respond to the sudden increase in demand for more information about intangibles, better models for measuring them, and better tools for managing them.[15] And investors have been saying that they want firms to tell them more about the intangible investments in their firms.[16]

Yet, despite all the apparent interest in the role of intangibles, most firms still fail to report much in the way of factual information about their intangible investments, or their strategies for managing them, in their public documents.[17] The result is a serious dearth of solid information about factors that appear to be driving the economies of developed countries in the twenty-first century.

THE MEASUREMENT PROBLEM

The Brookings task force concluded that the most important reasons why information about intangibles in the economy is so scarce and of such poor quality are the conceptual problems of deciding what things to measure and how to measure them. The transformation in the economy has been quite rapid, and businesspeople are only beginning to develop new models to help them understand the relationships between, say, investments in employee training and customer service,[18] investments in research and development (R&D) and the value of the resulting technology developments or patents,[19] or between advertising and brand loyalty. For purposes of considering the policy implications of the transformation in the economy, and specifically of the lack of good data on the factors driving economic growth and wealth creation in this new economy, the task force developed a framework for characterizing the conceptual problem.[20]

Characterizing Measurement Problems

A key factor in the problem of identifying and measuring intangible inputs into a productive process is the extent to which property rights over the intangibles are clear, or the nature of the intangibles is such that property rights could be assigned or clarified. Leif Edvinsson, former vice president and director of intellectual capital at Skandia AFS, took an early lead in developing extensive external reporting systems to describe and document intangible assets. He suggests that intangibles can be divided into "human capital" and "structural capital."[21] While "human capital is a critical component to the success of any company but one that walks out every evening," Edvinsson notes, "structural capital . . . is what's left in the company after the people go home . . . it can be owned."[22]

The task force adopted a similar distinction to identify three levels of measurement problems. At level 1 are assets that can be owned and sold. At level 2 are assets that can be controlled but not separated out and sold. At level 3 are intangibles that may not even be wholly controlled by the firm.[23]

Level 1. Assets Can Be Owned and Sold

Patents, copyrights, brands, and trade names are examples of assets for which property rights are, to some extent, defined and protected by existing legal systems. There may not be perfect clarity about property rights over these intangibles, but at least they are considered "property" under current law.

An asset must be well defined and delimited for property rights over the asset to be assigned. If the asset can be defined and delimited, and property rights are clear enough, then the asset can be sold. If an intangible asset or good has been purchased by or transferred to another party for consideration, that transaction provides an obvious, and useful, indicator of the value of the asset. An intangible asset that can be sold for consideration clearly meets the four accounting criteria for being recognized as an "asset" on the books of a company: It is well defined and sufficiently separate from other assets that it can be the object of a sales transaction; the firm has effective control over it and can transfer that control to someone else; it is (reasonably) possible to predict the future economic benefits from it; and it is (reasonably) possible to determine if its economic value has been impaired.[24]

In addition to intellectual property, certain business agreements, executory contracts, licenses, and databases may appear to qualify as assets (or liabilities) for accounting purposes; for example, mailing lists, operating licenses and franchises, media and other broadcast licenses, agricultural and other production quotas in regulated industries, and employment contracts. But these things are generally not included on the balance sheets of companies unless they have been the object of a transaction.[25]

If such assets are developed internally within a company, the expenditures associated with development are expensed immediately, and no asset is recorded. Income from the assets is treated as current income, but no depreciation charge is taken against it. If the assets are sold or transferred, the receipts from the transaction are recorded as a gain on sale, but there is no recognized reduction in balance sheet assets as a result of the sale. The firm that purchases the assets, however, will add the assets to its books. And if one firm buys another firm, and in so doing acquires a substantial bundle of such assets, the acquiring firm may add some goodwill to its balance sheet to reflect the difference between the price paid to acquire the firm and the estimated market value of the acquired firm's assets (after any allowable write-ups).

The task force noted that, while there are good reasons why information about these kinds of assets and their value to individual firms should be used more effectively within firms and made more widely available to investors, there are some problems that must be resolved to achieve this. One of the most important problems—and the one that is the focus of this chapter—is securing and clarifying property rights with respect to such assets.

Level 2. Assets Can Be Controlled But Not Separated Out and Sold

A more difficult set of problems arises in the attempt to identify, measure, and account for intangibles that are proprietary to a specific firm but would be very difficult to separate out and sell to another firm; for example, R&D in process, business secrets, reputational capital, proprietary management systems, and business processes. These intangibles may currently meet only one or two of the accounting criteria for "assets." The firm may have effective control over them—in that limited sense, the firm is understood to "own" the assets—and it may be possible to make some predictions about the economic benefits the assets provide. But it may not be possible to separate them out from other intangibles in the firm to determine their separate value or to convey them to some other party, unless they are bundled with the other factors to which they are tied.

Again, the task force identified problems that must be resolved in order to improve the flow of information about, and management of, assets at this level. One problem the task force recognized, but did not consider in detail, is the problem of establishing and clarifying property rights over these kinds of assets. Connected with that problem is a prior problem of developing clear definitions and consistent vocabulary for defining and delimiting these kinds of assets. The task force, however, recognized that certain techniques for giving firms stronger property rights over such assets (such as making "business processes" patentable and/ or strengthening the enforceability of "noncompete" clauses in employment contracts) might have other, undesirable effects on economic growth and efficiency, or on justice, or equity, or other social goals. Hence the group decided not to take up the question of whether public policy should strengthen property rights over these types of assets. Instead, it focused on ways to adjust property rights laws to add clarity and certainty, rather than to make property claims stronger or weaker. (In "The Brookings Proposals for Improving Intellectual Property Rights Protection" below we discuss these reform proposals in detail.)

Level 3: Intangibles May Not Be Wholly Controlled by the Firm

At this level are intangibles that have gone by such names as human capital, core competencies, organizational capital, and relationship capital. Although they do not meet any of the four accounting criteria for "assets," such factors clearly help to create value for corporations. But they are inextricably tied up with the people who work for firms and those who supply services or goods to them, such as consultants or networks of suppliers and others. Corporations do not have legal property rights over these intangibles.

There are at least two parties involved in the accumulation and utilization of human capital, for example: the employee and the firm. Investments in human capital differ from investments in tangibles, and even from investments in many categories of intangible assets, because workers can walk out the door at any time, taking their knowledge and skills with them. Although a firm may be able, at least for a limited time frame, to prevent former employees from competing with it and thereby capitalize on the knowledge or skills the employees took with them when they left, the firm cannot compel those employees to leave the knowledge and skills behind.

This does not mean that the firm has no influence over the development, retention, and utilization of such intangibles, however. In fact, a firm's personnel, management, and training policies may have a very large effect on the productivity, innovativeness, and profitability of a firm. Part of the value that gets recorded as goodwill in some corporate mergers may be due to such policies, rather than to level 1 or level 2 assets. Hence, even if it never becomes possible to measure such intangibles directly, assign property rights over them to third parties, or add them to the books of the firm, managers inside firms and investors outside might want to know a great deal more about them than they currently do.[26] Moreover, one of the important tasks for management is to try to convert level 3 intangibles to level 2 or level 1 assets, for example, by codifying the knowledge of employees, or formalizing management procedures and decision tools, or asserting property rights over the laboratory notes of researchers.

The problems that must be solved to improve the flow of information about intangibles at this level are almost exclusively conceptual, definitional, and measurement problems rather than problems in the regime of property rights laws.

The analysis implicit in this framework points to the central role played by property rights over intellectual assets in defining and delimiting the assets, in making it possible to determine their value, and in tracking their role in the economy. Later we discuss the role of the government in determining property rights, and thereby in creating intangible assets. But first, we briefly ask whether it matters if we are unable to quantify and measure intangibles in the economy.

Does It Matter That We Don't Have Better Measures of Intangibles?

In a sense, the whole premise behind the work of the Brookings task force was that it does matter, and a large section of the report is devoted to detailing the problems that we believe arise from not knowing.[27] We will not go into detail describing these problems in this chapter, but will note only that the task force concluded that the failure to understand the role of intangibles in the economy leads to:

- Mismeasurement of the national accounts and of data on such things as productivity, output, and inflation
- Faulty estimates of a variety of macroeconomic variables that are important in policies ranging from estimating the deficits or surpluses in government budgets, to preparing for the retirement of baby boomers
- Greater volatility of stock prices and of the financial markets in general
- Reduction in the confidence investors have that financial markets are transparent and fair
- Misallocation of capital across industries
- Misallocation of resources within companies
- Greater difficulties in designing a fair and efficient tax system

Although the Brookings task force suspected that there are biases in public policy that skew investments inappropriately toward, or away from, investments in intangibles relative to tangible assets, the group was unable to find convincing evidence of such biases in part because the measurement difficulties are so overwhelming. The report's policy proposals are limited to three areas.

First, the task force proposed expanded funding for, and reorienting the agenda of data collection agencies in Washington toward, building better data on intangibles. The report also stresses the important role the business community must play in developing suitable business models to guide such data collection. Second, it proposed an expansion of the disclosure goals of federal securities laws. Finally, the task force proposed a series of changes in intellectual property rights laws that the group believed would help to increase the certainty around the extent and degree of property right protection afforded to various kinds of intellectual property. In "The Brookings Proposals for Improving Intellectual Property Rights Protection," we focus our attention on the task force's proposals for reforming intellectual property rights laws.

THE ROLE OF GOVERNMENT IN DETERMINING PROPERTY RIGHTS OVER INTANGIBLES

The framework for analyzing the problems involved in measurement and valuation of intangibles outlined in the previous section highlights the important role played by property rights that are defined and protected by government.[28] Intellectual property rights laws, as well as the laws that govern corporations, contracts, and labor relations, are necessary to define which streams of benefits from which "assets" are protected as property and who gets the benefits of that protection. In other words, many intangible assets would not exist as assets at all without the starting point of a set of property rights defined and guaranteed at the state or federal level.

The founding fathers understood the establishment of property rights to be an important role for government and included in the Constitution a clause giving Congress the power "to promote the Progress of Science and useful Arts, by securing for limited Times to Authors and Inventors the exclusive Right to their respective Writings and Discoveries."[29] In 1790, Congress acted on this authority and enacted the first patent act. Thomas Jefferson was appointed as the first "patent examiner."[30]

The patent system is designed to foster ingenuity by promising an inventor that if she shares her invention with the rest of society, she will be awarded the right to exclude others from making, using, or selling the invention without her permission. Society, of course, receives the benefits of her hard work and may strive to improve on the invention, thus advancing that particular field of study in a manner that would otherwise not likely occur. Once a patent is granted to an inventor, that patent, just like any other form of personal property, may be transferred, sold, or licensed to others.

Nonpatented ideas that are in widespread use (the wheel, for example) may have enormous economic value, but most of this is captured in the tangible objects that incorporate these ideas. At the frontiers of knowledge, where technology is advancing rapidly, new ideas may have a great deal of value that has not yet been incorporated into tangible objects whose value can be estimated relatively easily. Once an intangible idea has been formulated into an invention having utility, it may be granted patent rights. And once those patent rights have been granted, the stream of economic benefits derived from that intangible idea is vested in the patent holder, who can exploit and protect those benefits. This makes it somewhat easier to estimate its value, but whereas tangible property may be owned, or at least controlled, by someone or some entity as long as it exists, property rights over intangible assets exist only to the extent that government creates them. They are highly contingent, generally harder to define, and usually limited by law to a certain period of time.[31]

In addition to patents on inventions, the federal government also provides trademark protection, which makes it easier for businesses to create and build reputational capital. Similarly, federal copyright protections give authors, composers, playwrights, film makers, sculptors, and other artists exclusive property rights over their creations.[32] And both patent and copyright law can be used to transform computer software into protected property.

Moreover, state statutory and common law governing agency, contracts, corporations, and the relationships between an employee and an employer also help to determine who is entitled to the benefits from information, ideas, and business opportunities developed on the job or in the process of pursuing some collaborative business enterprise. Thus the whole legal framework of property, contract, and business law helps to determine what is an "ownable" asset; who is entitled to realize the benefits of some idea, relationship, or opportunity; and how securely those benefits can be protected.

THE BROOKINGS PROPOSALS FOR IMPROVING INTELLECTUAL PROPERTY RIGHTS PROTECTION

As discussed above, one of the most important ways that existing government policy influences the creation and valuation of intangibles is through legal protections for intellectual property rights. Once an intangible good has been defined by the law as a piece of property, and the rights associated with that property have been delimited, it becomes easier to estimate a value associated with those property rights and to sell, transfer, or enter into other transactions involving that piece of property. Hence, anything that increases certainty or clarity in laws that determine the scope, nature, and enforceability of intellectual property rights should make it easier to assign a value to the intellectual asset in question. This section presents proposals that the Brookings task force made in its report for reforming intellectual property rights laws to respond to problems that the task force believes exist in the current system.[33]

Intellectual property may be difficult to evaluate for several reasons, including factors that are specific to the owner of the property. For example, someone who acquires intellectual property rights but does not actively license and enforce them will surely realize less value from the intellectual property than would an owner who does. Support for this notion is illustrated by Exhibit 4-2, which shows the top 20 damage awards for patent infringement in the United States.

Similarly, an owner of intellectual property who actively seeks out infringing parties for the purpose of soliciting licenses or settlement agreements incurs far greater costs in intellectual property right protection and enforcement than an owner who does not. An owner who can effectively exclude competitors so as to become dominant in a large profitable market, however, can achieve significant value. These issues are considered by companies in developing strategies for managing intellectual property and, when relevant to valuing that property, should be disclosed and discussed in their public documents.

Although these issues are important, members of the task force decided not to address them, since they are a product of individual corporate strategic decisions and not matters of public policy. Instead, the task force focused on questions about the operation of the intellectual property laws and systems.

The task force's recommendations focus primarily on intellectual property laws of the United States. In light of the ever-increasing significance of the global economy and marketplace and the exponential growth of the Internet as a medium for communicating and for conducting business, however, the task force also made some proposals on international law.

Patents

The establishment of the Court of Appeals for the Federal Circuit (CAFC) in 1982 has resulted in greater certainty and predictability of patent rights by funneling all patent disputes through a single appellate court of review. But the task force concluded that due to the increasing number of patent cases commenced, as well as the overall increase in intellectual property suits filed (see Exhibit 4-3), an additional step is needed to increase certainty and predictability in patent rights at the courts of first instance, the trial courts.

It therefore recommended the establishment of a specialized trial court to preside over patent cases. This could be accomplished through a single court with judges sitting for trials in various parts of the country or, alternatively, each circuit could have specialized patent judges who handle all such cases in that circuit.[34]

The task force considered the argument that specialized judges might be, or be perceived to be, too "pro-patent," in the sense of being predisposed to recog-

Top Damage Awards for U.S. Patent Infringement: 1–20
1982–February 2001

	Parties	Award	Date	Source	Court
1	Polaroid v. Eastman Kodak	$873,158,971	Jan–91	17 USPQ 2d 1711	D. Massachusetts
2	Cordis v. Boston Scientific	$324,400,000	Dec–00	Wall Street Journal	D. Delaware
3	Cordis v. Medtronic AVE	$271,100,000	Dec–00	Press Release	D. Delaware
4	Haworth v. Steelcase	$211,499,731	Dec–96	43 USPQ 2d 1223	W.D. Michigan
5	Smith International v. Hughes Tool	$204,810,349	Mar–86	229 USPQ 81	C.D. California
6	Procter & Gamble v. Paragon Trade	$178,000,000	Aug–98	Press Release	D. Delaware
7	Exxon v. Mobil Oil	$171,000,000	Aug–98	Houston Chronicle	S.D. Texas
8	Viskase v. American National Can	$164,900,000	Jul–99	Press Release	N.D. Illinois
9	Hughes Aircraft v. United States	$154,000,000	Jun–94	Wall Street Journal	Federal Claims
10	3M v. Johnson & Johnson	$129,008,502	Sep–92	24 USPQ 2d 1321	CAFC
11	Fonar v. General Electric	$128,705,766	Feb–97	41 USPQ 2d 1801	CAFC
12	Mobil Oil v. Amoco Chemicals	$120,000,000	Sep–94	Press Release	D. Delaware
13	Honeywell v. Minolta	$96,350,000	Jan–92	Business Week	D. New Jersey
14	Unocal v. Six Major Oil Companies	$91,000,000	Mar–00	Press Release	CAFC
15	Southern Clay Products v. United Catalysts	$78,037,430	Feb–01	Final Judgment	S.D. Texas
16	Stryker v. Intermedics Orthopedics	$72,750,704	Apr–97	42 USPQ 2d 1935	E.D. New York
17	General Technology v. Conoco	$68,750,000	May–00	National Law Journal	E.D. Virginia
18	Pfizer v. SciMed Life Systems	$68,000,000	Nov–95	Dow Jones News	CAFC
19	Durel Corporation v. Osram Sylvania	$63,110,000	Feb–00	National Law Journal	D. Arizona
20	Pfizer v. International Rectifier	$55,805,855	Jun–83	218 USPQ 586	C.D. California

Exhibit 4-2 Top damage awards for U.S. patent infringement: 1–20.
Source: Technology & Financial Consulting—James J. Nawrocki and Lance E. Gunderson.

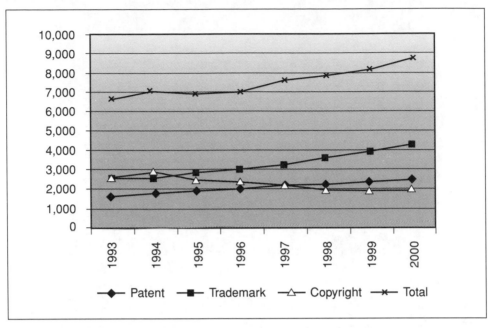

Exhibit 4-3   Intellectual property suits commenced in U.S. district courts 1993–2000.
Source: Technology & Financial Consulting—James J. Nawrocki and Lance E. Gunderson.

nize the validity or infringement of patents brought before them. They concluded, however, that a panel of specialized judges would be likely to become de facto experts in U.S. patent law issues and would therefore be more likely to bring a clear understanding of both the technical and the legal issues to the task. The result, it was felt, would be a fairer, speedier resolution of patent-related cases and controversies.

Taking the notion of specialized patent trial courts a step further, some members of the task force believed that the juries hearing cases in these specialized courts should be selected from a pool of specialized jurors, each having certain minimum technical qualifications. For example, a minimum educational level might be required for a person to be included within such a specialized jury pool. Presumably, jurors having more extensive educational backgrounds would be better able to grasp the complex issues that often arise in patent litigation.

Proponents of specialized juries argue that the more specialized the jury, the more consistent the results. At the very least, the litigants are more likely to have a jury that, albeit it does not come into court with an understanding of scientific subject matter, has the ability to hear evidence and to think critically while applying that evidence so that a fair and (presumably) more predictable outcome might be achieved.

While some members of the task force believe that this position is not without merit, it was believed so only up to a certain point. For example, a jury consisting only of experts in a particular field being litigated (e.g., semiconductor manufacturing), aside from being unduly burdensome in empanelling, might be less objective when hearing all the evidence. Such a jury would probably be more apt to find an invention was an "obvious" improvement over the prior art, and therefore the patent should be invalidated. In addition, it might be more inclined to view certain alternatives as "equivalents" under the doctrine of equivalents. In short, a jury panel of experts would not represent persons having "ordinary skill in the art," a standard often applied in patent cases.

Some members of the task force raised a concern whether the use of specialized juries was constitutionally permissible. Under Amendment VII, a party has a right to a jury of her peers. The issue is what constitutes the "peers" in the community. In other areas of the law unrelated to intellectual property, this has been generally construed to mean members of the community. Does the use of a specialized pool of jurors violate the provisions of Amendment VII? This issue was never fully addressed by the task force since there was disagreement as to the merits of this particular concept.

Since no consensus could be reached, no recommendation on specialized juries was made by the task force.

While we do not feel that specialized juries are necessarily required along with specialized trial courts for patent cases, establishing some type of minimum educational level requirement might be beneficial, and perhaps should be considered again in the future.

Another area of uncertainty and unpredictability in patent rights considered by the task force arises from the fact that patent laws vary from country to country. It was felt that the territoriality of patent rights must be broadened to respond to today's borderless marketplace, a product of the expansion of electronic commerce associated with the Internet. To that end, the task force recommended the establishment of an "international patent" that would harmonize international patent laws and provide patent owners with identical rights of exclusion in all countries that are signatories to such an agreement.[35]

The task force was not naïve in its assessment of the political and logistical difficulties of achieving such an international agreement on patents, however.

For example, some fundamental differences exist between the patent laws of the United States and those of many other countries. These differences would undoubtedly be the focus of controversy in attempting to arrive at an international agreement. One such difference is the United States' "first to invent" public policy in granting patent rights. In the United States, a party who is first to file a patent application and who may, in fact, be the first to have its patent granted may not have good claim to the rights conferred by the patent if they were not the first party to invent the subject matter of the patent. In the United States, a unique proceeding called an "interference" may be declared in order to resolve a controversy as to which party was first to invent the patented subject matter.[36] If the party who filed their patent application second can successfully prove they were first to invent the subject matter, they may be awarded the patent and all rights that go along with patent ownership while the party who was first to file loses all rights in the patent.[37]

The rest of the world follows a "first to file" policy which grants patent rights to the first party who actually files a patent application with that country's patent office regardless of who was first to invent. While the U.S. public policy is grounded in fairness, often the process of proving prior inventorship is quite expensive and unpredictable. This is one example of a difference in policy which would make an international patent difficult to arrive at, at least for the short term.

Hence, the Brookings task force recommended that, at least for the short term, the U.S. government should focus attention on negotiating a "regional patent," to at least extend the territoriality of patents to a geographical area beyond the United States and yet not quite one of "global" scope. For example, a "North American Free Trade Agreement patent," which would have uniform effect within NAFTA member countries, might be achievable in a relatively short time frame. Indeed, the European Union has already moved in this direction with the establishment of the European Patent Office, which issues EPO patents.

The task force also urged that the ultimate goal of harmonization of international patent laws be addressed by the World Intellectual Property Organization (WIPO), working with the U.S. Congress and the executive branch of the U.S. government, especially the U.S. Trade Representative.

Patenting Business Methods

The CAFC's decision in the 1998 case *State Street Bank & Trust Co.* v. *Signature Financial Group, Inc.* has been interpreted by the intellectual property community as removing barriers that might have existed to obtaining a patent on a so-called business method.[38] Since the decision was handed down, numerous patent applications have been filed that seek to protect methods of doing business. The Federal Circuit has recently reaffirmed its position that business methods are patentable subject matter in *AT&T Corp.* v. *Excel Communications, Inc.,* but the Supreme Court has not yet directly addressed the issue.[39]

There are two categories of business method patents. The first involves cases in which a specific method for achieving some business-related goal is implemented via software running on a computer system; for example, a specialized inventory-tracking system. The second category involves strictly conceptual or strategic business plans that have no reliance on any specialized computer- or software-based operation. In most of the Federal Circuit decisions addressing business method patents, the specific facts involved software; therefore, there is still speculation as to whether all types of business methods—including, for example, corporate business models and methods of providing services—will be found to be patentable subject matter.

Even prior to the *State Street Bank* decision, some of these methods of doing business might have been eligible for protection under trade secret laws. Those who argue that these business methods should remain an exception to patentable subject matter point to the vast field of state-level trade secret laws available in such cases. Patenting, however, generally provides stronger protection to the holder of the idea than is afforded to the owner of a trade secret.[40]

In one sense, the patenting of business methods would probably serve one of the important goals of the task force: the development and dissemination of better information about the role of intangibles in the economy. Were these methods to remain simply as trade secrets, they would be just that, secrets, with no real way of being evaluated and valued. Nonetheless, a number of members of the Brookings task force were cautious about this development in the law. In the end, the group recommended only that Congress and the USPTO monitor the issuance of business method patents over the next few years to assess the types of patents being granted, the additional burden on the courts, the impact on businesses, and the value of the additional information made available to the market by the patent process.[41]

One seemingly ameliorative measure taken by the U.S. Congress in light of the deluge of business method patents being granted was to enact the Intellectual Property and Communications Omnibus Reform Act of 1999. The Act includes a "First Inventor Defense," which is codified at 35 U.S.C. § 273. Section 273 seems to apply specifically to business method patents and provides a defense to an action for infringement to a person who, acting in "good faith," "reduced to practice" the subject matter of the invention at least one year prior to the filing date of the plaintiff's patent. In addition, the defendant must have "commercially used" the subject matter before the filing date of the plaintiff's patent.

As of October 2001, no court has taken § 273 into consideration; therefore, we can only hypothesize as to its construction. However, there is extensive legislative history suggesting the defense is intended to cover only "business methods."

As for the USPTO, it too has heard the complaints of industry and has taken some steps to address those concerns. In March 2000, the USPTO issued an action plan as part of its Business Method Patent Initiative. The action plan proposes an industry outreach program and improvements to the examination process to reduce the likelihood that "bad" patents will be issued. The industry outreach program proposes partnerships between the USPTO and the software, Internet, and e-commerce industries to discuss concerns and propose solutions to common problems. The examination process improvements include expanding the prior art databases available to patent examiners so that as broad and comprehensive a search as possible may be conducted at the examination stage.[42]

Trademarks

In the United States, state common law rules regarding territorial trademark rights were incorporated into federal trademark law under the Lanham Act.[43] Federal registration of a mark provides nationwide rights in the protected mark and constructive notice to potential users of that mark in commerce, thus prohibiting independent duplication of a registered mark or "innocent use" by unauthorized users. But federal registration does not provide constructive notice to the user of a duplicate mark outside the United States.[44] The lack of global protection for trademarks adds to the uncertainty surrounding the value of this type of intangible asset.

In response to this problem, the Brookings task force urged the United States to take the initiative in working with other countries to develop a centralized international registration system for trademarks. Here again, the task force recognized the enormous potential political obstacles to achieving such an international agreement—it took the United States 100 years to sign on to the Berne Convention on Copyrights, for example. But members of the task force felt that the rapidly growing use of the Internet in international trade is probably raising the stakes in this matter for many businesses both within and outside the United States. As a result, there might be a window of political opportunity for opening discussion of the issue in international forums, focusing first on the protection of trademarks used on the Internet. Hence, as a first step toward the longer-term goal of broader protection for trademarks used in international trade, the task force proposed that an international registration system be established for trademarks used on the Internet ("Internet trademarks").

The idea is that this registration system would supplement current national trademark rights and registrations. That is, each country that takes part in the centralized registration of Internet trademarks will maintain its sovereignty within its own borders. However, anyone from a participating country who wishes to post a mark on the Internet will be charged with having constructive notice of all other specially registered marks being used on the Internet. Initially, the resulting trademark protection would apply only to the use of marks on the Internet. Moreover, rights in an Internet trademark should be renewable, as for all trademarks under U.S. trademark law, so that rights are protected as long as the mark is in use on the Internet and as long as the owner polices the mark. Relatedly, the task force also proposed that Internet domain names alone, unless independently used as trademarks, should not be afforded Internet trademark status.

The task force also considered the problem of "cybersquatting." Cybersquatters are those who register a domain name knowing that it copies or imitates the trademark of some other party. Typically, the expectation is that the owner of the trademark will be forced to pay a substantial fee to the registrant in order to purchase the domain name containing its trademark. Cybersquatting has become a huge problem, and given the profits that have sometimes been made, it is not surprising that many have joined the game. A variant on this practice involves registering a domain name that is confusingly similar to a famous trademark (a common misspelling, for example), either to divert business from the trademark owner to the registrant or to confuse consumers into believing they have found the trademark owner's web site.

In order to address this problem, Congress passed the Anti-cybersquatting

Consumer Protection Act (ACPA), which went into effect in November 1999. In addition to prohibiting unauthorized individuals from registering domain names that imitate or include a trademark of some other party, the statute seeks to limit the ability of third parties to divert customers and potential customers through confusion about domain names.

In the first full year after the law was passed, hundreds of lawsuits were filed by trademark owners against parties who had registered similar-sounding domain names. By lowering procedural barriers and expanding the jurisdictional reach of the law,[45] the ACPA has made it possible for trademark owners to stop cybersquatters more quickly than they could before the law was passed.

The Brookings task force viewed this new legislation as an important step toward clarifying the extent and degree of protection that trademark owners have in cyberspace at least in the United States. But there were still concerns among task force members about whether trademarks used on the Internet could be adequately protected internationally. To address this problem, a Uniform Dispute Resolution Policy (UDRP) has been put in place by the Internet Corporation for Assigned Names and Numbers (ICANN). This became effective October 1999.[46]

This procedure results in an arbitration-like process for resolving disputes among multiple parties over the use of domain names. The current expectation is that these changes will greatly reduce the problem of cybersquatting internationally, but they may not eliminate it. Consequently, the Brookings task force concluded that cybersquatting practices should be monitored internationally. If they continue to be a problem, the international community should be engaged in developing and enforcing stronger laws and procedures to contain cybersquatting.

Trade Secrets

Trade secrets is a concept developed at common law in order to provide a remedy to those who have been economically injured due to the improper disclosure to competitors of secrets or other specialized information used in conducting business. The earliest trade secret laws were based upon such theories as breach of fiduciary duty or breach of implied contract. Needless to say, the laws governing trade secrets have varied greatly from state to state.

Over the years, a number of model laws have been proposed in an attempt to harmonize the various state laws. But because the states are under no obligation to adopt any of the proposed model laws, state laws continue to vary considerably. In the 1970s, the National Conference of Commissioners on Uniform State Laws again tried to harmonize state laws by drafting the Uniform Trade Secrets Act (UTSA). The UTSA has not been adopted by all state legislatures, however; at least 40, including the District of Columbia, have done so, but some have amended it to such a degree as to defeat the drafters' hopes of providing a uniform trade secret law.[47]

A problem that arises from the lack of uniformity across state borders, and that contributes to uncertainty in the protection of property rights in trade secrets, is the phenomenon called "forum shopping," whereby litigants choose the state in which they sue. Naturally, they select the state with laws most sympathetic to the facts of their case.

To address this problem, the Brookings task force recommended that Congress enact a "Federal Trade Secret Act" (FTSA), by virtue of its authority under the Commerce Clause. Members of the task force thought that UTSA should serve as a starting point in drafting the federal law, but did not endorse UTSA in all its particulars. The proposed Act would preempt inconsistent state laws under the Supremacy Clause and provide a high degree of certainty and predictability with regard to the legal treatment of trade secret cases. At the very least, task force members thought, it would put an end to forum shopping. That alone would increase the stability of trade secret rights, inasmuch as all litigants would know the law that would be applied to the facts and would presumably be more likely to settle their disputes. The task force suggested, however, that the field of trade secrets be revisited at some predetermined time after the enactment of a Federal Trade Secret Act, with the understanding that there will be room for improvement. After three to five years, for example, there would be ample evidence to show how the case law has interpreted the Act. Moreover, a revisitation of the issue would provide an opportunity to further harmonize trade secret laws on a larger scale and to harmonize the Act with the trade secret laws of other nations—perhaps enact an "International Trade Secret Treaty"—in much the same way as the task force proposed for patent law.

The task force acknowledged, however, that there is ambiguity in theory as to whether innovation and economic growth are encouraged more by strong trade secret protection or by weak protection. Empirical evidence on the question is equally indecisive. Hence, the task force chose not to make any specific recommendations about substantive trade secret law and emphasized that the scope of protection provided by any such federal law would need to be carefully considered in light of the theoretical and empirical controversies.

Copyrights

Copyrights enjoy the greatest degree of certainty and predictability of all the forms of intellectual property considered here.[48] The principal reason for the stability of copyright laws in the United States today is undoubtedly the fact that, since 1989, this country has been a signatory member of the Berne Convention.

Although copyrights are territorial and exist within the borders of a particular country, under the Berne Convention a territorial copyright automatically receives protection in all other member countries, according to the laws of the country where the infringement took place. When the copyright of a book first published in another country is infringed within U.S. borders, for example, that copyright, although of foreign origin, is conferred all the protections of a U.S. copyright under U.S. law.[49] This consistent treatment of copyrighted works within individual member countries, coupled with the fact that all member nations are required to make their own substantive copyright laws comply with certain minimum standards, has resulted in the relative uniformity of international copyright laws.

LESSONS AND CONCLUSIONS

Although there are many unknowns as we enter the third millennium, one thing seems clear. The significance of intangible assets in the new economy continues to grow because of the undeniable benefits they bring to the businesses which acquire them and foster their development. The focus of this chapter has been intellectual property, which begins as an intangible idea and which may be transformed into a bundle of rights in personal property, such as a patent, a trademark, a copyright, or a trade secret. Each of these forms of intellectual property, at least to some degree, is recognized as property that has economic value, contributes to the overall value of a business, and can be owned and sold.

As with any asset which tends to contribute to the value of a business, intellectual property rights, and legal mechanisms for protecting such rights, will undoubtedly become more important to the economy. The increased reliance by businesses, in general, upon the value generated by intellectual property highlights the need for better-defined rules within which such assets are acquired, owned, and transferred. The recommendations for change proposed by the Brookings task force are intended to increase certainty and clarity in some of the laws that determine the scope, nature, and enforceability of intellectual property rights. These reforms would help adjust the institutional and legal environment in the United States and internationally so that it will continue to support the kinds of investments needed in the economy of the third millennium.

NOTES

1. Professor Blair co-chaired the task force with Steven M.H. Wallman and drafted the final report, with inputs from seven specialized subgroups. Mr. Hoffman served as the chair of the intellectual property subgroup and drafted that subgroup's report. The final report of the task force, including a list of other participants, has been published as Blair and Wallman, *Unseen Wealth: Report of the Brookings Task Force on Intangibles* (Washington, D.C.: Brookings, 2001).
2. Purchased intangible assets may appear on the balance sheets of firms. But their value is often aggregated into a single catchall category, "goodwill." Intangibles acquired in mergers are likely to be accounted for this way, for example. Internally developed intangibles do not appear on a company's balance sheets at all.
3. The exception is software. Statisticians at the Department of Commerce who compile the national accounts recently began recognizing software as a separate asset category, and are developing methods to estimate the value of these assets.
4. Authors' calculations from Federal Reserve Flow of Funds Data. The net value of cor-

porate securities was computed as the market value of outstanding equities, plus the reported value of financial liabilities, minus financial assets. See Federal Reserve Board, Flow of Funds Data, Table L.102, various years. Data are available only since 1973, and are calculated in nominal dollar terms.

5. See Baruch L. Lev, "R&D and Capital Markets," *Journal of Applied Corporate Finance*, Vol. 11, No. 4 (Winter 1999), p. 21.

6. See Baruch Lev, *Intangibles: Management, Measurement and Reporting* (Washington, D.C.: Brookings, 2001), Figure 1-1.

7. See Robert E. Hall, "E-Capital: The Link Between the Stock Market and the Labor Market in the 1990s," *Brookings Papers on Economic Activity*, Vol. 2 (2000), pp. 73-118.

8. Robert Hall, *The Stock Market and Capital Accumulation*, NBER Working Paper 7180, June 1999.

9. By mid-March, 2001, the NASDAQ index had fallen by nearly two thirds from its peak the previous March, largely as a result of the collapse in prices of dot.com companies. But dot.com companies often had ratios of market value to book value at their peaks of 20:1, or even higher. The S&P 500, a much broader index, had come down from its peak by about 25 percent, suggesting there was still a substantial gap in most companies between market value and book value.

10. Bureau of Economic Analysis, National Income and Product Accounts, table 1.1, January 2001 (*www.bea.doc.gov/bea/dn1.htm*).

11. See Erik Brynjolfsson and Shinkyu Yang, "The Intangible Costs and Benefits of Computer Investments: Evidence from Financial Markets," Sloan School of Management, Massachusetts Institute of Technology, April 1999; and Timothy F. Bresnahan, Erik Brynjolfsson, and Lorin M. Hitt, "Technology, Organization, and the Demand for Skilled Labor," in Margaret M. Blair and Thomas A. Kochan, eds., *The New Relationship: Human Capital in the American Corporation* (Washington, D.C.: Brookings, 2000).

12. See Robert E. Hall, "The Stock Market and Capital Accumulation," Working Paper 7180 (Cambridge, Mass.: National Bureau of Economic Research, June 1999), p. 28.

13. See Carolyn Kay Brancato, "New Corporate Performance Measures," Report 1118-95-RR (New York: Conference Board, 1995); Carolyn Kay Brancato, "Communicating Corporate Performance: A Delicate Balance," Special Report 97-1 (New York: Conference Board, 1997); Brian Hackett, "Beyond Knowledge Management: New Ways to Work and Learn," Report 1262-00-RR (New York: Conference Board, 2000); and Brian Hackett, "The Value of Training in the Era of Intellectual Capital," Report 1199-97-RR (New York: Conference Board, 1997).

14. See Brian Hackett, *Beyond Knowledge Management: New Ways to Work and Learn*, The Conference Board Research Report, 1262-00-RR.

15. Cap Gemini Ernst & Young's Center for Business Innovation has sponsored several major research reports in the last few years on the correlation between intangibles and market value or financial results; see, for example, *Measures That Matter* (Cambridge, Mass., March 1997); *Managing the Success of the IPO Transformation Process* (Cambridge, Mass., June 1998); *The Value Creation Index* (Cambridge, Mass., June 2000). Cap Gemini Ernst & Young also co-published a book with the Organization for Economic Cooperation and Development (OECD) entitled *Enterprise Value in the Knowledge Economy: Measuring Performance in the Age of Intangibles* (Cambridge, Mass.: Center for Business and Innovation, December 1997). PricewaterhouseCoopers has developed a new business reporting model called "ValueReporting"; see Robert Eccles and others, *The ValueReporting Revolution: Moving Beyond the Earnings Game* (New York: John Wiley & Sons, 2001). And in August 2000, Arthur Andersen gave a $10 million grant to the Massachusetts Institute of Technology's Sloan School of Management to develop a "New Economy Value Research Lab." See Steffan Heuer, "The Bean Counters Strike Back," *The Standard*, August 21, 2000.

16. See Shelley Taylor and Associates, *Full Disclosure 2000: An International Study of Disclosure Practices,* London (October 2000) for survey information on the kinds of information investors say they want corporations to report and evidence on actual disclosure practices of 100 large international and domestic corporations.

17. A recent Boston Consulting Group study found that "high-quality information on companies, which is comparable across regions and sectors, is critical for investors to formulate accurate expectations and make informed choices. Unfortunately, this information is often not available." See *New Perspectives on Value Creation: A Study of the World's Top Performers* (Boston Consulting Group, 2000), p. 21.

18. Sears, Roebuck and Co. spent more than five years, for example, trying to develop a robust model of the connection managers believed existed between employee satisfaction and customer loyalty, and the further connection between customer loyalty and profitability. See J. Anthony Rucci, Steven P. Kirk, and Richard T. Quinn, "The Employee-Customer Profit Chain at Sears," *Harvard Business Review* (January–February, 1998).

19. See, for example, Baruch Lev, "R&D and Capital Markets"; Bronwyn H. Hall, "Innovation and Market Value," in Ray Barrell, Geoffrey Mason, and Mary O'Mahoney, eds., *Productivity, Innovation, and Economic Performance* (Cambridge University Press, 2000); and Bronwyn Hall, Adam Jaffe, and Manuel Trajtenberg, "Market Value and Patent Citations: A First Look," Working Paper 7741 (Cambridge, Mass.: National Bureau of Economic Research, 2000).

20. The next section is taken almost verbatim from *Unseen Wealth*, pp. 51–56.

21. Appointed to the post in 1991, Mr. Edvinsson is believed to have been the first "vice president for intellectual capital" at any company in the world. He is currently visiting professor in knowledge economics and intellectual capital at the University of Lund, Sweden, and president of Universal Networking Intellectual Capital.

22. Quoted in Brancato, "Communicating Corporate Performance," pp. 68–69.

23. For a related, but more detailed, parsing of the measurement problem, see Steven M. H. Wallman, "The Future of Accounting and Financial Reporting, Part II: The Colorized Approach," *Accounting Horizons*, Vol. 10 (June 1996), pp. 138–48.

24. See Financial Accounting Standards Board (FASB), "Elements of Financial Statements," Statement of Financial Accounting Concepts 6 (December 1985).

25. The accounting treatment of certain kinds of liabilities, such as maintenance, servicing, and environmental liabilities, and risk-hedging and financial instruments and derivatives, present similar problems.

26. There is evidence that outside investors do care about employment and personnel policies. Institutional Shareholder Services, a division of Thompson International that advises large institutional investors on proxy matters, recently endorsed an employee-led shareholder proposal at IBM urging that the company permit employees to choose whether to remain in a traditional pension plan or switch to a new cash-balance plan. IBM had initially announced that all employees would be required to switch to the new plan except those within five years of retirement, but under pressure from unhappy employees and negative publicity, it agreed to allow all workers age 40 and older and with at least 10 years of service to choose between the plans. See John G. Auerbach and Ellen E. Schultz, "Shareholder-Services Group Supports Workers Choice on IBM Pension Plan," *Wall Street Journal,* April 17, 2000, p. B6. To the extent that employees can be required or induced to switch to the cash-balance plans, IBM would probably be able to record higher current profits. Although many institutional investors apparently decided that the negative effect on employee morale would cost the firm more in the long run, other shareholders did not agree. The resolution won only 28.4 percent of the vote, and therefore was defeated. See Ellen E. Schultz and John G. Auerbach, "IBM Holders Defeat Pension Resolution," *Wall Street Journal*, April 26, 2000, p. A2.

27. See Blair and Wallman, *Unseen Wealth*, pp. 23–32.
28. This section draws heavily from Blair and Wallman, *Unseen Wealth*, Chapter 4.
29. U.S. Constitution, Art. 1, Sec. 8, Cl. 8.
30. See Donald A. Gregory, Charles W. Saber, and Jon D. Grossman, *Introduction to Intellectual Property Law* (Washington, D.C.: Bureau of National Affairs, 1994), p. 7.
31. Gregory, Saber, and Grossman, *Introduction to Intellectual Property Law*, p. 1.
32. The importance of copyright law in determining who is able to capture the economic value of artistic works has been dramatized by the legal fight over the operations of Napster, Inc. Napster operates a web site that allows users to share electronic copies of songs and other music recordings with each other. Napster attracted 23 million customers within a few months, but in late July, 2000, the U.S. District Court in San Francisco ruled that the company's operations violated the legal protection of the artists and record companies who held copyrights to the music being exchanged through the service. See Matt Richtel, "In Victory for Recording Industry, Judge Bars Online Music Sharing," *New York Times*, July 27, 2000, p. A1. In March 2001, a federal district court had issued a preliminary injunction ordering Napster to prevent the downloading, uploading, transmitting, or distributing of all copyrighted works identified as such by the recording industry. *A&M Records et al.* v. *Napster, Inc.*, 2001 WL 227083 (N.D. Cal. 2001). Subsequently in July 2001, Napster was ordered to remain shut down until it could ensure 100 percent effectiveness in filtering out copyrighted works from being distributed. As of October 2001, Napster remains shut down, has settled several lawsuits pending against it, and plans on launching a paid subscription service in the near future.
33. This section draws heavily from Blair and Wallman, *Unseen Wealth*, Chapter 6.
34. If the specialized patent court were based in a single location (say, Washington, D.C.), it might be prohibitively remote to some potential litigants. The idea of specialized trial courts for patent cases has been discussed by others; see, for example, Ernest Shriver, "Separate But Equal: Intellectual Property Importation and the Recent Amendments to Section 337," *Minnesota Journal of Global Trade*, Vol. 5 (Summer 1996), p. 449; Gregory D. Leibold, "In Juries We Do Not Trust: Appellate Review of Patent-Infringement Litigation," *University of Colorado Law Review*, Vol. 67 (Summer 1996), p. 648.
35. Former Commerce Secretary William Daley has also expressed support for this idea. See "Daley Calls for Renewed Effort to Negotiate Global Patent System," *Patent, Trademark and Copyright Journal* (September 16, 1999), pp. 552–53.
36. It should be noted that an interference may be declared by the USPTO before either patent is granted.
37. The party seeking to prove prior inventorship must show, without an unreasonable delay, when the idea was conceived and when the first device that embodies the idea was constructed.
38. 149 F.3d 1368 (Fed. Cir. 1998), cert. denied, 119 S.Ct. 851 (1999).
39. 172 F.3d 1352 (Fed. Cir. 1999).
40. See, for example, Claus D. Melarti, "*State Street Bank & Trust Co.* v. *Signature Financial Group, Inc.*: Ought the Mathematical Algorithm and Business Method Exceptions Return to Business as Usual?," *Journal of Intellectual Property Law*, Vol. 6 (Spring 1999), pp. 387–89.
41. The USPTO has recently instituted additional review procedures on business method patents.
42. See Sheila M. Ryan and John M. Bagby, "An Idea Whose Time Has Come: Patenting Software and Business Methods," *Business Law Today* (January/February 2001), p. 33.
43. 15 U.S.C. secs. 1051 et seq.
44. WIPO is well aware that international trademark disputes will proliferate because of the global nature of the Internet while trademark law only protects competing marks

in a common geographical area. See "Multimedia Developments of Note," *Multimedia and Web Strategist,* Vol. 4 (August 1998).

45. Plaintiffs can get injunctive relief even if only *in rem* jurisdiction can be established. This makes it possible to get an offending web site shut down, even if the site's owner is a foreigner or otherwise personally outside the jurisdiction of the U.S. court hearing the case.

46. The UDRP can be used against any dot.com, dot.net, or dot.org domain name registered with an ICANN-accredited registrar. The disputed name can be challenged in an administrative proceeding before an ICANN-approved dispute resolution provider, of which WIPO has been the most actively used. In general, in order for the complainant to be successful, he must show that the registrant's domain name is identical or confusingly similar to the complainant's trademark or service mark; that the registrant has no rights or legitimate interest in the domain name; and that the domain name was registered in bad faith. As of November 2000, over 4,000 proceedings have been commenced with approximately 80 percent favoring the complainant. See Sandra Edelman, "Cybersquatting Claims Take Center Stage," *Computer & Internet Lawyer* (January 2001), p. 1.

47. See Ian Ballon and Keith M. Kupferschmid, "Intellectual Property Opportunities and Pitfalls in the Conduct of Electronic Commerce," *Practising Law Institute/Pat,* Vol. 563 (June 1999), p. 103.

48. The recent controversies regarding the storing and sharing of music on the Internet has raised new questions that may eventually require a reexamination of the strength of copyright protection in this area.

49. See Brenda Tiffany Dieck, "Reevaluating the Forum Non Conveniens Doctrine in Multilateral Copyright Cases," *Washington Law Review,* Vol. 74 (January 1999), pp. 131–32.

ABOUT THE AUTHORS

Margaret Mendenhall Blair is a Sloan Visiting Professor of Law at Georgetown University Law Center (GULC), focusing on corporate finance and corporations. She came to GULC in 2001 from the Brookings Institution, where she was in residence as a scholar in the Economic Studies Program for the previous 13 years. She continues as a nonresident Senior Fellow at Brookings. She also serves as a director of Sonic Corp. Professor Blair is a renowned scholar in the field of corporate governance. She holds a PhD in Economics from Yale University, and is the author of numerous books and articles, including the internationally acclaimed *Ownership and Control: Rethinking Corporate Governance for the Twenty-First Century* (Brookings, 1995), which has been widely used by scholars and policy-makers working on enterprise reform and corporate governance problems in Europe and Asia. Professor Blair also co-directed the Brookings Project on Intangibles with Steven M.H. Wallman, SEC Commissioner from 1994–1997. This project culminated in 2001 with their publication, *Unseen Wealth: Report of the Brookings Task Force on Intangibles* (Brookings, 2001). Professor Blair's other areas of expertise include business ethics, organizational theory, human capital issues, the role of intangible assets, and financial market institutions.

Gary M. Hoffman chairs Dickstein Shapiro Morin & Oshinsky LLP's Technology Group of 65 attorneys. His practice focuses on intellectual property law, unfair competition, and computer law, including litigation, licensing, and acquisition of rights. In over 25 years of private practice, Mr. Hoffman has participated in more than 100 intellectual property lawsuits and has acted as lead counsel in over half of these. Mr. Hoffman has prepared more than 150 licensing agreements and has established programs for the acquisition and management of intellectual property rights.

Mr. Hoffman testified before Congress on intellectual property and international issues before the Subcommittee on Intellectual Property and Judicial Administration Committee on the Judiciary, U.S. House of Representatives. From 1967 to 1972, he was an examiner, U.S. Patent & Trademark Office, and served as a law clerk to the Board of Appeals, USPTO. He is co-editor of the Intellectual Property Section's book, *Patent Litigation Strategies Handbook*, published by Bureau of National Affairs in June 2000.

Salvatore P. Tamburo is an associate in the intellectual property practice of Dickstein Shapiro Morin & Oshinsky LLP. He joined the firm in September 1998. Mr. Tamburo's practice encompasses the drafting and prosecution of patent applications; the preparation of opinions on patentability, infringement, validity, and enforceability; and intellectual property litigation, as well as intellectual property licensing and counseling. Before joining the firm, Mr. Tamburo worked as an electrical engineer for 8 years with Signal Transformer Co., Inc., in Inwood, New York.

Part Two

Exploiting Intellectual Property

CHAPTER FIVE

Managing IP Financial Assets

Principles from the Securities Markets

by Alexander K. Arrow

PERSPECTIVES

Most companies are adept at prudently managing their tangible assets. Nonperforming physical assets that show up on a balance sheet, such as an unused plant, are generally sold, leased, or otherwise forced to perform by almost any competent business manager. The dramatic underutilization of intangible assets, particularly unused intellectual property rights to undeveloped technology, by contrast, has been a consistent and curious business failing. Nowhere is this deficiency more apparent than among public for-profit companies.

The problem may be due to the consistent failure of most otherwise rational managers to view selected IP rights under their control as financial assets. They are fixated on what Alexander K. Arrow calls "an anachronistic legal mind-set, in which managers view their patents as static legal documents, locked up and brought out for use only in the event of litigation." This is especially ironic, he contends, because IP assets, as a class, behave almost identically to another class of well-studied financial assets: call options. Now that IP assets are being viewed in this way, IP owners and investors are able to monetize some of their holdings through previously unavailable means.

"Options pricing," says Dr. Arrow, "underwent an outright transformation in 1973 with the advent of Myron Scholes's and Fischer Black's now-famous option pricing formula. The Black-Scholes formula, with the swift, precise, transparent, reproducible value it provides for each option contract, allows option traders to instantly post 'bids' and 'asks,' the prices at which they are willing to buy or sell options upon demand. The confidence with which the traders were buying and selling options at reasonable prices made it possible to do enough transactions that an exchange was needed, and the fledgling Chicago Board Options Exchange (CBOE) was created that same year as a result. Put another way, the reasonableness of the output of Black-Scholes' options pricing formula allowed confidence in quoted options pricing to grow, and this led to the robust, liquid options marketplace we enjoy today."

Dr. Arrow believes that a similar options pricing model can provide a more liquid and somewhat transparent market for trading patent assets, and facilitate their emergence as an important asset class.

MANY IP ASSETS ARE FINANCIAL ASSETS

Financial assets are the possessions of an entity which are held for purposes of producing revenue. Manufacturing plants are financial assets because they can be used to manufacture product, which is sold to produce revenue. Bonds are financial assets, because their owners receive a specific cash rate of return and can sell them outright for more cash when needed. Acquired goodwill—the amount by which the price paid for an acquired business exceeds its tangible value—is also a financial asset. Acquired goodwill costs money to obtain and is expected to generate a return in the form of customers' likeliness to purchase more goods, thereby creating more revenue. Financial assets, be they manufacturing plants, bonds, or goodwill, all cost capital to produce or acquire, and all are owned for purposes of generating a cash return.

So, too, are many intellectual property rights. Patents that secure ownership of a unique technology, product line, or process improvement are financial assets. That is because, very simply, they exist to give their owners rights to a future cash flow. Other IP rights, including brand trademarks, copyrighted text, or character likenesses, may not be so directly or specifically translated into cash. While it could be argued that these IP rights are also financial assets (otherwise they would not be maintained and defended with such vigor and resources by their owners), we will turn our attention to the more obviously financial IP assets for this chapter: patents on products, product improvements, and processes. To emphasize this, we will henceforth refer to them as simply *IP assets*.

Like conventional financial assets, IP assets require an outlay of cash to create or acquire. Unlike them, however, IP assets do not enjoy the same balance sheet treatment. They are, by decree of worldwide generally accepted accounting principles (GAAP), always recorded as zero value, while manufacturing plants, bonds, and even acquired goodwill are accounted for with nonzero values.

Securities analysts speculate about the discrepancy in the accounting treatment of IP assets and other types of financial assets. Many theories exist.[1,2,3] The two most popular, straightforward explanations for the discrepancy are likely that other financial assets have enjoyed greater corporate attention and priority than IP assets; and great differences exist in the mechanisms available to acquire and dispose of (buy and sell) IP assets compared with conventional financial assets. Both are changing now.

Change #1: Corporate management teams are giving IP assets the attention and resources previously afforded only to tangible assets. The resources being allocated to patents and the priority they are enjoying have risen sharply in the late 1990s, showing up in nearly every quantitative indicator (see Exhibits 5-1 and 5-2).

U.S. Indicators	Annual Increase
Total U.S. patents issued, 1998 [155,000], compared with 1997 [117,000]	33%
U.S. patents issued to IBM in 1998 compared with 1997[a]	54%
Total patents issued to U.S. universities 1997, compared with 1996[b]	26%
U.S. university IP license and option agreements ("technology transfer deals") concluded 1997[b]	21%
U.S. university licensing revenue, 1998 [US$611 Million]	cumulative 89% from 1993

[a]IBM Press Release, January 1999.
[b]IAssociation of University Technology Managers, Annual Review, 1999.

Exhibit 5-1   U.S. patent creation and licensing rose sharply in the late 1990s.

Worldwide Indicators	Annual Increase
Combined patents issued by U.S. Patent & Trademark Office, the European Patent Office, and the Japanese Patent Office, 1996 compared with 1995[a]	43%
Worldwide patent application filings, 1998	23%
Worldwide patent licensing revenue, 1998 [US$100 Billion]	12%

[a]Online data from the American, European, and Japanese patent offices.

Exhibit 5-2   Worldwide patent creation and licensing rose sharply in the late 1990s.

U.S. corporations are treating this recent IP prioritization so seriously that it is showing up in recently debuted corporate taglines, such as Hewlett-Packard, "Invent"; Sun Microsystems, "Powered by Innovation"; 3M, "Inside the Innovation"; and Apple Computer, "Great Ideas Powered by Great Technology."

Shareholders are speaking even louder than management teams. Approximately 83 percent of the collective market value of all publicly traded companies in the Standard & Poor's (S&P 500) index is now attributable to intangible assets; tangible assets (book value) account for the other 17 percent, a dramatic shift from 50 percent for each in the late 1970s.[4] Along with this greater corporate prioritization may come, perhaps with time, a more egalitarian accounting treatment.

Change #2:   Acquiring and disposing of IP assets (buying and selling) is becoming easier and safer. In fact, few industries on the planet are being changed by the arrival of e-commerce as much as the tech transfer industry—the network of patent licensing executives, inventor-scientists, patent attorneys, and technology brokers who make up the world's system for buying, selling, and licensing intellectual property.

For patents that are licensed or sold, the average transaction consumes three years and erodes 15 percent of the patents' potential lifetime value.[5] This destructive pace persists because the market for intangible assets has been inefficient. The market has been characterized by fragmented information and financial risk, which is to be expected, considering it has operated without the benefit of the financial tools that are standard to other disciplined financial markets.

The Internet has enabled, for the first time, the creation of information and financial tools that allow buyers and sellers of intellectual property to conduct their business in a more rational way. Some licensing officers who previously did business with only a narrow band of colleagues are now able to deal with the larger market. Those who previously could not close transactions for risk of patent invalidity or buyer credibility are making use of IP buyer and seller protection. Now a furniture company licenses a high-density ceramic created by an aircraft manufacturer. A wound care drug discovered in a small lab in Italy is licensed six weeks later by an American pharmaceutical company eager to add to its product pipeline. The IP transaction transformation is starting, and it looks like the kind of business-changing event that has not been seen since the founding of the Chicago Board of Trade in the late nineteenth century or the New York Stock Exchange (NYSE) a century before that.

With these two barriers to the treatment of IP assets as financial assets thus removed, the business of intellectual property asset management, and the ensuing selling and buying of patents and licenses, has the potential to grow quickly.

DEALING WITH FINANCIAL ASSETS: WALL STREET

Two centuries years ago, financial assets were risky to own and difficult to transact. They were risky to own because even the most stable, low-risk assets, such as bonds in established companies or government notes, could abruptly be declared worthless.[6] They were difficult to transact because there was no central exchange and no financial tools with which to sell or buy them. Worse still, sellers with phony assets and buyers with no intention of paying for their purchases abounded.

Selling shares of stock involved retaining a stock broker who, contrary to contemporary notion, was not a fast-talking wheeling-and-dealing portal to a stock market. Rather, a stock broker circa 1780 was simply a person who knew others with money or stock and therefore stood a chance of matching a buyer and seller.[7] To perform this service, the broker typically took claim to 30 percent of the value of the stock being transacted as a commission.

Wall Street's rules and structure, created out of necessity over a storied 210-year history, provide a robust set of risk-reducing financial tools that enable safe, dependable stock and bond transactions. This safety has led to the impressive volume of transactions the NYSE and other markets enjoy today, which in turn has created a sense that stock, bonds, commodities, real estate interests, and derivatives of these assets are tradable, liquid, and clearly financial. Financial assets can be traded in this way because they are securities—fractional ownership interests that exist for the purpose of profiting from the work of others. Also, Wall Street's financial tools and structure has made them *less risky to own and transact*—no one who buys bonds today fears that the bond certificates could be phony and potentially ruled worthless by a court, nor do sellers fear that a buyer will refuse to pay after the bonds they are selling have been delivered.

These two traits are shared by stock, bonds, commodities, real estate interests, and derivatives of these assets alike. Wall Street's institutions are the service industry that has evolved because of them.

By contrast, patents have had neither of these two important traits for most of the last two centuries. Unfortunately, intellectual property is not a security; patents are not broken into fractional ownership interests (yet). Buying and selling (and more practically, licensing) of IP assets is, however, for the first time, becoming safe. The Internet has made the mass application of financial tools to enable IP transactions possible. The first financial tool-enabled IP transaction closed in November 2000 between a U.S. seller and a German buyer,[8] marking what may be the beginning of a sea change in IP licensing. With the recognition that IP is actually a financial asset, and the resulting recognition that the safety of financial markets is therefore appropriate for IP, a large portion of Wall Street's infrastructure becomes applicable for IP assets. Its structure and tools become a template for the way IP can and perhaps inevitably will be transacted and internally managed.

LESSONS AND TEACHINGS OF FINANCIAL ASSET MANAGEMENT APPLY TO INTELLECTUAL PROPERTY

The two basic principles of financial asset management that any corporate manager should follow are:

1. Maximize the return on the company's assets by deploying them in those ways in which they are most valuable.
2. Sell off or otherwise dispose of assets that are generating an annual return below the company's cost of capital.

These principles are both well known and routinely followed by for-profit companies worldwide. Consider, for example, a company that manufactures both awnings and fume hoods, in which the manufacturing plant that produces fume hoods is responsible for $450 of revenue per year per square foot of space, while the plant that produces awnings is responsible for $45 of revenue per year per square foot of space. The prudent manager in this hypothetical company would, of course, stop producing awnings and use both plants to make fume hoods. If the company owns a third facility which is responsible for no product or revenue at all, the prudent manager would lease out the facility or sell it to dispose of such a nonperforming asset. Such thinking in business, and in microeconomics, is routine and assumed.

This type of reasoning is far from routine, however, in the world of IP asset management. For-profit companies that own thousands of unused and unlicensed IP assets are the norm. One might deduce that the logical way to manage a company in this common situation is to license out the unused IP assets, just as one would any other nonperforming asset. Instead, even while exhibiting extreme prudence and good asset management with their tangible financial assets, these companies typically do nothing with their IP assets. They constitute nonperforming assets—assets that have cost money to create, but which are not generating any return on the investment. They actually have a negative cash flow, because the company must pay their annual patent maintenance fees (an exercise which costs approximately $200,000 per asset for worldwide rights maintained over a 20-year patent life).[9]

Prudent managers should clearly want to maximize the return on financial assets in their company. As their IP assets are increasingly recognized as financial assets, good financial asset management is becoming possible. This includes making the decision to license or sell nonperforming assets rather than letting them lie as unused corporate reserves. It also includes making use of financial tools to maximize the safety of such transactions, the kind of safety that is standard in transactions for other financial assets on exchanges. In the next decade, prudent financial asset management of IP assets, including the selling or licensing of nonperforming IP assets, is likely to become not only possible, but expected.

PATENT VALUES AND CALL OPTION VALUES

Historically, patents have not been traded in any centralized marketplace despite their similarity to other financial assets.[10] In other words, stocks, bonds, and commodities are all publicly traded, while technology is not. This has obvious implications for technology liquidity—it is easy to buy or sell stocks, bonds, commodities, and options, but less easy for companies to buy, sell, or license a patent (hence the counterintuitive behavior of corporate IP managers discussed in the section above). The lack of liquidity has less obvious but equally important implications for patent value and, consequently, pricing.

It is trivial to find the fair market price (the value) of a stock, bond, or commodity by simply observing the latest price at which it has been bought or sold. This can be done using any of dozens of real-time computer data-feed programs like Bloomberg® or Reuters®, or by opening *The Wall Street Journal*. It is clearly far from trivial, however, to find the fair market price (the value) of a patent. The most recent patent sold or licensed is not identical to the one being valued, even if it does have an identifiable price. To make things more challenging, patent transactions are infrequent and large compared to other financial instrument transactions, which further confounds data collection.

For help, we can turn to the definition of a patent. Legally defined, a patent is the right to exclude others from manufacturing and selling a defined product, component, or process niche. Financially defined, however, a patent takes on an entirely different definition. When framed in a financial perspective, a patent is best defined as the right to a future series of cash flows that may or may not ever materialize. It requires its owner to expend money in order to obtain an underlying asset (create the product), and that asset may or may not turn out to be worth more than the money spent to obtain it. This defines the payout structure of the asset. And, like other kinds of assets, this payout structure gives us the key to its pricing behavior. Consider, for example, the payout structure of a bond, as shown in Exhibit 5-3.

A bond gives its owner a predictable cash flow over time with a large, predictable cash payment due at a specified end point in the future. The value of owning this instrument is a strict function of the value of its highly predictable cash payments, discounted to the present with a rate very close to the risk-free rate.

An instrument with a more volatile payout structure is a dividend-paying stock, as shown in Exhibit 5-4.

In this case, periodic cash flows during the initial period are variable, and the final value is also variable. When the expected cash inflows are unknown, the fair present value of the asset is reduced by the greater level of risk the asset brings.

A riskier asset still is a nondividend-paying stock, in which no cash flows are received while it is owned, and its ending value is an unknown, shown in Exhibit 5-5.

This type of highly risky, unpredictable asset appears to bear a similarity to owning an IP asset—an asset of uncertain future value. Before jumping to this conclusion, however, there is another type of asset with a payout structure which is an even better match with IP assets—call options, as shown in Exhibit 5-6.

The owner of a call option must pay out additional cash in order to receive

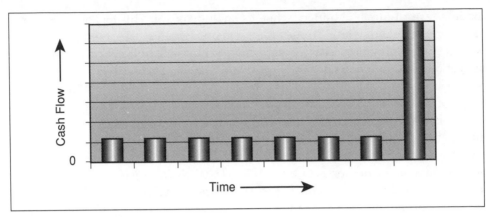

Exhibit 5-3　Payout structure of a bond.

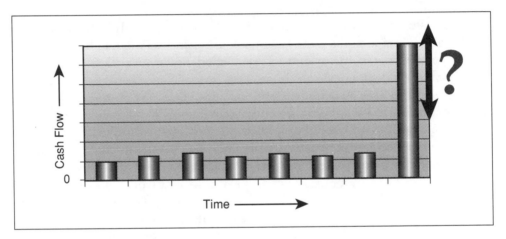

Exhibit 5-4　Payout structure of a dividend-paying stock.

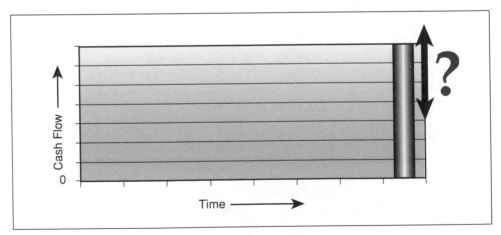

Exhibit 5-5　Payout structure of a nondividend-paying stock.

the cash value of the underlying asset. The future value of the underlying asset is variable and initially unknown; it may turn out to be less than the cash that must be spent to receive it (which is the case with an option that ends up out of the money). A call option, therefore, is the right to a future asset which may or may not have any value.

Every owner of a unit of intellectual property faces a familiar decision: whether to invest research and development (R&D) capital to transform the IP asset into a commercial product. The patent gives the owner the right to do this, knowing that he or she will own full rights to the cash flows from the eventual product, but it does not tell him or her whether these cash flows will amount to more or less than the cash outlay needed to effect the transformation. Indeed, the eventual value may turn out to be zero. In other words, a patent is the right to a future asset which may or may not have any value. Strikingly, this is a powerful match with the payout structure shown in Exhibit 5-6. IP assets have a nearly identical payout structure to another type of financial asset—a well-studied, well-quantified class of financial assets—call options.

Call options, one of the members of the innermost circle of liquid financial instruments, were not always as easily tradable (liquid) as they are today. In fact, as recently as the early 1970s, option trading was slow and infrequent, similar to the slow, infrequent pace of technology licensing today. Traders who made markets in these instruments were faced with comparing the price at which the option allowed its owner to buy stock (the strike price) to three other inputs after which they would have to post their asking price. To determine whether the option would expire worthless or be valuable, traders compared the strike price to:

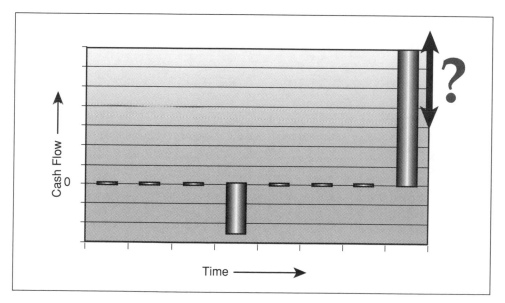

Exhibit 5-6   Payout structure of a call option.

- The price of the underlying stock
- The time remaining until the option expired
- The degree of volatility of the underlying stock

This is quite similar to the reckonings a corporate manager makes when faced with a decision about selling/licensing or buying/acquiring rights to a patented technology. To make a decision to either license/sell or not license/not sell—to transact or not transact—he or she must compare the predicted development cost to:

- The likely value of the underlying commercializable technology
- The time remaining until the product is commercialzed
- The degree of volatility of the value of the underlying commercializable technology

To make things worse, IP professions are beset by an additional problem—the predicted development cost, unlike the strike price of an option contract, is often a soft number. Companies have been known to spend six months of complex modeling and sensitivity analysis simply computing a predicted strike price for a new technology asset[11] when deciding whether to license it.

Even with a known strike price, a good stock option trader could do only a few of these complex computations in his or her head over the course of a day. This led to overly cautious options brokers who kept bids for option trades very low and asking prices very high, effectively to discourage business, for fear of offering mispriced options and suffering losses as a result. The same dilemma and fears face IP licensing professionals today and similarly diminish the volume of IP transactions.

THE BLACK-SCHOLES FORMULA

Options pricing underwent an outright transformation in 1973 with the advent of Myron Scholes's and Fischer Black's now-famous option pricing formula. The Black-Scholes formula, with the swift, precise, transparent, reproducible value it provides for each option contract, allows option traders to instantly post "bids" and "asks," the prices at which they are willing to buy or sell options upon demand. The confidence that the traders were buying and selling options at reasonable prices made it possible to do enough transactions that an exchange was needed, and the fledgling Chicago Board Options Exchange (CBOE) was created that same year as a result.[12] Put another way, the reasonableness of the output of Black-

Scholes' options pricing formula allowed confidence in quoted options pricing to grow, and this led to the robust, liquid options marketplace we enjoy today.

The thought process leading to the creation of the equation itself is revealing, and helps explain why the equation remained undiscovered for years after options contracts existed. Looking for a way to compute a fair present valuation estimate for a call option contract, Fischer Black, a one-time professor and Goldman Sachs economist with a penchant for theoretical physics, began with an assumption about the value of the underlying asset (or simply "the underlying," as he and other economists call the asset to which a call option gives its owner the right to purchase). He assumed that its motion was utterly random, and could therefore be described by the same equations Albert Einstein had used to describe the random movements of particles—Brownian motion.

The behavior of the value of a right to purchase an asset whose value is described by Brownian motion could be described, he reasoned, as the sum of multiple separate one-dimensional orthogonal (perpendicular) infinitesimal changes. He turned to a little-known theorem for characterizing value versus time for a function which depended on such a quantity. This theorem, Ito's Lemma,[13] applied to an option contract with an imposed boundary condition, that value is "risk neutral,"[14] gave Black, Myron Scholes, and Bob Merton the basis to derive an expression for the present value of an option, given several starting assumptions:

1. A "risk-neutral" owner
2. An underlying asset whose value fluctuated with short-term random movements
3. A lognormal distribution of returns

All fair assumptions, it turns out, for financial assets owned by dispassionate, reasonable managers or investors.

The formula that resulted (see formula on page 124) equated the present value of an option right to all the quantitative measurements of the option contract. The formula has since enjoyed a long and mathematically sound history as an indicator of fair options prices in the world's options markets. It receives praise which is afforded to few other innovations:

> Modern option pricing techniques are often considered among the most mathematically complex of all applied areas of finance. Financial analysts have reached the point where they are able to calculate, with alarming accuracy, the value of a stock option. Most of the models and techniques employed by today's analysts are rooted in a model developed by Fischer Black and Myron Scholes in 1973.[15]

The formula is referred to in financial circles with words that seem to imply that awarding the Nobel Prize to recognize it was an understatement:

> The economist Zvi Bodie likens the impact of The Black-Scholes Formula, which earned Scholes and Merton the 1997 Nobel Prize in Economics, to that of the discovery of the structure of DNA. Both gave birth to new fields of immense practical importance.[16]

Endorsements like these, and constant usage by financial institutions including the CBOE, as well as insistence on its use by major accounting firms such as Arthur Anderson, KPMG Peat Marwick, and Ernst & Young, has further cemented the Black-Scholes equation as the standard, universal mechanism for valuing rights to future assets that may or may not have value.

OPTIONS PRICING THEORY AND LIVE MARKET DATA

The Black-Scholes formula has been such a liquidity-enhancing tool for options that it is being used in other fields where option-like structures exist, including project decision making,[17] corporate asset purchases,[18] and even as a replacement for the popular Capital Asset Pricing Model for investments.[19] The formula is also widely used by technology-dependent corporations to evaluate research projects.[20] Academicians, noticing the growth of its use (and its misuse) and its impact on industries, have promoted it from a formula to a bona fide theory: Real Options Theory. In most cases, the use of the Black-Scholes equation has made pricing more predictable and transparent and made transaction volume grow.

Intellectual property assets, because of their potentially immense but highly uncertain value, present a unique case. Reaching an agreement on valuation of intellectual property is arguably the most difficult hurdle buyers and sellers must overcome in IP transaction negotiations. A seller is hoping to transform a sunk cost into a lucrative payback. A buyer is hoping to extract a lucrative return from a combination of the license price plus the time and money that will be spent after the transaction to develop a technology into a commercial product.

The seller tends to focus on the reward. The buyer tends to focus on the risk. While independent consultants may furnish suggested valuations, generally there has been no standardized formula for relating risk to reward. Therefore, each transaction entails two customized valuations for buyers and sellers that typically vary widely. If the parties are able to converge, a deal may result. If not, one more technology may languish unused and one more product pipeline may remain dry.

Today's IP licensing participants have an opportunity to use the Black-Scholes formula as a mechanism to help increase patent transaction volume as has been done in other industries before them. Unlike the hundreds of thousands of dollars an option trader may realize from a fortuitous option trade, a single patent sale or licensure can make or break an entire company.

Viewing Patents as Options

Given the similarity in payout structure shown in Exhibits 5-4 and 5-5, the progression of IP asset pricing practices need not be as slow as the original development of options pricing theory. The dynamic pricing challenges faced by early stock option traders, as recently as the early 1970s, effectively discouraged business until a uniform pricing methodology gained uniform acceptance. This fear of mispricing options was prevalent until 1973, when the options market underwent a transformation with the advent of Myron Scholes's and Fischer Black's Nobel prize-winning option pricing formula, as discussed in the previous section, which led to the robust, liquid options marketplace we enjoy today.

The intellectual property asset market has historically suffered from the same problems that plagued the options market in the 1960s—including having no clear way to set valuations. The use of the Black-Scholes formula, with an adjustment factor to account for the expiration date of the patent, makes pricing predictable and transparent for intellectual property just as it has done for call options on stock. Its use in valuing patents has recently been made possible because of the data stream translations of the Technology Risk-Reward Unit (TRRU®) valuation model.

The advent of the Intangible Asset Market[SM] (IAM) Index and the TRRU IP valuation model in 1999 brought, for the first time, many of the same techniques used in financial markets to the intellectual property market. Developed at The Patent & License Exchange (pl-x), the IAM Index uses live market data; TRRU Valuation uses both option pricing theory and live market data to objectively measure value associated with broad intangible asset markets and individual technology assets, respectively.[21]

Critics of the Black-Scholes formula's application to IP assets are quick to point out that one of the base assumptions of the formula may make it inapplicable for patents. They note that returns on stock prices, the assets underlying the call option contracts that the formula is traditionally used for, are lognormally distributed (skewed), and this lognormal data distribution is a prerequisite for the formula to be applicable.[22] By contrast, they assert that the distribution of returns on raw technology, the assets underlying patent call options, has an unknown distribution pattern, and is likely to be Gaussian (bell-shaped). Recent studies from Harvard Kennedy School of Government and the University of Munich, however, show that across a population of 4,000 technology assets studied in the United States and Germany, returns were highly skewed and, in fact, followed a lognormal distribution.[23] This type of statistical support, coupled with its impressive increase in usage,[24] has earned the TRRU model a special place in the evolution of IP asset valuation.

The Technology Risk/Reward Unit (TRRU®) Value of Patents

A new technology has the potential for creating significant value if successfully developed. It also carries the risk of being completely worthless. Great novelty allows for great potential value and great developmental risk. Balancing this risk/reward trade-off inherent in all IP assets, the TRRU® valuation calculation combines Real Options Theory with data from publicly traded, technology niche-specific companies to indicate *reasonable market values* for intellectual property assets.

The thesis of the system, and the likely reason for TRRU's recent popularity, is that a patent behaves financially as if it were a call option on a future technology asset. Built to replicate the way call options on stock are priced with the Black-Scholes formula, the call option's strike price (X), the price of its underlying stock (S), the time until the option must be exercised (τ), the variance, or variability (σ^2), and the risk-free rate of return (r), are used as its inputs.

$$c_i = S_i N(h) - X e^{-r\tau} N(h - \sigma\sqrt{\tau})$$

where:

$$h = \left\{ \ln\left(\frac{S}{X}\right) + r\tau + \frac{\sigma^2\tau}{2} \right\} / \sigma\sqrt{\tau}$$

Do not be alarmed by this formula. Even option traders who use it all day every day do not memorize it (they have hand-held machines that calculate it for them) and neither should you. They simply find the inputs X, S, τ, σ^2, and r; plug them into the formula; and use the output, c, as their fair value estimate.

To do this for IP assets the way it is done with call options on stock, the TRRU Valuation model uses measurable quantitative traits of an IP asset in place of each of the call option's measurable attributes used in Black-Scholes. For example, the strike price—the amount of money that the owner of a call option must spend in order to obtain the underlying stock—is analogous to the remaining product development cost, which is the amount of money that the owner of a patent must spend in order to obtain the finished product. Each of the Black-Scholes variables is similarly mapped, as is shown in Exhibit 5-7, and the result is an objective, transparent, market-driven intellectual property pricing formula known for its high correlation with results of lengthy licensing negotiations. In one forthcoming study, it was run against nine published real-world tech transfer transactions and the correlation coefficient between the technologies' TRRU suggested value and the actual deal closing value was greater than 0.9.[25]

The stock variable presents a challenge to map, since the analogy to the current price of the underlying stock would be the current value of the underlying

Black-Scholes variable for call options on Stock	TRRU Metrics analog variable for intellectual property
Strike price, X	Remaining development cost, X
Time in which the option must be exercised, τ	Remaining length of development, τ
Market price of underlying stock, S	Market value of underlying product, S
Variance of stock price return, σ^2	Variance of product value return, σ^2
Risk-free rate, r	Risk-free rate, r
Output: Call option present value, C	**Output: TRRU whole-asset value**

Exhibit 5-7   Variables used in Black-Scholes applied to call options on stock and IP assets.
Source: The Patent & License Exchange, Inc. (pl-x).

commercializable technology. Finding this value has historically been a vexing task as each technology is unique with no known value and no last trade. To run the equation, however, one must find a market-driven present value of the underlying technology to which the patent applies.

The underlying present value of early-stage products can never actually be known the way the present value of stock underlying a call option can. We are fortunate, however, that small-cap stock financial analysts and investors do us the convenient service of estimating the value of specific niche technologies in thousands of mini-sectors every day. They do this by buying and selling stock in very small publicly traded companies,[26] the kind with a single product in development and no revenues, providing a market-driven, reasonable estimate of diverse, specific technologies. Daily commercial product values of such obscure diverse technologies as viral vector-based gene therapy, automotive brake friction components, bar-code scanning technology, or wound-closing glues are generated in this way.

These market-driven technology values are processed to produce the mean enterprise value per product at launch in each of more than 350 technology niches adjusted forward or backward depending on when those products are due to launch.[27] The values are then discounted to the present to be used as the stock variable in the Black-Scholes equation. Since the small company stock prices change every day, the TRRU valuation calculation fluctuates on a daily basis. This dynamic fluctuation adds a sense of urgency and timeliness to each asset's final valuation.

In summary, TRRU Metrics uses the following variables to calculate continuously the present value of each unique technology asset:

1. Time until launch: τ is defined as the number of months it would likely take a well-funded corporate entity to turn the patent in its present state of development into a product ready for launch. The value of τ for most listings on the license market ranges somewhere between 0 (an already

launched product) to 120 (10 years of development and testing needed before launch).

2. Development cost: X is the estimated sum of the remaining funds needed to turn the raw technology into a commercial product, analogous to the strike price of a call option (the sum of money required to turn a call option into stock).

3. Market value of underlying product: S is the market-driven mean enterprise value[28] per product at launch from other "pure play" companies with products in the same niche technology category as the listed IP asset, discounted to the present day.

4. Variance: σ^2 is the variance of return plotted against time for market value of the underlying product (variable #3 above), just as variance in the Black-Scholes formula is taken from variance of return of the underlying stock price.

5. Risk-free rate: r is the offered rate on U.S. government Treasuries with comparable maturities.

Objections to Options Pricing Theory's Application to IP Assets

Objection #1: Subject matter experts are too important to leave out of the process of valuing IP assets.   Some have asked why the detailed analysis of a subject matter expert would not be a better input for S than the market-driven quantities used in options pricing theory. In other words, wouldn't an expert be a better judge of an IP asset's underlying commercializable value than the collective actions of relatively uninformed stock purchasers?

Aside from the obvious and trite answer that no two experts ever agree and taking one expert's opinion is a sure recipe for prolonged arguments, there is a more profound reason market-driven data is a superior input source, known in financial literature as the "Dumb Agent" Theory Standard. This popular modern financial theory holds simply that a large number of uninformed agents (such as investors) acting independently to guess any difficult-to-judge quantity (such as the proper value of stocks) will invariably be more accurate, collectively, than any individual subject expert trying to guess the same quantity.

Technology Risk/Reward Unit Valuation calculations comply with the Dumb Agent economic standard by virtue of the live per-product market data that goes into the S and σ^2 variable inputs. Specifically, S is determined by the collective wisdom of a large number of relatively uninformed people who buy and sell the stock of microcap technology niche–specific companies. These quantities are used in place of any subjective valuation assessment from subject matter experts, respecting and complying with the Dumb Agent standard.[29]

Objection #2: Options pricing for IP cannot be performed in an imperfect world, so don't try to do it.   Most business-minded IP professionals can agree that IP rights to a future product comprise a financial call option, but some cannot agree on uniform data inputs needed to run options pricing formulas. While each unique IP asset's "strike price" (its development cost) and "time until exercise" (its development time) can be estimated, the underlying asset market value (the technology, if it were instantly commercialized) is not obvious. All three are needed, as they are three of the five inputs into the Nobel prize-winning Black-Scholes options pricing formula. The need for data to feed the underlying asset variable has led to the creation of specific niche IP categories with live product value data. Naturally, this process has led some to question whether these categories can be made specific enough.

Those who focus on only one data feed into the options pricing equation may miss the forest for the trees. A typical question: "One of your 383 niche technology categories is motorcycle technology. Are you trying to suggest all motorcycle technologies have similar values? This is clearly not specific enough! Consider the difference between a new motorcycle engine and a new kind of motorcycle handlebars."

Market-driven options pricing IP valuation may be fast, transparent, and objective, but it is not precise. Even so, it is precise enough to differentiate between a new handlebar and new engine technology. This is because only two of the six inputs into the equation (mean product value at launch and daily variance) are affected by the choice of niche IP category. The other inputs—remaining development cost, remaining time to launch, and patent expiration dates—are likely to be different, leading to different resulting valuations.

Objections #3: "Breakthrough" technology IP assets cannot be valued using options pricing theory because no market-driven data is good enough. Some technology owners feel the unique qualities of their technology assets make them inapplicable to any kind of valuation model. They ask, "How does market-driven options pricing IP valuation value breakthrough technology? Where does TRRU Metrics get data for the stock variable if there are no similar 'pure-play' public companies?"

Every new technology worth licensing is unique and is therefore a "breakthrough" technology. Innovations that solve an old problem in a whole new way are nonetheless dealing with a similar, well-known target market or target patient population. An entirely new cardiovascular drug, for example, may function like no other blood pressure medication ever has, but still has roughly the same number of hypertension patients as its potential market. A new platform technology for public transportation may be completely unlike a car, bus, train, or anything else out there, but the same number of people still need transportation services. A whole new kind of engine lubricant that is nothing like any kind of oil we have ever seen is unique and distinct, but the number of total engines that need lubrication is still the same.

The value of a technology is determined by:

- The size of its market
- Its likelihood of leading its market

- The expense of developing the technology
- How long this development is likely to take
- The likelihood of the technology's value exceeding the cost to develop it
- The length of patent protection the technology enjoys
- The comparable financial returns available from using capital in investment choices other than buying technology

Options pricing theory (TRRU) IP value calculations take all of these factors into account except the second one, leaving negotiators free to concentrate on the likelihood of the technology leading the market, which is their natural expertise.

When an IP asset does not fit neatly into an existing data-rich technology niche category, a related category which is closest in size to its target market turns out to be an excellent proxy. This supplies the underlying asset input with a market-driven estimate of the average value of the average asset in a market of similar size, given the enormous diversity of individual technology niches, to its actual technology niche. With the final needed input thereby provided, the options pricing calculation can proceed along with the rest of the user's unique inputs. The result is a transparently derived, reasonable, market-driven asset valuation which takes into account the unique features of the asset.

A HEALTHY FINANCIAL MARKET FOR IP ASSETS

With the news that options pricing theory market-driven IP asset valuation has recently resulted in the first Internet financial tool IP transaction,[30] the next 10 years' IP transaction rates are likely to begin to look more like a financial market and less like the sporadic hit-or-miss industry they have been. Both the necessary financial tools and the necessary corporate attitudes are now in place.

The intention to treat IP assets with the prudence and management given any other financial asset, coupled with the tools now available, is a prerequisite for a meaningful financial market for IP assets. The appearance of these priorities in corporate agendas in the last two years is helping spawn a healthy financial market for IP assets. The process bears a striking similarity to the formation of inchoate stock exchanges of two centuries ago. Then, just as now, multiple channels of asset trade coalesced into a unified financial marketplace. Safety, volume, and transaction value has increased ever since and seldom looked back.

The Intangible Asset Market Index

Another natural outgrowth of the burgeoning financial market for IP assets is the appearance of IP asset-tracking indices. Just as the Dow Jones Index tracks value in the industrial economy and the NASDAQ composite index tracks the value of the high-tech new economy, the even newer intangible asset market (IAM) indices track the value of raw technology IP assets in various sectors.

The IAM indices track the value of intangible assets in the five fastest-growing IP sectors:

1. Advanced materials
2. Information technology
3. Automotive and transportation technology
4. Express package transport and logistics technology
5. Life sciences technology

These values, driven by the underlying value of intangible assets in IP-rich, technology-dependent sector-specific companies, form a telling indication of the relative value movement of differing IP sectors. This turns out to be true even in periods of rapid economic growth, as the IAM index segments from December 1999, depicted in Exhibit 5-8, suggest.

Following the trends illustrated by the individual sector indices can help both technology buyers and technology sellers formulate sound investment strategies, because the IAM indices may signal the right time to be acquiring, or offering for sale, different types of technology.

Each of the five IAM indices is calculated from the intangible asset values from 30 niche technology companies in an IP sector. Components in each index are rebalanced occasionally to account for changes in focus, mergers, or acquisitions.

These first five IAM indices correspond to the five broad intellectual property categories with the greatest growth.[31] With the addition of nine other sectors, the IAM index tracks 14 sectors thought to cover virtually all commercializable intellectual property today. The nine other IP sectors are:

1. Telecommunications technology
2. Software
3. Consumer products and apparel technology
4. Storage and environmental preservation technology
5. Basic materials and natural energy procurement
6. Firearms, explosives, and lasers
7. Building structure, manufacturing equipment, and civil infrastructure technology
8. Agriculture and food technology
9. Aerospace and defense technology

IP Asset Beta: A Measurement of Risk

The beta ratio is a standard measure of risk for any financial instrument and is published for all liquid financial instruments such as stocks, bonds, commodities, and options (see Exhibit 5-9). A beta greater than one signals a stock (or other financial instrument) that is riskier than the overall market. A beta less than one

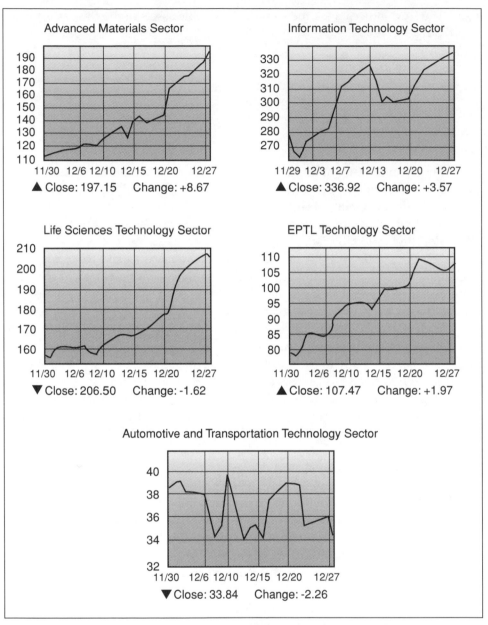

Exhibit 5-8   December 1999 index movements in the five fastest-growing IP sectors.

Source: The Patent & License Exchange, Inc. (pl-x)

Beta	Meaning	Example
>1	An asset with a riskier or more uncertain return than the board market	Biotech Stocks
1.0	An asset just as risky as the overall market	"Blue Chip" stocks
<1	An asset with greater predictability and less risk than the overall market	Government bonds

Exhibit 5-9   The meaning of beta.
Source: The Patent & License Exchange, Inc. (pl-x)

signals a stock that is less risky than the market, and a beta equal to one means that the stock's risk level is in lockstep with the market.

Stock beta is calculated as follows:

$$\text{Stock beta} = \frac{\text{Covariance of the stock price return with the market return}}{\text{Variance of the market return}}$$

In other words, beta is the covariance of the return of a stock with the return of the market, divided by the variance of the market. The combination of an intangible asset's market-driven options pricing theory-based value and the appropriate IAM index has made the same measure of risk now available in the intellectual property market.

In the IP market, the beta—or risk rating of a particular technology—is simply calculated with the same formula used by money managers examining a stock's beta. The return of the stock translates to the IP asset valuation return, and the variance of the market return translates to the variance of the corresponding sector's IAM index return.

$$\text{IP Asset Beta} = \frac{\text{Covariance of the IP asset's valuation return with the IAM index return}}{\text{Variance of the IAM index return}}$$

Using IP Asset Beta, buyers and licensees of intellectual property are able to quantitatively weigh risk levels of different assets they are considering acquiring. Participants in the intellectual property market, like their counterparts in other financial markets, are beginning to demand the right to make decisions based on the market price and risk of their potential investment, as well as consulting the appropriate IAM index. Indeed, the growth and publicity[32] of TRRU Metrics and the IAM index is a sign that this change is under way.

IP ASSET DERIVATIVES

In the past two decades, real estate investing spawned Real Estate Investment Trusts (REITs), and mortgage-backed securities. The unbundling of Treasuries in the 1980s released value by widening the range of investment options and allowing the creation of more targeted, focused fixed income financial instruments. So, too, a new class of derivatives based on intellectual property could have a similar effect on the nascent IP investment industry. The formation of a market for IP asset-backed derivatives may not be too far in the future, given the financial tools now available for IP assets and the historical precedent of previous derivative markets.

The key prerequisite for the formation of IP asset-backed derivatives is an objective IP asset valuation standard. Traditional discounted cash flow (DCF) valuations are unlikely to serve this purpose, as their revenue estimates and discount rates would lead to arguments that are nonconducive to asset trading. A market-driven options pricing theory based valuation system, as described above, is an objective standard.

Given a standard, objective IP asset valuation metric, the possible derivatives we may look forward to are positively exciting. Two illustrative examples are Technology Unit Investment Trusts (TUITs) and securitized IP options.

Technology Unit Investment Trusts

Technology Unit Investment Trusts are IP derivatives available for investing that could take the form of a bundle of a group of technology assets (similar in structure to REITs). The benefits to the investor are twofold: (1) to diversify away risk by combining into one security similar technologies whose returns are not directly correlated, and (2) to make investing in raw technology available to a broader audience of investors. The benefits to the technology owners who contribute IP asset to the TUIT are (1) the prospect of nearer-term cash receipts for assets that might otherwise take much longer to outlicense, and (2) a greater likelihood of sharing in the upside of a broad technology's success in exchange for relinquishing exclusive ownership of a specific asset.

Companies with technologies which are not generating cash could submit them for inclusion in a new TUIT. TUITs would be grouped around technology themes. One hundred patented products relating to silicon galadium arsenide semiconductors, 40 new kinds of wound-closing glues, 70 new materials relating to packaging perishable goods, 15 Internet-based business process patents could each be bundled into a single instrument labeled with its technology theme. The technology owners would not relinquish ownership of their technology, and no market maker would purchase the technologies, so no principal risk is incurred. Instead, each technology owner would retain an ownership interest in the TUIT equal to the computed valuation of the asset(s) he or she contributed divided by the sum valuations of all assets in the TUIT.

Investors could then purchase shares in each TUIT, representing fractional ownership in the instrument and a fractional claim to cash flows that result from future licenses. Technology contributors receive cash from investors according to their ownership interest in the TUIT.

Eight companies contribute 100 patented technologies relating to silicon galadium arsenide semiconductors

Company	Contribution	Total Value	% ownership in TUIT
Company A	6 patented technologies	$78.2 million	10.9%
Company B	17 patented technologies	$127.6 million	17.8%
Company C	1 patented technology	$8.1 million	1.1%
Company D	22 patented technologies	$266.8 million	37.3%
Company E	9 patented technologies	$10.7 million	1.5%
Company F	3 patented technologies	$1.6 million	0.2%
Company G	36 patented technologies	$141.8 million	19.8%
Company H	6 patented technologies	$80.3 million	11.2%

The TUIT is divided into 10,000 shares, initially priced at $71,510 each (1/10,000 of $715.1 million). Each share entitles the investor to 0.01 percent of all licensing revenues, less operating expenses, including legal fees incurred in collecting licensing royalties. After two months of posted availability and indication acceptance, the TUIT trader has indications to sell 50 shares at $45,000 each, 120 shares at $32,000 each, or 600 shares at $24,000 each. This is less than the $71,510 per share the assets theoretically warrant, but as the owners were previously receiving zero cash, it is welcome by the asset owners.

Feeling a sense of liquidity at the $24,000 level, the trader begins selling units: 50 @ $24,000 = $1,200,000 proceeds from the first sale. Assuming a 5 percent distribution commission ($60,000), the remaining $1,140,000 is paid to the technology contributors according to their ownership interest, as follows:

Results of the first sale

Company	Received from first sale	New ownership structure
Company A	$124,260	10.2%
Company B	$202,920	16.7%
Company C	$12,540	1.0%
Company D	$425,220	35.1%
Company E	$17,100	1.4%
Company F	$2,280	0.2%
Company G	$225,720	18.6%
Company H	$127,680	10.5%
New investors: 6.0% (600 shares)		

Companies A to H continue to serve as "selling shareholders" at the rate of $24,000/share, or higher if market demand dictates, until such time as all 10,000 shares are sold. When one or more of the patented technologies in the TUIT is needed by a corporate entity (to develop and sell a new product or product improvement), the corporate entity must pay a licensing fee to the TUIT, at a rate negotiated by the *Steward*, a technology consultant who negotiates on the TUIT's behalf for a percentage of the license royalties. This licensing revenue is passed through to the owners of the TUIT—this is the reason the new investors invested! Now that the TUIT's shares carry a cash flow with them (similar to a dividend-paying stock), they become more attractive to more investors and the market maker will likely do more business trading the shares.

Securitized IP Options

Puts and calls on a firm's intellectual property assets allow for more effective hedging of a company's risk. A "put" is a contract to sell a security at a specified price. It is used primarily by portfolio managers to achieve hedge risk. Puts and calls could also allow investors to make a more isolated bet on the value of a company's individual technologies, as well as broaden the investor base to include those speculating in either direction. Some fascinating examples arise: Imagine, for example, a put option offered on an IP asset owned by hypothetical "University A," which is not getting any use out of it and would like to outlicense it for $1 million.

"Small Company B" would like to license the technology from University A to develop and commercialize it. But the technology may or may not work, and the cost of licensing it plus the risk of developing it is just too much, so Small Company B passes on the opportunity. University A would like to get *some* cash for it, so to make it more attractive to Small Company B, University A offers a one-year $500,000 put option on the technology, along with the license to the asset. Small Company B now must spend $1 million to license it, but knows at the end of the year it can recover half its initial investment by choosing to exercise its option and return the technology to University A. Since universities are generally loath to ever return cash, University A should account for this by booking only half of the received $1 million, leaving the other $500,000 in a sequestered fund ready to return in case the put option is exercised by the technology owner.

Under these conditions, Small Company B licenses the technology and receives the put option from University A. Small Company B then wants to raise cash (to fund development), and can use the put option to help do this. If Small Company B reasons that it is confident it will succeed, it may come to believe that it will never need to exercise the put option—that the option will turn out to expire worthless. If it could find someone to purchase the worthless put option from it up front, this would be a source of essentially free cash inflow for Small Company B, since it believes it would be selling a worthless instrument.

Enter "Speculative Investor C," a hedge fund or other entity who believes Small Company B will fail to commercialize the technology. As long as Speculative Investor C really believes Small Company B will fail, it will be interested in purchasing the put option for $100,000. Why would Speculative Investor C be motivated to make such a purchase? Speculative Investor C believes the technology will fail and that Small Company B will therefore need to retrieve the put option, in order to recoup cash from University A. Since the cash Small Company B would recoup upon option exercise of the option would be $500,000, Speculative Investor C reasonably expects that it will be able to sell the put option back to Small Company B for $350,000, netting Small Company B $150,000 that it otherwise wouldn't have. Speculative Investor C stands to make a return of 3.5 times on the $100,000 it invested in buying the option—resulting in the first situation in which a company can raise funds by convincing investors that its technology will fail!

CONCLUSION

Without standard financial tools, it is little wonder IP assets have historically been severely underutilized. With no objective source of value—no market price—to gauge the risk and reward inherent in all technology, it is little wonder that valuation and financial risk has foiled so many negotiations, have left inventors with a glut of technologies, and have left many manufacturers with a shortage of products. Again taking a lesson from financial assets, wouldn't it be simpler if the same means of measuring value available in financial markets were available in the intellectual property marketplace as well?

The choices available to IP asset owners and licensors when IP assets are treated as the financial instruments they clearly can be are enormous. The pursuit of these choices leads to fabulous ramifications, including cash flow from otherwise nonperforming assets. Now that the tools are available to facilitate such treatment, licensing professionals are gaining relevance, power, and consequently prestige— a delightful and much-deserved result which has been 200 years in the making.

NOTES

1. B. Lev and P. Sarowin, "The Boundaries of Financial Reporting and How to Extend Them," *Journal of Accounting Research* (Autumn 1999), pp. 353–385.
2. B. Lev and T. Sougiannis, "Penetrating the Book-to-Market Black Box: The R&D Effect," *Journal of Business, Finance, and Accounting*, (April/May 1999), pp. 419–449.
3. D. Aboody and B. Lev, "The Value-Relevance of Intangibles: The Case of Software Capitalization," *Journal of Accounting Research*, Supplement, 1998, pp. 161–191.
4. R. Litan. *Corporate Disclosure in the Information Age*, Policy Matters 00-7. AEI-Brookings Joint Center for Regulatory Studies, May 2000.
5. The Patent & License Exchange, Inc. corporate brochure, January 2000.

6. The banking crash of 1837 is a good case in point, in which many dubious banknotes issued by fly-by-night banks in the western United States as well as the supposedly dependable bonds of the state of Pennsylvania were declared worthless.

7. John Steele Gordon, "Capital's Capital: How Wall Street Became 'the Street,'" *Worth* (November 1998), pp. 112–119.

8. Mark Voorhees, "The X Factor," *The Daily Deal* (December 12, 2000), p 4.

9. *Computer Patent Annuities*, corporate literature, December 2000.

10. Until the Patent & License Exchange opened the first viable financial market for IP assets in 1999.

11. M. Amram, N. Kulatilaka, *Real Options*, (Cambridge, Mass.: Harvard Business School Press, 1999).

12. Joseph O'Brien, a junior reporter at *The Wall Street Journal*, invented the options exchange as part of the Chicago Board of Trade (CBOT), which soon became the CBOE on April 26, 1973.

13.
$$dF = \left(\frac{\partial F}{\partial x} a + \frac{\partial F}{\partial t} + \frac{1}{2} \frac{\partial^2 F}{\partial x^2} b^2 \right) dt + \frac{\partial F}{\partial x} b\, dz$$

in which F is a function of x (the value of the underlying asset) and t (time). The resemblance between the result of applying Ito's Lemma to options pricing and heat diffusion expressions have contributed to the myth that the Black-Scholes formula was derived from the heat transfer equation.

14. Refers to the assumption that a 50 percent chance of receiving $2x and a 50 percent chance of receiving $0 is valued exactly the same as a 100 percent chance of receiving $1x.

15. Kevin Rubash, *A Study of Option Pricing Models*, Foster College of Business Administration, August 2000.

16. *Nova*, "The Trillion Dollar Bet," June 2000.

17. "Exploiting Uncertainty," *Business Week* (June 7, 1999), pp. 118–124.

18. "Get Real," Credit Swiss First Boston *Frontiers of Finance* series (June 23, 1999), pp. 1–29.

19. "Keeping All Options Open," *The Economist* (August 14, 1999), p. 62.

20. Ariane Reiss, "Investment in Innovations and Competition: An Option Pricing Approach," *The Quarterly Review of Economics and Finance*, Special Issue 2, 1998.

21. N. Kossovsky and A. Arrow, "TRRU® Metrics: Measuring the Value and Risk of Intangible Assets," *Les Nouvelles* (September 2000), pp. 139–142.

22. R. Jarrow and A. Rudd, *Option Pricing* (Irwin Press, 1983), pp. 89–95 and 117–145.

23. F. M. Scherer and D. Harhoff, "Technology Policy for a World of Skew-Distributed Outcomes," *Research Policy* 29 (2000), pp. 559–566.

24. From January 2000 to January 2001, the value of IP assets companies had valued using TRRU Metrics rose some 29,200 percent, from $162 million to $47.3 billion.

25. The Patent & License Exchange, Inc., Pasadena, California 91101.

26. Also known as "microcap" companies, a name indicative of these companies' small market capitalization.

27. "Intangible Asset Valuations," feature appearing every Wednesday in *The Daily Deal*, (2000-2001), p. 18.

28. Enterprise value, long defined as market value of a company less its book value (*EV = MV–BV*), is a commonly used parameter in securities analysis.

29. Greg Ip., "CSFB Strategist's 'Dumb Agent' Stock Approach Attracts Followers," *The Wall Street Journal* (September 1, 2000), p. C1.

30. A. Nyberg, "Intellectual Property—What's the Big Idea?" *CFO* Magazine (January 1, 2001), p. 28.

31. U.S. Office of Technology Assessment, 1998.

32. The Milken Institute and The Patent & License Exchange *TRRU Metrics Certification Program*, January 19, 2001, Santa Monica, California.

ABOUT THE AUTHOR

Alexander K. Arrow, MD, CFA, is Chief Financial Officer of The Patent & License Exchange, Inc., a 60-person company that transforms intellectual property into financial assets by providing the tools of financial markets. Customers include over 350 for-profit companies, IP consultancies, government labs, and IP law firms. Intangible assets under management exceed $83 billion. Board members include the former Commissioner of the U.S. Patent & Trademark Office (USPTO), and the former CEO of Mitsubishi Electric America.

Prior to joining pl-x, Dr. Arrow was Vice President, Research, at Los Angeles-based Wedbush Morgan Securities and led the firm's medical technology sell-side equity research team, which covered 14 companies and published industry reports on three sectors: (1) biotechnology in wound care, (2) point-of-care diagnostics, and (3) surgical automation, which are still quoted in the technical and business press. He is a frequent speaker at various investors' conferences. Dr. Arrow's background includes securities analysis, technology analysis, and life science research. Prior to Wedbush Morgan, he was a general surgery resident at the UCLA Medical Center, a management consultant at Arthur D. Little, Inc., a biotechnology analyst for Hambro Biofinance, Inc., and a biomaterials researcher at MIT. He is one of the foremost authorities on the wound care market and has participated in three initial public offerings. Dr. Arrow is a Chartered Financial Analyst; he holds an MD from Harvard University and a BA in Physics from Cornell University. He is on the Board of Directors of the Southern California Biomedical Council, and a member of the Association for Investment Management and Research.

The Patent & License Exchange (*www.pl-x.com*) provides a financial marketplace for valuing, marketing, and monetizing intellectual property. pl-x provides web-based business tools for creating value from intangible assets. pl-x offers IP owners, advisors, and inventors a comprehensive solution for marketing intellectual property, locating new technologies, and valuing patents.

driven intellectual property strategy generates innovations more under the guidance of marketing than technology, employing "marketing pull" rather than "technology push." Second, once the idea has been identified, protecting it with strong patents requires an integrated team of inventors, attorneys, and managers rather than the more traditional departmental "silo" approach. Finally, wrapping intellectual property around an invention becomes more of an ongoing and constantly evolving process, rather than static implementation. In this chapter, we will look at each of these three topics in turn. We discuss the transition of several companies from manufacturing-dominated to information-dominated business models and look at companies on the cutting edge of business-driven IP in the gaming and pharmaceutical industries, then consider an example from Walker Digital Corporation, a pioneer in marketing-driven IP, demonstrating in the process the risks and rewards of this important new paradigm.

THE MARKETING-DRIVEN APPROACH

In classical research laboratories, there often exists a virtual wall between research and marketing. As companies grow in size to achieve economies of scale, research and development (R&D) and marketing often become separate departments, with R&D tending to be located closer to manufacturing while marketing often resides within company headquarters. This means the groups may be located in separate buildings, in different states, or even in different countries. Multinational companies, for example, often operate with widely separated functions that interact only indirectly. In this classical paradigm, placing R&D groups near manufacturing sites was logical since the primary function of R&D was to improve upon existing products and design new ones. Likewise, having marketing functions centrally operated from headquarters was sensible since marketing typically operates across all of a company's products, developing a coherent overall brand/image.

This separation allowed R&D to concentrate on implementing the benefits of technological change—higher-quality goods that cheaply and efficiently incorporated the latest product enhancements. But as product quality and reliability steadily improves, differentiating products has become increasingly difficult. For this reason, many companies are turning to information content as a point of distinction. To illustrate, many delivery services can "get the package there overnight," so Federal Express created an Internet-based tracking system that allows users to know where their package is at any given time, becoming a package *confidence* business in addition to a package *delivery* business. Many companies manufacture toys, so Tiger Electronics created Furby, a toy that interacts with kids. Dozens of airlines can fly you to a given destination city, so American Airlines developed Sabre to sell information about flights. It now books $75 billion in travel annually; 40 percent of all reservations made in the world are now processed through Sabre.

As information begins to play a more important role in products, however, the old approach to intellectual property may have to be reexamined with an eye toward incorporating marketing thinking into the invention process, in addition to technology thinking. Given the virtually infinite range of possible information-based product improvements, marketing will play a key role in shaping innovations to meet the needs of customers. An engineer making a cell phone lighter, less power-consuming, or easier to use typically has a fairly clear idea of market interest in the solution. An engineer considering whether to develop a communication protocol to allow a microwave oven to communicate with a cell phone will need guidance from marketing to understand if this is something consumers actually want and, if so, how elaborate a system they want at what price.

In this new paradigm, an understanding of the needs of the market precedes and directs the development of innovations. Instead of researchers pursuing a technology in the hope of making product improvements, marketing experts analyze customer needs and then present these needs to the researchers. These consumer needs then act to filter out innovations without market motivation, resulting in fewer patents sitting on the shelf and fewer new product failures. To see the application of the two approaches (technology push versus marketing pull), consider the gradual transformation of the casino gaming equipment industry.

IP IN THE CASINO GAMING INDUSTRY

Driven by the high profitability of slot machines, the gaming equipment industry is constantly developing new devices. Dramatic growth occurred in the 1970s and 1980s as casinos spread from Las Vegas to Atlantic City to Native American reservations. Leading manufacturers have responded by directing significant resources to R&D. Research focused on developing gaming devices that lasted longer, broke down less frequently, and cost less to maintain. Patented innovations (driven more by technology than marketing) tended to focus on the mechanical elements of a slot machine, such as the spinning-reel mechanisms or coin-handling apparatus. But as the market for gaming machines slowed in the 1990s, slot machine manufacturers faced a market with sales driven increasingly by replacement purchases rather than newly installed machines. Mechanical innovations had relatively low value since most manufacturers had reached a high level of quality. Casino operators saw mechanical problems with machines as less of a distinguishing feature. Knowing that casino operators would tend to replace their machines only if higher profitability per machine were demonstrated, manufacturers were forced to come up with more radical innovations that would capture player attention and money. This shift from mechanical orientation to marketing-driven orientation is reflected in the slot machine patents filed during the last few decades.

Exhibit 6-1 compares mechanically oriented patents (related to increasing the mechanical effectiveness of machines) versus consumer-oriented (solving a cus-

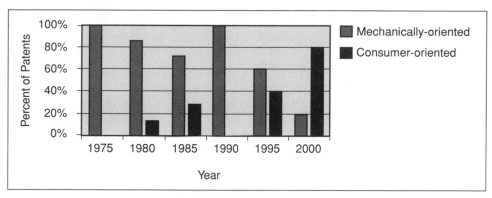

Exhibit 6-1   Slot machine patent evolution.

tomer need) slot machine patents issued over the last 30 years. A random sampling of patents from each of these years was taken and divided into the two categories. The chart shows that mechanically oriented patents have fallen from favor as consumer-oriented applications emerged in 1995 and 2000. Typical patents of the 1970s and 1980s included slot machine reel mechanisms such as a "replaceable plug-in reel module for game machines" and coin-handling mechanisms such as "electromechanical winnings distribution assembly for slot machines." By the 1990s, manufacturers began to file patents that were less about mechanical efficiency and more about solving customer needs. The patent for "gaming machines with bonusing" is typical, describing bonusing systems designed to attract and retain players. Another example is "method and apparatus for team play of slot machines." Rather than addressing mechanical efficiencies of the machine, this patent seeks to create a more social slot-playing experience. Note that the emphasis has shifted from the machine itself to the way that customers view and perceive the machines.

Within the casino environment, a number of questions suggest themselves. Why do players pick one machine over another? Why do they voluntarily end a gambling session (other than running out of money)? What aspects of the experience of playing slots frustrates them? Why do they play at one casino and not the one across the street? Do they gamble with friends or alone? Do they prefer frequent small wins or a few larger wins? Do they expect to lose, but have fun doing so? A thorough understanding of the answers to such questions reveal business-process targets for innovation. Rather than trying to develop an innovative new slot machine technology, inventive resources in the new methodology are deployed to find new ways to eliminate one or more of the reasons that players walk away from a slot machine. Ideas that do not solve this or other player needs can be deferred in favor of more marketable choices.

A good example of this approach is the work of inventor Ernest Moody. He recognized that video poker players were frustrated by only getting one chance to draw new cards to a starting hand of cards. When holding four cards of a royal flush, a player only had one chance to draw the missing card. Moody's inventive insight was to conceptualize a machine that could automatically display the same initial poker hand multiple times and thus let the player make the "exciting" draw repeatedly. His target was a certain kind of frustration, and the result was his patented Triple Play video poker. The game quickly became popular. Royalties to Moody are expected to exceed $100 million over the lifetime of the patent. Why did the game succeed? At least partly because it solved a real problem—limited excitement when more excitement was desired. Moody understood the frustrations of poker machine players, and invented a patentable game variation specifically designed to reduce that frustration. While there are other potential frustrations video poker players experience (cards not being dealt fast enough, payout tables that are too complex, etc.), Moody was able to isolate the frustration of not getting a second (or third) chance to improve a highly promising starting point. Identifying broad problems is not enough; the inventor needs to focus on a real and valuable problem.

Understanding the behavior of consumers does not have to be restricted to a casino environment. With many different industries solving computer needs, transplanting innovations from other industries into the gaming industry offers many possibilities. Frequent flyer reward programs, for example, were quickly emulated in the casino industry by giving players points for each dollar gambled, with points redeemable for food, drinks, rooms, and so on. The idea was a success because of a fundamental desire on the part of consumers to be rewarded for their patronage. The innovations of the airline industry may similarly be applied to many industries.

Casinos themselves have begun to recognize the value of intellectual property. Harrah's Entertainment, for example, operates 21 casinos in 17 different markets including Las Vegas, Atlantic City, Mississippi, Louisiana, and a number of riverboats. One of the largest gaming companies in the country, Harrah's faces increasing competition as the industry consolidates. This competition has forced the company to think more creatively, pushing it to reinvent itself. Harrah's response was to focus on one of its core strengths—providing a consistently high level of customer satisfaction at all of its properties. It developed a centralized database for tracking customers, allowing a player at one Harrah's property to get instant recognition and complementary casino perks such as free food or rooms at any of the other Harrah's properties. In 1998, the company received a patent called "national customer recognition system and method" which claimed a "computer-implemented method for rewarding patronage of a customer at a plurality of casino properties." It patented not the database itself, but rather a way to reward players through the use of a database. With this patent, it was able to prevent competitors from offering this uniform marketing solution. Note that this patent was not only marketing-driven, it fit well with the overall business direction of the company to provide a seamless player reward experience. Ultimately, this thinking led Harrah's to file other marketing-driven patents such as a system and method for "differentiating customers according to their worth to the casino." Investors looking to differentiate among gaming companies might want to seriously consider such patent filings, since the sustainable competitive advantages derived from patents should translate into higher returns to shareholders.

The increased tactical use of such patents in the gaming industry has led many companies to step up their commitment to intellectual property. Acres Gaming, for example, appointed a patent attorney as Vice President & Corporate Counsel, helping them navigate the increasingly complex maze of gaming patents. With a suit pending against Anchor Gaming to establish Acres's ownership of several secondary event gaming machines and a suit filed by Mikohn Gaming against them, Acres decided that it needed more IP expertise on its side. Such patent infringement suits are not uncommon in the gaming industry, the best-known example being the battle between International Game Technology (IGT) and WMS Gaming. IGT accused WMS of infringing the Telnaes patent, one of the most important in the gaming industry, and ultimately collected $27 million, which resulted in new lows for WMS stock. The Telnaes patent describes "virtual reel technology" in which the probability of a slot machine reel stopping on any given symbol is not uniform.

BUSINESS-DRIVEN INVENTING IN THE PHARMACEUTICAL INDUSTRY

The pharmaceutical industry, well known for highly technical biological formula patents, is also rapidly moving toward a more business-driven inventing process. Dominated by corporate giants capable of devoting billions of dollars to research budgets, the industry's initial efforts at drug discovery were largely a process of trial and error. Tens of thousands of compounds were tested for efficacy in the hope of a single success. Each compound might be tested against dozens of target diseases. Because of the expense of these research efforts, companies tried to move from a drug focus to a marketing focus. What were the biggest markets? How could they better identify targets? Rather than throwing thousands of drugs "against the wall to see what sticks," they began to analyze the genes associated with various maladies, hoping to understand the biological process of disease enough to describe what an effective drug might look like. For example, understanding the chemical structure of a key enzyme allows the characterization of drugs that could disable it. The companies' focus shifted away from manufacturing the product (the drug) toward identifying what the market (the disease process) wanted. With this shift in thinking came a corresponding change in intellectual property strategy, from patenting the drugs to patenting human genes. Companies like Celera Genomics were formed to provide a list of targets to the industry. Celera does not want to be the next drug company; it wants to be the *in-*

formation provider of the pharmaceutical industry. The company sequences genes and then sells access to the data to drug companies hungry for new drug targets. By patenting the gene sequences that it discovered, it has succeeded in becoming a content player with proprietary offerings. DoubleTwist, another biotech company, wants to be a portal to the genome. It provides no content of its own; instead it takes data from the public Human Genome Project, repackages it in a more useful form, and sells it to drug companies. To protect itself from competitors, it has patented its genomic processing software.

Note the overall evolution of the pharmaceutical industry. First companies patented drugs and then patented target genes, just as the gaming industry first patented slot machine components and then patented new ways for the machines to interact with customers. As we have already seen in the gaming industry, such marketing-driven inventions, while sometimes simple when viewed in hindsight, can actually be more complex than technology-driven inventions because the range of possible information interactions is so much greater.

The value of intellectual property to the pharmaceutical industry was underscored when, following the announcement by former president Bill Clinton and U.K. Prime Minister Tony Blair in March 2000 that certain genetic discoveries might not be patentable, some biotech stocks lost half of their value overnight. Smart investors realized, however, that the fundamental patent laws had not changed; biotech stocks have since regained some of the lost value.

We have seen the effect of the marketing-driven approach in the casino gaming and pharmaceutical industries. What are some of the implications of this new way of doing business? For one thing, companies may need to increase communication channels into and out of the marketing department, or even physically locate marketing so that it can better interact with other departments. Another point: companies should be prepared to invest more time in understanding the psychology of the customer, being careful to recognize the most important concerns and avoid expending resources solving minor problems. Finally, the new environment may ultimately lead to an evolution in who is considered an inventor. Those with an understanding of the marketplace and how to achieve market acceptance will become increasingly important members of the inventing team, alongside attorneys and inventors. Venture capitalists may become inventors as well, given their deep understanding of market needs and experience in developing business solutions. This leads us to investigate the business-driven process itself.

Generating an innovative idea is only the first step toward developing effective patent protection. The patent (or group of patents) needs to be written carefully so as to maximize its protective value. This involves a complex, lengthy, and challenging process. Managing this patent drafting process is typically the responsibility of patent attorneys, who interview inventors, research prior art, draft patent applications, incorporate comments and suggestions from inventors, and manage communications with the United States Patent & Trademark Office (USPTO). In some companies, attorneys also work with management committees to prioritize applications in the pipeline. Because all of these steps require a sophisticated understanding of intellectual property law, companies are often understandably content to let attorneys drive the process. (Commenting on claims or reviewing the specification of the patent to ensure that it conveys all aspects of the invention is difficult without years of legal training.) Empowering attorneys to handle patents fits with an overall corporate strategy of specialization, with each department focusing on its core competence. While this process has been very effective to date, the transition from manufacturing-driven to market-driven inventing may require new patent drafting processes.

The increased strategic importance of patents, for example, will also require greater attention to patent quality. Rather than simply being a potential source of licensing revenue or a chip to be bargained with competitors, business-driven inventions often develop from the core competencies of the company. While traditional inventions might be thought of as intangible assets added to the company, business-driven inventions emerge from the company. Like the patents behind Harrah's player tracking system, business-driven patents reflect the way the company serves the market. Because such patents may be crucial to building and maintaining competitive advantage, they should be of high quality.

THE BUSINESS-DRIVEN PATENT PROCESS

Companies can take a number of steps to ensure that business-driven inventions are turned into effective patents. Business processes can be adjusted to increase the amount of time each of the parties (attorneys, inventors, marketers) interacts with the others, and companies can provide intellectual property training to inventors and marketers. In brainstorming sessions, for example, having attorneys and marketers present in addition to inventors can help improve overall quality. Attorneys can provide advice at the inception of the idea, allowing for improvements to patentability before the idea has been fully formulated. Marketers also have the ability to ensure a good fit with business needs and have the opportunity to bring up other potentially addressable customer needs. The key here is to provide early feedback, before the inventor gets so far along in the process that course corrections are difficult.

Rather than having the inventor pass the invention baton to the attorneys, inventors and attorneys need to work closely together in drafting an application, editing multiple drafts to ensure that all of the inventive concepts are captured. Because subtle differences in embodiments of the invention can have a dramatic impact on how the market reacts to it, marketers should also be involved in commenting on drafts of the application. Even when negotiating with the patent office, inventors and marketers should be involved to ensure that any claim changes fit with the business needs of the invention.

Involving inventors and marketers more deeply in the patent process requires substantial training time for each, given the complexities of intellectual property law. Such training might enable a marketer to better understand patent claims, allowing him or her to provide feedback as to what embodiments are the most crucial to the commercial value of the invention. Such training might take the form of seminars conducted by the IP department, or books and articles relating to intellectual property.

The role of senior management in the patent drafting process should grow as well, since the patents being generated will ultimately support the business by providing sustainable competitive advantage. Only a solid commitment from top leadership at the company will lead to the investments that must be made to achieve successful patent protection. Senior management needs to understand the time commitment (in terms of both training and greater communications) that these integrated patent teams will require. While the direct costs are substantial, the opportunity cost of the time committed to patents is also significant, as those involved will have less time to participate in other important projects. Given the high quality of the employees involved, these opportunity costs may be especially high.

MANAGING THE RISKS

It should be noted that such added patent expenditures may not necessarily lead to improved protection for a business. There are many opportunities for setbacks along the way, some of which will be out of the company's control. For example, a company might invest significant resources to file 10 patents around a new business that it is launching, only to discover after all of the patents are issued that a legislative change has rendered the business opportunity worthless. Alternatively, the same company may instead find that the market for the new business opportunity has dried up with the surprise introduction of a new technology. Until someone invents a crystal ball, significant investments in IP will always carry considerable risk.

One way to manage such risks is to make patent investments in areas that are not changing as rapidly. For example, while there has been significant innovation on the part of grocery stores, the fundamental business has remained the same for decades. Yet Catalina Marketing was able to found a business based on small printers attached to the cash registers of grocery stores. When a customer buys one brand of soft drink, a coupon for a competing brand is printed. The company filed a number of patents around the process, ultimately licensing half of the grocery stores in the country.

A business should consider a number of factors before deciding to commit large resources to an aggressive business-driven IP effort. Will it own only a narrow slice of the invention? Will competitors be able to easily avoid the patents? Is the value of the invention small in comparison with the patent costs? Do competitors have a history of protracted litigation? Will filing patents significantly distract key employees from the job of managing and growing the underlying business? If the answer to one or more of the above questions is yes, a company should probably proceed carefully.

THE INVENTING TEAM

One benefit of the greater integration of the patent development team is that inventors, attorneys, and marketers all learn more about each other's roles—resulting in valuable cross-training and more satisfying work. As each participant of the team becomes more comfortable with the process, he or she may even begin to perform some of the functions of other team members—inventors proposing patent claims, attorneys spending time with customers to learn their needs, and marketers spending time inventing. As the teams become more integrated, and as intellectual property emerges as a higher priority at the company, the number of people engaged in the patent process is bound to dramatically increase.

In such an environment, the inventor role may be performed by a much larger portion of the workplace. As business drives inventing more, almost everyone involved in the business could be an inventor. Manufacturing-driven environments provided clear demarcation between inventors and noninventors. Those in R&D were inventors, the rest were not. As inventing becomes more business-driven, however, the line between who is or is not an inventor continues to blur. Managers and executives are increasingly likely to come up with innovations as they attempt to solve business problems and as they become more involved in the IP process. Information technology specialists may come up with ideas for innovations while creating software to implement an invention. Project managers within a recently launched business unit may develop new patentable directions to head in; sales representatives may report back with patentable ideas generated by conversations with customers in the field.

Inventors are even increasingly being found in nonprofit businesses. When the Mayo Clinic came up with cortisone in the 1950s, it decided not to seek patent protection, and ended up missing out on millions of dollars in royalties. Determined not to repeat the mistake, it created Mayo Medical Ventures to harvest and fund patentable ideas from within the research area of the hospital.

The number of inventors in a company may also grow dramatically as knowledge management software makes it increasingly easy for employees to collaborate on projects and share ideas. Will this make almost anyone in a company an inventor? Procter & Gamble, with that aim in mind, created InnovationNet, a central database for idea sharing that serves 18,000 employees. While such a network will almost certainly improve idea generation, it remains to be seen whether P&G will be able to handle the influx of new ideas. P&G already files 3,000 patents per year and pays $50 million annually in maintenance fees to keep the patents active. Is it willing to commit the resources to exploit these ideas? Without a program in place to manage the idea flow, such networks can overwhelm a company. An effective program would focus resources on only the most important ideas companywide, resulting in a rise in patent quality without a dramatic increase in the number of patents filed.

As the number of potential inventors at a company increases, companies will be forced to manage IP rights of employees (such as assignment obligations) more broadly, and will have to be even more diligent in protecting trade secrets. The use of nondisclosure agreements (NDAs) could multiply dramatically. The recent report that a graduate student requested that his professor sign an NDA before grading his homework shows how the IP environment is developing.

Another source of complexity arises when two companies collaborate on a joint project. Who owns the patents? Who owns the trade secrets? With joint ventures worth millions or potentially billions of dollars at stake, companies are going to have to be very careful in how they spell out such collaborative agreements. Perhaps we may see "knowledge walls" soon in the business world, similar to the "Chinese walls" seen commonly in the financial world.

AN ONGOING PROCESS

In many companies, the process of filing patents is a prelude to launching a new product or business. During launch phase, little attention can be spared for the pending patents. Once the patents issue, they are evaluated for possible tactical uses, for example as tools to stop competitors from entering the market. While this can be an effective strategy, business-driven inventing requires a more ongoing approach to intellectual property protection. Because business-driven patents are so tightly coupled to the core of the business itself, constant updates are needed as the business and the markets in which it operates change. Rather than representing a phase of development, patents may increasingly become the lifeblood of cutting-edge businesses, changing as the company changes to keep up with evolving markets. Patents will be filed throughout the life of the company, and claims will frequently be updated to meet current business needs.

An example of this kind of transformation from single-stage filing to ongoing process can be seen in the pharmaceutical industry. For decades, major pharmaceutical manufacturers have invested billions of dollars in research and development, recently as much as 20 percent of sales. With investments of this size, solid intellectual property had to be developed to prevent others from copying the resultant drugs. Such patents provided effective protection, but had a life span limited by the expiration date of the patent. Once drugs went off patent, drug manufacturers faced revenue losses of up to 90 percent as generic manufacturers moved in. In order to shore up declining revenues, drug companies looked for the next big drug in their pipeline, hoping to find another cash cow. Wall Street routinely analyzed patent expiration dates, punishing the stocks of companies that did not have promising pipelines to make up for drugs going off patent. While this strategy of patenting, earning profits until expiration, and switching to the next blockbuster was successful, it put tremendous pressure on R&D, and as drug discovery costs skyrocketed, this strategy became expensive and risky. What if the next big drug in the pipeline will not be ready for a couple years or if FDA approval is delayed? What is the sales team going to do during the down time? As Wall Street looked for more stable cash flows, pharmaceutical firms decided to try other strategies.

EXTENDING THE LIFE OF AN INVENTION

The pharmaceutical industry introduced the concept of "life cycle management." This entailed finding a drug that could be protected by a series of patents over time by finding other aspects of the drug process to patent, including developing patents for new uses, new coating technologies, new manufacturing methods, and anything else that could provide another avenue of protection. The approach was to look at every stage of the drug process as a potential "choke point" for further patents. When the base drug patent expired, companies reasoned that they could fall back on another choke point such as manufacturing, as long as there was some novel component to the way that particular drug was made. So while competitors might be able to copy the drug, they would have trouble avoiding the manufacturing patents. And if the filing date of the manufacturing patent was 10 years after the base drug patent, the company would in effect be able to retain the monopoly profits from their drug for an extra 10 years. With the strategic ongoing filing of patents, the companies were able to take some of the pressure off their R&D function, leveraging sophisticated tactical inventing to reduce reliance on the pipeline. In a way, the rest of the company becomes an extension to the pipeline of the company.

One of the more creative efforts in extending the life of a drug has been Schering-Plough's attempts to maintain some of the $3 billion per year earned by their allergy relief medicine Claritin. In thinking about choke points in the drug process, Schering-Plough discovered that Claritin was broken down by the body into a series of smaller molecules known as metabolites. So before the drug patent expired, it filed patents on one of the metabolites, potentially blocking any analogous competitive product that was broken down into the protected metabolite.

Such patent extension strategies are not exclusive to the drug industry. Any innovation that involves a complex series of novel steps can be similarly analyzed for choke points. Once identified, these choke points can be fed into an ongoing patent process that extends the lives of mission critical business-driven patents. For example, Henry Yuen founded Gemstar on the basis of a vision of what the world of television would be like in a high bandwidth future. With 500 channels to choose from, how would viewers navigate? How would they find what they were looking for? Yuen realized that he could capitalize on this opportunity by developing a portal—electronic guides to the channels that allowed a viewer simple and effective ways to search for a program. With more than 200 patents now issued around the process, Yuen has created a tremendous barrier to competitors. His intellectual property position allowed him to survive a takeover attempt from *TV Guide* in 1998, and in fact to turn the tables and take over *TV Guide*. Because cable companies have been largely unable to create similar electronic guides that avoid the Gemstar patents, Yuen has been able to extract not just patent licensing fees from cable operators but also a cut of the advertising dollars generated by his electronic guides as well. With licensing deals that stretch out in some cases for 20 years, Yuen will be earning money long after many of his patents have expired.

Looking at the approach taken by Yuen leads naturally to the question of whether core business insights such as the identification of a market need are patentable. For example, did Apple miss the opportunity to patent the look and feel of its operating system? Adobe Systems found themselves in a similar situation and decided to accuse Macromedia of infringing its "tab palette" patent, claiming that its products have a distinctive look and feel and that a major part of that is the tab palette, which allows users to customize the user interface of Adobe's products. With so many aspects of business becoming patentable, the opportunities for ongoing business-driven patents are plentiful. Venture capitalists, for example, would do well to perform periodic reviews of the potential intellectual property at companies in which they have investments, particularly before additional rounds of funding are provided. If the value of investments is to be maximized, companies should not be allowed to leave intellectual assets unexploited by failing to identify them.

Another driving force of this evolutionary move to a more continuous patenting strategy is feedback from new products or businesses. Once a new product hits the market, for example, data on consumers' likes and dislikes should be fed back into the innovation process. This sometimes triggers improvements to previously filed patents or reveals unforeseen novelty in technological implementation of patents focused on broad business methods or technologies. Although patents filed on implementation technologies might have narrower claims, the company still retains value in that they are more directly tied to the way the business is practiced and can be useful in more precisely highlighting infringing activity. While many have heard of Amazon.com's "one-click" patent, few realize that this patent is only a small part of a concerted effort to mine novel aspects of Amazon's business processes, developed over years of coordinated efforts to create a massive electronic commerce system. Already totaling 14 issued patents, the Amazon.com portfolio now includes patents to a customer referral system, methods for securely communicating credit card data, methods for collaborative recommendations, and an electronic gift certificate system. The point to remember here is that businesses often have multiple novel elements. By exploring all of the angles and patenting the strongest bottlenecks on an ongoing basis, a company can have virtually continuous patent protection. But unless a company is vigilant, such opportunities can easily slip through the cracks. How much more successful would American Airlines have been if it had patented the frequent flyer system? It had the opportunity to own a computer-controlled, miles-based frequent flyer system. While competing airlines might have been able to institute frequent flyer systems based on dollars spent or hours in the air, these alternative systems would likely have been rejected by consumers as inferior (given that these alternative systems are not currently in popular use).

As intellectual property begins to represent a larger portion of the value of a company, the need to cover all key aspects of an invention becomes vitally important. As the stakes rise, competitors are almost certain to devote greater resources to finding the weak link in any intellectual property armor. After analyzing a patent, they may attempt to find a way to achieve the benefits of your invention without infringing the claims. Such activity is known as "designing around" an invention, and involves carefully structuring a process to avoid the claims of a patent. As an example, witness the recent patent battles between Amgen and Transkaryotic Therapies. The business model of Transkaryotic is to make patented drugs through novel production methods, primarily by reverse engineering the drugs of other pharmaceutical companies and designing around their patents. In effect, the pipeline of Transkaryotic is the pipeline of every other drug company. Its first target was Amgen's anemia medicine EPO (erythropoietin), a drug with U.S. sales of nearly $2 billion in 2000. If Transkaryotic proves successful, it plans to target many other patented drugs, potentially destroying the value of patents worth billions of dollars. While such sophisticated attacks have only recently appeared in the pharmaceutical world, how long will it be before they show up in the semiconductor world? In business method patents? It is vital to anticipate how a competitor might design around your most valuable patents and then take account of these expected actions in subsequent patent filings.

We have seen how to extend the life of a patent. Yet, even if the company has successfully identified choke points, incorporated commercial feedback, and anticipated "design-arounds" by competitors, there is still no assurance that the patent position is strong. It is very easy to end up with bad IP because good patents look much the same as bad patents. It takes a true expert (or a costly infringement battle) to tell the difference. In many ways patents are like a new cryptographic algorithm. It takes an expert to know if the algorithm is secure, and even an expert may tell you that it might take years of testing by cryptographers to confirm its true strength. It is possible to take concrete steps to extend the life of a patent, but attorney expertise is also a critical factor.

WALKER DIGITAL CORPORATION: A BUSINESS-DRIVEN IP LAB

In order to illustrate some of the concepts discussed above, I will conclude by describing some of the thought processes behind the creation of one of the patents of Walker Digital Corporation, an IP lab devoted to inventing business solutions that has spawned several companies, including priceline.com and Retail DNA. We'll examine the various stages of the "dynamically priced upsell" innovation within the fast food industry.

The process began with the first of many brainstorming sessions. Inventors came into the sessions having broadly read on the subject at hand; some had significant industry expertise. Attending patent attorneys had already familiarized themselves with art in the topic area, and business managers were ready to draw upon past successes (and failures). Perhaps most important, all of these parties were well acquainted with Walker Digital's existing businesses and the needs of the market.

Attention quickly turned to the widespread problem of relatively low margins in the fast food industry, prompting a number of thoughts. Food is wasted as a result of being left too long under the warming lights; could any of this waste be avoided? Every store has a number of electronic point-of-sale registers, similar in many respects to a household PC; was there any way to harness this computing power? Most transactions involve cash; was there a way to economically introduce more advanced payment systems such as credit cards? Soft drinks and french fries drive profitability; was there any way to shift share into these categories? Was there any way to influence customer purchases to allow for more control over inventory? The group focused on the fast food business from the perspective of a franchise owner looking to improve profits. What were customers asking for? Rather than thinking about new technologies that could be implemented in fast food, the focus of the Walker Digital team was on the business needs of the stores. They focused on developing ideas that the market wanted, not solutions that were technologically interesting: idea generation guided by an understanding of marketing, not technology.

These issues and problems coalesced as the focus of attention turned to the conclusion of a transaction, when the cashier hands the customer her change. What if the store could retain the coin change in a typical transaction? Could it somehow upsell the customer on another item? Retaining the average 50 cents in change would go a long way toward improving margins, and directing an additional purchase to the customer would improve inventory control if multiple products could be selected from. A key insight came when it was suggested that the point-of-sale device could dynamically determine an item to upsell; it could choose a product to offer in place of the owed change. A customer buying a burger and drink for $2.65, for example, might be offered a small order of fries in exchange for her 35 cents in change. The customer gets a deal on the fries (they might retail for 95 cents) while the store keeps 35 cents for a product that cost it 10 cents to make. The calculations would be too complex for a clerk, potentially depending on available inventory, what products are currently selling well, and what the customer has already ordered—but a computer system could do it automatically and prompt the clerk.

Throughout the process, much time was spent considering not only how industry players might design around the claims of the invention, but whether or not those design around efforts were *economical*. For example, a cashier might be able to determine an upsell without the aid of the point-of-sale terminal by always offering to upsize a drink order. Such an offer is quick and simple, but does it maximize the profits of the store owner? Would customers begin to "game" the system by always ordering smaller drink sizes in anticipation of the upsell offer? If so, the store might actually lose money on the offer.

Once the initial brainstorming sessions were concluded, a team was put together to develop the intellectual property, including an inventor, an attorney, a researcher, and an entrepreneur with experience in retail. The inventor wrote detailed descriptions of the ideas and worked with the researcher to further explore the related arts. After many exchanged drafts of the application (and review with other inventors and business managers), the patents were filed. Around the same time, the entrepreneur led the effort to determine whether the invention merited the launch of a business, concluding that in this case it made sense.

The start up grew and additional applications were filed as the exact deployment plan was developed. The team expanded on the original idea and generated additional angles of coverage. As software was written and business plans refined, more patentable ideas were generated. Capital was raised, and the business ultimately grew into Retail DNA; its software is currently in operation at McDonald's, Burger King, Wendy's, and KFC.

CONCLUSION

While the above example makes business-driven inventing look simple and straightforward, the reality is that it takes long hours, dedication, a team of smart and experienced people, and a long-term perspective. As we have seen in this example and in the gaming and pharmaceutical industries, this new paradigm requires an inventing process driven by an understanding of the market, an integrated team to generate strong patents, and ongoing vigilance to ferret out additional novel opportunities. Moving from a technology-driven process to a business-driven inventing process requires significant investments and is not without risk. Often it entails significant procedural changes throughout the company under the direction of a committed senior management team. But those companies that succeed will reap a lasting sustainable competitive advantage in the emerging information economy.

ABOUT THE AUTHOR

James Jorasch is head of the inventing group at Walker Digital Corporation. He is named inventor on more than 100 issued patents and more than 200 pending patents. Fields covered by his inventions include telecommunications, financial services, electronic commerce, retail systems, video games, lottery, casino gaming, healthcare, and vending. Before joining Walker Digital, Mr. Jorasch was a management consultant with Deloitte & Touche Consulting in their San Francisco office working with high-tech clients such as Apple and Hayes Microcomputer Products.

Prior to that, Jorasch spent four years in Las Vegas as a Financial Analyst with the Tropicana Resort and Casino. He also acted as the games expert at the company, performing computer simulations of casino customer behavior and analyzing game variations, modifications, and risk for the casino. While at the Tropicana Jorasch co-developed Survival Dice, a patented three-roll dice game which was eventually sold to a number of other casinos. Mr. Jorasch received his MBA and Bachelor of Science in Applied Economics from Cornell University. Rarely turning down an opportunity to play in competitive games, he regularly plays in chess, poker, and backgammon tournaments.

Walker Digital is the world's leading inventor and developer of business method solutions. Founded in 1995 by Internet entrepreneur Jay Walker, Walker Digital has invented more than 300 Internet business methods, products, and services, and has launched several operating companies, including: priceline.com and Retail DNA. More than 100 U.S. patents have been issued to Walker Digital to date, with more than 300 additional patent applications currently pending at the U.S. Patent & Trademark Office.

CHAPTER SEVEN

Venture Investment Grounded in Intellectual Capital
Taking Patents to the Bank

by James E. Malackowski and David I. Wakefield

PERSPECTIVES

Venture capital and private equity investors are paying more attention to intellectual property than ever before. "What was only a summary recognition that a potential investment or target had patents,"
say venture capitalists James Malackowski and David Wakefield, "has
advanced to a detailed assessment of claim coverage and an involved
'gaps' analysis comparing patent coverage to the core business plan."
The authors believe that effective due diligence today must include
a thorough review of IP value and strategy options. Even so-called
failed investments may have an IP component that enables savvy
venture and private investors to salvage something from dot.com
wreckage. The key is knowing where to look and how to structure the
deal.

   While all private equity firms attempt to minimize the risk associated with investments, most venture capitalists do so by assessing
quality of management, business model risk, market opportunities,
and possible returns. Predicting returns in this manner is a difficult
and an inexact science, say Malackowski and Wakefield, especially with
early-stage start-up or later-stage technology-dependent companies.
A better understanding of intellectual capital and the value creation
it represents helps to manage investment risk. Even companies with
few tangible assets that can be used as collateral to obtain financing
may have great value in intangible or intellectual assets. "A prudent

investor will carefully consider the advantage a patent or other intellectual capital can have on identifying opportunities, developing strategies, and securing returns."

This chapter is designed to share strategies fundamental to venture investments that are grounded in intellectual capital (VIGIC). The discussion should be useful to companies and individuals seeking private equity, as well as to traditional venture capitalists who have until now rarely considered these issues. Specific topics addressed include:

- A review of techniques to generate patent-advantaged deal flow
- Unique elements of the due diligence process
- Investment theses developed around intellectual capital
- Novel investment-structuring issues

IN THE NEWS

We tend to have a bias toward business services, broadly defined. We think that the service sector has been the major growth engine over the last 20 years, and we think it's likely to be over the next 20, particularly where it leverages intellectual capital. Business services emphasizing proprietary knowledge and information are where we focus.

> — Bruce V. Rauner, Managing Principal
> GTCR Golder Rauner, LLC
> *The Wall Street Transcript*
> November 6, 2000

Commercialization of IP is not a short-term thing. There are opportunities for commercializing, selling, and licensing patents on the fringes of your portfolio that people call low-hanging fruit. But to really sustain this long-term growth rate, you have to have a long-term vision.

> —David A. Kennedy, Managing Director InteCap, Inc.,
> © 2001. Thomas, Kayden, Horstemeyer & Risley, LLP.
> *Legal Intelligence: Managing Your Intellectual Property*,
> Jeffrey R. Kuester and David A. Kennedy, Moderators.

As recent headlines in newspapers and magazines have made clear, the U.S. economy has been slowing over the past several months. Consumer confidence and other major economic indicators all point to the increased possibility of a recession this year. In light of these developments, it is more important than ever to make sure that your organization's intellectual property and research investments are being utilized as efficiently as possible. When performing these assessments, the first place to look to improve your return on investment should be your patent portfolio.

> — David C. Drews
> IPMetrics
> *The Benefits of Patent Donation*
> February 22, 2001

INTRODUCTION

The technologists' path to riches seems vivid, so matter of fact: simply invent, patent, obtain venture capital; build a business, grow it larger; and then go public. With so many great scientists and entrepreneurs, we're fortunate that we can avoid the long lines waiting to deposit the spoils of success in our local bank.

Although reality may not be so grand, it is clear that patents do provide a measure of competitive advantage that assists not only in building a business but also in obtaining venture financing. At its core, the competitive advantage patents offer may be seen through incremental market share, price premiums, or cost savings. The entrepreneur who can precisely relate his proprietary technology or process to these three parameters should have an advantage in obtaining funding.

Progressive investors appreciative of patent value develop strategic investment guidelines adopting traditional venture principles as well as additional parameters relating to portfolio intellectual capital. Most frequently thought of as patents and trademarks, intellectual capital extends to all intangible proprietary assets of a business. These assets often comprise a company's strongest market advantage or barrier to entry.

The purpose of this chapter is to share strategies fundamental to venture investment grounded in intellectual capital. The discussion should be useful to anyone who is seeking private equity as well as to traditional venture capitalists who have heretofore not fully considered these issues. Specific topics addressed include a review of techniques to generate patent-advantaged deal flow, unique elements of the due diligence process, investment thesis developed around intellectual capital, and novel investment structuring issues.

Discussions among private equity and venture capital firms regarding intellectual property are more frequent and in-depth today than ever before. What was only a summary recognition that a potential investment or target had patents has advanced to a detailed assessment of claim coverage and an involved gaps analysis comparing patent coverage to the core business plan. A simple Internet search of the terms *patent* and *venture capital* identifies investors who appreciate and affirmatively value intellectual property rights.

Are patents also appreciated by leading commercial banks? To assess interest, a survey of the largest 25 banks was executed with the following questions:

- Do you consider patents in your lending criteria?
- Do you seek to take a security interest in patents?
- Do you use patents in a way that will increase loan amounts or impact loan convenants?
- Have you taken possession and liquidated patent security interests?

Results here were not encouraging as most respondents did not have a defined policy regarding patent assets. Under the theory that more is better when discussing debt collateral, all were willing to secure significant intellectual property. Only one lender expressed an appreciation of a patent's ability to reduce costs or otherwise improve cash flow and therefore enhance lending amounts. None of the banks surveyed had yet taken possession and liquidated or disposed of any intangible asset. It appears as though the inventor seeking a patent-savvy financial partner must continue to rely on private capital to build and create value.

PATENT-BASED DEAL FLOW

Seldom do experienced venture capital firms wait for investment opportunities to approach them. It should therefore not be surprising that so few unsolicited business plans receive funding. Successful firms have a focused investment strategy and actively develop opportunities or targets. For the investor who appreciates the value creation patents offer, there are ready channels and tools to source opportunities.

Traditional networking opportunities with technology transfer and development professionals may be found by participating in select organizations. Three leading associations are the Licensing Executives Society (LES), the Association of University Technology Managers (AUTM), and the Commercial Development and Marketing Association (CDMA).

The Licensing Executives Society (United States and Canada), Inc. is a professional society engaged in the transfer, use, development, manufacture and marketing of intellectual property. Members include business executives, lawyers, licensing consultants, engineers, academicians, scientists, and representatives of government. The LES's main objectives are to hold meetings, seminars, and training courses for education, exchange, and dissemination of knowledge and information on licensing and intellectual property; to assist members in improving their skills and techniques; to inform the business community, public, and governmental bodies of the economic significance and importance of licensing; to monitor domestic and international changes in the law and the practice of licensing and protecting intellectual property; and to encourage the publication of articles, reports, statistics, and other materials on licensing and intellectual property.

The Association of University Technology Managers is a nonprofit association with membership of more than 2,300 technology managers and business executives who manage intellectual property. The association's members represent over 300 universities, research institutions, teaching hospitals, and a similar number of companies and government organizations.

The Commercial Development and Marketing Association is the world's leading professional association dedicated to fostering, promoting, and sharing business processes for long-term growth and value creation in the chemical and allied industries. The CDMA serves and educates its professional members in world-class practices of business development, corporate growth, business strategy, marketing, and related functional areas. Its focus is to conduct workshops, business conferences, networking forums, and local section activities for the purpose of educating members and other nonmember professionals.

Charitable organizations, such as the National Inventors Hall of Fame, provide a forum to identify leading technologists through the celebration of the creative and entrepreneurial spirit of great inventors. The creative genius of invention is showcased through exhibits and presentations that allow visitors to experience the excitement of discovery, creativity, and imagination. The National Inventors Hall of Fame is dedicated to the individuals who conceived the great technological advances which this nation fosters through its patent system. The purpose of the Hall is to honor these inventors and bring public recognition to them and their contributions to the nation's welfare.

With the advent of the Internet, several for-profit companies have been formed to act as a business-to-business exchange for patented technology. Leading examples include pl-x.com, yet2.com, techex.com, and IPnetwork.com. These companies function as a financial marketplace for intellectual property rights. They can assist in making nonintuitive connections, avoiding costly research and development (R&D) processes while simultaneously increasing speed-to-market and maximizing R&D profitability. The process is anonymous, confidential, and secure.

These sites also serve as an on-line trading floor where scientists and engineers can meet to exchange technology quickly, easily, and efficiently. For investment professionals, such a portal can help to realize maximum return through the simplification, integration, and management of the technology acquisition life cycle. Each offers unique search means, an option to secure rights on-line, and collateral services such as valuations, research, insurance, documentation, and news.

Patents can also be used as a further research tool to identify traditional investment opportunities whether proven technology, later stage, consolidations, management-based, or low-tech. Here again, a number of Internet sites exist to facilitate the investor including *www.uspto.gov*, *www.qpat.com*, *www.getthepatent.com*, and *www.delphion.com*.

Each investor will develop his or her own effective means to use these tools. Select developmental strategies include:

- *Proven technology.* In the current market, technology with two or more years of actual sales may be considered "later-stage" by the venture community. Often, such products are covered by existing patents. A search can identify which participants own the widest proprietary position. A review of all patents issued will allow a comparative evaluation of the target's technology as well as identification of leading candidates for partnership or investment.

- *Later stage.* Investments in traditional business enterprises are clearly not immune from competitive patent attacks, especially given the advent of recent trends involving business process patents. Products manufactured for years may now be subject to requests for expensive royalties or, worse yet, demands to cease operations. A review of newly issued process patents can identify the "have" from the "have not." Companies rich in process technology make more attractive investments.
- *Consolidations.* Consolidations should begin ideally with a platform firm rich in intellectual property. A search of competitive patents may indicate which targets offer complimentary technology or may require the platform's technology, facilitating a lower negotiated acquisition price.
- *Management.* Next to the chief executive, the senior technology officer is often the most important manager for the early-stage venture capital investor. A search by technology showing the most prolific inventors may identify a potential investment if not a more efficient recruiting strategy.
- *Low technology.* A review of patents related to the supply components of a targeted service provider may result in the identification of numerous investment candidates previously unknown. Such candidates often offer valuations outside of normal competitive bidding and provide immediate barriers to competition.

Each of the above strategies will generate additional data for review. The venture firm that can apply this data to existing investment criteria will benefit in the quality of its investment and the quantity of its return.

GENERAL IC-RELATED INVESTOR DUE DILIGENCE

The experienced venture investor receives well more than 1,000 funding opportunities annually. Of those, less than 100 (or 10 percent) may receive any noncursory review. Less than five will likely receive investment capital (IC). What, then, is the process for selecting the truly compelling investments? How does this process differ if intellectual capital is central to the investment rationale? For the private equity partner, the process is one of due diligence.

A general overview of the due diligence process is shown in Exhibit 7-1. The key to effective due diligence is to maintain an efficiency of time and focus. This template is divided into three phases based on the level of analysis and depth of issues explored. Each of the nine columns represents substantive areas of investigation. For each 1,000 deals received, less than 100 will enter the Phase I Review stage, 50 may advance to Phase II Evaluation and Development, and only 15 are likely to be the subject to an exhaustive Phase III Due Diligence.

Phase I Review

Portfolio	Intellectual Capital	Management	Business Model	Financial	Technology	Competition	Sales & Marketing	Deal Structure

Phase II Evaluation and Development

Portfolio Synergy	Existing IC	Executive Skill Set	Mission Statement	Profit %	Product Demo	Market Value	Market Size & Growth	Debt Leverage
	Future IC	Board of Directors	Partnership	Cash Flow	Tech Plan	Differentiate	Customers	Acquisition Strategy
	Competitive IC	Employee Skill Set	Mega-trend	Use of Funds			Outside Influences	Risk Factors
			Futuring	Valuation			Sales Strategy	

Phase III Due Diligence

Patent Doc	Employee Agreements	Supplier Relations	Debt	External Lab Review	Industry News	Customer Relations	Financial
Trademark Doc	Comp/ Incentive	Agreements	Tax Status & Planning			Distributor Relations	Legal
Trade Secrets	Employee Issues		Audit Review				
IC Threats	Shareholders		Property				

Exhibit 7-1 Due diligence process overview.

Although intellectual capital is listed uniquely as one of nine major verticals of consideration, a true appreciation of intellectual assets spans at least half of the remaining columns. Indications of such relevance are listed below:

- *Portfolio fit.* The venture firm's own intellectual capital should be assessed to determine the true fit of any investment. Expertise in particular industries or structures will affect advancement beyond the review phase.
- *Management.* The success of any business is strongly influenced by the knowledge, contacts, and experience of its management team. These intellectual assets should be explicitly identified and categorized at an early stage.
- *Business model.* The advent of process patenting suggests that all investments should be screened to see if their model is either unique or subject to the rights of others. See the Coolsavings.com case study.
- *Technology.* The technical plans and products of a business are obviously close to the heart of traditional intellectual property protection. Frequently, a mapping of the five-year technology plan to existing or pending patents shows potential competitive threat or market barriers not previously recognized.

CASE STUDY

Coolsavings.com Inc.

In 1995, Coolsavings applied for a business-methods patent. Soon after it received the patent, in 1998, the company began filing patent-infringement lawsuits against its rivals in the coupon distribution area.

Coolsavings, Inc. is an online distributor of coupons which is accustomed to generating more than $1 million in royalties for its patent process. The patent covers the process under which Coolsavings collects demographic information about consumers, such as age, income, and product preferences, and shares that information with advertisers.

Seven out of the nine lawsuits brought against companies considered to be infringing upon the Coolsavings process patent settled, agreeing to pay royalty fees to use the patent.

The remaining two competitors, however, have filed countersuits against Coolsavings claiming the patent is not valid. The countersuit alleges that Coolsavings knowingly withheld information about previous patents during its application process.

The patent, which has generated revenue for Coolsavings, is now at risk because of this re-examination. While Coolsavings downplays the importance of the patent, the initial public offering prospectus filed with the Securities and Exchange Commission (SEC) states: "Any ruling or legislation that reduces the validity and enforceability of our patents will seriously harm our business."

The Coolsavings example stresses not only the significance of patents to value creation, but also, and perhaps more important, the steps that an investor must take to ensure that all proper patent due diligence is completed and weighed in the consideration for investment.

Phase I

The first or Review Phase is designed to provide a quick indication of potential investment value. As Exhibit 7-2 shows, each of the major areas is addressed.

The Intellectual Capital column represents a need to determine existing or potential assets by type including: utility patents, process patents, brands, domain names, and a formal employee knowledge base. Commentary should simply address whether these items exist with a quick indication of quality. If not currently present, thought is given to the ability to create such rights and the related potential contribution to value.

Phase II

Those opportunities that pass the Review Phase enter a more detailed period of Evaluation and Development, or Phase II.

As shown in Exhibit 7-3, this second phase addresses existing, future, and competitive intellectual capital. Existing IC issues for investigation include the following:

- A review of key issued patents noting particular claims of interest. It is important to focus attention to the claims rather than the summary ab-

Portfolio Fit	Intellectual Capital	Manage-ment	Business Model	Financial	Technology	Competition	Sales & Marketing	Deal Structure

Exhibit 7-2   Phase I: Review.

Portfolio Synergy	Existing IC	Executive Skill Set	Mission Statement	Profit %	Product Demo	Market Value	Market Size & Growth	Debt Leverage
	Future IC	Board of Directors	Partnership	Cash Flow	Tech Plan	Differentiate	Customers	Acquisition Strategy
	Competitive IC	Employee Skill Set	Mega-trend	Use of Funds			Outside Influences	Risk Factors
			Futuring	Valuation			Sales Strategy	

Exhibit 7-3   Phase II: Evaluation and development.

stract of the patent. Only the claims are going to provide immediate barriers to entry and proprietary market positions for investment purposes. Here a patent attorney or consultant may be helpful.

- An understanding of the target's process for determining which patents to file and the steps taken in the prior art search. Such an analysis should provide guidance as to the breadth and depth of the claims reviewed above. The determination as to when and what to file may also yield cost reduction strategies or further areas for proprietary positioning.
- An assessment of the quality of the patent counsel the target retained.
- A review of the company's inventory of brands and domain names. The absence of an inventory showing corporate entity ownership and quality procedures for maintenance may be a cause for concern.
- A comparison between period of product introduction and patent number marking. Lax practices in this regard may greatly limit perceived competitive barriers.
- An investigation of cross-licensing activity noting both hidden rights and competitive permissions.

Future IC analysis should focus on a review of pending and potential future patent applications. Often, the presence of a pending application can provide tremendous near-term proprietary positioning. In fact, this right may be more valuable than the right the existing claims provide. Consideration should also be given to the budget for future IC development as shown internally, as well as in the target's funding pro forma statements. A declining future budget may be a means to improve overall profitability but at a cost of not preparing adequately for competitive threats. A rapid rise in budget may indicate an earlier-stage investment than originally believed. Competitive IC is the most overlooked aspect of the Evaluation Phase. Investors should allocate time to explore competitive patents as well as current processes to gather IC market intelligence.

Phase III

Only a few opportunities will advance to traditional due diligence (see Exhibit 7-4). When considering IC assets, it is at this stage that most investors will retain patent counsel or other advisors. This portion of the analysis comes after the venture capitalist has made a preliminary intention to make an investment, usually in the form of a term sheet.

Patent documentation begins with a complete inventory of existing and pending patents. A notation should be made as to whether or not the company is practicing the claimed technology and if the key inventor(s) remain with the business. All license agreements providing third-party rights can be similarly categorized. The correspondence between the company and the U.S. Patent & Trademark Office (USPTO) may prove insightful.

Patent Doc	Employee Agreements	Supplier Relations	Debt	External Lab Review	Industry News	Customer Relations	Financial
Trademark Doc	Comp/ Incentive	Agreements	Tax Status & Planning			Distributor Relations	Legal
Trade Secrets	Employee Issues		Audit Review				
IC Threats	Share-holders		Property				

Exhibit 7-4 Phase III: Due diligence.

Trademark documentation follows a similar effort with attention to cataloging all marks and domain names, checking for the use and availability of domain equivalents (e.g., www.cars4sale.com versus www.carsforsale.com versus www.cars4sale.net). A discussion with the target's trademark counsel may provide great insight on the status of any pending registrations. The investor may make a strong case for valuation discounts for any issues which are not as forecasted.

An analysis of trade secrets documentation usually begins with a copy of any existing trade secret policies and a review of key employee confidentiality and assignment agreements. Again, valuation discounts may be in order if documentation is not.

Lastly, IC threats should be listed and fully explored with management and counsel as infringement actions may be costly in both dollars and business flexibility.

PATENT INVESTMENT PARADIGMS

The methodologies used to capture value from intellectual capital are as varied as the investors who consider them. General strategies focus on a target's long-term ability to:

- Develop a patent portfolio based upon both core technology and proprietary business processes of target companies. Such strategies are often developed in conjunction with patent counsel or leading strategic consulting professionals.
- Combine proprietary technologies with existing products or service offerings to create incremental revenue.
- Generate competitive intelligence and advantage from public patent and pending patent databases.
- Proactively develop competitive barriers based on predictive reverse engineering efforts (i.e., filing of additional patent claims based upon third-party products).
- Leverage issued and pending patents discovering potential rights outside the company's field.

- Network with well-established contacts within the largest technology transfer trade associations to gather market intelligence or benchmarks known as best practices.

Specific investment paradigms include intellectual capital liftouts, levered consolidations, and executive partnerships.

Intellectual Capital Liftouts

Large corporate businesses may have a unique opportunity to increase shareholder value by contributing select technology and related intellectual capital to a new joint venture funded by a venture partner and led by an experienced entrepreneur (see Exhibit 7-5). Leading corporate business development offices now actively consider such partnerships.

This strategy requires that the investor work with senior management of an existing large entity to fund the productization of select intellectual capital. Typically, this process is intended to bring to market patented technology that was originally developed to support the company's core operation. The new entity is created either as a subsidiary of the parent company with the venture investment securing an equity interest in both operations, or as a separate joint-venture entity.

An example of an intellectual capital liftout investment is the spin-off of BigCo's operational software. The investor will work with BigCo to fund a joint-venture company leveraging millions of dollars in historical software development.

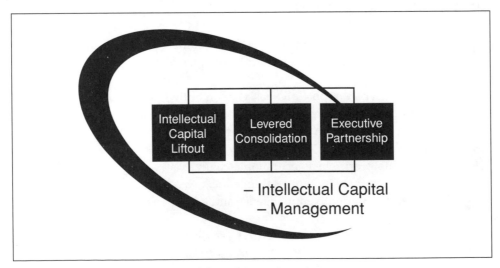

Exhibit 7-5   Intellectual capital-based investments.

The newly formed software company will continue to sell its patented products to BigCo, but would also sell its applications in a number of additional markets.

Levered Consolidation

Venture investors often seek to partner with the executive management of small to medium-sized existing businesses to fund the commercialization of a newly developed product, service, or technology. Concurrent with this vertical expansion, the equity sponsor and the target implement a strategic consolidation strategy to acquire competitive and/or complementary entities within the company's core industry. Building upon the newly assimilated revenue base, distribution channels, and customer access, the company is able to rapidly expand its new offering and position itself as a dominant market leader. Such a strategy will focus on technology application using cash flow to fund new technology. Exit valuations are protected from unsuccessful technology development as such expenses are an obvious add-back to purchase multiples.

An example of such a levered consolidation is the investment in the vertical expansion of ConsultingCo's newly developed ASP product. Leveraging the profits and relationships of its core business, ConsultingCo can rapidly accelerate the distribution of its new technology. The investor assists in identification and acquisition of complementary consulting practices with similar revenues and industry contacts to further accelerate ConsultingCo's growth.

Executive Partnerships

Private equity firms are known to team with outstanding chief executives possessing defensible intellectual capital to create a powerful new company in a rapidly growing industry. Investors typically seek management teams with previous successful large-scale business experience, a long history in their targeted market, and a strong barrier to entry. The author's experience with Dean Becker and ewireless, Inc. provides an example of such a partnership.

EXECUTIVE PARTNERSHIP CASE STUDY

ewireless, Inc.

In May 2000, VIGIC Services, LLC provided an equity investment to help launch ewireless. ewireless, Inc. holds the patents for abbreviated dialing, a direct advertising response that enables wireless phone users to respond to radio and outdoor advertising simply by dialing #333. The service developed by ewireless lets wireless phone customers connect toll-free with participating advertisers by dialing a four-digit code—#333—to receive more information when the customer sees a billboard or hears a radio announcement promoting a product or services.

VIGIC partnered with one of the leading executives in wireless technology, Dean Becker. After creating the largest telephone answering service in the Midwest, Dean Becker founded Becker Beeper, which became a regional powerhouse in wireless messaging, as well as the largest privately held radio paging and electronic messaging service in the country. VIGIC was eager to support an executive of Becker's caliber as well as lend financial backing to the patented business process that developed an entirely new category of wireless technology and marketing service that has changed how consumers and advertisers interact.

Together with the patent portfolio and the outstanding CEO, there was an immediate and defensible valuation increase in the business model. The combination of the two provided an opportunity to be the first and only business in this market.

PATENT INVESTMENT DEAL STRUCTURE

Intellectual capital-based investments are structured like all other transactions except that particular attention should be paid to the investor's security interest in the technology at issue. Key portions of a representative security agreement are attached at the end of this chapter.

Appreciative of the advantages that process-based intellectual property can provide any business, the author has filed for a patent related to private equity deal structure. The patent application relates generally to investment methods and systems. More particularly, the specification addresses a system and a method of risk minimization and enhanced returns in an intellectual capital-based venture investment based on the donation of secured intellectual capital.

Conventionally, investors can recoup losses from failed investments (regardless of whether or not the investment was directed to early-stage or technology-dependent companies) by taking a tax deduction for loss or worthlessness of the loan or investment. The amount, timing, and characterization of such a tax deduction differs depending upon whether the venture capital or private equity firm is treated as an "investor" or in the "trade or business of making loans." Typically, venture capital funds are treated as investors by the Internal Revenue Service (IRS). In such cases, the loss can be taken as a capital loss. In order to take advantage of this capital loss, the burden is on the secured party to demonstrate that the loan or investment is completely worthless. Generally, such a demonstration involves either the commencement of a lawsuit against the debtor to obtain a judgment and collection on the judgment or a strong showing that taking such legal steps would not result in any recovery of value or payment on the debt. The nature of the deduction, the timing of the deduction, and the manner of satisfying the secured party's burden of demonstrating worthlessness are all highly fact-sensitive and differ from investor to investor and transaction to transaction.

There is a need for a system and a method of risk minimization and enhanced returns in an intellectual capital-based venture investment as well as a need to recoup from losses incurred in investments other than taking a tax deduction for loss or worthlessness of the investment or loan. A solution exists in an investment risk minimization system providing an investment to a venture having an intellectual asset and receiving a security interest in the intellectual asset. The security interest secures an ownership right upon failure by the venture to meet established parameters. The method includes obtaining an ownership interest in the intellectual asset, valuing the intellectual asset, and transferring the intellectual asset to a charitable organization.

This method can include obtaining cooperation from a debtor and any secured parties having security interests in the debtor, receiving full ownership of an intellectual asset from the debtor in satisfaction of an obligation incurred from an agreement with the debtor, holding the intellectual asset for one year from receiving full ownership of the intellectual asset, donating the intellectual asset to a permissible charitable donee after one year from receiving full ownership of the intellectual asset, and reporting an appraised value of the donated intellectual asset to the IRS to obtain a tax deduction for the donation.

Donation to an Internal Revenue Code (IRC) Section 501(c)(3) charitable organization can offset earnings from other investments within an investment portfolio to reduce taxable earnings. While the rules governing charitable contributions are primarily covered by IRC Section 170(m), Revenue Ruling 58-260 provides the following specific insight into the deductibility of donated patents:

> The *fair market value* of an undivided present interest in a patent, which is contributed by the owner of the patent to an organization described in section 170(c) of the Internal Revenue Code of 1954, constitutes an *allowable deduction* as a charitable contribution, to the extent provided in section 170, in the taxable year in which such property was contributed. [emphasis added]

The appraised fair value of intellectual capital (e.g., a patent) at the time of disposal (e.g., donation) may be significant.

The investment may be generally broken into both an equity (majority) and debt (minority) transaction. The debt portion of funding is secured by the portfolio company's patent. This asset is reclaimed in the event of failure and then auctioned or donated. Not all patents are believed to have donation value. In certain cases, these assets may simply be held for future use or sale. In assessing the best disposition strategy, consideration should be given to the likely future market for the technology, the ability of other ventures within the same portfolio to benefit from the patent, and the competitive protection afforded other related ventures by restricting competitive access to the claimed technology.

An independent valuation of the patents to be donated must be done. As the value is market-focused, the prior business result of the portfolio company will not strictly limit the appraised valuation. The amount of a deduction for a charitable contribution of a patent is equal to the patent's fair market value on the date of the contribution, provided that certain requirements discussed hereinafter are met.[1]

"Fair market value" is the price at which the patent would change hands between a willing buyer and a willing seller, neither being under any compulsion to buy or sell and both having reasonable knowledge of relevant facts concerning the property.[2] To generate a full fair market value deduction, the donated property must be a capital asset in the hands of the donor and must have been held by the donor for at least one year prior to the transfer to the charitable donee. In the case of property received by a donor on the foreclosure of a security interest, the holding period begins on the date the donor becomes the legal owner of the property, not on the date the security interest was granted.

CASE STUDY

E.I. Du Pont De Nemours and Co.

E.I. Du Pont De Nemours and Co. donated three packages of intellectual property to the Virginia Polytechnic Institute and State University. The patents and know-how concerned thermoplastic composite sheets and was valued at $23 million.

The patents, which seemed destined to sit on the shelf, instead went to the university to benefit their research. DuPont lost all rights to the property, but gained more than an enhanced relationship with the university. The company was granted a tax break in accordance with IRS Revenue Ruling (58-260), which allowed DuPont to deduct, for tax purposes, the full fair market value of the intellectual property donated.

The opportunity to donate *shelved patents* fosters a mutually beneficial relationship between leading companies and academia. The company is able to donate the intellectual property that it no longer has use for, achieve a beneficial financial result from the donation, and benefit society by allowing research institutions access to conduct extensive research and development.

As to the measure of proof in determining the fair market value, all factors bearing on value are relevant including, where pertinent, the cost, or selling price of the item, sales of comparable properties, cost of reproduction, opinion evidence, and appraisals. Fair market value depends upon value in the market and not on intrinsic worth.

The cost or actual selling price of an item within a reasonable time before or after the valuation date may be the best evidence of its fair market value. Before such information is taken into account, it must be ascertained that the transaction was at arm's length and that the parties were fully informed as to all relevant facts. Absent such evidence, even the sales price of the item in question will not be persuasive.

It is expected that the donated value of the patent may exceed the original investment, allowing for complete fund recovery on an after-tax basis. The investor can use the tax advantages generated from donations of patents to offset income from successful investments. These tax savings values can be shared with the investor's limited partners by way of reduced management fees.

To give rise to a tax deduction, the contribution must be a transfer of money or property to a permissible donee without receipt of economic consideration or benefit in return. The interest of investor in the transferred property must be unencumbered. The contribution must be completed and documented in the manner in which the transfer of legal ownership of a patent is normally consummated. For example, the transfer can include execution of an assignment and the registration of the transfer with the USPTO. Whether the investor can utilize, in whole or in part, the deduction allowable under Section 170 to reduce income taxes depends on the situation.

Contribution of intellectual assets can be made to one of the following types of permissible donees: a state, a possession of the United States, any political subdivision of a state or possession, the United States, or the District of Columbia, so long as the contribution is made exclusively for public purposes; or an organization described in Section 501(c)(3) of the Internal Revenue Code, which is an organization not classified as a private foundation under Section 509(a) of the Internal Revenue Code. In the example of an entity described in Section 501(c)(3), a deduction is permitted only if the entity is created or organized under the law of any state, the District of Columbia, the United States, or any possession thereof. A contribution by a corporation to a trust, check, fund, or foundation is deductible only if it is to be used within the United States or its possessions exclusively for purposes specified in Section 501(c)(3)(3). The requirement that a corporation gift must be used within the United States or its possessions does not apply if the gift is made to an entity that is organized as a corporation under the law of any state, the District of Columbia, the United States, or a possession thereof.

The amount that may be deducted by a taxpayer in any year is limited under Section 170(b) of the Internal Revenue Code. In the case of an individual, a charitable contribution of property is generally allowable as a deduction to the extent that the aggregate of all such contributions for the year does not exceed 30 percent of the taxpayer's contribution base for the year; a carryover of the excess to each of the five succeeding taxable years is allowed. The term *contribution base* means the taxpayer's adjusted gross income computed without regard to any net operating loss carryback.[3] In the case of a corporation, the total deduction allowed for all charitable contributions for any taxable year may not exceed 10 percent of the taxpayer's taxable income, computed with certain adjustments listed in Section 170(b)(2).

A FINAL THOUGHT

In general, all private equity firms attempt to minimize the risk associated with investments. To date, most venture capitalists have attempted to minimize risk by assessing quality of management, business model risk, market opportunities, and possible returns. Nevertheless, predicting these returns can be a difficult and an inexact practice, especially with early-stage start-up or later-stage technology-dependent companies. Predicting success in such companies can be very challenging to say the least.

A better understanding of a target's intellectual capital and the value creation it represents can only help to manage investment risk. Even companies with few tangible assets that can be used as collateral to obtain financing may have great value in intangible or intellectual assets. A prudent investor will carefully consider the advantage a patent or other intellectual capital can have on identifying opportunities, developing strategies, and securing returns.

ABBREVIATED PATENT SECURITY AGREEMENT[4]

Following are relevant portions of a Patent Security Agreement for consideration in structuring venture investments with strong underlying intellectual capital. This document may also be used when attempting to benefit from potential donation of patents owned by failed investments. Please consult counsel before using or relying on the attached or any portions thereof.

<u>PATENT COLLATERAL ASSIGNMENT</u>
<u>AND SECURITY AGREEMENT</u>

THIS PATENT COLLATERAL ASSIGNMENT AND SECURITY AGREEMENT dated as of _____ (hereinafter called "Assignment") is made by _____, a _____ corporation, whose address is _____ (hereinafter called "Assignor") to _____, with a place of business at _____ (hereinafter called "Assignee") as agent for and representative of the lenders (together with each financial institution that may become a party to the Credit Agreement as therein provided, referred to herein collectively as "Lenders") which are parties to the Credit Agreement (as hereinafter defined).

R E C I T A L S

WHEREAS, Assignor and Assignee have entered into that certain Credit Agreement dated as of _____ (said Credit Agreement, as amended and as it may hereafter be amended or modified from time to time, being the "Credit Agreement"; the terms defined therein and not otherwise defined herein being used herein as therein defined);

WHEREAS, contemporaneously with the execution of this Assignment, Assignor and Assignee are entering into the Assignor's Pledge and Security Agreement and the Assignor's Trademark Collateral Security Agreement and Conditional Assignment each to Assignee on behalf of Lenders and each dated as of the date hereof (hereinafter called the "Security Agreements");

WHEREAS pursuant to the Security Agreements, Assignor is pledging, mortgaging, assigning, and otherwise transferring various of its assets as set out therein as collateral security for all Obligations (as hereinafter defined) owed to Assignee;

WHEREAS, in addition to tangible assets, Assignor has and may in the future have rights, title, and interest in various Patents (as hereinafter defined);

WHEREAS, Assignor intends to assign and otherwise transfer to Assignee its entire interest in existing and future Patents for the purpose of securing the complete and timely satisfaction of all of the Obligations owed to Assignee; and

WHEREAS, it is a requirement of the Credit Agreement that Assignor shall have granted the security interest and made the assignment contemplated by this Agreement.

NOW, THEREFORE, in consideration of the premises and in order to induce Lenders to make Loans under the Credit Agreement, Assignor hereby agrees with Assignee for its benefit as follows:

SECTION 1. <u>Grant of Security and Assignment</u>. To secure the complete and timely satisfaction of all obligations owed to Lenders now or hereafter existing under the Loan Documents, including, without limitation, the Credit Agreement and the Notes, whether for principal, interest, fees, expenses, or otherwise, and all obligations of Assignor now or hereafter existing under this Agreement (all such obligations under the Loan Documents and this Agreement being referred to herein as the "Obligations"), Assignor hereby pledges, grants, sells, transfers, sets over, conveys, and assigns to Assignee for the benefit of Lenders the entire right, title, and interest in and to all patent ap-

(continued)

plications and patents under any domestic or foreign law in which Assignor owns or controls an interest now or in the future (including without limitation, the patents and patent applications listed in Schedule A hereto), including all proceeds thereof (such as, by way of example and not by way of limitation, license royalties from the licenses listed in Schedule C attached hereto, and proceeds of infringement suits), the right (but not the obligation) to sue for past, present, and future infringements in the name of Assignor or in the name of Assignee, all rights (but not obligations) corresponding thereto and all re-issues, divisions, continuations, renewals, extensions, and continuations-in-part thereof (collectively called the "Patents"); provided that the rights and interests assigned hereby shall include, without limitation, rights and interests pursuant to licensing or other contracts in favor of Assignor pertaining to patent applications and patents presently or in the future owned or used by third parties, but in the case of third parties which are not Affiliates of Assignor only to the extent permitted by such licensing or other contracts and, if not so permitted, only with the consent of such third parties.

SECTION 2. Representations and Warranties. Assignor covenants and warrants as follows:

(a)   A true and complete list of all Patents owned, held (whether pursuant to a license or otherwise), or used by Assignor, in whole or in part, in conducting its business is set forth in Schedule A hereto;

(b)   Assignor has not assigned any shop right, license, release, covenant not to sue, or nonassertion assurance to any third person with respect to any patent or patent application;

(c)   Each of the Patents is valid and enforceable and Assignor is not aware of any past, present, or prospective claim by any third party that the Patents are invalid or unenforceable;

(d)   No claim has been made that the use of any of the Patents does or may violate the rights of any third person;

(e)   Assignor is the legal and beneficial owner of the Patents free and clear of any lien, security interest, charge or encumbrance including, without limitation pledges, assignments, licenses, shop rights and covenants by Assignor not to sue third persons, except for the security interest and assignment created by this Assignment and Liens permitted under subsection 6.2 of the Credit Agreement. No effective financing statement or other instrument similar in effect covering all or any part of the Patents is on file in any recording office, except such as may have been filed in favor of Assignee relating to this Assignment or for which duly executed termination statements have been delivered to Assignee;

(f) This Assignment will create in favor of Assignee a valid and perfected first priority security interest in the Patents upon making filings referred to in the clause.

SECTION 4. <u>Assignor's Covenants</u>. On a continuing basis, Assignor will, subject to any prior or prospective licenses, encumbrance,s and restrictions, make, execute, acknowledge and deliver, and file and record in the proper filing and recording places, all such instruments, including, without limitation, appropriate financing and continuation statements and collateral agreements, and take all such action as may reasonably be deemed necessary or advisable by Assignee to carry out the intent and purposes of this Agreement, or for assuring and confirming to Assignee the grant or perfection of a security interest in all Patents. Without limiting the generality of the foregoing sentence, Assignor (i) will not enter into any agreement which would or might in any way impair or conflict with Assignor's obligations hereunder without Assignee's prior written consent.

NOTES

1. Revenue Ruling 58-260, 1958-1 C.B. 126.
2. Treasury Regulations §1.170A-1(c)(2).
3. Internal Revenue Code §170(b)(1)(F).
4. This section is provided by Joel E. Lutzker of the New York Law firm Schulte Roth & Zabel, 919 Third Avenue, New York, NY 10022, for the sole use in the chapter "Venture Investment Grounded in Intellectual Capital: Taking Patents to the Bank," written by James E. Malackowski and David I. Wakefield.

ABOUT THE AUTHORS

James E. Malackowski is a founding Principal of VIGIC Services, LLC, a GTCR Golder Rauner, LLC company. Prior to partnering with GTCR, he spent 15 years as a consultant focused on intellectual capital valuation and strategy. On several occasions, Mr. Malackowski has served as an expert in Federal Court on questions relating to accounting, financial, and economic matters, including the subjects of business valuation and damages. He is frequently asked to participate as a member of the Board of Directors for leading technology corporations. Mr. Malackowski is a director of ewireless, Inc., Insignis, Inc., Infocast, Inc., Evince, LLC, and Solutionary, Inc. He is also President-elect of the Licensing Executives Society, the leading IP organization, a Director of the National Inventors Hall of Fame, and a Resident Advisor for the U.S. Department of Commerce and U.S. Information Agency on matters relating to intellectual capital. Mr. Malackowski is a summa cum laude graduate from the University of Notre Dame majoring in Accountancy and Philosophy. He is a licensed Certified Public Accountant in the state of Illinois.

David I. Wakefield is an analyst at VIGIC Services, LLC. Mr. Wakefield previously worked with Morgan Stanley & Co., New York. Mr. Wakefield earned a BA in History with Minors in Political Science and Modern Languages and Literatures from Fairfield University.

VIGIC Services, LLC is a GTCR Golder Rauner, LLC company focused on venture investments with an intellectual capital-based competitive advantage. GTCR, based in Chicago, manages more than $4.5 billion in capital provided by pension funds, endowments, investment advisors, portfolio company executives, and GTCR principals. Equity funds and mezzanine funds allow it to provide both debt and equity funding. The opinions expressed herein are those of the authors and do not necessarily represent the views of VIGIC Services, LLC or its parent company, GTCR Golder Rauner, LLC.

CHAPTER EIGHT

From Tech Transfer to Joint Ventures

Building a Business Model for Research

An interview with Jack Granowitz of Columbia Innovation Enterprises, Columbia University

PERSPECTIVES

By monetizing research through patent licensing and equity participation in selective joint ventures, some universities are turning technology transfer into a cottage industry. These institutions of higher learning have learned how to capitalize on their intangible assets through partnerships with private sector businesses and are in some cases reaping abundant rewards for inventions they are unlikely or unable to commercialize on their own.

Transferring technology rights to businesses like pharmaceutical companies hungry for new products makes a lot of sense for universities and research institutions, which are better equipped to identify and develop early-stage inventions than to risk commercializing them. If recent tech transfer successes are any indication, businesses may be able to learn a thing or two from their academic cousins. Universities generated almost a billion dollars in royalties from science and technology for fiscal 2000. This income is still only a fraction of the royalties attributed to giant patent licensors such as IBM ($1.6B for 2000) and Qualcomm ($705B for fiscal 2000). However, it is far more than 95 percent of private sector companies, many with billon-dollar research and development (R&D) budgets and staffed by professional inventors. (See "Licensing Revenue: Universities and Research Institutions" in the Data Bank section of this book.)

Most public companies are notoriously guarded about their patent and other IP licenses. For-profit corporations do not always agree on the value of outlicensing their proprietary rights. However, most will agree that the profit margins on IP royalties can be extraordinary. Many companies prefer to use their patents defensively to protect key technologies, rather than to "rent" them to noncompeting companies—let alone to direct competitors. Most universities, however, as well as some research institutions such as hospitals and foundations, are less interested in commercializing and manufacturing products. Their strategy has been to advance an invention far enough to attract corporate interest and, ultimately, royalty payments. Lacking the infrastructure and access to the capital markets necessary to commercialize inventions, they concentrate on what they do best and leave the greatest risk to the pharmaceutical giants and others which have the resources to mitigate it.

The emerging importance of university licensing over the past several years is of interest to all patent owners. It demonstrates that well-focused research programs can result in excellent profitability without necessarily high risk. It also shows that valuable research talent can be retained through a combination of financial incentives and freedom to pursue independent interests that also reflect institutional objectives. The catalyst for these activities was passage of the Bayh-Dole Act in 1980, permitting universities to benefit from government-sponsored research. Shortly after, in 1982, the Court of Appeals for the Federal Circuit (CAFC) was established, which is devoted to hearing patent appeals. This gave more consistency both to patent holders and to those wishing to challenge or invalidate patents.

Columbia University, through its Columbia Innovation Enterprise (CIE) unit, has, since 1983, amassed more than 400 U.S. patents and has secured more than 1,000 active licenses, of which more than 50 are currently generating royalties. From 1993 to 2000, the university's annual patent licensing income grew sevenfold, from about $20M to more than $143M. Columbia has emerged as a patent royalty leader among both research institutions and most for-profits, where technology licensing results are seldom detailed. According to the Association of University Technology Managers (AUTM), total revenue for U.S. universities for 1999 was $641M. Hospitals and other research institutions represent another $150M. Columbia's $89.1M in licensing for 1999 represents better than 15 percent of all university income from patents. Its licensing successes significantly outpace those at such institutions as Stanford, the entire University of California system, and MIT.

Columbia has accomplished this level of success by relying on more than one or two "home run" patents. Columbia Innovation Enterprise (CIE) generates royalties from patents covering health sciences, engineering, information technology and chemistry. For FY 2000, Columbia took in $143.6 million in royalty income and an additional $22.7 million in research income from innovation-seeking companies such as

Amgen, Johnson & Johnson, Biogen, Genentech, and Pharmacia, a 46 percent increase over the previous year. Significant income has been derived from co-transformation and other biotechnology patents and from patents covering such drugs as Xalatan®, ReoPro®, and Remicade®. Healthcare products in which the university's patents play a major role include pregnancy tests, screening agents, pediatric feeding solutions, transgenic animals, reagents, medical devices, and instruments. A number of software programs have been licensed, including MacroModel, Delphi, and Switcap, as well as products involving oil exploration and robotics.

Publicly held businesses can learn from CIE, whose goals are to leverage technology and science for the benefit of the institution, the faculty, and society. Columbia is attempting reproduce its success with patents by instituting a program to license the content of its faculty's lectures, research, and writing. It intends to collect royalties on copyrighted material from other institutions of higher learning and private sector businesses in a manner similar to CIE. This program to mine its professors' knowledge and expertise, which it owns a significant portion of, through a for-profit company focusing on copyrightable content is expected to be spun off as an independent company called Digital Knowledge Ventures (DKV).

The primary architect of Columbia's licensing strategy is Jack Granowitz. Mr. Granowitz, a chemical engineer and former executive director of CIE, joined Columbia in 1983, when the university's technology transfer program had just been launched. Prior to that he was an executive with IPCO Corporation, American Cyanamid, and Pfizer Inc. He was involved with the development and marketing of medical and pharmaceutical products, including the first surgical scrub brush and the first total hip prosthesis. He holds several patents related to medical and surgical devices. I spoke with Mr. Granowitz about developing a successful business model for exploiting technology, and what the private sector might learn from this experience.

The following discussion with Jack Granowitz, now a Special Advisor to CIE, was conducted in January 2001, with subsequent discussion and e-mail exchanges in April 2001.

More opportunities may be on the horizon for universities and other research institutions to raise serous capital. In August 2000, BioPharma Royalty Trust, formed by an Ivy League university to securitize the licensing revenue from its patent on the HIV medication Zerit®, raised $115 million in senior and mezzanine notes and equity. (See Chapter 22, "New Patent Issue: BioPharma Royalty Trust.")

Mr. Berman gratefully acknowledges the assistance of Sam Adler, JD, legal editor and journalist, who participated in the preparation of this transcript.

BB: What factors are most responsible for CIE's success in patent licensing?

JG: Columbia is renowned as an academic center. Its researchers are some of the best people in their fields and work in a broad range of technologies, including medical, chemical, engineering, and digital technology. After Bayh-Dole, universities had to decide what to do with their intellectual property. The university knew that it had an opportunity to own and commercialize the inventions that were being developed in its labs. It chose a strategy of bringing in people from industries who understood the use of patents and had a business focus. Columbia's success is directly related to its focus on finding commercial partners who can develop technology into marketable products.

BB: Isn't that what most universities did with their research?

JG: Most universities took academics that were already working at the university and put them into the offices that had to be set up under Bayh-Dole. These people were very strong technically, but they were usually not businesspeople. That is what set Columbia apart from many other universities.

BB: How do you identify technologies for research?

JG: The way Columbia and most other academic institutions work is that the researcher applies for various types of federal, state, or other types of government or foundation grants based on his or her interests. Any inventions that he or she makes are reported to the university. CIE then takes the necessary steps to protect these inventions and find commercial partners. In terms of corporate support for research, generally this develops as part of the license agreement. Often, Columbia has a technology which is available for license to a corporation which desires to support this particular research and obtain additional rights to license new inventions.

BB: In addition to NIH [National Institutes of Health], NSF [National Science Foundation] and DoD [Department of Defense], who funds your research?

JG: Pharmaceutical and other private sector companies. Last year [FY 2000] about $22 million of our $167 million in revenue was attributed to corporate-sponsored research. Usually, this involved a corporation licensing some of our intellectual property and, as part of the licensing agreement, wanting us to undertake some additional research, which they would fund in exchange for certain additional rights. Under Bayh-Dole, universities are permitted to mix private sector and federal funds and to grant a company the rights to any inventions that may result.

BB: Because you receive federal funding for which they are ineligible, do private sector companies sometimes feel that you not competing fairly?

JG: I don't think a corporation would give us funds if they could easily do the research themselves. We provide something that they don't have. When Columbia started this program in the early 1980s, biotechnology had just burst onto the scene. Most of the knowledge for biotechnology was located within academic centers. All of the start-ups were basically academic people. Large pharmaceutical companies didn't have this technology or the researchers available in their laboratories to do this type of research. We are not competing because we are actually ahead of the curve for most technologies. An academic center should be able to anticipate future innovations and the direction of technology . . . Columbia's technology transfer business is finding commercial partners who will develop and market products for our technology, innovations, and intellectual property.

BB: The University of California's research budget was $1.8 billion in FY 1999 [this includes nine medical schools]; Columbia's was $279 million. But your licensing revenue for FY 1999 was $89.2 million versus $71 million for UC. To what do you attribute the difference?

JG: I think that we've done a better job of bringing the technology we've developed to the attention of the corporate sector and of setting up the deals to move it downstream.

METHODOLOGY FOR INNOVATION

BB: Do you have a methodology for identifying and organizing innovation? For example, do you have a program to advise professors and researchers about how to determine what's patentable and what's not?

JG: Absolutely. We meet with them individually and at department meetings and put information on our web site. We encourage them to come to us if they are not sure about something. We also advise them to fill out an Invention Report, a standard form for reporting innovations. They can download it from the CIE web site.

We have a variety of ways of making sure that we stay on top of inventions that are being developed throughout the university, and of identifying what might be unique. We have CIE people who work very closely with the departments to find out what new things are happening. We also use some faculty members on a consulting basis to keep us advised of new things going on in their departments. We tell all department chairmen and faculty who we are and why it's beneficial for them to interact with us. Then we regularly review the list of faculty members from each department to make sure we have contacted them. So we use a variety of different ways to try to make sure we're on top of all the technology and innovations.

BB: How many people are on the staff at CIE?

JG: Approximately 30, which includes both full-time and part-time people.

BB: How involved is CIE staff in the inventing process?

JG: CIE has a group of people who work with inventors from the point at which they either submitted an idea to the CIE office or we made contact with them, to the point when a commercial deal is completed. Having one CIE person involved from start to finish ensures continuity. It's also good because when a corporation comes on the scene, it only has to work with one person at CIE. I think Columbia is one of the few schools that does it this way. Most of the time, if a corporate person comes in, he has to work with a licensing person and if he wants to go do a research project, he has to work with a research person, etc. There's a discontinuity that develops. This is also the most efficient way to work with our faculty.

We try to make it really simple for the corporate world. As for CIE's ongoing interaction with inventors, we have a monthly inventors' review meeting where the inventors meet with a group comprised of CIE people, our outside patent counsel, and some advisors we use to help us determine if an invention is patentable, if it has commercial value, whether we should file a patent application or have the inventor to do some more work, and whether our licensing strategy should involve forming a start-up or partnering with an established company. All of these questions are answered as we work our way through the process—and the inventor is involved all along the way because his input is extremely valuable.

BB: You may be discussing these issues before you're even sure you have something that's patentable?

JG: Many inventions that are reported are marketed without a patent being issued or even applied for.

FROM RESEARCH TO REVENUE STREAM

BB: Walk us through a successful license from research to revenue stream.

JG: One such license is Xalatan, which is licensed to Pharmacia Inc. This project dates back to the early 1980s when our inventor discovered that a prostaglandin compound could be used to treat glaucoma. Research was carried out in the Columbia lab and several patent applications were filed. A number of companies were contacted to commercialize the technology and Pharmacia was selected. Over the years, Pharmacia supported research in our laboratories and did the work in its own laboratories to develop a product which was taken through clinical trials and FDA approval. The product is now marketed worldwide and is the leading drug for treating glaucoma.

BB: What's the policy on sharing licensing revenues with faculty members?

JG: Columbia has a standard formula for distributing the licensing revenues it receives from corporations. Up to $100,000, the inventor gets 40 percent of the gross amounts for himself personally and 20 percent for his research lab. Over $100,000, he gets 20 percent for himself personally and 20 percent for his lab. This funding is open-ended and remains the same as long as revenues are received from the licensee and is considered very generous. It's far different from what the corporate world has. Of course, the private sector has equity which it can distribute to their inventors in a similar way. If Columbia takes equity in a start-up or a corporate partner, we also distribute that to the inventor. But that's our standard formula for any gross receipts that come in, whether from front-end payments, milestones, royalties, or equity. There should be some way to reward inventors who do not want to get involved in commercialization and technology development.

BB: Some say that incentivizing researchers to invent (and patent) in areas that are lucrative might pollute the waters of academic freedom by introducing too strong a profit motive. Can aggressive business partnerships discourage pursuit of other less financially rewarding research?

JG: Based on our experience, our most successful researchers, in terms of receiving licensing revenues, have continued to file for grants, conduct [basic] research, and publish their results. There does not appear to be any slackening of interest or effort on the part of researchers who are receiving revenues from corporate licenses.

BB: What prevents a faculty member from going into business on his own or leaving for a better university post?

JG: Nothing. However, under federal laws, a researcher must report any inventions that have been made during his research. The law does allow a faculty member to request a license from the university for a start-up with which he may become involved, within university guidelines.

SPIN-OFFS

BB: Not-for-profit research institutions like SRI International (originally a part of Stamford University) and MIT occasionally work with partners to "spin-off" technologies into companies in exchange for equity. Has Columbia pursued spin-offs?

JG: Yes, Columbia has an active program for creating new start-ups. Early on, we focused on the licensing aspect because start-ups were just coming into play. By the early 1990s, however, faculty members had become more interested in doing start-ups, so we've moved more into that area. We now have about 50 companies that have started up with university technology and we have an equity position in most of them [a listing of these companies can be found on the CIE web site, *www.columbia.edu/cu/cie.com*].

A good example is Pharmacopeia, which combines combinatorial chemistry technology, high throughput screening, and the use of modeling, simulation, and information management software to address key challenges in the drug discovery process.

BB: What did CIE realize from that?

JG: An equity position and some milestone and royalty payments. It was an interesting deal because it was done in combination with Cold Spring Harbor Laboratory and we had some joint patents that we had licensed together. Our combined equity interest was slightly more than 10 percent, which was subsequently diluted down when they went out and raised money. We had options to acquire additional shares, which we did.

But I think the reason that Columbia's technology transfer has been successful is that, at the beginning, we focused on licensing rather than start-ups. Second, we realized that the pharmaceutical industry was tremendously interested in patents and licensing. It was also the early days of biotechnology so we had something very unique, which we could put on the table. So part of what Columbia did well was to ascertain what strengths we had that we could take out to the corporate world. The deals done in the 1980s led to the development of products that by the 1990s were producing large royalty streams.

Some of our start-ups pay us royalties; some have milestone payments. We try to get a flow of revenue. But the major sorts of money will come from royalties when the product is introduced, in combination with the equity interest. . . . Sometimes you get front-end payments which are spread out over a period of time. In addition to milestone payments, there could be performance payments. Sometimes on the start-up we will also do research, for which we receive funds. All of this allows some money to flow into the university which we can distribute back to the researcher.

BB: What's the downside to start-ups?

JG: Low annual revenues. MIT, for example, has a lot of joint venture partners, but if you look at their [licensing income] ranking [reported by the AUTM, the Association of University Technology Managers], their royalty revenues are not that high. That's the nice part about licensing: If you can get some good patents that cover products, you can generate a nice steady income stream.

BB: Is the revenue that Columbia's licenses generate concentrated in one or two "home-run" patents or are they based on revenue from many patents?

JG: Columbia has had several home-run patents, but there is also a number of other technologies which are generating substantial income. Significant income has been derived from the co-transformation patents and from patents covering such drugs as Xalatan®, ReoPro®, and Remicade®. In addition, significant revenues are coming from MPEG-2 patents. MPEG is a worldwide standard covering encoding and decoding of data, widely used in set-top boxes for television and for DVD players. Also, there are a number of smaller sources of revenue coming from a variety of other inventions and innovations.

BB: What would you say is your most successful patent in terms of licensing revenue?

JG: The co-transformation patents for biotechnology. They are used to make complex proteins, such as tissue plasminogen activator, erythropoietin, growth colony stimulating factor, Factor VII, Pulmozyme, Cerezyme, and ReoPro. A variety of products have come out of some of the patents in this area. One of the technologies generated a nonexclusive patent license which we licensed to more than 30 companies. It's generated several hundred million dollars to date.

BB: Do you license the patent or technology separately from the know-how or does it all go together?

JG: What we try to do is create a package of patents and research information so the company can build the best patent portfolio covering the products. That's what companies want to do. In fact, many times when we license technology, the company will support research leading to additional patents that will enhance their position covering the product. Also, you have to remember that academic researchers publish most of their results. This is the case for all the corporate research collaborations in which we have been involved. We are interested in doing joint ventures and start-ups.

BB: Has Columbia had to enforce its patents against infringers?

JG: Yes. To maintain a viable licensing program, it's necessary from time to time to take legal action against infringers—to show that you mean business and to defend your patents. This is true of all businesses that rely on patents.

BB: Is it awkward for a university to sue potential for-profit competitors?

JG: Under Bayh-Dole, we're obligated to protect our intellectual property. So, yes, we do defend our patents. We've been involved in several litigations concerning our co-transformation patents. Also, with our nonmedical patents, we're involved in litigation against infringers.

PATENTS PENDING

BB: Can private sector companies replicate what Columbia does in leveraging IP?

JG: Many do. More and more corporations are outlicensing inventions which are not part of their core technologies . . . Initially, most of our licensing was generated by the medical school because of the molecular biology, but now it's broadening out. For example, in the digital technology area, we have some patents covering the standards for MPEG-2, and seven or eight other companies, including Sony, Mitsubishi, Matsushita, and Phillips, also had some patents covering this standard. We entered into a pooling agreement where we would go out and market them as a package. We formed a new start-up company for this purpose called MPEG LA, LLC.

We are very innovative in that we are willing to develop new ways for a university to deal with industry other than the straight license, the start-up, or the combination of licensing and research. We have formed partnerships with other academic centers or corporations such as the MPEG2 [patent] pool. That was innovative in that we were willing to put together our technology with those of commercial businesses for a similar objective. (See "Licensing Revenue: Universities & Research Institutions" in the Data Bank section of this book.)

BB: Was the pool your idea?

JG: We were one of the early originators of the patent pool, and our organizing activities helped to make it a reality. It was a good example of international cooperation that was able to bring a group of patents to the commercial markets. Other interesting collaborations have been with Pharmacopeia and the British Diabetes Association, which was working with Oxford University and a group that included Pasteur [Institute] and Eli Lilly and Company. The research involved looking at type II diabetes. We're expanding our partnerships with other universities to bring in different technologies.

BB: How do you let companies know that a particular technology available for license?

JG: The Web is a very powerful marketing tool. Before we had a web site, we would publish lists and mail them out. Or someone would call us and ask what technologies we had and we would send them out a list. They would take the list and mark off items of interest and we would send them non-confidential pieces describing it. Then they would say whether they were interested in going further. This would take months and months. Now if someone is interested in a certain area of technology or innovation, they just go to our web site and look it up. They can click on it and get a brief description of the technology and, usually, a reference for the patent. They can see the patent and the inventor. It's all linked. With the Web, you can very quickly make someone aware of a new technology. On our home page, we list key technologies that we're featuring. We feature new inventions each quarter. Another thing we do is contact companies that we know of or have done a deal with, such as Guidant with whom we developed a heart stent. We might go back to them and say "Look, we've got something new, are you interested?" We've staffed CIE with business people who have ties to industry. A lot of times the inventors themselves have contacts.

BB: Columbia's Digital Knowledge Ventures (DKV) sounds like another potentially innovative leveraging of IP. While its focus is primarily information and content as opposed to inventions, licensing is still a primary objective.

JG: Basically, it's set up to do in the new media area what CIE does in life sciences and technology—develop licensing opportunities and start-up companies. The first company that's been started by DKV is Fathom, which is a portal for distant learning. In addition to using existing content, DKV also is attempting to develop its own new content that will be marketed through the portal. Like CIE, the idea behind DKV and Fathom is to leverage existing resources in the form of licensing, rights, and equity.

BB: At the end of the day, what has the technology transfer program meant to Columbia?

JG: It's a healthy ecology. Revenues generated though research that flow back to the university in the form of payments, partnerships, and equity provide the basis for funding new research and education, which, in turn, create opportunities for innovation and new inventions. It helps the university to remain relatively independent and to prosper. But in order for it to work, it needs to be managed and marketed like a business.

CHAPTER NINE

Making Innovation Pay
Aligning Patent Rights with Business Strategy

by Stephen P. Fox and Guy J. Kelley

PERSPECTIVES

"Innovative companies have been thrust into an intellectual property 'arms race,'" say Stephen Fox and Guy Kelley of Hewlett-Packard Company. As a result, some companies are in danger of creating an obsession with patent quantity at the expense of quality. Disruptive technologies, which can make some patents obsolete, argues Mr. Fox, Director of Intellectual Property and Associate General Counsel at HP, may pose a huge threat to the unwary company that relies on the traditional patent portfolio built around a core technology, rather than one that responds to markets.

Mr. Fox's responsibilities at HP include identifying and capitalizing on innovation through patents. One of his most important challenges is to facilitate the development of innovation and encourage his company's inventors and other employees to turn innovation into legally enforceable assets. Like Jeffrey Brandt, former head of IP at Walker Digital Corporation and priceline.com (Chapter 3, "Capturing Innovation: Turning Intellectual Assets into Business Assets"), Mr. Fox believes in the value of market-based inventing. For active innovators like HP, which spent $2.6 billion on R&D in fiscal 2000, or 5.4 percent of net revenue, this represents a change in focus whose effects are just beginning to be felt on the bottom line. Economists and consultants who focus on patent portfolios, say Fox and Kelley, have tended to look at what has been created, not at what needs to be. "The investor," they conclude, "should know when a company has a sustainable futuristic approach to protecting innovation."

Mr. Fox and his staff have developed a systematic approach to align IP protection with HP business strategy. (Part of HP's redesigned

corporate logo is the word "invent.") Needless to say, ongoing communications between engineers, strategists, and management is
essential. Fox's series of worldwide "InventShops" and "Innovation
Workshops" enable him, according to HP's 2000 annual report, "to
plumb HP inventors for promising IP they're developing, helping
them identify market-leading technology and ideas that require protection." Early indications are that these workshops are beginning to
pay off. HP's worldwide patent applications for 2000 exceeded 3,000,
a 30 percent increase over the previous year. With HP's impending
acquisition of Compaq, an earlier acquireror of Tandem and Digital
Equipment, the company's patent estate is likely to expand even
faster.

INTRODUCTION

If you were to ask an economist about intellectual capital management (ICM), you
would likely hear about the importance of appropriating value in intellectual property by increasing the rents to the company through patent licensing. If you were
to ask a consultant in one of the big accounting firms about ICM, you would likely
hear about the importance of doing an IP audit to see what patents the company
owns. These are solid concepts, but they focus on what has already come out of
the company's patent pipeline. It is important to recognize that what you get out
of the pipe depends on what you put into it. In other words, how is a company's
intellectual property captured and codified? The purpose of this chapter is to provide perspective on how to drive innovation so knowledge is moved from the
minds of inventors to legally enforceable patents.

BACKGROUND

Patents are part of a company's intellectual capital, which comprises two broad
categories: *human capital* and *intellectual assets*. A component of intellectual assets
is the intellectual property of the company, which in turn includes patents. A
company's patent portfolio can be both important and valuable. A company can
choose to protect its intellectual property in a variety of ways, such as patents, trade
secrets, copyrights, trademarks, or mask works. However, it is the patent portfolio that often becomes the major consideration in understanding the value of an
innovative company.

The value of a patent portfolio lies in both its composition and management.
What is in the portfolio and how the company uses it are both important. An innovative company needs a program that addresses both of these issues. Much has
been written about using a patent portfolio in ways to generate revenue for an

innovative company, but there has been less discussion on how to actually build the portfolio. Hewlett-Packard Company has been transforming the way it builds the patent portfolio using a variety of techniques and strategies.

The patenting life cycle is composed of four phases. The first phase is generating invention disclosures. This includes the precursor act of conceiving the invention. The second phase is processing and evaluating invention disclosures, which includes docketing the disclosures and identifying patent coordinators, who are technologists that can work with the patent attorney. The third phase is converting selected invention disclosures into filed patent applications and prosecuting those applications until they are issued by the government patent offices in various countries. The fourth and last phase is to manage the patent portfolio. This includes knowing the composition of the portfolio and being able to identify offensive, defensive, and collaborative areas of opportunity.

Regarding the first phase, creating a traditional patent portfolio is straightforward and relatively easy using traditional techniques that patent professionals and intellectual property managers know well. In earlier years, many companies went about patenting on an ad hoc basis. In effect, it was a sequential waiting process: first waiting for an engineer to dream up a nifty invention, then waiting for the inventor to get around to writing an invention disclosure (if ever), then waiting to see if the invention makes it into a product (if it ever does), then determining whether the invention made a significant contribution to the product, and finally patenting it. Over time, this approach resulted in a semirandom assortment of patents on nifty inventions. Like the infinite number of monkeys typing on the infinite number of typewriters, a sufficiently large number of talented engineers working for a sufficiently long time in a sufficiently specialized technology can eventually yield enough nifty patents to give the company a reasonably good patent position in that specialty.

As one can see, the traditional method of building and maintaining a patent portfolio has been to identify and file patent applications on inventions that have already been conceived, reduced to practice, and developed into a product or service, where the product and service have a planned commercialization date. To build the traditional portfolio, the patent professional simply needed to wait and identify the company products ready to be released. Once the products were identified, then the inventions in those products were identified and disclosed. After disclosure, the inventions were evaluated for the appropriate type of protection, such as patents or trade secrets. In the case of patent protection, often the commercialization date is before (but not more than one year before) the filing date of the resulting patent application. This forecloses patent protection everywhere in the world except the United States, due to more restrictive laws in other countries.

It must be recognized that the concept of the traditional patent portfolio has not remained static. It has gone through several major evolutions. For example, 15 years ago, software patents were relatively new and they became a topic of heated debate. Many software inventors predicted that patenting software would destroy the freedom to create; software development would come to a standstill. As typical in many new areas of technology which become subject to patent protection, just the opposite happens. Patenting encourages investment and development in the new technology. Now patents that cover inventions embodied in software are a standard part of the traditional portfolio of all companies involved in software technology.

In the traditional method, some of the criteria for evaluating an invention disclosure are:

- Whether the invention is in or going to be in the company's product
- Whether the invention can be discovered through reverse-engineering
- Whether the invention is going to be or has been publicly disclosed
- Whether the invention could be used in future products
- Whether the invention solves a general problem
- Whether the invention solves a problem peculiar to the company's product not found in other products in the market

Generally, applying these criteria will build a good patent portfolio of the kind that has been adequate in the past. It may still be adequate for many companies, depending upon their particular business and market. For instance, if the products of the company have relatively long useful and commercial lives—four years or more—the traditional method may build the appropriate patent portfolio and serve the company well.

Frequently, as part of this traditional process, the company would provide financial incentives to inventors in order to encourage the disclosure of the invention so that it could be evaluated. Additional incentives often followed upon acceptance of the invention disclosure or the filing or issuance of a patent application. These incentives would help to make sure that a reasonable number of inventions embodied in the company's products or services would be identified and disclosed. While incentives provide the motivation to identify more of the inventions in a product, incentives alone do not change the type of inventions ultimately protected in the patent portfolio and thus do not change the kind of inventions disclosed and protected. The patent portfolio may get relatively larger, but usually does not change much in nature.

While this method has been adequate in the past, it may not be appropriate for many companies in either the new economy or high technology. In a company involved in fast-paced technology with typical product life spans measured in months rather than years, there is a need for different methods in order to preserve its design freedom, maintain competitiveness through proprietary products and services, and take advantage of realizing an appropriate level of income from its intellectual capital.

Building a patent portfolio according to the traditional method may leave gaps in the portfolio. At any given time, the product offerings of a company may not span the entire market. The company may want to bring out a product in an area that fills a gap in its product line in the future. The issue may be whether the patent portfolio has sufficient patents to provide protection and design freedom in the case of a new gap-filling product.

PROBLEMS WITH THE TRADITIONAL APPROACH

Innovative companies have been thrust into an intellectual property arms race. Competitors are moving faster and faster. There are three forces at work. First, a company's patent portfolio may have lost value due to a spin-off or the recognition that many of its patents cover short-lived and now-irrelevant old technologies or simple productivity enhancements for specific products. Second, the increase in patenting in many markets may threaten to leave a company behind. Third, it is clear that the for-profit licensing and outside-the-box use of a company's patent portfolio will be the mark of a successful company in the future. Besides this "arms race" between companies, disruptive technologies may pose an even bigger threat to the unwary company that relies on the traditional patent portfolio built around a core technology rather than a more market-based portfolio.

Many innovative businesses find that much of their revenue is due to products or services that have been introduced into the market within the last two years. This means that much of their revenue two years from now will come from products that have not yet been put on sale. Innovative businesses competing with other innovative businesses may find that waiting until an invention has been fully developed into a commercial product does not provide an adequate patent portfolio. Indeed, there is no legal reason to wait so long to seek patent protection. Historically, there may have been financial reasons, which are no longer valid for an innovative business. In the past, companies wanted to save money and only file patent applications on the inventions determined to be in the final product.

We now know that simply because an invention does not make it into the final product does not mean it has no value. In fact, in many cases, it means that the invention is merely ahead of its time. The invention will likely be in a future product. Waiting for such an invention to be developed into a future product may result in the invention losing its novelty. By the time the invention is disclosed and evaluated, other companies may have come up with similar if not identical inventions in the meantime. Waiting to protect the invention until it has been implemented in a particular form may result in narrower protection because the general broader idea has already been either publicly disclosed or patented by someone else.

Moreover, with short-lived products that need to be replaced every two years or sooner in order to stay competitive, the inventions embodied in those products may have ephemeral usefulness. By the time a patent application is issued protecting such an invention, the technology may have taken a different direction, making the invention obsolete. Only a fraction of the inventions in a current product may have value beyond that product.

Correspondingly, inventions that were not chosen to be in the current product may be overlooked or undiscovered under the traditional process, even though those inventions may eventually make it into succeeding generations of products or even other product lines of the innovative business.

Another problem with the traditional approach is the failure to take advantage of the protection available, at least in the United States, for innovations in business methods and Internet marketing and selling. Such innovations may not be embodied within the product per se and might be overlooked.

Still another problem is the inability to forecast and provide the appropriate level of design freedom for future products that will need to be developed in converging or intersecting markets. This could be especially problematic for a company that has essentially no presence in one of the two markets that converges or intersects the company's existing market. The consequence at best would likely be pricey license agreements and at worst costly patent fights.

Finally, in an innovative environment, the traditional patent portfolio may have limited value when confronted with a disruptive technology.

No doubt, an innovative company will get some benefit from building a traditional patent portfolio, but in today's environment, much more is needed.

GOING BEYOND THE ORDINARY

A company in an innovative industry needs to develop tools to identify and create inventions as well as obtain protection well before the decision is made to incorporate the invention into a product or service that will be offered to the public.

An innovative company does not merely produce more of the same types of patents that came out of the traditional approach. The patent portfolio of an innovative company will include different kinds of patents, not just more of them. For example, everyone talks about the ability to protect business method and Internet-related inventions, as well as patenting inventions to cover future products and converging markets. Simply knowing that patents can protect these types of inventions is one thing, but actually creating and incorporating these patents into the company's portfolio is quite something else. The innovators who produce these types of inventions must be informed, trained, and encouraged to identify and disclose them. Otherwise, while the company may create those types of inventions, they will not find their way into the company's patent portfolio.

For futuristic, gap-filling, and strategic inventions, potential inventors must be given the time and opportunity to be creative, in addition to being given the training and encouragement to identify and disclose such inventions. Invention concepts alone may make good lunchtime discussion among in-house counsel, but they offer no practical value to the company's patent portfolio. More is needed. Inventions must be created and protected well before they are developed into products. It is imperative to protect not only inventions in present products, but also inventions that will be needed to compete with future products. New markets created out of converging or intersecting markets must be anticipated. Innovations across the business must be identified and protected.

Various tools have been developed to create, identify, disclose, and evaluate inventions that will allow a company to protect its design freedom for present products as well as for the future market. Implementation of the tools alone is not sufficient to create an adequate patent portfolio for the innovative business. Changes must be made in the evaluation process and criteria. For example, actual use of the invention in a current product becomes less significant. Also, different types of inventors need to be sought out, not just among product design engineers, but also in the marketing, support, sales, and finance functions. Furthermore, complementary assets surrounding an invention should be identified. Protecting them can be as important as protecting the innovative nugget itself, especially in markets subject to potentially disruptive technologies.

THE TOOLS AND THE WORKSHOPS

InventShop

Two techniques in various formats have been developed to generate the gap-filling, futuristic, strategic invention disclosures necessary for the patent portfolio of the innovative company. They serve different purposes, but they complement each other. First, there is a workshop called an InventShop. This workshop typically is a half-day event and is very flexible in terms of the size of the group. It works well for groups from 10 to 100 participants. The only limiting factor is the size of the room available and the logistics of scheduling and inviting the participants. Often, snacks, drinks, or lunch are provided to encourage attendance as well as active participation of inventors.

The InventShop begins with distribution of invention disclosure forms to each participant. As an introduction, everyone is told that it is fine to write an invention disclosure at any time during the event. Present at the event are one or more patent attorneys and perhaps a facilitator with an evangelistic message about the importance of patents. Not much guidance is given except that everyone is considered an inventor and, in fact, has probably already made an invention and has probably come to the workshop with at least three inventions already in mind. An expansive definition of invention is presented to include futuristic, gap-filling, and preemptive inventions rather than just the inventions embodied in current products. Also, participants are informed of the need for business-method inventions and Internet-related inventions. If the participants are generally from one area of technology, the strategic areas of importance are presented for that area of technology and market. This does not limit the types of inventions disclosed in the workshop. Instead, the workshop encourages the disclosure of all inventions. A primary purpose is to train participants on how to fill out invention disclosures. Experience has shown that an InventShop will produce many irrelevant and nonnovel inventions, but it also serves to encourage the participants to recognize that they are, indeed, inventors and gives them the training to submit invention disclosures as they recognize more relevant inventions in the course of their work.

Next, the InventShop covers the importance of patents to the company, the financial incentive program, and the training in writing an invention disclosure. It should also cover the company's interest in building a broad patent portfolio with emphasis on company interest in inventions that cover the products not only of competitors but of complementors, substitutors, downstream customer's customers, and upstream suppliers.[1] The InventShop presentation typically lasts between 40 to 60 minutes depending on the makeup of the group and questions from participants. In essence, the presentation part of this workshop is not much different from a dog and pony show or a coffee talk on patents.

The rest of the time is spent on writing invention disclosures and sharing ideas. The patent attorney roams the room and answers questions. Depending on the size of the group, often the participants will circulate each others' invention disclosures and this will prompt more ideas and, thus, more disclosures. Sometimes smaller groups will form around common technology areas and further discussions will lead to more invention disclosures. The synergy among energized participants can be an exciting thing to watch.

This type of workshop will also help build the traditional patent portfolio. The participants could be a group that has just released a product. They can use the workshop as an opportunity to harvest all of the inventions that went into the product. When given permission to go beyond that, the participants also can disclose many inventions that were rejected from incorporation into the product, but nevertheless were created during the project.

Innovation Workshop

The second technique is called an Innovation Workshop. It is typically longer than an InventShop—two days, for example—and has fewer participants—say 6 to 12 people. In addition, the group includes one or two facilitators, a patent attorney, and a technographer. The workshop involves much more time and administrative effort to organize and conduct than does an InventShop. The Innovation Workshop is also much more targeted and focused in a given area of technology.

The targeted technology area can be a result of an analysis of the existing patent portfolio and the gaps in it. Often included are an analysis of future products (preemptive), as well as an analysis and investigation into different markets (convergent or intersecting markets). The participants are carefully selected for their expertise related to the targeted technology and whether their expertise would be merely redundant or whether it would complement the other participants' expertise.

In essence, an Innovation Workshop is a structured and guided brainstorming session of six to eight future-oriented innovators, scientists, and engineers over a two-day time period. The purpose of the session is to generate invention disclosures describing futuristic inventions that have not yet been reduced to practice. Indeed, the inventions that result from such a session may not even have been conceived prior to the session.

In addition to its primary purpose, an Innovation Workshop provides other valuable benefits:

- The participants learn to think creatively about the future.
- The participants learn to work together more effectively as inventors.
- New research directions and even new products can be discovered and explored.
- The patent attorney for the business entity acquires a better understanding of the entity's technology.
- The entity's patent coordinator gains a better understanding of the strategic thinking of research and development (R&D) management.
- The entity's R&D manager gains a better insight into the future market from the perspective of some of the entity's best innovators in the technology.

In more detail, the participants of an Innovation Workshop are:

- One client (R&D manager or equivalent)
- Six to eight brainstormers
- Two facilitators (or one experienced facilitator-teacher and two trainees)
- One technographer
- One patent attorney

The client is a representative of the business entity for which the workshop is being conducted. Usually, he or she is a manager or a patent coordinator. The client should understand the entity's technology and should have some knowledge of the present and future business directions of the entity.

The brainstormers are imaginative, future-thinking innovators, engineers, and scientists who understand the entity's technology and processes. Although they may be drawn entirely from the entity, it is often advantageous to draw some of them from other related entities in the company or from the central research group of the company.

The facilitators are trained in facilitating Innovation Workshops. The company may want to retain an outside consultant who specializes in conducting Innovation Workshops. A properly chosen consultant can also train others in the company to conduct such workshops. For a company that wants to make Innovation Workshops a regular tool in patent portfolio management, it is good to identify several employees with an aptitude for facilitating other types of group meetings. These employees can be trained to facilitate Innovation Workshops.

The technographer may be compared to a court reporter. The technographer captures the proceedings of the workshop in a word processor in real time for printing and distribution to the participants during the workshop. Although verbatim transcription is not needed, accuracy in capturing the essence of what is said is important to capture simple sketches as well as words. It is desirable for the technographer to be able to print out and copy documents during the workshop.

The patent attorney is usually the company attorney who handles patent work for the entity. In some cases a different attorney, or even an outside counsel, may be used. The attorney can use the proceedings to learn more about the technology of the entity, as well as help prepare invention disclosures during the final hours of the workshop. Sometimes he or she may even join in the discussions of the brainstormers.

It is important that all participants be committed for the entire duration of the workshop. Certainly, they should not be distracted with phone calls or other business matters. If necessary, a substitute participant who can devote his or her full time and attention to the workshop should be arranged beforehand in case a nominated participant is put in a position of having to divide time between the workshop and a conflicting simultaneous activity.

Preferably, adequate time is allowed for planning the workshop to help insure its success. However, when it is important and the businesspeople are sufficiently motivated, a Workshop can be put together in a matter of days. Ideally, to reduce stress and provide a reasonable amount of time for planning and availability of attendees, about six weeks should be allowed between the time a decision is made to hold an Innovation Workshop and the actual workshop session.

A preliminary planning meeting of about an hour should be held four weeks in advance between the facilitators and the client, optionally with patent attorney participation. The sponsoring business entity should decide which (if any) other business entities might profitably be invited to participate. A focus area should be selected. Then the client and the facilitators hold the preliminary planning session, optionally with the patent attorney. During the planning session, the focus area is refined and a final list of brainstormers is prepared.

A premeeting of all involved should be held about a week prior to the session, although the premeeting can also be held the afternoon immediately preceding the session if some of the participants are not local.

Most workshops run for two consecutive days. During the last part of the second day, invention disclosures are written, so there should not be any required work after the session. Sometimes, disclosures come in after the workshop, and for these, the patent attorney is available to help keep track of them.

It is critically important that the participants devote their full time and attention to the workshop session. For this reason, it is highly recommended that the session be conducted at a remote site. Experience has shown that it is very difficult to hold 100 percent of the participants' attention if the session is held on site at a company facility. Depending upon the site and the commitment of the managers and attendees, some Innovation Workshops have been successfully held on site, but the session should be in a building far removed from the building where the participants' offices are located.

A large conference room is needed. Even though the actual number of people in the session is only 10 to 12, the session does not work effectively unless the participants have plenty of room to spread out. Also, a lot of wall space is needed for putting up easel paper. A room that is rated for 40 to 50 people is about the right size. It is better not to serve meals in the meeting room. The session is intense, and a break to a different location (even if only the next room) for lunch is very helpful in refreshing the participants.

The room should be equipped with a whiteboard or blackboard and several easels (ideally five or six) with lots of easel paper, Magic Markers, and masking tape or pins for posting sheets of easel paper on the walls. A computer with printer should be provided for the technographer.

The Innovation Workshop is a particularly valuable tool that HP is using to develop strategic market-based patents. Such a workshop typically yields 15 to 45 futuristic inventions that can be patented, thereby providing a key competitive advantage, particularly over others who are not so forward-thinking.

The company's inventors, marketers, managers, and attorneys all have a role to play in identifying future market-based patent opportunities in an innovative company. This is not an extracurricular activity for those with excess time on their hands. On the contrary, this activity serves as a catalyst among some of the most creative people in the company; the activity may have a bearing on a company's survival and, hence, the worth of its stock. This should be reason enough to hold Innovation Workshops.

The relationship between InventShops and Innovation Workshops is shown in Exhibit 9-1. The bare-bones InventShop presents the case for patents, trains the participants on writing invention disclosures, and sets them loose to write inven-

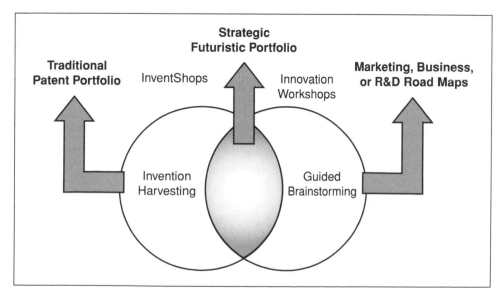

Exhibit 9-1 InventShops versus Innovation Workshops.

tion disclosures. This format harvests the inventions that the participants bring into the workshop and will help build the traditional patent portfolio. However, the InventShop can do more. The priorities of business management can be presented to help guide brainstorming. Also, the invention disclosures can be shared and informal discussions can be encouraged. InventShop formats can be designed to combine invention harvesting and guided brainstorming, even though they come from a strong heritage of invention harvesting. Conversely, the basic Innovation Workshop format is designed to lead a group through a rigorous guided brain-storming session focused on a particular topic. This pure creativity and problem-solving session can be used for a variety of purposes to generate business plans, road maps, and potential solutions, and the results can be harvested as in an InventShop.

As can be seen, both Innovation Workshops and InventShops can be used to generate futuristic, strategic, market-based patents. The three essential elements are:

1. A technology focus statement
2. Adequate training of participants to write usable invention disclosures
3. Time for discussion, whether it is serial, parallel, formal, or informal

RESULTS OF THE WORKSHOPS

First, regarding InventShops, they have proven to be easy to schedule and run. Also, they are productive. A rule of thumb for an InventShop is that three invention disclosures per participant will result from one workshop; however, there is a definite learning curve. Participants who attend a second InventShop produce more disclosures and those produced are more relevant. For example, participants who attend their first InventShop produce about two disclosures each, while a group of second-timers produces almost six disclosures each.

InventShops are an excellent way to train groups who have not been histori-cally included in the patent process. Participants gain clear insight on what makes a good disclosure and on what is a relevant invention based upon the feedback from the evaluation of their disclosure at a later patent coordinator meeting. InventShops raise the level of knowledge within an organization to the importance of business-method patents as well as the need to include in the patent portfolio inventions that may be relevant to a supplier or customer rather than being lim-ited to the inventions in the company's products.

The workshops are very convenient to do for first-time inventors and for in-ventors who have not in the past thought that their inventions were patentable. Experience has shown that with inspired and enthusiastic inventors, a collection of about 50 InventShops generated over 1,600 invention disclosures, even though most inventors were new at the process.

While these workshops can produce hundreds of disclosures, many are not actually turned into patent applications. Patent filing rates of 40 to 60 percent are common. This is lower than either the Innovation Workshop or the traditional processes, which usually have filing rates of 95 percent.

The strength of the InventShop is that it provides training to a large number of people in a relatively short time and is an effective tool for reaching first-time inventors. Because of the large number of disclosures produced, even with a relatively low relevance rate, there results a significant number of important strategic inventions that would not otherwise have found their way into the patent portfolio. The InventShop provides visibility to many inventions that would otherwise go unnoticed and thus unprotected by patents.

Another strength of the InventShop is its flexibility. The approach can be used in a more traditional way to harvest inventions from project teams that have soon-to-be released products. InventShops can be used with marketing and financial business groups that have traditionally not been asked to disclose their inventions, in order to obtain different types of patents not usually included in the more traditional portfolio. Also, an InventShop can be used with the more traditional inventor community, asking them to think about the future and about inventions that they wished they could put into a product, but were not able to do so at the time.

Offsetting all the benefits of the InventShop is the fact that many of the resulting disclosures are of questionable relevance and diffuse. Hence, substantial time may be needed to filter the invention disclosures to find significant ones.

In contrast to the InventShop, the Innovation Workshop produces a very high percentage of relevant inventions. Most Innovation Workshops have filing rates of 80 to 90 percent and produce 15 to 45 disclosures immediately after the workshop and another 25 to 40 disclosures within a couple of months after the workshop, all of which are related to the technology statement the client generated. By way of example, over 2,000 invention disclosures have been generated from about 40 Innovation Workshops, and a sizable number of those disclosures have been filed as patent applications with many more to be filed in due course.

The Innovation Workshop also has its own type of flexibility. The kind of invention disclosure sought is usually on futuristic, strategic, market-based inventions, but this workshop can provide other results besides invention disclosures. The process of the Innovation Workshop adapts itself well to any group that wants to explore the strategic direction of a business; investigate different business strategies; and evaluate different potential products with respect to different potential markets and futures. It would not be uncommon that the results of an Innovation Workshop could help provide the R&D road map for an entity.

Innovation Workshops may not always produce useable invention disclosures. This issue can be addressed in several ways. At the beginning of the Innovation Workshop, the participants are trained on writing invention disclosures. Alternatively, participants may be asked to attend an InventShop before they attend an Innovation Workshop. Also, a patent coordination meeting (explained below) is scheduled soon after the workshop so that the context is not forgotten and the workshop coordinator can follow-up on an inadequate disclosure immediately, while the invention is still fresh in the mind of the inventor.

From a process standpoint, there are similarities in how invention disclosures from an InventShop or an Innovation Workshop are handled to codify the intellectual property content. An effective process is shown in Exhibit 9-2. A business or technical manager reviews disclosures at a Patent Coordination Meeting. Each disclosure is assessed in light of recommendations from engineering managers and IP attorneys who attend the meeting. In addition, the assessment reflects priorities contained in a survey form business general managers submit. Also, the assessment conforms to certain Evaluation Guidelines designed to help facilitate the Patent Coordination Meeting. The result is a triage: For each disclosure, there is a decision to file a patent application, keep the invention as a trade secret, or publish the disclosure to put it in the public domain.[2]

The primary result of incorporating these workshops into the patent portfolio management process is the significant increase in invention disclosures and patent application preparation and prosecution. Of course, a collateral result is the need for additional capacity to handle such an increase effectively and efficiently. One should expect that the capacity issue is something that will need to be addressed on a continuing basis.

SHAREHOLDER PERSPECTIVE

In order for an investor to be comfortable with a long-term investment in a company competing in an innovative business environment, it will be critical that the investor know and have evidence of the institutionalized processes that assure ongoing capture of innovation. The investor needs to know when a company has made it a standard mode of operation or whether it is a one-shot approach that is not sustainable. Asking the right questions as an investor or potential investor can

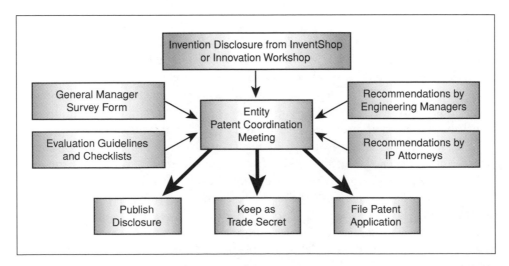

Exhibit 9-2   Invention review process.

determine whether a company can survive and thrive in an innovative industry. The investor should know when a company has a sustainable futuristic approach to protecting innovation.

If it is determined that a company is in an innovative market, how can one tell whether that company has an adequate patent portfolio or at least is making efforts to build one so that it can continue to design products and compete successfully in that market? Are inventors included in all areas of the company: marketing, finance, IT, inventory control, manufacturing, as well as R&D? Are there patent coordinators (patent ambassadors) who are in the entities and meet with their patent attorney in regularly and routinely scheduled meetings? Does the company's patent portfolio include inventions that have not been in the company's current or past products? Are those inventions relevant to future products; relevant to related markets that may converge or intersect their present market? What is the company doing now to continue producing such futuristic strategic preemptive inventions?

The single most important aspect of succeeding in this fast-paced environment is the conversion of tacit knowledge to codified form through the creation of durable and effective processes that capture new innovations and adequately protect them. The potential rewards in terms of competitive advantage, profitability, and shareholder value are unprecedented.

NOTES

1. For a more complete discussion of this concept, see Chapter 11, "Intellectual Property Management: From Theory to Practice," by Stephen P. Fox in *Profiting from Intellectual Capital*, ed. Patrick H. Sullivan (New York: John Wiley & Sons, Inc., 1998).
2. Additional details regarding this process are contained in Chapter 11, ibid.

IP DIALOGUE: "HP INVENTS NEW WAYS TO MANAGE ITS INNOVATION"

Hewlett-Packcard Corporation's Director of IP, Stephen Fox, is interviewed by Bruce Berman. (This interview originally appeared in the "IP Dialogue" column of *Corporate Legal Times* in July 2000. It is reprinted with permission.)

The evolution of Hewlett-Packard Co.'s logo reveals much about the company's attitude toward innovation. In 1999, the $42 billion in annual sales company, the largest manufacturer of computer peripherals in the world, added a single word under its well-known HP imprint—Invent.

HP is among the 15 companies that are issued the most U.S. patents. In 1999, the company received 850. More than 3,000 pending patent applications have been filed in the United States alone.

The company's patent count increased 50 percent, from 530 to 804, between

1997 and 1998. In the critical period preceding that increase, R&D spending jumped from $1.5 billion in 1995 to $2 billion in 1996 to approximately $2.5 billion today. This is still almost half of what GE spends and almost a third of IBM's outlay.

Stephen Fox, HP associate general counsel and director of intellectual property, is emblematic of a new breed of intellectual property directors and chief patent counsels at Fortune 500 companies. He is a business strategist as well as a legal manager.

According to Fox, you can expect to see more dot-com thinking at HP.

Fox served as 1999 president of the Association of Corporate Patent Counsel, which comprises Fortune 1,000 chief patent executives. Fox has been with HP for 32 years.

BB: How does HP's IP strategy support its business objectives?

SF: The strategy has three components. First, we seek to protect the company's ideas and innovations using the intellectual property laws. Second, we seek to obtain design freedom for the company in the creation of new products and processes without interference from the IP rights that other companies or individuals may own. Third, we seek to manage and promote the company's interest in IP, its ownership of IP, and the transfer of IP rights. This includes extracting value from IP in a variety of ways, whether it's out licensing, cross-licensing, or technology transfer.

BB: How are IP activities aligned with overall goals?

SF: They're closely linked to the business units. Our businesses are well aware of the legal services we offer in the IP area.

It's useful to consider some of the more recent IP trends. First, there is an increasing demand amongst our client businesses for more in-house knowledge of our products and our technology and expertise in the IP area. We seek to accomplish more futuristic positioning on behalf of the company to pre-empt the competition in securing IP rights.

There's also more emphasis on trademarks and branding, and we are doing more complex system deals with other companies. We want to make sure that we have the assurance of the right to compete in the marketplace.

It is important that we use IP rights to discourage so-called free riders in markets where there are low barriers to entry.

Coming to Market Quickly

BB: Is trade-secret protection frequently relied upon?

SF: We are a company where more than half of the sales in any given year come from products just introduced in the last two years. So there is a very rapid product-development activity. These products come to market very quickly.

As soon as they come to market, generally the trade-secret aspect of them are lost, because they are out there where folks can see them.

So, relative to the other forms of protection, trade secrets are not as high a priority. But certainly we do have key processes we like to maintain as trade secrets.

BB: Is HP's use of patents for defensive and strategic purposes, as well as revenue generation?

SF: There are primarily two ways we use our patent portfolio. One is defensive, and there are two aspects to that. The first is to obtain patents on our own developments before somebody else does, and the second is to build an arsenal of good patents we can use as a counterattack in the event somebody asserts their patents against us where we don't agree with the scope of their asserted coverage or the validity of their patents. That's the defensive side.

Then the offensive side, which we also employ, is using our patents to protect our markets against free riders in the marketplace.

The $100 Test

BB: Patent management, or IP asset management, has emerged as an important initiative for many companies. What are some of HP's elements of IP management?

SF: We start with the notion that there is a tight linkage between the IP legal department, our technologists, and our business units. On a periodic basis, typically once a year, we survey our key technologists and the general managers of our businesses with a formal survey to determine which technologies and products they think are the most important ones for them in the next five years. This is done on a business-by-business basis.

After they list their most important technologies, we ask them to prioritize on a top-down basis by applying what we call a $100 test to their list of technologies. In other words, if you had only $100 to allocate to protect all the technologies you listed, how would you spend it? That gives us a feeling for which ones they think are the most important and how important each one is. It's a weighing activity.

The third aspect of the survey is to ask these businesspeople which countries they think are the most important, as far as protection is concerned, outside the United States. We then use that input to determine where in the world we file our patent applications. These are just the first steps in patent management.

BB: For many companies, patent strategy seems to have become more "marketing-centric," or focused on the needs of the market, as opposed to what the bench scientists come up with and what the lawyers think are patentable.

SF: That's absolutely correct. In most portfolios, there are a certain group of patents that we call low-value patents. Those are the ones that relate to very specific inventions and perhaps just productivity-enhancing solutions for marketed products. Over time, these patents become obsolete and are relegated to a low value. There is another category, which includes patents on more strategic technology and processes. These, in turn, can be divided into two parts. One part is what we call the corporate-based technical or crown jewels, so to speak, relating to core technologies, core products, and those are fairly easy to spot. Certainly, the patents we have protecting our inkjet printing technology are valuable and would fall into this category. They serve to protect our position in the marketplace. There is another category of high-value patents that we in HP call our "market-based patents." These are intended to cover the goods of our competitors, substitutors and complementors of our products, as well as downstream customers' products and upstream suppliers. We do look more and more at the market-based aspects of things, whether it's in the product area or in the process area. These strategic patents have a high value.

BB: Have the importance of business method patents increased for HP?

SF: Yes, there are a lot of Internet applications that are patentable as business methods. For example, HP has a new initiative that we recently introduced to the market called E-speak. It is a technology that is particularly suitable for Internet use and we have devoted quite an effort to protect those innovations within the E-speak environment in a variety of way's including what you might call business-method patents.

BB: What does E-speak do?

SF: It is a way for a user to selectively integrate a variety of applications that affect his or her daily life. One of the examples often used is if you are on your way to catch a flight to another city for an appointment where you've made car and hotel reservations, lunch reservations or whatever, and you find that you are delayed because of traffic on the way to the airport, you can use your cell phone, and an integrated Internet link, and through just a few clicks of the appropriate key command set in motion a number of applications that will change your flight, your hotel and car reservations, notify someone that you are going to be late and change your lunch reservations, all on an integrated basis. It can all be put into action, with just a few simple commands. That all requires integrated applications of systems in the Internet environment.

BB: How far are you from the market?

SF: We are just introducing some of these concepts now.

BB: How many lawyers in the IP department at HP?

SF: HP is in the processing of spinning off a piece of the company. HP as we know it today is the computing and imaging company. The part we are spinning off is the test and measurement company, and it is called Agilent Technologies. Following the split, about a quarter of the attorneys went to Agilent and the rest stayed with HP. We currently have about 75 professionals in the department and about 50 of those are in the United States. The others are in Europe and Asia.

Three Challenges

BB: What are some of the techniques and tools you use to facilitate IP management?

SF: We have three challenges as a knowledge-based company: The first is to get the innovations from the innovators. Number two is to build an arsenal of quality patents, and number three is to extract value from those patents through licensing, cross-licensing, or protecting our position in the marketplace.

To facilitate patent analysis we use Aurigin Systems' Aureka software, which is used both by the legal and R&D departments. We use it to determine which other companies might be active in a particular technology class and to see who is active in leveraging off of our own technology.

Aureka is useful for patent-citation analyses. Its graphical interface, large patent database, and secure in-house installation make it highly worthwhile. Also, there is a comfort level to having all of your search and review analysis activity taking place from behind a firewall secure within the company.

ABOUT THE AUTHORS

Stephen P. Fox has overall responsibility for the intellectual property section of Hewlett-Packard's legal department comprised of approximately 100 professionals in Europe, Asia, and the United States. He is based in HP headquarters in Palo Alto, California. Mr. Fox, who joined the company in 1968, is a member of the executive committee and past president of the Association of Corporate Patent Counsel; a member of the board of directors of Intellectual Property Owners, Inc.; and a member of the Licensing Executives Society, the American Intellectual Property Law Association, and the American Bar Association.

He received a bachelor's degree in electrical engineering from Northwestern University in Evanston, Illinois, and a juris doctorate from George Washington University Law School in Washington, D.C. Publications he has authored or co-authored include "Intellectual Property Management: From Theory to Practice," a chapter in *Profiting from Intellectual Capital* by Patrick H. Sullivan (John Wiley & Sons, Inc., 1998), "Establishing an Out-Licensing Activity" by Patrick H. Sullivan and Stephen P. Fox, a chapter in *Technology Licensing*, edited by Russell L. Parr and Patrick H. Sullivan (John Wiley & Sons, Inc., 1998), and "How to Get the Patents Others Want," pp. 3-8, in *Les Nouvelles*, Journal of the Licensing Executives Society, Volume XXXIV, No. 1, March 1999.

Guy J. Kelley is a managing counsel for Hewlett-Packard Company. He supervises patent attorneys who conduct patent application preparation and prosecution for Hewlett-Packard facilities in six states, including his home state of Colorado. Mr. Kelley graduated from the University of Denver College of Law in 1988. Prior to becoming an attorney, he graduated from the University of Colorado at Boulder with a Bachelor of Arts in physics (1977). He worked for 10 years as an engineer and manager in the integrated circuit industry for National Semiconductor, Motorola, and Hewlett-Packard. Kelley is actively involved in politics, higher education, and intellectual property activities. He served on the State Board of Regents for the University of Colorado system from 1993 to 1999, chairing the board from 1994 to 1995. In 1996, Kelley ran for U.S. Congress. As a candidate, he fully supported a strong patent system with the USPTO retaining all of the funds it collects, believing that "patents provide the fuel of interest to the fire of genius."

Hewlett-Packard Company is a leading global provider of computing and imaging solutions and services. The company focuses on making technology and its benefits accessible to individuals and businesses through simple appliances, useful e-services, and solutions for an Internet infrastructure that's always on. Hewlett-Packard's portfolio of end-to-end, Internet-enabled hardware, software, and services helps companies transform their businesses and increase profit. The company's 17 product categories include computing systems, imaging and printing systems, and IT services. Hewlett-Packard employs more than 90,000 people and has major sites in 28 U.S. cities and in Europe, Asia Pacific, Latin America, and Canada. The company sells its products and services through about 600 sales and support offices and distributorships in more than 135 countries, as well as through resellers and retailers. In the year 2000, Hewlett-Packard was awarded over 900 U.S. patents. Corporate headquarters are in Palo Alto, California.

CHAPTER TEN

Patent "Brands"
Positioning IP for Shareholder Value

by Bruce Berman and James D. Woods

PERSPECTIVES

When it comes to using patents to provide more brand and shareholder value, some companies may be getting in the way of their own success.

Consumer products giants, such as Procter & Gamble, L'Oreal, and Coca-Cola, often have at least a few and as many as hundreds of patents that play a role in the development of their corporate brand equity. Some of these patents are associated with inventions that are vital to product performance. Tide®, for example, is a leading detergent due in no small part to the many U.S. and foreign patents associated with its formulation, manufacture, and distribution. Disney, a strong trademark enforcer, with a brand value of $32.5 billion and a market value of $60 billion, received 110 utility patents between 1990 and 1999, only 22 of which were design patents. (Expect to find more than Mickey Mouse value here.)

In this chapter, Bruce Berman and James D. Woods, intellectual property consultants who focus on communications and finance, say the importance of these patents may be overlooked and under-communicated because of the nature of low-cost, mass-produced products that most branded companies sell. Exploring the relationship between two different types of IP, trademarks and patents, they examine the opportunity to increase shareholder value by linking a brands to patents and vice versa. They show that companies known for their brands frequently have accumulated proprietary innovation and know-how worth taking seriously, even if they escape the scrutiny of most Wall Street analysts. Those companies with strong consumer brands that do not exploit this side of their intangible asset profile may be doing themselves and their shareholders a serious disservice.

Similarly, companies known for their advanced technology and strong patent estate that fail to capitalize on their intangible assets and other intellectual capital by creating a sufficient level of brand awareness may find these crown jewels underexploited. Mr. Berman and Dr. Woods show how strong branding, such as Intel Inside® or Teflon®, can complement certain patents and patent groups and help to maximize their licensing potential, enforcement, and shareholder value.

"Especially affected by a lack of communication concerning the value of IP are innovative technology or patent-intensive companies that are overlooked or misunderstood because of their business-to-business focus," say the authors. "The other group of companies whose market value may be negatively affected by a lack of IP brand awareness is, ironically, consumer brand companies . . . The multiples of these companies suffer, too, when they appear to be 'Old Economy' or without a critical mass of proprietary inventions, designs, and business methods, when, in fact, they are in many cases significant innovators."

"The World's 100 Most Valuable Brands" and "Highest Market Capitalizations + Patent Awards" charts in the Data Bank section of this book help to show why Berman and Woods contended that while patents may be worth more to some companies than others, they almost always are worth something in the right context. Data from both charts are accompanied by individual summaries of U.S. utility and design patent grants from 1990 to 1999, a good indication of the seriousness (or lack of it) that some large "nontech" companies, including those in finance, regard their innovation.

Wall Street has always been interested in how a company creates value for its shareholders. Until recently, value had been defined primarily by profitability, tangible assets, and reputation. Now that intangibles, including patents, trademarks, and other IP, have been revealed as major drivers of value for businesses, comprising up to 75 percent of companies' wealth, money managers, investment bankers, and others are taking intellectual property more seriously. An illustration of financial community interest in IP is reflected in the increased scrutiny of the topic in the business media. From 1996 to 2000 the number of articles mentioning "intellectual property" in *The Wall Street Journal* increased 250 percent, to more than one article every business day. (See Exhibit 10-1.) As IP volume, value, and strategic importance increase, intelligent investors are asking questions they did not even consider a few years ago: "What are the firm's intellectual property assets?" "What does the IP mean in terms of performance and competitive advantage?"

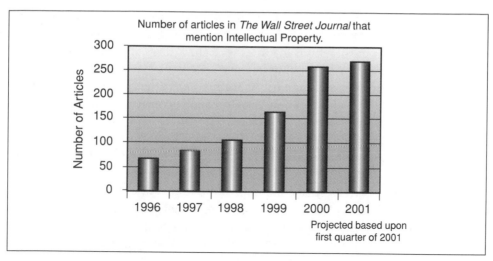

Number of articles in *The Wall Street Journal* that mention Intellectual Property.

Projected based upon first quarter of 2001

Exhibit 10-1   IP is receiving more attention.
Source: Dow Jones News Retrieval.

"How are inventions, processes, content, names, and other innovations being managed?" and "Which IP benchmarks reveal company performance?" In today's knowledge-dominated economy, perception counts. It is not enough for firms to identify and properly nurture their IP. They also must convey IP strengths to key audiences in the hope of establishing a strong IP "brand." While a few firms have worked quietly (or not so quietly) to establish and maintain IP brand-awareness, unfortunately, most still do not believe that it is necessary to do so.

The primary focus for IP has been on IP management, the identification, classification, and exploitation primarily of patent rights. While these functions are important, it is often difficult for market participants such as investors to translate their results into information that they can readily evaluate. Perhaps equally as important as successfully identifying and classifying IP, maybe even more important, is conveying the results of IP management to key audiences in a meaningful way. Firms that underestimate the interest and intelligence of investors regarding IP and fail to educate, quantify, and communicate, are going to be in for a rude awakening. The failure to convey IP strengths—such as number and types of patent assets, strategy, licensing revenue and transactions, competitive IP position, and successful enforcement actions—can be a major impediment for companies that wish to establish or to reinforce how their inventions and other innovations are perceived. These firms run the risk of being misunderstood in the product marketplace and on Wall Street, or, even worse, understood too late.

Especially affected by a lack of communication concerning the value of IP are innovative technology or patent-intensive companies that are overlooked or misunderstood because of their business-to-business focus. These firms include chemical companies like Eastman Chemical, technology hardware suppliers like Halliburton and Texas Instruments, and the extremely powerful Fujitsu, one of the leading IP companies in the world. Valuations for many of these types of companies suffered bitterly at the height of the Internet frenzy, despite proven patent assets and a strong proprietary position in key market areas.

The other group of companies whose market value may be negatively affected by a lack of IP brand awareness is, ironically, consumer brand companies. Their strong focus on inexpensive consumer products tends to lead investors to believe that all of their innovation is in marketing. Organizations like Philip Morris, General Foods, McDonald's (which relies significantly on trade secrets), and Black & Decker are more IP-rich, or at least patent-aware, than their public image conveys. The multiples of these companies suffer too, when these firms appear to be "Old Economy" or without a critical mass of inventions, designs, and business methods, when, in fact, they are in many ways significant innovators. Companies like IBM, Intel, DuPont, and Pfizer benefit uniquely from using their consumer brand-awareness to reinforce their patent brand and, in turn, to strengthen their corporate bond. Realizing the power of their strong brand awareness to imbue their patented innovations with added value, Microsoft, Dell, Compaq, Sun Microsystems, and others have gotten IP "religion" over the past few years and are patenting at an unprecedented rate.

A systematic approach to conveying information about a firm's patent strengths—patent branding, if you will—can itself be a source of value in the same way other firm intangibles create value. Typically, firms communicate information about a wide variety of important developments related to their current and future prospects. For example, they announce new products, new senior manager appointments, management's outlook on economic conditions, and overall firm strategy. They also spend tens of millions of dollars in advertising to position their products and personae, to create awareness, and to reinforce credibility. From these communications, market participants develop opinions about the value of a business. If the firm does not include information about IP in its communications, it is leaving out an important aspect of the investment public's information set. IP-savvy firms convey a coherent IP message to their constituents, either explicitly or implicitly. They realize, for example, that it is dangerous to assume that stakeholders in patent-intensive companies are uninterested or incapable of understanding a relative position of strength.

In a recent news article, "Auto Makers See Future Features as Current Assets,"[1] automobile manufacturers took the opportunity to position innovations yet to be implemented in their vehicles. The article discusses how General Motors Corp., Ford Motor Co., and Daimler Chrysler AG are touting technology-based features today that will be available for sale several years from now. These firms are likely displaying technology that is not yet available for mass production to accomplish several goals, including defusing comments that characterize the industry as a laggard on issues such as safety, fuel economy, and environmental protection. However, a subtler objective is to offer a glimpse of the proprietary technology that each has developed (and presumably protected) to secure its future market position. Disclosing this information early allows investors to assign higher values to technological leaders in the industry.

Firms interested in maximizing value need to communicate selected information about their proprietary innovations and IP strategy. This can be challenging because patents and IP strategy can be abstract and difficult to describe to those without a technical background or to those who are unfamiliar with IP's role in a particular industry. Additionally, published financial statements and other public disclosures do not generally include information about IP assets. Moreover, there is little framework and no common language available to help firms communicate about IP. A possible solution is for a firm to systematically educate and convey information about its IP assets, value, performance, and its role in the firm's overall business strategy.

The remainder of this chapter discusses IP branding as a value-enhancing business strategy, focusing primarily on patents. The first section discusses the increasing pervasiveness of IP in corporate America and how IP communication is important for all firms, but more important for some. The second section show how brand management has moved beyond the consumer products industry to include a wide variety of product and service industries, some with intangible assets. The third and fourth sections show how IP branding activities might work, and the fifth, and final, section discusses obstacles that may have to be overcome in establishing patent branding activities.

FIRM VALUE DEPENDS ON IP VALUE

Firms in traditional technology industries such as computers, semiconductors, and pharmaceuticals spend large sums, often a billion dollars or more, on research and development (R&D). (IBM, for example, spent $4.3 billion in 2000.) However, significant R&D spending is not limited to what are typically thought of as technology-intensive firms. (Exhibit 10-2 illustrates the high level of R&D spending at nontechnology-based firms.) Companies like Unilever, Procter & Gamble, Ford, and Boeing each spend in excess of $1 billion annually on R&D. Significant R&D expenditures often result in the creation of valuable IP. Patent issuance data seem to support this conclusion. Exhibit 10-3 shows that Procter & Gamble, Caterpillar, and L'Oreal SA—which are not normally thought of as technology leaders—spent significant R&D dollars in 2000 and were, in fact, awarded more patents than 3M, Compaq, and Merck.

The traditional role of brand in patent strategy is essentially separate and linear (see Exhibit 10-4). Brand activity occurs near but apart from the deployment of IP rights, resulting in separate revenue-generating civilities. Under a more enlightened or integrated view (see Exhibit 10-5), brand and IP rights are brought together for common activities, potentially yielding greater shareholder value.

Many firms that are not traditionally thought of as technology firms develop significant IP without reporting large R&D expenditures. These firms innovate

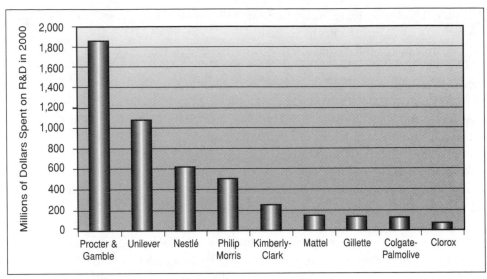

Exhibit 10-2 Spending at top consumer product firms.
Source: SEC Form 10-K

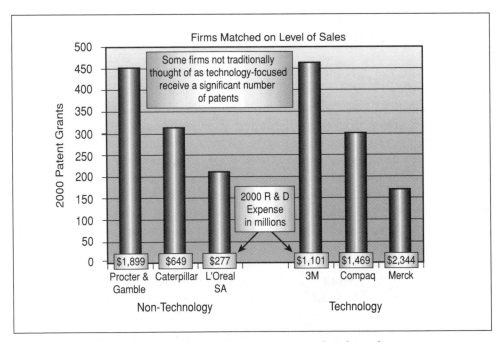

Exhibit 10-3 Patents are important to some nontechnology firms.
Sources: Brody Berman Associates, Deloitte & Touche LLP, SEC Form 10-K, USPTO

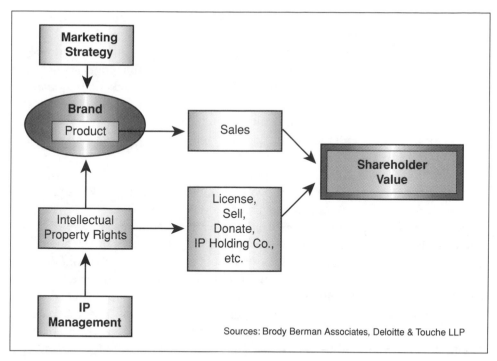

Exhibit 10-4 Traditional IP role.

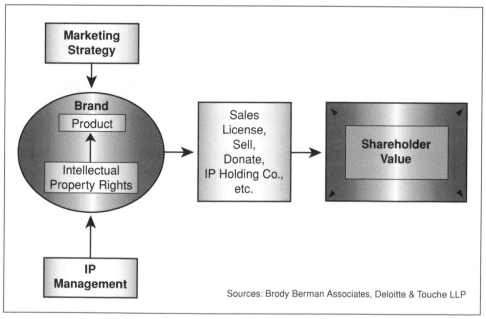

Exhibit 10-5 IP "branding" strategy.

through less formal means than traditional technology firms, but have recognized
the importance of protecting their innovations. The list shown in Exhibit 10-6 contains several large consumer products firms that have a significant number of
design and utility patents. Additionally, there is evidence that suggests firms, including Coca-Cola, McDonald's, and KFC (Kentucky Fried Chicken), frequently do
not seek patent protection for many inventions, choosing to avoid the disclosure
requirements of patent filing, maintaining their key processes as trade secrets,
which are protected under state law. It is very possible that IP is more pervasive
and important in the economy than the evidence indicates.

   Are investors aware of IP's importance? Take, for example, the consumer
products industry. As illustrated above by Unilever and Procter & Gamble, consumer product companies spend heavily on research and development. This R&D
appears to result in patents that are used not in advanced hardware or life science
products, but to protect elements of these firm's valuable and highly branded consumer product lines. An examination of the label on common household products
indicates that significant IP rights underlie these products. Procter & Gamble's
Tide® is protected by 18 patents; the Clorox Company's SoftScrub® label discloses
four patents, and it has been said that diapers are among the most heavily patented
consumer products, with as many as 1,000 patents covering everything from the
amount of elastic around the legs to the Velcro tabs used as fasteners.[2] (Kimberly-
Clark's Huggies® label discloses 25 patents.) Additionally, the business processes
used to manufacture these products effectively and efficiently are also often patented. If firms that market well-known and valuable brand-name products have
significant patent portfolios that are not well understood by investors or, at least,
not associated with the branded product lines, then these firms may be inaccurately

Company	2000 Sales (in millions)	Utility Patents	Design Patents	Total
CitiBank NA	$111,826	29	0	29
Philip Morris	63,276	320	24	344
Nestlé SA	50,254	635	19	654
Walt Disney Co.	25,402	88	22	110
Coca-Cola, Inc.	20,458	250	119	369
PepsiCo, Inc.	20,438	51	12	63
McDonalds, Corp.	14,243	0	1	1
Anheuser-Busch, Inc.	12,262	10	4	14
H. J. Heinz Co.	9,408	4	0	4
Nike, Inc.	8,995	67	970	1,037
Kellogg Co.	6,955	24	7	31

Exhibit 10-6   Patent awards for consumer brand companies.
Sources: SEC Form 10-K, IFI CLAIMS

valued. The misvaluation may occur because investors lack awareness of the importance of patents' roles in establishing and protecting a brand and making it profitable. Successful consumer products are rarely the product of aggressive advertising alone. Investors may be unable to assess the difficulty competitors would have replicating the beneficial attributes of branded products due to the protection afforded by the patents and the firm's demonstrated willingness to enforce its proprietary rights. This protection reduces the risk of competition, and this reduction in risk increases the value of the firm.

Consumer product firms with successful R&D programs may have a unique advantage in profiting from their patents: The value of their patents may be enhanced by their association with a successful branded product. One theory of the value of a brand relies on consumer's ability to distinguish easily the branded product and its beneficial features from competing products. Consumers see the brand and know what to expect from the product they are purchasing. A coherent IP marketing-communications program tied to the brands supported by the patents may increase the value of the IP. Obviously, a potential IP licensor would not want to diminish the value of his brand by introducing competition in his market space. However, if, for example, P&G's Tide contained a patented surfactant that could be used in nonlaundry applications, P&G may increase its licensing revenue by disclosing the importance of the patent in its successful Tide product to potential licensees. This disclosure may help the licensee value the technology covered by the patent and may ultimately lead to a higher royalty rate. A coherent presentation of all of the firm's strengths, in this case patents and brand value, directed to stakeholders—investors, potential licensees, current and potential shareholders, even employees—conveys value-enhancing information.

FIRM VALUE ALSO DEPENDS ON BRAND MANAGEMENT

Just as it is true that patent management is not uniquely important to traditional high-technology firms, it is also true that brand management is not uniquely important to traditional consumer product firms. Virtually all firms are interested in shaping the way outsiders see the firm's activities and perceive its credibility and value. Many firms rely upon a "brand" image to facilitate perception of who they are and what they stand for. While consumer product companies typically develop an entire stable of brands, each aimed to achieve particular goals, as well as an overall corporate brand, nonconsumer product firms generally develop their brand image around a few or, most likely, one concept. This concept is usually then branded with the firm name and a logo.

Several nonconsumer product firms have been extremely successful at creating brands. Corporate Branding LLC compiles an annual Corporate BrandPower™ score, a measure of familiarity and favorableness, for the largest publicly traded companies in the United States. According to the 2001 report,

Microsoft Corporation has the highest score, followed closely by The Coca-Cola Company and The Walt Disney Company.[3] There is also evidence to suggest that these brands are extremely valuable. According to Interbrand, Microsoft, IBM, General Electric, Hewlett-Packard, and Cisco Systems rank in the top 15 of the most valuable brands with an estimated total value of over $200 billion.

Intel provides a convenient case study of how nonconsumer product firms can develop a brand identity that increases patent asset value and shareholder value. In 1991, Intel planned to spend about $125 million over 18 months to launch its brand image to the consumer market.[4] Intel developed a logo and a slogan, "Intel Inside®," and encouraged computer manufacturers to place small decals on their computer cases. The purpose was to let computer users know that the computer had an Intel microprocessor. Later, this campaign was extended to support the introduction of the Pentium product line and was expanded to include a three-tone identifier and men in clean-room suits dancing as they assemble multimedia-capable Pentium chips.

Some industry observers thought Intel's campaign was inappropriate because traditionally consumers were not major purchasers of microprocessors. Additionally, others argued that consumers did not understand the differences between microprocessors from various manufacturers. However, this is precisely the reason the Intel Inside campaign was successful. It reinforced the qualitative difference (or, at very least, the perception of one) between their microprocessor and others for an audience which heretofore did not care. The brand awareness developed by the campaign helped discourage computer manufacturers from adopting competing microprocessors as the market for personal computers matured. This brand awareness also may have created an opportunity to increase the licensing value of the patents supporting Intel's microprocessors through their association with the "microprocessor of choice" in consumers' minds.

Branding has become so important and ubiquitous that even service companies that market their products to other businesses now consider it extremely important. PricewaterhouseCoopers (PwC) and more recently Accenture have both undertaken massive advertising campaigns and developed images of themselves, their goals, and objectives. In 1999, PwC hired 11 well-known photographers to capture images of its partners and staff, and placed advertisements in 150 publications in 30 languages to roll out its new brand image. Similarly, at the beginning of 2001, Accenture spent $175 million to introduce itself after its split from Anderson Worldwide.

WHY ESTABLISH AN IP BRAND?

There is little doubt of the value of branding products. The product behind the world's most valuable brand, Coke, is essentially carbonated sugar water, yet the brand is estimated to be worth $72.5 billion. Similarly, McDonald's, American

Express, Nescafé, and Heinz are all valuable, widely recognized brand names that are associated with products low in (apparent) technical sophistication. Much of the value ascribed to these brands derives from their ability to simplify the purchasing decisions consumers make. The images and attributes created by the brand are linked to the product, thereby building a relationship with consumers that engenders not only their immediate purchase decision, but also their continued loyalty. Reputation and awareness which reinforce consumer loyalty is worth more to a company than anything. In essence, the brands create value by improving the communication between the seller and the buyer of goods.

Examined under a similar light, communication between management and investors, a firm's investor relations, needs to ensure that the value of the firm's costly IP is fully reflected in the firm's valuation. Firms whose patent assets, performance, and strategy are not clearly articulated to investors and other key audiences may be inaccurately valued because investors must wait until the products that result from R&D come to market and prove profitable before including their value into firm value. Similarly, attributes of a firm's product may be effectively protected by a well-staked patent or series of patents. However, if these protections are not understood by market participants, then the observed valuation may never fully reflect the value of the product line because the observed value will include a discount for the possibility of competitors entering the market. In the best case, failure to communicate IP strengths and strategies results in an unnecessary delay between value generation and stock price appreciation. In the worst case, failure results in permanent stock market undervaluation.

Brands create value when they, and a firm's reputation, are properly managed. They also may be helpful in improving communication about intellectual property. Associating a firm's IP with a brand may be an efficient means of establishing a meaningful communication channel with the investing public. A branding program that reveals the strength of a firm's technology in an efficient and consistent manner makes business sense. If this program also ties the brand, whatever it may be, to the appropriate patents and other IP, it makes even more sense. The linkage between the brand and the IP provides a mechanism for the consumers of information to classify and store relatively complex information. This mechanism allows the consumer to better use the information—that is, to make better decisions. This mechanism also allows consumers to recall information faster, and therefore, firms can develop complex messages with repeat exposures over time. This is precisely how firms currently handle brand names.

An IP branding program that conveys the firm's patent prowess, its IP savvy, if you will, could even become an asset in itself much like a brand name can become an asset detached from the product it originally represented. When the brand owner affixes the brand to a particular piece of IP, say a patent, the IP's value would be enhanced by this "stamp of approval." The value would derive from the performance and reputation of the brand, and could include past enforcement or licensing successes, as well as product successes.

WAYS OF BRANDING IP

To operationalize the concept of branding IP, firm managers must answer four deceptively simple questions:

1. Who are the members of the target audience and what do they want to know about the firm's IP?
2. How should audiences quantify measures of the firm's IP?
3. Which methods best communicate the brand message?
4. Which IP information can and cannot be disclosed?

These questions are easily stated but difficult to answer. They put the burden on management to define how IP fits into the firm's overall strategy, as well as to prove its value and performance without disclosing sensitive information. Doing so requires an integration of the goals and energies of several departments, including legal, research and development, marketing, and finance. Only through a high level of integration can management develop and communicate a coherent IP strategy that will be the foundation of much of the value created through patent branding.

As a first step, managers must determine the composition of the audiences the firm wants to reach—and what BTG CEO Ian Harvey calls their "patent literacy." (See Chapter 25, "Creating Tomorrow: IP and the Future of Business.") Establishing the makeup of the audience and its literacy with regard to IP allows managers to determine what the audience needs to know and how best to convey the information. Generally, audiences are made up of the various firm stakeholders, such as investors, customers, suppliers, and employees. Audiences may also include potential infringers of the firm's IP rights and other firm competitors, as well as potential licensees or purchasers of the firm's IP. Audiences will most likely want to know the role IP assets play in a firm's profits and what the company is doing to secure new IP. Much of this information is found through traditional IP management activities such as identification and classification of IP and by analyzing research and development activities.

Second, while identifying the correct audience and explaining the role of IP may be helpful, it is probably insufficient to support an IP branding effort. Participants in today's marketplace desire statistics to quantify the information that is being presented before it is incorporated into their decision-making process. To satisfy this desire, firm managers should provide the audience with measures to quantify aspects of the IP portfolio that managers determine are important. Additionally, to provide a frame of reference for the audience to gauge the various IP statistics, management should provide a set of suggested benchmarks or peer group statistics. These points of comparison should illustrate management's conclusions concerning IP and their IP strategy. The benchmarks also would be helpful in highlighting areas where the firm has been successful and areas that may need more attention.

Selecting the statistics and the benchmarks can be problematic. There is no single metric for measuring the important aspects of all IP portfolios. For example, in the pharmaceutical industry, total R&D spending may be a good predictor of the value of the patent portfolio, while in the semiconductor industry, the total number of patents may be an important measure. Given that there is no one single measure, managers must select the best measures. The key is for managers to select a set of measures and to effectively communicate these measures to the audience.

Recent evidence suggests that technology indicators related to patents can predict stock market performance. It confirms that selecting and communicating the correct measures related to IP strength is important. This evidence implies that measures of IP strength correlate with overall firm value. CHI Research Inc. has developed and is marketing an index, Investor Tech-Line®, that appears to be useful in selecting undervalued equity securities. (See Chapter 14, "Using Patent Indicators to Predict Stock Portfolio Performance.") The index relates three indicators of patent "quality":

1. The number of times the firm's patents are cited by other patents
2. The number of scientific papers cited by the patents
3. A measure of the speed of innovation to market.

(The DataBank at the end of this book includes two sample reports that illustrate CHI's Patent Profiles that are used to in compiling the stock performance index.)

Firms touting their IP may benefit by developing similar criteria to demonstrate the value of their IP or how their IP strategy differs from their competition. A properly constructed index may quantify and support vague and difficult-to-quantify claims such as "leading edge R&D" and "IP leadership." Providing quantitative information to support claims of IP value can substantially increase the perceived value of a firm's IP in general and help to develop an IP brand.

Other statistics may be helpful in quantifying a patent portfolio's performance and reputation over time so that a brand may develop. The academic literature contains articles and recent working papers indicating that patent renewals, the level of foreign patent filings, the addition of new PTO classifications, R&D spending, and various industry characteristics may be helpful in determining the value of a firm's patents. Additionally, Part Three of this book entitled "Measuring Intellectual Property Performance" contains chapters that may help managers select the applicable measures of the strength of their firm's patent portfolio.

Third, managers must determine the most effective communication vehicle for information about IP value and performance. Management must carefully select the medium used to convey the information. Firms that can help investors understand IP in, for example, a section of their annual report will help themselves. Such communication is relatively inexpensive since it would be part of a generally required document that is distributed regardless. Additionally, most large firms have a review procedure established for ensuring that the information contained in the report accurately portrays management's strategy and goals. While the annual report is an excellent communication opportunity, it is not the sole medium available. Press releases, analyst conference calls, websites, advertisements, and product labels all provide opportunities to brand the firm's patents.

It is entirely possible that IP branding is best accomplished implicitly through actions and not by overly detailed explanation. Rather than disclose explicitly the firm's IP strategy, it may be optimal to allow the firm's day-to-day business activities, including acquisitions, transactions, and joint ventures, to communicate its IP message. A steady stream of carefully worded and strategically targeted press releases concerning patent grants, licenses completed, litigation initiated, litigation victories, and the relationship between IP and the firm's products can, over time, help to develop an IP brand. For this technique to be successful, managers must decide beforehand on the strategy and then consistently follow through to the media to ensure the message is consistent.

It is possible to view management's actions at IBM as an example of branding IP through actions. While it does not appear that IBM consciously brands its patent assets by conveying information about its highly profitable patent licensing program, the company does seem to manage carefully how its activities in this area are viewed. (See sidebar "IBM: A Compelling Patent and Royalty 'Story.'") IBM has imbued the IBM brand on its vast patent holdings and ability to innovate in support of its business objectives. IBM uses measured communication to project its image as a technology driver. It tailors its message to the marketplace to ensure that the IBM brand stands for technological leadership by weaving a fabric of Nobel prize-winning discoveries, leading-edge new product announcements, and contests between computers and chess champions. Much of IBM's current success can be traced to the early 1990s when the firm determined that it was not doing enough to protect its IP. The increased patenting efforts that resulted from this decision landed it atop the list of patent recipients for the last eight years. IBM has leveraged the resulting strong patent position through active enforcement and licensing programs that complement one another. While difficult to enumerate, IBM's strategy works to project IBM's IP forcefully in the marketplace. This strategy should allow IBM to secure favorable licensing agreements and ultimately to generate superior returns through IP for its shareholders.

As an alternative to the indirect approach described above, firms may communicate their IP brand directly. This campaign would be similar to the traditional brand campaign discussed above for PricewaterhouseCoopers and Accenture. The managers would explicitly describe how the firm's IP fits into its products and strategy. From this information, stakeholders could evaluate the value of the firm's IP and place an appropriate value on the firm as a whole. Under either strategy, it is critical that the firm managers carefully determine their IP strengths and IP goals. Since the goal of branding is increasing the value of the firm, and the value of branding derives from improved communication, it follows that branding IP only works if the firm has clearly identified its IP strengths and is working to accomplish profitable goals.

IBM: A Compelling Patent and Royalty "Story"

IBM generated approximately $1.6 billion in IP-related royalty payments in 2000. This is believed to be the most income of its kind by any company. While IBM had been generating respectable payments from its intellectual property since early in the 1990s, according to Salomon Smith Barney (SSB) analysts John B. Jones, Jr. and Craig A. Ellis, additional focus and resources were placed on patents when Louis Gerstner became CEO in 1994. Since then, it has been granted the most U.S. patents of any company, a total of more than about 13,000. The company has about 34,000 patents worldwide. Of the U.S. total for 2000, nearly 1,000 were awarded for software, 400 for storage, and 1,000 for microelectronics.

Since 1994, IBM has increased its yearly royalty payments, which include software and trademark licensing, more than threefold. Current projections are based on an estimated 15 to 20 percent growth rate per year and two times corporate revenue growth, or $1.8 billion and $2.1 billion, for 2001 and 2002 respectively. This represents a very lucrative source of payments—with operating margins of 97 percent—since the only real cost is a team of attorneys and licensing managers. See Exhibit 10-7.

According to Jones and Ellis, "Patent and other royalty revenues are passed back to the divisions that generate the IP, with the bulk (Salomon Smith Barney estimates 80 percent-plus) used to offset SG&A expenses and the re-

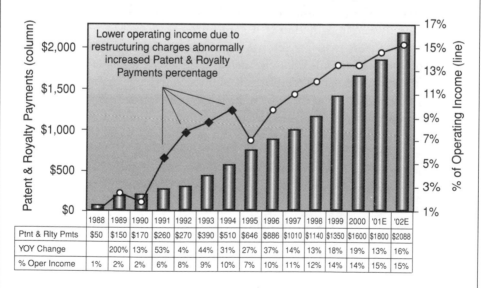

	1988	1989	1990	1991	1992	1993	1994	1995	1996	1997	1998	1999	2000	'01E	'02E
Ptnt & Rlty Pmts	$50	$150	$170	$260	$270	$390	$510	$646	$886	$1010	$1140	$1350	$1600	$1800	$2088
YOY Change		200%	13%	53%	4%	44%	31%	27%	37%	14%	13%	18%	19%	13%	16%
% Oper Income	1%	2%	2%	6%	8%	9%	10%	7%	10%	11%	12%	14%	14%	15%	15%

Exhibit 10-7 Effect of patent royalty payments on operating income at IBM.

Source: Salomon Smith Barney

maining used to offset R&D expense. Each $100 million of incremental patent and royalty revenue decreases operating expense as a percent of revenues by 0.1 percent. These cost offsets are part of each division executive's P&L plans and provide both divisional and personal incentives to increase the amount of patent and royalty payments."

Additional noncash intellectual property benefits include cross-licensing the inventions generated by the company's more than 3,400 researchers worldwide. Often, this is a win-win for IBM and the licensee or licensor, since each gains access to the IP that would otherwise be very costly or impossible to duplicate.

Finally, management must determine what information can be released. Managers must ensure that the costs of information disclosure are offset by the benefits of patent branding. Disclosing complete information about how patented technology provides benefits will help market participants place an accurate value on the patent brand, but doing so may also provide competitors with information about how to reverse engineer or to design around inventions by creating competing products. Managers must avoid the propensity to err on the side of extreme caution and to hide all details about the firm's IP and IP strategy. Successful patent branding requires management to disclose sensitive information. Without such disclosures, managers cannot capture the attention of the audience since modern corporate finance teaches that all public information is already reflected in the firm's valuation. Managers must use their skill and understanding of the marketplace to identify the information that is required to be released to develop the patent brand.

Highly proprietary information, such as the specific terms of licensing transactions and royalty rates, will require that some sensitive information be withheld. However, detailed transaction information abounds in the unregulated private equity and venture capital markets because it is in the best interests of the parties to communicate. Intellectual property disclosure is in almost all cases positive for business. It has been proven time and again that transparency facilitates markets rather than impedes them. Without self-regulation regarding IP assets, management, and performance, agency regulation will not be far behind. After a company starts talking in detail to investors about its IP, or once investors demand it, it will be very hard to go back to the limitations of GAAP "goodwill" disclosures regarding intangible assets, whether the SEC will eventually require that more information be conveyed about IP assets or not. (This issue is discussed in greater detail in Chapter 4, "Clarifying Intellectual Property Rights for the New Economy.")

OBSTACLES TO BRANDING IP

While there is little doubt of the value of IP and the importance of brands and brand management, there appear to be few examples of firms that have attempted to brand IP. The lack of IP branding potentially results from several obstacles. Some of these obstacles involve the nature of IP itself, others are internal to the firms that own IP, and others involve the environment outside these firms. One of the biggest obstacles is that since IP, particularly patents, is abstract and difficult to define, developing a brand image requires the right language and tools. The term *IP* has different meanings depending on the type of proprietary right, the context in which it is used, and especially the industry. This ambiguity makes developing a consistent brand image difficult. However, this difficulty is exactly the reason branding IP could be valuable. It is up to managers to construct how they want their audience to view the firm's IP. The use of the concept of branding can help present this image coherently and to frame its presentation by the goals of the organization.

Another potential obstacle to IP branding is the differing role IP plays in various industries (see Exhibit 10-8). For example, in the pharmaceutical industry, R&D expenditures are high and since pharmaceutical patents cover the manufacture of substances shown to be effective in treating specific diseases, the ratio of patents to products is low. This implies that one would expect to find that pharmaceutical patents are relatively easy to value and that this value can be quite large. This conclusion is supported by the blockbuster status of drugs such as Lipitor and Prozac, which have earned their owners billions of dollars. Contrast the pharmaceutical industry and its expensive (but effective) "home run" patents with the semiconductor and related industries, where a great deal of cross-licensing typically occurs. Exhibit 10-9 shows the total number of patents received by the top

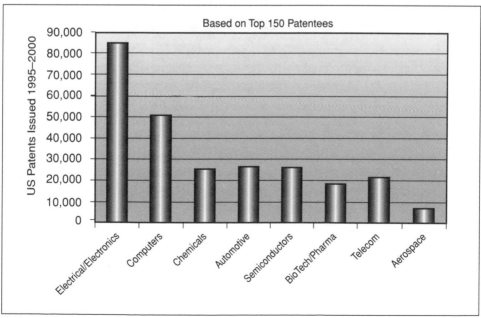

Exhibit 10-8   U.S. patent grants: Key industries, 1995–2000.
Source: MIT Technology Review

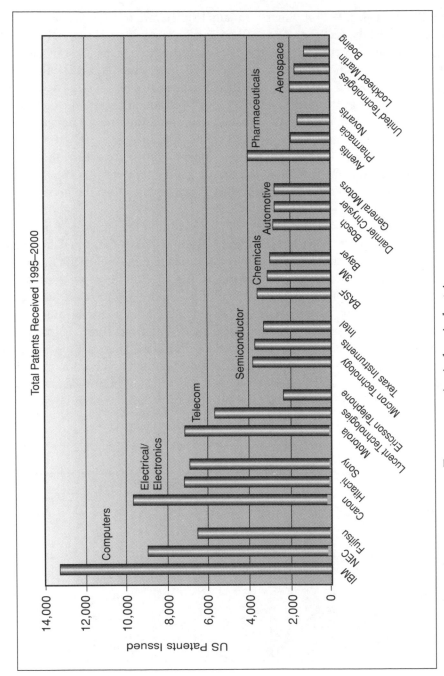

Exhibit 10-9 U.S. patent grants: Top companies in key industries.

Source: MIT Technology Review

patenting firms from 1995 through 2000. There is a wide variance in the number of patents earned by each industry, with the computer-related firms generally earning the largest number of patents. The computer-related firms also have the largest variance in number of patents earned between firms. These differences indicate that the various firms are pursuing different IP strategies. If these strategies are not conveyed in proper context, then it may be difficult to develop a patent brand.

Not only are the number of patents different, but the R&D cost per patent varies as well. Exhibit 10-10 indicates that manufacturing firms' cost per patents varies widely. While pharmaceutical patents may be more expensive than average, the variance between cost per patent at each firm is relatively small. To effectively develop a brand, management must help investors understand why these differences occur. This requires communication about the goals and progress of the R&D department and information about the firm's patent strategy. Since releasing this information may help the firm's competitors determine their best strategy, management may, as a matter of course, resist releasing this information.

Finally, current views and biases held by the public affect firms' ability to communicate the value of their IP. Often, IP only attracts attention when litigation is involved. Patents are only seen as valuable when it is observed that their existence "makes someone pay." On average, investors pay dearly. Indirect costs asso-

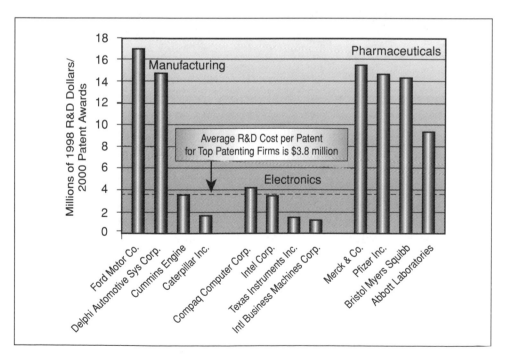

Exhibit 10-10 Average amount of R&D spent per patent awarded.
Sources: Brody Berman Associates, Deloitte & Touche LLP, SEC Form 10-K, USPTO

ciated with litigation include the bad publicity or "pitchfork effect" (as opposed to the halo effect) that follows conflict and strife. For example, one study showed that the combined market-adjusted value of the firms fell by an average of 3.1 percent within two days of their reported involvement in a patent suit. Another study found a 2 percent drop. The latter study, which sampled 530 Massachusetts companies, showed an average loss of shareholder wealth of $67.9 million and median loss of $20 million.[5]

While the enforcement aspect of patents is important, the most valuable result of owning a patent is the clear market space that it may create for the patentee. For every patent supporting a multimillion-dollar patent infringement award, there are several other patents of significant but less obvious value protecting their owner's market from direct competition. This protection provides superior profits and the opportunity to provide technology leadership to an industry segment. If the current emphasis on developing and valuing IP is to continue, the nonlitigated group of patents must be taken as seriously as the litigated group. This narrow focus on the litigated value of IP discourages the sharing of IP through license agreements and stands as an obstacle to branding IP to increase the value of the firm.

Each of these obstacles is actually good a reason to brand patents. The main goal is to communicate clearly the attributes of the firm's IP and IP strategy to ensure that their value is reflected accurately. Investors face many obstacles like valuing patent licenses and discerning IP strategy when they are assigning a value to the firm. If management can help investors overcome these obstacles, then their firm's valuation can be increased and the opportunity to create an IP brand is enhanced.

CONCLUSION

Many of the obstacles to branding IP such as the different meanings of IP and the variances across firms and industries are also reasons why it must occur. Market participants' misconceptions, and opaque corporate decision-making processes, create an environment where well-structured and consistent messages about intangible assets are valuable, if not rare. Yet, many firms do not disclose even the most rudimentary and benign information about their IP or IP strategy. It is naïve to think that by saying as little as possible about a firm's ability to innovate successfully and to articulate its IP position, investors will not form an opinion. Extraordinary sales, earnings, and share price often speak for themselves. However, performance is rarely that black and white. In an increasingly knowledge-dependent economy, investors need help understanding the role intangibles play in company success. Sophisticated stakeholders (investors, both internal and external, executives, competitors, dealmakers, and potential infringers) form opinions about a firm's IP regardless of whether or not management chooses to strategically communicate the value of the firm's intangible assets. In the absence of information, investors will value the firm based upon their vague or misguided opinions of value regardless of whether these impressions are well informed or not.

Given the success of branding consumer and industrial goods, branding key intangibles, such as patents, proprietary lists, content, names, and even trade secrets, is a logical next step. The development of a coherent IP brand image provides a foundation that supports stakeholders' impressions and opinions of the IP strength and value of a firm. The image creates a structure that allows managers to deliver complex messages over time and provides an opportunity to ensure that the firm is correctly valued. Considering the difficulties associated with defining intangible assets in general, IP branding provides an efficient method that helps key audiences process important information that is sure to play a role in their investment decisions. Just as IP can be an asset, so too can IP information. Actively managing information flow fosters a positive IP image and minimizes misconceptions. At the end of the day, firms that fail to identify and manage information associated with innovation and proprietary knowledge can expect to see a material decrease in their valuation and performance—a scenario for which no manager or investor would care to be held responsible.

NOTES

1. Josep B. White, "Auto Makers See Future Features as Current Assets." *The Wall Street Journal*, May 1, 2001.
2. Tara Parker-Pope, "Cleaning Up: Stopping Diaper Leaks Can Be Nasty Business." *The Wall Street Journal*, April 5, 1999.
3. "Top Ten Corporate Brands Announced; Microsoft, Coca-Cola, and Walt Disney Top Annual List; P&G Falls Off." *Business Wire*, March 29, 2001.
4. Jamie Beckett, "Intel Rolls Out $125 Million Advertising Campaign." *The San Francisco Chronicle*, November 2, 1991.
5. Josh Lerner, "Patenting in the Shadow of Competitors," *The Journal of Law & Economics*, Vol. 38, 1995.

ABOUT THE AUTHORS

Bruce Berman is president of Brody/Berman Associates, Inc. in New York, the leading marketing and communications firm for intellectual property owners, advisors, and investors. Brody/Berman's clients include technology and life sciences companies, consulting organizations, law firms, and financial institutions worldwide. Over the past 15 years, Mr. Berman has implemented public relations, investor relations, and marketing programs on behalf of more than 200 businesses and professional organizations, including law firms and financial institutions. He conceived and edited *Hidden Value: Profiting from the Intellectual Property Economy* (Euromoney-Institutional Investor), a critically acclaimed anthology that was published in 1999. (See *www.brodyberman.com*.)

Mr. Berman is on the Editorial Board of *Patent Strategy & Management* and is a member of the Financial Markets Committee of the Licensing Executives Society

(LES). His articles have appeared in many periodicals, including *The National Law Journal, BuySide, Corporate Legal Times, The New York Times,* and *EuroBusiness.* Media that have quoted him on technology and IP-related issues include *Buyouts, Reuters, Asset Sales Report, BondWeek, Crain's New York Business, PR Week,* and *EE Times.* He is a member of the Advisory Board of xpressMD Technologies. His pro bono work includes the Brookings Institution's *Unseen Wealth,* a study on the potential impact of intangible value and the International Intellectual Property Institute.

Mr. Berman received a Masters degree in film scholarship from Columbia University, where he also completed course and comprehensive requirements for his PhD. He received his Bachelor of Arts with honors in literature from The City College of New York.

James D. Woods, PhD, is a Senior Manager in the Financial Advisory Services group of Deloitte & Touche LLP in Houston, Texas. He has helped scores of attorneys and business leaders determine the value of trademarks, copyrights, patents, and trade secrets in a variety of contexts, including joint venture formation and dissolution, licensing negotiations, litigation settlement discussions, and expert testimony. Since earning his PhD in finance, he has valued trademarks in diverse industries such as confectionary, oil field equipment, and supply chain management. Previously, he was with another Big Five consulting organization. Dr. Woods has testified as an expert witness concerning the value of architectural copyrights and patent damages in a wide variety of industries. In addition to his work at Deloitte & Touche, Dr. Woods also serves as an adjunct professor of finance at the University of St. Thomas in Houston, Texas. He is a co-author of "Identify and Convey IP to Reveal True Firm Value," a chapter in *Hidden Value: Profiting from the Intellectual Property Economy* (Euromoney Institutional Investor, 1999).

Deloitte & Touche LLP provides accounting and auditing, tax, and related services through 23,000 professionals in more than 100 U.S. cities. The Financial Advisory Services group works with its clients to solve complex problems ranging from developing reorganization plans to emerge from bankruptcy protection to valuing intangible assets in acquisitions. Expressed opinions in the above chapter are those of the authors and not necessarily of Deloitte & Touche LLP.

CHAPTER ELEVEN

New Economy Innovations from an Old Economy Giant

How Procter & Gamble Is Maximizing the Hidden Value of Its Intellectual Property to Redefine Competitive Advantage

by Jeffrey D. Weedman

PERSPECTIVES

A strong argument for utilizing patents as strategic assets comes from the Procter & Gamble Company (P&G), an organization known for the management of many of the world's most valuable brands. While P&G is not known for its technology, the company, in fact, rivals many leading businesses in patent volume and utilization. With nearly $40 billion in global sales in fiscal year 2001, and more than 250 brands marketed in 130 countries, P&G is considered by many to be the world leader in the packaged goods industry. However, as with many consumer goods companies, the depth and breadth of P&G's technology is almost universally underestimated. Perhaps it would be well served to apply a portion of its advertising dollars to a branding campaign for its patent portfolio?

The company employs more than 8,900 research and development (R&D) professionals, including more than 1,200 MDs and PhDs, at its 18 R&D facilities in eight countries on four continents. Procter & Gamble's R&D investment, nearly $2 billion in FY2001, represented 4.5 percent of its sales, a ratio similar to those of "technology leaders" like General Electric, DuPont, 3M, Dow, and Canon. The company holds more than 27,000 active patents worldwide and is granted more than 3,000 new domestic and international patents per year.

Why should a company that owns a number of the most valuable brand names be regarded as a leading inventor? It takes more than an aggressive advertising campaign to make Tide®, Crest®, Cover Girl®, or Pampers® valuable to an organization. What helps to maintain the quality, consistency, and profitability of these products are dozens, if not hundreds, of unique technologies and manufacturing processes, most of which are protected by patents. Traditionally, companies like P&G and, to a lesser extent, Philip Morris have felt they needed to operate in a stealth mode, maintaining an extremely low profile with regard to their intangible patent assets, despite the fact they were might be worth a lot to the company if licensed. Part of P&G's problem was perception—self-perception, as well as Wall Street's.

"P&G's secretive and protective culture controlled the company's patent policy," writes Jeffrey Weedman in his revealing profile of his company's new thinking about utilizing its technological resources and patent assets. "There was minimal business involvement in upstream research and the company's patent policy focused on internal utilization, rather than maximizing value externally."

Licensing or joint ventures were also of little interest to the company. Licensing was largely a reactive response to cases of patent infringement, focusing on its legal, rather than business, aspects. The company also preferred to maintain arm's length relationships with the majority of its suppliers. "The result of this insular corporate culture," concludes Mr. Weedman, "was a limited value extraction of P&G's intellectual property, a situation that began to catch the eye of corporate managers in 1996 as they looked for new ways to generate value for the company."

Today, P&G has an active patent licensing program, under its External Business Development & Global Licensing organization (EBD&GL). The company has learned that it needs to actively manage its inventions and the patents that give them value, as it does its consumer brands. The goal, says Weedman, is to quantify patent performance in order to position P&G's innovation in the marketplace and investment community.

In 1994 Procter & Gamble engineers Tom Lange and Art Koehler walked into Los Alamos National Laboratories in New Mexico, one of the most rigorously guarded strongholds of U.S. national security and the birthplace of the Atomic Age. Fifty years earlier, under the leadership of Dr. J. Robert Oppenheimer, the scientists of the Manhattan Project were in a race against the clock to develop the technology

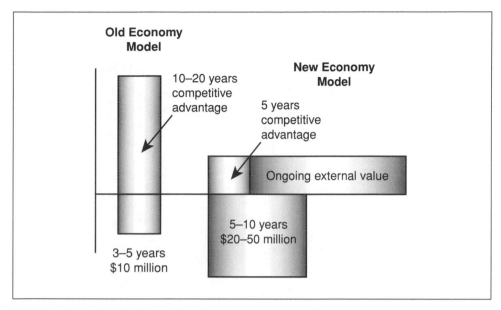

Exhibit 11-1   Technology development cost vs. value.

nor can it support the ever-broadening range of technological resources necessary to keep moving ahead.

4. There's a growing opportunity to reapply P&G technology. Other industries, and indeed even the company's competitors, can benefit from technologies P&G has developed, without threatening its existing competitive advantages.

These factors led to the realization that P&G could increase the return on its investment in intellectual property. However, early experience pointed to a need for genuine cultural and strategic changes in order to achieve that objective.

From 1996 through 1998, what was then known as the company's Global Licensing Unit focused almost exclusively on patent licensing, with little attention to trademarks or know-how. It achieved success with several deals, more than covering its costs, but only scratching the surface of its potential.

"Despite our limitations, we knew from the very beginning that we had to look for opportunities where the licensee, the retail customer, and the consumer could all benefit," remembers Steve Baggott, an EBD&GL director and one of the company's licensing pioneers. "To be able to generate meaningful return for P&G, in most cases, a deal would have to deliver important financial return to the licensee, produce new sales and profits for the retail customer, and deliver a genuine benefit to the consumer. The intersection of those three sets of benefits is the sweet spot (see Exhibit 11-2) where licensing works best. It's where our early successes came from, and it's where we continue to look for opportunities."

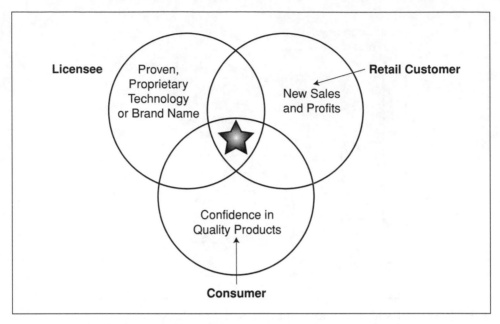

Exhibit 11-2   The licensing sweet spot.

Notable among those early successes was the licensing of P&G's calcium ci-trate malate (CCM) technology, which fortifies drinks and other products with calcium. The technology was successfully licensed to Tropicana for use in its or-ange juices and to General Nutrition Centers for use in nutrition supplements.

CCM was an ideal candidate for licensing because it met several key criteria—criteria that have become benchmarks for subsequent deals. It was a proven tech-nology; CCM had been, and continues to be, successful in P&G's own Sunny De-light drink products. It had an outstanding portfolio of clinical studies in support of its effectiveness. It had a strong proprietary position in terms of the patents protecting it. It had a clear potential in other products; P&G knew, for example, that in orange juice it overcame taste and appearance obstacles that were troubling juice companies. And finally P&G had no intentions of extending its own use of CCM into other fruit juice or nutrition supplement products, so licensing for those uses presented no competitive problems internally.

But successes like CCM were limited until 1999, when P&G applied the les-sons learned in the previous three years to create a new approach to licensing, based on four key principles:

1. P&G redefined its profit policy for external commercialization. Profits from licensing agreements would now flow back to the business unit that had developed the technology. Returning profits to business units pro-vided unit managers with motivation to seek external commercialization opportunities, motivation they hadn't had before.

2. All technologies became candidates for externalization. In a decision that was made at the very highest levels of P&G management, patent licensing became the "default" position on all technologies. Specifically, a technology is available for licensing—even to competitors—within three years after it is introduced to the market or five years after a patent is granted. For packaging technologies, all patents are available immediately. Any exception to this rule must be driven by hard data that demonstrates greater value by keeping the technology exclusive to P&G as opposed to licensing.

   This new patent policy has effectively redefined how P&G views competitive advantage (see siebar on page 240), and it also serves as a strategic rationale for:

   - Increasing the pace of innovation. In effect, P&G is "obsoleting itself," forcing it to innovate faster than ever before.
   - Increasing its speed to market. The company is generating returns not only from latent, back-burner technologies, but also from new, cutting-edge discoveries faster than before.
   - Increasing return on investment. By shifting its focus from "internal only" to external as well, P&G is able to generate additional returns on technology investments over a longer period of time.

3. The company established a new, more broadly based licensing organization. The new profit policy justified expansion of the licensing unit itself, as well as multifunctional organizations within each of P&G's five Global Business Units and key corporate functions.

4. It broadened its scope beyond patent licensing. EBD&GL now includes licensing P&G trademarks and know-how (from engineering to marketing to building customer relationships), plus new commercialization models such as equity investments in existing companies, formation of spin-offs or other new entities, and technology donations to universities and research institutions.

"This represents a genuine shift in the company's culture," says Steven Miller, Vice President and General Counsel, Patents, P&G Worldwide. "It means we're now actively managing our intellectual property—patents, trademarks, copyrights, know-how—much as we do our hard physical assets. We're treating technologies and business methods as key assets. We're addressing—and I believe leading the way in—the New Economy concept that the intellectual assets of a company can be more valuable than the physical assets. It's not just our R&D folks who are inventors now; everyone is a potential inventor. That includes customer business development people, marketing, finance, and IT. We are also developing new licensing relationships with suppliers and even with competitors that we previously viewed as patent infringers."

The results of this new approach to business development have been dramatic. Since implementing the new approach, P&G has increased the number of deals it closes fourfold, it's generating more than a sevenfold increase in annual income, and it believes it's "just scratching the surface" in maximizing the value of P&G's intellectual property.

Redefining Competitive Advantage at Procter & Gamble

Old Economy Definition:

I've got it . . . you don't.

New Economy Definitions:

- I've got it . . . you've got it . . . I've got it cheaper.
- I've got it . . . you've got it . . . I've got it with no (or less) capital.
- I've got it . . . you've got it . . . I've got it with 18 months' lead time.
- I've got it . . . you've got it . . . now you follow my technology.
- I've got it . . . you've got it . . . and I got to market two years faster than I could have alone.
- I've got it . . . you've got it . . . I make money when I sell it, *and* I make money when you sell it.

REAL-WORLD SUCCESSES AND OPPORTUNITIES

Licensing Patents and Technologies

The licensing of P&G's CCM technology, outlined earlier in this chapter, is a classic example of straightforward licensing, where the primary benefit comes from the royalties the license generates. But the company also generates other forms of value from technology licensing.

As an example, EBD&GL Associate Director Norma McDonald cites a pricing problem at a discount merchandiser.

"The customer was selling P&G's Liquid Tide detergent in proprietary, 300-ounce, self-dispensing bottles," Ms. McDonald says, "alongside competing detergents in conventional 200-ounce bottles. The larger bottles exaggerated Tide's per-ounce price premium, despite the added consumer convenience of the self-dispensing feature. Sales were lagging behind projections.

"The solution? We worked with the retailer and its Customer Business Development [P&G sales] team to prepare a licensing proposal for our competitors. We proposed licensing the 300-ounce bottle to them. We outlined the benefits all around: consumers would get the larger, easier-to-use package; the competitor's less expensive product would still enjoy a price advantage over Tide; and the retailer would benefit from increased overall sales.

"With the competitor selling its product in the same size bottle, the playing field was leveled for Tide, which could then compete successfully, based on its superior formula and brand equity, despite the premium price. Our business has grown markedly as a result."

Ms. McDonald is currently working on a speed-to-market licensing proposal to partner with one or more companies in developing what P&G has dubbed "Nodax" biodegradable plastics technology in recognition of Dr. Isao Noda, the P&G researcher who has led the initial development.

"Nodax is the result of our search, beginning in the late 1980s, for a biodegradable disposable diaper," McDonald explains. "Dr. Noda and his colleagues have filed more than 30 patents on the technology, which can produce a biodegradable plastic that can be extruded, blow-molded, injection-molded, produced as a fiber or as a nonwoven for a wide variety of uses.

"Our own potential use of the technology in diapers is extremely limited, compared to the wide range of uses we see in other industries: compostable trash bags; agricultural films; fertilizer; disposable, safely biodegradable biomedical devices; disposable plates, cups, and utensils. The list goes on and on, and it reaches far beyond P&G's core businesses.

"That's why we're seeking development partners, companies who can work with us to accelerate this technology to market, and who will then profit along with us from that acceleration."

Licensing Trademarks

P&G has built some of the strongest brands in the world—Tide®, Crest®, Pampers®, Folgers®, Mr. Clean®, Cover Girl®, and many others—so leveraging the value of those brands through targeted licensing has become a key strategy for EBD&GL.

"As with technology licensing," EBD&GL Director Steve Baggott emphasizes, "we search for that sweet spot where the interests of the consumer, the licensee, and retailer all intersect. In this case, we also need a fit with our brand equity. Our return includes royalties, certainly, but even more important is building the equity of the brands we license. We look at the process as one where the licensee borrows equity from the brand's equity 'bank account,' then pays that equity back with interest."

The Pampers brand provides an excellent example. A new licensing agreement with Dana Undies places the Pampers brand name on a line of high-quality infant and toddler underwear. The synergies of this agreement generate benefits for all the parties, including the retail customers (supermarkets and discounters) that sell the product to consumers. The Pampers brand name assures consumers of the clothing's quality. Dana gets not only the brand, but also access to additional retailers through P&G's sales network. Retailers place the products near the Pampers diapers in the store, where parents can easily make the brand connection and purchase decision. P&G gets the brand-equity interest of meeting consumers' needs one more time with a quality product through a convenient source. And P&G technologists, who have studied infant anatomy for decades, were able to provide Dana with new insights that led to innovative design features, such as a cut-out for the umbilical cord on the newborn size.

In a different type of agreement, a license with Universal Group for use of the Noxzema and Old Spice brands enables P&G to make the most of what might otherwise be underutilized brand equities. P&G's focus on Noxzema cleansing creams and Old Spice deodorant and fragrances had created orphan products in the brand families, notably the brands' shaving creams. Through the license, shave-product specialist Universal Group is able to give these products the development, distribution, and marketing attention they need to succeed—including development of Noxzema and Old Spice gels, a growing market segment, but one outside P&G's focus.

"Again, it's a win-win-win," says Baggott. "Consumers get traditional and new Noxzema and Old Spice products they can depend on; Universal Group gets brands with built-in equity, and P&G gets royalties, plus the equity interest that comes with retaining loyal consumers and reinforcing our brand positionings."

Licensing Know-How

In addition to patents and brands, P&G's worldwide experience in creating, manufacturing, and marketing a broad range of packaged goods has created a vast storehouse of know-how—expertise ranging from manufacturing processes to business management systems to market research and consumer understanding. It's a huge area of untapped intellectual-property potential.

A prime example is Reliability Engineering, P&G's proprietary technology for improving manufacturing efficiency.

Michael Hock, now an associate director of EBD&GL, was a Reliability Engineering pioneer at P&G as early as the 1970s. "At that time," he remembers, "process engineers throughout the company, across our full range of product categories and in facilities around the world, were focusing on process reliability as a means of lowering the cost of production. We accumulated a tremendous amount of knowledge about the ways production efficiencies impact bottom-line results and about how to improve those efficiencies to build the bottom line.

"By the 1980s, we had adopted many efficiency-building procedures throughout our worldwide operations. We were viewing reliability as a science, and in the early 1990s we developed the formal concept of Reliability Engineering, a set of 'tools' that could be applied to systems in any product category anywhere in the world.

"When P&G simulation engineers like Tom Lange and Art Koehler began working with their counterparts at Los Alamos National Laboratories, we were able to add the final piece of the puzzle: computer models that could predict the reliability of specialized manufacturing systems. Reliability Engineering has helped enable P&G to cut our typical start-up time for a new manufacturing system from six months to two months—with 85 percent process reliability. We can show how that efficiency alone saves the company millions of dollars per year. When we add improved process reliability, reduced capital investment, accelerated time to market, and reduced maintenance costs, Reliability Engineering's benefit to the company over the past decade climbs into the billions. If we can do that for P&G, we can achieve similar results for almost anybody. That's what makes the concept of licensing Reliability Engineering so exciting."

P&G's initial targets in this licensing endeavor are its own suppliers and customers, companies whose relationships with P&G will be strengthened by enhancing their own production reliability; but Hock is energized by the confidence that Reliability Engineering can be effective "almost universally." It consists of a toolbox of 23 technologies, such as state-of-the-art simulation, equipment testing, product quality testing, and maintenance optimization, aimed at improving existing systems, reducing project costs, accelerating project start-ups, and predicting system performance. And it is designed to be implemented in discrete phases: "due diligence" (with steps such as opportunity assessment, recommendations, and estimates), "demonstration" (small-scale prototyping and evaluation), and "corporate rollout" (full-scale technology transfer).

The technological expertise behind Reliability Engineering is just one example of the know-how in P&G's intellectual property treasure trove, and Reliability Engineering's licensing model is just one of many external commercialization models the company is exploring.

In the marketing field, P&G has brought its 160 years of global marketing leadership and expertise to a partnership with Worldwide Magnifi in a new company, Emmperative. Emmperative will provide other companies with best-practice marketing know-how (e.g., strategy development and deployment, concept development and testing, pricing strategy, package design, advertising development, media planning, direct marketing, interactive marketing, and sophisticated new tools for Internet-enabled product development and testing), marketing tools (e.g., applications for research, forecasting, testing, media planning and buying, and market simulation techniques that launch from the desktop), and patented software and global infrastructure. Initial Emmperative customers include the Coca-Cola Company, BBBO Worldwide, and Philips Domestic Appliance and Personal Care division.

Technology Donation

Last year, EBD&GL launched an additional innovation, a technology donation program designed to extract value from, and realize the further development of, promising technologies the company has elected not to pursue. The program donates all the patents and know-how related to a given technology to a university or other research institution that specializes in that research field.

Thomas Minnick, P&G's director in charge of the donation program, notes that, in addition to the initial tax benefit that any donation carries with it, the program achieves several other strategic objectives.

"By donating technologies, P&G fosters development work that can deliver whole new revenue streams for universities and research institutions," Minnick says. "And the donations result in further development of important new technologies that otherwise may not have been commercialized.

"Reaching out to institutions with our high-potential technologies gives the next generation of scientists real-world experience, and it connects them to P&G's culture of scientific innovation."

The donation program is founded on four key principles that enhance its value to P&G, to the research institution, and to consumers who stand to benefit from the technology's commercialization:

1. Each technology P&G donates has real, demonstrable potential value.
2. The selection of each recipient institution is made with the consultation of independent experts. This process ensures that the recipient has the best possible capability—including a recognized expert professor who will champion the research—to maximize the technology's value in terms of both development and commercialization.
3. Each donation includes full disclosure to the recipient institution, including ownership of all related patents and documentation, as well as an in-depth scientific information transfer, through which P&G researchers familiar with the technology bring the institution's researchers up to speed on all the work done to date.
4. Follow-up support to help ensure success, including a high-level public event announcing the donation (typically including the university's chancellor or president, plus the state's governor). The event builds awareness for P&G, and for the institution and its research programs, in the academic, scientific, and business communities. P&G also provides restricted cash grants to the research institution to cover initial patent maintenance and/or research and development costs.

In its first year of operation, the program donated 10 promising technologies—prototype tooling, photobleach, anti-inflammatory drug therapy, water-softening technologies, and others—to such research institutions as the University of North Carolina, Vanderbilt University, Case Western Reserve University, and the Milwaukee University School of Engineering.

MARKETING P&G'S INTELLECTUAL PROPERTY

Given P&G's well-earned reputation as "the world's largest advertiser," it may come as a surprise to learn that mass media advertising plays no part in the company's IP marketing plan. Instead, EBD&GL has adopted the philosophy that

IP marketing is best accomplished by making one-to-one connections with potential customers and partners.

As Exhibit 11-3 shows, this process of "connecting" incorporates both proactive and reactive elements. On the proactive side, two key resources are P&G's retailer customers and its suppliers. Customers often manufacture their own products, so they're potential licensees. They're experienced at selling licensed products, so they understand licensing and are excellent sources of business-building ideas and additional contacts. And they're companies that already have top-management relationships with P&G, eliminating layers of corporate bureaucracy.

Suppliers are also excellent sources of diverse application ideas; they're already knowledgeable about P&G technology, and they're often already active in licensing themselves. Cold-calling has been effective, too, but it works best when it is targeted to a prospect with a clearly defined application for a particular technology or trademark.

General awareness of P&G's licensing effort, generated through public relations and corporate communications, is as close to mass media communications as the program comes. The primary public relations tools are public announcements of licenses or donations (always made with the licensee's permission and participation). Most notable have been the public events announcing technology donations, which, although the events are always conducted by the recipient institu-

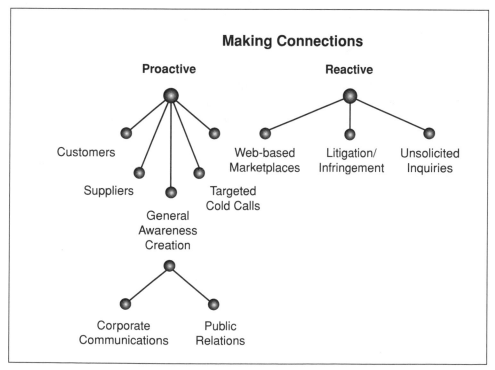

Exhibit 11-3 Marketing P&G's intellectual property.

tions, place substantial emphasis on P&G's worldwide technological leadership. Corporate communications, from the annual report to executive speeches, continue to focus on the company's innovation leadership and "open for business" licensing organization.

Reactive connections also have come, perhaps surprisingly, from such unlikely sources as patent-infringement litigation. The simple fact in these cases is that the other party is clearly interested in a P&G technology or trademark; and opting to license can create a win-win for both parties. Unsolicited inquiries are always welcome, too; but they require a robust process to capture, catalog, and respond to each inquiry appropriately.

Perhaps the most intriguing point on the diagram is the one where proactive and reactive connections intersect: Web-based marketplaces. The Internet represents the very essence of the New Economy, a global community where time, distance, and other traditional barriers to business and communication no longer apply, where both risk and reward can be great.

A key vehicle in which the company has invested in the Web-based marketplace is yet2.com. Established by a worldwide group of founding companies and institutions that include P&G, DuPont, Dow, Honeywell, NTT, TRW, Toyota, the Battelle Memorial Institute, and many others, yet2.com is the first global forum for buying and selling technology on the Internet. Although yet2.com is still young and relies on user pull to generate inquiries, it presents a potentially effective business model, time- and cost-efficient. Licensing and acquiring leading-edge technologies via the Internet is simply the next logical step in the process of knowledge sharing that continues to expand the depth, breadth, and value of P&G's intellectual property—a process that can be traced back at least as far Lange and Koehler's 1994 visit to Los Alamos.

"The Internet is an amazing medium for this phase in our company's growth," says EBD&GL Associate Director Wally Murray, "just as the rise of broadcast television was for our work to create a mass audience for consumer products. The Web has a fantastic ability not only to provide a global audience for our licensing efforts, but also to facilitate technology acquisition. It can be both the medium and the message."

But while P&G views the Web as a powerful tool for creating a more efficient technology-transfer marketplace, it's the approach to sharing intellectual property, not the channels through which it is shared, that the company sees as the real break between Old Economy and New Economy.

"The real breakthrough for us is related to strategic perspective, not simply to the Internet," Mr. Murray says. "The New Economy is a world not only where information is value, but also where information creates new value only when it moves, not when it's static."

At P&G, the New Economy is bringing together technology, consumers, and corporations in an ever-accelerating expansion of business models. The growth of EBD&GL attests to P&G's emergence as a company that is redefining "competitive advantage" and innovating to succeed in the New Economy by maximizing the value of its Old Economy roots.

ABOUT THE AUTHOR

Jeffrey D. Weedman is Vice President-External Business Development & Global Licensing for the Procter & Gamble Company (*www.pgtechnologytransfer.com*). He is responsible for external business development, including licensing and commercialization of Procter & Gamble's 27,000+ patent technology assets, over 300 global trademarks, and extensive processes and know-how. Mr. Weedman was a founder of this entrepreneurial Procter & Gamble start-up in 1996. He had previously served as Vice President/General Manager, Laundry and Cleaning Products-Canada. Mr. Weedman also serves as an observing Board Member of yet2.com, an Internet-based business-to-business company, focused on creating a global intellectual property marketplace. Mr. Weedman's career at P&G is quite diversified, with marketing and general management responsibilities across brands such as Tide, Dawn, Mr. Clean, Downy, Crisco, Folgers, Crush, and others. His assignments have covered retail, institutional, club, and direct store delivery channels. Mr. Weedman has also had experience in marketing, sales, and global strategic planning. A native of Anderson, Indiana, Mr. Weedman joined Procter & Gamble in 1977 in Brand Management after receiving an AB degree from Albion College and an MBA from the University of Michigan.

Part Three

Measuring Intellectual Property Performance

CHAPTER TWELVE

Measuring Intellectual Property Portfolio Performance

by Walter Bratic, Brent Bersin, and Paul Benson

PERSPECTIVES

Prior to the formation of the Court of Appeals for the Federal Circuit (CAFC) in 1982, 75 percent of patent claims were denied. By way of comparison, today approximately 75 percent of patent claims are upheld, with only 25 percent denied. In addition, the number of patent suits filed annually has nearly doubled within the last 10 years.

In the following chapter Walter Bratic, Brent Bersin, and Paul Benson examine the limitations of traditional intellectual property performance metrics and the evolution of emerging approaches that IP stakeholders may wish to consider in order to evaluate the effectiveness of an organization's patent portfolio and patent management.

"IP portfolio management is undergoing constant review and evolution," observe the authors. "No one single indicator or yardstick of performance is sufficient to give a comfort level as to whether the organization is effectively managing its IP portfolio. Qualitative and quantitative factors are and will be coupled together as a matrix of performance review to help management evaluate how effectively it is managing and exploiting its IP portfolio."

This chapter reflects the opinions of the authors and not those of Intecap, Inc. The concepts and theories covered by this chapter are not intended to be all-inclusive on the topic of measuring intellectual property portfolio performance. They are for illustrative purposes and may not necessarily represent approaches the authors or InteCap would recommend in any particular matter. The reader should keep in mind that each situation should be evaluated in light of its own facts and circumstances.

Relying on a single IP metric, such as licensing royalties, to evaluate asset value, strategy, and research and development (R&D) effeiciency is potentially shortsighted. While companies such as Lucent Technologies, Dow, and Qualcomm are generating hundreds of millions of dollars from their patent licensing activities, it does not mean that companies that use patents less proactively, or for defensive reasons, are using them imprudently. The authors' discussion of alternative methods for IP evaluation, includng the use of holding companies, internal benchmarking, and citation analysis, goes a long way to explaining the depth and complexity of IP assets and the potential dangers inherent in analyzing their performance.

INTRODUCTION

Well into the last decade IP management and measurement was a subject matter to which few organizations had allocated significant resources. It had been common practice for many organizations to view their IP portfolios as a defensive asset. Historically, organizations have placed responsibility for IP management with their in-house legal department, and often did not view it as an integrated, multidisciplinary function.

However, we have observed a notable change from this traditional view to one that deals with the strategic issue of IP portfolio management and exploitation from an offensive perspective. Many organizations now aggressively seek to maximize and profit from their IP assets. This has led these businesses to focus on seeking new ways to profit from their existing IP portfolios beyond directing R&D efforts toward the creation of innovative and profitable new technologies.

The increased focus on exploiting IP assets is highlighted, in part, by the significant increase in R&D spending, with the collective expenditures of U.S. companies totaling $550 billion between 1994 and 1998.[1] The observed growth in R&D spending is attributable to increasing international competition, sustainable profitability, and significant new IT capabilities, among other factors.[2]

Organizations have also become increasingly aggressive in protecting and enforcing their IP rights. The establishment of the U.S. Court of Appeals for the Federal Circuit (CAFC) in 1982 has had a significant impact on such enforcement actions. Prior to the formation of CAFC, 75 percent of patent claims were denied. By way of comparison, today approximately 75 percent of patent claims are upheld, with only 25 percent denied.[3] In addition, the number of patent suits filed annually has nearly doubled within the last 10 years.[4]

In this chapter we will discuss how organizations are increasingly capitalizing on their IP portfolios and review the traditional measures of success of IP portfolio management. We will then examine the limitations of traditional IP portfolio management and measurement and the emergence of additional approaches that the reader may wish to consider in order to evaluate the effectiveness of an organization's IP portfolio management.

IMPLEMENTATION OF IP STRATEGY

An effective IP management strategy can provide an organization many benefits. These benefits include increasing competitive advantage through expansion and improvement of products, anticipation of technology and market shifts, incremental revenue from technology transfer, and enhancement of brand equity. A well-placed IP portfolio strategy can also defend against competitive threats and assist in identification of new market opportunities. Such benefits will, in turn, improve financial performance through IP transaction opportunities, increase sales and profits, and enhance shareholder value.

The implementation of an effective system to develop and manage an IP portfolio has become a vital business strategy for many organizations. Organizations that desire to successfully capitalize on the advantages conferred by IP must typically follow several action steps. First, an organization must proactively solicit, review, and implement ideas from all areas of the business. Second, once developed, the IP portfolio must be effectively managed and protected. Further, the organization's IP strategy should be clearly and routinely conveyed to personnel at all levels of the organization. In addition, an organization should consider advising its investors about its IP position.

Although the development of an effective IP strategy can be rewarding, it may not be an easy undertaking and can often be difficult to implement and monitor without an effective plan. However, experience has shown that organizations that develop and maintain successful IP portfolios generally follow similar steps.

The first step in implementing a successful IP portfolio strategy is for an organization to assess its existing IP portfolio. This assessment would include evaluating the nature and breadth of its patents, copyrights, trademarks, and trade secrets. While this step appears somewhat obvious, some organizations have little familiarity with the intricacies of their IP portfolio. A practical approach to this assessment is to conduct an IP audit. In order to conduct an IP audit, organizations should assemble a cross-functional team with legal, accounting/financial, technical, marketing, and consulting expertise to assess and catalog their IP assets.

Once an organization has identified and cataloged its IP portfolio, it should explore avenues to exploit and extract value from this portfolio. A 1998 survey by BTG International revealed that 67 percent of U.S. companies have technology assets that they fail to exploit. The study found that American organizations, on average, squander in excess of 35 percent of their patented technologies because they have no immediate use in their products, with the value of the unused technology assets estimated at approximately $115 billion.[5]

IP VALUE EXTRACTION

There are a number of avenues through which an organization can derive value from its IP portfolio. First and foremost, an obvious way for a firm to extract value is to develop new products and services which incorporate its IP. The organization should also attempt to improve existing products with newly developed technologies leveraging off the IP portfolio. The continuous focus on using the IP portfolio to create new and improved products provides the organization with a competitive edge it might not otherwise possess.

Technology transfer is another opportunity for organizations to take advantage of their IP portfolios. An organization may have some amount of IP that is not essential to its core products or service lines, but potentially have significant value to other companies. In addition, an organization may realize incremental revenue by licensing to third parties that can reach additional markets and customers that are not reachable by the organization or within its core product or service market. Value may also be extracted via cross-license agreements where mutually beneficial technologies are exchanged between two organizations, enhancing the offensive and defensive position of the existing IP portfolio.

Organizations can also use their patent portfolios as leverage to form strategic alliances in order to gain access to additional markets. Organizations can similarly gain tax benefits from the donation of nonstrategic or nonessential IP, an example of which would be the donation of patents to a university.

Securitization of patent portfolios is another avenue for organizations to create an additional source of capital. An article in *Forbes* magazine stated that underutilized IP may offer organizations attractive new opportunities:

> Here is a way for corporations to generate cash, bundle patents and patent portfolios into investment grade instruments [and] identify forgotten or underutilized patents with economic potential. Just as corporate divisions can sell minority stakes to partners, there is no reason patent portfolios could not be treated in exactly the same manner.[6]

These securities are based on the expected future cash flows associated with the commercialized IP portfolio giving the holder of the security an income stream similar to a corporate bond. The securities holder is entitled to share in the cash flow from the commercialization, but is not entitled to ownership or recourse against the patents.

An example of an IP securitization transaction is Prudential Securities' successful issuance of $55 million in bonds backed by the future royalties from rock star David Bowie's records in 1997.[7] While securitization may be available for some companies, it is generally not practical where the revenue derived from the subject IP assets is not relatively consistent and predictable.

Another way to exploit an organization's IP assets is by leveraging the IP portfolio in order to secure debt financing, in part by pledging the borrower's IP as collateral. Lenders traditionally required collateralized assets that have a reasonable and ascertainable value and are readily identifiable, durable, marketable, and reasonably liquid. This form of collateral offers potential for organizations to raise additional capital, since in technology and knowledge-based organizations the IP portfolio often represents the bulk of the entity's value.

CONVENTIONAL IP PERFORMANCE METRICS

Once an organization has implemented an IP management program, various methods may be employed to track and measure the results of its efforts. In our experience, there are several methods by which organizations have historically measured the results of their IP management programs.

The primary measuring stick for the success of an IP management program has been the number of patents issued annually to the organization and the size of its active patent portfolio. Organizations likewise have traditionally compared their R&D expenditures to the patents they have received as a measure of success.

In addition, organizations with active licensing programs often view success based on the corresponding licensing revenue derived from their IP assets, or their ability to facilitate technology-sharing with other organizations via cross-license agreements. We discuss these various metrics in more detail below.

Patent Issuance

Both patent applications and issuances have grown significantly across all sectors of the U.S. economy within the last decade. From 1990 to 1999 there were over 1.2 million patents issued and over 2 million patent applications filed (see Exhibit 12-1).[8]

In fact, in 1999, 169,148 patents were granted—a 70 percent increase over the 99,219 patents issued in 1990.[9] Over the last decade, IBM, Canon, and Toshiba have been the leading organizations to which U.S. patents were issued (see Exhibit 12-2).[10]

A preliminary estimate of the top 10 U.S. patent recipients for 2000 is shown in Exhibit 12-3.[11] IBM, for the eighth year in a row, received more U.S. patents than any other organization.

The ongoing trend of increasing U.S. patent applications and issuances to many businesses reflects the fact that the rate of patent issuance is an important indicator of success. This objective measurement for assessing the results of an organization's R&D efforts facilitates, in part, benchmarking against industry peers and provides some measure of representation to upper management that the organization's R&D efforts are being directed in a presumably profit-enhancing manner.

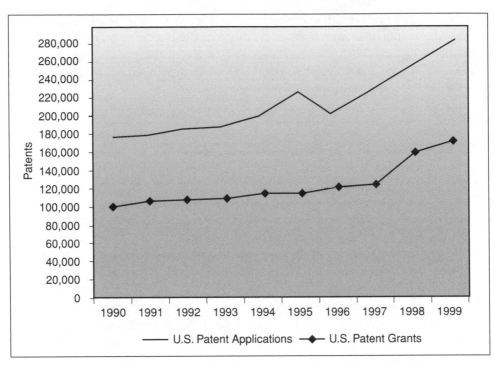

Exhibit 12-1   Annual U.S. patent applications and grants, 1990–1999.

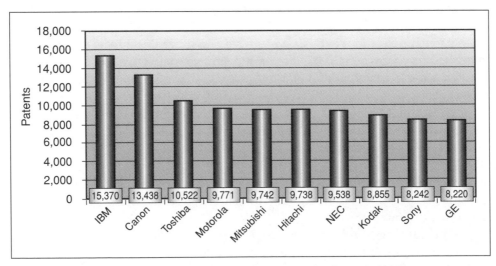

Exhibit 12-2   Top ten recipients of U.S. patents issued, 1990-1999.

Organization	Patents Issued
IBM	2,886
NEC	2,020
Canon	1,890
Samsung	1,441
Lucent	1,411
Sony	1,385
Micron	1,304
Toshiba	1,232
Motorola	1,196
Fujitsu	1,147

Exhibit 12-3 Top U.S. patent recipients in 2000.

R&D Expenditures Compared to Patents Received

Another prevailing measure of IP portfolio performance is the linkage of the patents received by an organization to its corresponding investment in R&D efforts on an annual basis. Similar to tracking patent issuance, such analysis is often benchmarked by organizations against industry peers. Exhibit 12-4 shows four leading recipients of U.S. patents from 1995 to 1999 and the corresponding percentage of revenue reinvested in R&D.[12]

For example, IBM was granted over 13,000 patents from 1993 through 1999,[13] becoming the leading recipient of U.S. patents issued for each of these years, having invested almost $34 billion in R&D expenditures[14] during the same time period (see Exhibit 12-5). Based on this measurement criterion, IBM is an organization that appears to have been quite successful in the management of its IP assets.

Certainly, the successful alignment of R&D efforts with an organization's patent strategy can increase an organization's ability to create innovative products and enhance shareholder value. One study performed in the 1980s suggests that for each dollar a company spends on R&D, its market value is increased by $18.70.[15] Stated another way, one dollar invested in R&D yields, on average, a return to investors of $18.70. The comparison of R&D expenditures to patents issued received continues to be a metric widely used by organizations across a variety of industries in an attempt to evaluate the performance of their IP portfolios.

Company	1995	1996	1997	1998	1999
IBM	5.8%	6.1%	6.2%	6.2%	6.0%
Canon	6.5%	6.5%	6.7%	6.9%	7.6%
Motorola	8.1%	8.6%	9.2%	9.8%	11.1%
Sony	5.9%	5.2%	4.9%	5.9%	6.3%

Exhibit 12-4 R&D expenditures as a percent of revenue.

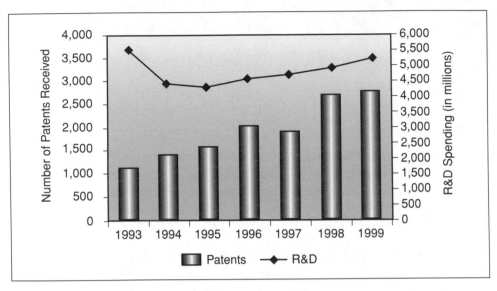

Exhibit 12-5　IBM R&D expenditures compared to patents.

Licensing Revenue

Licensing revenue is another traditional measure of the success derived from managing an IP portfolio. IP licensing revenue provides a palpable measure of the success of an IP portfolio to an organization with respect to patents in particular. This measure can be of particular value to organizations with active licensing programs.

For example, IBM, the leading recipient of U.S. patents during the last decade, has also emerged as the organization with perhaps the most significant licensing revenue stream. IBM's annual patent licensing revenue has soared to excess of $1 billion today.[16]

In addition to IBM, many organizations have implemented successful, revenue-generating licensing strategies. Some examples of successful licensing programs include the following:

- Lucent Technologies launched a licensing program that is already earning several hundred million dollars per year.[17]
- Dow Chemical completed an IP audit in 1994 and has subsequently seen its licensing revenue rise from $25 million to over $125 million today.[18]

In addition, there are examples of organizations that receive, or intend to receive, a significant portion of their overall revenues from licensing activities. In this situation, the company typically maintains a significant portfolio of patents that are not utilized internally in the manufacture and sale of products or services incorporating the patented technology. Rather, the company licenses the use of these patents, generally on a nonexclusive basis, to organizations that desire to utilize the technologies to develop and market licensed products.

An example of such a company is Qualcomm, Inc. Previously, the company manufactured cellular subscriber equipment as well as cellular handsets for consumer use. However, the company sold its subscriber equipment business to Swedish cellular giant, Ericsson, Inc. in May 1999.[19] In February 2000, Qualcomm sold its cellular handset business to Kyocera Corporation.[20]

The sale of these business units has allowed Qualcomm to focus on the strategic licensing of its significant number of cellular patents that embody the code division multiple access (CDMA) digital cellular standard technology, a digital wireless standard that encodes each call uniquely. In fact, Qualcomm's technology licensing business unit recognized total licensing revenue of $705 million in the fiscal year ended September 30, 2000. This represents a 55 percent increase in licensing revenue over the $454 million licensing revenue reported the prior year. Furthermore, Qualcomm's technology licensing unit realized a healthy pretax profit margin of 90 percent in fiscal year 2000, compared to pretax profit margins in the 30 percent range earned by its other business divisions during the same period.[21]

Another example of a company executing an IP strategy similar to Qualcomm is Rambus, Inc. Rambus is an organization that develops, but does not manufacture, semiconductor technologies. The primary way in which a "design house" such as Rambus can create shareholder value and exploit its IP portfolio is to license its technologies to third parties.

Unlike the measures previously discussed, licensing revenue generated by specific IP assets is a more easily quantified measure of success. It also provides a potentially more direct measure of the return on R&D investment to the extent that it can be linked to the development of the licensed asset or assets. Furthermore, licensing revenue is likely the most readily identifiable indicator of a successful active licensing program and provides an indication, to management and shareholders alike, of the dollars flowing to the corporate "bottom line" from the use of the organization's IP portfolio.

Cross-Licensing

Yet another method organizations often utilize to measure the results of IP management is the level of success in cross-licensing their IP assets. Cross-licensing involves the sharing of technologies between two organizations for mutual benefit. Cross-licensing can occur on a royalty-free basis or include a "balancing payment" to either party to the agreement.

Cross-licensing is particularly widespread in the semiconductor, cellular, and other high-tech industries where competitors wish to have the freedom to operate or mutually share necessary technologies to a standard, among other reasons.

Companies such as Intel, IBM, AT&T, and TI are examples of companies that have been particularly active in the area of cross-licensing.

While cross-licensing success is often difficult to quantify in hard statistics or figures, the ability to actively enter into cross-license agreements can indicate that an organization owns important technologies that are both desirable and necessary to third parties. Furthermore, it provides an organization that is IP-rich access to technologies that have not otherwise been developed in-house through a type of high-tech barter transaction. This provides an element of R&D cost savings to the organization by capitalizing on its existing IP portfolio to license complementary technologies with little or no additional monetary investment.

Patent Landscape Analysis

Another approach to determine the efficacy of an organization's IP portfolio management is to perform patent landscape analysis, also known as patent mapping. A patent landscape analysis is analogous to a bibliographic reference that may be performed on academic publications to assess their value or importance (see Exhibit 12-6).

The rationale behind a patent landscape analysis is that, similar to an academic publication, the number of times a patent is cited is indicative of its possible importance. This is known as mapping "forward" citations. These citations can be "mapped" similar to branches on a tree, and the more branches, the more important the invention (or inventions) is perceived to be in the marketplace. Further, if

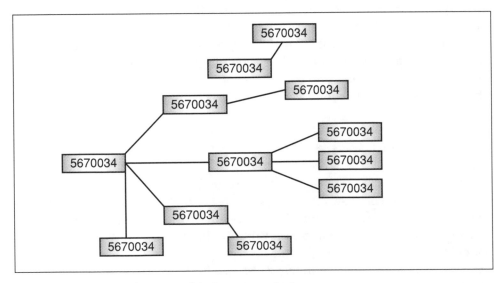

Exhibit 12-6   Sample patent landscape analysis.

an organization owns a number of frequently cited patents, it would indicate that it is creating innovative technologies that are yielding successful products or that it possesses technology that is important to third parties.

Conversely, a landscape analysis can be performed in order to determine the prior art cited by the subject patent (or patents) when it is under development. Such analysis can provide insight as to whether the organization is citing more recent, innovative prior art or is relying more on mature, older technologies. Generally, rapidly innovating organizations will cite more recent, leading-edge technologies.

Limitations of Conventional IP Metrics

Although a number of traditional metrics described above assist in measuring IP portfolio performance, there are limits to their ability to communicate relevant information to an organization. Furthermore, there are risks to viewing these measures in a vacuum, as none of the measures is by itself necessarily indicative of success or failure. In fact, relying solely on such metrics could result in ill-advised decisions that are expensive or which can negatively impact market share, sales, and shareholder value and could result in filing and maintenance of patents with little or no commercial value.

In our opinion, there is no textbook solution to measuring the success of an IP portfolio, because IP contributes to an organization in a number of ways, some of which are not easily quantified. Some of the contributions not easily measured or captured include the legal protections afforded by IP, product differentiation, increased productivity, and ability to be a price setter.

It can be similarly difficult to measure the impact of IP assets other than patents, such as trade secrets and know-how, which can provide significant value, yet whose value often cannot be directly measured. As discussed earlier, organizations have typically attempted to measure success through comparison of patents issued on a stand-alone basis relative to their R&D expenditures. This yardstick measurement device, however, fails to capture the value contributed by an organization's confidential or proprietary information and know-how that are not otherwise disclosed.

Microsoft's situation is representative of the potential pitfalls of the use of such metrics. During the period from 1993 through 1999, Microsoft spent approximately $11 billion on R&D activities[22] and received only 1,106 patents[23] (see Exhibit 12-7), as compared to the 13,000 patents IBM received relative to its corresponding $34 billion in R&D expenditures during the same period.[24]

Based on this stand-alone analysis, an observer could incorrectly conclude that Microsoft has been unsuccessful in managing its IP portfolio. However, during this period Microsoft has experienced phenomenal growth in sales, market share, and market capitalization. This success can be attributed, in large part, to

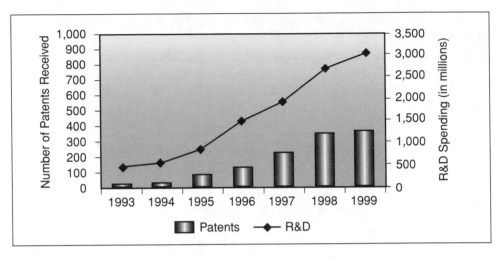

Exhibit 12-7   Microsoft R&D expenditures compared to patents.

Microsoft's incorporation of its leading-edge proprietary technology into numerous software products and operating systems, in particular its Microsoft Office suite and Windows operating system, both of which have become the industry standard for personal computers.

The above example also highlights the ongoing difficulty in attempting to link an organization's IP portfolio to its stock price and performance. Part of the reason such linkage remains elusive is that stock pricing models are generally based on publicly disclosed information regarding a company's R&D activities, which is often coarse and inadequate for the purpose of investment analysis. Similarly, investors can rarely discern the differences in innovations and technical capabilities among various companies based solely on publicly disclosed information.

In addition, a fundamental matching problem exists in attempting to correlate patents received with R&D expenditures in a given time period. There is always a lag between patent application and issuance, with R&D expenditures generally unrelated to patents actually issued during the same time period.

For example, an organization might have invested R&D dollars from 1990 to 1992 in developing a technology for a patent application that is filed in 1992. However, the resulting patent may not issue until 1995—three years later. Therefore, the R&D dollars spent in 1995, or even 1993 and 1994, would not correlate with the patent issued in 1995.

Licensing revenues can also be a less useful measure to an organization that has not implemented an active licensing program or uses a significant number of its patents for defensive purposes. An organization may not wish to license its technologies and know-how to competitors if it believes this course of action will be detrimental to its ability to compete and prosper. Furthermore, organizations that utilize defensive or blocking patents as competitive tools would find this measure of minimal value.

Difficulties in benchmarking an organization's licensing revenues to that of one's competitors arise in discerning the differences in type and amount of intellectual property, the relative importance of the IP assets to third parties, and the royalty payment structures of the license that may include milestone payments or the exchange of IP for equity in the licensee. Cross-license provisions incorporated into a license agreement can often offset some amount of the value of the technology being transferred by the organization to a third party. This increases the difficulty in measuring the value or benefit obtained from the technology transfer exclusive of the two-way transfer of technology. Furthermore, much of this type of competitive information is often restricted and confidential, which can hamstring such benchmarking efforts.

Cross-licensing, as described earlier, is difficult to quantify and not easily compared to the activities of competitors. In addition, unless an organization is able to identify companies it can mutually benefit from in terms of technology sharing, cross-licensing activity may be limited.

A confluence of factors are often involved in consummating a cross-license agreement, which makes it difficult to value the technologies exchanged by the parties, in particular from a benchmarking perspective. Perceived inequities in the technologies exchanged are often reconciled by a negotiated "balancing" payment to the one of the parties to the agreement. However, the technologies exchanged by the parties, and any resulting balancing payment, is often the consequence of negotiations that often involve factors other than simply the technologies at issue, such as cooperative agreements and the relative bargaining positions of the parties to the cross-license.

EMERGING MEASUREMENT APPROACHES

As discussed above, traditional methods of measurement are often limited in their ability to communicate relevant information regarding IP management success. In fact, attempts to directly assess the economic value of the contribution of IP rights to an organization can be quite problematic. Further complicating the matter is that there are no accepted or recognized accounting practices under generally accepted accounting principles (GAAP) to assess the economic value of IP assets.

Consequently, tools and approaches to assessing the effectiveness of IP management continue to evolve. Emerging approaches of IP measurement tend to emphasize the relative effectiveness and importance of the IP assets in the context of an organization, rather than just quantify the value contribution in absolute accounting or economic terms. In addition, organizations are undergoing initiatives to correlate relative corporate value creation with the underlying IP assets.

As tools for measuring IP and evaluating the role of IP in an organization evolve, any measurement approaches used to assess the effectiveness of an organization's IP strategy should be sanctioned by top management. Once approved and adopted, the results of the measurement process using these indices or tools should be reported at regular intervals to all relevant constituencies within the organization on a routine basis.

In this section, we will examine some emerging approaches to managing and evaluating IP portfolio management that the reader may wish to consider.

IP Holding Companies

One of the approaches that has gained renewed popularity in the last few years for the management and evaluation of IP asset performance is through the creation of an IP management holding company (IPHC). Upon the creation of an IPHC, all of an organization's IP assets are transferred into a separate corporate subsidiary, placing all the IP assets under one umbrella. This is a critical step to implementing an effective IP management program. The IPHC is then charged with the categorization and management of the organization's entire IP portfolio and aligning it with overall corporate goals and strategy.

The IPHC often classifies an organization's IP portfolio according to corresponding business units and products or service lines. The IP assets held by the IPHC can be licensed at arm's length to internal business units or to third parties. The IPHC can also be charged with investing and monitoring in R&D activities for the organization's business units and for new product development. The IPHC can also facilitate the sharing of required technologies by entering into joint ventures, strategic alliances, and cross-licenses with third parties.

A number of companies have recently formed such IPHCs:

- Boeing created a separate subsidiary and divided its patent portfolio into 30 different technology categories. Boeing then proceeded to mine its existing portfolio for existing "jewels" and potential licensing opportunities. The company also created licensing groups for each business unit, as well an IP Best Practices Team charged with development of its patent strategies.[25]
- Xerox Corporation formed a separate business unit to manage its IP, Xerox Intellectual Property Operations (XIPO). With the creation of this unit, Xerox intends to grow its licensing revenue from the $10 million it realized in 1999 to $180 million by 2002.[26]
- Ford Motor Company established a separate IP holding company called Ford Global Technologies, Inc. (FGTI). FGTI is charged with making available all of Ford's IP for licensing, with the exception of those technologies critical to the company's competitive position. Along those lines, FGTI actively solicits licensees for IP both inside and outside the automotive industry. The fact that a manufacturing company, such as Ford, has established such a business unit is indicative of the benefits of an IP strategy across any number of industries.[27]

There are a number of benefits resulting from the formation of an IPHC. First, with this approach both the costs and licensing revenues associated with the organization's IP can more readily be identified and measured. Similarly, an IPHC can provide a truer picture of R&D expense within the various business units because R&D costs could be allocated to current products or service lines. In addition, the business units are freed up so they can concentrate on managing and selling products and services, while the IPHC focuses on managing the firm's IP and corresponding return on R&D investment.

Overall, the return on R&D investment and the results of IP management would be more effectively measured within the confines of the IPHC. In summary, the value of the IPHC could approximate the value of the organization's IP, and as a profit and loss center, the success of IP management can more readily be identified, managed, and measured.

Internal Benchmarking

Setting internal benchmarks for an organization's IP program is generally a more practical and meaningful approach to measuring IP performance than attempting to benchmark performance against that of its competitors. The formation of an IPHC discussed above readily facilitates such benchmarking.

An organization's IPHC, for example, would set certain quarterly or annual budgets or goals against which its performance would be measured, similar to a profit and loss center. For example, if an organization has an active licensing program for certain intellectual assets, it can set a budget for corresponding licensing revenue for which its managers would be accountable. An organization might also set a goal related to the number of commercially viable patents that it expects to develop and receive in a given time period.

Further, given that an IPHC can often directly link R&D spending to specific products and related business units, the organization can set internal goals for the number of successful new products or services it creates. This would more readily facilitate the determination of the typically elusive return on R&D investment. It would also provide a mechanism to evaluate how IP managers are contributing to an organization's bottom line and the efficiency of the R&D group.

In a recent paper, Lex Van Wijk, Patent Counsel for Siemens AG, proposed a new model of evaluation indices to measure the effectiveness of an organization's patent assets.[28] Mr. Van Wijk's model focuses on proposed indicators that are categorized into four areas:

1. Employee competence
2. Internal structure
3. External structure
4. Alignment of strategies[29]

An organization could choose among Mr. Van Wijk's proposed indicators and select those most relevant to its internal patent strategy. The value of the proposed indicators is not the ability to assess the contribution of an organization's patent assets in absolute economic terms. Rather, the intent is to identify the effectiveness of an organization's patent strategy and how closely it is aligned with overall business objectives through periodic reports to upper management.

Employee competence indicators are intended to reflect the innovativeness of the organization's R&D staff, dependence on key personnel, and the potential relevance of new inventions. Highlights of proposed indices include the number of reported inventions/R&D employee and the number of inventors/number of reported inventions.

Internal structure indicators purport to represent the size and maturity of an organization's patent portfolio, its growth, and the extent to which legal protections are sought. Such indices include the average age per patent (years) and the total number of patented inventions.

External structure measurements represent the extent to which the patented inventions have been commercialized or utilized in the marketplace. Such indices include the percentage of patented inventions which are commercially used by the company and the percentage of patented inventions licensed to others.

Finally, indicators based on the alignment of strategies provide information regarding the extent to which an organization's patents are used as strategic business tools. The indices are also intended to represent the effectiveness of a company's R&D efforts in the creation of strategic patent assets and the alignment with its business and R&D strategies. Proposed indices include the percentage of total sales protected by patent rights and the sales protected by patent rights/R&D expenditures.

Setting internal benchmarks, such as those described above, provides a basis to measure and communicate relevant and useful information to an organization's executive management. It can also alleviate some of the limitations of typical IP metrics and associated competitor benchmarking. The objective is to create multiple yardsticks of organizational performance related to the management of the IP portfolio across several different disciplines. These yardsticks can be coupled with some or all of the traditional tools of IP measurement (discussed earlier in this chapter) to facilitate an assessment of an organization's management of its IP assets that is as comprehensive as possible.

OTHER NONFINANCIAL METRICS

On January 16, 2001, CHI Research, Inc. (CHI) was issued U.S. patent no. 6,175,824 (the 824 patent). This patent embodies a mathematical algorithm and process for evaluating technology stocks based on various patent indicators. In short, the '824 patent teaches a process for ranking and scoring technology companies according to the growth rate of an organization's patents, citations to company patents from later patents, the references from company patents to earlier patents and research papers, and historical stock appreciation.[30]

The patented technology attempts to address some of the pitfalls of traditional

IP measurement noted in this chapter. The '824 patent looks fundamentally to non-financial information for stock evaluation given the inventor's view of the limitation of publicly disclosed information as to an organization's R&D activities. According to CHI, patent disclosures and patent landscape analysis provide a wealth of information regarding the nature of the impact on shareholder wealth of technologies owned by the patentee.

CHI's patented stock selection process relies on three key indicators for assessing attributes that underlie technology strength[31]:

1. *Citation impact.* The influence of a company's patents is based on how frequently they are cited by other patents.
2. *Science linkage.* The number of scientific papers cited in a company's patent filings. This indicates whether a company's technology is building on cuttig-edge research.
3. *Technology cycle time.* The median age of the patents cited in all of a company's recent patents. This indicates whether a company is innovating rapidly.

As the thinking about IP portfolio measurement has evolved, organizations have started to link financial information with nonfinancial information to create performance metrics in order to assess a stock's performance potential, which in turn reflects on the performance of the IP portfolio itself.

CONCLUSION

It is said that the one constant in business is change. This tenet is remarkably evident in the so-called New Economy, which is dominated by talent, innovation, and knowledge, all of which is reflected in an organization's IP portfolio.

It is, therefore, incumbent upon organizations not only to extract value from their IP assets, but to continually measure IP portfolio performance in a meaningful and relevant manner. The ongoing process of innovation and evaluation can, in turn, enhance an organization's return on its investment in R&D, increase the speed of new product or service development and commercialization, and prolong product life cycles.

The concept of IP portfolio management is undergoing greater awareness as the tools and metrics used to evaluate its efficacy are evolving quickly. No one single indicator or yardstick of performance is sufficient to give management a comfort level as to whether the organization is effectively managing its IP portfolio. Qualitative and quantitative factors are, and will be, coupled together as a matrix of performance review to help management evaluate how effective it is at managing and exploiting its IP portfolio. Expect ongoing innovation and evolution in the critical thinking of how IP can and does contribute to the value of an organization.

More and more organizations are beginning to realize that traditional or "textbook" formulas for the measurement of IP have limitations. Organizations are also realizing that "custom-made" IP portfolio measurement and management programs should be developed that focus on the business objectives and strategies of the organization. This involves bringing together a multidisciplinary team of in-house and outside professionals to design, implement, and monitor the customized IP portfolio management and measurement system, which reflects the unique characteristics of the organization and the industries and markets it competes in.

NOTES

1. *Biotech Patent News*, June 1, 1998.
2. National Science Foundation web site.
3. Kevin G. Rivette, and David Kline. *Rembrandts in the Attic*, (Boston: Harvard Business School Press, 2000), p. 43.
4. Erik Espe, "Friendlier Courts, Higher Stakes Unleash Patent Suits." *The Business Journal of San Jose*, July 5, 1999.
5. IPR Market Benchmark Study, June 1998.
6. Jeffrey Young, "Investing Money." *Forbes Digital Tool*, February 9, 1998.
7. "Bowie Bonds Purchased by Prudential Insurance." *Wall Street Journal*, February 11, 1997.
8. "All Patents, All Types." *TAF Special Report*, January 1977–June 2000, and USPTO, U.S. Patent Statistics, 1963–1990.
9. "All Patents, All Types." *TAF Special Report*.
10. Ibid.
11. "USPTO Releases Annual List of 10 Organizations Receiving Most Patents." *USPTO Website*, January 10, 2001.
12. "All Patents, All Types." *TAF Special Report*; company 10-Ks.
13. "All Patents, All Types." *TAF Special Report*.
14. IBM 10-Ks.
15. Zvi Griliches, Ariel Pakes, and Bronwyn Hall. "The Value of Patents as Indicators of Economic Activity." *Economic Policy and Technological Performance*, Partha Dasgupta and Paul Stoneman, eds. (Cambridge: Cambridge University Press, 1987).
16. IBM 1999 Annual Report. *1999: The Highlights*.
17. David Rubenstein, "Patent Profits: How Lawyers and Engineers Milk the Intellectual Property Cash Cow." *Industry Week*, November 2, 1998.
18. Rivette and Kline. *Rembrandts in the Attic*, p. 67.
19. "Qualcomm and Ericsson Close Agreements." May 24, 1999 Press Release; Qualcomm web site.
20. "Qualcomm and Kyocera Close Agreement for Terrestrial CDMA Phone Business," February 22, 2000 Press Release; Qualcomm web site.
21. Qualcomm 10-K.
22. Microsoft 10-Ks.
23. "All Patents, All Types." *TAF Special Report*.
24. IBM 10Ks.
25. Robert Sprouse, "Case History: Integrated IP Management." *Les Nouvelles*, June 1999.
26. Rivette, and Kline. *Rembrandts in the Attic*, p. 127.
27. Henry Fradkin, "Launching a Licensing Program at Ford Motor Company." *Les Nouvelles*, September 1999.

28. Lex Van Wijk, "Measuring the Effectiveness of a Company's Patent Assets." *Les Nouvelles,* March 2001.
29. Ibid.
30. U.S. Patent No. 6,175,824. "Method and Apparatus for Choosing a Stock Portfolio, Based on Patent Indicators." *USPTO web site.*
31. Brody Berman Associates, "U.S. Patent Awarded to CHI Research for Technology-Driven Stock Selection Method"; "Company Develops Patent-Based Stock-Picking Method." *EETIMES.com*, March 19, 2001.

ABOUT THE AUTHORS

Walter Bratic is the Vice Chairman and Managing Director of InteCap, Inc., where he has directed numerous litigation, valuation, and strategic consulting engagements. His experience includes consulting to small firms and Fortune 500 companies in a variety of high-tech, manufacturing, retail, and service industries. Mr. Bratic was previously a partner with PricewaterhouseCoopers LLP from 1998 to 1999 and a partner with Price Waterhouse LLP from 1989 to 1998. While at PricewaterhouseCoopers, Mr. Bratic was Global Director of Intellectual Property Services for the Financial Advisory Services practice. Mr. Bratic holds a MBA from Wharton Graduate School, University of Pennsylvania, and a BA from the University of Pennsylvania. He writes and speaks both in the United States and abroad about damages, trade secrets, performance, and other IP issues. He is a Certified Public Accountant, licensed in the state of Texas.

Brent Bersin is Director in the Houston office of InteCap, Inc. Mr. Bersin is experienced in providing litigation support services to legal counsel involving a variety of commercial litigation and intellectual property matters. Mr. Bersin has also performed numerous valuations of specific intangible assets such as patents, trademarks, and noncommercialized technology, as well as the valuation of entire businesses. He has also been involved in providing consulting services in a variety of corporate reorganizations and restructurings. Prior to joining InteCap, Mr. Bersin was a consultant with PricewaterhouseCoopers and Arthur Andersen. He holds a BBA in Accounting and is a Certified Public Accountant, licensed in the state of Texas.

Paul Benson is an Associate in the Houston office of InteCap, Inc. Mr. Benson has consulted in a number of intellectual property disputes and has experience with IP assets. He holds a BBA in Finance from Baylor University. Mr. Benson is a level II candidate in the CFA program.

InteCap (*www.intecap.com*) is an international consulting firm dedicated to advising clients and counsel on economic, valuation, licensing, and strategy issues related to intellectual property and complex commercial disputes. The firm's client base is comprised of entrepreneurs, start-up companies, Fortune 500 corporations, and the law firms that represent them.

CHAPTER THIRTEEN

IP Leverage
Facilitating Corporate Value Creation

by Russell L. Parr

PERSPECTIVES

While intellectual property and intangible assets dominate our economy, not all companies know how to exploit them. According to Russell Parr, a well-known IP valuation specialist and author, IP, particularly patents, dominates even more than most people think. Mr. Parr says that IP and intangibles represent almost twice the value of fixed assets (43 percent vs. 24 percent) among the relatively "Old Economy" Dow Jones 30 Industrials. Mr. Parr says that understanding the importance of intellectual property is the key to future stock market rewards. "The New Economy is not all that new," he contends. "Companies still need to develop great ideas into [commercial] products and deliver them with excellent customer service." It is not only the innovation, but how it is managed and exploited that makes a discernible difference in value creation. The management of IP is as much a part of the innovation equation as science and technology.

"Understanding the importance of intellectual property is key to future stock market rewards," says Mr. Parr, who often serves as an expert witness in patent damages trials. "Finding companies that possess, create, and have access to IP is the first step. Then identifying those companies which are nurturing and rigorously managing these assets will lead investors to stocks that are likely to grow and provide attractive investment returns."

Patents, trademarks, and copyrights are now the central resource for creating value in almost all industries. This chapter will discuss the emerging corporate strategy that focuses on intellectual properties and their management.

BETTER THAN GOLD

The foundation of commercial power has shifted from capital resources to intellectual property. Once intellectual property received little if any attention. As an example, patents were obtained only for defensive purposes to be used in patent infringement lawsuits, should the need arise. Currently, intellectual property is at the forefront of corporate strategies. In fact, if you do not have these assets, you are going out of business.

The definition of capital resources is shifting. No longer does the term "capital resources" bring to mind balance sheets of cash or pictures of sprawling manufacturing plants. The definition of capital now revolves around intellectual property such as technological know-how, patents, copyrights, and trade secrets. Corporations once dominated industries by acquiring and managing extensive holdings of natural resources and manufacturing facilities. Barriers to entry were high because enormous amounts of fixed asset investments were required to attempt to displace well-entrenched players. Today, companies that once dominated industries are finding themselves fighting for survival. Companies are creating new products and services based not on extensive resource holdings or cash hordes but on intellectual property resources and innovation. Ownership of intellectual property is the most important asset that any company can possess. It's better than a bank vault of gold, and proper management of these properties will define the winners from the losers in the decades ahead.

In a time period shorter than 10 years, corporations have been faced with technological advances including the continued miniaturization of electronics and widespread communications without wires. Surgical equipment manufacturers are facing increased use of noninvasive surgical techniques. Computer makers have seen their mainframe businesses literally reduced to, and replaced by, a laptop model, which are now facing competition from palm-sized devices and personal digital assistants (PDAs). Also in the past 10 years, companies have been required to incorporate disparate technologies into their products. The equipment used to decode the human genome, such as the automated gene sequencers manufactured by Perkin Elmer, uses a broad variety of technologies from the different sciences including fiber optics, computers, software, chemistry, biotechnology, robotics, and electronics. As a result, all corporations need more innovation technology, and it is often of a kind they do not possess.

Change is coming fast and it keeps coming—all driven by technology. Time to gain expertise in all the different technologies required to compete does not exist. There is no room for the old "not invented here" mind-set. The pace of change does not afford any company the luxury of developing expertise in all the divergent technologies that it needs. It is even doubtful that such a wide-ranging goal could be accomplished.

The Intellectual Property Age is on us and the new paradigm is yet to be fully played out, but clearly the trend is away from independence and toward a vital need for the talents of others. Interdependence is at the root of the paradigm shift that is taking place. Technology management in the future will center on leveraging technology that is owned to gain access to technology that is needed. Sharing technology is a concept many will find difficult to accept but accept it they must. Denis Waitley writes in *Empires of the Mind*, "The leaders of the present and the future will be champions of cooperation more often than of competition. While the power to maintain access to resources will remain important, 'the survival of the fittest' mentality will give away to survival of the wisest, a philosophy of understanding, cooperation, knowledge, and reason."[1]

Access to vital resources has changed because the nature of the most important resources is no longer embodied in fixed material assets. Gaining access to technology and new innovations means cooperating with other companies, even competitors, in order to gain access to their knowledge-based resources. Independence is again being replaced by interdependence. Mr. Waitley succinctly explains, "The future leaders will only get what they want by helping others get what they want."

Along with the demise of self-sufficiency is the death of captive internalization of technology. The past saw technology commercialized solely by its developer. Corporations conducted research and focused efforts on promising discoveries. Additional effort brought about innovative new products, and the new products were brought to market by the originator. This has changed for all industries.

VALUE OF INTELLECTUAL PROPERTY

Intellectual property and intangible assets comprise the lion's share of value for almost all company stocks.

In 1997, Coopers & Lybrand (since merged into PricewaterhouseCoopers) conducted a study of the market capitalization of all publicly traded companies. They found that two thirds of all the then $7 trillion of market value could only be counted as intangible assets and intellectual property.[2] The study looked at the value of companies and then accounted for the value of the assets presented on their balance sheets. After allowing for the value of cash, inventories, accounts receivable, land, buildings, machinery, office furnishings, and all other forms of equipment and fixed assets, Coopers & Lybrand found that over 66 percent of the value of the companies was unallocated. They rightly attributed this value to intangible assets and intellectual property—the soft assets that allow for innovation and the creation of value.

Exhibit 13-1 depicts another analysis that focuses on the 30 companies that comprise the Dow Jones Industrial Average. The overall value of these companies is allocated among the different asset categories of the business enterprise, leaving 43 percent of the value for intangible assets and intellectual property.

The 43 percent figure is depressed by the presence of several companies that are not dominated by technological innovation. Retailers, financial services provid-

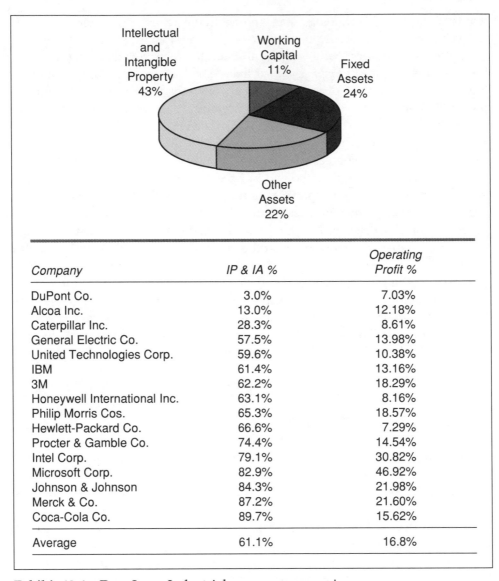

Exhibit 13-1   Dow Jones Industrials average companies.

Company	IP & IA %	Operating Profit %
DuPont Co.	3.0%	7.03%
Alcoa Inc.	13.0%	12.18%
Caterpillar Inc.	28.3%	8.61%
General Electric Co.	57.5%	13.98%
United Technologies Corp.	59.6%	10.38%
IBM	61.4%	13.16%
3M	62.2%	18.29%
Honeywell International Inc.	63.1%	8.16%
Philip Morris Cos.	65.3%	18.57%
Hewlett-Packard Co.	66.6%	7.29%
Procter & Gamble Co.	74.4%	14.54%
Intel Corp.	79.1%	30.82%
Microsoft Corp.	82.9%	46.92%
Johnson & Johnson	84.3%	21.98%
Merck & Co.	87.2%	21.60%
Coca-Cola Co.	89.7%	15.62%
Average	61.1%	16.8%

ers, and long-distance communications companies are part of the Dow Jones Industrial Average (DJIA). While they possess and use technology, they are not high-
growth businesses leading the economy based on the development of technology
and innovation. These companies tend to use innovation, but do not create it. If we
look at innovative companies from the DJIA, we can see that the soft intellectual
property assets dominate these companies to a much greater degree. Also included
in Exhibit 13-1 are companies that are part of the DJIA and for which intangible
assets and intellectual property are critical for their continued prosperity. For these

companies, over 60 percent of their market value is associated with the intangible assets and intellectual property that spur innovation. We can also show that companies dominated by intangible assets and intellectual property (as measured by the percentage of total value that is ascribed to intellectual property and intangible assets) have a corresponding higher level of profits as measured by recent operating profit margins (see Exhibit 13-2).

SOURCE OF IP VALUE

An example of the power of intellectual property can be found in the drug industry. Just compare the prices for proprietary (patented) and generic drugs.

  Business Week reported that the patent protection for the ulcer drug Tagamet was about to expire and "Mylan Laboratories is planning a clone of Tagamet for half the price."[3] This represents a 50 percent discount off the price of the product while under patent protection. In the same story, *Business Week* said, "Gross margins for generics are 50 percent to 60 percent versus 90 percent to 95 percent for branded products . . ."[4]

  Forbes reported that patent protection for Naprosyn, a $500 million (1992 annual sales) arthritis drug made by Syntex, expired in December 1993.[5] Prior to the loss of patent protection the company introduced a generic version of the drug in October 1993 to try to ease the loss of its market share. A few months after the launch of Syntex's generic version, five other generic drug companies entered the market. Forbes said, "Soon the generics were selling at one tenth [10 percent] of Naprosyn and had over 80 percent of the market."

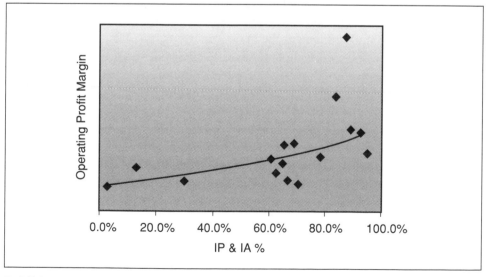

Exhibit 13-2   IP & IA and profits.

Pharmaceutical Business News, a medical and health industry publication, reported, "Generic drugs typically cost 30 percent to 50 percent less than their brandname counter parts."[6]

The price advantages associated with patented drugs is enormous, and most, if not all, of the price advantage goes directly to bottom-line profits.

Trademarks can have a similar value. Manufacturers often can set higher prices for products that are emblazoned with well-known trademarks. Consider the lowly T-shirt. An all-cotton, plain white T-shirt can be purchased for $10. When the same shirt is decorated with a popular trademark, it can easily to be sold for $25, a 150 percent increase. More subtle but equally important is the competitive use of a trademark. Two products of equal utility are being compared for purchase. Prices for the two items are close. Which one do you want, the product carrying the well-known brand or a brand that you never heard before? Most people pick the product with the brand like Sony, Procter & Gamble, Hickey Freeman, Nike, Thomasville, Toro, Kitchen-Aide, and Rolex. Are the comparative products inferior? Probably not, but the presence of the brand makes the sale. Generally consumers are not alone is this regard. Corporate buyers have a saying when it comes to spending millions of dollars on large computer system: "No one ever got fired for buying IBM."

A BUSINESS ENTERPRISE FRAMEWORK

While there is a great deal of talk about the existence of a New Economy, not so much has really changed. Converting ideas into revenues, profits, and value requires a framework of integrated complementary business assets. Complementary assets are required to convert intellectual property into a product. These assets are also needed to produce the product, package it, sell the product, distribute it, collect payments, and implement the many other business functions that are required for running a business. Companies must still possess the traditional business enterprise framework regardless of wanting to call the present economy new or old. In a year-end review, *The New York Times* said, "Perhaps the biggest lesson for alert investors in 2000 was that the new economy looks a lot like the old economy . . . "[7]

Exhibit 13-3 shows the composition of a typical business enterprise as comprised of working capital, fixed assets, intangible assets, and intellectual property. It represents the collection of asset categories that all companies use to participate in an industry and generate profits. Regardless of the contribution of e-commerce, companies still operate as they always have operated. They create innovative products, produce them, and deliver them to customers along with great customer service.

Working capital is the net difference between the current assets and current liabilities of a company.[8] Current assets are primarily composed of cash, accounts receivable, and inventory. Current liabilities include accounts payable, accrued salary, and other obligations due for payment within 12 months. The net difference

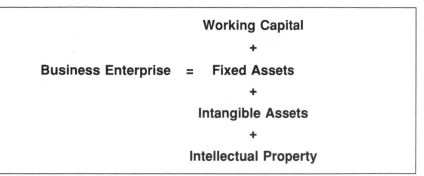

Exhibit 13-3 Composition of a business enterprise.

between current assets and current liabilities is the amount of working capital used in the business.

Fixed assets include manufacturing facilities, warehouses, office equipment, office furnishings, delivery vehicles, research equipment, and other tangible equipment. This asset category is sometimes referred to as hard assets.

Intangible assets and intellectual property are the soft assets of a company. Generally, intellectual properties are those the law creates; trademarks, patents, copyrights, and trade secrets are some of the examples. Intangible assets are of a similar nature. Often, they do not possess a physical embodiment but are nonetheless still very valuable to the success of a business. Customer lists, distribution networks, research and development capabilities, regulatory compliance know-how, clinical trial know-how, and manufacturing practices are examples. A more detailed summary of these soft assets can be found in the notes to this chapter.

So if the framework for conducting business has not changed, what has changed? The answer to this question is the central focus that is placed on the soft assets of the company. These are the assets that are used to continue the process of innovation. In turn, this leads to new products, which capture market share. Profits come from the growing revenues and value created. Let's look at the value that is placed on these soft assets.

Detailed Business Enterprise Framework

Exhibit 13-4 presents a more detailed illustration of the business enterprise framework. The intangible assets and intellectual property of a business are the assets that allow for the creation and exploitation of innovative products and services.

LICENSING ROYALTY RATES

Large multinational corporations are looking at their intellectual property portfolios as key assets that deserve specialized management. They are establishing sub-

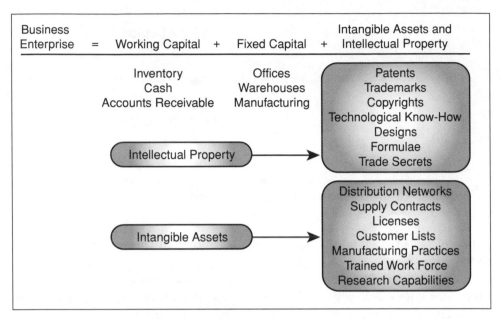

Exhibit 13-4   Business enterprise framework.

sidiaries with the sole purpose of managing and licensing their technology. Others are using their technology as the basis for new businesses and strategic alliances. Many other companies are using their new technologies to establish industry standards. All of these forces are driving the royalty rates to new levels.

Exhibit 13-5 summarizes royalty rates across all the industries covered in *Royalty Rates for Technology*, 2nd edition, published by Intellectual Property Research Associates (*www.ipresearch.com*). The royalty rates reported are grouped by rate as a percent of sales and graphed by the frequency of their appearance, providing the distribution shown in the exhibit. Excluded from the graph are two instances where royalty rates were 30 percent of sales; two instances with royalty rates of 35 percent; and one instance where a royalty rate was 40 percent. Also excluded from this graph are instances where royalty rates were specified on a per unit basis.

INNOVATE, PROTECT, AND LEVERAGE

Innovate, protect, and leverage is the mantra all companies follow that wish to create value in the future. These are the companies whose stock you want to own.

Innovation involves the continued creation of new products and services that are smaller, faster, more efficient, and work better. Protection involves guaranteeing exclusive rights to exploit the innovations. Leverage is the proactive management of the protected innovations. This is the new formula for corporate success. The remainder of this chapter will discuss the three components of this strategy and emphasize the importance of leverage.

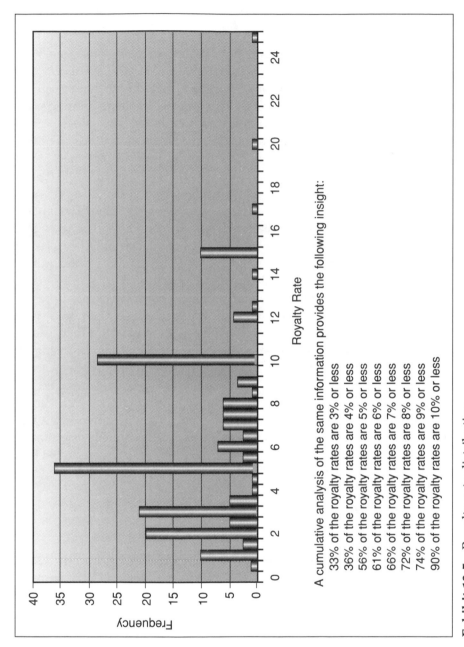

A cumulative analysis of the same information provides the following insight:

33% of the royalty rates are 3% or less
36% of the royalty rates are 4% or less
56% of the royalty rates are 5% or less
61% of the royalty rates are 6% or less
66% of the royalty rates are 7% or less
72% of the royalty rates are 8% or less
74% of the royalty rates are 9% or less
90% of the royalty rates are 10% or less

Exhibit 13-5 Royalty rate distribution.

279

Innovate

Continued innovation has long emblazoned the path to success. Stone tools were replaced by metal. Muscle power yielded to steam power. Travel evolved from foot power to horsepower to jet power. Communications started with smoke signals, became cans united by string, and currently is accomplished using orbiting satellites. Nearly disposable calculators have replaced the abacus. Saw blades are losing out to laser beams. Robots perform repetitive tasks and hundreds of photographs can be carried around on several plastic disks, three and one-half inches square.

Part of the human condition apparently is driven by a desire for innovation. One side of the innovation equation is the need to create innovation. The other is a desire to utilize innovation. This equation yields an economy where those that continually create advanced products and services enjoy continued success. A downside for some is that the absence of continued innovation stalls the growth of an innovative company and leads ultimately to its demise.

As previously discussed, innovation has become more complex, requiring the combination of a broad variety of scientific knowledge derived from innovation that has gone before us. Gone are the days when exciting new products can be developed inside a garage. Innovation requires the integrated use of the intangible assets and intellectual property that companies have collected over the past 100 years. For these fortunate companies, continued innovation is quite possible, but the cost of maintaining and using these innovation assets is high. This leads to reinforcement of the patent protection system and yields a new requirement. As innovation becomes more complex and more expensive, full economic exploitation of newly created innovations is absolutely necessary, and this has led to the new corporate strategy of innovate, protect, and leverage.

Protect

Protecting the fruits of labors is also not new and has long been practiced by companies and individuals. On September 5, 1787, the Committee on Detail reported to the Constitutional Convention that Congress should have the power "To promote the progress of science and useful arts, by securing for limited times to authors and inventors the exclusive right to their respective writings and discoveries." That recommendation was unanimously adopted without recorded debate, and the provision was incorporated into the final draft of the Constitution. Such a constitutional clause is highly unusual in that it instructs Congress how to promote the progress of the useful arts; namely, by securing to inventors the exclusive rights to their discoveries. But America was not the first to recognize special rights for inventors. "The patent institution was established by the medieval Venetian state, which articulated the basic feature of the law today: spur innovation through the incentive of limited-time exclusivity by demanding the demonstration to the public of a working model and promising to seize and destroy counterfeit product."

Patent rights arise because inventing is an expensive process and costs must be recouped to provide incentives to invest. If others can cheaply appropriate an inventor's innovation, calling it their own without having invested time and energy in it, investments in innovation will not be made.[9] ". . . Venice institutionalized the right of patent in 1474 in a statute that contained all the main features of contemporary patent law, including requirements that the device be novel, be actually constructed (reduced to practice in modern jargon), and be made public. It also required that it be examined (although the examination was rather informal), that there be term limits to exclusive rights, and that there be remedies for infringement. Finally, the Venetian statute declared that the inventor must teach others how the invention worked and be granted exclusivity in return."[10]

Society has long regarded innovation as being so important that it has willingly provided innovators with limited-time monopolies as a reward for the time, effort, and expense associated with inventing. Companies have routinely applied for patent protection, but as discussed next, they have not until recently proactively used the protection of their innovations as a primary strategic business tool.

Leverage

This is where the money is made. Assertive use of well-protected innovation rights is the source of value creation. Over time, we have seen implementation of this strategy evolve from something that was simple and straightforward into elegantly complex efforts. This final section will illustrate the different levels of leverage that companies are using to create value. They are often referred to as "carrot and stick" licensing strategies. Sometimes the incentives for taking a license are sold with a positive spin. Other times, the avoidance of harm is the main selling point. Each of the strategies discussed below shows elements of the carrot-and-stick incentives that are used to create value.

Leverage—Simply Defensive

Protection of profits and markets is the first and most common objective of this strategy. A portfolio of intellectual property is maintained to hold competitors at bay. The legal department is often the central force of this strategy. They prosecute patents and maintain them to use against competitors who are making inroads into business markets of the company. This strategy has evolved from the crumbling of traditional barriers to entry. In the past, distribution networks, manufacturing capacity, and large bank accounts of cash have made it difficult for competitors to steal market share. Today, these barriers are easily eroded, leaving the legal rights associated with intellectual property as the most powerful wall remaining between a strong market position and crumbling market share.

A defensive strategy is simple. Patent everything in sight and threaten competitors with infringement litigation when they come too close to making products or doing business in a similar fashion. Licensing income is not a goal that is part of this strategy. In some cases, licensing occurs but usually as part of settlement of infringement litigation.

This same IP management model can also serve to protect companies from infringement litigation. In the event that a competitor comes after a company for infringing one of their inventions, a portfolio of patents may contain one or more patents that can neutralize the threat. A countersuit may be appropriate, or a cross-licensing of the respective patents may make the entire problem disappear.

This defensive IP management strategy is a passive strategy of maintenance and monitoring. Maintenance of the portfolio is the primary activity coupled with monitoring the activities of competitors for encroachment on your market share. This aspect of the strategy is not really a leveraging action, but it is the first step in intellectual property management.

Leverage—Defensive with Cost Control

One step up from the defensive strategy just described is the allocation of the costs of maintaining the intellectual property portfolio among the different business units that benefit from the portfolio. Maintaining a large portfolio of patents and trademarks requires that the owner pay annual fees for each patent. The fees are not limited to the United States so protecting an invention around the world can become expensive. Multiply the fees by the thousands of patents that many companies maintain and the annual expense gets real big, real fast. At this level of effort, companies start to focus on the usefulness of some components of the portfolio. Usually a study is conducted to identify patents and trademarks that are not economically beneficial. Once assets of questionable economic value are discovered, they can be abandoned with the result being a significant savings of maintenance fees. Think in terms of real estate. Companies are not likely to maintain a shuttered manufacturing facility that will never be used again. They sell it or give it away if necessary and save maintenance costs, insurance costs, and property taxes.

Market positions around the world need to be analyzed to implement this strategy, but savings can be achieved quickly. Often, companies will find that they are paying to maintain patent protection for countries in which they no longer operate. There may be a conflict between prosecuting patents and global operations. The patent department might be seeking global domination with a patent portfolio, while business units may be exploiting markets more prudently. As a result, the company is protecting innovations in countries where it does not currently, and may never, operate. This is the reason that costs are allocated to the various business units. Profit and loss statements have a way of getting the attention of business unit managers. When they start paying for something, they will start asking questions. The answers may lead to the discovery of cost savings.

Leverage—Income Generation from Licensing

Producing income directly from an intellectual property portfolio is an added goal at this level of leverage management. Generally, the defensive goals are still part of the overall strategy but here is where additional income-producing goals come into play. The new objective here involves the generation of income directly from intellectual property. This can be accomplished by licensing patents, inside and outside of the industry in which the assets are used. Outright sale of these assets is also a means by which to generate profits.

Licensing technology to competitors is probably the easiest first step. This may sound like advocating the diminution of a company's last remaining competitive barrier, but this is not always the case. Entering into the income generation management strategy requires a shift in corporate philosophy. The previous two philosophies focused on keeping technological advantages for exclusive internalization. The profit center model requires you to consider whether you wish to allow competitors to use the company's inventions against you. In a small two-player market, where salespeople go head-to-head on a regular basis, this might not want be a prudent option. In large markets with several players, a different viewpoint can allow a company with intellectual property to generate new sources of income. This philosophical shift requires admitting your company will never dominate 100 percent of the market. You must admit that you are always going to lose a certain portion of the market to your competitors. However, why not get a piece of their sales each time they beat you out for a new customer?

IBM does not hesitate to license its industry technology, and as a result the company earns $1 billion per year in patent royalties. Texas Instruments (TI) also broadly licenses its patents and currently earns around $800 million from this activity. Since beginning its licensing effort, TI has earned more than $4 billion from licensing.[11] Other companies that are now outlicensing their patents include General Electric, Honeywell International, DuPont, Lucent Technologies, Xerox Corporation, Nissan, Qualcomm, and AT&T Wireless. These efforts are not sideline businesses. They are conducted by a full-time staff of highly experienced professionals with support from all other business departments of a company including research, marketing, legal, and finance. Michael Greene, Vice President of Intellectual Property for Lucent Technologies, has a full-time staff of 266 professionals and support personnel. Of his task he says ". . . with 12 percent of [Lucent's] $30 billion in annual revenues devoted to R&D, it's important we get a good return on that investment."[12]

This level of a leverage strategy allows a company to earn income from internalization of its innovation properties and also earn income from its use by others.

Leverage—Pure-Play Licensing

Instead of participating in an industry and licensing to other participants, some companies are now focusing their activities solely on the development of innovative technology and then licensing it to others. Direct participation through manufacturing and distribution of products is not part of their strategy. For these companies, licensing has become the sole activity and backbone of their businesses.

Rambus Inc. develops and licenses scalable bandwidth, chip-connections technologies that enable semiconductor memory devices and ASICs to keep pace with faster generations of processors and controllers. Rambus technology is incorporated onto dynamic-random-access-memory (DRAM) chips and the logic devices that control them to deliver more than 10 times the performance of conventional DRAMs. A single Rambus® DRAM device, referred to as an RDRAM® device, transfers data at speeds up to 800MHz and beyond over the Rambus Channel to Rambus-compatible ICs.

Rambus chip-connection technology is an open standard, accessible to all semiconductor companies. Rambus provides licensees with a full range of design, documentation, and system-engineering services. In exchange, IC companies pay an up-front license fee and royalties. System companies buy Rambus-compatible ICs from licensed semiconductor companies; they do not pay separate royalties or license fees for using Rambus technology. Rambus technology addresses a wide range of computer, consumer, and communications systems, including system memory, PC graphics, multimedia, workstations, video game consoles, and network switches.

Rambus interface technology is broadly licensed to over 30 semiconductor companies, which include the leading DRAM, ASIC, and PC controller and chip set manufacturers. Eight of the world's top 10 semiconductor companies license Rambus technology. Recently Rambus struck a deal with Samsung, the largest memory manufacturer in the world with nearly 21 percent of the market. Overall, the license agreements possessed by Rambus provide the company with the possibility of making one dollar for every desktop, laptop, or server sold.

MIPS Technologies, Inc. designs and licenses high-performance, high-value, embedded 32- and 64-bit intellectual property and core technology for digital consumer and embedded systems market. MIPS Technologies' reduced instruction set computing (RISC) designs are licensed to leading semiconductor suppliers, foundries, ASIC developers, and system original equipment manufacturers (OEMs) for use in products such as set-top boxes, digital cameras, video game systems, routers, and handheld computing devices.

MIPS Technologies' intellectual property can be found in a wide range of digital consumer applications ranging from video games including PlayStation and the Nintendo 64 game consoles; handheld personal devices running Microsoft Windows CE including IBM WorkPad, Samsung PalmPC, and NEC MobilePro™ 750c, and digital set-top boxes from General Instruments, EchoStar Communications, and WebTV. Additional applications include arcade games and communication devices. MIPS Technologies' architecture is also used extensively in traditional embedded applications. The MIPS architecture powers applications such as laser printers from Hewlett-Packard, Okidata, and Lexmark; numerous copiers; as well as routers from Cisco, Bay Networks; and network computers from Tektronix and Network Computing Devices, Inc.

MIPS has license agreements with:

- Alchemy Semiconductor
- Altera Corporation
- ATI Technologies, Inc.
- Broadcom Corporation
- Centillium Communications, Inc.
- Chartered Semiconductor Manufacturing
- Conexant Systems Inc.
- EmpowerTel Networks, Inc.
- ESS Technology, Inc.
- General Instrument
- IDT
- inSilicon Corporation
- LSI Logic Corporation
- Metalink Inc.
- NEC Corporation
- NeoMagic Corporation
- NKK Corporation
- Philips Semiconductors
- QED, Inc.
- QuickLogic
- SandCraft
- SiByte
- Synova
- Texas Instruments
- Toshiba Corporation
- TSMC
- Virata

Both Rambus and MIPS have a pure-play intellectual property business where the focus is on creation of new inventions and then licensing the new properties to others to manufacture and distribute.

Leverage—Charitable Donation Strategies

Tax savings are another and indirect source of income. A penny saved is a penny earned, and if paying less income tax saves it, the income is even more gratifying. Implementation of the cost savings strategy probably identified patents that are not providing an economic benefit to the company. This does not mean that the underlying invention is valueless. In such cases, an asset has been identified for sale outside your company. In other cases, a patented technology may not yet be commercially viable without further development. An embryonic technology still has value even if other corporations are not currently willing to pay for needed developmental costs. In such instances, companies are donating their unused technology to nonprofit institutions and taking a charitable deduction on the value of the technology. Procter & Gamble provides an example that was reported in *Licensing Economics Review* and is reprinted below[13]:

> The link between corporations and universities goes beyond cash contributions and research grants. Corporations also give patented technology to universities. In return the corporation gets a tax write-off equal to the value of the donated technology. The university obtains a technology that may eventually become a generator of royalties from licensing. Society gains access to a new technology that might have otherwise been closely held by the corporation or not commercially developed at all. Recently Procter & Gamble announced that is donating more than 40 U.S. and international patents along with the accompanying intellectual property to the Milwaukee School of Engineering (MSOE), a world leader in rapid prototyping systems. MSOE will realize all future licensing revenue from the patents.
>
> The patents make up P&G's proprietary PHAST (prototype hard and soft tooling) technology, which radically reduces the time it takes to design and develop molded parts across a wide variety of fields. PHAST helps products go to market sooner. The reason for choosing MSOE was explained by Gordon Brunner, P&G chief technology officer, "A world-class technology such as PHAST needs a world-class leader in rapid prototyping to develop it. MSOE was selected because it is uniquely qualified to realize the PHAST technology's full potential," said Brunner. "MSOE is the only university in the world with machines that use each of the four leading types of rapid prototyping techniques," he added.
>
> "Beyond that, MSOE has a proven ability to bring technologies to the marketplace through a consortium of companies for which they've already developed products." According to MSOE President Hermann Viets, "PHAST technology will revolutionize the tool and die industry. PHAST is a great example of the technical and scientific innovation for which P&G is known. With further development, this technology can be applied to everything from cooking utensils to children's toys to high-tech tennis shoe soles."

Rapid prototyping is a process that enables a three-dimensional product model to be created quickly and automatically from computer data. PHAST is a series of steps that accelerates standard rapid prototyping processes and produces mold inserts for prototypes more quickly, helping products get to market faster.

PHAST can make prototypes up to five times faster than other conventional mold-making techniques. For example, prototype injection-mold tooling can be produced by PHAST in just one-and-a-half to three weeks, compared to an industry average of six to eight weeks when using conventional methods. PHAST is particularly helpful because product developers can get initial samples off a mold much faster than before. It provides developers quick and inexpensive working samples that can be tested with consumers, and then revised as needed and tested again quickly. In addition to being quick, PHAST technology is simple to use and does not require computer systems or designs like other rapid prototyping processes. Therefore, PHAST can be taught to workers with basic tool-and-die skills, and it can be used in low-tech companies or developing countries that produce patterns by hand rather than computer.

This donation to MSOE marks the beginning of a broad initiative by P&G to donate technologies to universities and research. P&G invests more than $1.7 billion in research and development each year. Sometimes the intellectual property that comes from this research effort does not fit with P&G's strategy. Brunner said, "Donating these commercially viable patents and the accompanying intellectual capital to leading universities and research institutions will help us make important new connections. It will also extend the value of the technology more broadly to the world, so that more consumers can benefit much sooner."

To make this gift, P&G engaged an independent expert to find a worthy recipient of the PHAST technology. It also engaged an outside firm to determine the value of the gift for use in filing its income tax return.

Leverage—Securitization

A different kind of intellectual property is revolutionizing the bond market. Intellectual property is serving as collateral for bonds and bank loans. As fixed assets become less important to companies, they will keep less of these assets around. Banks wishing to lend to IP-dominated companies are coming to grips with the new character of these companies and are willing to accept IP as loan collateral. Music copyrights have recently been used as collateral for fixed income securities.

In September 1999, The Pullman Group LLC announced the exclusive signing of Ron Isley and his Isley Brothers for completion of another groundbreaking

Pullman Bond music royalty securitization deal.[14] There are over 300 songs in the Isley catalog and over 50 charting R&B classics including published hits like "Shout," "Twist & Shout," "It's Your Thing," "Fight The Power," "That Lady," "Who's That Lady," "Work To Do," and recorded hits like "Rock Around The Clock," "Love the One You're With," "Lay Lady Lay," "Spill the Wine," and "Summer Breeze." The group is also highly respected for pioneering the ownership of record labels by black artists.

The Pullman Group's music royalty securitization with Ron Isley and the Isley Brothers' catalog joins the ranks of other prestigious transactions created by David Pullman, including the Bowie Bonds, Holland Dozier Holland (Motown Hit Machine) Bonds, Ashford & Simpson Bonds, and James Brown Bonds. The Pullman Group, as principal, specializes in financing and securitizing music publishing, writer's share record masters, artist and record royalties, film and television libraries, TV syndication, literary estates, and other entertainment royalties. The Pullman Group's experience includes well over $1 billion in transactions through 2000.

Not far off in the future will be securities that are backed by trademarks, patents, and possibly technological know-how.

Leverage—Strategic Alliance Entry Fees

This strategy adds the concept of making strategic decisions regarding IP to the defensive costs savings and profit objectives. Entering into joint ventures and strategic alliances is part of this level of intellectual property management. Cost savings and profit center goals continue to be important, but at this stage intellectual property becomes an integral part of the overall corporate strategy. It becomes the driving force behind key decisions.

Entry into new strategic alliances and joint ventures is not easily accomplished without something special to contribute. Cash and manufacturing capacity are not so scarce that potential joint venture partners will give up a significant financial interest to obtain access to them. Intellectual property, patent rights, and technical know-how are currently the coin of the realm. Using intellectual property for the creation of new products and services in combination with another company is becoming a necessity. Products are becoming more complex. Many require expertise in a broad range of different technologies. Rarely does one company possess all of the required expertise. This results in more strategic alliances, but entry into the game requires that you contribute intellectual property. A new approach to management of intellectual property will open up these opportunities. Biotechnology and pharmaceutical companies have practiced this strategy using IP as the foundation. They are no longer alone. Complex electronic products like high-definition television, wireless communication, medical instruments, and computers are requiring the establishment of alliances. Your IP is the ticket into this new arena.

Qualcomm is using its mobile phone intellectual property to gain equity ownership in new companies. Standard CDMA (code division multiple access) technology licenses require a multimillion-dollar license fee payment to Qualcomm in addition to running royalty payments. Start-up companies often do not have extra funds for such an initial payment, preferring to use such funds for product development and activities that will build the new company. In such cases, Qualcomm has begun a program to accept equity from the start-ups.

A very powerful example of an IP-oriented joint venture was recently announced. Two consumer product giants are joining forces. Together, they plan to succeed where alone they have stagnated. Procter & Gamble Co. and Coca-Cola Co. are going to combine some of their most valuable intangible assets. P&G and Coca-Cola are planning to form a joint venture that combines their well-known juice, drink, and snack businesses. Each company will contribute products lines with annual sales of $2 billion, making the joint venture a $4 billion company. Coke and P&G will equally share ownership of the new limited liability company being formed. Coke will contribute its Minute Maid juices, Hi-C drinks, Five Alive, and Fruitopia. P&G will contribute Sunny Delight and Pringles. So far, all that has happened is another combination of well-recognized brand products. The real magic comes from other assets. P&G is going to benefit by having access to Coke's unbeatable international distribution system. The P&G products have not had significant international exposure, but Coke will be able to get the P&G products around the world with an ease that P&G can only dream about. Coke's secret benefit is that P&G's extensive scientific research capabilities will be available to the joint venture. P&G is a juggernaut of innovative new products. New research for the joint venture is expected to focus on the development of nutrition-enhanced juice drinks. Coke could not even begin to accomplish this feat alone.

This joint venture is a unique combination of trademarks, research capabilities, and a powerful distribution network. Cash had little to do with this deal. The driving force behind this deal was intellectual property.

CONCLUSION

Understanding the importance of intellectual property is key to future stock market rewards. Finding companies that possess, create, and have access to IP is the first step. Then identifying those companies, which are nurturing and rigorously managing these assets, will lead investors to stocks that are likely to grow and provide attractive investment returns. The New Economy is not all that new. Companies still need to develop great ideas into products and deliver them with excellent customer service. The major change that is sweeping across all industries involves optimizing the exploitation of these assets. Intellectual property is the key to survival and success for as far into the future as anyone can see. Those possessing intellectual property are very fortunate, but aggressive exploitation of these innovation assets is vital, and this has led to a new three-pronged corporate strategy of innovate, protect, and leverage. All must be diligently integrated. When they are managed well, impressive stock performance will result.

NOTES

1. Denis Waitley, *Empires of the Mind—Lessons to Lead and Succeed in a Knowledge-Based World*, (New York: William Morrow and Company, Inc., 1995), p. 8.
2. Coopers & Lybrand, "Maximizing the Value of Intellectual Property" (brochure, 1997).
3. *Business Week*, "A Big Dose of Uncertainty—An Industry Plagued by High Costs Faces Healthcare Reform," January 10, 1994, p. 85.
4. Ibid.
5. *Forbes*, "Drug Wars," August 29, 1994, p. 81.
6. *Pharmaceutical Business News*, "Market Forces Usher in a Golden Age of Generic Drug," November 29, 1993, published by Financial Times Business Information, Ltd., London, UK.
7. Gretchen Morgenson, "A Year Underachievers Everywhere Can Be Proud Of," Market Watch, Section 3, *The New York Times*, December 31, 2000, p. 1.
8. Current assets are defined by generally accepted accounting principles as assets which are expected to be converted into cash within 12 months of the date of the balance sheet on which they appear. Current liabilities are financial obligations that are expected to be satisfied within 12 months of the same date.
9. Michael P. Ryna, *Knowledge Diplomacy, Global Competition, and the Politics of Intellectual Property* (Washington, D.C.: The Brookings Institute, 1998), p. 21.
10. *Ibid*, page 24.
11. Kevin G. Rivette and David Kline, *Rembrandts in the Attic* (Cambridge, Mass.: Harvard Business School Press, 2000), pp. 125–126
12. Ibid.
13. Reprinted from *Licensing Economics Review*, Vol. 5–6 (1999), p. 26.
14. "Music Securitization," *Licensing Economics Review*, February 2000, page 6.

ABOUT THE AUTHOR

Russell L. Parr, CFA, ASA, is President of Intellectual Property Research Associates, Inc. He is an expert in determining the value of intellectual property. His books are published in Japanese, Korean, Italian, and English. He is dedicated to the development of comprehensive methods for accurately defining the value of intellectual property.

Mr. Parr is responsible for completion of complex consulting assignments involving the valuation and pricing of patents, trademarks, copyrights, and other intangible assets. His opinions are used to accomplish licensing transactions, mergers, acquisitions, transfer pricing, litigation support, collateral-based financing, and joint ventures. Mr. Parr also conducts customized research into industry-specific factors that drive royalty rates. He advises banks about the use of intangible assets as loan collateral and has served as an expert witness regarding intellectual property infringement damages.

Mr. Parr founded the highly respected *Licensing Economics Review* (LER) in

September 1990 for reporting royalty rate information from around the world. He served as the editor-in-chief through August 2001. LER is dedicated to reporting detailed information about the economic aspects of intellectual property licensing and joint venturing.

Recent assignments have included the valuation of the Dr. Seuss copyrights and the patent portfolio of AT&T. Mr. Parr has also conducted valuations and royalty rate studies for communications technology, pharmaceuticals, semiconductor process and product technology, automotive battery technology, lasers, agricultural formulations, biotechnology, computer software, drug delivery systems, medical products technology, incinerator feed systems, camera technology, flowers, consumer and corporate trademarks, motivational book copyrights, and cosmetics.

CHAPTER FOURTEEN

Using Patent Indicators to Predict Stock Portfolio Performance

by Francis Narin, Patrick Thomas,
and Anthony Breitzman

PERSPECTIVES

The science of analyzing scholarly citations, bibliometrics, has been applied to many disciplines, from literature to gene splicing. Dr. Francis Narin of CHI Research and his collaborators, Dr. Patrick Thomas and Anthony Breitzman, track the citation frequency of patents and scientific papers that establish quantitative patent indicators. They then use these indicators to identify companies with high-quality patent portfolios, which in turn form the basis for identifying companies whose patent portfolios are undervalued by the stock market. Investing in this manner over the past 10 years would have given investors returns far in excess of Dow Jones (DJ), Standard & Poor's (S&P), and NASDAQ indices. In 2000, for example, CHI's technology-heavy Tech-Line Index® outperformed the NASDAQ 23.7 percent to −39.3 percent.

". . . Background research," say the authors, "provides a strong rationale for the expectation that companies with strong patent portfolios [with patents that are frequently cited by other patents, that are more frequently renewed] will perform better in the stock market. A method devised to accurately measure the quality of company technology should therefore have a significant predictive effect on company stock performance. Furthermore, information of this type should be particularly valuable because it is not currently available to market analysts, leading to a strong likelihood that the quality of company technology might not be properly valued in the market.

"Deng et al. showed that companies with high-quality patent port-folios had market-to-book valuations that were 25 percent higher than other companies in the same industries with lesser-quality port-folios, both contemporaneously and for a number of years in the future."

A patent for "Method and Apparatus for Choosing a Stock Portfo-lio Based on Patent Indicators" (Pat. No. 6,175,824) was awarded to CHI on January 16, 2001. In the chapter that follows, Dr. Narin and his colleagues define patent quality indicators and show how they can be play an important role in identifying investments, measuring com-pany performance, and quantifying merger and acquisition targets.

INTRODUCTION

There is a growing awareness that the intellectual property owned by companies can be an important factor in their commercial success. Intellectual property, par-ticularly in the form of patents, provides the technological foundation upon which new products and services are built. Revealed here are models that use quantita-tive patent citation indicators to identify companies with high-quality patent port-folios and also companies whose patents the stock market has undervalued. Invest-ing in such companies would have produced impressive results from 1991 through the early part of 2001. Over this period, stock portfolios containing the companies with the highest-quality and most undervalued patents would have outperformed major market indices by a wide margin.

Over the last two decades, the analysis of company patent portfolios has become an increasingly important part of competitive intelligence activities, as well as a key tool in analyzing national, regional, and company technology strengths. Implicit in these analyses is the idea that identifying a company's intellectual as-sets, specifically those intangible assets that patents protect, is tantamount to iden-tifying areas of strength within a company.

Underpinning the groundswell of interest in the valuation of a company's intellectual property is the idea that this unseen wealth will eventually enhance shareholder value. Recent discoveries by CHI Research indicate that high-quality patent portfolios, a prime example of company intellectual property, are long-term predictors of a company's stock market performance. Two different but related approaches using patent citation indicators to measure the quality of a company's patent portfolio both lead to this conclusion. These models are described in detail here.

In our *Technology Quality Model*, we show that companies with strong patent indicators have substantially larger increases in their stock values for a number of years in the future compared with competitor companies with weaker-quality patents. In our *Technology Market Model*, we compare companies' actual market valuation with a technology valuation derived from a combination of their patent indicators. Companies whose actual market valuation is lower than their technology valuation have been shown to rise in price substantially over the next few years. Using both the technology-quality and the technology-market approaches, we have created stock portfolios whose performance has exceeded that of standard market averages over a number of years.

BACKGROUND: IDENTIFYING QUALITY PATENTS

The idea of a patent is simple. An inventor or his/her company is granted a 20-year monopoly on an invention, in return for detailed disclosure of how the invention works. Rather than stifle innovation, the idea is that patents should spur innovation. Through the patent system, inventors get 20 years of exclusive control of their inventions, while the public is able to see how the current inventions work and can therefore build and improve upon them without the pitfalls of starting from scratch.

When an inventor applies for a patent, s/he must show that the invention is novel, useful, and nonobvious to someone with average expertise in the same industry. To achieve this, the inventor will cite to earlier patents and explain why the new patent improves on the earlier inventions. The patent examiner may also add earlier inventions that limit the scope of the new invention. A U.S. patent typically cites seven or eight earlier patents in the "references cited" section of its front page. These references cited—also called "backward citations"—in essence identify the important prior art that has contributed to or limits the claims of the just-issued patent.

The fundamental idea of patent citation analysis is that when a patent is highly cited (by many later patents), it is likely to contain important technological advances upon which many subsequent developments have built. In other words, highly cited patents are regarded as markers for important new ideas, identifying quality assets in a company's patent portfolio. A number of previous studies have provided support for this assumption. Carpenter et al.[1] found that patents related to IR 100 invention awards are cited twice as often as typical patents. Similarly, Breitzman and Narin[2] showed patents assigned Pioneering Patent status were cited much more often than average, as were patents accorded Hall of Fame status by the U.S. Patent & Trademark Office (USPTO). In another study, Albert et al.[3] in cooperation with Eastman Kodak Laboratories reported that patents Kodak's staff saw as important were more frequently cited than patents they regarded as less important.

There is also evidence to suggest that patent citations may have some validity as a proxy for patents' commercial value. A study by Harhoff et al.[4] showed that patents regarded as commercially valuable by their owners are more highly cited than patents regarded as less valuable. In addition, a study by Thomas[5] revealed that highly cited patents are more likely to be renewed than patents that receive fewer citations (U.S. patents must be renewed 4, 8, and 12 years after their issue date). Given that patent assignees must pay renewal fees at each of the three renewal points, the decision to renew patents is an economic one. Patent assignees will only renew patents if they expect the commercial returns on those patents to exceed their renewal fee. The finding that highly cited patents are more likely to be renewed therefore suggests that patent assignees expect higher commercial returns from these patents.

Companies that have large numbers of these patents thus have strong patent portfolios and would be expected to do better in a technologically competitive area than a company with a patent portfolio of lesser quality. Narin et al.[6] studied 17 U.S. pharmaceutical companies and uncovered a significant positive correlation between patent citation frequency, concentration of company patents in a few patent classes, and company profits and sales. Pakes[7] examined the relationship between patents, research and development (R&D) dollars, and the stock market rate of return. He found that unexpected changes in R&D expenditures or patent applications were both significantly correlated with changes in stock market value. In the economics literature, Comanor and Scherer[8] studied the relationship between patents granted and sales from product innovation, and patent applications and sales from product innovations. They found that they could explain 26 percent and 24 percent of the variation, respectively. More recently, Deng et al.[9] showed that companies with high-quality patent portfolios had market-to-book valuations that were 25 percent higher than other companies in the same industries with lesser-quality portfolios, both contemporaneously and for a number of years in the future.

In summary, background research provides a strong rationale for the expectation that companies with strong patent portfolios will perform better in the stock market. A method devised to accurately measure the quality of company technology should therefore have a significant predictive effect on company stock performance. Furthermore, information of this type should be particularly valuable because it is not currently available to market analysts, leading to a strong likelihood that the quality of company technology might not be properly valued in the market.

DATA

The sample of companies used for this study contained all U.S. companies listed on U.S. stock exchanges at the end of 1999 that had been granted at least 50 U.S. patents over the previous five years. The analysis was restricted to U.S. companies listed on U.S. exchanges to remove the effect of any differences among worldwide stock exchanges. The minimum patent threshold was used to focus the analysis on companies in which patents are an important source of future success. There is little point in producing patent-based evaluations of companies that do not produce patents on a regular basis. This is often the case in industries such as banking and retailing. The final sample contained 308 companies.

The patent data for these 308 companies was taken from CHI Research's Tech-Line® database, which contains the patents of the 1,400 leading worldwide patenting organizations. The Tech-Line® database pieces together the corporate structure of each of these companies in order to produce accurate patent lists for each company, including all of their subsidiaries. This unification of the companies' various components is not a trivial process. After the standard clean-up of patent assignee names, there are still more than 20,000 different components of the 1,400 companies, all of which are carefully assigned in the Tech-Line® database. In the course of each year, all 1,400 companies are reviewed for new mergers, acquisitions, and divestitures, so that the corporate structures remain accurate over time.

Patent data were collected from the Tech-Line® database on an annual basis for the period from the end of 1990 to the end of 1998. For each company, this data included counts of patents and measures of patent growth, along with a number of patent quality indicators, which were normalized using industry averages. The indicators included in the model are described in the next section.

One characteristic of the sample should be noted at this point. The 308 companies in the sample were all in operation at the end of 1999 and had each been granted at least 50 patents in the previous five years. However, not all of these companies were in the sample for all years. Some of them were not in existence throughout the period being analyzed. Others did not meet the minimum patent threshold in previous years and so were not included in the model. The minimum number of companies in the sample was 192 in 1990.

KEY INDICATORS

In our various models of our stock market performance, CHI uses five specific patent indicators and one nonpatent indicator, R&D intensity (R&D expenditures as a percent of sales). The five patent indicators are:

1. *Number of Patents.* The number of patents granted to a company, including its subsidiaries, in the previous year. This is a measure of the technological productivity of a company.
2. *Patent Growth.* The percentage growth in the number of patents granted to a company in the previous year, compared to the year before. This indicator shows trends in a company's commitment to technological innovation.
3. *Current Impact Index (CII).* The CII shows the impact of a company's patents on the latest technological developments. The CII is a measure of how often the previous five years of a company's patents are cited by patents issued in most recent year, relative to all U.S. patents. A CII of 1.0 shows that the last five years of a company's patents are cited as often as

expected, compared to all U.S. patents. A CII of 1.1 indicates 10 percent more citations per patent than expected, and so forth. Note that CII is a synchronous indicator and moves with the current year, looking back five years. As a result, when a company's patents from recent years start to drop in impact, this is picked up quickly as a decline in the current year's CII.

4. *Science Linkage (SL).* Science linkage is a measure of the extent to which a company's technology builds upon cutting-edge scientific research. It is calculated based on the average number of references on a company's patents to scientific papers, as distinct from references to previous patents. Companies whose patents cite a large number of scientific papers are assumed to be working closely with the latest scientific developments.

5. *Technology Cycle Time (TCT).* In general, companies that are innovating rapidly tend to be more successful in product development than companies relying on older technologies. This leads to another citation indicator, the technology cycle time (TCT). TCT is a measure of the median age of the U.S. patents cited on the front page of a company's patents. A tendency to cite older patents is an indication that a company utilizes older technology. The average TCT is as short as three or four years in rapidly evolving industries, such as electronics, and as long as 15 years in industries that change more slowly, such as shipbuilding. Similarly, the average company in the biotechnology industry has a science linkage of around 15 patents to reference on a company's scientific paper, while the average automotive company has a science linkage of less than one.

In order to account for these differences, the Tech-Line® database divides companies into 26 industry groups, and calculates industry averages for each patent indicator. Industry-normalized indicators are computed by taking the indicator value for a particular company and dividing by the average for that company's industry. By removing the industry effects, it is possible to identify the companies that have strong patent indicators relative to other companies in their industry. For example, an automotive company with a science linkage of four is more science-linked relative to its industry than a biotechnology company with a science linkage of eight.

THE TECHNOLOGY QUALITY MODEL

CHI's Technology Quality Model is the basis for our recently issued U.S. Patent (#6,175,824) for a "Method and Apparatus for Choosing a Stock Portfolio, Based Upon Patent Indicators." The purpose of the Technology Quality Model is to identify the companies with the strongest patent portfolios in their industry. The rationale for this is that the strength of their patents will enable these companies to achieve, or maintain, a position of technological leadership. In turn, this position will lead to a strong market position for these companies, causing investors to view their stock favorably. Although this may be seen as a somewhat simplistic and mechanistic view, the idea of investing in companies that are technological leaders in their industry remains a sound one.

The Technology Quality Model examines the relationship between the five patent indicators discussed earlier and future stock price changes. Its aim is to identify combinations of patent indicators that are related closely to stock price appreciation. To identify these combinations, we used a two-stage Monte Carlo method. In a Monte Carlo analysis, a finite number of variables are entered into the model, along with upper and lower limits for their coefficients. A random set of coefficients is then generated, and the results recorded. In this example, the variables are the five patent indicators, and the result recorded is the stock market returns produced by the companies with the highest scores based on the coefficients assigned to these indicators.

In the first stage, we randomly selected coefficients for each normalized patent indicator, with the following upper and lower limits: between −100 and +25 for normalized TCT, −50 and +50 for normalized science linkage, −25 and +25 for normalized growth, −25 to +100 for normalized CII. The coefficient for number of patents was set to zero, since we wanted to identify companies with strong patents, not necessarily those with large numbers of patents.

We then ran 50,000 random simulations, each with a different combination of weighting coefficients for the patent indicators. For each simulation, the patent indicators of each company in the sample were entered and its technology score was calculated using the formula:

$$\text{score} = \sum_{i=0}^{k-1} \alpha_i x_i$$

where the α_i are the weighting coefficients and the x_i are the five patent indicators. Note that many of the α_i may be 0.

For each combination of coefficients, we identified the 25 companies with the highest technology scores at the end of every year between 1989 and 1998. We then calculated the change in the value of a portfolio containing these 25 stocks in the subsequent 12 months. We recorded all combinations of coefficients that produced portfolios of companies providing an average return of at least 25 percent annually for the 10 years.

By studying the outputs of this analysis, we determined that it was possible to narrow the range of coefficients to the following: TCT −100 to 0, normalized science linkage −15 to 15, CII 0 to 25, normalized growth −10 to 10. This narrower set of coefficients allowed us to focus on the combinations of coefficients that were most likely to produce the highest returns. We then ran 200,000 random simulations within those ranges and recorded equations that produced portfolios of stocks with the best returns.

The models offering the highest returns had two characteristics in common. The first was a positive coefficient for CII. This suggests that companies with highly cited patents are likely to be attractive investment opportunities. The second characteristic was a negative coefficient for TCT. This shows that companies that innovate quickly also tend to experience higher stock market returns. One of the models that produced the highest returns was

$$\text{Technology Score} = 2 \times \text{CII} - 9 \times \text{TCT}$$

This equation is used for purposes of illustration in this description of the Technology Quality Model.

To show the results of this model, we entered the patent indicators for each company in the sample at the start of each year into this equation. The 25 companies with the highest scores each year were then identified. Equal dollar amounts of stock of these 25 companies were hypothetically purchased at the beginning of each year and then sold at the end of the year. The funds were then reinvested in the top 25 companies at the beginning of the next year. Exhibit 14-1 shows that a portfolio of stocks chosen in this manner would have appreciated at three times the rate of the S&P 500 over the period 1989 to 1998.

Given that the model was built based on data from 1989 to 1998, it is not surprising that it performs so well over that in-sample period. However, if the model is to be of use, it must continue to perform in the out-of-sample period since that time. This has indeed been the case. In 1999, the Technology Quality Model returned over 63 percent, its highest return over the entire period. This performance was better than the S&P 500 and the Dow Jones Industrial Average (DJIA), but not as strong as the NASDAQ. However, it should be noted that the Technology Quality Model does not include any of the Internet companies that drove the NASDAQ's strong performance in 1999. This turned out to be a blessing in the year 2000. Many of the so-called dot.com stocks that performed so well in 1999 lost most of their value in 2000. As a result, while the NASDAQ lost over 39 percent in 2000, the Technology Quality Model gained 14 percent. This was a much stronger performance than the S&P 500, which lost 10 percent in 2000, and the DJIA, which lost 6 percent in 2000.

Setting the portfolio size for the Technology Quality Model at 25 was an arbitrary decision. Other portfolio sizes could also be used. We have found that portfolios of fewer then 25 stocks would produce higher average returns, but with a greater degree of volatility. Portfolios of 20 to 25 stocks seem to be fairly stable and provide consistent yield. As the number of stocks is increased beyond this point, the portfolio performance tends to decrease toward the market averages.

Also, additional constraints may be added to the portfolio selection process to change its focus. For example, instead of merely optimizing for overall performance, the algorithm can be designed to select portfolios that not only provide superior returns, but also have other desirable traits for a particular investment style. Some examples include picking portfolios that have a low amount of vola-

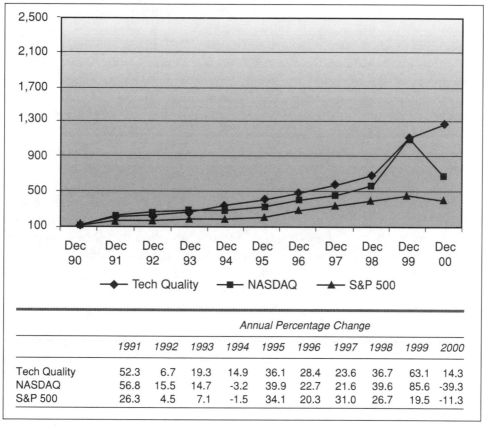

	1991	1992	1993	1994	1995	1996	1997	1998	1999	2000
Tech Quality	52.3	6.7	19.3	14.9	36.1	28.4	23.6	36.7	63.1	14.3
NASDAQ	56.8	15.5	14.7	-3.2	39.9	22.7	21.6	39.6	85.6	-39.3
S&P 500	26.3	4.5	7.1	-1.5	34.1	20.3	31.0	26.7	19.5	-11.3

Exhibit 14-1   Returns on the Technology Quality Model 1990–2000.

tility, companies that are suitable for short-term or long-term investment, companies that mainly come from specific industries, and so on.

THE TECHNOLOGY MARKET MODEL

The purpose of the Technology Market Model is to identify companies whose high-quality patented technology is not fully valued by the stock market. This model is the basis for CHI's Investor Tech-Line® product. There are two stages in this model. The first stage develops a valuation of companies based on the quality of their technology and their commitment to R&D. In the second stage, these valuations are compared to the companies' actual valuation in the market. This two-stage process facilitates identification of companies that are under- and overvalued in the stock market. To demonstrate the validity of the model, we reveal the performance of investment portfolios containing the most undervalued and overvalued companies.

Developing Technology-Based Company Valuations

In order to produce technology-based company valuations, the five raw patent indicators and five industry-normalized patent indicators, along with companies' R&D Intensity (R&D Expenditure/Sales)[10] were mapped against companies' stock market valuations using multiple regression analysis. The stock market valuation used as the dependent variable in the regression equation was companies' market-to-book (MTB) ratio.[11]

The MTB measures the relationship between the market value of a company (share price × number of shares outstanding) and its book value (the value of the assets it has on its balance sheet). For example, if a company has a book value of $10 million, and has five million outstanding shares priced at four dollars each, it has an MTB of two ($20 million/$10 million). The average MTB of companies in our sample at the end of 2000 was around five, showing that these companies' tangible assets only accounted for 20 percent of their market value.

A high MTB reveals that the stock market believes a company has value over and above the assets revealed on its balance sheet. This value may emerge in part from the quality of a company's technology, which is not explicitly shown in any of its financial statements.

Eight separate regression analyses were carried out for the end of each year between 1990 and 1997. The purpose of the regression analysis was to identify the combination of patent and R&D indicators that was most closely related to companies' MTB valuations at a given point in time. The regression analysis revealed that the number of patents and patent growth were not significantly related to companies' market-to-book ratios. The coefficients associated with these variables were therefore set to zero and the regressions rerun. Setting the coefficient associated with the number of patents to zero means that there is no inherent bias in the model toward large companies with extensive patent portfolios. The model depends on the quality of companies' patent portfolios, not their size.

To varying degrees, the coefficients for the other variables changed each year. However, there was a high degree of consistency across years in four of the variables. Specifically, there was a positive coefficient for normalized CII and a smaller positive coefficient for nonnormalized SL. There was also a negative coefficient for normalized SL and a small positive coefficient for R&D. In most years, there was a negative coefficient for TCT, showing that companies that innovate quickly tend to have higher market-to-book valuations. However, the TCT coefficient was less stable than those associated with the other variables.

A new regression analysis was run for each year using only the four variables whose coefficients were relatively stable. The means of the coefficients for each variable were then combined to produce a single equation covering the period 1990 to 1997. Sensitivity analysis was carried out on this equation, with each of the coefficients being changed up to 10 percent in each direction to establish whether alternative equations would produce values that correlated more closely with the dependent variable. Small changes were made in the coefficients as a result of this analysis.

Applying an exponential function to the final equation (to reverse the effect of the earlier transformation using natural logs) produced an MTB valuation for a company based on a combination of patent indicators and R&D intensity. This valuation is defined as the Technology MTB, and has the formula:

$$\text{Technology MTB} = e^{(a + b1 \times \text{CIInormed} + b2 \times \text{SL} + b3 \times \text{R\&D} - b4 \times \text{SLnormed})}$$

The average R^2 value of the eight regression equations was 0.08. F statistics revealed that five out of the eight models were significant at the 1 percent level, and a further two models were significant at the 5 percent level. However, the R^2 value is relatively low, suggesting that the relationship is a very noisy one. This is a reflection of the complexity of stock market valuation, which leads to a high level of noise in any model of the stock market. For example, Lev and Sougiannis[12] reported a similar R^2 between earnings, a widely used stock market indicator, and MTB.

Relating Technology MTB and Actual MTB Values

Based upon the relationship between actual MTB and technology MTB valuations, it is possible to define whether a company, based upon its technology, is overvalued (actual MTB>technology MTB) or undervalued (technology MTB>actual MTB).

The most undervalued and overvalued companies are of particular interest. To identify these companies, all companies in the sample were placed into percentiles according to their technology MTB, with 100 assigned to the company with the highest technology MTB and 1 to the company with the lowest technology MTB. Companies were then placed into percentiles according to their actual MTB, with 100 representing the highest actual MTB.

For each company, the actual MTB percentile was subtracted from the technology MTB percentile. Companies were then placed into percentiles on the basis of the resultant differential, to produce the investment potential of each company. The highest investment potential (100) was assigned to the company with the largest positive differential, and the lowest investment potential (1) to the company with the largest negative differential.

The investment potential of a company reflects how its valuation in the stock market compares to a valuation of it based solely upon its technology. A company with an investment potential of 100 has strong technology that is not recognized by the stock market. Meanwhile, a company with an investment potential of 1 has a valuation in the market that cannot be justified on the basis of its technology (although there may be other factors that explain its high valuation). A company with an investment potential of 50 is regarded as fairly valued, based upon the quality of its technology.

The usefulness of a model of this type depends upon its ability to forecast future changes in stock market valuations. In this analysis, we paid particular attention to the companies at the two ends of the investment potential distribution—the companies that are most under- and overvalued. Exhibit 14-2 shows the returns that investors would have received if they had invested equal dollar amounts in two annually updated portfolios—the 20 most undervalued companies and the 20 most overvalued companies. Each year the portfolio is sold, and the funds are invested in the new portfolio of stocks. Exhibit 14-2 reveals that an investment of $1,000 in December 1990 in an annually updated portfolio of the 20 most undervalued stocks would have returned over $21,000 by December 1999. This portfolio significantly outperformed both the NASDAQ Composite Index and the S&P 500. Meanwhile, the portfolio of overvalued stocks returned only $3,000 over the same period, underperforming both the NASDAQ and the S&P 500.

The stock market performance of the most undervalued stocks was particularly strong in 1999, with a return of 99 percent. This strong performance was achieved without any of the Internet-related companies that drove the strong performance of the NASDAQ in 1999. The strong performance of the Technology

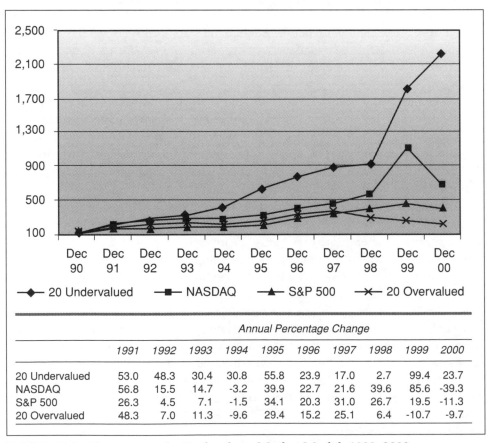

	1991	*1992*	*1993*	*1994*	*1995*	*1996*	*1997*	*1998*	*1999*	*2000*
20 Undervalued	53.0	48.3	30.4	30.8	55.8	23.9	17.0	2.7	99.4	23.7
NASDAQ	56.8	15.5	14.7	-3.2	39.9	22.7	21.6	39.6	85.6	-39.3
S&P 500	26.3	4.5	7.1	-1.5	34.1	20.3	31.0	26.7	19.5	-11.3
20 Overvalued	48.3	7.0	11.3	-9.6	29.4	15.2	25.1	6.4	-10.7	-9.7

Exhibit 14-2   Returns on the Technology Market Model, 1990–2000.

Market Model continued in the year 2000, with a return of 23 percent. This was in a market that saw large falls in all three major stock market averages.

CONCLUSION

The effect of intellectual property on the valuation of companies has been widely discussed recently, complete with many general statements about intangible assets as fundamental drivers of company value. Among the most tangible of these intangible intellectual property assets are patents. We have shown here that the quality of a company's inventive technology, as revealed by its possession of high-impact patents, may be an important indicator of future stock market performance.

We have outlined two distinct approaches to stock selection, both of which have indicators of patent quality at their core. Using combinations of such indicators, we have developed models that have outperformed standard market averages over the past 10 years. It should be noted that beating the S&P 500 index is a significant achievement. The S&P 500 index has outperformed 90 percent of all actively managed mutual funds over the last 3-, 5-, and 10-year periods.[13]

The analysis presented here is not purely an academic exercise. Since June 1999, CHI has managed part of its pension portfolio using the techniques presented here. This part of the pension fund has outperformed the standard market averages since that time.

The models outlined here represent a pioneering attempt to examine the relationship between patent quality and stock market performance. This analysis has produced some promising results. CHI believes that there are a number of possible future developments that may lead to improved forecasting power for the models.

The most important development of the models may be the addition of financial indicators. The models presented here contain solely patent and R&D indicators. Therefore, they make no reference to the financial health of companies. For example, many of the companies selected by the Technology Market Model have low market valuations. This may be for a number of reasons, such as poor management, falling sales, and failure to meet analysts' earnings estimates. These factors are not taken into account in this model. It may be possible to improve the performance of this model by including some financial indicators.

A second development may be to reduce the minimum patent threshold. The current threshold of 50 patents over five years tends to restrict the analysis to relatively large, established companies. It therefore excludes many new high-tech companies whose success is closely linked to the quality of their technology, but which do not currently have enough patents to meet the threshold. However, reducing the threshold has the potential drawback of reducing the stability of the models, given that the patent indicators for the additional companies would be based on smaller numbers of patents.

Adding companies may also facilitate the development of separate models for each industry. In this chapter, companies from all industries are entered into the same model, although their patent indicators are normalized to reduce the effect of differences between industries. This is because, in many industries, there are insufficient companies in the sample to produce robust models. Developing separate models for each industry may allow for industry-specific stock market factors to be taken into account.

Finally, the models only consider U.S. companies listed on U.S. exchanges. The relationship discovered here between patent portfolios, R&D intensity, and stock market returns may occur in other countries. It may be possible to produce similar models based on other stock exchanges.

NOTES

1. M. Carpenter, F. Narin, and P. Woolf, "Citation Rates to Technologically Important Patents," *World Patent Information,* Vol. 3 (1981), pp. 160–163.
2. A. Breitzman and F. Narin, "A Case for Patent Citation Analysis in Litigation," *The Law Works*, Vol. 3 (March 1996), pp. 10–11, 26–27.
3. M. Albert, D. Avery, F. Narin, and P. McAllister, "Direct Validation of Citation Counts as Indicators of Industrially Important Patents," *Research Policy*, Vol. 20 (1991), pp. 251–259.
4. D. Harhoff, F. Narin, F. Scherer, and K. Vopel, "Citation Frequency and the Value of Patented Inventions," *The Review of Economics and Statistics*, Vol. 81 (1999), pp. 511–515.
5. P. Thomas, "The Effect of Technological Impact Upon Patent Renewal Decisions," *Technology Analysis & Strategic Management*, Vol. 11 (1999), pp. 181–197.
6. F. Narin, E. Noma, and R. Perry, "Patents as Indicators of Technological Strength," *Research Policy*, Vol. 16 (1987), pp. 143–155.
7. A. Pakes, "On Patents, R&D, and the Stock Market Rates of Return," *Journal of Political Economy*, Vol. 93, No. 2, (1985), pp. 390–409.
8. W. Comanor and F. Scherer, "Patent Statistics as a Measure of Technical Change," *Journal of Political Economy*, Vol. 77 (1969), pp. 392–398.
9. Z. Deng, B. Lev, and F. Narin, "Science and Technology as Predictors of Stock Performance," *Financial Analysts Journal*, Vol. 55, No. 3, (1999), pp. 20–32.
10. Taken from Schonfeld & Associates R&D Ratios and Budgets.
11. Regression analysis is based on the assumption that the dependent variable approximates to a normal distribution. Preliminary analysis revealed that the distribution of MTB values in each year was positively skewed. These values were therefore transformed using the natural log function. Kolmogorov-Smirnov tests revealed that the natural logs of the MTB values were normally distributed in each year.
12. B. Lev and T. Sougiannis, "The Capitalization, Amortization, and Value-Relevance of R&D," *Journal of Accounting and Economics*, Vol. 21 (1996), pp. 107–138.
13. P. Coy, "Can You Really Beat the Market?" *Business Week*, May 31, 1999.

ABOUT THE AUTHORS

Francis Narin is recognized as one of the leading experts on science and technology analysis, and he has acted as an expert witness in patent litigation. He has presented his work at many meetings and conferences around the world. His recent speaking engagements include the National Science Foundation, the Australian Research Council, the Licensing Executives Society, and the Council for Chemical Research. His work with CHI Research, Inc., has also been reported in *The New York Times, Business Week* and *MIT Technology Review*. Dr. Narin has a BS in Chemistry from Franklin and Marshall College, an MS in Nuclear Engineering from North Carolina State College, and a PhD in Bibliometrics from Walden University.

Patrick Thomas, who joined CHI Research, Inc., in 1998, has worked extensively as Project Manager on science and technology evaluation projects for a variety of Fortune 500 companies and governmental agencies. He is also a central figure in CHI's development of products aimed at the financial community. He is responsible for the design, implementation, and maintenance of CHI's Investor Tech-Line® product, which identifies companies whose patented technology is undervalued by the stock market. He has also been instrumental in developing CHI's models used to select stocks for the Patent Select Quality Trust, a unit trust sold by Nike Securities LP. Dr. Thomas was educated in the United Kingdom, and prior to joining CHI, he was employed as Lecturer in Quantitative Methods at Southampton Institute in the United Kingdom. He earned a BS in Management Science from the University of Manchester Institute of Science and Technology; an MS in Computer Science from the University of Birmingham and a PhD in Management Theory and Bibliometrics from Nottingham Trent University.

Anthony Breitzman joined CHI Research, Inc., as an associate analyst in 1993, and in 1996 he became the youngest vice president in the company's 30-year history. He has three major responsibilities at CHI: working as a competitive intelligence consultant for commercial clients, generating new business for the company, and steering the technical direction of the company. He has worked with many Fortune 500 companies. He is co-inventor with Dr. Francis Narin of CHI's 1084 patent for selecting a stock portfolio based on patent indicators. Mr. Breitzman has a BS in Mathematics from Stockton State College; an MA in Mathematics from Temple University; and an MS in Computer Science from Drexel University. He recently completed his PhD in Computer Science at Drexel University.

CHI Research, Inc. (*www.chiresearch.com*), analyzes competitive technology strength by tracking patent citations and other key indicators. The company, established in 1968 by Dr. Francis Narin, maintains a database of all U.S. and European Patent Office patents, with special emphasis on the 1,400 largest patenting companies—those with 45 patents or more over a five-year period. Included in the database are 350 publicly traded U.S. companies. CHI's products include Investor Tech-Line®, a monthly ranking of public companies for their investment potential available by subscription, and a unit trust based on CHI indicators, the Patent Quality Select Trust, introduced by Nike Securities in August 2000. CHI's clients include institutional investors, professional money managers, large companies, and domestic and foreign government agencies. The technical leadership of CHI of Haddon Heights, New Jersey, has been recognized in more than 125 peer-reviewed academic journal papers over a 30-year period, including a recent paper in *The Financial Analysts Journal*.

CHAPTER FIFTEEN

Patenting Activity as an Indicator of Revenue Growth

Five Industries

by Darlene Slaughter

PERSPECTIVES

Patent strength is not easily measured. Amassing large numbers of patents, an often cited and readily available statistic, while meaningful, does not necessarily reflect outstanding performance or value. Many factors determine the success of a company's patent portfolio, including timing and demand for the inventions covered, as well as the quality of the proprietary rights and how they are managed. Patent filing trends that indicate increased activity within the U.S. Patent & Trademark Office's (USPTO) ever-changing filing classifications are looked upon as reliable indicators of innovation and likely industry growth. Mapping these trends facilitates comparing similar companies or, at least, patentees competing in the same industry. This is important because, as the author of the following chapter, Darlene Slaughter, points out, "different industries have characteristic patenting behaviors." Comparing a pharmaceutical company with a software company can be confusing because the nature and number of their patents can differ widely. However, comparing unlike companies with the same PTO classification filings may indicate more about their future direction and competitive position.

In this chapter, Ms. Slaughter, an executive and analyst with IFI CLAIMS® Patent Services, looks at relative patent activity in the context of company revenue among five important PTO classifications: Telecommunications (class 455), Semiconductor Manufacture (class

438), Molecular Biology or Biotech patentees (class 435), Drugs (class 514), and Business Methods (class 705), a relatively new and controversial class.

Concludes Ms. Slaughter: "While a rise in patent holding is not a guarantee of future income or growth, a continuing decline or even a leveling off of patent growth is often a signal that a company's revenues may be at risk."

INTRODUCTION

Investors use a variety of methods to decide which companies are most likely to survive and grow over the long term. For many industries, patents are a significant factor in the success of an enterprise.

Those who invest in companies often rely on revenue forecasts to judge a company's potential. No matter how much a corporation's marketing campaign promises, the bottom line is still the ultimate gauge of quality. Stockholders eventually will withdraw their support if the company is losing ground to its competitors and does not have assets that will give it an edge over similar businesses.

Patents are assets that can provide the needed advantage, enabling companies to generate revenue by selling the unique products of their research. These patents afford protection from potential rivals who may only produce and sell products that do not infringe the patented technology of others in the marketplace.

Patents are evidence of innovation—certification from a patenting authority that something new and improved has been awarded patent protection. They indicate that a company has invested time and resources in developing an advantage it believes is worth defending from others.

Simple ownership of a patent does not guarantee success. Many factors determine the value of a company's patents, including the marketability of the patented product, the strength of the patent portfolio protecting the technology, and the skill with which that portfolio is managed. As a comparative measure, though, does a company's rate of patent growth indicate its degree of success relative to others in the same field?

FINDING THE GROWTH AREAS: FIVE INDUSTRIES

If innovation is linked to industry growth, it seems logical that the latest technologies will show the highest rate of growth in patenting activity. Exhibit 15-1 shows the increase by year in U.S. patents granted in five areas of technology, as defined by USPTO classifications: business methods (class 705), telecommunications (class 455), semiconductor manufacture (class 438), molecular biology, or biotech (class 435), and drugs (class 514). (The patent information in this chapter is from the

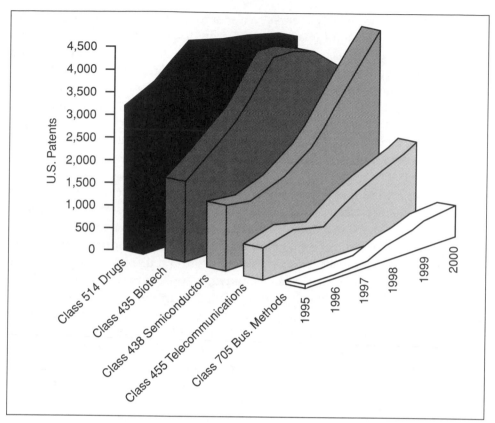

Exhibit 15-1 U.S. patents by class, 1995–2000.

Patent Intelligence and Technology Report and U.S. patent databases published by IFI CLAIMS® Patent Services.)

While all five sectors exhibit a rise in patents issued, a steep growth curve appears in the semiconductor class, with an overall increase of 197 percent since 1995. In fact, more patents were issued in this class during 2000 than in any other class of technology.

The telecommunications group displays a 189 percent increase for the same period, following closely behind the semiconductors, although the year's total patents in the telecom class were less than half the semiconductor count.

Patenting in biotech has also risen quickly, with a 138 percent increase from 1995 to 2000, after drifting down from a peak in 1998. The biotech growth spurt began about 10 years earlier, in 1985, when the patent level climbed steadily from 935 patents for the year to an annual total of 3,579 in 2000. Drug patents are currently in a slight decline but are still 23 percent ahead of their 1995 level.

The rate of increase is even more pronounced for patents on automated business methods, a 529 percent gain, from 118 patents in 1995 to 742 patents five years later.

If we look more closely at these five areas of technology, we see that the relationship between patenting activity and growth of revenue varies depending upon the nature of the technology and the products. In the semiconductor field, for example, product cycles tend to be short, and the innovation protected by a patent may become obsolete long before the term of the patent expires. On the other hand, pharmaceuticals tend to have much longer product cycles, and successful drugs are marketable for many years, even after their patent protection has lapsed. A patent for a new drug usually represents a greater investment in research, as well as a potentially longer payback period, than a patent for a semiconductor chip improvement.

A comparison of revenue growth to increases in patenting activity within these two industries shows that fluctuations in patenting activity have a more noticeable effect on the revenues of semiconductor businesses than they do on the revenues of pharmaceutical companies. The pharmaceutical industry, of course, is more mature and less cyclical than semiconductors, but there is more to the story.

Based on the number of patents granted, it appears that the semiconductor powerhouse is Micron Technology (see Exhibit 15-2). In 1995, it was in seventeenth place among companies acquiring patents for semiconductor manufacturing. By the year 2000, it had leaped to the top position with 410 patents, holding a lead of 34 patents more than its nearest competitor in the class, Advanced Micro Devices (AMD) (see Exhibit 15-3). Micron's performance in related areas was equally impressive. All told, it received 1,306 US patents in 2000, moving up to seventh among all companies getting U.S. patents. Other leaders in the semiconductor area, including Intel and Advanced Micro Devices, show a similar upward trend in both patenting and income (see Exhibit 15-4).

In a growing industry such as this, it is important for companies to keep pace with competitors by maintaining a similar rate of research and patenting activity. One company that has languished recently in patenting as well as in income is National Semiconductor Corp (see Exhibit 15-5). In 1995, it received more patents than either Micron or AMD, but its patenting activity remained at virtually the same level for the next five years. Over the same five-year period, overall revenues decreased to a level below their 1995 income.

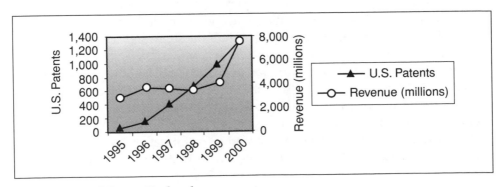

Exhibit 15-2   Micron Technology.

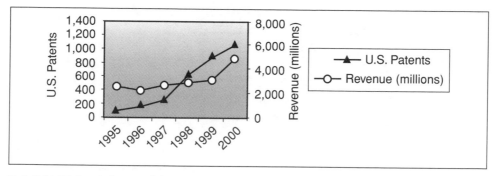

Exhibit 15-3 Advanced Micro Devices.

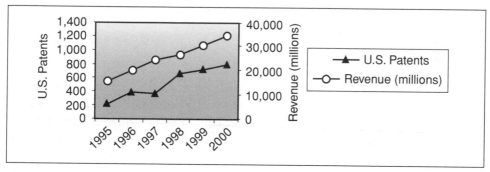

Exhibit 15-4 Intel.

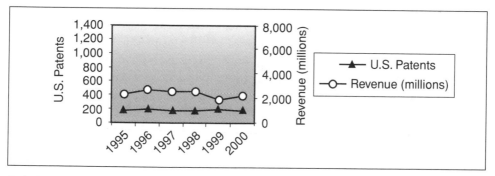

Exhibit 15-5 National Semiconductor Corp.

A small decrease in patenting in one year is not necessarily a sign of trouble, but a continuing trend deserves closer evaluation. In the case of LSI Logic Corporation, the total U.S. patents they received in 2000 dropped about 5 percent below their total for 1999 (see Exhibit 15-6). For the same period, however, the number of patents held by LSI in their core technology, semiconductor manufacturing, rose by more than 20 percent, so the reduction in overall output could be a temporary dip or perhaps a shift in focus. If the patenting rate remains flat or continues its downward trend, though, National Semiconductor's performance suggests that the future revenue growth of LSI might be in danger.

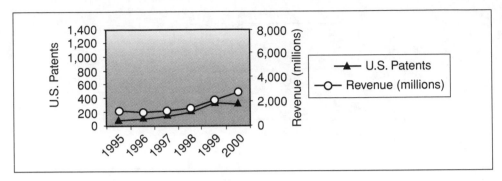

Exhibit 15-6   LSI Logic Corporation.

PHARMACEUTICALS

The requirements for a successful drug patent are more rigid than those for a product that does not directly affect human health. A marketable drug not only must cure, treat, or prevent an illness, but it must do so without harming the patient. Pharmaceutical products are subject to strict government regulation; rigorous testing by the Food and Drug Administration (FDA) will often uncover problems serious enough to deny approval for a new drug's use. If a patented product is not salable, a pharmaceutical company may decide that the relevant patents have no value to the company and there is no reason to pay maintenance fees to keep them active.

Patents for other types of products, such as computer hardware, may be more easily adapted to a variety of applications. If the first product incorporating an invention is not a success, the invention may still be useful in another application, or the patent may serve as the basis for more marketable improvements.

Because of the typically slow and steady rates of patent production by drug companies, the rate of patent issuance is quite stable, particularly since most pharmaceutical companies are well established and depend almost exclusively on patenting to maintain a profitable product line.

While the research and development phase for a pharmaceutical patent is both lengthy and expensive, the return on each patent is also higher than most. For the year 2000, the average revenue per active patent for six pharmaceutical companies ranged from $6.5 million for Eli Lilly, up to $25 million for Merck's patents (see Exhibits 15-7 through 15-10). Semiconductor companies, having a relatively large number of patents compared with pharmaceutical companies, showed a much lower return per patent, from $1.2 to $8.4 million per patent on average (see Exhibits 15-11 and 15-12).

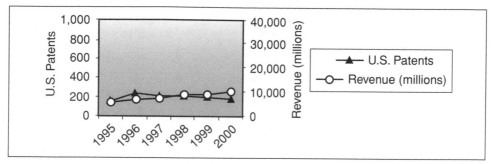

Exhibit 15-7 Eli Lilly and Company, Inc.

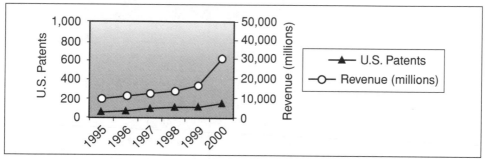

Exhibit 15-8 Pfizer Inc.

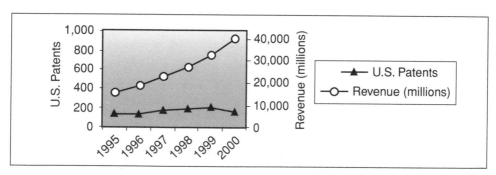

Exhibit 15-9 Merck & Co. Inc.

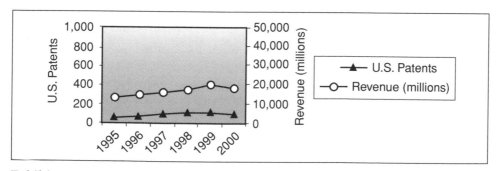

Exhibit 15-10 Bristol-Myers Squibb Co.

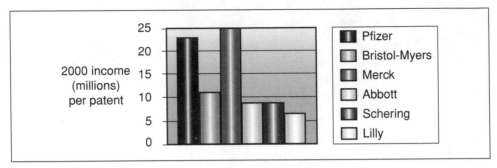

Exhibit 15-11   Income per patent—pharmaceuticals.

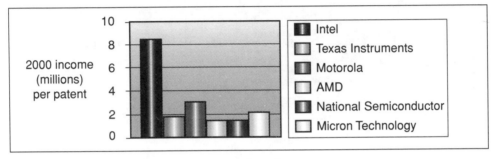

Exhibit 15-12   Income per patent—semiconductors.

BIOTECHNOLOGY

The biotechnology industry has characteristics of both the semiconductor and pharmaceutical industries. Like semiconductor technology, biotech is an area experiencing rapid growth. The growth curve in patenting is a result of increasing numbers of patents issued to companies already active in the area, as well as patents acquired by companies just starting research in the biotech area.

However, the number of pure biotech companies in the top rankings in the USPTO class for molecular biology is relatively small. The following list shows the top patenting organizations for USPTO class 435, Molecular Biology and Microbiology, where many biotech patents are classified. Established pharmaceutical companies, universities, and research institutes hold many of these patents.

Unlike many other high-growth tech sectors, there are relatively few non-U.S. companies in this group. The United States seems to have a clear lead in biotechnology patenting activity.

USPTO Class 435 Chemistry: Molecular Biology and Microbiology

Class 435 Patents in 2000	Patent Assignee
98	Incyte Pharmaceuticals Inc.
86	Smithkline Beecham Corp.
79	California, University of Regents
59	ISIS Pharmaceuticals, Inc.
57	Novo Nordisk A/S DK
39	Smithkline Beecham PLC GB
38	U S of America Health & Human Services
37	Johns Hopkins University
34	Chiron Corporation
32	Genentech, Inc.
29	Millennium Pharmaceuticals Inc.
28	Human Genome Sciences Inc.
25	Institut Pasteur FR
25	Roche Diagnostics Gmbh DE
25	Leland Jr. Stanford University Trustees
23	Abbott Laboratories Inc.
23	General Hospital Corp.
23	Rockefeller University
22	Eli Lilly and Co., Inc.
22	Ludwig Institute for Cancer Research
22	University of Michigan
21	Merck & Co., Inc.
19	Ajinomoto Co. Inc. JP
19	Columbia University
19	Dade Behring Marburg Gmbh DE
18	Affymetrix, Inc.
18	Becton Dickinson & Co.
18	President and Fellows of Harvard College
17	University of Texas System
16	Heska Corp.
15	Cornell Research Foundation Inc.
15	Genencor International Inc.
15	Institut National De La Sante et de la Recherche Medicale FR
15	The Scripps Research Institute

The question, of course, is whether patenting activity can help to predict income growth and future stability of a biotech company. The answer depends partly on the type of product being produced.

Most biotech products fall into one of three categories:

1. Treatments for disease
2. Agricultural products
3. Equipment, methods, and databases for doing genetic research

The first two categories, in particular, are subject to rigorous regulation and may require years of research and patenting before the first product is ready for market. The high barriers to entry and lengthy product development period typical of the pharmaceutical industry suggest that biotech companies developing therapeutic products will have patenting records similar to traditional drug companies.

One route to success for a biotech company in one of these two categories is acquisition by a larger company with existing product lines in those areas. The merger is mutually beneficial. The traditional pharmaceutical or chemical company acquires a ready-made biotech research unit with specialized equipment, expertise, and a patent portfolio. The biotech company benefits from the deep pockets as well as the product development and marketing experience of the larger company. A strong patent portfolio is an important asset when a company looks for acquisition candidates, particularly in the area of genetic research.

Two companies with successful drugs on the market are Genentech and Amgen (see Exhibits 15-13 and 15-14). While both have been steadily acquiring patents, their total patent holdings may be more significant than year-to-year variations. A solid collection of patents is important to future revenue growth for companies planning to market pharmaceutical or agricultural products, although the

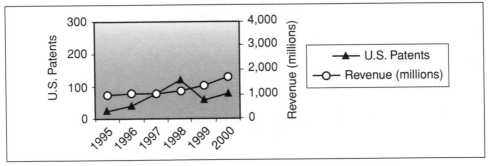

Exhibit 15-13   Genentech, Inc.

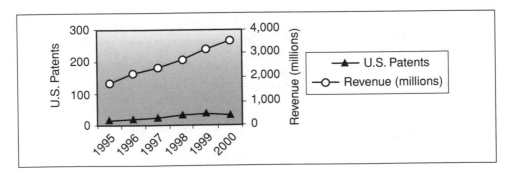

Exhibit 15-14   Amgen, Inc.

revenue may not be apparent for a number of years. Both Genentech and Amgen are in the following list, showing some of the top patent holders among biotech companies.

Total U.S. Patents

671	Genentech, Inc.
561	Incyte Pharmaceuticals Inc.
502	Pioneer Hi-Bred International, Inc.
406	Chiron Corporation
352	Isis Pharmaceuticals, Inc.
236	Amgen, Inc.
198	Zymogenetics Inc.
173	Immunex Corporation
165	Human Genome Sciences Inc.
135	Genzyme Corp.
71	Affymetrix, Inc.

In addition to companies producing therapeutic and agricultural products through genetic research, there are other companies that are selling the tools for genetic research. The market for these tools includes traditional pharmaceutical and agricultural chemistry companies, as well as biotech companies that are doing research in molecular biology.

While it is much easier to get these tools to market, it is important to protect the technology with patents, since competitors can also find a ready market for such tools. Incyte has been marketing databases of their patented genetic libraries for several years, and Affymetrix has patented DNA chips that a number of companies use (see Exhibits 15-15 and 15-16). Both Incyte and Affymetrix have shown steady patenting growth over the past five years, and will need to continue the trend to maintain a secure position in their businesses and stay ahead of the competition (see Exhibits 15-17 through 15-21).

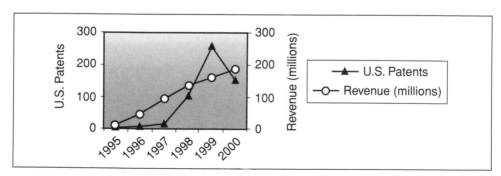

Exhibit 15-15   Incyte Pharmaceuticals.

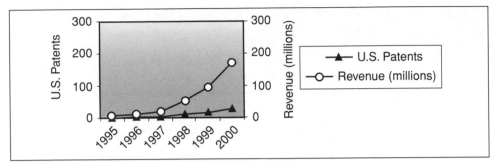

Exhibit 15-16   Affymetrix.

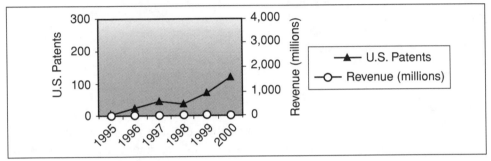

Exhibit 15-17   ISIS Pharmaceuticals.

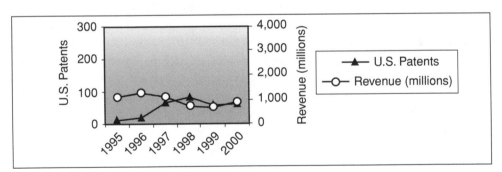

Exhibit 15-18   Chiron.

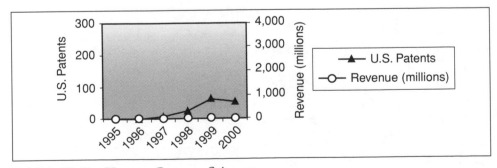

Exhibit 15-19   Human Genome Sciences.

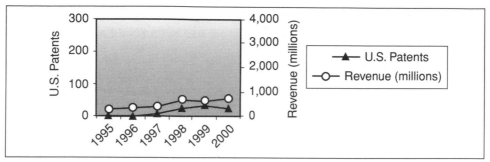

Exhibit 15-20 Genzyme, Inc.

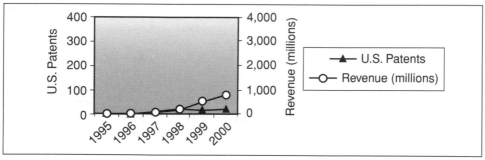

Exhibit 15-21 Immunex.

TELECOMMUNICATIONS

The telecommunications sector is rapidly expanding, as systems become more sophisticated and the demand for instant communication grows. Patents are a good indicator of technological strength for companies in the telecom business, particularly for those participating in the newer markets for wireless communication.

The relationship between patenting activity and revenue growth for companies in communications resembles that for the semiconductor businesses, with increases in patenting usually accompanied by rising income. The patenting leaders, including Nokia, Motorola, and Ericsson, all show this trend (see Exhibits 15-22 through 15-26).

Because of the rapid changes and diversification within the communications area, companies can often succeed by finding and exploiting a niche in the new technology. With this approach, smaller companies can focus on patenting within a narrow specialty to lock in much of the profit from that segment.

Qualcomm is leveraging its patents for Code Division Multiple Access (CDMA), digital wireless communications standard that encodes each call uniquely, by licensing this technology to all companies that need the CDMA technology in their wireless businesses. To guard against obsolescence, Qualcomm holds patents on several variations of the CDMA standard and is reaching into other segments of the business as well.

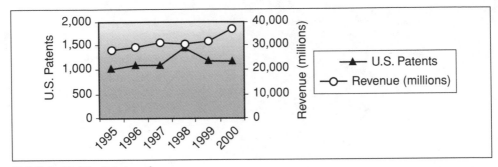

Exhibit 15-22 Motorola.

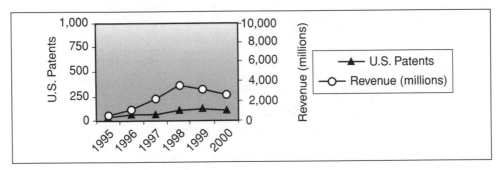

Exhibit 15-23 Qualcomm, Inc.

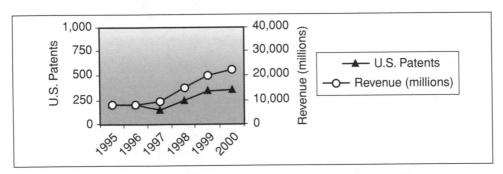

Exhibit 15-24 Nokia.

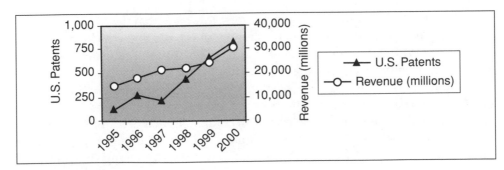

Exhibit 15-25 Ericsson.

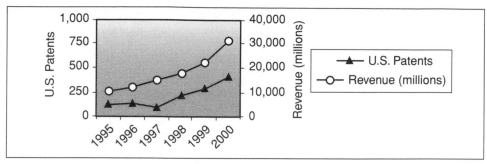

Exhibit 15-26   Nortel.

With a narrowly focused patenting strategy, however, Qualcomm and others risk losing their competitive advantages if an improved technology replaces the need for their patented systems. Companies with larger and more diversified patent portfolios, such as Motorola, are much less vulnerable to such changes.

PATENTS FOR AUTOMATED BUSINESS METHODS

In the United States, one can obtain a patent on a computer-implemented method of doing business. The USPTO has established class 705, titled Data Processing: Financial, Business Practice, Management, or Cost/Price Determination, for categorizing many of these business method patent applications.

Because patents in class 705 often relate to the Internet and e-commerce, one might expect that young Internet companies would own most of them. A look at the list of top patent holders in this class shows that most are owned by large, well-established tech companies, including IBM, Microsoft, and AT&T. Companies that sell business systems and machines are the best positioned to patent inventions for business methods, and investors should expect to see these companies grow. These patents can give a company an edge over others in the competitive e-commerce industry, and they can also be licensed or sold to others who need the new technology.

705 - Data Processing: Financial, Business Practice, Management, or Cost/Price Determination

Patents in 2000	Company
50	International Business Machines Corp. (IBM)
36	Pitney-Bowes Inc.
12	Fujitsu Ltd. JP
11	AT&T Corp.
11	Hitachi Ltd. JP
10	Microsoft Corp.
10	Citibank N A

Patents in 2000	Company
9	Walker Digital LLC
8	AT&T Global Information Solutions Co.
8	NCR Corp.
7	Lucent Technologies Inc.
7	Nortel Networks Corp. Ca
7	Walker Asset Management L P
6	Health Hero Network Inc.
6	Matsushita Electric Industrial Co. Ltd. JP
5	Electronic Data Systems Corp.
4	Gilbarco Inc.
4	Verifone Inc.
4	Mitsubishi Corp. JP
3	The Dow Chemical Co.
3	Francotyp-Postalia Ag & Co De
3	Hewlett-Packard Co.
3	Micron Electronics Inc.
3	Sun Microsystems Inc.
3	Toshiba Corp. JP

While larger companies are actively patenting technology in class 705, most of the patent holders in this class do not have large patent portfolios. Of the nearly 1800 companies with patents classified and cross-referenced in 705, over 1,300 own only one patent in the class. Some of those companies have patents in other technologies, but for others, this single patent represents their entire portfolio.

Unless a company owns a key patent that can be licensed or used to give the owner a clear business advantage, the acquisition of a single patent for a business method will probably not significantly affect the company revenues. Venture capitalists may look at intellectual property holdings, however, to judge the technical and IP savvy of a company, even if there are no revenues.

For some other businesses that do not usually hold patents, including banks, brokerages, greeting card companies, and mortgage companies, patent ownership is generally a positive indicator. Owning patents in the computer-aided business area shows that the companies are beginning to invest in intellectual property and are using the benefits of networking and computerization that will be a requirement for success in almost every business in the future.

SUMMARY

Patenting activity can be a useful indicator of company growth, particularly as a comparative measure. Because different industries have characteristic patenting behaviors, results are most meaningful when comparing similar companies within similar technologies.

While a rise in patent holdings is not a guarantee of future income growth, a continuing decline or even leveling off of patent growth is often a signal that a company's revenues may be at risk. Even a company that was a leader in its field can quickly lose ground to competitors when its level of patent protection begins to slide.

When viewed with the proper care and knowledge, a company's patent position can reveal much about the strength of its technology base as well as its prospects for steady revenue growth.

ABOUT THE AUTHOR

Darlene Slaughter, Manager of Technical Operations for IFI CLAIMS® Patent Services in Wilmington, Delaware, has been working in the patent information industry since 1975. She is involved in the production and development of IFI's specialized chemical patent database and is also active in customer service and training for clients who use IFI databases for patent research.

IFI CLAIMS® Patent Services (*www.ificlaims.com*) has been providing value-added U.S. patent information to the public for over 45 years. The CLAIMS online patent databases offer searchable access to over 3 million U.S. patent records granted since 1950. The databases include references to post-grant Patent Office actions that can affect the status or ownership of a patent, including premature expirations, term extensions, reassignments, and reexaminations. Since 1975, IFI has been publishing the annual *Patent Intelligence and Technology Report*, a statistical summary of the latest six years of U.S. patenting activity for over 1,600 companies. The report shows which companies are the most active in each technology or USPTO classification, as well as company trends.

CHAPTER SIXTEEN

The Economics of Patent Litigation

by Samson Vermont

PERSPECTIVES

Unreliable information about patent disputes often leads to poor business decisions. Poor decisions cost companies and shareholders. A science of decision making, a subdivision of the field of operations research called quantitative decision tree analysis, can make life a little easier for those affected by costly patent disputes. "Decision tree analysis helps us determine whether we should litigate or settle and for what amount," says Samson Vermont, patent attorney and writer.

Specifically, decision tree analysis applies mathematical and financial rigor to an area often obscured by emotions. It enables parties to (1) unbundle a problem into parts simple enough to comprehend, (2) weigh the relative significance of those parts, (3) systematically assign probabilities to them, (4) recompile all of our judgments about those parts, and (5) distill the problem to a few numbers, such as the dollar value of settling versus the dollar value of litigating.

Mr. Vermont's chapter is loaded with surprising statistics about the economics and probabilities of patent litigation, which deserve greater scrutiny by senior management and serious investors. A few facts:

- Applicants spend roughly more than $4.5 billion every year obtaining U.S. patents.
- At any give time, over 95 percent of patents are unlicensed and over 97 percent are generating no royalties.
- On average, large companies obtain one patent for every $4.26 million they spend on research and development. IP-intensive companies spend $2.08 million in R&D for every patent.

- Patent suits filed in 2000 will generate roughly $4.2 billion in legal fees before they are resolved.
- In the last five years 11,000 patent suits were filed in the United States. More than half failed to settle within the first 12 months.
- Awards for patent damages are growing rapidly. The total amount awarded in the 1990s was double the total amount awarded in the 1980s, and the average of all the awards from 1996 to 1999 was 55 percent higher than the average of all the awards from 1992 to 1995.
- For reported cases, the average award over the 1990s was $14 million. Reported awards, however, tend to be higher than unreported awards, which outnumber reported awards by almost four to one. (Patent awards have run as high as $1 billion.)
- A company's market value can drop by 2.0 to 3.1 percent within two days of a report of its involvement in a patent suit. One study found an average loss of shareholder value of $67.9 million.
- Only 6.9 percent of patent suits were tried in the last 20 years. However, virtually all of those that settle are settled in light of what would likely happen at trial. (All bargaining takes place in the shadow of the law.)

INTRODUCTION

Seventy-six percent of patent suits settle,[1] but not before each side incurs more than $1 million in direct legal fees and indirect expenses.[2] Usually what we could have settled for at the outset is no better or worse than the deal we accept down the road.[3] So the question arises: if most of us are going to settle anyway, why not do so before incurring the costs?

This appears to be easier to say than to do because in the last five years, 11,000 patent suits were filed in the United States[4] and more than half remained unresolved after the first 12 months.[5] The difficulty in settling early stems from divergence between the parties in information and expectation.[6] Theory and evidence suggest that parties tend to litigate when at least one side is overly optimistic about its case[7]; they tend to settle when their information and expectation converge, at the point they both become realistic.[8] When approached conventionally, this convergence comes slowly since each side must first gradually develop a feel for, or a judge's ruling must indicate, which way the case might go at trial.[9]

Again, one reason for this delay is sheer optimism and bias.[10] For example, intellectual property damage experts say that patent owners often dramatically overestimate the recoverable damages and defendants typically underestimate them.[11] Litigants are not disabused of these false hopes early in the process. Although 85 percent of patent attorneys claim to start valuation of the case before filing, damage experts are hired before filing only about 19 percent of the time.[12]

(All patent litigators agree that a damage expert must be hired prior to the close of discovery.[13] In fact, one third generally hire more than one damage expert.[14])

Another reason the feel for case value is tardy is that the human mind is bad at manipulating large numbers of interrelated and uncertain variables.[15] Indeed, the average person cannot hold, much less manipulate, more than seven things in his mind at once, which is one reason that phone numbers have seven digits.[16]

Ben Franklin articulated these cognitive limitations in 1772:

> When those difficult cases occur, they are difficult, chiefly because while we have them under consideration, all the reasons pro and con are not present to the mind at the same time; but sometimes some set present themselves, and at other times another, the first being out of sight. Hence the various purposes or inclinations that alternately prevail, and the uncertainty that perplexes us.[17]

These obstacles have given rise to a science of decision making, a subdivision of the field of operations research called decision analysis. This chapter introduces a subdivision of that subdivision—quantitative decision tree analysis. Decision tree analysis helps us determine whether we should settle or litigate and if the former, for what amount. If the latter, it helps us focus and strategize.

More specifically, decision tree analysis enables us to:

1. Decompose a problem into parts simple enough for our minds to wrap around
2. Weigh the relative significance of those parts
3. Systematically assign probabilities to them
4. Recompile all of our judgments
5. Boil the whole problem down to a few numbers, such as the dollar value of settling versus the dollar value of litigating[18]

We'll first evaluate the general costs and benefits of patents and patent litigation. These evaluations serve as vehicles for the presentation of little-known patent facts and statistics,[19] some of which we will later plug into our decision trees—Baby Tree, Mama Tree, and Papa Tree. We'll then take a short break from the onslaught of numbers and review the basics of decision analysis. Finally, we'll set up a hypothetical patent suit and climb into the decision trees. The sections of the chapter devoted to the trees also double as vehicles for the presentation of facts and figures. The object is to learn the numbers while learning how to manipulate them.

THE LAST BARRIER

Patents are more important than they used to be[20] because the confluence of the Internet, global venture capital, and cultural changes have eroded other traditional barriers to entry. Eroding barriers include:

- *Capital formation.* It used to be that the biggest bank account would often win because the competition simply couldn't gather the funds to build factories, finance start-up operations, and so on. Capital formation is easier now.
- *Recruiting and retention of key employees.* Never have employees been so mobile and quick to jump ship for a slightly better offer.
- *Proprietary distribution systems.* Even when competitors developed better products at a better price, they often lacked access to customers; they lacked the requisite bricks and mortar facilities to physically put the product in front of the buyer.
- *Proprietary supplier relationships.* Big companies, or companies established in a niche, used to incur relatively low supply costs because they could buy in bulk and/or enjoyed close relationships with vendors. Now, via aggregation through the Internet and other means, new entrants can also buy at a discount.[21]

So companies are wringing more out of intellectual property.[22] Accordingly, while about 108,000 U.S. patent applications were filed in 1980, about 289,000 were filed in 1999,[23] and the rate of increase is increasing. From 1990 to 1994, a five-year period, filings increased 17 percent (meaning that the number of patents filed in 1994 was 17 percent higher than the number filed in 1990). From 1997 to 1999, a three-year period, filings increased 25 percent and issuances increased 61 percent.[24] Aside from an economic downturn,[25] there is no reason to expect this to stop. Nor is the phenomenon limited to the United States, although filings in most other countries have risen less dramatically. For example, filings in the European Patent Office (EPO) increased 40 percent from 1990 to 1999.[26]

Licensing revenues have risen even faster than patent filings. From 1980 to 1999, U.S. patent licensing revenues increased about 4,000 percent.[27] Patent suits are also giving chase. The number of patent suits is growing more than three times faster than the number of nonpatent civil suits.[28] For example, in 1991 just over 1,178 patent suits were filed.[29] Throughout the 1990s, patent suits increased on average about 8 percent each year[30] such that, in the year 2000, 2,486 were filed.[31]

Awards are also up. The total amount awarded in the 1990s was double the total amount awarded in the 1980s,[32] which well exceeds the cumulative inflation from the 1980s to the 1990s of about 30 percent.[33] Also, the cumulative average of all awards from 1996 to 1999 was 55 percent higher than the cumulative average of all awards from 1992 to 1995.[34]

PATENT COSTS AND BENEFITS

Nevertheless, patents are not always a good investment. They're often narrowed substantially during prosecution through the Patent Office,[35] ending up much narrower than people think. In some areas, such as software, the technology may

be moving so fast that it overtakes the prosecution process. The average time in prosecution for all patents is 2.8 years, the median is 2.2 years.[36] (For patents that end up being litigated, it's 3.6 years on average and 2.7 years at the median.[37])

Other disadvantages of patents include: they expire; competitors can often design around them in just a few years; to enforce them you must litigate or at least threaten to litigate; and they're often invalidated in litigation. Companies must, of course, recoup the expenses of R&D, but studies indicate that more is recouped from the inherent lead time that R&D garners and by the complementary sales and services it facilitates.[38] Plus, patents disclose a great deal of proprietary information that may be better protected through secrecy, which lasts forever and can provide broader protection than patents, which cannot protect unoriginal subject matter.[39] Trade secret misappropriation is also easier to prove in many cases.[40]

On the other hand, trade secrets must remain secret. So, they cannot be marketed or directly enhance company valuation. They also provide no protection against independent development. If some other company develops the same subject matter, only a patent can stop that company from using, selling, or making it. Finally, since maintaining secrecy can impose onerous procedures and increase bureaucracy, the costs of trade secrets are very indirect and may therefore be underestimated.

In contrast, the legal fees for patents are more conspicuous, and surprisingly reasonable. Unlike litigation, which must always be customized for the client, patent prosecution is something of a commodity in that it entails well-defined, standard procedures that predictably result in specific products (patents). In other words, market forces can fully work their magic because law firms can tacitly or overtly bid against each other and because companies can meaningfully compare those bids.

Accordingly, it is well known that patent prosecution has lower margins than other legal specialties. When you think about it, it's moderately remarkable that a professional—with degrees in both law and science, good writing skills, and at least two bar memberships—will spend a whole week or two intensively drafting your patent and only charge you $3,000 to $12,000.[41] (To prosecute the application to issuance generally costs about another $2,000 to $7,000 in attorney fees[42] and $2,500 in Patent Office fees. The Patent Office maintenance fees on an issued patent cost another $3,000 for the first 11.5 years and $3,000 for the remaining life of the patent's 20-year term. But only about 37 percent of patents are maintained until the end of their term,[43] and the Patent Office fees are cut in half for small entities having fewer than 500 employees.[44])

It is also true that the nation's aggregate costs of patent prosecution are dwarfed by its aggregate patent license revenues. Applicants spend about $4.5 billion every year obtaining U.S. patents.[45] In 2000, annual patent license revenues reached about $130 billion.[46] At very first glance, this implies a profit margin of 2,900 percent (i.e., $130/4.5 = 29 \times 100$ percent). The real costs behind patents, however, are not the legal fees, but the R&D that creates the inventions on which those patents are based. On average, spending on intellectual property is only 2.5 percent of spending on R&D.[47] Arguably, the value of patents is only the difference between the value of the technology if patented and the value if not patented, minus the cost of the patents.

At any given time, over about 95 percent of patents are unlicensed and over about 97 percent are generating no royalties.[48] This is often because the technology the patents protect is not useful, feasible, or marketable. Many are never licensed, however, because the companies that own them secure more value by monopolizing the technology than by licensing it out.[49]

In other words, many people would argue that most of the value of patents comes not from what you actually collect from licensing but from the market advantage they secure. The real value lies in all the things your competitors could not do: they could not move into market X, they could not offer feature Y. Indeed, most areas of the law share this dynamic. For example, only about 1 percent of taxpayers is audited, and the real value of audits is not the revenue collected directly therefrom but the revenue collected from the rest of us who fear an audit.

At least one study suggests that, apart from effects due to licensing income, there is a positive, albeit marginal, relationship between companies' stock prices and the quality of their patent portfolios.[50] In fact, a patent for a method of picking stocks based on patent quality recently issued. The owner (CHI Research, Inc.) claims its approach generated an average annual gain of 38 percent over 10 years, compared to the S&P 500 Index average annual gain of 16 percent and the NASDAQ's 25 percent.[51]

Another piece of evidence that patents are worth more than their licensing potential is the fact that 37 percent of U.S. patents are renewed 11.5 years after they issue.[52] Since far fewer than 37 percent of patents are licensed, licensing cannot be everything.

Some say that intangible assets now account for two thirds of corporate value.[53] Others say it's more than 85 percent.[54] Unfortunately, no one knows what portion of that two thirds or 85 percent is attributable to patents as opposed to trade secrets, copyrights, trademarks, customer lists, know-how, goodwill, and the like. There is a crude way, however, to roughly estimate the value of patents. On average, a large company obtains one patent for every $4.26 million it spends on R&D.[55] (IP-intensive companies spend $2.08 million in R&D for every patent.[56]) Therefore, the average patent cannot be worth more than $4.26 million.[57] Actually, it must be worth much less because most of the benefits of R&D are appropriated through other means, such as secrecy and first-mover advantage.[58]

On the other hand, we also know that the average patent cannot be worth much less than the average cost of filing and prosecution, which is about $20,000 (including everything) for the roughly 80 to 85 percent of U.S. patentees who don't file a corresponding application overseas.[59] If patents *were* worth much less, people wouldn't apply for them. As a starting point, therefore, we know with some certainty that the average value of patents is somewhere between $20,000 and $4.26 million.

We can narrow this range. Since U.S. patents provide an "implicit subsidy" (a return) on R&D of about 15 percent,[60] the average patent should be worth somewhere around $640,000 ($4.26M × .15).[61] This figure of $640,000 is probably not too far off. There are about 2.75 million patents that issued less than 20 years ago and about 1.3 million of them are active,[62] meaning their maintenance fees have been paid. If patent licensing revenues are $130 billion per year, then the average patent would seem to generate $100,000 per year from licensing alone ($130 billion/1.3 million). Now consider that the average *effective* life of a patent—that is, the average time until the product or feature it covers in the marketplace is replaced by a better product—is only about five years from the date it issues. Assuming licensed patents are licensed for four of those five years[63] and discounting *pro rata* to present value at 10 percent from a date four years from today, we obtain a lifetime licensing value of $326,000 for an issued patent.[64] If the market advantage of patents generates as much value as patent licensing, then we're up to about $640,000 (2 × $326 = $652,000).

It's a self-evident truth, however, that all patents are created unequal. One study found that the bottom 50 percent of patents account for only about 10 percent of aggregate patent value, while the top 10 percent of patents account for at least 40 percent of it.[65] (This is probably too generous to the bottom 50 percent.[66]) In other words, to say the average patent is worth around $640,000 is misleading because the vast majority are worth very little. High values skew up the average. Recall your middle school math teacher: If you add together the income of 99 people who each make $30,000 per year and one other person who makes $100 million per year, the *average* income for this group is over $1 million.

Thus, companies should avoid patent portfolio socialism. To the extent they can predict which of their inventions will be important, they should spend a great deal more for patent applications on those inventions—at least three times more. For important inventions, applicants should perform prior art searches[67] before filing,[68] and the applications should be detailed, containing around 50 claims or so.[69] As a rule of thumb, if your attorneys are charging you less than $15,000 to draft each important application, then the applications probably aren't good enough.

The numbers in the last two sentences ought to be doubled for important biotech, chemical, and pharmaceutical applications because a number of studies show that patents in these areas are almost twice as valuable as patents for electrical, mechanical, and business method inventions.[70] One reason is that discovering, testing, and obtaining approval for "the microscopic inventions" is extremely expensive, difficult, and slow—on average it takes $500 million and 14 years to go from discovery to government approval of a new drug[71]—but making them is relatively cheap, easy, and fast. So for these inventions, the protection patents afford is more valuable.

The greater value is also due to the fact that the microscopic inventions often stand alone as buyable products, so if a patent covers the invention, it covers the whole product that is sold. In contrast, electronic devices often contain a multitude of parts from a multitude of manufacturers, so a patent on any one part cannot monopolize the device. Accordingly, applicants spend almost twice as much for biotech, chemical, and pharmaceutical patents[7]; these patents are litigated almost twice as often[73] (except chemical); and they take almost twice as long to get through the Patent Office.[74]

PATENT LITIGATION COSTS

Only 1.1 percent of all U.S. patents are ever litigated,[75] but when they are it's notoriously expensive.[76] For instance, by the time they're all disposed of, the patent suits filed in 2000 will alone generate roughly $4.2 billion in legal fees.[77]

Patent litigation is expensive for three main reasons. First, patent law is one of the most ever-changing and vexing areas of the law, [78] and patent litigation entails legal and technical issues that are subtle to the point of evanescence.[79] Its complexity is reflected in the length of patent trials. Patent cases make up about 0.57 percent of all civil cases in the federal courts, but over 9.4 percent that require a trial of 20 days or more.[80]

Second, the stakes are often so high that the legal fees do not seem high *in comparison*; so companies put the legal pedal to the metal. This modus operandi is justified insofar as the additional legal costs generate commensurate litigation advantages. (This is not a given since attorney effort often exhibits diminishing returns and, like anything, the pareto principle applies—20 percent of the work generates 80 percent of the results.[81]) This approach is unjustified, however, insofar as it reflects the framing effect—a cognitive bias by which people become less price-sensitive with regard to relatively small purchases when making relatively large purchases. For example, people are less resistant to buying a fancy car stereo when buying a car because the stereo purchase seems small in comparison to the car purchase. They are more price sensitive when buying only a stereo even though, all other things equal, they have more disposable income (because they did not also buy a car).[82] Accordingly, when a plaintiff is trying to "buy" a $20 million verdict and the defendant is trying to "buy" the opposite, monthly legal bills for $100,000 don't seem so bad.

Third, some attorneys divorce litigation from their clients' business goals.[83] This afflicts every type of litigation (except perhaps contingency fee litigation). One reason is that lawyers benefit more from protracted litigation than early settlement. This is not to say that lawyers consciously avoid settlement. Rather, it may simply be a matter of professional evolution. Firms that facilitate early settlement make less money and, all other things equal, may eventually be selected out of the financially competitive world of law.[84] Another reason is that lawyers arguably do too good a job. Long ago lawyers created for themselves a crowning but ultimately self-serving virtue: "A lawyer should represent a client zealously."[85] In other words, there shall be no such thing as purposefully mediocre legal representation. No lawyer may sell Ford Escort representation; every client must receive Cadillac representation (or none at all[86]). This demand for quality, which has been the battle cry of guilds throughout history,[87] encourages some lawyers to adopt an aggressive, absolutist, cost-be-damned approach. For them, every fact must be checked, rechecked, and checked again. For them, every possible argument, legal theory, and cause of action must be pressed, and the fact that some have but a minuscule chance of success is almost irrelevant as long as they have some chance.

Alas, the median legal fees for litigating a patent case through trial is about $2 million per side and increasing.[88] We will revisit these costs in much greater detail.

DECISION ANALYSIS PRIMER

Only 6.9 percent of patent suits were tried in the last 20 years and only 4 percent or so will be tried in the coming years.[89] But 100 percent of those that settle are settled in light of what would likely happen at trial. All bargaining takes place in the shadow of the law. Therefore, determining possible judgments and the chances of obtaining or avoiding them is the best indicator of settlement value. Each party must estimate the outcome and its chances, and value the former in light of the latter. Just as a gambler should understand that a one-in-four chance of winning $100 is worth $25, a litigant should understand that a 25 percent chance of winning a $100 million judgment has an "expected value" (probability-weighted average value) of $25 million, assuming no transaction costs, no discounting (e.g., for the time value of money), and no other possible benefits or costs.

Decision analysis helps determine expected value in complex situations and can account for discounting risk aversion and less conspicuous benefits and costs. The essence of decision analysis is to divide and conquer, in order to clarify uncertainties, evaluate risks, grapple with tough trade-offs, and make a series of linked decisions in the right sequence.[90]

As shown in the exhibits, time flows from left to right in a decision tree. At the root of the tree is a "decision node" (usually square), from which emanates option branches such as "litigate" or "settle." These option branches are typically followed by a series of circular "chance nodes" that signify uncertainties and from which emanate "event branches" such as "valid" versus "invalid." Each path through the tree eventually ends with a triangular "terminal node" representing a final outcome or payoff, like a $5 million judgment.

Probabilities are assigned to branches emanating from chance nodes and are placed below the branch line of the event they represent. The probabilities must sum to 100 percent. They should be assessed as "conditional" probabilities. That is, probabilities should be assigned to particular branches under the assumption that the events and decisions to the left of the branch in question have already occurred.

To calculate or "roll back" a decision tree, one works backward, from right to left. The value of each node is determined as follows:

- The value of a terminal node is equal to the value of its payoff.
- The value of a chance node is equal to its expected value, which is found by (a) taking the value of the node located immediately to the right of

each event branch emanating from the chance node, (b) multiplying each node value by its event branch's probability, and then (c) adding the products together.

• The value of a decision node is equal to the value of its best option. Thus, if a plaintiff's two options are "litigate" and "settle," and if the expected value of litigating is $5 million and the value of settling is $4 million, then the value of the decision node is $5 million.[91]

In sum, the first goal is to build a tree that visually depicts the major choices, the events that could follow, the probabilities of those events occurring, and the consequences if they do.

Of course, these are the bare bones of tree analysis. A full exploration of the field of decision analysis is far beyond the scope of this chapter. Nevertheless, following is a sampler of common decision analysis issues, tools, and techniques.

Scope of Analysis

A good decision analysis is straightforward and flexible, acknowledges both subjective and objective factors, blends analytical with intuitive thinking, and requires only as much information and analysis as is necessary to resolve the particular dilemma.[92] A good decision analysis also focuses on fundamental ends and takes care not to confound them with their means. Otherwise, double counting inflates the importance of those ends.

Decision analysts universally recommend keeping it as simple as possible. For example, Marc Victor's guiding principle is that the tree should mirror the judge's or jury's level of analysis, and should avoid capturing the minutiae that lawyers often spend much time exploring but which judges and juries won't use to arrive at their ultimate rulings and verdicts.[93]

Studies show that decision trees are quite robust and, except for one or two crucial variables, small alterations in estimated probabilities or payoffs won't reverse the overall superiority of one option over another. Fine tuning is more justified, however, when the options are not a simple yes or no but involve a continuous variable[94] with no clear boundaries, as in "How much money should we offer?"

An acceptable decision tree can usually be drawn up in 1 to 10 days if the experts and decision makers are available, but in complex and very high stakes cases it may take several weeks.[95]

Countering Biases

Analysts must mitigate motivational and cognitive biases[96] such as overemphasis on recent data; availability (which refers to considering events that are easy to visualize as more probable)[97]; representativeness (which refers to placing more confidence in a single piece of information that is considered representative rather than in a larger body of generalized information); ignoring regression to the mean (which refers to expecting extremes to follow extremes)[98]; overestimating the probability of conjunctive events (e.g., not appreciating that if seven independent events are each 90 percent likely to occur, the chances of all occurring is only 48 percent, i.e., $.9 \times .9 \times .9 \times .9 \times .9 \times .9 \times .9$); misjudging the probability of disjunctive events (e.g., not appreciating that if 10 machines have a $1/100$ chance of failing, the odds that one will fail is almost $1/10$); supra-additivity (when asked for large numbers of *mutually exclusive* and exhaustive probability assessments, the sum of subjects' assessments often exceeds 100 percent)[99]; and others.

Anchoring is one of the most prevalent biases.[100] It refers to the fact that people tend to cluster their answers around an initial number. For example, imagine you ask an expert "Given these conditions, what is the award amount that is at the 50th percentile, at which half of awards fall below and half fall above?" You then say "What is the amount at the 60th percentile?" And then "What is the amount at the 70th percentile?" Many studies show that the estimate of the 60th, 70th, and every percentile thereafter will tend to be closer to the 50th percentile than if, for example, you first asked "What is the amount at the upper 90th percentile?" This bias is so robust that even when a computer generates a random number, and the subject is told it's random, the subject will still tend to cluster answers around it. To counter anchoring, analysts initially avoid the medians and jump around unpredictably in their questioning. For example, they start at the 95th percentile, then ask about the bottom 10th, then about the 65th, and so on.

Another prevalent bias is overconfidence, especially with regard to underestimating the range of probabilities.[101] In other words, people usually estimate ranges that are too narrow. To counter this, analysts postulate extremely favorable and unfavorable results, and then ask the expert to work backward to explain the chain of events that could lead to those results. Indeed, if the expert hasn't thought through the bases for his or her estimates, they're of little value. Therefore, before eliciting probabilities, analysts commonly prime experts by asking them to create comprehensive lists of reasons that support or underlie estimates they will soon proffer.[102]

Studies show that even when we're aware of biases, they still affect us. So if you plan to incorporate your own estimated probabilities, do so before you hear others' estimates of probabilities, but preferably after you hear their list of reasons.[103]

Clarity

Obtaining good probabilities requires unambiguous questions and numerical answers. Do not ask: "Do you think the event is very likely, likely, unlikely, or very unlikely?" People ascribe decidedly different meanings to terms such as likely, probably, doubtful, expected, and possible. In one study, participants were asked to rank 10 such terms in decreasing order of uncertainty. "Likely" ranged from second place to seventh place, while "unlikely" ranged from third to tenth.[104]

Also, avoid asking for percentages when you're inquiring about increases or decreases. For example, imagine some legal outcome has happened 10 percent of the time historically, but a new court decision makes that outcome more probable. If you ask lawyers "By what percent did the decision increase the chances of the outcome?" some might say "20 percent" and mean that the initial 10 percent will increase by 20 percent to become 12 percent ($1.2 \times .10$). Others will say "20 percent" and mean that the 10 percent will triple to become 30 percent (10 + 10 +10). Others will say "20 percent" and mean that the 20 percent *replaces* the 10 percent, thereby doubling the initial 10 percent.

When possible, frame probability questions in terms of frequencies: "If it occurred 10 times out of 100 before, how many times out of 100 will it occur now?"

Weighting Averages

In major litigation, it's best to obtain probability estimates from up to (but usually no more than) five individuals.[105] Since some individuals are more experienced and have better judgment than others, analysts must sometimes[106] determine who has the best judgment and to what extent to weight it, using factors such as the individual's confidence in his own particular judgment; colleagues' confidence in the individual's judgment; the analyst's confidence in the individual's judgment; and objective indicators such as years of experience and other credentials. For our decision trees, we'll use actual average and median figures, rather than quantifying the judgment of an expert.

Sensitivity Analysis

It's usually the case that some variables are much more important or volatile than others. Sensitivity analysis entails holding every variable constant except one, and then changing the value of that one to measure its effects on overall expected value.

Sensitivity analysis prunes issues by telling us which uncertainties are most crucial and where we should focus on eliciting more realistic probabilities. It also tells us where to allocate legal resources to change outcomes. In a patent suit, for example, sensitivity analysis may indicate that the possibility of infringement under the doctrine of equivalents is 10 times more crucial than the possibility of willfulness damages, which counsels in favor of shifting attention from the latter to the former. Or, we may want to know how much of an increase in the probability of infringement liability is justified per unit decrease in the probability of lost profit damages (as opposed to reasonable royalty damages).[107]

In a real case, sensitivity analysis is a must. "Its importance cannot be overstated."[108]

Value of Control

To determine how much to spend on various pre-trial activities, analysts ask: "What is the most we would be willing to pay a wizard to guarantee a certain holding or outcome?"[109] For example, how much would we pay to guarantee that our patent will be deemed valid? To determine this value, analysts who have performed an initial tree analysis change the probability of the event to 100 percent and then roll back the tree again. This gives the expected value of the tree with perfect control, which, when subtracted from the original expected value of the tree, leaves the value of perfect control.

To determine the value of imperfect control, they ask, for example, "How much would we pay to decrease the possibility of liability by 15 percent?" Analysts then change the original probability of the event (X percent) to the new value (X – 15 percent) and roll back the tree.

Value of Information[110]

Determining the value of information is particularly useful in patent suits because discovery accounts for the brunt of their costs. Paying lawyers to pursue discovery is nothing more than purchasing information and evidence. As with any other purchase, we should estimate the value of what we're purchasing.

Determining this value begins with determining the value of "perfect" information. That is, after we've constructed a decision tree, we pick a chance node we're interested in and we ask, "If a clairvoyant could tell us with perfect certainty whether an event will occur, how much would that information be worth?" That worth is determined by a technique similar (but not identical) to the technique for determining the value of perfect control.

The value of perfect information sets a ceiling. If you're spending more than the value of a particular batch of perfect information to discover that information, you're spending too much. Analysts estimate the value of imperfect information by discounting the value of perfect information by the estimated quality of the imperfect information.

Software

In the pages that follow, we'll run through tree analyses more or less manually, doing most of our own arithmetic. Decision analysis computer programs can automate some of these calculations. Such programs include @RISK, Precision Tree, Expert Choice, DPL, HIVIEW, and others. By far the most popular package among lawyers is DATA by TreeAge Software Inc., screen shots from which constitute the exhibits shown later in the chapter.

Other Tools

Analysts use a variety of devices to visually depict or elicit probabilities. The most common is the probability wheel, which is simply a pie chart with two pie slices, one of which can be adjusted to decrease or increase its size relative to the other slice. One slice represents the probability that the event in question will occur; the other slice represents the probability that it won't. The analyst changes the size of the first slice until the expert intuitively feels that it represents the correct probability. Despite its goofy simplicity, research shows that it's the best way to obtain a realistic probability. Computer programs such as DATA often include electronic probability wheels.

A HYPOTHETICAL CASE

Imagine we represent a company that recently filed a patent suit, in which the defendant just offered to settle for $500,000.[111] (In 15 percent of cases, alleged infringers file declaratory actions and are technically plaintiffs.[112] By "plaintiff," however, I mean the patent owner, also called the patentee or patent holder.) We'd like to avoid legal fees and expenses so we start thinking about the case's settlement value, but soon find ourselves deluged by innumerable variables and fundamental uncertainties.

Fundamental legal uncertanties that usually arise include those surrounding claim interpretation, literal infringement, infringement under the doctrine of equivalents, prosecution history estoppel, patent validity, and inequitable conduct. All of these issues contain subissues. For example, patents may be invalidated on various grounds, including those that relate to the one-year statutory bar, prior art, failure to name the correct inventor, failure to disclose the best mode of the invention, failure to enable an ordinary artisan to make the invention based on the disclosure in the patent, and other reasons. Similarly, patents can be rendered unenforceable (effectively invalid) for inequitable conduct if the plaintiff can show that the defendant withheld material information from the Patent Office, that the withholding was intentional, that the Patent Office didn't already have equivalent or better information, and that the defendant has "clean hands" (is not the bad guy). Of course, all of these subissues contain their own myriad of sub-subissues.

Damages, which *must* be estimated to determine settlement value, raise another host of questions. Will the damages be based on lost profits, reasonable royalties, or both? Will there be willfulness damages? What is the amount of lost revenues, the appropriate market share for the plaintiff, the definition of the market, the elasticity of demand, the portion of the infringing product attributable to the patented invention, the going license royalty in the precise market at issue, the appropriate prejudgment interest rate, and so on, for a good long while? And there are always numerous questions about evidence and procedure.

So we turn to decision analysis. Our goal is to determine and compare the expected value of litigation and the value of settlement. Thus, the option branches in all of the trees are "litigate" and "settle." Baby Tree is simple, overly so. Mama Tree refines both the chances of success on the merits and likely outcomes. Papa Tree focuses mainly on outcomes and costs. It models not only what the plaintiff stands to gain, but also what the defendant stands to lose—its expected value (cost) of litigation and settlement. Thus, as discussed below, Papa Tree is really two separate trees. By the time we finish the Papa Trees, we will have taken almost everything imaginable into account with regard to outcomes and costs.

For pedagogical reasons, we'll look at what happens generally by using the average and median numbers available in the empirical literature on patents, which is sparse and scattered. Most of the numbers represent the combined and weighted statistics from both judge and jury trials.

Note that the use here of median and average money damages is not an endorsement of using them when evaluating a real case. For success on the merits (the chances of a verdict of infringement or invalidity), median and average numbers *are* informative. Before a defendant gets too excited about its inequitable conduct defense, it should know that only about 11 percent of all patent trials ultimately result in a finding of unenforceability.[113] Median and average award numbers, however, are less useful for estimating likely damages in a particular case because damages are so variable. They can range from one dollar to $1 billion depending entirely on circumstances such as the size of the companies and the market at issue.[114] In a real case, therefore, the judgment of experts *should* be quantified for success on the merits, but it *must* be quantified for damages.

Baby Tree

Baby Tree has two option branches (litigate or settle) and two event branches (win or lose). At the terminal node of the settle branch is the defendant's offer of $500,000 (see Exhibit 16-1).

Recent research shows that patentees prevail 58 percent of the time *at trial*.[115] More specifically, they prevail 51 percent of the time in a bench trial and 68 percent of the time in a jury trial.[116] (Although the number of trials is fairly evenly divided between judges and juries,[117] this is going to change as this recently unearthed disparity becomes widely known. After all, alleged infringers win less than one third of the time before juries. Recent research also shows that plaintiff win rates vary enormously depending on the forum and whether the patent owner or alleged infringer first files the case.[118]) So we put 0.58 under the win branch and 0.42 under the lose branch. The tree is now complete with regard to probabilities of success on the merits. We must now determine the outcomes to which these probabilities are applied.

The average award over the 1990s for reported cases was $14 million.[119] The award amounts for reported cases, however, tend to exceed the award amounts for unreported cases, but there are almost twice as many unreported as reported

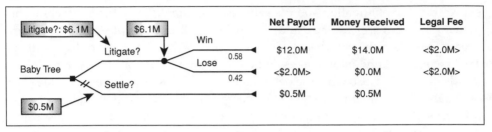

Exhibit 16-1   Baby tree.

cases.[120] Plus, in 1990 Polaroid slapped Kodak with an $873 million judgment,[121] which skews the average over the entire decade from $10 million to $14 million. For the last few years, however, the average reported award has been around $20 million[122]; so $14 million is probably a reasonable figure and we'll use it.

Consistent with the simplicity of Baby Tree, we take the average patent award of $14 million and subtract the median legal costs of $2 million for a first-scenario net payoff of $12 million. We then put the legal fees at the terminal end of the "lose" branch for a second scenario net payoff of negative $2 million. (The negative values are enclosed in greater/less than symbols.)

Now we roll back the tree. We multiply the first net payoff by 0.58 percent, the result of which is $7 million. We then multiply the second payoff by 0.42 percent, which is –$840,000. To determine the expected value of litigating, we add together these two products. Since the result, $6.1 million, exceeds the $500,000 offer, Baby Tree indicates the plaintiff (us) should continue litigating.

MAMA TREE

Validity

The first uncertainty (chance node) in Mama Tree is between validity and invalidity. At trial, plaintiffs face a 33 percent chance that their patents will be invalidated.[123] We may adjust this figure downward, however, because about 15 percent of cases are thrown out by judges before trial,[124] and roughly half of that 15 percent (8 percent) are thrown out for invalidity.[125] Also, 38 percent of all validity-related verdicts are appealed.[126] The Federal Circuit overturns these validity-related verdicts 22 percent of the time.[127] Much of this 22 percent, however, constitutes successful appeals by the alleged infringers—all that matters here is the difference between the rate of reversal for decisions that invalidate patents and the rate of reversal for those that validate them. It turns out that when the appellate dirt settles, patentees get a little over two thirds of this 22 percent.[128] When all these validity-related numbers are run through a separate decision tree (not shown), patentees lose another 2 percent overall. Thus, at best,[129] patentees face a 65 percent chance (67 − 2 = 65) that their patents will ultimately remain valid if they are fully litigated.

Note that in a real case, at least before the defendant filed its answer, we'd subdivide the validity node into a series of nodes representing the main bases for invalidating a patent. One study showed that when patents are invalidated, the grounds for invalidity break down as follows:

- Obviousness (42 percent)
- Section 102 untimeliness-related statutory bars (31 percent)
- Section 102 substantive lack of novelty (27 percent)
- Failure to disclose the best mode of the invention (12 percent)
- Failure to describe or enable the invention (9 percent)
- Indefinite claims (6 percent)
- Double patenting (4 percent)
- Four rarer grounds (2.8 percent)[130]

The total exceeds 100 percent because many patents are invalidated for more than one reason.

Enforceability

When inequitable conduct is an issue at trial, plaintiffs face about a 12 percent chance that their patents will be held unenforceable for inequitable conduct.[131] Before trial, they face roughly a 2 percent chance.[132] Also, 32 percent of enforceability-related decisions are appealed,[133] and the Federal Circuit overturns one quarter of this 32 percent.[134] Assuming the reversal pattern for validity-related appeals carries over to enforceability-related appeals, patentees should get a little over two thirds of that quarter of 32 percent.

Factoring in appeals and pretrial dismissals brings the chances of unenforceability down by 1 percent overall. Thus, assuming a patentee is going to litigate through trial, from the outset of the case it faces about an 11 percent chance that its patent will ultimately be held unenforceable, or an 89 percent chance that it will be enforceable.

Infringement

Sixty-six percent of trial verdicts find infringement.[135] Before trial, plaintiffs probably face roughly a 5 percent chance of a dispositive finding of no infringement.[136] Thirty-seven percent of infringement-related verdicts are appealed, and the Federal Circuit overturns 20 percent of them.[137] Unlike validity and enforceability, however, no published data or rationale justifies assuming that patentees win more of these appeals than they lose. Factoring in only the pretrial dismissals brings patentees' chances of a verdict of infringement down to 63 percent.

Reality Check

Our overall chance of success appears to be worse now than it was in Baby Tree. In Baby Tree, we had a 58 percent chance of success; now it seems we're down to 36 percent: 65 percent valid times 89 percent enforceable times 63 percent infringed equals 36 percent ($.65 \times .89 \times .63 = .36$). One reason is that we've accounted for the 15 percent of cases dismissed before trial. Accounting for this, however, should only bring plaintiffs' chances down to 49 percent (($100 - 15) \times .58 = .49$). The other factor is that the rulings overlap—many of the patentees lost on more than one ground. When considering both validity and infringement, judges rule in the same party's favor on both issues 74 percent of the time.[138] Juries do so 86 percent of the time.[139]

With more complete data about this overlap, we could extrapolate the percent chance of validity, enforceability, or infringement in light of each other, as in "Given that the patent has been held valid, what is the chance of validity?" For now, we can correct for the overlap, in a sense, by increasing the success figures proportionally until their product equals the actual overall chance of success (49 percent). Although these individual probabilities are strictly inaccurate, they still reflect their *relative* importance and therefore well inform the allocation of resources. Raising the numbers proportionally until their product equals 49 gives 74 percent valid, 90 percent enforceable, and 73 percent infringed.

Average or Median Award

In Baby Tree, we used the average award of $14 million. The median award, however, is only about $1 million.[140] In other words, 50 percent of judgments are for less than $1 million. Since the average award greatly exceeds the median, we know that high awards are skewing up the average, which raises questions about whether the average award is the appropriate one to use. In fact, even after throwing out the billion-dollar Polaroid verdict, 56 percent of the total money damages go to just 5 percent of the litigants, and 90 percent of the money damages go to just 16 percent of the litigants.[141]

Of course, the awards aren't random. If the infringer is very small, it's impossible for it to damage a plaintiff to the tune of hundreds of millions of dollars, and even if a plaintiff obtained such an award, a small infringer couldn't pay it. In a real case, we'd have a much better idea of the likely range of damages. Here, however, we pretend not to know much about the plaintiff (us). We do know, however, that our odds of an award in the neighborhood of $1 million are much better than our odds of hitting the "average" $14 million jackpot. So let's use the median award for now.

Chances of Collecting

Fifty percent of all new businesses go belly up within five years.[142] Of the top 100 companies in 1917, only 15 are in business today.[143] It is true that a defendant who can actually fund litigation through trial probably has the resources at the end of the trial to pay the median award. In some senses, however, we should pretend we're going trial and in others we should not. For this issue, it behooves us to consider the possibility of business failure starting from the outset of the case.

The precise rate of failure among the 12 million U.S. businesses is unknown,[144] but census data indicates that across industries, almost 10 percent of business establishments are closed down every year.[145] Most of this 10 percent, however, represents start-ups and businesses too small or fleeting to infringe patents on a noticeable scale. A conservative but substantial estimate of the annual failure rate of an alleged infringer in a patent suit is probably more like 3 percent. Interestingly, there is an almost[146] equal chance that *our* company will fail and not be around to prosecute the suit to judgment. If we assume litigating through trial takes about five years on average,[147] and if we assume an annual failure rate for patentees of about 2 percent per year, then the chances of either or both the plaintiff and defendant failing before a verdict is rendered is 22 percent. Discounting the $1 million by 22 percent results in $780,000.

Taxation

Including federal, state, and local taxes, corporations pay an average of 40 percent of their income in taxes.[148] Presumably, 40 percent of the adjusted award of $780,000 would go to taxes, bringing our expected value down to $468,000. Forty percent of the settlement also goes to taxes, bringing it down to $300,000.

Time Value of Money

Now we discount for the time value of money.[149] Discounting the adjusted median award of $468,000 at 10 percent[150] for five years results in an overall discount for the time value of money of 37 percent. Thus, the present value of the award to the plaintiff (and present cost to the defendant) is now $295,000.

Legal Costs

In Baby Tree, we used the average cost through trial of $2 million. Here, this $2 million cost figure would imply that each party alone spends much more than either party likely stands to gain or lose. In reality, the legal costs correspond to the amount at risk.[151] When less than $1 million is *at risk* (not the amount awarded), which is true about 5 percent of the time,[152] the direct legal fees and expenses cost each side an average of about $500,000 to litigate through trial.[153] When the stakes range from $1 to $10 million, which is true about 43 percent of the time, it costs each side about $1.3 million.[154] When $10 to $100 million is at stake, which is the case about 46 percent of the time, it costs about $2.9 million.[155] When more than $100 million is up in the air, true about 8 percent of the time, it costs about $6.5 million.[156]

Since the unadjusted median award of $1 million falls between the cost when less than $1 million is at risk and the cost when $1 to $10 million is at risk, we could use an intermediate figure of $900,000 in legal costs (($500,000 + $1.3 million)/2 = $900,000).[157] (All the legal costs can roughly be halved for the 93.1 percent of cases that do not go to trial,[158] but we're pretending we're going to trial in Mama Tree.)

Some may point out that we just disparaged average numbers above and now we're relying on one. But this average is not really *the* average; it's the average around the median. Plus, legal costs are not as volatile as awards. In 1990, Polaroid socked Kodak with an $873 million judgment. No legal fees can approach those kinds of numbers (except perhaps contingency fees) because attorney effort exhibits diminishing returns, which is why litigating a case where more than $100 million is at stake costs only 16 times more than litigating a case where $1 million is at stake as opposed to costing 100 times more.[159]

Roll Back

As shown in Mama Tree (see Exhibit 16-2), when the DATA program discounts the median award in all the ways described above and subtracts the legal costs and rolls back the tree, our expected value of litigating is –$760,000. This indicates we should accept the offer.

PAPA TREES

If you and a friend are hiking and a bear starts chasing you, you don't have to outrun the bear, just your friend. Similarly, to justify further litigating we don't need an expected value of litigation that exceeds a defendant's offer; we just need a defendant's offer that's slightly less painful than the defendant's expected cost of litigation. In other words, we may want to hold out or counteroffer for an amount that is slightly better for the defendant than what it believes is the alternative.

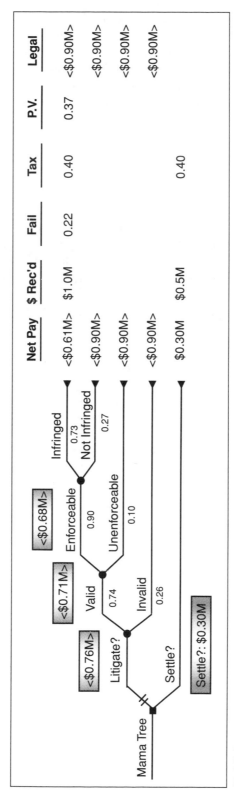

Exhibit 16-2 Mama tree.

So Papa Tree focuses on outcomes for both the plaintiff and defendant. Accordingly, it's really two trees. Papa Tree One depicts the plaintiff's expected value of litigating versus its value of settling. Papa Tree Two depicts the defendant's expected cost of litigating versus its cost of settling. Again, the purpose of Papa Tree Two is to determine how the defendant might value the case. If Papa Tree Two showed, for instance, that the defendant's expected value is a negative $3 million, we might want to hold out for a better offer, even if the current offer of $500,000 is better than our expected value of litigation.

Taxation of Awards and Settlements

One reason that the defendant's expected cost is not simply the plaintiff's expected value with a minus sign in front of it is that only the defendant may deduct the award or settlement as a business expense. The plaintiff must pay taxes on it as regular income. Thus, we must deduct for the defendant 40 percent of whatever it pays and take from the plaintiff 40 percent of whatever it receives. (It appears defendants can also deduct payments for willful infringement damages.[160])

Legal Fees Redux

Both parties may deduct legal fees and expenses from income as regular business expenses. (Indirect costs, discussed below, are nondeductible.) With a 40 percent corporate tax rate, a conservative estimate of each side's real median legal fees for litigating through trial is roughly $540,000 ($900,000 × .60). (The *average* fees are $1.2 million, that is, $2 million × .60. In major litigation, each party can expect to pay $3 to $15 million.[161])

Due to space contraints, in Papa Tree One and Two the legal fees (combined with Indirect Costs under the "Admin" column) already include this 40 percent deduction for taxes, unlike the 40 percent tax rate on awards and settlements, which appears in Papa Tree One in its own column entitled "Tax."

Indirect Costs

Indirect and intangible costs, such as lost opportunity and diversion of management and technical personnel, are nothing to sneeze at.[162] Research results on the opportunity costs of patent litigation, sponsored by the National Academies Board on Science,[163] should be available by the very end of 2001. While the research is preparatory as of the time of this writing, it tentatively appears that, although lost opportunity costs probably do not exceed by and large direct costs, they are in the same ballpark.[164]

Other indirect costs include the bad publicity or "pitchfork effect" (as opposed to halo effect) that follows conflict and strife. For example, one study showed that a biotech company's market value drops by an average of 3.1 percent within two days after its involvement in a patent suit is reported.[165] Another study found a 2.0 percent drop.[166] The latter study, which sampled 530 Massachusetts companies, showed an average loss of shareholder wealth of $67.9 million and median loss of $20.0 million. (Of course, if we assume we've already filed suit, then this cost is sunk.)

It would be foolish to ignore the indirect costs since they are substantial and an analysis that ignores them is simply inadequate. In lieu of better information and in light of the fact that legal costs are the best proxy for a suit's activity level and therefore its indirect costs, let's assume the indirect costs constitute a substantial but conservative figure of two thirds of the adjusted legal costs of $540,000. Taking these indirect costs into account, therefore, adds another $360,000 for suits through trial.

Due to space contraints, in Papa Tree One and Two the indirect costs are combined with the legal costs under the "Admin" column. Thus, $900,000 ($540,000 + $360,000) appears in every scenario under the "Admin" column except the settlement scenario.

Note that indirect costs do not include payments for such things as graphic artists, document managers, trial automation providers, mock trial and jury consultants, expert witnesses, court reporters, and copy services. These are encompassed by the direct legal costs. Surprisingly, these non–law firm expenses account for 45 percent of the direct legal costs.[167]

Patent Invalidation

If our patent is invalidated or held unenforceable, it may endanger existing flows of license income and open the doors to other infringers, leading to a loss of market advantage. We should account for this potential loss, but how?[168]

We estimated earlier that the average value of the average patent is probably somewhere in the neighborhood of $640,000, but we also saw that patent values are highly skewed. Just as the top 10 percent of patents account for at least 40 percent of the value of all patents, the top 1.5 percent (which are the ones that are generally litigated) probably account for a disproportionate share of that 40 percent. On the other hand, if our patent is invalidated, it stands to reason that it wasn't that valuable to begin with—because market value will reflect its perceived validity.

It also stands to reason that the amount the plaintiff spends prosecuting the suit should generally set a floor for the value of its patent; generally people won't spend much wielding something of little worth. Again, therefore, in lieu of better information, let's assume the cost of patent invalidation constitutes a substantial but conservative figure equal to the Admin costs, $900,000. At the terminal ends of the invalidity and the unenforceability branches, let's place –$900,000 in the "Admin." column.

Presumably, the defendant gains nothing from the patent's demise—the defendant is already infringing. Indeed, it's possible that the defendant would be harmed because other companies may enter the former duopoly.

Injunctions

Plaintiffs request preliminary injunctions in only 19 percent of patent suits; only half of those requests end up being heard by a court; and only half of those hearings result in a preliminary injunction.[169] As such, preliminary injunctions are granted in only 5 percent of cases. Plaintiffs who end up winning money damages, however, almost always win a permanent injunction barring the defendant from making, using, selling, or contributing to the infringement of the invention. Although it varies enormously based on the circumstances of each case, a popular educated guess is that permanent injunctions are usually at least equal to the money damages.[170]

Are money damages a good starting point for valuing injunctions? It stands to reason that a court's damage calculations (excepting perhaps enhanced damages) often approximate what the plaintiff loses from infringement and sometimes approximate what the defendant gains from it, but there are many variables. For example, if the patentee prevails early in the patent's 20-year term, the money damages will generally be lower because the defendant could not have infringed for very long, but the injunction will be more valuable because it will bar the defendant from using the invention for the large remaining portion of the patent's life. Conversely, if the patent is old, then the money damages will tend to exceed the value of the injunction.

Research shows that for the average litigated patent, final judgment is not rendered until after the midpoint of the patent's term, 12.3 years after the patent is filed.[171] (The median is about 7.5 years.[172]) Research also shows that the average effective life of a patent—that is, the average time until the product or feature it covers in the marketplace is replaced by a better product—is only about five years from the date it issues.[173] This suggests that permanent injunctions usually have little value because the invention is often obsolete by the time of final judgment.

How do we square this with experts' intuition that injunctions tend to be at least as valuable as money damages? First, only about 1.1 percent of patents[174] are ever litigated, and since it stands to reason that a litigated patent is usually more important[175] than the average licensed patent, a litigated patent's effective life is likely to exceed five years. Second, 12.3 years to final judgment is an average, and it may be that injunctions granted in cases filed shortly after patent issuance are disproportionately valuable. Since the value of injunctions granted late cannot be less than zero, the early injunctions may skew up the average value. Third, the pitchfork effect is exacerbated by injunctions because customers don't like it when suppliers tell them a product is no longer available. Fourth, the defendant loses the sunk investment in its facilities. For example, if it tooled up a factory to make a device and was later enjoined, the tooling up will have been for nothing and changeover costs will be incurred in retooling for something else.

Putting a value on these things, however, is rendered even more difficult by the fact that injunctions tend to harm defendants more than they help plaintiffs. Also, injunctions provide prospective relief after final judgment, so we would have to discount for time, starting at five years and amortizing for the patent's remaining years of life. This is beyond our ken, but leaving out the value of injunctions altogether seems foolish because they are clearly valuable. For example, in some alternative legal fee arrangements, which are partly based on performance, if the patentee's lawyers obtain an injunction against the infringer, the lawyers receive a bonus that exceeds their take from the money damages. Under one prominent firm's (sample) agreement, if the firm represents the defendant and an injunction is granted, the firm eats 20 percent of its hourly fees for the entire litigation. If the firm represents the plaintiff and only wins money damages at trial, the firm's bonus ranges from zero to $3 million.[176] If the plaintiff wins a preliminary injunction, the firm gets an additional $500,000 bonus; if it wins a permanent injunction, the firm gets another $2 million. These bonuses are on top of whatever money damage bonus the firm receives. Since the money damage bonus will usually be less than $2 million, it appears that plaintiffs value injunctions at least as much as money damages, or they wouldn't be agreeing to these terms.

In lieu of better information, let's assume a substantial but conservative value to the plaintiff equal to half of the discounted money damages and a cost to the defendant equal to the discounted money damages. (The injunction values in the Papa Trees are shown prior to discounting, but are discounted during the roll-back.)

Enhanced Damages

Willfulness damages add to the compensatory damages an additional zero to 200 percent[177] of the compensatory damages. Judges and juries find willful infringement about 29 percent of the time.[178] (Enhanced awards are trebled 35 percent of the time.[179]) But proving willfulness and obtaining damages for willfulness are not the same. To wit, only 42 percent of that 29 percent results in willfulness damages, resulting in a total of 12 percent of all judgments being enhanced. When awards are enhanced, the mean enhancement is 69 percent.[180]

Willfulness damages account for about 22 percent of total money damages[181] per year, but awards are not enhanced uniformly. As compensatory awards cross the $1 million mark, judges and juries appear to lose their nerve. For example, the mean enhancement for all awards that are trebled is only $3.4 million, whereas the mean enhancement for all awards that are doubled is $9.4 million. These low numbers imply that the base compensatory award is less[182] than $1.13 million for most trebled awards and less than $4.7 million for most doubled awards. (An alternative hypothesis is that small companies, which almost necessarily generate lower compensatory damages, are more likely than large established companies to engage in outlandish behavior.)

Thus, awards around the median are more likely to be enhanced. More specifically, it seems that about 50 percent of award amounts around the median tend to consist of enhanced damages (as opposed to only about 15 to 20 percent of award amounts well above the median). Thus, for every ten $1 million awards, about $5 million of their total sum is likely to be due to willfulness.

Note that a real case could incorporate the possibility of enhanced damages into the tree. Here, however, we're using amounts based on real awards, which already include willfulness damages. If we considered willfulness damages here, we'd be double-counting. We don't count attorneys' fees here for the same reason. In any event, they're only awarded in 7 percent of all tried cases,[183] and they only account for about 3 percent of total damages every year.[184]

High, Low, and Median Damages

In important decision tree analyses that involve continuous variables like money, each final chance node is usually split into three branches: high (top 90th percentile), median (50th percentile), and low (bottom 10th percentile). Mathematicians discovered that these particular discrete percentiles (based on the Gaussian quadrature and McNamee-Celona methods[185]) approximate distributions of continuous variables fairly well. Note that these "90-50-10" percentiles refer to the size of the outcomes, not their probability. As shown in the trees, the "90-50-10" method requires that the outcomes be assigned probabilities of .25, .50, and .25 respectively.

As discussed earlier, the median outcome is $1 million. The outcome at the top 90th percentile is probably about $30 million.[186] (The top 95th percentile is more like $100 million.) The bottom 10th percentile is about $100,000.[187]

Rollback—Papa Tree One

Based on all the values and adjustments in Exhibit 16-3, Papa Tree One indicates that our value of settling is $300,000; our expected value of litigating is $600,000.

Rollback—Papa Tree Two

The defendant's cost of settling is –$300,000. Mainly due to its vulnerability to an injunction, however, its cost of litigating is –$3.2 million. Arguably, therefore, accepting the offer is not ambitious enough; the plaintiff should hold out for almost $3.2 million (see Exhibit 16-4).

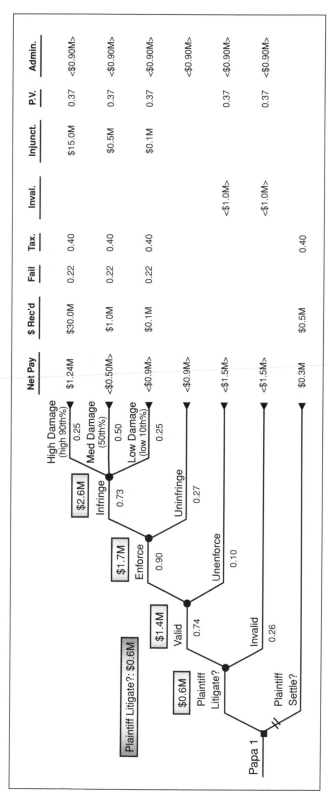

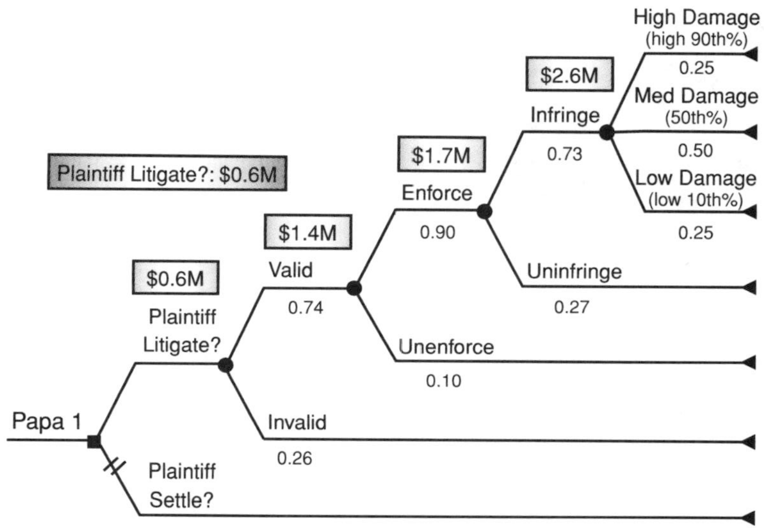
Plaintiff Litigate?: $0.6M
$0.6M
Plaintiff
Litigate?
Papa 1
Plaintiff
Settle?
$1.4M
Valid
0.74
Invalid
0.26
$1.7M
Enforce
0.90
Unenforce
0.10
$2.6M
Infringe
0.73
Uninfringe
0.27
High Damage
(high 90th%)
0.25
Med Damage
(50th%)
0.50
Low Damage
(low 10th%)
0.25

Net Pay	$ Rec'd	Fail	Tax.	Inval.	Injunct.	P.V.	Admin.
$1.24M	$30.0M	0.22	0.40		$15.0M	0.37	<$0.90M>
<$0.50M>	$1.0M	0.22	0.40		$0.5M	0.37	<$0.90M>
<$0.9M>	$0.1M	0.22	0.40		$0.1M	0.37	<$0.90M>
<$0.9M>							<$0.90M>
<$1.5M>				<$1.0M>		0.37	<$0.90M>
<$1.5M>				<$1.0M>		0.37	<$0.90M>
$0.3M	$0.5M		0.40				

Exhibit 16-3 Papa tree one.

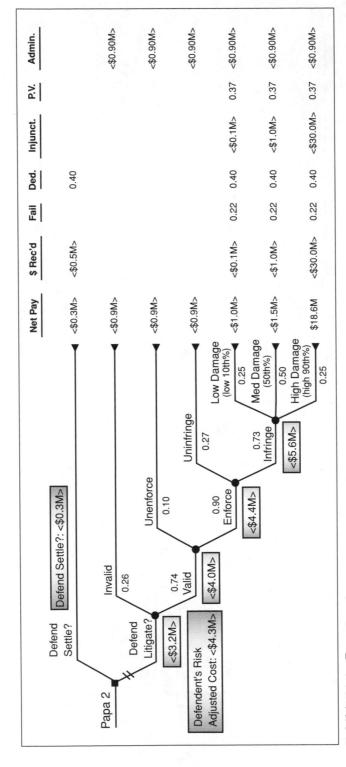

Exhibit 16-4 Papa tree two.

Adjustment for Risk

Most people and companies are averse to risk. For example, imagine that your life savings is $500,000 and you're offered the opportunity to make a bet with the following odds: 90 percent chance of losing $500,000, 10 percent chance of winning $10 million. Although the expected value of the bet is $1 million, almost everyone would refuse it.

Decision analysts have techniques for determining a person's or company's risk profile. Assuming a settlement offer is already on the table, however, ignoring the risk profile normally shouldn't change your decision about whether the offer is favorable unless the potential risk exceeds 15 percent of net worth.[188] Since the *average* patent litigant is a large company with about 12,000 employees and annual sales of about $2.6 billion,[189] and since we're considering the likely awards, which tend to be on the lower end of the award distribution, the majority of litigants need not consider their own risk profile. About 28 percent of litigants, however, are small entities with fewer than 500 employees[190] and less than $50 million in annual sales. If a litigant falls into this 28 percent or is otherwise small or shaky enough to be risk-averse in the face of an unfavorable verdict, it should adjust its expected value for risk. The amount that is left over is the "certain equivalent."

To the extent it's possible, determining the *opponent's* certain equivalent is also useful. For example, a large plaintiff may, after estimating a small defendant's certain equivalent, reject an offer, not because its terms aren't favorable but because analysis of the defendant's risk profile suggests better terms can be extracted. For pedagogical purposes, let's assume in our scenario that (1) we are a large company that is not risk-averse because 15 percent of our net worth is not reasonably at risk, and (2) the defendant's net worth is about $100 million.

The complete method for determining the certain equivalent is beyond the scope of this chapter. Fortunately, there is a shortcut that handles almost all cases. The certain equivalent is equal to: expected value $-^1/_2$ (variance/risk tolerance). We've already determined the expected value (cost) for the defendant, –$2.8 million. We must now determine the variance and risk tolerance.

The variance is equal to the square of the standard deviation: (each outcome – expected value)^2 × (probability of outcome). Intuitively, the variance refers to the spread of the awards—are they clustered around the median or do they range from $50,000 to $1 billion? As we've seen, it's the latter. Specifically, the awards tend to break down as follows:

- About 43 percent of awards are between zero and $800,000
- About 11 percent are between $800,000 and $1.7 million
- About 27 percent are between $1.7 million and $8.5 million
- About 7 percent are between $8.5 million and $17 million
- About 12 percent exceed $17 million.[191]

Of that 12 percent, about half falls below $50 million; about one third fall between $50 million and $150 million; and the rest are between about $150 million and $350

million. A range of zero to $350 million, however, is never the range in any particular case. So these numbers don't help us. Fortunately, with a simple press of a
button, DATA calculates the standard deviation of the values already in Papa Tree
Two. Squaring the standard deviation gives a variance of $32 million. This variance
reflects injunctions, legal and indirect costs, and the other adjustments discussed
herein.

Decision analysts may determine a company's risk tolerance by asking a representative—one who has a good feel for the company's risk attitude—the following (initially cryptic) question: what is the *most* money the company would pay (R)
for you to be comfortable having a 50/50 chance of winning R or losing half of R?
When R is low, there is little or no aversion to risk; as R rises, aversion increases.
For example, if R equals $1,000, and a company has a 50/50 chance of winning
$1,000 or losing $500, the expected value of this bet is $250 and almost every company would accept it. On the other hand, if R equals $100 million, and a company
has a 50/50 chance of winning $100 million or losing $50 million, many smaller
companies won't accept the bet, even though its expected value is $25 million.

After eliciting a value for R, it's best to corroborate the company's risk attitude with a graph of the probability distribution (or histogram) that visually depicts the risk. As shown in Exhibit 16-5, pursuant to Papa Tree Two the defendant
faces an 88 percent chance of a judgment it can swallow and a 12 percent chance
of a judgment for $19 million, which could kill the company. If the company representative is uncomfortable with the distribution, the analyst should keep asking
the question about R until the answer matches the representative's intuition about
the graph.

On the other hand, Marc Victor, the pioneer of litigation risk analysis, relies
directly on intuition:

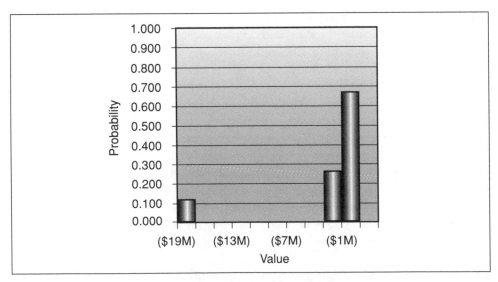

Exhibit 16-5   Probability distribution at "Defendant Litigate."

If a company has not already defined its risk tolerance for use in making major business decisions, I don't want to try to do it with the Board of Directors or the CEO (which is the level at which it really should be done) for the very first time in the corporation's history in the context of a lawsuit. It's so much easier—and I think better—just to show the top corporate people the histogram for their real lawsuit and tell them (assuming the bar chart in Exhibit 16-6): "You know, the expected value may be just under $3 million, but you can see that this consists of a small probability of a large hit. Are you comfortable taking that risk if you can't get the case settled for less than $3 million? If not, how much of a premium would you offer above the $3 million to insure against the 12 percent chance of $19 million?" They don't need to go through some brand-new, and strange, set of questions to determine R. They always find it easier just to look at the real histogram and say "I can live with that degree of risk" or "I can't, but I'll only pay a premium of $X—more than that, and I'm better off taking some risk, since I might win and owe $0."

Since we've assumed the defendant's net worth is $100 million, and since we're using the popular guideline that risk aversion kicks in at about 15 percent of net worth, let's assume that R equals $15 million. Plugging into the certain equivalent formula $15 million for R and $32 million for the variance results in a certain equivalent for the defendant of about –$4.3 million, indicating that the defendant's risk-adjusted cost of litigating is much lower than its non–risk-adjusted cost. (The $4.3 million is shown in the "Risk-Adjusted" box located near the root of the defendant's litigate branch in Exhibit 16-4.) Arguably, therefore, we should hold out for an offer of almost $4.3 million.

Note that as events occur the expected values change. For example, if the patent were found valid, enforceable, and infringed, but damages were not yet assessed, the defendant's expected cost at that point would be –$5.6 million. The variance would be about $56 million and the certain equivalent would be about –$7.5 million. As shown in Exhibit 16-6, the probability distribution would then indicate a one in four chance of a company-killing judgment.

Note also that it's possible that a small defendant or plaintiff will *seek* risk, and this can be rational. For instance, since it's rumored that small high-tech and Internet start-ups have a failure rate around 80 percent, does it makes sense for the CEO to bleed away $3.2 million in vital funds to avoid a 12 percent chance of a company-killing judgment? In such a case, the certain equivalent could *exceed* the expected value.

FINAL THOUGHTS

Many patent suits are poor investments. A very large minority of them exhibit negative expected values for plaintiffs as well as defendants. Yet the number of

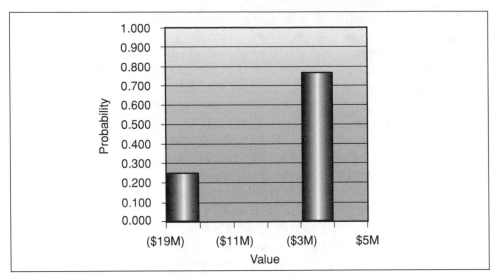

Exhibit 16-6   Probability distribution at infringed, valid, and enforceable.

patent suits has been increasing about 8 percent per year on average for the last 10 years and shows no signs of stopping. Is this a dubious trend?

Apparently not. The raw fact that a cottage industry has arisen to finance patent litigation is consistent with the notion that patent litigation can be a good investment.[192] More telling, however, are the overall cumulative numbers: from 1990 to 1999, 925 patent cases went to trial[193]; about 450 of those resulted in damage awards and 250 of those damage awards were reported.[194] The 250 damage awards total $3.5 billion. Since patentees prevail 49 percent of the time, we can assume that these 250 awards resulted from about 510 cases (250/.49 = 510). Since reported cases are usually higher-stakes cases and since all of these cases went through trial and some through appeal, I will, despite inflation and increasing fees, assume legal fees for the plaintiffs near the high end at $2 million per case. Thus, these plaintiffs spent around $1 billion (510 × $2 million) and gained $3.5 billion, resulting in a combined net gain of 250 percent[195] (ignoring any discounting and adjusting). Even if we throw out the Polaroid verdict as an outlier, the net gain is still about 200 percent.[196]

Furthermore, reputational and deterrent effects are often at play.[197] To start with an analogy: If a burglar breaks into a house and steals a VCR, the total damages may only be a few hundred dollars. Nevertheless, the state is prepared to spend thousands to apprehend, try, and perhaps incarcerate the burglar. Should the state refuse to prosecute any time the cost of prosecution exceeds the damages from the particular crime? No, because for every prosecution many other such crimes are deterred. If the state adopted the shortsighted approach, then property crime would increase dramatically because criminals would simply make sure that whatever they steal or destroy that day is worth less than, let's say, the $30,000 it costs to incarcerate someone for a year.

Similarly, if companies with large patent portfolios earn a reputation for aggressive enforcement, would-be infringers will tend to steer clear. In the long run, aggressive patentees may end up filing fewer suits and enjoying lower legal costs and increased license revenue.[198] In other words, a good offense is the best defense, and the fact that a particular suit is not cost-effective on its own terms does not always militate against pressing it.

Consultants/Lawyers

Novices can execute tree analyses that generate insight, but "it is difficult to avoid serious biases without having an analyst present."[199] In difficult or important cases, it's best to hire a decision analyst versed in law or a lawyer versed in decision analysis. This is especially true if you want to create more detailed trees, elicit probabilities from more than a few experts, incorporate sensitivity analysis,[200] determine risk profiles and the value of information, or employ Monte Carlo simulation.[201] Furthermore, in a real case where we know the particulars, we could consider many other uncertain variables such as measure of damages, admissibility of expert testimony, waiver of attorney-client privilege, and many more. Significant but certain variables, which affect probability estimates but are not modeled in the tree (because they're not uncertain), include venue, type of technology, citizenship of litigant, the judge's politics and past decisions, whether a jury trial has been requested, the presence of insurance coverage, and the asserted grounds of invalidity, some of which stand a much better chance of invalidating a patent than others.[202]

If the consultant is not versed in the law, he won't know what to focus on, what probabilities to elicit, and how to obtain information about variables such as those listed above. Also, he won't be able to provide the second opinion—on the merits and outcomes of the case—that can be so useful when it comes from a knowledgeable observer with a fresh, more disinterested perspective. Having the attorney-client privilege is also nice. However, precious few decision analysts are versed in the law, perhaps because there is little cross-pollination between law and operations research.[203] In fact, there appear to be only two such consultancies[204] in the entire country; they are one-consultant operations and only one is run by a lawyer.[205]

Courage of Our Predictions

Companies don't start multimillion-dollar projects without some analysis and forecasting, and they shouldn't enter multimillion-dollar litigation without the same.

It's not hard to get people to agree to this general statement, but there's a mighty big slip between the cup and the lip. When the fate of millions of dollars hinges on subjective judgments about multiple uncertainties, there's a tendency to turn away and lapse into mindless emphasis on details, endless refining of what we already know,[206] and excessive gathering of information[207]—what might be called "careless caution."

Acting rationally given the information available is the most that anyone can ask for, but even when it's encouraged, it takes courage.[208] Fear and cognitive limitations—such as the tendency to ignore uncertain outcomes—cause decision makers (in general but particularly in litigation) to focus too much on immediate and direct costs, and too little on expected revenue.[209] So executives must remember to distinguish good choices from good outcomes. Responding to the odds rationally doesn't mean you won't be hammered. If there's a 60 percent chance you'll win a bet, there's a very good chance you'll lose. Buck up and take the bet.

NOTES

1. Kimberly A. Moore, "Judges, Juries, and Patent Cases—An Empirical Peek Inside the Black Box," 99 *Mich. L. Rev.* No. 2, November 2000. See also Eugene R. Quinn, Jr., "Using Alternative Dispute Resolution to Resolve Patent Litigation: A Survey of Patent Litigators," 3 *Marquette Intell. Prop. L. Rev.* 77 (1999). The percentage of cases settling will probably increase. See *infra*, notes 88–89.
2. Most patent litigants—93.1 percent—do not litigate through trial. Moore, "Judges," *supra*. The legal fees for the average litigant, who usually settles after or well into discovery, are about $1 million. The figure of $1 million derives from the *American Intellectual Property Law Association Report of Economic Survey 1999* (hereinafter, "AIPLA 1999"), which found a median amount for litigating through discovery of $800,000. Enhancing this by 30 percent (for reasons discussed below) results in a total of $1 million in direct legal costs. By taking into account indirect expenses (discussed later), I added $500,000 to the $1 million to obtain $1.5 million. It is a coincidence that this $1.5 million is the same as AIPLA 1999's finding of a median of $1.5 million in direct legal costs to litigate through trial.
3. See James J. Foster, "How to Manage the Cost of Patent Litigation—Suggestions of Trial Counsel," 68 *J. Patent and Trademark Office Soc'y* 131, No. 3 (March 1986). Also, 80 percent of what you know by the time of trial was usually available at the beginning of the litigation from your own people and documents. James L. Ewing IV, "Patent Litigation Management and Alternative Billing," in *Patent Litigation 1999* (Practising Law Institute 1999), p. 1062.
4. *Trends in Patent Infringement Lawsuits 1990–1999,* Navigant Consulting Inc. (2000) (available from Dr. William O. Kerr, Washington D.C.).
5. Kimberly A. Moore, "Forum Shopping in Patent Cases: Does Geographic Choice Affect Innovation?" 79 *N.C. L. Rev.* (2001) (forthcoming at time of this writing). Moore's study indicates an average time to resolution of 1.12 years. Lanjouw and Lerner find an average case pendency of about 1.4 years. Jean O. Lanjouw and Joshua Lerner, "Preliminary Injunctive Relief: Theory and Evidence from Patent Litigation," Table 3, NBER Working Paper No. 5689 (NBER 1996).
6. And divergence in stakes. See generally Joel Waldfogel, "Reconciling Asymmetric Information and Divergent Expectations Theories of Litigation," NBER Working Paper No. 6409 (Feb. 1998); Bruce L. Hay and Kathryn E. Spier, "Litigation and Settlement," in *The New Palgrave Dictionary of Economics and the Law* (Stockton Press 1998);

Leandra Lederman, "Which Cases Go to Trial? An Empirical Study of Predictors of Failure to Settle," 49 *Case W. Res.* 315 (1999). See also Jean O. Lanjouw and Mark Schankerman, "Stylized Facts of Patent Litigation: Value, Scope and Ownership," NBER Working Paper No. 6297 (NBER 1997).

7. See generally Richard A. Posner, *The Economic Analysis of Law*, 5th ed., 554–560 (Little Brown & Co. 1992). Or when the stakes are higher for one side. See generally Moore, "Judges," *supra*; Lederman, *supra*.

8. The stakes, unlike information or expectation, rarely converge.

9. Only about 25 percent of cases settle without any court action. See Moore, "Judges," at fn 79. See also Quinn, *supra* at 12, Fig. 13.

10. See generally David P. Hoffer, "Decision Analysis as a Mediator's Tool," 1 *Harv. Negotiation L. Rev.* 113 (Spring 1996); Lionel Tiger, *The Biology of Hope* (Kodansha Int'l 1995).

11. William O. Kerr, Penta Advisory Services, personal e-mail communication (April 9, 2001); anonymous IP damage expert, personal telephone communication (April 2001).

12. Quinn, *supra* at 30–34.

13. Ibid.

14. Ibid.

15. Carl S. Spetzler and C.A. Stael Von Holstein, "Probability Encoding in Decision Analysis," 22 *Management Science* No. 3 (Nov. 1975). Daniel Kahneman, Paul Slovic, and Amos Tversky, *Judgment Under Uncertainty: Heuristics and Biases* (Cambridge University Press, 1982); Amos Tversky and Daniel Kahneman, "Judgment Under Uncertainty: Heuristics and Biases," 185 *Science* 1124–1131 (Sept. 26, 1974); Paul Goodwin and George Wright, *Decision Analysis for Management Judgment,* 2nd ed. 55–72 (John Wiley & Sons 1998).

16. G.A. Miller, "The Magical Number Seven, Plus or Minus Two: Some Limits on Our Capacity for Processing Information," 63 *Pyschological Review* 81–97 (March 1956).

17. Benjamin Franklin, letter sent from London on September 19, 1772, to Joseph Priestly.

18. See generally the following articles by Marc B. Victor, "How Much Is a Case Worth?" 20 *Trial* 48 (July 1984); "The Proper Use of Decision Analysis to Assist Litigation Strategy," 40 *Business Lawyer* 617 (Feb. 1985); "Risk Evaluation in Intellectual Property Litigation," in *Intellectual Property Counseling and Litigation* (Matthew Bender 1988); "Litigation Risk Analysis and ADR," ch. 17 in *Donovan Leisure Newton & Irvine ADR Practice Book*, John H. Wilkinson, ed. (John Wiley & Sons 1990); "A New Use for Decision Analysis: Choosing an Optimum Fee Arrangement," 94–8 *Managing Litigation Costs* (Aug. 1994); "Decisions Trees Take the Guesswork Out of Contingency-Fee Proposals," 2–11 *Managing Litigation Costs* (April 1995); "Evaluating Legal Risks and Costs with Decision Tree Analysis," ch. 12 in *Successful Partnering Between Inside and Outside Counsel* (West Group/American Corporate Counsel Association 2000) (Victor's best article on the subject). See also Alexander I. Poltorak and Paul J. Lerner, "Litigation Risk Analysis in Patent Infringement Lawsuits," *Managing Intellectual Property* (May 2001); Bruce L. Beron, *Litigation Strategies & Risk Management Primer* (LRMI 1996); *Litigation Strategies & Risk Management Seminar Materials* (LRMI 2000); Robert D. Behn and James W. Vaupel, *Quick Analysis for Busy Decision Makers* (Basic Books 1982) (especially chapters 6 and 9); Stephen C. Glazier, *Patent Strategies for Business*, 3rd ed., p. 83–97 (LBI Institute 2000); Hoffer, *supra*; Goodwin and Wright, *supra*; Robert T. Clemen, *Making Hard Decisions: An Introduction to Decision Analysis*, 2nd ed. (Wadsworth Publishing Co., 1996); David C. Skinner, *Introduction to Decision Analysis*, 2nd ed. (Probabilistic Publishing, April 1999).

19. Some of the figures are very rough and ready, meaning that I derived, deduced, or inferred them from sources and combinations of sources that do not themselves state

the figures. In many cases, I had to make more than one arguable assumption or informed guess to get from A to B. When the derivation reached a point that a reader might not see how the cited reference implies the result, I put the word "derived" after the citation, as in "Moore, Judges, *supra*—derived." The following illustrates the kinds of calculations and guesses I had to make: To determine the average likelihood of any random patent being held unenforceable due to inequitable conduct, I took the total number of trials in Moore's study (Moore, "Judges," *supra*) that found inequitable conduct and divided it by the total number of all trials in her study to obtain a figure of 12 percent. But Moore did not take into account cases that were thrown out, by judges *before* trial on pretrial motion. Since her study indicates that 6.9 percent of cases go to trial and since another one of her excellent papers (see Moore, "Forum," *supra*) indicates that 76 percent of cases settle, the difference of 17 percent must represent cases that are transferred, thrown out or otherwise dismissed before trial. In personal communication, Moore confirmed that at least 15 percent of cases were thrown out by judges on pretrial motion. But what portion of this 15 percent is attributable to findings of no inequitable conduct as opposed to findings of invalidity and lack of infringement? Well, the 12 percent figure is a weighted statistic that reflects the findings of both judges and juries. So, using data in her study, I divided the number of trials where judges found inequitable conduct by the total number of judge trials to determine that judges find inequitable conduct a little more often than juries, 15 percent of the time, to be exact. I then made the somewhat reckless assumption that this pattern would more or less hold before trial, i.e., that 15 percent of the 15 percent of cases thrown out by judges before trial are thrown out for inequitable conduct. Fifteen percent of 15 percent is 2 percent. Next, I adjusted the base number going to trial from 100 percent of cases to 85 percent of cases, thereby effectively bringing the 12 percent down to 10 percent ($.85 \times .12 = 10$). Adding the 2 percent thrown out before trial to this 10 percent brought it back to 12 percent—a wash. Taking into account reversals on appeal, however, reduces this number by about 1 percent, resulting in an overall chance that a patent will be held unenforceable of 11 percent (assuming we view the case from its outset and assuming that it will be litigated "all the way").

20. In total, but not necessarily individually, because the rate of increase of patent filing *now* may be greater than the rate of increase of licensing revenue.

21. Kevin Rivette, "Innovate, Protect and Leverage," presented at Patent Strategy & Management Seminar (Tysons Corner, VA: November 2000).

22. Patent efficiency—the number of patents per million dollars of R&D—increased 18 percent from 1997 to 1998. *1999 Intellectual Property Metrics Report*, PriceWaterhouse Coopers (1999). See also *2000 Intellectual Property Metrics Report*, PriceWaterhouse Coopers (2000).

23. *www.uspto.gov/web/offices/ac/ido/oeip/taf/us_stat.pdf.*

24. Ibid.; IP News, 6 *Intellectual Property Strategist* 8 (October 2000).

25. R&D is the first thing to go in a recession.

26. Fons Theis, Phillippe Bautier, and Annette Simes, "Germany Is by Far the Most Active Member," *//europa.eu.int* (March 2001). Also EPO 1997 application information, available at the EPO web site, shows an increase of 10 percent from 1993 to 1995 and 22 percent from 1995 to 1997.

27. Emmett J. Murtha, "Licensing As a Business," in Jack Barufka and Michael Einschlag, *Patent Strategy & Management Seminar Handbook*, Samson Vermont (ed.), pp. 1–25 (American Lawyer Media Inc., November 2000); Kevin Rivette and David Kline, *Rembrandts in the Attic: Unlocking the Hidden Value of Patents* 4–6 (Harvard Business School Press 2000). Patent license revenues increased about 700 percent in the last eight of those years.

28. William O. Kerr and Gauri Prakash-Canjels, "Some Evidence of the Influence of Patent Law on Innovation and Technology," p. 3 (Penta Advisory Services 2000); Quinn, *supra* at 7–8; "Survey Predicts More, Costlier IP Disputes in Future," *Patent Strategy & Management* (June 2000).
29. See generally "Trends," *supra*; Kerr and Prakash-Canjels, *supra*.
30. Ibid.
31. Welcome Page, Patent Enforcement and Royalties Ltd., *www.peralltd.com*. See also Phillip A. Beutel, "Is the Tide Turning in Defendant's Favor? Evidence from Recent Judgments in Patent Cases," 12 (NERA Dec. 2000). But see Mark Lemley, "Rational Ignorance at the Patent Office" 9, Working Paper No. 2000-16 (U.C. Berkeley Law and Economics Working Paper Series 2000).
32. See generally Ronald B. Coolley, "Overview and Statistical Study of the Law on Patent Damages," 75 *J. Patent and Trademark Office Soc'y* 517 (No. 7, 1993); See generally "Trends," *supra*. But the *proportion* of money awards is about the same. Beutel, "Is the Tide," *supra* at 13.
33. See inflation table at *www.orst.edu/dept/pol_sci/fac/sahr/cv95.htm*.
34. See generally "Trends," *supra*; Kerr and Prakash-Canjels, supra; Margaret Cronin Fisk, "Juries Giving Til It Hurts," *Patent Strategy & Management* (March 2001).
35. Prosecution refers to drafting the application and shepherding it through the Patent Office.
36. Mark A. Lemley and John R. Allison, "Who's Patenting What? An Empirical Exploration of Patent Prosection," 52 *Vanderbilt L. Rev.* 2099, 2101, 2118 (2000).
37. John R. Allison and Mark A. Lemley, "Empirical Evidence on the Validity of Litigated Patents," 26 *AIPLA Quarterly J.* 185, 237 (No. 3) (Summer 1998).
38. Richard C. Levin et al., "Appropriating the Returns from Industrial Research and Development," 3 *Brookings Papers on Economic Activity* 783 (1987); Wesley M. Cohen, Richard R. Nelson, and John P. Walsh, "Protecting Their Intellectual Property Assets: Appropriability Conditions and Why U.S. Manufacturing Firms Patent or Not," NBER Working Paper No. 7552 (2000); Ashish Arora, Marco Ceccagnoli, and Wesley Cohen, "Intellectual Property Strategies and the Returns to R&D," Working Paper (Nov. 2000).
39. Peter J. Toren, "Protecting Inventions as Trade Secrets: A Better Way When Patents Are Inappropriate, Unavailable," 2 *IP Law Weekly* (May 24, 2000); Patents v. Trade Secrets, in Barufka and Einschlag, *supra* at 293–330.
40. Ibid.
41. AIPLA 1999, *supra* at 63–64.
42. AIPLA 1999, *supra* at 64–65; Lemley, Rational, *supra* at fn. 14.
43. Office of USPTO spokesperson Brigid Quinn, personal e-mail communication (Jan. 11, 2001). See also Lemley, "Rational," *supra* at 12.
44. USPTO fee schedule, Oct. 1, 2000.
45. Lemley, "Rational," *supra*.
46. Rivette and Kline, *supra*—derived; Murtha, "Licensing," *supra*—derived.
47. 2000 U.S. Law Department Spending Survey 44, PricewaterhouseCoopers (2000).
48. See Emmett J. Murtha, personal e-mail communication (April 16, 2001); Murtha, "Licensing," *supra* at 13. See also Lemley, "Rational," *supra* at 16. These numbers are probably too generous because entire or large portions of patent portfolios are often licensed as a package even though the licensees care about only one or two of the patents, so the tagalong patents get credit they don't deserve.
49. Michael B. Einschlag, "Speech," Patent Strategy & Management Seminar (Tysons Corner, VA Nov. 3, 2000). If you could make a 50 percent margin and instead you license at a 5 percent royalty, the licensee has to sell over 10 times what you could sell to make it worthwhile. See also Reiko Aoki and Jin-Li Hu, "Imperfect Patent Enforce-

ment, Legal Rules and Settlement," Working Paper (1999); But see Murtha, "Licensing," *supra* at 13 (roughly less than 5 percent of patented inventions are used by the company that owns them).

50. See Mark Hirschey, Vernon J. Richardson, and Susan W. Scholz, "Value Relevance of Nonfinancial Information: The Case of Patent Data," *papers.ssrn.com* (1998). See also Bronwyn H. Hall, "Innovation and Market Value," NBER Working Paper 6984 (NBER 1999).

51. Samson Vermont, *Patent Strategy & Management* (April 2001) (U.S. Patent No. 6,175,824).

52. Office of USPTO, *supra*. See also Lemley and Allison, "Who's Patenting," *supra* at 2128.

53. Kevin Rivette, David Kline, and Gerald Mossinghoff, "Wall Street's Untapped Patent Opportunities," in *Hidden Value: Profiting from the Intellectual Property Economy*, p.127, Bruce Berman (ed.) (21st Century Books 1999).

54. Russell L. Parr, "Valuing and Determining Royalties for Technology," in Barufka and Einschlag, *supra* at 49.

55. 2000 Intellectual Property Metrics, *supra* at 44. But see Murtha, "Licensing," *supra* at 13. Murtha says it's more than $10 million in R&D for every patent.

56. 2000 Intellectual Property Metrics, *supra* at 13.

57. Patents can't be worth more than their underlying costs because that would mean creating something out of nothing. More precisely, if ever there were a time when each patent (which costs about $20,000 to get) was worth more than $4.26 million (price), then filings would increase dramatically (supply) until the value of patents decreased to the point that they reflected their actual cost.

58. Levin et al., *supra*; Cohen, Nelson, and Walsh, *supra*.

59. This figure was derived by comparing EPO application filing data with USPTO application filing data: In 1997, Americans filed about 20,400 EPO patent applications in the EPO and about 130,000 U.S. patent applications in the USPTO. (Foreigners also filed about 102,000 U.S. applications in the USPTO in 1997.) Assuming that these EPO applications had a U.S. counterpart application, which would generally be the case, then at least 16 percent of the U.S. applications (20,400/130,000 = .16) have an EPO counterpart application.

60. Jean O. Lanjouw and Mark Schankerman, "Characteristics of Patent Litigation: A Window on Competition," p. 3 Working Paper (March 2000).

61. She confirmed this interpretation (not the R&D numbers). Lanjouw, personal e-mail communication (April 13, 2001).

62. Office of USPTO, *supra*.

63. Ted O'Donoghue, Suzanne Scotchmer, and Jacques-Francois Thisse, "Patent Breadth, Patent Life and the Pace of Technological Progress," 7 *J. Econ. & Mngmt. Strategy* 2, No. 1 (Spring 1998). Samson Vermont, "Patent Math as Experienced Through a Cost-Benefit Analysis of Reacting to *Festo*," *Patent Strategy & Management* (January 2001).

64. See also Jin-Li Hu and Reiko Aoki, "Time Factors of Patent Litigation and Licensing," Working Paper (2000).

65. Jean O. Lanjouw, "Patent Protection: Of What Value and For How Long?" NBER, Working Paper No. 4475 (NBER 1993).

66. See Dietmar Harhoff, Frederic M. Scherer, and Katrin Vopel, "Exploring the Tail of Patented Invention Value Distributions," Discussion Paper (Social Science Research Center, 1997).

67. "Prior art" generally refers to all technology that existed at least one year before the application was filed. Typically, however, only prior art patents are searched, not all prior scientific literature.

68. Searches by the EPO are superior to searches by U.S. examiners, and it may be advisable to commission a search there before filing in the United States because changes made after filing result in reduced claim scope.

69. For technical legal reasons stemming from a controversial patent decision, *Festo Corp. v. Shoketsu*, arguably at least 10 of those claims should be "independent," a term of art for a claim that stands alone in a patent application and for which the Patent Office charges extra if you exceed three in one application.

70. Levin et al., *supra*. See also Arora, Ceccagnoli, and Cohen, *supra*; Lemley, "Who's Patenting," *supra* at 2125–2132.

71. Ellen Licking, John Carey, and Jim Kerstetter, "Bioinformatics," 50 *The Business Week* 167 (Spring 2001).

72. AIPLA 1999, *supra*.

73. Lanjouw and Schankerman, "Stylized," *supra*; Lanjouw and Schankerman, "Window," *supra*; Josh Lerner, "Patenting in the Shadow of Competitors," 38 *J. Law & Econ.* 463 (Oct. 1995).

74. Lemley and Allison, "Who's Patenting," *supra* at 2125–2127.

75. Lanjouw and Schankerman, "Stylized," *supra* at 3.

76. It's become so expensive that even some beneficiaries of the expense, the patent and trial attorneys, are calling for change. For example, every year the AIPLA, whose membership comprises about 12,000 IP attorneys, hosts a symposium on reducing the costs of patent litigation. See also Tom Arnold, "Why ADR," in *Patent Litigation 1999* (Practising Law Institute 1999); Ewing, "Patent Litigation," *supra* at pp. 1057–1070 (Practising Law Institute 1999); see also Lucy J. Billings, "Managing Patent Litigation," in *Patent Litigation 1999*, p. 1047–1054 (Practising Law Institute 1999). It's also hard to estimate the expense. About 50 percent of the time, the costs will exceed their estimate by more than $500,000 or go under the estimate by more than $250,000. Similarly, in about half of cases, the length of suit will exceed the estimated length by more than two years or go under it by more than one year. Tom Arnold, *supra* at 1017.

77. Derived from Lemley, "Rational," *supra* at 10. I'm trying to use conservative but forward-looking numbers. Lemley comes up with $2.1 billion using legal costs from 1999 and the number of suits filed in either 1992 or 1996 depending on whether one relies on the Derwent Litalert database or the Administrative Office of the U.S. District Courts.

78. "Understanding patent law is a tricky business. The history of American patent law has been relatively chaotic compared to other laws providing for exclusive rights to property. Major changes in patent law occur on a yearly and sometimes monthly basis. The frequent changes in patent law are a symptom of the confusion that surrounds it. The difficulty does not arise because the general goal of the law is unclear or hard to understand. . . . The difficulty comes in understanding exactly how the patent system helps the economy and how particular rules contribute to that goal." John W. Schlicher, *Patent Law: Legal and Economic Principles*, pp. viii–ix of preface (West 1992, updated annually).

79. "Patents and copyrights approach nearer than any other class of cases belonging to forensic discussions, to what may be called the metaphysics of the law, where distinctions are, or at least may be, very subtle and refined, and, sometimes, almost evanescent." Justice Story in *Folsom v. Marsh*, 9 F. Cas. 342, 344 (C.C.D. mass. 1841) (No. 4901); *Barret v. Hall*, 2 Fed. Cas. 914, 923 (No. 1047) (C.C.D. Mass. 1818). *See* also Judge Gee's opinion in *Rohm & Hass Co. v. Dawson Chemical Co.*, 599 F.2d 685, 706 (5th Cir. 1979) (agreeing with Story's assessment).

80. Moore, "Forum," *supra*.

81. Ewing, *supra* at 1062.

82. Amos Tversky and Daniel Kahneman, "The Psychology of Preferences," *Scientifica America* 132–242 (1982). Goodwin and Wright, *supra* at 65–72.

83. Billings, *supra* at 1052, appears to agree with this statement.

84. See generally Samson Vermont, "Memes and the Evolution of Intellectual Dishonesty in Law," 22 *Legal Studies Forum* 655 (1998).

85. Canon 7, ABA Model Code of Professional Responsibility.
86. The pro bono ethic is a quasi-recognition of this problem. It's "quasi" in that it reflects an unrealistic and overly tidy view that if the pie is just sliced and diced the right way everyone can have everything: attorneys can be perfectionists and those who can't afford perfectionists will get them nonetheless. But pro bono work is too paltry to have this effect. Arguably, it's a token gesture which sustains the illusion of high-mindedness without making any serious dent in the pocketbook. (This is not to say that lawyers who perform pro bono work think this way.) See generally Vermont, "Memes," *supra*.
87. See Richard A. Posner, *"Overcoming Law"* 33–67 (Harvard Univ. Press, 1995).
88. The 2001 AIPLA Economic Survey was not available at the time of this writing. However, since the fees and related expenses increased 30 percent from 1997 to 1999, and since the last two years have seen dramatic increases in associate salaries, I assumed a 30 percent increase from 1999's average figure of $1.5 million. (Law firm partners are eating some of this salary increase, but some will come out of increased hourly rates. See also AIPLA 1999, *supra* at 86; the table is vague but appears to show billings increasing about 25 percent per year.) Also, patent suits are increasing about 8 percent every year, whereas the number of judges and patent trials will remain fixed. See generally "Trends," *supra*; Kerr and Prakash-Canjels, *supra* at 2–3; Quinn, *supra* at 5. This will increase the length of suits, which invariably increases fees. Work expands to fill the time allotted for it. Cyril N. Parkinson, *Parkinson's Law* (1957). If you have two weeks to complete a task, you'll tend to complete it in two weeks. If you have two days to complete the same task, you'll tend to complete it in two days. Therefore, since attorneys generally charge for their time and not by the task or according to value added, increasing the time interval in which they work invariably increases costs. This is especially true in litigation which, when protracted and open-ended, drinks attorney billables with abandon. And no litigation is thirstier than patent litigation.
89. By looking at Quinn, *supra* at 6, one can see that the number of patent trials is likely to stay constant at about 100 per year. In 2000, 2,486 patent suits were filed. (One hundred is 4 percent of 2,486.)
90. John S. Hammond, Ralph L. Keeney, and Howard Raiffa. *Smart Choices: A Practical Guide to Making Better Decisions,* pp. viii–ix (Harvard Business School Press 1999).
91. See generally Marc B. Victor, *Getting Started with DATA 3.5—for Litigators* 9–12 (TreeAge Software Inc. 1999); Goodwin and Wright, *supra* at 19–22, 145–179.
92. Hammond, Keeney, and Raiffa, *supra* at 4.
93. Victor, "Evaluating Legal Risks," *supra* at 12–42.
94. Continuous is the opposite of discrete. For example, a light switch has a discrete variable—it's either on or it's off, there is no in-between. Money, on the other hand, is a continuous variable because it increases or decreases incrementally forever.
95. Marc B. Victor, personal telephone communication (April 2001). Compare Goodwin and Wright, *supra* at 156–162.
96. See generally "Symposium: Legal Implications of Human Error," 59 *S. Cal. L. Rev.* 225 No. 2 (January 1986); Spetzler and Von Holstein, *supra*; Kahneman, Slovic, and Tversky, "Judgment," *supra*; Kahneman, Slovic, and Tversky, "Science," *supra* at 1124–1131; Goodwin and Wright, *supra* at 248–273.
97. Vermont, "Memes," *supra*; and "Why Law and Economics Is Not the Frankenstein Monster," 15 *Economics & Philosophy* (1999).
98. See Goodwin and Wright, *supra* at 254–255.
99. See Ibid. at 284–285.
100. Skinner, *supra* at 204.
101. In one study, subjects who were asked to estimate ranges wide enough to have a 90 percent chance of including a true value—such as the actual distance from England to

Chile—estimated ranges that included the true value only 57 percent of the time. Goodwin and Wright, *supra* at 259–260.

102. Marc B. Victor, personal telephone communication (April 2001).

103. Hammond, Keeney, and Raiffa, *supra* at 52.

104. See P.G. Moore and H. Thomas, *The Anatomy of Decisions*, 2nd ed. (Penguin 1988); Goodwin and Wright, *supra* at 73–74.

105. See generally Goodwin and Wright, *supra* at 298.

106. Research shows that simple averages usually produce overall outcomes that are as good as weighted averages. See Goodwin and Wright, *supra* at 298–300.

107. See generally Beron, "Seminar," *supra*.

108. Goodwin and Wright, *supra* at 275.

109. See generally Beron, "Seminar," *supra*.

110. See generally Goodwin and Wright, *supra* at 227–243.

111. This number is not based on anything.

112. See Moore, "Forum," *supra*; Lanjouw and Schankerman, "Stylized," *supra* at 9. Moore reports 14 percent; Lanjouw and Schankerman report 16 percent.

113. Moore, "Judges," *supra*—derived. The 12 percent figure refers to all patent suits filed, whether inequitable conduct was a real issue or not. In suits where inequitable conduct was tried, 27 percent of patents were held unenforceable.

114. Median and average award figures can be useful, however, for analyzing large portfolios of patents.

115. Moore, "Judges," *supra*.

116. Ibid.

117. Ibid.

118. Ibid.

119. See generally "Trends," *supra*.

120. Moore says 55 percent of cases are reported. She also says "reported" means reported to the PTO or Administrative Office of the U.S. District Courts. It does not mean "published," as in a published opinion resulted. Personal telephone communication with Kimberly A. Moore, June 2001. See also Moore, "Judges," *supra*; "Trends," *supra*.

121. *Polaroid Inc. v. Eastman Kodak Co.*, 228 USPQ 305 (D.Mass 1985), *aff'd* 229 USPQ 561 (Fed. Cir. 1986).

122. See generally "Trends," *supra*.

123. Moore, "Judges," *supra*—derived.

124. Kimberly A. Moore, personal e-mail communication (March 27, 2001). Note that, for our purposes, 15 percent is an absolute *minimum*. If all patent cases proceeded as far as they could go, that is, if none ever settled, then certainly judges would throw out additional cases before trial. In other words, in the real world most cases settle before all opportunities for pretrial disposal have been exhausted. If they didn't settle, invariably many would be disposed against the plaintiff before trial, so that more than 15 percent of all filed suits would be dismissed before trial.

125. Moore, "Judges," *supra*—derived. I shifted some percentage points from infringement to validity on a hunch that the trial pattern for infringement is too high for pretrial and that the pattern for validity is too low. This is based on the view that infringement issues are more fact intensive and because Allison and Lemley's validity study indicates that the pretrial invalidation rate is high. See Allison and Lemley, "Empirical," *supra*.

126. Moore, "Judges," *supra*—derived. Compare Allison and Lemley, "Empirical," *supra* at 241. According to Allison and Lemley, about 54 percent of published decisions that invalidate a patent are appealed, whereas 44 percent of published decisions that validate a patent are appealed.

127. Moore, "Judges," *supra*—derived.

128. Allison and Lemley, "Empirical," *supra* at 241—derived.

129. See *infra* note 124.

130. Allison and Lemley, "Empirical," *supra* at 208. Allison and Lemley only examined reported decisions. They did not account for the likely fact that decisions of invalidity are much more likely to produce published opinions than decisions of validity. Thus, the study is not a solid basis for estimating the likelihood of a patent being invalidated. With respect to the *grounds* for invalidity, however, published decisions probably don't differ from unpublished decisions.

131. Moore, "Judges," *supra*—derived.

132. Moore, "Judges," *supra*—very derived. See *infra* note 19, explaining how percentage held enforceable was determined.

133. Moore, "Judges," *supra*.

134. Ibid.

135. Ibid.

136. Ibid.—derived.

137. Ibid.

138. Ibid.

139. Ibid.

140. See generally Moore, "Judges," *supra*; Coolley, *supra*. This figure mainly comes from Moore as derived in light of inflation and the fact that her award amounts don't include interest, attorneys' fees, or enhanced damages. Also, as discussed *infra*, enhanced damages constitute a larger portion of these lower awards. See also "Trends," *supra*; Kerr and Prakash-Canjels, *supra* (median award for reported cases was $2.8 million in the 1990s).

141. Coolley, *supra* at 517—derived. See also Norman L. Balmer, "Alternative Dispute Resolution in Patent Controversies," Franklin Pierce Law Center (online) (March 5, 2001).

142. Bernard Siskin Staller, Jerome Staller, and David Rorvik, *What Are the Chances?* 115 (Signet 1993).

143. *Forbes* 130–140 (July 7, 1997).

144. Neil DiBernardo, Dunn & Bradstreet, personal telephone communication (Spring 2001). D&B tracks businesses that file bankruptcy or that go out of business owing substantial sums. But this amounts to only about 100,000 businesses per year and does not include the much larger number of business "discontinuances," which is apparent considering that if only 100,000 of the 12 million U.S. businesses fail annually, the failure rate would be less than 1 percent.

145. "Establishment" means a physical place of business, not necessarily an entire business.

146. The failure rate should be higher for infringers because they form a different statistical population; the infringement itself may stem from financial desperation. Also, the very fact of the suit itself will undermine confidence in the defendant company and further increase its chance of failure.

147. An appeal takes about another year, but losing infringers must normally post a bond upon appeal. Thus, only successful appeals by patent owners matter here. Since most appeals do not result in more money damages for the patentee, appeal time can be ignored.

148. KPMG Corporate Tax Rate Survey, January 2000; Ronald Blasi, Georgia State University School of Law, personal e-mail communication (March 26, 2001); unofficial spokesperson for National Economics Research Associates (NERA), personal e-mail communication (March 26, 2001).

149. Courts award prejudgment interest, but that has already been taken into account because these amounts are based on real awards. By the way, prejudgment interest tends to be low, around the prime rate. Thus, it's generally about half of the true discount rate.

150. Determining the appropriate discount rate is a complex area. Goodwin and Wright,

supra at 200. The company CFO is probably a better source for the discount rate than the decision analyst.

151. "At risk" means what potentially could have been lost, not what was actually lost.

152. AIPLA 1999, *supra* at 75.

153. Ibid.—derived.

154. Ibid.

155. Ibid.

156. Ibid. The legal costs also correspond to the actual award amounts, not to just the amounts at risk. See generally Moore, "Judges," *supra*. Moore's numbers don't include willfulness damages, which account for about half of the amount of lower damage awards.

157. If one of the two parties were going to fail before the end of five years of litigation, the legal costs expended prior to bankruptcy would be somewhat less, so one could also decrease the legal costs based on the annual rate of failure. Marc B. Victor, personal e-mail communication (May 2001).

158. Moore, "Forum," *supra*.

159. However, since diminishing returns later on means logarithmic returns early on, legal fees cannot go as low as awards either. The plaintiff might win only one dollar, but there is a certain minimum legal effort that any case demands, even when the representation isn't particularly zealous.

160. I received contradictory answers about the deductibility of willfulness damages. I eventually asked two tax law professors, two IP damage experts, and a bunch of patent lawyers. No one knew for sure and I couldn't find any case law on it. Since you can't prove a negative, I concluded that they must be deductible like regular punitive damages. Regular punitive damages are deductible so long as they derive from a business purpose. Camilla Watson, personal e-mail communication, University of Georgia School of Law (March 26–27, 2001).

161. ClickNSettle.com provided the $15 million figure.

162. See generally William F. Heinze, "Patent Mediation: The Forgotten Alternative in Dispute Resolution," 18 *AIPLA Q.J.* 333, 334 (1991); Steven J. Elleman. Note, "Problems in Patent Litigation: Mandatory Mediation May Provide Settlements and Solutions," 12 *Ohio State J. on Dispute Resolution* 759 (1997).

163. For further information on this research, visit *www.nationalacademies.org/ipr*, or contact: Craig Schultz, Research Associate, 2200 The National Academies Board on Science, Technology, and Economic Policy (STEP), or at cschultz@nas.edu.

164. See also Balmer, *supra*.

165. See also Sanjai Bhagat, James A. Brickley, and Jeffrey Coles, "Comparing the Cost of Outside and Inside Counsel," 8 *Corporate Counsel's Quarterly* 80–89 (1994).

166. Lerner, "Shadow," *supra* at 471–472.

167. See James L. Ewing IV, "In-House Participation in Patent Litigation," *Patent Strategy & Management* (Oct. 2000).

168. Sophisticated econometric studies of the average values of patents are all over the map. See generally Ariel Pakes, "Patents as Options: Some Estimates of the Value of Holding European Patent Stocks," NBER Working Paper No. 1340 (NBER 1984); Jean O. Lanjouw, Ariel Pakes, and Jonathan Putnam, "How to Count Patents and Value Intellectual Property: Uses of Patent Renewal Data and Application Data," NBER Working Paper 5741 (NBER 1996); Harhoff, Scherer, and Vopel, *supra*.

169. Lerner and Lanjouw, "Preliminary," *supra* at Table 3—derived. Although the chances for patents that have been litigated before are much better. Thomas Pavelko, Stevens Davis, Miller & Mosher, personal communication (April 10, 2001). About 40 percent of patents in litigation have been litigated before. Lerner and Lanjouw, "Preliminary," *supra*—derived.

170. William O. Kerr, Penta Advisory Services, personal telephone communication (Spring

2001); Thomas A. Turano, Testa Hurwitz & Thibeault, personal e-mail communication (March 12, 2001). See also Mark Schankerman and Suzanne Scotchmer, "Damages and Injunctions in the Protection of Proprietary Research Tools," NBER Working Paper No. 7086 (NBER 1999). The following article title is very telling: Alan Ratliff, "It's Not Just About Injunctions Anymore: An Overview of Money Damages in Intellectual Property Litigation," 7 *IP Litigator* 2 (No. 3, March 2001).

171. Allison and Lemley, "Empirical," *supra*.

172. Lanjouw and Schankerman, "Stylized," *supra* at fn. 8.

173. See infra note 63.

174. Ibid.

175. Ibid.

176. It cannot exceed 20 percent of $15 million ($3 million). Ewing, "Managing," *supra* at 1064–1066.

177. When damages are trebled, the plaintiff gets three times the compensatory damages, not three times the compensatory damages plus the original compensatory damages.

178. Moore, "Judges," *supra*. Coolley indicates 43 percent of the time, but Coolley only looked at 152 *reported* cases. See Coolley, *supra*.

179. Ibid. Coolley shows 38 percent. Coolley, *supra*.

180. Moore, "Judges," *supra*.

181. Prejudgment interest accounts for 11 percent and attorneys' fees accounts for 3 percent. Coolley, *supra* at 519.

182. "Less than" because we're looking at the *mean* enhancement but we're referring to the absolute number of awards. Since high awards can skew the mean upward far more than low awards can skew it downward—because an award can't go below zero but it can go into the hundreds of millions—we may assume that most trebled and doubled awards are for amounts a good bit lower than, respectively, $1.13 million and $4.7 million.

183. Moore, "Judges," *supra*—derived.

184. Coolley, *supra*.

185. Skinner, *supra* at 208. There are other methods, such as the Extended Pearson-Tukey approximation (95-50-5) and the Extended Swanson-McGill technique (30-40-30). The latter is used when the distribution is very skewed.

186. This figure can be roughly deduced by comparing values available in "Trends," *supra* and Coolley, *supra* at 517.

187. Derived from Coolley, *supra* at 516, in light of "Trends," *supra*.

188. Skinner says one sixth of net worth. Skinner, *supra* at 227. Beron says one fifth. See Beron, "Primer," *supra*.

189. Lanjouw and Lerner, "Preliminary," *supra* at Table 2—modified to account for inflation.

190. I assume that because 28 percent of patent owners are small entities, about 28 percent of litigants are also small entities. See also Allison and Lemley, "Empirical," *supra* (small inventors more, not less likely to sue).

191. Moore, "Judges," *supra*—derived in light of Coolley, *supra* and "Trends," *supra*. Awards have doubled since the 1990s and Moore pools together amounts from both the 1980s and 1990s. To account for downward skewing by the 1980s, I increased her award categories by 33 percent. See also Beutel, "Is the Tide," *supra* at 14–17.

192. These litigation financiers, however, only take the strongest cases. Also, they may have less to lose because it's not their patent that could be invalidated, which alters the cost-benefit analysis.

193. Moore, "Judges," *supra* at 120.

194. "Trends," *supra*.

195. Although this would probably have to be discounted somewhat based on an average risk profile.

196. Also, according to Dr. Nir Kossovsky: "The greatest challenge to decision tree analysis is that the mathematics assume that any of the branches are pursued to completion, whereas in reality, there exist managerial options to abandon a track. If you were to analyze the same tree using real options theory, you would tend to get higher values for litigation, and that fact may also explain why parties are more likely to litigate than not even if a rational decision tree analysis shows that the value proposition for litigation is zero. See Martha Amran, "Real Options" from Amazon *www.amazon.com/exec/obidos/ASIN/0875848451/starshopcom/107-0244459-9764573*. Nir Kossovsky, personal e-mail communication (April 26, 2001). The author does not really know what to make of this statement. For a different (theoretical) take on why patent litigation may be more valuable to plaintiffs than it seems, see Reiko Aoki and Jin-Li Hu, "Imperfect Patent Enforcement, Legal Rules and Settlement," Working Paper (Nov. 1999).

197. See generally Lanjouw and Schankerman, "Stylized," *supra.*

198. Lerner found that companies with high legal costs stay out of highly litigated areas of technology. See Lerner, "Shadow," *supra.*

199. Spetzler and Von Holstein, *supra* at 356.

200. For example, performing sensitivity analysis with DATA is tricky and subtle. Victor, "Getting Started," *supra.*

201. Monte Carlo simulation is used when there are very large numbers of interrelated variables. It may be useful for combining the many factors used to determine reasonable royalties.

202. See Allison and Lemley, "Empirical," *supra.*

203. Glazier, *supra.*

204. Marc B. Victor's *Litigation Risk Analysis* (Kenwood, CA, formerly Menlo Park, CA) (*www.LitigationRisk.com*); Bruce Beron's Litigation Risk Management Institute (Palo Alto, CA).

205. Victor's *Litigation Risk Analysis.*

206. Out of sight, out of mind is a major obstacle to good decision making. See Goodwin and Wright, *supra* at 160–167.

207. See generally Beron, "Primer," *supra*; Skinner, *supra* at 14, 73–97.

208. Some claim that "minimization of regret," not maximization of utility, is what people strive for. See generally Robert E. Scott, "Error and Rationality in Individual Decision-Making," 59 *S. Cal. L. Rev.* 329, (January 1986); Jeffrey J. Rachlinski, "Gains, Losses, and the Psychology of Litigation," 70 *S. Cal. Rev.* 113 (November 1996).

209. Lucy F. Ackert, Ping Zhang, and Bryan K. Church, "Uncertain Litigation Costs and Seller Behavior: Evidence from an Auditing Game," White Paper (Federal Reserve Bank of Atlanta 1998). See also Skinner, *supra* at 111.

ABOUT THE AUTHOR

Samson Vermont is a patent attorney in the Washington, D.C., office of Hunton & Williams, a U.S. law firm with more than 700 attorneys serving clients in 80 countries from 15 offices around the world. Mr. Vermont is the founder, columnist, and editor of the monthly periodical *Patent Strategy & Management*; and an advisor and columnist for the monthly *The Patent Journal*. Mr. Vermont has written numerous articles about IP, including "A New Way to Determine Obviousness: Applying the Pioneer Doctrine to 103(a), 29," *AIPLA Quarterly Journal* (Summer 2001); "The Economic Logic Underlying the Patent System," *www.law.com* (October 2000); "Turning Knowledge Into Gold I: Patent Strategy Goes Mainstream," *IP Law Weekly*

(March 2000); and "Strategies for Avoiding Willfulness Damages," *Intellectual Property Strategist* (December 1999). He has also authored journal papers concerning the intersection of law, economics, philosophy, cognitive science, and/or evolution, including "Why Law and Economics Is Not the Frankenstein Monster," *Economics & Philosophy* (1999); and "Memes and the Evolution of Intellectual Dishonesty in Law," *Legal Studies Forum* (1998). He received a BA in philosophy and psychology from Rhodes College in 1990; a J. D. from the University of Georgia School of Law in 1994; and completed graduate coursework in chemistry at Georgia State University in 1997. The author is grateful for the assistance with this chapter. Special thanks goes to Marc Victor, president of Litigation Risk Analysis, Inc., and a pioneer in applying decision analysis to litigation, for his insights and invaluable guidance. For their helpful comments, Mr. Vermont also thanks Kimberly Moore of George Mason University School of Law; Phillip Beutel of NERA; Emmett Murtha of Fairfield Resources International Inc.; William Kerr of PENTA Advisory Services; Nir Kossovsky of The Patent & License Exchange; Bruce Beron of Litigation Risk Management Institute; and Morris Raker of TreeAge Software. The author also thanks Ms. Moore for granting early access to her patent studies.

CHAPTER SEVENTEEN

Avoiding Transaction Peril
Value-Based IP Due Diligence

by Mark Haller, Edward Gold, and Brian Blonder

PERSPECTIVES

Intellectual property rights are now among the most significant components of many business transactions. Still, the overwhelming focus of most deals is not IP but tangible assets like real estate and inventory. The reasons for this are complex and include the traditional difficulties about the language used to describe and discuss patents and other intangibles, as well as misconceptions about the value and strategic importance of IP. In the final analysis, many companies simply do not fully understand the IP they are acquiring (or divesting) and the impact on the current and ongoing value of the deal. This has proven a costly mistake.

"Synergies between the operations of the buyer and target are often a prime motivator for deals," says PricewaterhouseCooper's (PwC) Mark Haller. "Yet how often is pre- or post-deal analysis of the fit between the IP portfolio of the buyer and target conducted? Not often. As a result, the acquiring party subjects itself to greater risk and is far less likely to reap the benefit of the combination of the portfolios, or to discover valuable but off-strategy assets that can be offloaded to reduce the cost of the acquisition. Here we suggest a new approach to IP due diligence—an approach beyond the legal—a business, value-based approach that addresses the current deficiencies to achieve better decision making, lower risk, and increased value in these transactions."

In their chapter, Mr. Haller, Mr. Gold, and Mr. Blonder address issues to consider in defining the scope of any IP due diligence process, provide guidance on steps and approaches for addressing these issues, and address issues in due diligence surrounding intangible assets other than IP. They also include a discussion of the latest techniques and advanced methodologies for analyzing IP assets, particularly patents. Their list of acquirer's key questions and of target/seller's questions would serve many owners and advisors well.

Mr. Haller, Mr. Gold, and Mr. Blonder cite Rivette and Kline in a *Harvard Business Review* article, "Discovering New Value in Intellectual Property," regarding how thoroughly IP is being regarded on Wall Street. ". . . One would be hard-pressed to find a major investment bank that employs even one individual with experience in evaluating patent portfolios." In this context, conclude the authors, "do you want to rely on an IP due diligence process still rooted in the industrial age or one that recognizes the realities of the new economy and the changing source value?"

INTRODUCTION

Today more than three quarters of the total market value of Standard & Poor's (S&P) 500 corporations derives from intangible assets, as total book value has declined to one quarter of market value; down from three quarters in 1989.[1] But with as much as 75 percent or more of the value of major corporations now represented by intangible assets, has the process for conducting due diligence in business acquisitions changed? "Not enough" is the answer, and the negative results can be significant.

In any business acquisition, among the most identifiable and significant of the intangible assets are the target's intellectual property. Together with related know-how, these codified and legally protected intangible assets often represent the fruit of tens of millions of dollars of research and development (R&D).[2] In addition, their existence and proper application may be both the source of and protection for the lion's share of the target's revenue, income, or cash flow. These assets alone may have such impact on the predicted cash flows and on the risk of those cash flows occurring as to render assessments of the price of the deal perilously deficient without proper consideration. Yet the due diligence process typically focuses on tangible assets and historical results. Intellectual property and related intangible assets are typically considered late in the game and then often only to the extent of ticking off items on a list and assessing the veracity of the legal bona fides of ownership.

Synergies between the operations of the buyer and target are often a prime motivator for deals. Yet how often is pre- or post-deal analysis of the fit between the IP portfolio of the buyer and target conducted? Not often. As a result, the acquiring party subjects itself to greater risk and is far less likely to reap the benefit of the combination of the portfolios or to discover valuable but off-strategy assets that can be off-loaded to reduce the cost of the acquisition. Here we suggest a new approach to IP due diligence—an approach beyond the legal—a business, value-based approach that addresses the current deficiencies to achieve better decision making, lower risk, and increased value in these transactions.

THE PRESENT STATE

Today, due diligence is often deficient in the review of the underlying benefits and risks associated with the related IP and other intangible or intellectual assets (IA). In a recent article on IP value, the authors go as far as to state that ". . . unfortunately, many managers would be surprised to discover just how abysmal most due diligence efforts regarding intellectual property are" and go on to say ". . . one would be hard-pressed to find a major investment bank that employs even one individual with experience in evaluating patent portfolios."[3] In fact, they quote one senior executive of a leading Wall Street Investment bank as stating, "Most M&A [managers and acquisitions] companies, including ours, simply don't look closely at the patent portfolios involved, either for valuation issues or for exploitation possibilities."[4]

Based on our experience and our discussions with others involved in due diligence matters, it is evident that due diligence related to IP, if it occurs at all, is often limited to a focus on legal aspects of the IP. A review of the recent literature confirms that IP due diligence is often limited to addressing whether:

- The IP rights are owned by the seller
- There are technical defects in these rights
- The rights are valid
- The rights are enforceable (all legal factors)[5]

However, even if the answer to each item on the list above is "yes," there are many other factors that might lead one to conclude the IP is of little or no business value. Other intangible assets, like associated know-how, typically receive even less attention during the due diligence process.

This practice is surprising, considering the ever-increasing importance of IP and other intangible assets as a motivating factor behind corporate mergers and acquisitions. A recent article noted that "Increasingly, the value and importance of intangible assets are the driving force behind these mega-mergers and are playing a greater role in terms of assets received through mergers, acquisitions, and take-overs."[6] In fact, intangible assets may end up being the most valuable assets acquired in a transaction. Even if the basis for the transaction is access to a product or a service, the success of that product or service is often dependent upon the legal protection and support of intangible assets, including IP.

OUR MISSION

Here we take a closer look at additional reasons why a due diligence review should include a more thorough consideration of the rights to intangible assets being transferred as a part of the transaction, and provide examples of specific situations signaling the need for a more precise IP due diligence effort. We step through three overall phases of the IP due diligence review:

Phase I—Strategy and Scope

1. Understand Transaction Objectives and Plan Due Diligence
- Understand the transaction objectives.
- Develop critical questions.
- Pick the IP due diligence team.

2. Characterize IP Culture and Fit of Acquirer and Target
- Will the cultures mesh easily?
- What impact does this have on the scope and depth of IP due diligence effort?

Phase II—Inventory and Review

3. Inventory Products and Services Changing Hands
- What is needed to make the integration a success?
- What is core to the deal, what is extra?

4. Inventory IP Changing Hands
- Consider all intellectual property changing hands including trade secrets.
- Conduct interviews to uncover full list.

5. Inventory Contractual Obligations
- Are the contracts transferable?
- Are there other important restrictions?

6. Inventory Other Intangible Assets Changing Hands
- Which key employees must be kept?
- Which key relationships (customers, distributors, etc.) must be maintained?

Phase III—Analysis and Response

7. Link Intellectual Assets and Related Intangibles to Products and Services and Evaluate Impact
- Identify strengths and weaknesses in protection. Can weaknesses be corrected, indemnified?
- Is there surplus IP of value?

8. Evaluate the Competitive Landscape and Other External IP/IA Influences
- Are third-party licenses needed?
- Will acquirer receive IP that can be offensively used against competitors?
- Consider industry, customer, competitor, antitrust, and regulatory trends for IP/IA.

9. Estimate the Value to Enable Pre- or Post-Deal Action
- Consider key risk and value drivers from above.
- Consider value from internal and external exploitation.
- Formulate and execute actions.

Exhibit 17-1 Nine IP due diligence steps to transaction success.

1. Strategy and Scope
2. Review and Inventory
3. Analysis and Response

Exhibit 17-1 takes the reviewer through the nine key IP due diligence steps to transaction success.

We also address issues to consider in defining the scope of any IP due diligence process, provide guidance on steps and approaches for addressing these issues within the defined IP due diligence scope, and address issues in due diligence surrounding intangible assets other than intellectual property.

In addition, we include a discussion of state-of-the-art techniques and advanced methodologies that have improved the due diligence process. Finally, we address why IP due diligence provides benefits, including those that directly support the analysis of the proposed transaction and those indirect additional benefits that result from the IP due diligence process, which far outweigh the cost.

PHASE I—STRATEGY AND SCOPE

Objectives and Planning

The goal of due diligence is to provide the party proposing the transaction with sufficient information to make a reasoned decision as to whether or not to complete the transaction as proposed. Due diligence should provide a basis for determining or validating the appropriate terms and price for the transaction incorporating consideration of the risks inherent in the proposed transaction.

Generally, the desire to complete the transaction is based on one or more objectives to be achieved as a result of the transaction. A key first step in any due diligence effort is to develop an understanding of the purpose for the transaction.[7,8] Take for example, a situation where the transaction target is the subsidiary of another company and is being acquired because the buyer desires access to a particular cost-reducing manufacturing process the target owns. The acquirer's due diligence should be designed to determine not only whether, and to what extent, the process is owned (for example, patented), but also whether or not this cost reduction goal will be achieved within the acquirer's existing manufacturing operations through the transaction (portability) and what risks are inherent in completing this transaction. Intellectual property due diligence that does not consider portability and risk falls far short of addressing whether or not the transaction will achieve its objectives and whether or not the risks of the transaction will outweigh the benefits. In this first step, the planning of relevant inquiry should be determined to support information gathering that will be key to the due diligence process.

Some examples of critical questions concerning the IP may include:

Acquirer's Questions

1. Will the patented subject matter be adaptable to the acquiring company's products, services, and/or processes?
2. What effect will the protected process/features have on the quality and marketability of the acquiring company's product?
3. What activities are ongoing at competitors that may lessen the value of the obtained protected process/feature?
4. Could the patented subject matter be adapted to other products manufactured by the acquiring company?
5. Is there a right (and value) to both exclude others from the practice as well as to practice without infringement upon the rights of others?
6. Is there an opportunity to license the IP to others (those who do or do not compete with the acquiring company)?
7. Are competitors developing next-generation products or do they have IP that will lessen the impact or relevance of the acquired IP?
8. Are there key engineering or manufacturing individuals working for the target who are critical to the success of implementing the patented technology at the acquiring company?
9. What additional value is the acquirer obtaining from the other IP in the target's portfolio that might redefine the objective or strategies driving the transaction? Can this IP be sold for value that decreases the cost of the deal?
10. Is this the best technology (and most cost-effective means) for solving the problem or are there better/cheaper alternatives?
11. What additional IP risks is the acquirer inheriting through the purchase of the target?
12. Have the above issues been analyzed to determine their effect on the overall value of the transaction?

Seller's Questions

1. Does the seller have a good understanding of all of the IP being sold as a part of the transaction (i.e., an IP inventory)?
2. Do other subsidiaries or divisions of the seller currently utilize the IP being sold as protection or competitive advantage which requires license back?
3. Are the other subsidiaries or divisions aware of the sale of the IP and the right to practice the process or use the technology and what losing the rights might do to their future plans?
4. Is there an opportunity to license the IP to others who do not compete with the target company?
5. What other IP of the target included in the sale is currently or might potentially be used by other subsidiaries or divisions of the seller's parent?

6. What additional nonIP intangible assets are being transferred from the target to the acquirer and what value is being given away?
7. Are there key employees of the target who should be retained rather than becoming employees of the acquired company?
8. Would licensing the patented process to others while maintaining ownership of the targeted subsidiary provide a better long-term return to the parent than selling the subsidiary to the acquiring company?
9. Are there potential shareholder liability risks associated with selling the subsidiary?
10. Are there existing legal obligations to others associated with the IP?
11. Have the above issues been analyzed to determine their effect on the overall value of the transaction?

Ensuring that the objectives of the transaction are met and the risks associated with the transaction have been carefully considered requires a scope of IP due diligence much broader and more detailed than the traditional scope of due diligence. This broader and more detailed level of due diligence must be understood and planned in order to address questions such as the ones listed above. In the remainder of this chapter, we assume that the traditional due diligence will be performed and focus on the *additional* due diligence tasks required to respond to questions such as those listed above.

THE CULTURE OF IP MANAGEMENT[9]

Just as companies analyze other aspects of the business synergies of a merger or acquisition, it is important to determine if the target has an IP culture and IP assets that will integrate well with the acquiring company. While this step is of particular importance for the acquirer, the seller may also be able to justify a high selling price by helping the acquirer see the synergies from a good fit.

For example, it is important to determine if the two companies place similar importance on the role of technology in the success of their business. If the target focuses on cost control and low price marketing as the basis for differentiating its products in the marketplace, there may be cultural clashes with an acquiring company that differentiates its products through developing state-of-the-art, high-quality products focused on the high-end premium-priced market. It is important to consider how the plans of the target blend or mesh with the plans of the acquiring company.

Another component of the IP culture due diligence involves comparing the seller's and acquirer's methods for developing, perfecting, maintaining, and enforcing IP rights. A considerable difference between the two parties signals that the target may not be a proper fit for the acquiring company or that provisions need to be made in the integration process. This difference could lead to the loss of expected synergy or might require significant additional integration time and cost to change the culture and generate the work process parity. On the other hand, it is possible that the acquirer may see hidden value in what would result from improving the methods utilized by the target.

Apart from any specific considerations of IP or intellectual assets, most would accept that it is important to determine what factors make the target a success in the market and to confirm that integrating the target into the acquiring company will not place these factors at risk. The key question to ask is "Will the IP culture of the combined firm be able to support the target's product and services at the level required to ensure their continued success after they are integrated into our company?" To begin to answer this question, the reviewer should consider whether or not the IP management cultures will mesh well and create a combined entity that will successfully work together. This point often impacts the scope and depth of the IP due diligence effort. Most likely, the greater the disparity in the cultures (and in particular the more disorganized the IP process), the greater the effort needed to ensure that hidden risk will not severely diminish the value of the acquisition.

PHASE II—INVENTORY AND REVIEW

Products and Services Changing Hands

Generally, as a part of the overall due diligence effort, a review of the products and services involved in the transaction will be available, since that is often the reason for the merger effort in the first place. The IP due diligence team must gain an understanding of the complete inventory of the products and services being transferred. While due diligence will often focus on primary products and services, we recommend that the parties not limit the inventory in this manner but strive to acquire or develop as complete a list as possible. Also consider the existing inventory of products and services of the buyer that are expected to be complementary or associated. As will be explained in greater detail below, there is no way to know what potential risks or hidden value is resident within the transferred products and services, even among those appearing to be insignificant on a stand-alone basis.

Inventory Intellectual Property

Whether from the position of the acquirer or the target, it is important to develop a complete list of all IP changing ownership as a result of the transaction.[10] A key starting point in any transaction involving the acquisition of an interest in intellectual property is the identification and categorization of the intellectual property assets involved. Without knowledge of what IP is being transferred, it would be near impossible to have a reasonable sense of what value is being transferred and what risks are being created due to the transaction. Also, if both parties perform an IP inventory and agree as to the assets in the IP inventory as part of the due diligence process, the likelihood that there will be issues posttransaction related to what IP assets were included in the transaction is greatly reduced.

It is worth noting that this is the point in the typical IP due diligence review where most of the traditional questions are answered. Once the list of IP rights being transferred is known, the IP review team traditionally checks the documentation supporting the validity and enforceability of the IP. These steps are certainly an integral part of a broader IP due diligence review. While most transactions involve such process, we suggest that it is not sufficient to stop here. Still, even as it relates to this basic step, costly oversights are not at all uncommon.

To demonstrate the impact of a failure to carefully inventory the transferred IP, consider the example of a company named Maximizer that decided to acquire Tracker Software Australia Pty. Ltd. (TSA) from the company's administrator in a bankruptcy procedure in 1997. The object of the purchase was to acquire the rights to Connexion, a new contact management software product. However, after Maximizer had taken possession of the software, the parent company of TSA, Track Software International (TSI), claimed it had the intellectual property rights to Connexion and that shareholders of TSI were contemplating legal action to have the sale reversed.[11] Had the parties agreed to an IP inventory performed prior to completion of the transaction, this dispute would have been avoided. Numerous other examples abound.

Sometimes the surprise is a positive one. For example, a company that manufacturers laptop computers was acquired, but the buyer was not aware of the fact that the target owned a patent covering the basic clamshell construction of a laptop. Several months later, the buyer discovered the patent and the result was an unexpected treasure of licensing royalties due to the implementation of an aggressive licensing program.[12] Still, the reward could have been much greater. While the buyer did eventually reap the considerable benefits of the discovery, it took them months after the transaction was completed to identify the IP rights linked to the laptop product. Had the IP rights been discovered as a result of IP due diligence prior to the completion of the transaction, the acquirer could have initiated its license royalty program many months sooner than it actually did and reaped significant additional royalty revenue.

And what about the seller? Surely they could have obtained a much higher price for the transaction had they done the proper due diligence and uncovered this laptop patent. One wonders what the reaction of the sellers were when they learned about the licensing revenues that the acquirer earned by enforcing the laptop patent rights transferred through the transaction.

The nature of the transaction can put the inventory at center stage. This was the case with Mostek, a company that owned semiconductor chip patents. While Mostek did not try to enforce these patents, SGS-Thomson saw an opportunity to gain significant revenues through ownership and enforcement of the patents. SGS-Thomson purchased Mostek for $70 million in the mid-1980s but collected $450 million in licensing revenues from the purchased patents over the next seven years.[13] It was not possible to successfully evaluate the benefits and risks of the transaction without a complete list of IP assets being transferred (and of course the examination of the value of these assets more broadly).

These examples beg the questions:

- How many acquirers might never have discovered this IP right linked to the acquired product?
- How many times is such incremental value in these deals never identified?
- How many good deals never get done due to the failure to identify this type of IP value?
- How many opportunities exist for astute buyers to get a better deal or even a windfall by identifying a valuable IP asset that the seller didn't even know they had through careful due diligence?

Care must be taken in preparing the list of IP assets to be transferred, as not all IP assets require legal or official registration and may be easily uncovered. For example, as the seller or target, it may be important to review ongoing R&D projects to gauge the potential value hidden in these activities. It may be a good idea to file invention disclosures and patent applications before the divestiture. Similarly, there may be considerable value in identifying and documenting the target's trade secrets and know-how before negotiations commence, so that they can be articulated for value.

Interviewing key employees is one way to uncover these nonregistered or potential IP assets in process. For example, interviewing individuals in charge of research projects may provide useful information concerning potentially patentable discoveries. Interviews with individuals in development or marketing may uncover plans to create a valuable trademark to support a new product launch. In addition to interviews, nonregistered IP assets may be identified through documents including reviews of customer agreements, internal memoranda, business plans, or system design specifications.[14] Even if for some reason this process is not practical before the close, it should be done immediately postclose in order to identify and locate valuable assets and to aid in maximizing the transaction benefits through integration cycle reduction and synergy value.

Contractual Agreements Affecting IP Rights

Another area of focus for the inventory in even more traditional IP due diligence is consideration of the risk associated with contractual agreements and terms affecting the IP rights of the parties to the contract. Intellectual property due diligence must consider limitations and constraints on rights resulting from contractual agreements. For example, the acquirer may purchase a target with products that are dependent upon IP rights obtained from third parties. However, the target may not be able to transfer those rights to others, so the acquirer may discover that it has paid for rights it does not obtain.

As an example, St. Jude Medical acquired Ventritex in a transaction valued at $365 million.[15] Ventritex had a line of implantable cardiac rhythm management devices (generically known as implantable pacemakers and defibrillators) that St. Jude wanted in order to more effectively compete with market leaders Medtronic and Guidant. The problem is that the courts have held at this point that a necessary license to key patented technology does not transfer to St. Jude, subjecting it to a patent infringement verdict of $140 million.[16]

Other examples of risks related to IP contractual rights include representations, warranties, indemnification, university agreements, government agreements, assignment restrictions, geographic restrictions, other restrictions, and noncompete agreements. In general, these contractual terms are signals to additional risks associated with the transaction and, depending upon the terms of the agreement, may be borne by the seller or the acquirer. These risks can be made even more difficult to analyze due to the recent onslaught of joint ventures and alliances, as well as the complexities and nontraditional boundaries of Internet-related businesses.

The traditional IP due diligence may uncover these risks. It is much less likely that the expected financial effect of these risks on the transaction (e.g., the expected value of the future costs associated with an indemnification clause) is fully evaluated and considered in the decision as to whether or not to pursue the transaction. In fact, considering the material nature of most of these contractual terms, it is surprising how rare it is that these risks are evaluated in economic terms.

Other Intangible Assets and Intellectual Capital

The due diligence team will also want to review and understand the broader set of intellectual assets and intellectual capital that may be linked or related to IP. Intellectual assets extend beyond IP to those intangible assets that are not legally protected but are articulated or codified and can be transferred and applied (i.e., a description of formulas, processes, or other codified knowledge). Intellectual capital is that uncodified intangible value found in the minds of employees or emanating from relationships and culture. Short shrift should not be given to these other intangible assets in the due diligence process. In fact, these assets alone or as an enhancement or necessary component with IP, may be the most valuable part of the deal.

For example, a company in the pharmaceutical industry completed a hostile takeover of a competing pharmaceutical industry company to enhance its product offerings in a particular pharmaceutical market. While obtaining the patents and the brand name associated with the target's product line, the acquirer failed to consider the impact of not retaining certain key employees in the R&D function. These inventors were the primary contributors to the technology that was key to the strategy of the merged firm. A number of key inventors (not immediately recognized as such) left the company shortly after the closing. A subsequent general program of "rightsizing" and early retirements added to the problem and left the technological future of the enterprise in question (and a good measurer of the purchase price paid for naught).

Had proper due diligence been performed, the acquirer would have likely analyzed the contributions of the various intellectual capital components of the targeted company and their relative contributions to the success of the product line of interest. This multifunctional due diligence could have uncovered the importance of the target's inventor group to the success of the current product line and future direction of the company, and identified the risk and effect associated with an exodus after the takeover. This would have allowed the acquirer to determine, prior to the takeover, what incentive plan, benefits, or other program would motivate the right inventors to remain.

In contrast, another company cross-matched the detailed descriptions of technological competencies necessary to support the company's strategic plan with the documented credentials and demonstrated past success of its inventors to determine what resources were essential to retain and which could be lost with little or no real impact.[17]

Examples of other areas to consider in performing due diligence of the broader set of intangible assets include:

- Research and development efforts under way related to potential new products or potentially patentable discoveries
- Manufacturing and business process know-how
- Sales force components with key technical knowledge and/or customer contacts
- Information technology and systems supporting the company's business

This is not an exhaustive list or a complete review of issues related to appropriate due diligence of intangible assets other than IP. However, it is important to point out that these other intangible assets are often critical and require careful consideration in the IP due diligence process.

PHASE III—ANALYSIS AND RESPONSE

Products and Services Linked to IP

Now that the important intangibles and the products and services being transferred are identified, the two should be associated to ensure future protection of the value of those products and services and to identify critical gaps. The inventory of products and services allows the review team to assess what IP rights are necessary to protect those products and services. The inventory of IP, as well as the inventories of contractual rights and obligations and other intangible assets and capital, teaches the review team what rights will be available posttransaction. Holes in the protection can now be identified, areas of strength can be exploited, and extraneous assets can be dropped from the transaction.

Again, without being able to determine what IP rights can or need to be transferred to support/protect the business's products and services, it is virtually impossible to assess the risks and value impact of not obtaining particular IP rights. With this knowledge one can not only assess the likelihood of the occurrence of adverse events, but also quantify an adjustment in transaction value based on the risk assessment.

In addition, other valuable assets that will be acquired and that can be exploited or off-loaded to reduce the cost of acquisition can also be identified. Although it may be easy to imagine the potential risks that can arise if one acquires a product line that is inadequately protected by IP, it may be less obvious that linking products and services to the acquired IP can uncover these otherwise hidden gems. Assume the target is being acquired for its manufacturing capabilities in one particular product line. The IP due diligence team is shown a portfolio of manufacturing patents that it determines, after the linking analysis, support the production of some acquirers' existing products. The acquirer may learn that these patents represent an opportunity to take a more aggressive stance with its existing competitors. Only the effort of linking the patents to the target's secondary product lines revealed this incremental value. The careful buyer will match the inventoried IP to its own product and service portfolio to identify additional value or risk mitigation.

The Competitive Landscape and Other Risks

Most of the due diligence discussed up to this point has focused on reviewing the IP assets of the target and the acquirer. However, these two parties do not operate within a vacuum, separated from any outside influences. It is important that the IP due diligence also consider the IP held by competitors and other third parties, as well as the implications of IP-related government regulatory requirements and the influence of industry consortiums and standard-setting bodies.

Failure to do adequate IP due diligence has also been shown to be the precursor to nasty lawsuits. For example, a competitor of your company may be waiting in anticipation for you to complete your acquisition of the target. What the competitor may know that you do not is that your target's product infringes patents held by the competitor. The competitor may prefer to wait to file a lawsuit until you become the manufacturer and marketer of the infringing product and the inheritor of the target's liability for past infringement. Intellectual property due diligence of the target's product and research into the patents related to the product including those of competitors would help to prevent this from happening. Intellectual property due diligence can also provide information on the likelihood of success of any potential infringement claim. Judging in advance not only the existence of potential claims and legal likelihood of them prevailing, but also the potential financial impact is important. That impact may be far greater than monetary damages paid to another party and include the impact of an injunction, reduction in profit margins due to requirement to pay royalties, loss of market share, and tarnished reputation.

One example of this involved due diligence efforts of a venture capital firm, Adams Capital, related to a possible investment in CoreTek. Adams Capital discovered that a Stanford University professor held a patent covering one of CoreTek's technologies. Because of the due diligence efforts, CoreTek was able to negotiate a license with the Stanford professor and obtain the needed patent rights. Adams decided to become an early investor in CoreTek. Coretek was later sold to Nortel Networks providing Adams Capital with a hefty return on its investment.[18]

Adams Capital recognized the importance of doing a "landscape" analysis of intellectual property critical to the success of the business. Because Adams Capital performed broader IP due diligence including a landscape analysis of others' existing patents related to the CoreTek business, a messy patent dispute was avoided. This example also demonstrates that risks to the success of the transaction may not necessarily come exclusively from competitors.

Risk may come in the form of third-party blocking patents, improvement patents, obsolescence, trade secrets, design-arounds, and/or ongoing development. Therefore, the landscape analysis should not be limited to reviewing patent documents. The analysis should include review of recent popular publications, Internet searches, consultants' reports, industry studies, trade publications, competitor annual reports, and other disclosed competitor documents.

New analysis tools that cross match vast amounts of information quickly to facilitate better-informed decision-making are appearing on the scene. For example, through a technology landscape analysis conducted with our Multi-Term Frequency Analysis™[19] one of our clients determined that the joint venture partner with whom they were about to strike a deal was in fact not the best partner. Instead, it was revealed that there was nonobvious partner that would arm the joint venture with a far superior technology position; the basis for our client's interest in a joint venture in the first place.

The IP due diligence landscape analysis also needs to consider the impact of regulations and industry standards. Tax regulations, government industry regulations, and product or technology standards existing or pending can have a significant impact on value. For example, a company purchasing a target with a portfolio of patents related to computer hardware might find that the value of this portfolio is linked to whether or not the computer industry chooses to adopt the patented technologies as part of the industry standard. The portfolio may be of little value if alternative methods are adopted.

A final example of the importance of due diligence of the IP inventory of the acquirer is demonstrated by the events in the *SCM Corporation v. Xerox Corporation* case in which the court concluded that antitrust implications arose when a company as a result of an acquisition, enhanced its already powerful patent portfolio. The court concluded that the acquired IP, in addition to the already owned patents, provided the company with a monopoly position in that industry.[20]

In addition to IP, the parties to the transaction will also want to consider the impact that outside influencers have on the combined entity's other intellectual assets and intellectual capital. Trends such as new distribution media, customers' alternatives for inputs to production, regulatory issues and other broad-based factors that influence demand are important to the question of valuation and therefore should be considered to the extent that they intersect with intangibles. Where is this intersection likely to occur? Almost all facets of firm activities include intangibles. Customer, supplier, and distributor relationships, manufacturing know-how, government and lobbying contacts, and human capital are some of the intangible assets that make a firm successful but might make a transaction unsuccessful.

Finally, a growing trend in litigation is the increasing threat of corporate liability to shareholders related to the failure to perform appropriate IP due diligence. This threat includes lawsuits related to the liability of the corporate board of directors as well. For example, a recent article discusses the issue of lawsuits over "IP wasting" and points out that the "failure to steer R&D away from potential infringement problems" is at the root of many lawsuits involving Silicon Valley companies.[21]

Estimating the Value and Impact

The value of a product within a business may not be the same as the value of the patents or other IP. A business captures only a portion of the entire market, but retains all the profits from that business. In contrast, a patent may be able to extract value from the entire market but only lays claim to a portion of the profits from each business within that market. Other IP as well as factors such as entrepreneurial talent, land, and labor must collect their shares of the market's total profits.

Patent portfolios, for example, face unique risk factors that may be the main discrepancy between the parties in a negotiation. These risk factors include such issues as the probability of issuance (if pending), the ability to enforce the property rights, the penetration of the technology into a market, and the alternative technologies available to the potential targets. Other risk factors related to the scope of market potential are the fraction of the market that will adopt a particular technology, the risk of a standard bypassing the technology, and the value of other technologies that must also be adopted.

A critical assessment of the above issues relies in a large part on access to information and detail that can be collected during the due diligence process. Because assessing the value of a patent involves legal, financial, marketing, industry-specific, and economic issues, this step is often best executed by a multidisciplinary team comprised of IP counsel, corporate employees involved with the technology, and financial experts knowledgeable of the industry and market dynamics.

We generally recommend developing a valuation model that is capable of being quickly adjusted to incorporate new information or different assumptions and will be useful in the negotiation process with potential partners or investors. To this end, when the value justifies the effort, developing a dynamic model that separately quantifies many of the risk elements that would likely have been collapsed into one discount factor in traditional valuation models is more useful. All of the key risk factors that have been uncovered during the aforementioned steps of the due diligence review can be explicitly incorporated to the valuation model.

One of the principle reasons for estimating the risk factors in greater detail than in a traditional valuation is to best prepare for the questions that typically arise in a negotiation. By first quantifying the specific elements that form the key underpinnings of value, the negotiator can develop his or her own assessment of the opposing side's reservation price by learning how the opposing side would quantify those key variables. One also can be more attuned to differences in opinion that could otherwise lead to a breakdown in the negotiation or an unfavorable deal. And, when reasonable parties are negotiating with the intent of reaching a win-win business deal, a carefully crafted model can reduce the negotiation time by allowing both sides to more rapidly come to agreement on the impact of certain assumptions.

Advances Supporting Due Diligence

Many of the due diligence tasks and activities outlined in the previous sections of this chapter might seem challenging and unwieldy. However, the advances in methodologies and technologies available to support due diligence efforts make these efforts practical and cost effective.

For example, state-of-the-art techniques have been developed that have greatly improved the quality, speed, and effectiveness of the information archive and retrieval efforts related to registered IP rights. These technologies allow for automated means for reviewing history and trends in patent citations, filing and compiling information on the technology portfolios of targets and competitors, analyzing large portfolios of technology through attribute clustering of like technologies based on user-defined groups, and graphically comparing the overlap with target or competitor portfolios. Many tools are secured via the Web. The automation of information available from IP registration authorities like the United States Patent and Trademark Office (USPTO) or the World Intellectual Property Office (WIPO) have further stimulated the advance of online analysis for IP.

Due to the ever-increasing importance of IP assets in the success of business, IP assets have received considerably more economic and financial scrutiny than in decades past. The result is that advances have also been made in methods for analyzing the value or financial contributions of IP assets.

Those unfamiliar with these technological and financial analysis advances related to IP assets will be happy to learn that consulting firms (such as

PricewaterhouseCoopers) provide these services, including some that are proprietary in nature or protected via patents, as part of their offerings to clients. These consulting firms are often "on the leading edge" of developments in IP due diligence technology and methodologies.

Benefits Outweigh Costs

Some may be concerned about the potential cost of performing IP due diligence despite the many advances in improving the efficiency and lessening the cost of steps in the due diligence process. As with all expenditures, the extent of the costs must be balanced against the potential benefits to be gained. It is virtually a sure bet that these costs are a far better alternative than the costs associated with uncovering IP-related defects after the transaction has been finalized. Would you rather learn before or after the deal closes that:

- There exists a patent blocking your ability to produce the key product acquired through the transaction and forcing you to negotiate a license when you are "under the gun"?
- Employee-related trade secret issues could lead to years in court fighting over those trade secrets?
- The future cash flows that you were using in your value calculations are not sustainable because key IP protection is soon expiring?
- Your newly acquired product line is not protected by patents and can easily be copied by competitors?
- Third-party contractual agreements limit the IP rights of the targeted company?
- The patents you threw in to sweeten the deal are, in fact, a key offensive weapon for the acquirer?

It is not difficult to envision these or many other examples where the costs of an effective IP due diligence pales in comparison to the risks and potential costs of failing to complete the IP due diligence *before* completing the transaction.

Avoiding these posttransaction cost nightmares provides enough support for the need to perform detailed IP due diligence. However, one should not ignore the fact that completion of detailed IP due diligence, as described in this chapter, provides many additional benefits to the company above and beyond ensuring the transaction objectives are met and the risks are evaluated.

One benefit of the IP due diligence efforts arises from the resulting inventory of IP assets developed as part of the IP due diligence process. Notwithstanding the benefit of better integration, the existence of this IP asset inventory may also enhance the company's ability to utilize the IP portfolio in corporate financing efforts. In fact, it may be possible to use the inventory of IP assets as collateral to raise the money needed to finance at least part of the cost of the acquisition.[22]

Another possible benefit is that the acquirer may be able to justify a higher price for the target because the IP due diligence effort has uncovered considerable additional value in the IP assets of the target. Therefore, the acquirer may enhance the likelihood that a transaction can be completed because the acquirer can offer a price that incorporates consideration of this additional value instead of the lower price that would result from very limited knowledge of the IP assets of the target.

And there are many more examples of benefits from the IP due diligence process. Some examples are listed below:

- Creating the foundation for a strategic plan
- Helping to define the future direction of the company and long-range planning
- Learning more about products in the pipeline and discoveries on the drawing board
- Identifying key factors in the company's success
- Discovering untapped market opportunities for the company
- Uncovering hidden IP jewels
- Discovering alternate revenue sources through licensing or sale of IP
- Unearthing new competitive weapons that stem from the combination of portfolios
- Improving the company's ability to negotiate more favorable transaction terms
- Ensuring that the company receives the appropriate level of value for its purchase (or the right price for its divestiture)
- Improving the company's management of the assets it is acquiring (or its understanding of how to succeed without divested assets)
- Enhancing knowledge of key trends in the industry, market, and regulatory environment
- Enhancing knowledge of the company's own IP portfolio
- Enhancing the company's understanding of the link between its own IP portfolio and its products and services
- Improving the company's knowledge about the IP portfolio and IP strategies of its competitors
- Acquiring into potential strengths and vulnerabilities of competitors
- Improving the company's understanding of contractual agreements and obligations in existence and their effect on the success of the company
- Reducing merger integration time and cost
- Acquiring "insurance" against a catastrophic IP-related event that can have severe financial consequences and may even result in shareholder action and director and officer (D&O) liability

Even if only a few of the above items are obtained from the detailed IP due diligence, the benefit received should more than compensate for the costs associated with the process.

The New Reality

The value and importance of intellectual property and other intangibles have grown to vastly surpass that of hard assets. The stakes are high when deals are being done, and today many more deals are based on the value proposition surrounding the intangibles, supported by IP, than are tangible asset-based propositions. The shift to an intellectual asset-based economy is opening up vast new opportunities for companies to convert these intangible assets into millions, even billions of dollars of corporate value. In particular, patents and other intellectual property are being increasingly recognized as critical components of corporate strategy and the foundation of competitive advantage. Through activities such as strategic patenting, portfolio management, competitive intelligence, proactive enforcement, and licensing, companies are seeking innovative new approaches to better create, manage, and exploit these critical assets. With this growing focus, do you want to rely on an IP due diligence process still rooted in the industrial age or one that recognizes the realities of the new economy and the changing source value? And if you don't approach the task at hand from a new perspective, who is to say that the other guy will not? If that happens, you may well do a deal only to have a "deal" done on you in the process. In our opinion, there is no debating the cost benefit—it is clear. Improving the IP due diligence process and adopting a business, value-based approach will bring great benefit. Stick to the status quo at your peril.

NOTES

1. A recent PricewaterhouseCoopers study.
2. IP, the associated know-how, and other useful codified knowledge taken together are increasingly referred to as the company's "intellectual assets." This classification is distinguished from the additional intangibles, such as the assembled workforce or R&D staff—assets that cannot be held or walk out the door each day. Together, the intellectual assets plus the value incorporated in these less transferable, or less "ownable" assets are referred to as the "intellectual capital" of the enterprise.
3. Kevin Rivette and David Kline, "Discovering New Value in Intellectual Property," *Harvard Business Review*, January/February 2000, p. 54.
4. Ibid.
5. Gerson Panitch, "Strategic Due Diligence." *The National Law Journal*, May 15, 2000, p. B7.
6. Lanning Bryer and Scott Lebson, "Intellectual Property Plays Major Role in Mergers," *National Law Journal*, February 7, 2000, p. B11.
7. Ethan Horwitz and Heather Wilde, "Doing Diligence with Trademarks," *New York Law Journal*, January 18, 2000, p. S6.
8. Panitch, "Strategic Due Diligence."
9. Many companies actively manage all intangibles rather than just IP, following a broader program of intellectual asset management (IAM).
10. Richard Raysman, "Carrying Out Effective Intellectual Property Due Diligence," *Corporate Counsellor*, January 1997, p. 1. Leader Publications, Inc., a division of the New York Law Publishing Company.

11. William Boei, "Maximizer Disputes Notion Purchase Might Be Reversed," *Vancouver Sun*, June 17, 1997, p. D2.
12. John H. Coult, "Payoffs for Buyers Who Probe a Target's Intellectual Property," *Mergers and Acquisitions: The Dealmakers Journal*, June 1, 1999, Securities Data Publishing.
13. Kevin Rivette and David Kline, "Discovering New Value in Intellectual Property," *Harvard Business Review*, January/February 2000, p. 54.
14. Richard Raysman, "Carrying Out Effective Intellectual Property Due Diligence," The Corporate Counsellor, January 1997, p. 1. Leader Publications, Inc., a Division of The New York Law Publishing Company.
15. *St. Jude Medical Amend Merger Agreements*. St. Jude Medical, Inc., press release dated March 31, 1997.
16. *Jury Verdict Announced in St. Jude Medical Patent Lawsuit*. St. Jude Medical Inc. press release dated July 3, 2001.
17. This company used MTFA™ to cross-match detailed competencies with strategic needs and the demonstrated skill base of the inventors (see note 19).
18. Peter Loftus, "A Little Digging Can Unearth Skeletons," Dow Jones News Service, Jerry Mahoney, *Austin American-Statesman*, October 16, 2000, p. D2.
19. Multi-Term Frequency Analysis (MTFA) is a PricewaterhouseCoopers patent pending methodology that can be used to cross-tabulate massive amounts of patent and/or other data to discover and score relationships in a time frame that is useful to inform decision-making and reduce risk.
20. 645 F.2d 1195 (2d Cir. 1981) *cert. denied*, 445 U.S. 1016 (1982).
21. Rivette and Kline, "Discovering New Value in Intellectual Property."
22. Judith L. Church, "Resolving IP Issues in Mergers and Acquisitions," *Practicing Law Institute, Patents, Copyrights, Trademarks and Literary Property Course Handbook Series*, May 1999.

ABOUT THE AUTHORS

Mark W. Haller is a partner in the Financial Advisory Services practice of PricewaterhouseCoopers in Chicago, Illinois. He is the founder and leader of the PricewaterhouseCoopers Intellectual Asset Management (IAM) practice. Mr. Haller specializes in helping corporations leverage the value of their intellectual assets (IAs) to increase shareholder value. He works with corporations to enhance internal organization and business processes, design and implement portfolio management systems, and develop and conduct financial and business analyses to extract greater value from corporate intellectual asset portfolios.

Mr. Haller counsels clients on the business and financial issues surrounding transactions and other business arrangements such as licenses, joint ventures, joint development, and strategic partnerships where intellectual assets are an essential driver of value. In the context of transactions, he often determines royalty rates, develops offer prices and frameworks to evaluate alternative offers, evaluates the economics of substitute technologies, and formulates and executes negotiation strategies. His experience also includes determining incremental value of IA rights in M&A transactions, the purchase and sale of technology, and the donation of intellectual property rights. Additionally, Mr. Haller assists clients with the economic and financial impacts of intellectual property in infringement litigation, and has served as an expert on numerous matters. He is a frequent speaker on IA and IP issues. Mr. Haller is a member of the Licensing Executives Society and is a licensed CPA. He received a Bachelor of Science in accounting and finance from Miami University and his Masters degree in Business Administration from the University of Chicago.

Edward Gold is a Director in the Financial Advisory Services practice of PricewaterhouseCoopers, LLP, and a member of the Intellectual Asset Management practice. He has assisted clients in the formulation of negotiation strategies as they relate to intellectual property licensing, sale, or joint ventures. He has estimated the value of intellectual property under different market conditions, evaluated the financial alternatives facing the patent holder, formulated negotiation strategies to optimally position the patent holder, and directly participated in the negotiations. Dr. Gold has also presented on this topic to legal and industry representatives in a variety of forums.

Dr. Gold has applied economic theory and econometric methods to liability and damages issues in litigation matters involving patent infringement, antitrust issues including innovation, technology and product markets, reasonable royalty determination, false advertising, price discrimination, real estate financing, fair lending, and breach of contract. In addition, he has experience with a wide range of liability and damage analysis in employment litigation issues including hiring, earnings, promotion, training, and termination. Dr. Gold received his PhD in Economics from the University of Rochester in 1993.

Brian L. Blonder, after 15 years with PricewaterhouseCoopers, left his partnership position in the Washington, DC, office to become the Managing Director of intellectual property services in Washington for Micronomics, a subsidiary of InteCap, Inc. Mr. Blonder has extensive experience in analyzing the business aspects of patents and patent portfolios as well as other types of intellectual property. His experience includes providing assistance and intellectual asset management services to intellectual property owners desiring to value, market, or better manage their intellectual property portfolios. Mr. Blonder has testified in court as to damages, harm, and the value of intellectual assets in matters involving infringement or misappropriation of intellectual property.

His emphasis in litigation engagements, both those involving intellectual property and those involving other matters, has included the preparation of expert testimony and/or testifying on matters involving lost profits estimation, reasonable royalties, damage estimation, analysis of financial performance, financial condition, cost accounting, historical business transactions, and quantitative and statistical analysis. Mr. Blonder has an undergraduate degree in finance from Wayne State University and a Masters in Business Administration with concentrations in finance and computer information systems from the University of Michigan. He is a licensed Certified Public Accountant and Certified Fraud Examiner.

PricewaterhouseCoopers's Intellectual Asset Management Practice works with a broad range of clients in delivering sophisticated solutions across the IAM life cycle. The IAM consulting practice is comprised of professionals with industry, business, legal, and R&D expertise who offer cutting-edge approaches to strategy and performance improvement, organization and operational effectiveness, financial and transaction support, advanced analytics and metrics, and information technology. Intellectual Asset Management is a part of the Financial Advisory Services (FAS) practice of PricewaterhouseCoopers. Financial Advisory Services is composed of one of the largest dispute analysis and investigations, business recovery services, and corporate value consulting practices in the world; one of the highest-rated corporate finance and investment banking practices; and the second largest project finance and privatization practice. PricewaterhouseCoopers (*www.pwcglobal.com*) is the world's leading professional services organization with 150,000 people in 150 countries.

CHAPTER EIGHTEEN

Leveraging Brand to Generate Value

by Jeffrey Parkhurst

PERSPECTIVES

Trademarks, like patents, must be registered with the United States Patent & Trademark Office (USPTO). For their owners to maintain their rights, trademarks must be actively enforced. A not-too-distant cousin of patents, trademarks offer similar challenges when it comes to valuation. While patents protect inventions and processes, trademarks cover symbolic innovation, such as names, images, and logos. Marks are most valuable when they are readily associated with successful brand names, such as Jeep®, Bayer Aspirin®, IBM® or Tide®, which are registered with the USPTO and in other countries. The artful science of valuing trademark-protected brands, a type of intangible asset, which are often licensed or merchandized, has evolved over the past 20 years. Components of a valuable brand include advertising, product differentiation, perceived quality, and consumer loyalty.

Brand recognition plays an important role in shareholder value. Corporate branding found that a strong corporate brand can add anywhere from 5 percent to 7 percent of a company's stock price in a bull market, and can mitigate losses in a down market. An Ernst & Young study says that corporate brand knowledge and reputation accounts for 30 percent of a company's stock price (*PR Week*, April 23, 2001). Brand valuation provides a measure at a point in time. If a company does a great job differentiating itself and establishing customer loyalty, while retaining prudent capital expenditure and reasonable margins, it can expect to have a premium brand value. Brand valuation helps to communicate this story for everyone. However, says Jeff Parkhurst, director of brand valuation for Interbrand U.S.,"It is what

you do with the measure that can lead to higher profits and ultimately shareholder value."

Coca-Cola, says Parkhurst, is an interesting brand story with stock
implications. From 1983 to 1998, its shares appreciated 23 percent
annually versus 14 percent for the S&P 500. At the end of this run, its
market capitalization approached $200 billion, with roughly 92 percent
of it tied to intangible assets. "Why," asks Mr. Parkhurst, "would anyone want to invest a dollar only to be rewarded immediately with
eight cents of tangible assets or book value, and 92 cents of something that they cannot touch or feel, let alone explain in an articulate
way?" (This question also might be asked of biotech companies, like
Celera Genomics, which own a handful of promising patents.)

A person became a shareholder because he saw significant forward
earnings streams tied to those intangibles, of which brand was a
major component. During this period, the company strategy employed generated significant cash flow. Capital expenditure was prudent. Focus was provided with the brand. Interestingly, Coca-Cola's
performance from 1974 to 1982, and since 1998, has generally lagged
the S&P 500, indicative of the fact that "great branding still requires
great execution."

In the following chapter, Mr. Parkhurst provides methodologies for
how brands and companies are valued and provides a list of "The
World's Most Valuable Brands."

BRANDS AND SHAREHOLDER VALUE

For nonbrand enthusiasts, branding can come across as soft and nebulous. Serious
brand managers believe that great brands command differentiation and loyalty,
which ultimately can lead to higher profits. As branding is part art, the question
is always raised of how it relates to shareholder value. While our focus with this
chapter is the emergence of brand valuation, it is important to answer the shareholder value question first.

As a starting point, one well-chronicled story is Coca-Cola. From 1983 to 1998,
its stock appreciated 23 percent annually versus 14 percent for the S&P 500. At the
end of this run, its market capitalization approached $200 billion, with roughly 92
percent of it tied to intangible assets (see Exhibit 18-1). Why would anyone want
to invest a dollar only to be rewarded immediately with 8 cents of tangible assets
or book value, and 92 cents of something that they cannot touch or feel, let alone
explain in an articulate way?

They became shareholders because they saw significant forward earnings
streams tied to those intangibles, of which brand was a major component. During

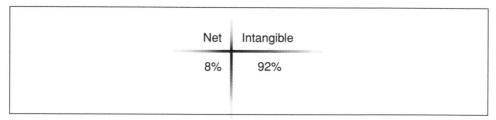

	Net	Intangible
	8%	92%

Exhibit 18-1   Coca-Cola share of market capitalization.

this period, the company strategy employed generated significant cash flow. Capital expenditure was prudent. Focus was provided with the brand. Interestingly, Coca-Cola's performance from 1974 to 1982 and since 1998 has generally lagged the S&P 500, indicative of the fact that great branding still requires great execution.

Exhibit 18-2 provides another glimpse at how brand equity ties to shareholder value. Good branding delivers differentiation and loyalty. Success with these drivers leads to higher market share and/or selling price. In some cases, it can lower costs of good sold. Any of these three, barring poor marketing investment, can lead to higher earnings. Higher earnings, over time, net higher shareholder value.

An alternative game seen in some industries is the combination of incremental capacity, incremental volume, and a lower selling price. While this strategy

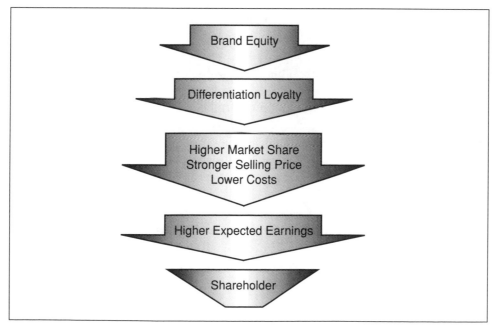

Exhibit 18-2   Brand equity and shareholder value.

grows earnings, the added capacity has a limited life span, the free cash available after capital employed is lower, and riding the price curve down to variable cost clearly has an unfavorable conclusion.

In the early 1990s, economic value added (EVA) became a mainstream financial measure. In a nutshell, EVA can be defined as net operating profit after tax less an invested capital charge. Stern Stewart and Company, which played a pioneering role with EVA, successfully demonstrated a higher correlation between standardized EVA and market value added ($R^2 = 50\%$) versus more traditional financial measures: Return on equity ($R^2 = 35\%$); cash flow growth ($R^2 = 22\%$); earnings per share growth ($R^2 = 18\%$); dividend growth ($R^2 = 16\%$); and sales growth ($R^2 = 9\%$).[1] Intuitively, this makes sense: Net cash in your hand at the end of the day is more meaningful financially than how high your sales were or how you set up your operation. It is interesting to note that it took until the early 1990s to recognize free cash flow as a mainstream measure. Where were all the financial analysts in the 1970s and 1980s? Where are they today?

In 2001, Interbrand looked at a sample of companies to understand the relationship between market value add, an EVA proxy, and role of brand. The role-of-brand measure quantified what percentage of the intangible earnings stream was due to the brand and its influence on the purchase decision. When they combined EVA with role of brand versus market value add, the correlation with shareholder value increased. While this work is emerging, it demonstrates directionally that firms that manage their invested capital efficiently and that can secure a more intimate customer relationship through sustainable branding can win big.

Let's finish the discussion on shareholder value by introducing the subject of brand valuation. Initially, brand valuation provides a measure of one's brand value at a point in time. If you have done a great job generating differentiation/loyalty while retaining prudent capital expenditure and reasonable margins, you can expect to have a premium brand value. Brand valuation helps to communicate this story for everyone.

But importantly, it is what you do with the measure that can lead to higher profits and ultimately shareholder value. With this measurement insight in hand, there is a growing list of ways in which in you can leverage it (see Exhibit 18-3).

Hopefully, we have brought you encouragement on the link between the art of the brand and shareholder value:

- There are best-practice examples like Coca-Cola
- There is a commonsense link between brand equity and shareholder value
- There is a fact-based evolution of financial measures that correlate with value
- Once you have brand value, you can leverage it to increase profits and ultimately shareholder value over time

Near-Term Profits	Long-Term Profits	Investor Relations
• More optimal media spending • Higher licensing and royalty rates • Better M&A deals • Better contracts in joint ventures • More co-branding ventures • Increased leverage for ingredient brands • Basis of negotiation to lower the cost of goods sold • Lower cost of debt	• Focused organization on increasing brand value with a scorecard • More optimal go-to-market organizational structure, including brand architecture • Internal best practices • New product development • Internal licensing • Trademark protection	• Communicating hidden value • Illustrating path to shareholder value growth

Exhibit 18-3   Leveraging brand valuation.

THE NATURE OF BRANDS

"Brand" derives from the old Norse word *brandr*, meaning literally to "burn." Branding was then, and remains today, the principal means by which owners of livestock marked their animals. It has, on occasion, also been used to mark thieves and wrongdoers. In similar fashion, producers of whisky placed identifying marks on to wooden whisky casks which handily display the maker's mark. Today, a brand is still the means by which a business differentiates its goods and services from those of its competitors.

Despite what appears to be a brand renaissance over the last 10 years, there is still a common misunderstanding as to what brands actually are.

Brand success stories seem to be the exception rather than the rule, and one could easily conclude that many companies have seemingly forgotten why they have or should have brands, or they do not completely understand what their brands mean or stand for. A research study[2] entitled "Brand Asset Management in the 1990s" substantiates this view. According to this study, "more than one third of companies polled indicated that the most critical threat to the long-term success of their brands is an internal lack of understanding of what the brand represents." One can imagine that short-term sales orientations and corporate-profit pressures do not give much help to the long-term brand prognosis either.

Brands, and the art of branding, are anything but a new phenomenon. It is interesting to note that a client commenting on the topic of his own corporate brand identity recently made the statement that branding was, in his judgment, faddish. This view misses the point. Brands are indeed topical, and rightly so given the increasing percentage of total corporate worth represented by these important intangible assets (see Exhibit 18-4),[3] but they are not faddish. Indeed, branding is quite old despite the apparent renaissance, and dates back centuries. If it is a fad, it is an enduring one.

At the simplest level, brands serve a functional purpose: They are a way to identify and distinguish one item (or service) from the next. This functional benefit has relevance to both brand owner and brand purchaser alike.

For the brand owner, a brand (as communicated by the trademark or symbol, the trade name, or a combination of these elements) identifies property and provides a certain level of legal protection. Most countries in the world today have trademark laws on their statute books that allow the owners of brands to claim the title to their brand names and logos through trademark registration. Legal systems now recognize that brands (along with other forms of intellectual and/or intangible property) are indeed protectable, similar to tangible property such as land, buildings, and equipment.

For the consumer, brands also provide important functional benefits. Even in the earliest of times, brands served as a guarantee of homogeneity and as a signal of product quality. Potters in medieval trade guilds in Europe, for example, identified their products by putting a thumbprint, a fish, cross, star, or other differentiating mark into the wet clay of their wares. The expectation was, presumably, that customers would seek out their particular brand of goods if satisfied by the original purchase.

This particular benefit of branding became increasingly important over time as manufacturers and sellers of goods lost face-to-face contact with their custom-

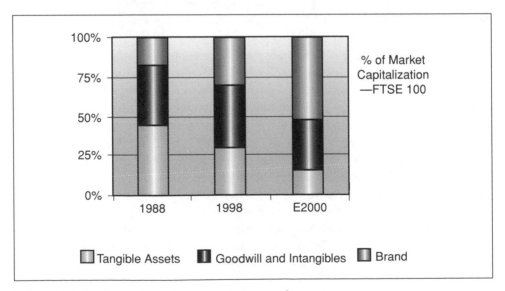

Exhibit 18-4   Percentage of corporation worth.

ers. This development was brought on most notably in the nineteenth century with the advent of railways, and later with the internal combustion engine, both providing a means of distributing products across wide traveling areas. Good news for product sales volumes, bad news for maintaining close customer relationships and ongoing seller-buyer dialogue!

In the absence of a direct, face-to-face supplier-customer relationship, a brand serves as a means of assuring product authenticity and consistency of quality—it is, in effect, a promise or pact between manufacturer and buyer. The brand name assures us that the features, functions, and characteristics of the brand will remain invariable from purchase to purchase. In this way, the brand provides its maker with the means to consistently provide the consumer with intrinsic value, the illusion of such value, or both.

Brand management must now, out of necessity, be increasingly concerned with creating a Gestalt for the brand, defined as being "the unified physical, psychological, or symbolic configuration or mix of elements that, when combined, are greater than the sum of the parts." This is no easy task, particularly in the identification and blending of the relevant mix of psychological values that a brand needs to embrace and reflect. Even when properly done, successful brands require considerable time and significant financial investment and, of equal importance, the consistency of a well-managed brand-identity program to effectively take root in the minds of consumers.

Products are tangible. As such, the ability to develop and sustain distinct or superior competitive differentiation at the product level is, today, a shot-lived proposition. Even where a patent or copyright would seem to hold promise for longer protection, commercial reality may limit its power.

The painful truth is that most new and seemingly innovative products can, and often are, copied or cloned in a matter of months—sufficiently different from a technical point of view to evade copyright infringement, but virtually indistinguishable in form, function, or benefit to most customers. By themselves, features and functions of products or services are not the best foundation from which to build strong, enduring brands. This is not to suggest that the generic product or service is unimportant to the totality of the brand concept. Clearly, a truly innovative product, or one of superior performance, exceptional quality, or high value should be at the core of any brand. But these dimensions of a brand, while extremely important, are now table stakes in many respects; they are the minimum requirements of virtually all product, service, or corporate brands, if any marketplace success is to be expected.

A brand is much more than its name or the object it identifies. BMW is not just a corporate name of an automobile manufacturer; for hundreds of thousands of people, BMW is a way of life rich in imagery, attitude, meaning, and distinctive, expressive, and central values. This phenomenon of "name equals brand" seems to be most prevalent in companies that have, historically, operated as manufacturing-driven organizations and where business success has come simply from meeting market demand.

One of the recent key shifts in management is ownership and responsibility for the brand or brands. Brand management can no longer be viewed as the sole purpose or responsibility of the marketing department. It makes little sense to hand over responsibility for what are often the corporate jewels to a junior brands manager. It is for this reason that CEOs are increasingly assuming the charge and challenge of being brands stewards—a development truer of monolithic corporate brand-dominant organizations than fast-moving consumer goods (FMCG) multibrand companies (for pragmatic reasons), but a positive step nonetheless.

Only the CEO or chairman in these instances can effectively set course for the brand—articulating the reason it exists, its values and beliefs—and, importantly, ensuring that all appropriate initiatives are put in place to realize the brand's long-term ambition. If brands are the most valuable assets of many corporate holdings, then who better to monitor and guide their well-being?

Brand development cost is one reason why there is movement toward having fewer brands with greater "stretch" potential in many company brand portfolios. Companies that can stretch their brand shrewdly while retaining relevance, differentiation, and credibility net significant increases in brand value. Case examples in the 1990s would include Virgin, Disney, Swiss Army, and Harley-Davidson.

Maximizing brand sales, which has been the focus of the past three decades, is no longer the most profitable objective. It is actually possible to increase sales without increasing profits where the cost of customer acquisition offsets gains in achieved production or service provision! Unless you are the lowest-cost producer in a respective category with price as the principal business driver, this is not a sustainable strategy. Low price may stimulate short-term sales, but it does little to foster long-term brand loyalty.

Building strong, differentiated brands and loyal brand franchises will increasingly come to rest on the brand owner's ability to create vision for the brand and a reality in which people can share. It will require that the brand's meaning rises above physical attributes, characteristics, functional benefits, and an overall fact-based foundation, to a more socially aware, philosophical reason for being—a more humanistic entity with a particular view on the world and accompanying core values. Leadership brands will convey a sense of self, a spirit, and consciousness—a brand life force—in addition to the expected dimensions of high quality, reliability, impeccable service, overall good value, and so forth.

Creating leadership brands requires that brand meaning is understood throughout the internal organization and lived in daily practice. Only then will the brand be able to communicate convincingly to the external world, attract and retain consumers who share in its vision, stand apart from others, and ultimately increase in its economic value as an asset.

A BRIEF HISTORY OF BRAND VALUATION

In 1988, Interbrand first became involved in the unexplored world of brand valuation when the London firm was asked to assist Ranks Hovis MacDougall (RHM) to defend itself against an unwelcome takeover bid by Goodman Fielder Wattie (GFW), the Australian foods group. That first brand valuation exercise demonstrated the value of RHM's brand portfolio and helped them repel the GFW bid. In the course of Interbrand's close relationship with RHM, they developed, in collaboration with the London Business School, an innovative model for brand valuation.

The industry for brand valuation expanded in the 1990s with new players including FutureBrand, Brand Finance, Young & Rubicam, an occasional boutique effort, and periodic assignments seen with classic management consultancies.

There are four reasons why the brand valuation market is growing today:

1. Brand-related earnings continue to increase as a percentage of the total earnings stream.
2. Branding continues to offer a basis for sustainable differentiation.
3. Applications for brand valuation continue to expand.
4. The marketplace continues to improve their understanding of what brand valuation can do for them.

CASE HISTORIES

Invariably, brand valuation can be viewed as an academic exercise at first pass. To demonstrate how brand valuation ties to bottom-line results, here are just a few case histories that have taken place since 1988:

- In 1993, a global market leader in computers retained a brand that the competition regarded more highly than the corporation itself did. As a result, individual business units wanted their own brand and assumed that the corporate brand was someone else's problem. This resulted in more than 100 agency relationships, each with its own refined message. A brand valuation was conducted and proved that the role of the brand has common attributes across business lines and that the decentralized approach was not advantageous to the value of the brand. As a result, all advertising was consolidated behind one brand and one message.
- Although this company had already developed into the most successful new brand in a European mobile telecommunications market in the mid-1990s, a brand valuation study identified a tremendous amount of unrealized potential with the brand. In the eventual sale, the company realized a purchase price of $33 billion, representing a $21 billion price premium over a competitive brand, which retained similar customer numbers. The valuation helped support the sale with added insight; without, significant money may have been left on the table.
- Facing the acquisition of a premier automobile brand, an U.S. automobile manufacturer conducted a brand valuation in order to identify a fair price for the brand. As a result, the company was able to negotiate a significantly lower price for the multibillion-dollar brand.

- When a U.K.-based FMCG company acquired a U.S.-based FMCG company for $5.8 billion, a valuation was conducted on the U.S. company's brands to reassure analysts and shareholders that the purchase price was justified. Results showed the difference between the purchase price and the tangible assets was most accounted for by the value of the brands, resulting in broad support from the street for the acquisition.
- In 1998, a major U.S. high-technology firm was facing inconsistencies in the value-add of its brands throughout the organization. Threatened by a fragmented brand strategy, a brand valuation was conducted to assess where value resided with the master brand. Ultimately, one business was spun off and the master brand was refocused.
- The largest brewing company in the Pacific Rim installed a computer-based brand value management system for the management of the company's extensive brand portfolio. In addition to monitoring the investments in the brands, the management uses the brand valuations actively for managing its investor relations through balance sheets and discussion with financial analysts.
- When a major telecomm company entered a consortium with three Regional Bell Operating Companies (RBOCs) to create a national wireless service leveraging their brand, a brand valuation was conducted to assess the value the brand would contribute to such a venture and to mitigate risks to the brand. The valuation concluded that the brand should not enter the joint venture. The valuation team continued to work with the company to enhance the value of the brand portfolio and eventually helped maximize the price paid for the company at a later date.
- In the late 1990s, at about the same time as a merger, a major West Coast U.S. bank conducted a brand valuation to understand the value of their brand. They confirmed that they retained one the best bank brands in the business, which helped lay the groundwork for an updated master brand across the entire company.

BRAND VALUATION TECHNIQUES

An asset may be valued on a going concern or on a liquidation basis. It may be valued on an open-market basis or in the knowledge of special circumstances. For example, the valuer may be briefed to account for the incremental value of an asset to a given business. He may have been commissioned to estimate any one of the following: a fair value, a fair market value, a commercial value, an investment value, or a tax value.

Each of these is subtly different from the others. *Inter alia* it is necessary to prepare a valuation after making assumptions concerning the physical, functional, technological, economic, or legal life of the asset, each of which will, obviously, be different.

The value of an asset tends to differ depending on the assumptions made in the valuation exercise. It is clear that a taxpayer might want to use assumptions, which produce valuations at the lower end of expectations, while a seller might want to use assumptions, which produce valuations at the higher end. A professional valuer must use his, or her, independent judgment as to the reasonableness of assumptions used and to disclose them and their effect on the resulting valuation.

In addition to agreeing to the assumptions, it is necessary to determine the most appropriate valuation method. There are fundamentally different ways of arriving at a value, and each may be appropriate under different circumstances. The three commonest approaches are: cost-based, market-based, and income-based. Which of the various bases is most appropriate to a brand valuation?

Cost-Based Valuations

It is possible to value a brand on the basis of what it actually cost to create or what it might, theoretically, cost to re-create. Such valuations are sometimes used in legal cases where compensation awards are under consideration.

In the case of a historical creation cost, it may be possible to look back over the years since the brand was originally launched and restate actual expenditure to a consistent, current monetary value. This represents the current value of the amount spent on getting the brand to its current state and condition. For example, it is often possible to look at the history of advertising expenditure in building brand awareness and loyalty, render it into current monetary terms, and summarize the total amount invested.

The same can be done for each of the other costs that have gone into building the particular brand, and it is possible to arrive at a total figure. Such an approach may be meaningful in the context of a new brand, where the time period for study is short and the costs are readily available. However, actual costs of creation, even if they are collectible and translatable into a single amount, are of little use in expressing the current value of any particular brand. It would be relatively easy to estimate the development costs of Verizon, a fairly new brand identity. However, an exercise of this kind is of limited use. In the case of many brands, the actual costs of creation may have been very low while the ultimate value may be high. Above all, historical expenditure is not a guide to current value.

In the case of current re-creation cost, one argument is that it is possible to estimate the costs involved in re-creating a brand. This could, theoretically, be attempted on a restoration cost basis (re-creating an identical brand) or on a replacement cost basis (re-creating a brand with similar economic value to the owner). The obvious difficulty is that both these approaches are theoretical, as the objective is to replicate a unique brand. The method is more likely to be found in the valuation of a tangible piece of equipment in a factory. Its application to intangible assets is inappropriate. By definition, unique brands cannot be re-created easily. There is no such thing as a standard, similar, or identical brand. Virgin and Body Shop are just two examples of this phenomenon. The reason brands have such value is because they are unique. By their very nature they are not comparable nor are they replicable. Therefore, attempting to estimate replacement cost is, in general, a futile exercise.

Market-Based Valuations

This approach is based on the assumption that there are comparable market transactions (specific brand sales), comparable company transactions (the sale of specific branded companies), or stock market quotations (providing valuation ratios against which a comparable branded entity can be valued). A valuation may, therefore, be based on disposal of comparable individual brands, specific branded divisions, or whole companies where adequate information is made publicly available (see Exhibit 18-5). Were this sort of information available, it might be possible to estimate directly one brand's value by comparison with the value of another brand. As an example, it is possible to determine a brand value by calculating the total business value based on comparable stock market multiples, then deducting known tangible-asset values from that implied stock market value, leaving a residual value representing the intangible assets, including the brand. It may then be possible to estimate what proportion of the total intangible-asset value the brand represents.

The main difficulty with this deductive approach is that few companies or divisions operate with one brand alone. In practice, they frequently trade with several brands, together, possibly, with some unbranded product. Separating out the brand to be valued without access to internal information, therefore, can prove difficult. Alternatively, it may be possible to simply apply a comparable market multiple to post-tax brand earnings. However, this also presupposes that it is possible to identify individual brand earnings from a divisional, or company, brand portfolio. In practice, there are few brand sales which are directly comparable. Even where there is information concerning the sale of specific brands or branded businesses, details are not often widely available. The terms of the sale usually remain confidential, although press headlines may suggest otherwise. Without details, it is impossible to make sensible comparisons. In addition, the notion of comparability again assumes that brands are similar or identical, which is unlikely. Using supposedly comparable transactions, such as stock market ratios or multiples, is unsatisfactory as the primary method for valuing a brand. However, market comparisons can be useful to test the primary valuation method for reasonableness.

Income-Based Valuations

Again, a number of alternative methods are available. The two most frequently used of those are royalty-relief method and discounted cash flows.

2001#	Brand	2001 Brand Value ($MM)	% change (2001 vs. 2000)	2000 Brand Value ($MM)	% change (2000 vs. 1999)	1999 Brand Value ($MM)	Brand Leverage (2001)	Industry	Country of Origin	Parent Company
1	Coca-Cola	68,945	-5%	72,537	-13%	83,845	4.18	food & beverages	US	Coca-Cola
2	Microsoft	65,068	-7%	70,197	24%	56,654	3.16	software	US	Microsoft
3	IBM	52,752	-1%	53,184	21%	43,781	0.67	technology	US	International Business Machines
4	GE	42,396	11%	38,128	14%	33,502	0.38	industrial	US	GE
5	Nokia	35,035	-9%	38,528	86%	20,694	1.37	telecoms	Finland	Nokia
6	Intel	34,665	-11%	39,049	30%	30,021	1.15	technology	US	Intel
7	Disney	32,591	-3%	33,553	4%	32,275	1.91	travel and leisure	US	Disney
8	Ford	30,092	-17%	36,368	10%	33,197	0.27	automotive	US	Ford
9	McDonald's	25,289	-9%	27,859	6%	26,231	0.75	retail	US	McDonald's
10	AT&T	22,828	-11%	25,548	6%	24,181	0.39	telecoms	US	AT&T
11	Marlboro	22,053	0%	22,111	5%	21,048	2.28	leisure goods	US	Phillip Morris
12	Mercedes	21,728	3%	21,105	19%	17,781	0.59	automotive	Germany	Daimler Chrysler
13	Citibank	19,005	1%	18,810	N/A	N/A	0.86	financial services	US	Citigroup
14	Toyota	18,578	-1%	18,824	53%	12,310	0.23	automotive	Japan	Toyota
15	Hewlett-Packard	17,983	-13%	20,572	20%	17,132	0.41	technology	US	Hewlett-Packard
16	Cisco Systems	17,209	-14%	20,068	N/A	N/A	1.01	technology	US	Cisco Systems
17	American Express	16,919	5%	16,122	28%	12,550	0.80	financial services	US	American Express
18	Gillette	15,298	-12%	17,359	9%	15,894	3.89	personal care	US	Gillette
19	Merrill Lynch	15,015	N/A	N/A	N/A	N/A	0.63	financial services	US	Merrill Lynch
20	Sony	15,005	-9%	16,410	15%	14,231	0.29	electronics	Japan	Sony
21	Honda	14,638	-4%	15,245	37%	11,101	0.31	automotive	Japan	Honda
22	BMW	13,858	7%	12,969	15%	11,281	0.54	automotive	Germany	BMW
23	Nescafe	13,250	-3%	13,681	N/A	N/A	2.72	food & beverages	Switzerland	Nestle
24	Compaq	12,354	-15%	14,602	N/A	N/A	0.33	technology	US	Compaq
25	Oracle	12,224	N/A	N/A	N/A	N/A	1.35	software	US	Oracle
26	Budweiser	10,838	1%	10,685	26%	8,510	1.70	alcohol	US	Anheuser Busch
27	Kodak	10,801	-9%	11,822	-20%	14,830	0.86	leisure goods	US	Kodak
28	Merck	9,672	N/A	N/A	N/A	N/A	0.26	pharmaceutical	Germany	Merck
29	Nintendo	9,460	N/A	N/A	N/A	N/A	2.11	leisure goods	Japan	Nintendo
30	Pfizer	8,951	N/A	N/A	N/A	N/A	0.57	pharmaceutical	US	Pfizer
31	Gap	8,746	-6%	9,316	18%	7,909	1.32	retail	US	Gap
32	Dell	8,269	-13%	9,476	5%	9,043	0.37	technology	US	Dell

Exhibit 18-5 The world's most valuable brands.

2001#	Brand	2001 Brand Value ($MM)	% change (2001 vs. 2000)	2000 Brand Value ($MM)	% change (2000 vs. 1999)	1999 Brand Value ($MM)	Brand Leverage (2001)	Industry	Country of Origin	Parent Company
33	Goldman Sachs	7,862	N/A	N/A	N/A	N/A	0.27	financial services	US	Goldman Sachs
34	Nike	7,589	-5%	8,015	-2%	8,155	0.99	leisure goods	US	Nike
35	Volkswagen	7,338	-6%	7,834	19%	6,603	0.20	automotive	Germany	Volkswagen
36	Ericsson	7,069	-9%	7,805	-47%	14,766	0.27	telecoms	Sweden	Ericsson
37	Heinz	7,062	N/A	N/A	N/A	N/A	2.54	food & beverages	US	Heinz
38	Louis Vuitton	7,053	2%	6,887	69%	4,076	2.77	luxury	France	LVMH
39	Kellogg's	7,005	-5%	7,357	4%	7,052	1.16	food & beverages	US	Kellogg's
40	MTV	6,599	3%	6,411	N/A	N/A	2.55	media	US	Viacom
41	Canon	6,580	N/A	N/A	N/A	N/A	0.30	business services	Japan	Canon
42	Samsung	6,374	22%	5,223	N/A	N/A	0.23	electronics	Korea	Samsung
43	SAP	6,307	3%	6,136	N/A	N/A	1.19	software	Germany	SAP
44	Pepsi	6,214	-6%	6,637	12%	5,932	0.88	food & beverages	US	Pepsico
45	Xerox	6,019	-38%	9,700	-14%	11,225	0.36	business services	US	Xerox
46	IKEA	6,005	0%	6,032	N/A	N/A	0.79	retail	Sweden	IKEA
47	Pizza Hut	5,978	N/A	N/A	N/A	N/A	0.87	retail	US	Tricon
48	Harley Davidson	5,532	N/A	N/A	N/A	N/A	2.17	automotive	US	Harley Davidson
49	Apple	5,464	-17%	6,594	54%	4,283	0.76	technology	US	Apple
50	Gucci	5,363	4%	5,150	N/A	N/A	4.00	luxury	Italy	Gucci
51	KFC	5,261	N/A	N/A	N/A	N/A	0.87	retail	US	Tricon
52	Reuters	5,236	7%	4,877	N/A	N/A	1.40	media	UK	Reuters
53	Sun Microsystems	5,149	N/A	N/A	N/A	N/A	0.37	software	US	Sun Microsystems
54	Kleenex	5,085	-1%	5,144	12%	4,602	2.08	personal care	US	Kimberley-Clark
55	Philips	4,900	-11%	5,482	24%	4,421	0.15	electronics	Netherlands	Philips
56	Colgate	4,572	3%	4,418	24%	3,568	2.00	personal care	US	Colgate-Palmolive
57	Wrigley's	4,530	5%	4,324	-2%	4,404	2.36	food & beverages	US	Wrigley's
58	AOL	4,495	-1%	4,532	5%	4,329	0.65	media	US	AOL Time Warner
59	Yahoo!	4,378	-31%	6,300	258%	1,761	4.42	media	US	Yahoo!
60	Avon	4,369	N/A	N/A	N/A	N/A	0.86	personal care	US	Avon
61	Chanel	4,265	3%	4,142	32%	3,143	2.03	luxury	France	Chanel
62	Duracell	4,140	-30%	5,885	N/A	N/A	1.79	leisure goods	US	Gillette
63	Boeing	4,060	N/A	N/A	N/A	N/A	0.09	industrial	US	Boeing
64	Texas Instruments	4,041	N/A	N/A	N/A	N/A	0.38	technology	US	Texas Instruments
65	Kraft	4,032	N/A	N/A	N/A	N/A	1.05	food & beverages	US	Kraft

Exhibit 18-5 (continued)

Rank	Brand	Value	Change	Value	Change	Value	Ratio	Sector	Country	Parent
66	Motorola	3,761	-15%	4,446	22%	3,643	0.11	telecoms	US	Motorola
67	Levi's	3,747	N/A	N/A	N/A	N/A	1.17	leisure goods	US	Levi's
68	Time	3,724	N/A	N/A	N/A	N/A	0.89	media	US	AOL Time Warner
69	Rolex	3,701	4%	3,561	47%	2,423	2.76	luxury	Switzerland	Rolex
70	adidas	3,650	-4%	3,791	5%	3,596	0.94	leisure goods	Germany	adidas
71	Hertz	3,617	5%	3,438	-3%	3,527	0.79	travel and leisure	US	Ford
72	Panasonic	3,490	-7%	3,734	N/A	N/A	0.08	electronics	Japan	Matsushita
73	Tiffany & Co.	3,483	N/A	N/A	N/A	N/A	2.33	luxury	US	Tiffany & Co.
74	BP	3,247	6%	3,067	3%	2,985	0.04	oil	UK	BP
75	Bacardi	3,204	1%	3,187	10%	2,895	2.90	alcohol	Bermuda	Bacardi
76	amazon.com	3,130	-31%	4,529	233%	1,361	1.26	media	US	Amazon
77	Shell	2,844	2%	2,786	4%	2,681	0.02	oil	UK	Royal Dutch/ Shell
78	Smirnoff	2,594	6%	2,443	6%	2,313	2.75	alcohol	UK	Diageo
79	Moet & Chandon	2,470	-12%	2,799	0%	2,804	2.29	alcohol	France	LVMH
80	Burger King	2,426	-10%	2,702	-4%	2,806	0.24	retail	US	Diageo
81	Mobil	2,415	N/A	N/A	N/A	N/A	0.04	oil	US	Exxon Mobil
82	Heineken	2,266	2%	2,219	2%	2,184	1.27	alcohol	Netherlands	Heineken
83	Wall Street Journal	2,184	0%	2,185	N/A	N/A	1.60	media	US	Dow Jones
84	Barbie	2,037	-12%	2,315	N/A	N/A	1.74	leisure goods	US	Mattel
85	Polo Ralph Lauren	1,910	4%	1,834	11%	1,648	1.14	luxury	US	Polo Ralph Lauren
86	Fedex	1,885	N/A	N/A	N/A	N/A	0.12	business services	US	Fedex
87	Nivea	1,782	N/A	N/A	N/A	N/A	1.06	personal care	Germany	Beiersdorff
88	Starbucks	1,757	32%	1,330	N/A	N/A	0.90	retail	US	Starbucks
89	Johnnie Walker	1,649	7%	1,541	-6%	1,634	2.36	alcohol	UK	Diageo
90	Jack Daniels	1,583	7%	1,480	N/A	N/A	1.91	alcohol	US	Brown Forman
91	Armani	1,490	2%	1,456	N/A	N/A	1.36	luxury	Italy	Armani
92	Pampers	1,410	1%	1,400	-2%	1,422	1.71	personal care	US	P&G
93	Absolut	1,378	N/A	N/A	N/A	N/A	4.57	alcohol	Sweden	Vin&Sprit
94	Guinness	1,357	11%	1,225	-3%	1,262	0.48	alcohol	Ireland	Diageo
95	Financial Times	1,310	14%	1,149	N/A	N/A	1.72	media	UK	Pearson
96	Hilton	1,235	-17%	1,483	12%	1,319	1.33	travel and leisure	US	Hilton Corp/ Hilton Group
97	Carlsberg	1,075	N/A	N/A	N/A	N/A	0.51	alcohol	Denmark	Carlsberg
98	Siemens	1,029	N/A	N/A	N/A	N/A	0.02	industrial	Germany	Siemens
99	Swatch	1,004	N/A	N/A	N/A	N/A	1.57	leisure goods	Switzerland	Swatch
100	Benetton	1,002	-1%	1,008	N/A	N/A	0.95	retail	Italy	Benetton

Exhibit 18-5 (*continued*)

2001#	Brand	2001 Brand Value ($MM)	% change (2001 vs. 2000)	2000 Brand Value ($MM)	% change (2000 vs. 1999)	1999 Brand Value ($MM)	Brand Leverage (2001)	Industry	Country of Origin	Parent Company
P1	Johnson & Johnson	68,208	N/A	N/A	N/A	N/A	2.61	portfolio	US	Johnson & Johnson
P2	P&G	45,435	-6%	48,352	-2%	49,193	1.27	portfolio	US	P&G
P3	Nestle	41,688	4%	40,250	4%	38,769	0.92	portfolio	Switzerland	Nestle
P4	Unilever	37,847	2%	37,100	9%	33,929	0.94	portfolio	UK	Unilever
P5	L'Oreal	17,798	N/A	N/A	N/A	N/A	1.66	portfolio	France	L'Oreal
P6	Diageo	15,004	3%	14,557	6%	13,704	1.41	portfolio	UK	Diageo
P7	Colgate-Palmolive	14,361	5%	13,636	20%	11,333	1.71	portfolio	US	Colgate-Palmolive
P8	Danone	13,583	N/A	N/A	N/A	N/A	1.13	portfolio	France	Danone

Figure 18-5 (*continued*)

*Brand Leverage reflects Brand Value in relation to the previous year's Branded Sales. The higher the Leverage the more value is being generated from each $ of sales. In this way the relative size of one business over another is neutralized. Since this is often a function of the industry (its margins and how brands operate within the category) this is best viewed at an industry level. The numbers have been indexed to 1.00 such that they reflect a position above or below the average for the set of global brands shown.

Source: Interbrand, Citigroup, Businessweek

The royalty-relief method is based on the theoretical assumption that an operating company owns no brands and needs to license them from a nonoperating brand owner. If a brand has to be licensed from a third-party brand owner, a royalty rate on turnover will be charged for the privilege of using the brand. By owning the brand, such royalties are avoided. Ownership of the intangible assets therefore "relieves" the company from paying a license fee (the royalty rate), hence the term "royalty relief." The royalty-relief method involves estimating likely future sales and then applying an appropriate royalty rate to arrive at the income attributable to brand royalties in future years.

The idea with discounted cash flows (DCFs) is to take the stream of expected cash flows, arising at different times in the future, and identify their value to an investor now. This is conventionally achieved by identifying a discount rate that takes account of the risks inherent in the predicted cash flow. A high-risk cash flow, such as that on sales of Nintendo games, would be discounted much more heavily than the cash flow from a less risky product, for example, Lego. The former is volatile, and a sensible investor would mark down the value of the future cash flows, while the latter is likely to be safe and reliable. Using the DCF approach, the valuer discounts future royalties, at an appropriate discount rate, to arrive at a net present value (NPV)—the brand value.

The advantage of the royalty-relief approach is that there are many examples of royalties in use by companies that are licensing brands to one another. The brewing sector abounds with examples of brands licensed between major players. Some brands that are well known in one industry are also licensed into others. The Dunhill name is famous as a cigarette brand, but it is also licensed for use on clothes and luxury goods. The franchising sector is another ready source of information on rates charged for franchising certain brands, particularly in the retail sector. The valuation departments of several major accountancy firms (notably Ernst & Young and Coopers & Lybrand) have preferred the royalty-relief method of valuation. They argue that, after years of compiling comparable royalty rates, they have large databases of appropriate rates from which they can produce reliable valuations. Their view appears to be shared by some courts.

The royalty-relief method has, historically, been popular in legal and tax cases because of the belief that comparable data are available to form a sound judgment. For example, a 1995 case in the U.S. Tax Court, *Nestlé v. IRS*, involved the determination of what was an appropriate transfer value for the total worldwide trademark portfolio of the Carnation corporation. This had been sold by the U.S. subsidiary (Carnation) to the Swiss parent company (Nestlé). The judge accepted a relief-from-royalty approach as the basis for final judgment. An expert witness had demonstrated to the court's satisfaction that the range of likely royalties for prepared and packaged food products would be in the range of 1 to 5 percent. The bottom rate of 1 percent would relate to weaker brands while 5 percent would relate to the strongest. The total Carnation portfolio, because of its strength and longevity, was valued on a 4 percent implied royalty rate. However, detailed information on royalty rates is not often widely available, nor are the terms on which the royalties are based. Rates often incorporate payments for the use of patents, copyrights, or shared marketing costs. They vary, depending on tax considerations, expected profits, and market circumstances from time to time. They are often highly complex, with differential rates at the varying sales levels, margin split clauses, and many other noncomparable terms. More important, the rate charged for an established brand in one sector or geographical region will differ when that brand is being licensed into a new market sector or region. For example, the rate charged for the use of the Shell brand in an established market such as the U.K., where the brand is already well known and commands strong consumer loyalty, would be quite different from the rate that would be appropriate in an undeveloped market, such as China, where the Shell brand may be little known. It can, therefore, be extremely difficult, if not impossible, to identify an appropriate royalty rate for a particular brand valuation.

Economic use valuations are the most popular approach to brand valuation. Such valuations consider the economic value of a brand to the current owner in its current use. In other words, they calculate the return that the owner actually achieves as the result of owning the brand—the brand's net contribution to the business, both now and in the future. This can be measured by estimating the increase in gross profit attributable to selling a branded rather than an unbranded product or service. However, brand valuations are more commonly based on net, fully absorbed profits by identifying the excess net earnings attributable to ownership of the brand. Such valuations draw on internal information, supplemented by external market research. They do not consider the value of the brand in use by a different owner or any "hope value" based on new uses of the brand.

Economic use valuations were used by Interbrand to value the RHM portfolio and have been applied to many hundreds of brands since. Initially, they were based on a multiple of historical brand earnings. However, multiples of historical earnings tend to be unreliable because past performance is not necessarily an indication of future performance. Such valuations are also volatile because of the reliance on a small number of years used in the calculation. For example, in 1992, Financial World estimated that the Marlboro brand was worth $51.6 billion. In 1993, after cutting its price to retain market share, Marlboro was revalued at $33 billion. Many observers would argue that Marlboro was actually stronger and more valuable after cutting price than before. What we really want to know is the value of future earnings stemming from the brand's pact with its consumers.

It is, therefore, increasingly common for economic use valuations to be based on the discounted value of future brand earnings. This approach depends on the accuracy of future sales and earnings projections. However, the royalty-relief method noted above is equally dependent on accurate sales forecasts. Theoretically, the economic use approach should use pure cash flows from future brand sales. However, it is more straightforward to use an adjusted profit and loss account figure as an approximation of the pure cash flow. This has the benefit of simplicity. The approach uses the future-earnings stream attributable to a brand after making a fair charge for the tangible assets employed (both maintenance and financing costs). The result is earnings attributable to the intangible assets as a whole. A charge is also normally made for tax at a notional rate. The resulting "excess" earnings are discounted back to a NPV representing the current value of the brand in question. Typically, such brand valuations are based on earnings forecasts of five to 10 years prepared on an annual basis. In addition, an annuity is calculated on the final year's earnings on the assumption that the brand continues beyond the forecast period, effectively in perpetuity. As brand rights can be owned in perpetuity, and many brands have been around for over 50 years, this is not an unreasonable assumption in many instances. Just as analysts now value shares on the basis of sustainable cash flows from the business, putting a value on that cash stream, the economic use brand valuation process is essentially a cash flow valuation. In fact, this type of cash flow approach has been endorsed by the Accounting Standards Board.

There is no single method of brand valuation which is appropriate under all circumstances. Courts sometimes prefer to use a cost or a royalty-relief basis. Tax authorities sometimes prefer a deductive approach, starting with a market-based valuation of the whole enterprise. Bankers generally prefer either a multiple of historic profits, or an evaluation of discounted future cash flows. In many cases it is necessary to use a number of benchmarks to substantiate the primary valuation basis. However, it seems that the approach which is being used as the primary measure of brand value more and more is the economic use basis calculated by discounting future brand earnings.

THE INTERBRAND APPROACH

The Interbrand methodology believes that brand value is most effectively measured similar to the way that financial analysts assess the value of any business, that is, on the basis of the discounted free cash flows they produce. Cash flows produced by the brand are discounted to their present value using a discount rate that reflects the risk of those cash flows being realized.

Because brand value is created at the point of contact with the customer, the Interbrand approach to measuring it is designed to capture any variation in the way the brand operates. Branded revenue streams are divided into segments in which customer decision-making processes are broadly homogenous. This takes into account the behavioral patterns of a purchase decision and the role that the brand plays: They are likely to differ depending on the purpose of use and channel through which the product is purchased. Through our experience we have found that this "bottom-up" approach is the most effective way of valuing a brand because it is able to capture the difference between customer groups in terms of how they use the brand. These are the basic building blocks of the brand's value.

The first step in any valuation is to establish sufficient understanding of the market (or markets) in which the brand (or brand portfolio) operates. Interbrand analyzes the level of customer involvement, key long-term trends, and the market's competitive situation, among other indicators, in order to derive the most appropriate segmentation. Once a segmentation analysis is completed, the value of the brand is calculated in an extensive process including financial analysis, market analysis, and brand analysis before being integrated into an overall brand value (see Exhibit 18-6).

Financial Analysis

The first phase of the Interbrand analysis is to derive the business earnings for each unit within the segmentation. This is based on historic and forecast profit and loss (P&L) data that are adjusted to approximate free cash flow over time. A charge is made to remunerate for tangible capital employed and an appropriate level of tax. This is calculated for each unit of the segmentation to derive the intangible or economic earnings (in effect, the EVA). By constructing a range of potential financial scenarios at this stage, it is possible to explore the implications on brand value of different business strategies.

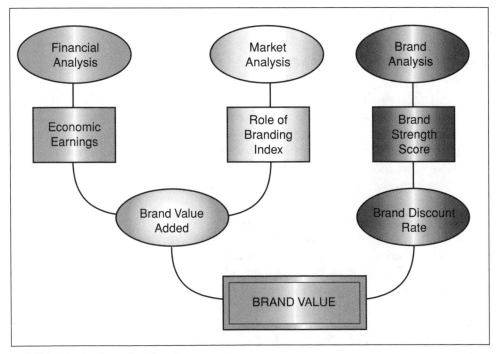

Exhibit 18-6   Brand valuation.

Market Analysis

The second phase of the analysis is designed to determine the brand earnings (brand value added, or BVA). This is achieved by means of our proprietary Role of Branding analysis (see Exhibit 18-7). This separates the economic earnings the brand generated from those generated by the other intangibles of the business. The Role of Branding Index represents the percentage of economic earnings that is attributable to the brand. It is based on an assessment of the individual key drivers that generate branded revenue and the influence the brand has on each of them.

There are then two distinct steps in assessing the role that branding plays. The first is to identify what it is that drives the business (what contributes to competitive success) and weight these for their relative importance. Each driver is analyzed, weighted, and ranked relative to all the others in the business. The second is to ask to what extent is this driver dependent on the brand? One of the best tests to apply during this process is to consider how effective, or otherwise, the driver would be were the brand to be taken away. If the driver would be just as effective without the brand, then that is a fairly strong indication that the brand has no role. If, on the other hand, the driver would be neutralized, then it suggests that the brand plays a very strong role. Importantly, these questions need to be examined in relation to a homogenous market or product segment. Even within a defined segment, there may be substantial differences between territories or customer groups.

We identify the Role of Branding through an in-depth analysis of marketing and consumer market research data supported by executive interviews with appropriate key management personnel.

We calculate the BVA by compounding the Role of Branding Index with the economic earnings within each segment. This then represents the specific economic

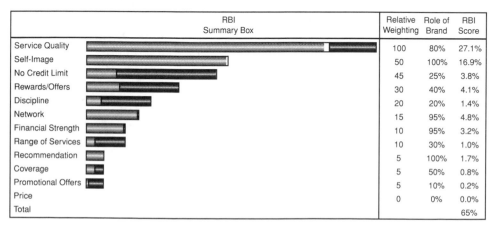

RBI Summary Box	Relative Weighting	Role of Brand	RBI Score
Service Quality	100	80%	27.1%
Self-Image	50	100%	16.9%
No Credit Limit	45	25%	3.8%
Rewards/Offers	30	40%	4.1%
Discipline	20	20%	1.4%
Network	15	95%	4.8%
Financial Strength	10	95%	3.2%
Range of Services	10	30%	1.0%
Recommendation	5	100%	1.7%
Coverage	5	50%	0.8%
Promotional Offers	5	10%	0.2%
Price	0	0%	0.0%
Total			65%

Exhibit 18-7   Role of branding analysis.

earnings within each business segment that can reasonably be attributed to the brand.

Brand Analysis

The third phase of the analysis calculates an appropriate risk rate to apply to the brand earnings going forward. This is converted into a discount rate, which is applied to forecast brand earnings in order to effect a net present value calculation of the overall brand value. As with the first two phases, this analysis is conducted segment by segment. The risk assessment is, in essence, a measure of the likelihood that the brand will continue to exert its influence going forward. Again, Interbrand has a proprietary method for assessing this value for a specific brand earnings forecast. This is the Brand Strength Analysis.

The principle behind the Brand Strength Analysis is that a strong brand provides a high level of confidence that brand earnings will be maintained over time and is manifest in a lower discount rate. Two examples of a strong brand in recent years would be MTV and IBM, serving very different types of customers. Conversely, a weak brand gives a lower level of confidence in future earnings, so the discount rate is higher to reflect this increased risk. As with the Role of Branding, the Brand Strength Analysis examines a combination of market data, consumer research evidence, and executive interviews and collectively assesses the brand and the market in which it operates in accordance with a number of predefined criteria. These include market, brand stability, leadership, trend, support, geography, and protection. These individual assessments are combined and weighted according to an Interbrand proprietary construct (S curve) and ultimately converted into an appropriate discount rate.

While a Brand Strength Analysis considers a number of the factors that contribute to a brand's equity, it should be remembered that its main thrust is to assess the brand's capacity to deliver future earnings. The bottom line is that if one accepts a definition of brand equity as "the set of brand-related assets and liabilities that add to, or subtract from, the value (in the nonfinancial sense) provided to the customer by the product or service itself," then brand equity represents an assessment of the brand's influence from a consumer perspective, while brand strength represents an assessment of the brand as an engine of profit from a management perspective.

Having calculated the appropriate discount rates, they are applied to the forecast brand earnings, which are then combined to arrive at the net present brand value.

QUALITY CONTROL

In general, brand valuations require projections of three to five years, although they may be for periods of between five and 10 years, depending on the nature of the sector and the brand under review. If it is not possible to forecast at least three to five years, there has to be a doubt about the susceptibility of that particular brand to reliable valuation.

In addition, the discount rate used in the valuation of a brand operating in a highly volatile sector will be greater than the discount rate applied to a brand operating in a less volatile sector. The higher discount rate depresses the valuation, thereby reducing the impact of volatile brand earnings forecasts.

Management approaches to forecasting can be characterized in a number of different ways, examples of which follow.

Central Forecasting

Many organizations prepare long-term forecasts centrally, for treasury and for strategic decision-making. They are often produced without much reference to local or specific brand management. The purposes for which they are prepared may not require a great deal of sensitivity to specific brands within a whole portfolio.

Departmental Forecasting

Financial and marketing departments frequently produce forecasts quite separately from one another. Sales forecasts are often geared more to the needs of the current sales target than to a medium- or long-term planning horizon. Reconciling assumptions and overcoming departmental biases toward pessimism or optimism can often be difficult.

Which forecast should the valuer depend on? Forecasts are inevitably affected by the attitude of the preparer to risk, by current sentiment in the industry, by the use of the forecast within the organization, by the time period over which it is prepared, and so on. Does this state of affairs make brand earnings forecasts (and therefore brand valuations) a waste of time? Some argue that it does. However, it is possible to synthesize different management forecasts credibly and use them to value brands reliably. It is possible to benchmark and analyze the data in a number of ways to reduce the margin of error.

Disclosure of assumptions is a critical issue. If the user of a brand valuation is aware of the forecast data and assumptions used in producing the valuation, it becomes a useful technique for comparing many different brands with different cash flow patterns in a consistent manner. Although brand valuations may change from time to time, disclosure of assumptions allows a clear reconciliation and explanation of changes in brand value. In fact, such reconciliations are often as useful as the absolute valuation itself.

However, the vital safeguard is the brand valuer's critical review. Brand forecasts must be subjected to detailed scrutiny by the valuer to ensure that they make sense in terms of historical data, internal and external market intelligence, and relationships within the data.

In addition to testing assumption and facts in a number of ways prior to producing three-, five-, or even 10-year forecasts, the brand valuer typically reviews the results by considering the sensitivity of the forecast to changes in the assumptions. Some changes in assumptions have minimal impact on the outcome of the valuation; others have a major impact. These are tested and reviewed both internally and externally to arrive at the most sensible result in terms of both forecast and ultimate valuation.

SUMMARY

Leveraging the brand to generate value has been in play for more than 150 years, dating back to the first brand, Bass Ale. Brand valuation has been emerging since the 1980s.

As brand-related value continues to grow as a percentage of total firm value, brand value management will become increasingly relevant (see Exhibit 18-8). Great branding is iterative and requires continual focus. The Coca-Cola story showed the power of branding on shareholder returns. It also showed that it is difficult to sustain perfect momentum, although I would be personally proud of a 15-year run.

To close, brand valuation provides a reasonably straightforward basis to drive branding forward. Besides the growth of intangibles, it is also gaining mainstream acceptance because it is the only measure that truly ties financial performance with the role of the brand.

What is also great about brand valuation, as a tool, is that you can make money with it directly. Spend a dollar on brand valuation and get 12 to 15 dollars back within 6 to 18 months. To date, there are more than 15 ways to do this.

NOTES

1.   Thomas P. Jones, "The Economic Value Added Approach to Corporate Investment," Stern Stewart and Company.
2.   "Brand Asset Management in the 1990s." Kuczmarski & Associates, Chicago.
3.   1998 Interbrand analysis of Financial Times Stock Exchange (FTSE 100).

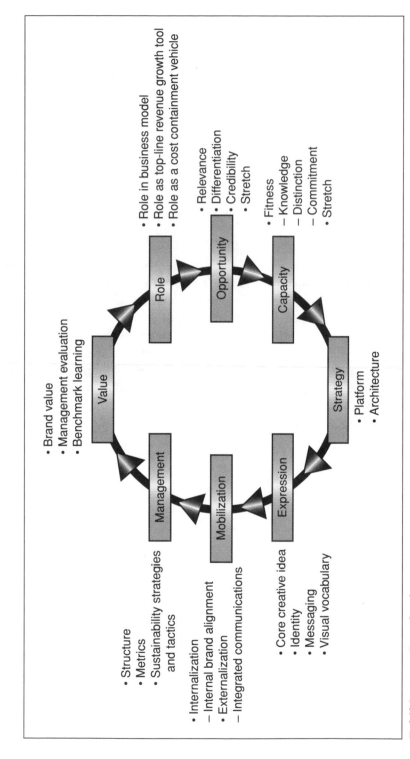

Exhibit 18-8 Brand value management.

ABOUT THE AUTHOR

Jeffrey Parkhurst is the Director of Brand Valuation at Interbrand for the United States and Americas, one of the leading brand consultancies. Mr. Parkhurst, who is based in New York, has conducted a broad range of brand valuations in a variety of industries and business situations. Prior to joining Interbrand, he spent 17 years with The Procter & Gamble Company, Kraft Foods, and AT Kearney in marketing, sales, technology, and strategy. He has an MBA with honors from the University of Chicago in Finance, an MBA from Xavier University in Marketing, and a Bachelor of Computer Science from the University of Minnesota. Mr. Parkhurst's work or opinion has been cited in *BusinessWeek*, *The New York Times*, *USA Today*, ABCNEWS.com, Broadchannel, and a host of other national and regional publications.

Interbrand (*www.interbrand.com*) is the leading international brand consultancy, combining the rigorous strategy and analysis of a management consulting practice with the entrepreneurial and creative spirit of branding and design. Founded in 1974, Interbrand has 25 offices in 19 countries and clients from among the most respected names among traditional and new economy businesses. The company is owned by the Omnicon Group and offers comprehensive capabilities that guide clients in the creation, enhancement, maintenance, and valuation of their most valuable asset—their brands. Service offerings include: brand valuation, naming, corporate identity, brand identity, package design, research, environmental design, interactive branding, and trademark law.

Part Four

Intellectual Property Transactions and Finance

CHAPTER NINETEEN

The Basics of Financing Intellectual Property Royalties

by Joseph A. Agiato

PERSPECTIVES

"Suppose you owned a stock, and the stock was selling for $50 a share," says Joseph Agiato, an expert in intellectual property valuation. "After a year the stock is selling for $65 a share. You decide that you do not want to sell the stock, but you do want to protect your gains, so you buy what is called a 'put' option. Simply stated, a put option gives the holder the right to 'put' the asset to a specific buyer for a contractually agreed upon price within a given time frame."

If an investor buys a contract to put the stock to a buyer at $65, and the stock actually decreases to $60, he or she can require that the owner of the put purchase the stock at $65. He "puts" the stock to them for $65, the contractually agreed upon price. If the stock in the example rose to $70, then the investor would simply choose not to exercise his put option and let the option expire.

Intellectual property royalty financing essentially creates a "put" option on the investment, says Mr. Agiato, and, similar to an insurance policy, "creates a floor on what an IP owner will receive on their asset." Once the borrower has received a loan on their IP, he or she is protected from downside risk not only from a financial perspective, but also from the perspective of keeping the IP from being impaired.

IP royalty financing is nonrecourse debt financing. A licensor of IP can take the future cash flow expected from a license agreement, and receive an "up-front" cash payment representing the present value of the future cash flows. This allows the owner of the IP to leverage income today that they expect to receive in the future, and thus add another weapon to their IP exploitation arsenal. Financing a royalty stream can provide much-needed capital to those faced with limited options and limited funds, such as research institutions, small and mid-cap companies, and individual inventors.

The purpose of Mr. Agiato's chapter is to explain the concept of intellectual property royalty financing, its advantages, and when it might make sense for a company to finance its future royalties. It will also detail how intellectual property may be financed and what is the process for IP royalty financing. By using royalty financing, the owner of the intellectual property can actually transfer a considerable amount of risk that comes from owning the intellectual property and at the same time increase their return on their intellectual property portfolio.

INTRODUCTION

It started with mortgages, credit cards, and even student loans. Now, with the substantial increase in licensing revenues, the era of issuing securities backed by intellectual property has arrived. While the concept may sound foreign, it is consistent with the strategy taken by many companies of treating proprietary intellectual property rights such as patents, copyrights, and trademarks as a discrete asset. While IP assets do not appear on the balance sheet of most companies, they need to be actively managed and exploited much like tangible assets. If you were purchasing real estate, would you take a mortgage out on the property or purchase it for cash? Of course, you would most likely take out a mortgage, because you would want to leverage your assets to increase your return.

Indeed, with the number of intellectual property exchanges and web sites dedicated to assist licensors and licensees find each other, the beginnings of a free and open trading of intellectual property rights is starting to evolve. Once an open exchange matures, valuations will be more reliable and thus leveraging your intellectual property becomes a logical tool for an intellectual property owner to use in managing assets.

The purpose of this chapter is to explain the concept of intellectual property royalty financing, its advantages, and when it might make sense for a company to finance their future royalties. It will also detail how intellectual property may be financed, and what is the process for IP royalty financing. Additionally, by using royalty financing, the owner of the intellectual property can actually transfer a considerable amount of risk that comes from owning the intellectual property, and at the same time increase their return on their intellectual property portfolio.

WHAT IS IP ROYALTY FINANCING?

IP royalty financing is nonrecourse debt financing. A licensor of IP can take the future cash flow expected from a license agreement and receive a cash payment up front, representing the present value of the future cash flows. This allows the owner of the IP to leverage today what they expect to get in the future, and thus add another tool for IP exploitation. Often faced with limited options and funds, financing a royalty stream can provide much-needed capital to research institutions, small and mid-cap companies, and individual inventors.

This type of financing is not particular to any specific type of IP. It includes patents, copyrights, trademarks, and trade secrets. Unlike other types of financing, IP royalty financing allows the owner of the IP to retain all of the upside in asset value. IP royalty financing is a unique source of capital collateralized by IP royalties. This is an extremely attractive vehicle for companies with robust royalty streams and a need for capital. Given the many advantages this type of debt financing offers, as discussed below, companies have a strong incentive to choose IP royalty financing over traditional financing means. Further, every responsible IP manager needs to investigate IP royalty financing as a way of lowering a portfolio's risk and leveraging the IP's return.

Creating a "Put" Option on Certain IP Assets

Suppose you owned a stock, and the stock was selling for $50 a share. After a year, the stock is selling for $65 a share. You decide that you do not want to sell the stock, but you do want to protect your gains, so you buy what is called a "put" option. Simply stated, a put option gives the holder the right to "put" the asset to a specific buyer for a contractually agreed upon price within a given time frame. Following our example through, if you buy a contract to put the stock to a buyer at $65, and the stock actually decreases to $60, you can require that the owner of the put purchase the stock from you at $65. You "put" the stock to them for $65, the contractually agreed upon price. If the stock in the example rose to $70, then you would simply choose not to exercise your put option and let the option expire.[1]

IP royalty financing essentially creates a "put" option on the intellectual property and creates a floor on what an IP owner will receive on their asset. Once borrowers receive loans on their IP, they are protected from downside risk not only from a financial perspective, but also from the perspective of keeping the IP from being impaired.

DEBT VERSUS EQUITY

One common mistake made by most licensors is assuming that they are actually selling their royalty stream, which is an incorrect assumption. When using IP royalty financing, the licensor retains the entire upside benefit from the IP if the royalty stream actually exceeds the projections of the lender. The only "upside" realized by a lender is the interest rate. In fact, it is safe to assume that lenders want their collateral to exceed expectations so that they are protected. There are several other advantages to debt financing over equity financing which are described in Exhibit 19-1.

Issue	Retain	Sell Interest in Royalty Stream	IP Royalty Financing
Risk Profile	Retain risk of product recall, competition, infringement, invalidity, etc.	Transfer these risks to purchaser.	Transfer these risks to the lender up to the loan amount (nonrecourse).
Upside Potential	Retain all royalty cash flow.	Sell entire royalty cash flow regardless of actual performance. Performance beyond projections benefits purchaser.	Obligation is solely interest and principal on the loan. Excess cash flows are remitted to the borrower.
Economics	Receive cash over time based on sales. Assume all risk of product performance and catastrophic loss.	Receive up-front payment based on conservative projections and equity discount rate (30+%).	Receive up-front proceeds based on loan-to-value calculation. Cash flows support interest and principal.
Ability to Enforce/ Insurance	Enforcement limited to budgeted funds.	Not Applicable	Enforcement for the borrower's benefit is included in financing.
Tax Advantages	None. Royalties are taxed as received.	None. There is a gain on sale of the asset.	Royalties are taxed as received and interest is tax deductible.

Exhibit 19-1   Comparison of debt and equity financing.

WHAT IS THE MARKET?

The IP licensing market has grown an estimated 700 percent, from $15 billion in 1990 to well over $100 billion in 1998.[2] Patent licensing revenue is predicted to top half a trillion dollars annually by 2005.[3] Additionally, the number of new U.S. patents issued in 1998 reached nearly 155,000, a 33 percent increase over 1997, and the total number of patents is expected to reach 6 million by 2015.[4] Already, there is more than $3.5 trillion in intellectual property value held by the Standard & Poor's (S&P) 500 and NASDAQ traded companies.[5] However, many creators of IP are small companies, offering mostly one type of product with some variations.[6]

Year	Amount (in Millions)	Collateral
1991	$480	Borden Trademark[7]
1992	$400	Disney Copyrights[8]
1995	n/a	General Electric Trademark[9]
1996	n/a	Nestle Trademark[10]
1997	In excess of $1 billion	Universal Studios[11]
1997	$325	Dream Works Copyrights[12]
1997	$55	David Bowie Copyrights[13]
1998	$280	Cecchi Gori Copyrights[14]
1998	$30	Holland-Dozier-Holland[15]
1999	$30	James Brown Copyrights[16]
2000	$25	Bill Blass Trademark[17]

Exhibit 19-2 Forms of IP collateral.

The worldwide IP revenue, therefore, is distributed across many companies and, with a few exceptions, is mostly below $10 million annually, per company.

With the technology IP asset wealth of U.S. companies recently estimated at a staggering $1 trillion coupled with the recent upsurge of licensing activity, patents and other forms of IP are increasingly recognized by their owners as their most valuable business assets. Nonetheless, the true value of these assets has seldom been accurately quantified on businesses' balance sheets, and to date these assets have not been widely used as collateral for debt financing. Various forms of IP have been used as collateral in the recent past, such as those listed in Exhibit 19-2.

However, patents, long recognized as the largest IP asset base, have not yet been widely used as a valid form of collateral for debt financing.[18] The most likely reasons for this is the very detailed due diligence process, general lack of understanding in the financial community of the importance of patent protection, and the fact that, until recently, there was not really enough money being generated to capture the interest of Wall Street. As more intellectual property is being created, more royalty revenue is being generated. The generation of royalties creates a cash flow that is of interest to Wall Street. Perceiving an enormous potential market, lending institutions and specialty finance companies have begun to structure nonrecourse financing collateralized by IP.

The major obstacles most companies face with obtaining this kind of financing are organizational. The IP law department usually is tasked with filing and enforcing patents. The research and development (R&D) group is interested in and compensated for basic and applied research. The business managers tend not to have formal technical or engineering training and have difficulty understanding the technical merits of a licensed technology, nor may they actually care, since the technology is actually already licensed.[19] Basically while you would get consensus from the entire organization that IP is crucial to the business's success, other than perhaps the licensing department, no one is singularly responsible for exploiting and leveraging the IP.[20]

The next major obstacle stunting the growth of IP financing is the lack of understanding by IP managers. Most IP managers do not understand the financial instruments enough to know that they can actually increase shareholder value by leveraging their royalty stream. In fact, usually the capital structure, hence the borrowings of a company, are controlled by the CFO. That notwithstanding, there are several potential uses of IP royalty financing that need to be considered by potential borrowers.

Potential classes of borrowers include:

- U.S. and foreign corporations that are looking for funds for expansion, to fund research, or for working capital
- Universities or nonprofit research institutions that are looking to accelerate the payments on their royalties and leverage intellectual property
- Venture capital investors who are looking to refinance an investment or who would be interested in leveraging the IP to satisfy a round of financing
- IP management companies who are seeking to become financially independent from their parent corporations
- Individual inventors who are looking to retain the upside value of their IP while satisfying an immediate cash need or to diversify their risk

While the market as defined by potential borrowers is diverse, so are the potential industries that this type of financing applies to, including:

- Patented technologies in the pharmaceutical, medical device, electronic, chemical, mechanical device, and computer hardware industries, among others
- Copyrights in the movie, literature, and computer software industries
- Trademarks in the entertainment, fashion, and sports merchandising industries

CLIENT MOTIVATIONS, FILLING A MARKET NICHE

Why would someone want to borrow against their royalty stream? Several reasons. First, IP represents another asset owned by a company that can borrow against. Since the borrowing is secured only by a royalty stream, it is attractive to many companies. But there are other reasons for borrowing against your royalty revenue stream.

- *Low-cost funding.* Given that interest rate pricing on IP royalty financing is based on the creditworthiness of the licensee(s), the borrower stands to benefit from the credit quality of its licensee(s) by receiving a lower cost of funding than normally obtainable. Therefore, companies that may not otherwise be able to obtain debt financing may now be able to do so at very attractive borrowing rates. This will be addressed more later in the chapter.

- *Long-term, fixed rate funding.* Companies can now borrow long term and at a fixed rate based on an assessment of the company's royalty stream. Most loans are fixed rate loans ranging from 5 to 10 years in length. Intellectual property royalty financing allows the borrower to "lock in" at an attractive long-term fixed-interest rate, regardless of the quality of the borrower's future financial performance as a whole. The main criteria used to establish the amount of the loan is the level of credit, the anticipated strength of the royalty stream, the credit rating of the licensee, and the strength of the intellectual property. Further, with a quality licensee, the borrower can leverage the credit rating of the licensee into a more favorable borrowing rate since the lender's credit risk is that of the licensee and not the borrower.

- *Creating a floor value and floor return for the IP.* If you are able to borrow a percentage of the future cash flows and employ that capital today in projects that exceed the cost of borrowing, then you are profitably leveraging your IP. If, at the same time, you can reduce the overall risk of the portfolio, and thus lower the risk of the organization, you have generated an above-average return to the investor and increased shareholder value.

- *Nondilutive capital.* While venture capitalists commonly acquire an equity interest in exchange for capital, IP royalty financing does not dilute a borrower's equity. This allows a company or individual access to funds without having to give up more equity in the company or partial ownership of the IP. With smaller companies, a cost of equity of 35 percent is not unusual. Clearly, in a situation where the alternative financing is raising capital at a 35 percent cost of equity, a typical borrowing rate is much more appealing.

- *Nonrecourse financing.* With IP royalty financing, in the event that the borrower is unable to repay the principal and interest on the loan, the lender will not seek compensation through the borrower's personal or company assets; the debt is secured only by the borrower's royalty cash flows and IP. This means that the loan is not secured by any personal or corporate guaranty, and a portion of the risk is transferred to the lender. Risk transference is discussed more later in the chapter, and is a significant benefit to most borrowers.

- *Unrestricted use of proceeds.* The loan proceeds can be used in any manner that the borrower so chooses; for borrowers that are corporations, the proceeds can be distributed to partners, stockholders, and/or lenders, as well as reinvested into R&D, marketing, or patent procurement. For borrowers that are inventors, the capital can be used for estate planning purposes and/or investment opportunities.

- *Freedom from restrictive covenants.* Unlike stringent bank loan covenants,

IP royalty financing does not require company-specific covenants or events of default. Additionally, there are no working capital or liquidity ratios that need to be maintained.

- *A lending decision based upon royalty the revenue streams.* The lender's focus is only on the royalty streams and not the traditional institutional focus on net income or net cash flow.
- *Perfectly matched funding.* The royalty revenue generated by the license agreement is used to pay down the borrower's debt, and the payment schedule and loan amortization are tailored to the timing of expected royalty payments. Therefore, the loan can be back-ended with regard to principal; amortized on a straight-line basis; or can even use a traditional mortgage amortization.
- *Tax advantages.* Interest is fully tax-deductible.
- *Dedicated funding for the IP management company.* The debt financing is independent from its parent company's funding sources.
- *Independent IP valuation.* The lender's valuation of the IP asset enhances the overall company valuation and supports transfer pricing.
- *A potential hedge against product obsolescence.* One potential use of IP royalty financing is as a hedge against technological obsolescence. If a technology becomes outmoded quickly, it may no longer be used. By having nonrecourse debt, you are protected against this risk up to the amount you have borrowed.

ABILITY TO SETTLE COSTLY INFRINGEMENT LITIGATION

Another use of IP royalty financing is the settlement of costly infringement litigation. Often, a case can settle if the licensee (infringer) would be willing to take a paid-up license, especially if the infringement is not in an area where the patentee and the infringer actually compete. By using a debt structure, the licensor can propose a royalty paid over time and then have that royalty stream used as collateral on a loan. By using this technique, the patentees can maximize their return from the IP and receive their money in a lump sum. As always, once the loan is paid off and royalties received by the lender exceed the amount of the loan payment, the additional funds are remitted to the borrower.

A related use in litigation matters is to package historical damages and an ongoing license into a financing so that the historical damages can also be paid over time. For example, assume the following facts:

- Patent Co. owns the rights to certain technology.
- Infringer Co. has been determined to be an infringer.
- Patent Co. and Infringer Co. do not compete in the market.
- Historical damages have been determined to be $10 million.
- Patent Co. wants Infringer Co. to take a paid-up license for $20 million or will not allow it to use the technology in the future.

- Infringer Co. would accept the proposal if it had the cash. In lieu of taking the deal, Infringer Co. is forced to offer an above-market-value royalty rate to settle the entire dispute.

In the above hypothetical, the deal can be financed using a debt structure if the parties would be willing to cooperate. The entire $30 million ($10 million historical and $20 million for a paid-up license) can be financed. Patent Co. would receive the entire $30 million today, thus making settlement a very attractive option, and Infringer Co. would pay a royalty per a typical agreement, except instead of paying Patent Co., it is paying the financing company. As always, if the royalties exceed the loan amount, the additional royalties are paid to the borrower, who in this case is Patent Co. Since the above scenario is not uncommon, it is anticipated that royalty financing can be used to settle a substantial number of IP litigation cases.

CATASTROPHIC RISK REDUCTION

There are always certain risks associated with owning IP. Many of the risks are catastrophic in nature, meaning that if they occur, the IP can be rendered useless or the value may be severely impaired. While these risks may be unlikely, they are not insignificant. Additionally, most lenders cannot reasonably price the occurrence of a catastrophic event such as those detailed below.

Patent Invalidity

A primary benefit to IP royalty financing is risk transference. There are certain events, which, if they occur, would result in the lender having to write off the remaining loan balance. For example, if a borrower had its patent declared invalid, the licensee would no longer be obligated to pay royalties. Since the debt is non-recourse, the lender would be out the remaining balance of the loan. Thus, the risk of patent invalidity in a royalty financing transaction is shifted in large measure to the lender, in that a patent being challenged and declared invalid would represent total write-off of the loan. The probability of a patent being declared invalid, while small, is not insignificant.

Potential Infringers

Another risk that is transferred in an IP royalty financing is the risk of infringement litigation. Assume for example that Small Co. holds a patent in a basic technology that is profitable and throws off a robust royalty stream. Assume further that after a loan is made, Large Co. decides to enter the market and, as a result, the royalty payment to Small Co. decreases substantially. Assume further that Large Co. is infringing Small Co.'s patent position. This again is not an infrequent occurrence, and Small Co. in the example is not usually in a position to adequately fund patent infringement litigation. If the royalty stream has been financed, then the licensor-patent holder has already received a significant portion of the anticipated revenue stream and therefore is not at risk for a substantial portion of the anticipated lost revenue resulting from an infringer entering the marketplace. In fact, in this specific instance it is in the financing company's best interest to pursue the infringer, which is indeed what happens. When an IP royalty financing is initially funded, the borrower usually retains the option of going after potential infringers in order to protect the royalty stream. This benefits the borrower in several ways. First, the borrower does not have to pay any legal fees; it is only obligated to cooperate with the lender in prosecuting the litigation. Second, most small companies do not have a so-called war chest to pursue litigation and therefore are not in any position to deal with a larger company and be caught up in a multiyear litigation. Finally, the ability to have the cash available from the financing allows the borrower to continue business as planned, while the financing company funds the litigation and pursues the infringer. The risk of the litigation has now been transferred to the financing company.

Potential Infringment

The above situation can be reversed also where Large Co. actually sues Small Co. for patent infringement litigation. Now Small Co. needs to defend a costly patent litigation and faces many of the risks cited above, now including potential temporary or permanent injunction. In this situation, as before, it is the financing company that assumes much of the risk. If the borrower's patents actually read on the patents of Large Co., then Small Co. may be considered an infringer, which is a risk that the financing company is assuming when it makes the loan. Most loans from financing companies will require the finance company to defend the borrower in the event of a patent infringement litigation, which again transfers a risk that most companies do not want to assume—whether they are large or small companies.

TRANSACTION PROFILES

What types of transactions are actually best suited for IP royalty financing? It depends on contract language, terms, and the parties to the transaction.

Model Transaction

The model transaction, which is not the most common transaction, involves the following:

- The patent holder has a technology currently being licensed.
- A license has several years remaining.
- Technology obsolescence is not a factor.
- The license agreement has been in place for two or three years and the royalty payments have been increasing.
- The licensee is a highly rated company from an investment standpoint.
- The IP can be protected in the event the borrower goes bankrupt.

Although the above represents a framework that the finance companies like to work from, few transactions actually do fit the "model transaction." In fact, every transaction seems to have its own particular nuance; whether it be no royalty history, or a noninvestment-grade licensee, or even an unrated licensee, there is usually some obstacle to the transaction that needs to be worked through by a quality IP financing company such as Licent Capital, LLC. You should expect your IP financing company to work with you in dealing with a specific deal. More often than not, there is a way of completing a transaction.

Ability to Separate IP from the Company

The IP finance company is going to want to make the IP, its only collateral, safe from a bankruptcy by creating what is known as an SPV. An SPV, or special purpose vehicle, is a wholly owned subsidiary of the patent holder. As will be seen later, the SPV is actually the borrower in the transaction. In the event that the IP cannot be separated from the patent holder, then other structural changes may need to be made to the loan.

SAMPLE FACT PATTERNS FOR IP ROYALTY FINANCING

As suggested, there are a number of different types of transactions that can be financed if the specialty finance company can offset additional risk with a more creative loan structure. Representative transactions include:

- A company that has orphan drug status (and therefore no patent protection) and manufactures an active ingredient in its licensee's product applies for financing. The licensee is an AA-rated company. In this financing, there is no way to separate the IP from the licensor, nor is there even a patent to hold as collateral. The transaction amounts to financing a supply agreement, which can be accomplished by the IP financing company by creating a specific loan structure that will account for the attendant risks and mitigating the risk by using IP royalty financing techniques.
- A fund that purchases royalty streams is looking to increase their returns and lower overall risk in the portfolio. They take a discrete royalty stream

from a technology that they have purchased the rights to and use that discrete stream to secure a loan at 10 percent. Since their return on investment for the portfolio is 35 percent, borrowing at a fixed interest rate of 10 percent allows the fund to have less capital at risk in a specific transaction, and earn a 25 percent return with no capital at risk. For example, if the initial investment was $100 million, and from that the fund earned about $35 million per year, the fund would return 35 percent. If the fund then finances $50 million, they still earn $35 million, but on an investment of $50 million, which yields a return of 60 percent on the portfolio.[21] This return is realized, while at the same time the overall risk of the portfolio is reduced as a result of the risk transference that takes place in the financing.

- A company wants to enter into a license agreement with another organization and wants all of the payments up front. In this situation, there are no historical royalties, but the financing company can step in and convert the payments into an up-front payment if certain conditions are met. By working with the financing company, the parties are able to negotiate a deal where the payments get directed to the financing company that has lent the money up front to the licensor. After the nonrecourse loan is paid off, the remaining funds are transferred to the licensor.

- Sample Co. has an ongoing patent litigation with Infringer Co. Infringer Co. is found to infringe the patent of Patent Co. and now wants to settle the case and take a license going forward. Historical damages now been agreed to be $10 million. Patent Co. wants the historical damages and another $20 million for a paid-up license. Infringer Co. works with the specialty finance company and finances the entire $30 million over seven years. This allows Infringer Co. to settle the litigation and continue to manufacture the product, while not having to deplete its current cash position.

- Company A has a royalty that it has been receiving for three years. In an effort to transfer the risk of possible litigation which it could not defend due to costs, it opted to finance its royalties for the remaining term of the agreement.

How the Transaction Actually Works

The way the loan is actually made may vary from company to company, but the basic structure is meant to mitigate a few basic risks that a lender might face. Assuming the standard licensor-licensee relationship is already in place, the lender will attempt to do two things:

- Make the intellectual property bankruptcy remote. In a typical licensor-licensee relationship, the licensed property is actually owned by the borrower (licensor). In a financing transaction, the intellectual property is assigned to a bankruptcy-remote wholly owned subsidiary of the borrower. The reason for this is simple: The licensor does not want its collateral tied up in a bankruptcy proceeding.

- Redirect the royalty payments to the lender. In a typical financing transaction, the royalty payments from the licensee are going to be redirected to a lockbox under the control of the licensor. The licensor then funds the transaction out of the royalty payments only. To the extent a royalty payment from the licensee is not enough to fund the loan, the lender has no recourse.

Exhibit 19-3 shows the details of the transaction. To the left is a typical licensor-licensee relationship. As you can see from this figure, the actual transaction is made between the financing company and the SPV, as the SPV is the assignee of the intellectual property. The licensee is actually making its royalty payment to the lockbox instead of the licensor. The funds paid into the lockbox are used to fund the loan, including principal, interest, loan reserves, and loan sinking funds. The actual loan agreement is between the SPV and the financing company, which enables the lender to protect its collateral in the event of bankruptcy.

TRANSACTION PROCESS

The transaction process is actually pretty straightforward (see Exhibit 19-4). Initially, the applicants contact the finance company and speaks in general terms about the type of intellectual property they have and how their royalty agreement

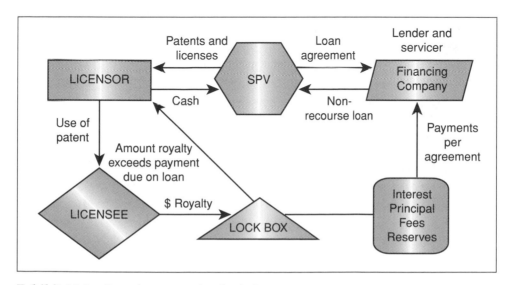

Exhibit 19-3 Sample transaction logistics.

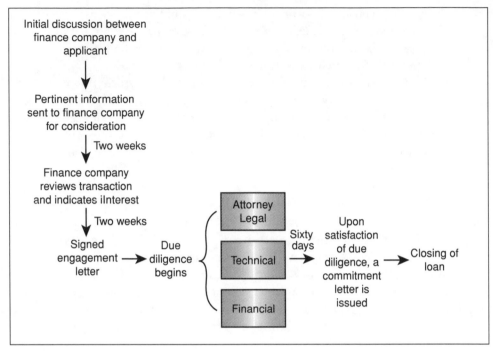

Exhibit 19-4   Transaction process.

with the licensee is structured. The reason for this detailed discussion up front is that the finance company needs to have an interest in the collateral, but also needs to understand what type of loan structure needs to be investigated. For example, a licensee with a AAA credit rating may allow the finance company to pursue a different loan structure than a noninvestment-grade licensee in a transaction where the separation of the collateral from the borrower is difficult.

If the lender thinks that a transaction is possible, then the parties may enter into a nondisclosure agreement, and the patent holder would send some basic information to the lender that would give more details than the initial discussion and provide some support for what has already been represented by the patent holder. After the initial review, which should take no longer than two weeks, the finance company should be able to indicate whether it has an interest in doing a deal and be able to indicate to the borrower the basic structure and cost of the transaction. A term sheet from the finance company will be presented to the borrower, with the terms and conditions of course being subject to the necessary due diligence process.

If the parties wish to continue, then it is customary for the borrower to engage the financing company and pay the initial due diligence fees that are necessary to complete the transaction.[22]

Due Diligence

The due diligence process for this type of transaction is detailed and thorough. The due diligence depends on the expertise of independent scientists, patent attorneys, and valuation professionals. This process, which should be complete in 60 days assuming full cooperation, is very important for the lender, and thus ultimately for the borrower. By having a multidisciplinary team in place, the finance company can complete its due diligence with minimal disruption to the business of the borrower. As the borrower, you can expect the due diligence to include:

- Does the borrower actually own the patent being licensed?
- Does the license agreement with the licensee actually cover the patents being pledged as collateral?
- Are all of the royalties being received from the licensor that has licensed the subject technology?

The due diligence process also reviews other risks being assumed by a lender that may not be as obvious such as:

- How difficult would it be for the licensee to actually design around the patent being licensed?
- Is the licensee actually manufacturing according the patent, or has the licensee's manufacturing process actually evolved to the point that the manufacturing process in no longer dependant on the licensed technology?
- What is the innovation in the field currently, and what is the expected technology life cycle of the product?

Having a multidisciplinary team is crucial. Without the expertise of each discipline, it would be very difficult to complete a transaction.[23] The level of expertise that the finance company can bring to bear on the transaction is also something that a potential borrower should consider before engaging a particular finance company.

SETTING UP AN INTERNAL PROCESS

Every company needs to have well-defined internal management processes with regard to its IP management. The issue of IP royalty financing should be addressed at that level, and it needs to be addressed from three different perspectives:

1. Deals currently in place
2. Deals that could be in play if a financing were done
3. Future licensing deals

Deals Currently in Place

For deals currently in place where the company is a licensor, the company may want to review the following:

- If the remaining term of the agreement is financed, can I adequately employ the funds and generate a return in excess of the borrowing cost?
- Can I get use the financing to hedge the risk of litigation, patent invalidity, and other catastrophic risks?

For deals currently in place where the company is a licensee:

- Can I convince the licensor to give me a buyout of future royalties due with a current cash settlement?

Deals That Could Be in Play

There may very well be deals that are currently in process that can be better constructed and economically more beneficial if the IP royalties are financed. Some things companies need to consider are:

- Can I as a licensor now negotiate a higher royalty rate by allowing the licensee to pay over time instead up front?
- Are there agreements that would have been advantageous to enter into except the terms were inconsistent with the organization's cash needs? If so, is it worth revisiting those opportunities?

Future Licensing Deals

It makes logical sense to attempt to construct licensing transactions that can be leveraged and financed, if not today then in the future. There is tremendous upside available to a deal that can be financed and leveraged. Organizations should set up an internal process and have standard language inserted into their agreements that would allow future deals to be financed. Organizations can create at no cost an agreement that can potentially be a source of capital, but equally as important, they can and should look to lower the risk of their patent portfolios, thereby increasing shareholder value.

This form of financing is quickly becoming very popular, and is expected to have a significant impact on IP exploitation in the future. Investigating the possibilities with a finance company may provide a key to capital for many organizations, which necessitates an internal process to evaluate the financing and risk transference opportunities.

NOTES

1. Options and option pricing is actually a very complex topic. There is also a cost for purchasing the "put" option, which is not figured into the example in order to keep the example simple.
2. Kevin Rivette and David Kline, *Rembrandts in the Attic: Unlocking the Hidden Value of Patents* (Boston: Harvard Business School Press, 2000).
3. Capital District Business Review (Albany), August 14, 2000, *http://albany.bcentral.com/albany/stories/2000.*
4. Constance Parten, "Intellectual Property Market Untapped by Insurers, Rife with Litigation." *Insurance Journal, www.insurancejournal.com/html/ijweb/publications/IJWest/w112700/intellectprop.htm.*
5. Ibid.
6. This actually just increases the values previously given as far as IP values go since all of the small companies and inventors are excluded from the NASDAQ and other market capitalization calculations.
7. *Financial World,* 1 September 1992.
8. *Euroweek,* 16 October 1992.
9. Mark Bezant, "The Use of Intellectual Property as Security for Debt Finance," Intellectual Property Group, Arthur Anderson.
10. *Financial World,* 6 December 1996.
11. *The Financier,* Vol. 4, No. 5, December 1997.
12. *Best's Review,* February 2001.
13. *The Times,* 7 February 1997 (London); *Daily Telegraph,* 5 February 1997.
14. Fitch IBCA Research Report, *Finance for an Italian Library of Movies plc,* 30 April 1998.
15. *Financial Times,* 4 August 1998.
16. *Reuters,* 26 June 2000.
17. *Mergers & Acquisitions,* 1 January 2000.
18. Most banks do take the IP as part of the collateral for bank loans, but do not attribute much value to the IP as collateral. In this instance, the lender is usually getting something for nothing.
19. I was actually at a Fortune 100 company known for its great management and the business manager told me that although his division was technology-based and he had hundreds of patents that had issued, he had no time or resources to go through the patents to see if they were even valuable.
20. Over the last few years, certain companies, such as Dow Chemical, have created positions for intellectual asset managers. These managers are responsible for exploiting a company's IP.
21. The calculation is $35 million return less interest of $5 million on the loan results in a $30 million net return on investment. With the investment lowered from $100 million to $50 million, the portfolio actually returns 60 percent.
22. If you are in process of structuring a license agreement that you would like to be able to finance, most finance companies will assist you in the licensing transaction at no cost to the borrower.
23. Interestingly enough, one of the common outgrowths of rigorous due diligence is more licensing opportunities. Patent holders are not used to someone coming in from the outside and looking at their technology. We have found that often, by undergoing such a process, new applications may actually be found for issued patents.

ABOUT THE AUTHOR

Joseph A. Agiato, MBA, CPA, ASA, FIBA, is a Managing Director of Licent Capital, LLC. He focuses on financing intellectual property royalty streams and assisting in the negotiation of licensing agreements on behalf of clients. Mr. Agiato has performed over 2,000 intellectual property valuations in various industries and has assisted individual inventors, Fortune 500 companies, and universities in their licensing management and intellectual property strategy development.

Mr. Agiato's distinguished career includes serving as the National Practice Leader of the Intellectual Property Services Group for KPMG and a consultant and advisor to Deloitte & Touche's intellectual property department. Mr. Agiato holds undergraduate degrees in accounting and economics from Mt. St. Mary's College, and Master's degrees in finance from C.W. Post University and in valuation sciences from Lindenwood College. He holds five professional designations including CPA and ASA (Accredited Senior Appraiser) and served as a technical review editor on this book. He is an active member of 10 professional associations and has held 16 professional committee positions over the last 12 years. Among these committee positions were liaison between the AIPLA (American Intellectual Property Law Association) and the AICPA, member of the board of directors of the National Patent Board, and member of the Appraisal Standard Board's Issues Resource Panel, established by the United States Congress. Mr. Agiato has written and lectured extensively on valuation, intellectual property, and licensing. He has been retained as an expert in licensing and damages on numerous occasions and has been the court's own expert in over 60 cases by 23 different judges in three different states. He has been called a "foremost authority on intellectual property" by the AICPA.

Licent Capital (*www.licentcapital.com*) is the first specialty finance company to provide nonrecourse debt financing for the licensors of all intellectual property, including licensed patents. IP finance is Licent Capital's only business. The company was co-founded by members of Merrill Lynch & Co.'s Asset Backed Finance Group.

CHAPTER TWENTY

Credit Analysis of Intellectual Property Securitization

A Rating Agency Perspective

by Jay H. Eisbruck

PERSPECTIVES

While intellectual property royalties may never trade as broadly as mortgage-backed securities, they represent intangible assets with vast financial potential. From 1990 through 1999, asset-backed securitizations, in general, totaled more than $750 billion. Intellectual property–related transactions of this type were less than $5 billion, most of which were focused in copyright publishing and future film royalties. However, for the right owner, under the right conditions, securitizations—including those associated with patent licensing— can be uniquely rewarding.

Intellectual property rights, such as trademarks, copyrights, and licenses associated with them, often generate significant revenues. As with other types of assets, the income streams associated with cash flow can be securitized or packaged as a tradable security. In recent years copyright royalties from music publishing (e.g., so-called Bowie Bonds) to licensing revenues associated with clothing designer Bill Blass have been successfully leveraged in this way. Patent royalties pose special problems because of the complex and often changing nature of the rights and the inventions they cover. Still, experts say that this market is likely to grow much larger as companies learn to communicate to underwriters and shareholders the value of their inventions and the rights that cover them. Broad and efficient monetization of intangible assets is certain to become a shareholder expectation.

"One characteristic that differentiates IP transactions from other types of future cash flow transactions (such as the securitizations of future cash flows generated by an oil pipeline)," says Jay Eisbruck, a Senior Vice President of Moody's Investors Service Asset-Backed Finance Group, which rates bond quality and issuer creditworthiness, "is that they are highly dependent on popular tastes or technological change, adding a layer of complexity and risk to the analysis."

In addition to the lack of education, motivation is a potential detriment to IP securitizations. Many of those companies with the greatest critical mass of securitizable assets, the Fortune 500, are highly creditworthy. The cost of borrowing for these giants is little more than treasury rates. Even AA-rated companies that need capital and do not want to dilute shareholder equity can easily access the bond market. However, companies and universities that need capital and that generate significant licensing cash flow, such as Xerox, Lucent, and small to mid-size biotech businesses, may be in an excellent position to securitize their licenses, depending on the borrowing environment and the state of the equity markets.

Though only one pharmaceutical patent securitization has been completed to date, a $100 million transaction backed by the revenues generated by a university's patent (see Chapter 22, "New Patent Issue: BioPharma Royalty Trust"), "this market has huge potential," says Mr. Eisbruck. "The licensing of patented technology is a $100 billion annual business involving thousands of companies. Whether this market develops will depend on the financing needs of the holders of these patents, as well as their willingness to develop transaction structures that protect against the risks of these assets . . ." Mr. Eisbruck sees the potential for "pooling" IP collateral, not unlike the popular collateralized loan obligations (CLOs).

"We do not expect that education will develop overnight because there is little standardization among these assets," asserts Mr. Eisbruck. "Consequently, issuance volume in this subsector of the securitization market is unlikely to rival the $50 billion annual issuance of traditional asset-backed collateral types in the near to medium term. However, we expect issuance volume to increase steadily during the next two years, as at least some issuers are likely to find this type of financing to be more attractive than current forms."

INTRODUCTION

Intellectual property[1] securitization has taken a variety of forms since its creation in the mid-1990s. These have included music royalty, future film, and trademark licensing receivables transactions. In analyzing the credit quality of those securities, Moody's adapted its general asset-backed securities analysis to the many unique characteristics of the different IP businesses. This chapter explains those special characteristics and how they affect the credit analysis of the transactions.

Transactions backed by IP are one form of future cash flow transactions. As with any future cash flow transaction, Moody's analysis draws on expertise not only with the structuring and the particular assets being securitized, but also with the overall industry of which they are part. However, one characteristic that differentiates IP transactions from other types of future cash flow transactions (such as the securitization of future cash flows generated by an oil pipeline) is that they are highly dependent on popular tastes or technological change, adding a layer of complexity and risk to the analysis.

The transactions done to date, totaling under $5 billion, represent only a thin slice of the potential IP securitization market. They also represent a tiny percentage of the total securitization market, which has completed over $750 billion over the same period (see Exhibit 20-1). Since the use of IP continues to grow as a portion of the economy as a whole, the intellectual property arena represents a vast potential market for securitization.

The extent to which other intellectual property assets can be successfully securitized will depend in part on the degree to which a broad spectrum of investors becomes educated about their unique attributes. We do not expect that education will develop overnight, because there is little standardization among these assets; consequently, issuance volume in this subsector of the securitization market is unlikely to rival the $50 billion annual issuance of traditional asset-backed collateral types in the near to medium term. However, we expect issuance volume to increase steadily during the next two years, as at least some issuers are likely to find this type of financing to be more attractive than current forms.

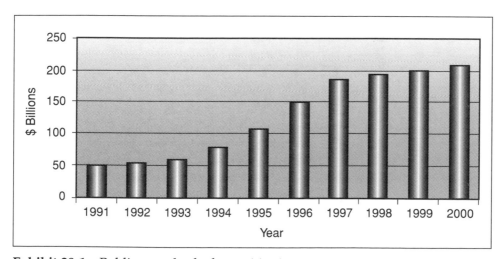

Exhibit 20-1 Public asset-backed securities issuance.

A BRIEF EXPLANATION OF SECURITIZATION

Securitization is the process of using the cash flows generated by an asset or pool of assets to support the issuance of debt. It is an offshoot of traditional secured debt, whose credit is supported by a lien on specific assets. With conventional secured issues, the primary source of repayment remains the issuer's earning power, but in a securitization, the burden of repayment is shifted away from the issuer to a designated pool of assets. Bondholders are protected from the operating performance of the issuer through features in the securitization's structure. These include the right of bondholders to replace the issuer as manager or servicer of the assets if it has difficulties. Securitizations also use bankruptcy-remote special purpose vehicles (SPV) that prevent other creditors of the issuer from making claims on the securitized assets. These features allow securitizations to achieve higher bond ratings than the senior secured rating of the issuer.

Securities that use this structure are generally referred to as asset-backed securities (ABS) (see Exhibit 20-2). Since the first ABS transactions were completed in the mid-1980s, the market has grown dramatically. Over $200 billion of new issuance was completed in 2000 and there is nearly $1 trillion in outstanding securities. As the securitization market has grown, it has broadened to include a progression of new assets, with IP being one of the most recent types under development. The following sections describe the credit risks associated with different types of IP securitization and what can be done to mitigate them.

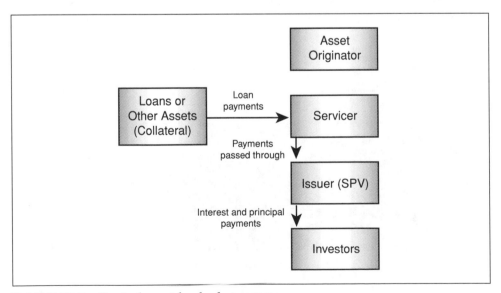

Exhibit 20-2   Typical asset-backed structure.

PATENT LICENSING REVENUES

Patent revenues is an IP asset class that a number of market participants are attempting to securitize. Through securitization, companies holding patents can accelerate the realization of the revenues generated by the licensing of a patented product or process, enabling them to more quickly recoup the often significant research and development costs incurred in creating the asset.

Though only one patent securitization has been completed to date, a $100 million+ deal backed by the revenues generated by a university's patent for an HIV/AIDS medication, this market has huge potential. The licensing of patented technology is a $100 billion annual business involving thousands of companies. Whether this market develops will depend on the financing needs of the holders of these patents, as well as their willingness to develop transaction structures that protect against the risks of these assets. Though it is difficult to gauge the current needs of these companies, the following sections highlight the risks that will need to be addressed to complete highly rated patent revenue securitizations. These risks include:

- Technology marketing and acceptance
- Technological obsolescence
- Licensee payment risk
- Servicing risk
- Legal risks

Technology Marketing and Acceptance

New products using patented technology experience a period following their introduction that determines their market demand and the ability of their owner to meet that demand. Predicting the success or failure of a new product can be difficult and is speculative by its nature. This risk can be reduced by having licensing agreements lined up in anticipation of the granting of the patent, but even this does not guarantee the level of future sales or the abilities of the licensee and licensor to fulfill their obligations under the agreement.

As a result, it is difficult to accurately predict future revenues the patent will generate if there is no history of past revenues or performance. Patents in this stage of their lives will rarely be good candidates for highly rated securitizations. For a transaction to be completed at this early point in the product life cycle, a performance guaranty from a highly rated third party will probably be necessary.

A better candidate for securitization is a patent that has moved past this stage and has demonstrated multiple years of collected revenues from one or more licensees. The chances of success for the transaction would be further enhanced if the agreements with the licensees extend into the future and if there is demonstrable evidence that there are additional uses for the technology.

Technological Obsolescence

Even if the technology has gained market acceptance and has demonstrated performance in the past, there is a risk that a superior technology will be developed during the life of the securitization that makes the benefits of the patent obsolete. This risk is most acute in high-technology industries, such as semiconductors and pharmaceuticals, where the pace of innovation is rapid. If this occurred, royalties generated by the patent, which are generally paid as a percentage of sales, could decline rapidly from the levels of earlier years. This risk could render historical revenues irrelevant.

To analyze this risk, Moody's evaluates the factors that might limit the asset's exposure to obsolescence during the life of the transaction:

1. *Short term of the securitization.* As mentioned earlier, all new products need time to achieve market acceptance. The period when a competing patent first enters the market could provide a window during which an established patent's revenues are not threatened. If the term of the securitization is confined to this window, the risk of obsolescence is reduced.

2. *Large cost of replacement technology.* Licensees often need to make a substantial financial or marketing investment in order to bring products to market using licensed patents. That provides a high barrier to entry for potential new products, limiting the exposure of existing patents to obsolescence. This fact could also discourage competitors from developing competing technologies, further reducing the risk.

3. *Brand recognition.* Superior technologies often have difficulty overcoming the popularity of existing brands. Therefore, patent income from products with strong brand recognition and loyalty would be more resistant to erosion from new technologies.

4. *Alternative use.* Patented technology can potentially be applied to a variety of different uses. Development of new uses reduces exposure to a technological advance in one application and expands the patent's revenue-generating potential.

In each case, an analysis of the specific patent will need to be performed to determine how well each of these factors applies. In some cases involving highly technical expertise, independent industry experts may be consulted to assist in the analysis.

Licensee Payment Risk

Even if the patented technology gains acceptance and remains technically viable, cash flows may not reach investors if licensees default on their payment obligations. A large group of diverse, highly rated licensees mitigates this risk in a patent license fee transaction.

Another potential risk is the expiration of current license agreements during the term of the securitization. The terms of subsequent agreements can be difficult to predict, which will make the level of royalties these agreements generate difficult to predict as well.

Servicing Risk

In some licensing agreements, the patent holder has significant ongoing obligations to the licensee. For example, the licensor could be required to manufacture a necessary component of the final product, or further develop the technology over time, and/or provide marketing or technical support. Noncompliance with any of these obligations could cause the agreement(s) to be dissolved and interrupt the revenues paid to the securitization.

The licensor also needs be able to properly account for and collect the revenues. If not, revenues the patent generates will inevitably be missed.

As in a typical securitization, the best way to mitigate this risk is to hire a backup servicer to perform these obligations if the original servicer/licensor should experience difficulties. However, it could be more difficult to find a qualified backup servicer for a patent securitization, since the technical skills needed might be difficult to replicate. Servicing risk can also be reduced by minimizing the licensor's obligations in their agreements, which would limit the impact of a possible disruption in the event of a bankruptcy.

Legal Risks

There are a variety of legal risks that can threaten the revenue stream generated by a patent. These include:

1. *Product liability.* Use of the patented technology could result in damage claims for environmental, personal injury, or other forms of negligence that a securitization could be responsible for.
2. *Patent challenge or infringement.* Challenges to the validity of the patent can be made by third parties causing all or part of it to be overturned. In addition, nonlicensed entities could attempt to use the technology without paying royalties.
3. *Expiration.* By law, patents are valid for only 19 years after the date of grant.
4. *Bankruptcy.* Other creditors of the licensor could attempt to claim patent revenues in the event of the licensor bankruptcy.

The extent of the first two of these risks can be assessed through a review of the history of the patent. If a patent has been in existence and has been generating revenues for a number of years without these problems, it is less likely to experience them in the future. A long view must be taken on the risk of product liability, since it could take time for evidence to accumulate and scientific studies to be completed assessing damage and causes. Active monitoring by patent compliance specialists can also be done to reduce the risk that unauthorized use of the technology does not occur.

Even if the patent has a long history, these risks cannot be eliminated completely. Here too, an extensive analysis of potential liability and patent challenges by an independent industry expert might be needed to assess this risk. The use of a third-party insurer to cover this risk is another alternative.

Another factor that can impact the revenue streams from patent licensing is the expiration of the patents. Both the expected negative impact on the future cash flows and the increased uncertainty around those postexpiration cash flows need to be evaluated for patents that are scheduled to expire during the life of the transaction. This risk is mitigated to the extent the securitizations hold patents whose remaining lives last well into, or exceed, the term of the transaction.

The risk of seller bankruptcy is a common one for securitization. As mentioned earlier, it is usually covered through the sale of the assets to a bankruptcy-remote special purpose vehicle (SPV). The use of a SPV is designed to insulate the assets from other creditors of the seller in the event of bankruptcy of the seller. If properly structured, this risk can be greatly reduced, if not eliminated, and allow for the rating of the securitization to be greater than that of the seller.

TRADEMARK REVENUE SECURITIZATION

Trademarks, much like patents, are a right granted by the government to control the use of a logo or brand name. The risks of securitizing these rights are also similar to patents. A major difference between the two is that future revenues will be at risk in trademark deals if the image falls out of fashion or popularity, as opposed to the technological obsolescence risk of patents.

One securitization backed by trademark licensing revenues was completed in 1999. The transaction securitized the future revenues generated by the trademark licensing business of the fashion designer Bill Blass. Bill Blass has been a prominent designer for 40 years, with a long history of licensing his name across a wide variety of different product lines. These include men's and women's apparel and housewares.

In addition to traditional forms of asset-backed credit enhancement, the transaction had features that enabled it to receive a rating of Baa3. (The purpose of Moody's credit ratings is to provide investors with a simple system of gradation by which the relative investment qualities of bonds may be noted. Gradations of investment quality are indicated by rating symbols. There are nine symbols used to designate the least investment risk [i.e., highest investment quality] to that denoting the greatest risk [i.e., lowest investment quality]. The following symbols are used: Aaa, Aa, A, Baa, Ba, B, Caa, Ca, C.) This rating is significantly higher than Bill Blass Ltd.'s underlying credit. This was despite significant obligations of the issuer to assist in the generation of future revenues in its role as servicer of the assets.

The first feature was a series of triggers built into each structure related to the financial condition of the servicer/issuer. Essentially, these triggers gave investors the right to take control of the assets and place them with a backup servicer, before they lose considerable value and place future debt repayment at risk. In this case a qualified backup servicer with specialized industry knowledge was in place at closing to take over management of the assets, should the original servicer/issuer underperform expectations or fall into financial difficulty. Since the backup servicer had specialized industry knowledge, the risk of a significant drop-off in asset performance due to a servicer/issuer bankruptcy was reduced.

Secondly, the amount of debt financed in relation to the asset's appraised value, or its loan-to-value (LTV) ratio, was low enough to provide a sufficient cushion for bondholders to be able to liquidate the assets in order to repay the bonds if they underperform specified trigger levels. This further protects investors in the case the best efforts of the backup servicer are still unable to improve performance.

MUSIC ROYALTIES

One of the first forms of intellectual property to be used as collateral to back a securitization was music royalties. The first securitized music royalty transaction—for the Jones/Tintoretto Entertainment Corporation (JTEC)—closed in February 1997. That transaction was backed by future royalties generated by the music of pop artist David Bowie, and was rated A3 by Moody's. Since the close of the JTEC transaction, Moody's has rated a number of other deals in this asset class (see Exhibit 20-3).

The approach that Moody's has used to rate the music royalty transactions to date encompasses three broad topics:

- Asset credit quality
- Structural cash flow allocations
- Legal issues

In the following sections, we will describe the specific issues that arise in music royalty transactions under each of the broad topics.

Asset Credit Quality Analysis

In traditional ABS, involving auto loans or credit card receivables, asset credit quality is assessed by studying a pool of loans, and determining to what extent

Transaction	Artist or Company	Approx. Closing Date	Rating	Placement Agent
Jones/Tintoretto Entertainment Co., LLC	David Bowie	February 1997	A3	Pullman Group
Brian Holland LP	Brian Holland	June 1998	A3	Pullman Group
Lamont Dozier LP	Lamont Dozier	June 1998	A3	Pullman Group
Edward Holland LP	Edward Holland	June 1998	A3	Pullman Group
Nick-O-Val, LLC	Ashford and Simpson	November 1998	A3 (Class A)	Pullman Group
Universal Credit Trust 1999-A	SESAC Inc.	May 1999	Aaa	CAK Universal Credit Corp.
IMH Holdings	Iron Maiden	July 1999	Baa1	Daiwa Securities
Universal Credit Trust 2000-A	Curtis Mayfield	April 2000	Baa3	CAK Universal Credit Corp.
Music Finance Corp.	Chrysalis Inc.	March 2001	Private	Royal Bank of Scotland

Exhibit 20-3   Music royalty-backed transactions rated by Moody's.

those loans will pay as promised. This is generally done by examining historical data, current industry trends, and company operations (such as underwriting and servicing) to come up with an expected loss on that pool of loans and a level of anticipated variability around those expectations.

In contrast, for music royalty-backed transactions, receivables typically do not exist at the inception of the transaction, but instead are to be generated during the life of the security. As a result, the asset quality analysis becomes a two-step process, involving analyses of both the potential amount of assets that will be generated and the extent to which the receivables will be paid once generated.

To evaluate how much revenue a particular music catalog, or portfolio of songs, could generate in the future, it is necessary to understand first the nature of the assets, including the sources that will generate the revenue. The assets in music royalty transactions fall into two major categories: record sales/master royalties and music publishing royalties.

Record sales royalties are paid for the sale of a specific song or album. They are also called *record master rights*. Since the level of royalties depends on the number of records sold, predicting future sales is a critical part of the asset quality analysis. That analysis will depend on whether the albums are relatively new or "seasoned" and the performer's historical market power, which affect both the expected level of sales and the uncertainty surrounding those expectations.

Music publishing royalties are paid to the writer of a song. Those royalties, which are protected by copyright law, are based on the use of songs on albums or CDs ("mechanicals"), the use in performances or broadcasts, and the use as background in TV shows, movies, and commercials. In estimating the potential for future music publishing royalties, Moody's analyzes the proven popularity of the catalog of work and the degree to which that catalog has been fully utilized in the past.

Historical data are an important component of the valuation of all music royalty rights. The value of the data depends on the length of time covered and the level of detail. In addition to information provided by the issuer, it can be useful to receive an independent third-party valuation of a catalog by an industry expert. However, Moody's puts all historical data in perspective through an understanding of the current environment, including an assessment of the strategies, resources, and abilities of the participants in the transaction, including the record company, the publisher, the artist(s), and the performing rights societies, which monitor and collect fees for the use of works in a catalog.

Structural Cash Flow Analysis

Structural cash flow analysis focuses on how the cash flow collected and losses incurred by the transaction are allocated among the parties to the transaction. In most ABS transactions, this includes an analysis of the "payment waterfall," which determines the order of distribution of the cash collected. Generally, credit quality is enhanced by waterfalls that allocate payments to bondholders first.

However, Moody's also evaluates the cash flow allocation mechanism for its ability to provide for continuing incentives for the other participants in the transaction to continue performing necessary functions. For example, to evaluate the likelihood of maintaining an adequate level of servicing throughout the life of the transaction, Moody's analyzes the incentives provided to the servicer by its fee structure.

Other sources of payment, such as cash reserve funds, guarantees from highly rated third parties, and subordination, can provide additional credit and liquidity support to the deals. All of these traditional ABS enhancements can be included in a music royalty transaction.

In typical ABS transactions, the size of a deal is usually stated in terms of, and compared with, the amount of receivables. However, in music royalty transactions, as in all future flow transactions, there are no receivables, per se, at the start of the transaction. Instead, the deal is usually sized in terms of an estimate of the current value of the assets, often obtained from a third-party valuation. In general, the smaller the transaction relative to the value—that is, the lower the LTV ratio—the higher the rating possible. However, the rating will, of course, depend on numerous other factors, including the quality of the valuation.

The transaction will also be evaluated for the level of future revenue projections versus the transaction's debt service coverage. Obviously, the higher the debt service coverage above expected revenues, the better the potential rating as well.

Legal Analysis

As mentioned earlier, in evaluating the credit quality of any ABS deal—including music royalty-backed transactions—Moody's analyzes its legal structure to assess the risk that, in the event of a bankruptcy of the originator, cash flows earned by the assets may be subject to claims from creditors of the originator and diverted away from the ABS investors. This risk is particularly relevant to transactions in which bankruptcy is relatively likely, such as when the parties to the transaction have a low rating or are small, thinly capitalized entities.

As in other ABS transactions, it is also important to determine that there are no preexisting liens on the assets to be securitized. An artist's previous financial arrangements, pending lawsuits, or divorce settlements could have a bearing on this issue. These issues are typically addressed before the close of the transaction by conducting thorough lien searches.

FUTURE FILM RECEIVABLES

Another form of IP securitization that has gained acceptance over the past five years is the securitization of the future revenues from previously unreleased films. Including the two transactions that closed in 2000, Moody's has rated over $3.5 billion in the term and asset-backed commercial paper markets. The ratings on these transactions have ranged from as high as Aaa to as low as Baa3.

These transactions have numerous benefits to the issuing movie studio. These include:

1. The transfer of a portion of film-performance risk to bondholders
2. Access to an alternative and possibly lower cost of funding
3. Earlier reimbursement of capital invested in the production of films
4. Off-balance sheet accounting treatment

The rating approach places particular emphasis on the financial strength of the issuing studio because of its substantial ongoing obligations and because the transfer of the assets is usually not a legal true sale. This analysis is layered on top of an evaluation of the historical performance of a studio's films and the likelihood that the studio will be able to achieve similar performance in the future. The structure of the transaction is also analyzed to gauge the potential benefits of structural features such as triggers.

Basic Structure

The basic structure of future film securitizations is as follows: From the proceeds of the offering, a pool of cash is created for the purchase of films once they are completed ("in the can") and ready for release. Since the trust only purchases films when they are in the can, the trust does not take film completion risk.

It is customary that a studio's entire future slate of completed films, subject to a loose set of eligibility criteria, is sold into the trust in order to limit its ability to "cherry-pick" the films that have a greater chance of success. The cost to the trust to purchase the film is its negative (production) cost plus corporate overhead and capitalized interest allocated to the film, subject to limits. Caps are also placed on the cost of an individual film to prevent a concentration of the trust's funds in a small number of (expensive) films.

In exchange for the purchase price, the trust receives ownership of the film and is entitled to receive all revenues it generates. These revenues are then allocated according to the payment waterfall among debt service, distribution expenses, and other transaction costs. Most deals have a revolving structure through which revenues on earlier films are reinvested to purchase additional films for the trust until a specified date or until an early amortization trigger is hit.

The studio is typically licensed back the marketing and distribution responsibilities for the film. Because of its past experience distributing films, the studio is generally best qualified to insure that the film is distributed and promoted properly so that revenues generated are maximized. These obligations are equivalent to servicing responsibilities in traditional asset-backed deals.

Asset Quality Analysis

The asset quality analysis of a future film securitization focuses on two areas:

1. Fundamental analysis of the studio
2. Film performance analysis

Fundamental Analysis of the Studio

In contrast to most asset-backed transactions, the issuer (the studio) must continue to generate new assets following the closing date for future film securitizations. In addition to producing the films, the studio is also obligated to distribute and market the films in order to maximize their revenues. As a result, it is necessary to analyze the financial condition of the studio to determine the likelihood that it will be able to fulfill these responsibilities for the period it takes to create a diversified portfolio of films.

For studios with a rating, Moody's view of the studio's financial condition is relatively easy to determine. For unrated studios, it is necessary to perform a shadow rating analysis to assess this risk. All of the six major studios, which account for approximately two thirds of 2000 domestic box office, are divisions of larger rated entities. Their ratings are as follows:

Studio	Corporate Parent	Rating
Columbia	Sony Corp.	Aa3
Warner Brothers	AOL Time Warner	Baa1
Universal	Vivendi	Baa2
20th Century Fox	News Corp.	Baa3
Buena Vista	Disney	A3
Paramount	Viacom	A3

The other film studios include so-called independents like Miramax (Buena Vista) and New Line Cinema (Warner Brothers), which are actually wholly owned subsidiaries of the majors' corporate parents, as well as true independents such as DreamWorks, MGM, and Artisan. None of the independents is currently rated, but it is believed that in most cases their ratings would be below investment grade.

Because of their greater stability, well-developed film pipeline, and established distribution network, the major studios are best able to create future film securitizations that can achieve high ratings. It is not surprising that these companies were the first to enter this market and have issued the lion's share of the transactions. For unrated or lowly rated studios, it is possible to structure a future film transaction that can achieve ratings higher than the studio. How this can be achieved is explained below.

Film Performance Analysis

In the 1990s, as home video and cable television became more common throughout the world, the potential revenues that a film generates have increased dramatically. Though domestic box office receipts, also referred to as theatrical rentals, are often considered the barometer of a film's success, they usually equal only 15 to 20 percent of a film's lifetime revenues. The other 80 to 85 percent of total revenue generated by the exhibition of the film is composed of international rentals, domestic and international home video, pay and free television, and nontheatricals (see Exhibit 20-4). Further revenues can be earned through various other forms of merchandising.

Because of the variety of revenue sources available, it has become less difficult in recent years for a studio to recover its production cost on a film. Accord-

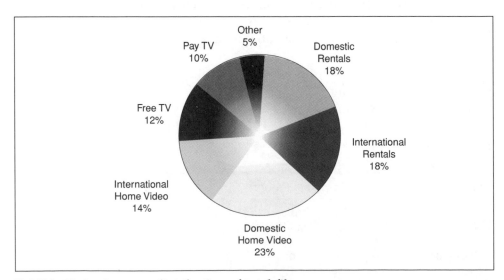

Exhibit 20-4   Average distribution of total film revenues.

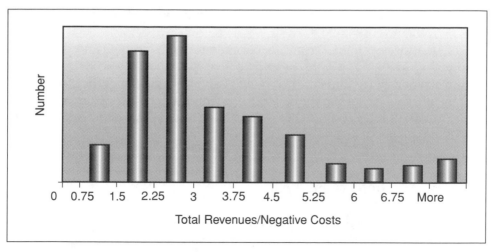

Number

0   0.75   1.5   2.25   3   3.75   4.5   5.25   6   6.75   More

Total Revenues/Negative Costs

Exhibit 20-5   Histogram of sample historical film performance.

ing to the available data, the average film produced by the major studios in the 1990s has generated revenues that cover its negative costs more than two and a half times.

This high average coverage level is a key factor in lowering the risk of securitizations of future film revenues. Since the transaction finances only the film's production costs, average film performance would usually more than cover the securitization's debt service. Additional film expenses like prints and advertising (P&A) costs, which can reach over 50 percent of a film's negative costs, are typically funded by the studio and are generally repaid in a position that is subordinate to bondholders. This exposure to expenses and subordinated position in the cash flow structure aligns the studio's interest with that of the bondholders and provides it with a strong incentive to distribute the films properly.

Although average film performance is generally sufficient to more than cover debt service, individual film performance is highly variable, with coverage levels often falling below one time and sometimes reaching above six to seven times for major blockbusters (see Exhibit 20-5). To reduce this risk, future film securitizations cross-collateralize the revenues of a portfolio of films.

The benefit of this is to reduce the probability of a string of unsuccessful films with low coverage levels. If a studio can demonstrate that its performance can match the industry average, modeling of portfolios of films has found that a portfolio of approximately 10 films can achieve a level of diversity that supports investment-grade ratings. With smaller portfolios, there is a higher likelihood that a limited number of films will all be weak performers, which increases the transaction's expected loss and lowers the rating.

This was determined by using a Monte Carlo simulation that randomly selected film revenues from a distribution created with historical data for slates of different sizes. The revenues generated by these slates are then fed through the transaction waterfall to determine the expected loss for the pool. If the studio's performance is below average, the number of films needed to sufficiently lower film performance risk increases.

In most transactions, the portfolios of films at the start of the transaction are smaller than necessary to achieve sufficient diversification. However, in such cases, Moody's will evaluate the financial stability and track record of the studio to assess the likelihood that the studio will be able to produce a sufficient number of films. Attention is also paid to the studio's production pipeline to determine the length of time it will take to create the portfolio.

Legal and Structural Analysis

Due to the obligation of the studio to continue to produce the films on an ongoing basis, as well as its exposure to film performance risk because of its investment in P&A costs, the transfer of the assets by the issuing studio is not deemed to be a legal "true sale." The trust does, however, receive a perfected security interest in the films and the revenues they generate, which characterizes the transaction as a secured financing and not a securitization. In the traditional corporate finance context, the security pledge would normally enable the transaction to achieve a rating one notch above that of the issuer, but Moody's has determined that, through the use of structural enhancements in future film deals, it is possible to achieve a larger separation.

These structural protections normally take the form of a set of triggers related to both the financial condition of the studio and the performance of the included films. The triggers are designed to protect investors from a bankruptcy of the studio by increasing the likelihood that the bonds will be fully repaid prior to a potential filing.

Typical results of the triggers include early amortization events and reorderings of the priority of payments in the waterfall to reduce future payments to the studio. In addition, a clawback feature, which requires the studio to return funds paid to it in prior periods to cover principal and interest shortfalls, can also be included.

In Moody's analysis of the transaction, the relative strength of the triggers is evaluated in combination with the film performance analysis discussed earlier to determine how much benefit they add to the final rating.

Despite the benefits that the triggers add to the credit profile of the transaction, Moody's does not believe that the risk of company bankruptcy can be completely eliminated. As a result, even with the strongest set of triggers, the rating of the transaction is still limited by the credit quality of the studio.

THE FUTURE: POOLED TRANSACTIONS AND OTHER IP ASSETS

All of the IP deals rated by Moody's have been backed by a single pool of collateral owned by a single individual or company; however, market participants suggest that the next step could be a transaction backed by a pool of different catalogs. Such a transaction would take a group of separate financings to owners of individual pools of collateral and pool them into a larger securitization. In theory, this structure would be similar to that used in commercial real estate transactions or collateralized loan obligations (CLOs).

These transactions could benefit from the diversity created by having a large pool of loans, which may allow the pooled transaction to achieve a rating higher than that of the ratings of the individual loans. In addition, this structure could also be used to tranche the bonds into various classes, with senior classes possibly achieving as high as a Aaa rating. Such a high rating would typically be difficult to reach if the loans were securitized separately.

Moody's believes that, in principle, IP transactions could benefit from the diversification achieved through the pooling of assets; however, this might be difficult to achieve in practice. The amount of any credit for the diversification of having loans backed by a variety of different forms of IP will be evaluated on a case-by-case basis. In addition, for meaningful credit to be given for diversification, the pool must include a large number of loans, without significant concentration in any individual loan.

Since this asset type is not as homogeneous as corporate loans, it will be necessary, at least at the inception of the market, for each loan in a pool to be evaluated on an individual basis to determine its credit quality. The credit quality can then be assessed using a CLO-like analysis. Given the current slow pace of loan origination in the market, underwriters or issuers will have to be prepared to warehouse their loans until the pool reaches the critical mass of loans that makes a pooled transaction most economical.

Other IP Assets

Many other forms of IP have been suggested as potential candidates for securitization, such as existing movie libraries, book publishing rights, and licensing and endorsement agreements. It is expected that the general approach outlined above can be applied to these assets as well.

CONCLUSION: IP ANALYSIS MUST BE FINE-TUNED

The securitization of intellectual property assets is an area that has already included a variety of different industries and asset types. Moody's incorporates the specific risks posed by these assets into its traditional approach to rating asset-backed securities, providing a consistent way in which to analyze the asset quality, structural cash flow, and legal risks of the securities. In many cases, these transactions are future flow transactions, which require an additional layer of analysis beyond the traditional assessment of the risks of existing receivables, to include the risks involved in generating receivables in the future.

For the foreseeable future, the analysis of each proposed transaction will be tailored to the particular asset being securitized and will need time to be properly analyzed. This chapter has outlined a number of the major issues that can be identified at this point and has indicated how they could affect Moody's analysis. In doing so, it is hoped that the market will factor in these issues when attempting to structure transactions in what can be a sizable market covering a variety of different industries.

NOTE

1. For the purposes of this chapter, intellectual property is defined as the ownership and control over the tangible or virtual representation of ideas.

ABOUT THE AUTHOR

Jay H. Eisbruck is a Senior Vice President in Moody's Investors Service Asset-Backed Finance Group, where he has worked since 1991. During this time, Mr. Eisbruck has evaluated transactions backed by a variety of assets, including credit cards, auto loans, manufactured housing, entertainment-related, sports, and intellectual property assets. He currently directs Moody's New Assets Group and is responsible for maintaining rating consistency across all structured finance assets. Mr. Eisbruck has also contributed to a number of articles on structural innovations and general trends in the asset-backed market and is a frequent speaker at industry conferences and seminars. He earned both an MBA in Finance and a BS in Economics from New York University's Stern School of Business, where he was a Racoosin Scholar.

Moody's Investors Service, a leading global credit rating, research, and risk analysis firm, publishes credit opinions, research, and ratings on fixed-income securities, issuers of securities, and other credit obligations. Moody's publishes rating opinions and research on corporate and governmental obligations issued in domestic and international capital markets, structured finance securities, and commercial paper programs. Credit ratings and research help investors analyze the credit risks associated with fixed-income securities. Ratings also create efficiencies in fixed-income markets and similar obligations, such as insurance and derivatives, by providing reliable, credible, and independent assessments of credit risk. Moody's has rated intellectual property-backed securities since the market's inception in 1995. The company has been involved in several bellwether deals including the David Bowie music royalty securitization, both DreamWorks SKG future film transactions, and the Bill Blass trademark licensing deal.

CHAPTER TWENTY-ONE

Asset-Backed IP Financing
Strategies for Capitalizing on Future Returns

by Douglas R. Elliott

PERSPECTIVES

For CFOs and other managers, intellectual property rights, especially patents, are fraught with danger. Creating intellectual property assets consumes cash, shortens the balance sheet, and reduces current earnings, which threaten stock value. "Coming to grips with the fiscal-strategic paradox of intellectual property is likely to take center stage early on in the new millennium," says IP strategist Doug Elliott, who has venture capital, engineering, science, legal, and inventing experience. "For an economy increasingly based on knowledge, intellectual property must serve up more value than ever to keep companies competitive."

Asset-backed securities are governed by common principles, which include the cost of capital and an issuer's creditworthiness. These irrefutable laws permeate financial transactions the way physics permeates the universe. Scientific physics, says Mr. Elliott, preoccupies itself with the relationships of force, matter, and energy. The physics of investment banking plots a course according to the laws of economic behavior, more commonly known as fear, greed, knowledge, and ignorance. "The validity of any transaction, no matter how novel or virtuous, can no more escape the consequences of these laws than planets and stars can defeat the force of gravity. The laws of economics are continuously revealed in the history of the markets, which can be a useful perspective when considering IP asset derivatives."

Mr. Elliott's chapter focuses on monetizing IP from a banker's and a borrower's perspective. He concludes that the timing is right for IP securitizations, including patents, to work, but that most companies fail to consider them seriously because they and their advisors do not understand them. The pros and the cons of IP asset-backed transactions, as well as their history and evolution, are considered in Elliott's reflective chapter, elements of which include:

- A brief history of finance: Where have we been? Where are we going?
- Asset financing: an investment banking perspective
- Investment banking mechanics for IP assets
- Technology IP sales
- Royalty trusts
- IP debt leveraging
- Synthetic license monetizations: sale and back-license
- IP financing strategies: pros and cons

Where should we look to find the new generation of IP investment banking money wizards? Not on Wall Street, says Elliott—at least not yet. Look on Main Street, in the companies and universities that line the American landscape. Look in the licensing departments because that is where the skills and intuitions can be found to translate IP into a twenty-first-century financial currency. "Converting the inventory of intellectual properties into cash-generating corporate assets will ultimately turn on the ability to convince CFOs and CEOs that putting technology into play, financially speaking, is a win-win proposition . . . Intellectual property derivatives will be successful only if they can make, hold, and deliver market value."

INTRODUCTION

Some CEOs recognize that creation of intellectual property is one strategy that can lift stock market values. For CFOs, intellectual property can seem like a money pit. Creating intellectual property consumes cash, shortens the balance sheet, and reduces current earnings, which threaten stock value. Coming to grips with the fiscal-strategic paradox of intellectual property is likely to take center stage early on in the new millennium. For an economy increasingly based on knowledge, intellectual property must serve up more value than ever to keep companies competitive.

If history is an indication of the future, recruiting the investment banking community to the cause of intellectual property would be one remedy of choice. But such a transition will require a new financial tool kit arrayed with intellectual property derivatives that build balance sheets as well as stock prices. To pull it off will take a new breed of investment banker—visionaries with a knack for understanding intellectual property assets and revenue streams derived from licensing.

Where should we look to find the new generation of IP investment banking money wizards? Not on Wall Street—at least not yet. Instead look on Main Street, in the companies and universities that line the American landscape. Look in the licensing departments, for that is where the skills and intuitions exist to translate IP into a twenty-first-century financial currency. In other words, look for licensing executives.

Converting the inventory of intellectual properties into cash-generating corporate assets will ultimately turn on the ability to convince CFOs and CEOs that putting technology into play, financially speaking, is a win-win proposition. There must be a significant upside potential and negligible risk. The financial tools employed must also convince investors that derivatives backed by intellectual property are reliable assets capable of income production or asset appreciation. Intellectual property derivatives will be successful only if they can make, hold, and deliver market value.

Like an iceberg, the vast bulk of a proprietary intellectual property rights is submerged from view. Extracting market value from internal IP assets is a great challenge and even greater opportunity for licensing professionals. Success will depend on the ability of licensing executives to visualize IP from the investment banking perspective. Devising solutions will involve business methods which use variations of a proven investment banking technique—asset-backed financing—to transform IP into attractive financial real estate.

Asset financing is a trusted method for selling tangible assets in exchange for future financial returns. By definition, an asset-backed financing is the sale of a financial interest in any property that can generate future revenues. To be an attractive investment, an IP-backed asset financing must address five essential issues:

1. Pricing the IP asset portfolio
2. Defining the term and payout of IP revenues
3. Maintaining continuity with existing business practices
4. Satisfying the multiple market needs of IP owners, IP users, and financiers
5. Creating practical entry and exit strategies

The mechanics of licensing transactions satisfy the first three requirements for IP asset financing. Investment banking provides the final two elements. The result is a set of straightforward rules for the design, deployment, and distribution of IP asset-backed derivatives. Doing so creates a value relationship that directly connects CEO and CFO strategies to the wealth effect of IP.

Developing a game plan for IP asset-backed financing requires perspective, and it will be helpful to look, if only briefly, at a variety of topics:

- A brief history of finance: Where have we been? Where are we going?
- Asset financing: an investment banking perspective
- Investment banking mechanics for IP assets

- Technology IP sales
- Royalty trusts
- IP debt leveraging
- Synthetic license monetizations: sale and back-license
- IP financing strategies: pros and cons

From royalty trusts to sale-license backs, IP is adaptive as well as durable. By comparing and contrasting several approaches to IP investment banking, the reader can gain an appreciation of strategies and tactics that will raise the table stakes of IP in the world of high finance.

A BRIEF HISTORY OF FINANCE

This chapter is mostly concerned with the mechanics and strategies of asset-backed financing as it relates to intellectual property. Before we start, it is worth remembering that asset-backed deals, like stocks or bonds, are governed by common principles. Those principles permeate investment banking the way physics permeates the universe. Scientific physics preoccupies itself with the relationships of force, matter, and energy. The physics of investment banking, on the other hand, plots a course according to the laws of economic behavior. These laws manifest themselves in behaviors more commonly described as fear, greed, knowledge, and ignorance. I mention this now because the validity of any transaction, no matter how novel or virtuous, can no more escape the consequences of these laws than planets and stars can defeat the force of gravity. The principles are continuously revealed in the history of the markets. This can be a useful perspective when considering IP asset derivatives.

The story of investment banking unfolds in market cycles, and the 1990s was clearly the decade of the Great Bull Run. Americans saw their stock markets double—twice. We witnessed the arrival of the NASDAQ as a new financial engine for technology stocks. More IPOs and more billionaires were birthed in the 1990s than in the entire previous history of capitalism. Greed when exploited to this level becomes a cauldron of financial invention, and the Great Bull Run witnessed the arrival of many new investment banking products. Of these, none was more innovative than the so-called Bowie Bonds, a moniker derived from the name of the 1970s rock musician, David Bowie.

The performer best remembered as the "Man Who Fell to the Earth" set another milestone as the "Man Who Sold Himself" for approximately $55 million in 1997. What Bowie sold was the present value of his personal intellectual property—that is, the expectation of future royalty income, less a discount, from Bowie's music and entertainment copyrights. Bowie was not alone. From 1991 to 1998 nearly $3.5 billion in Bowie-like royalty instruments[1] were sold by other musicians (Rod Stewart), media conglomerates (Disney, Dreamworks, Universal), and branded marketers (Calvin Klein, Borden, and GE Capital). It's not surprising that much of this innovation was overlooked in the Great Bull Run. Compared to the trillions created in new market capitalization, $3.5 billion seems like a mere pittance. Still, these securitizations proved that property need not be tangible to have asset value.

If a bull runs long enough, it will tire out, slow down, and get eaten by a bear. Somewhere around March 2000, the Great Bull Run of the 1990s began to peter out and, needless to say, the bears got their claws into the stock markets. Like the crash of 1987, this bear market will pass, but not before it wrings loads of cash out of stock and bond holder expectations. Like the crash of '87, there are lessons and opportunities to be harvested from the millennial bear market. Eventually a cornucopia of wisdom and folly will be revealed on how investors factored their perceptions into market strategies. At times like these, it's worth remembering two things. First, that to ignore history is to repeat it. Second, the seeds of the future are always planted in the topsoil of history. In this regard, the market correction of October 1987 is instructive.

The 1987 crash was the result of another great idea—junk bonds—going beyond its economic limits. In the end, greed overreached fear. A junk bond was (and is) a brilliant technique for injecting cash into businesses whose assets are carried on the books at a steep discount to their replacement value. A junk bond is an unsecured, unrated debt security. The junk bond was also the cure for the inflation wave of the 1970s. In exchange for inflation-level interest rates, junk bonds pumped money into the hands of buyout artists. The newly crowned junk bond kings, in turn, pledged to sell off the highly undervalued assets of the companies they sought to acquire. This retired much of the junk bond debt. Why were the assets undervalued? Inflation. Because banks were stuck with the *book value* of corporate holdings rather than *replacement value*, most 1980s corporations were severely underleveraged, undercapitalized, and undervalued. The leveraged buyout boom was largely borne on the backs of hapless corporations unable or unwilling to issue junk paper on their own to compensate for inflationary devaluation of their balance sheets.

The sunny side of the junk bond craze was the tremendous shift to the buy side as leveraged buyout (LBO) funds and corporate raiders relentlessly outbid each other to acquire the undervalued assets of corporate giants. Buyers outnumbered sellers and the stock markets soared. But Wall Street is never modest when a party is going on. Junk bond mania came to an abrupt end in October 1987, when a combination of thievery and greed conspired to over-reach the bond markets' ability to pay for overpriced and oversubscribed debt issues. The cascade of defaults triggered a massive sell-off and the markets corrected. The end became inevitable because of company and investor ignorance about assets.

The 1980s didn't completely preoccupy itself with junk bond mania. A basic retooling of American and global business interests was also taking place. It was a retooling based on microprocessors, computers, and the software to run them. These were the seeds of the 1990s Great Bull Run. Computing technology proliferated due to personal computers, and workforce productivity soared. With it, the economics of asset deployment also changed. Smart assets create more throughput than dumb assets. Smart throughput meant fewer assets were producing more goods and services than ever before. It also meant that companies could be technically undervalued according the old market-to-book ratios (stock market value divided by the book value of company assets). There was an inference that companies producing the means for this jump in productivity had to been especially valuable; in other words, their market-to-book ratios should be even higher than the average market indices. These were the New Economy companies of the NASDAQ.

One corollary to the technology-driven market value is high sales growth. Another corollary is the accelerator effect on profit growth, particularly where there is high asset productivity. When coupled together, these principles are catalysts for capital appreciation—or at least they should be. Decoupling technology from sales and profit growth had a disastrous effect on the Great Bull Run. It was called the Internet.

For a few years, investors were willing to forgo their knowledge of the sales-profit growth paradigm in exchange for a portfolio of technology-based "market spaces" on the Internet. Market space was a virtual business hypothesis that assumed that the laws of economics had changed—sort of like declaring gravity null and void in the physical universe. It framed the New Economy notion that a technology is valuable by virtue of its existence. In the Old Economy, technology is valuable when it does something useful. The Old Economy was right. Failure to learn from history led to the wholesale extermination of most Internet start-ups. Pricing intellectual property in a dot.com vacuum did not prove to be a viable solution for the New Economy.

What seeds were planted in the Great Bull Run that can be growth engines for the twenty-first century? One of them is a seed of discontent—a growing distrust in the appreciation power of stocks. With it should come a renewed interest in income securities. The investor shift from stock to bond preferences will intensify in the coming decade. As American baby boomers retire, they will need real cash flows to fund their golden years. Another seed was the invention of intellectual property derivatives. The hybrid of these two seeds is enormous synergy. This raises a question: If knowledge assets become the twenty-first century's first financial gold rush, will licensing executives become the twenty-first century's preeminent investment bankers?

Converting the reservoir of existing IP assets into financial derivatives is a potent opportunity for corporate finance. Asset financing opens an opportunity to market IP to a huge and complementary clientele—institutional investors. Institutional investors represent the legions of individual investors in the form of retirement accounts, insurance companies, mutual funds, and pension funds. How businesses and institutions approach this windfall is first a function of education and second a function of financial strategy.

Is IP financing a mere novelty? Perhaps. More likely it is an opportunity to access the larger economic possibilities of intellectual property. But what portents does it hold for the future of technology, licensing professionals, and the companies and clients they represent? A key to success in IP asset financing will be in perfecting the transaction. In investment banking, transaction equals strategy.

ASSET FINANCING: AN INVESTMENT BANKING PERSPECTIVE

The language of investment banking is money. A meaningful dialogue with investment bankers requires translation of IP assets and payouts into the literature of cash flow. To recap, in an asset-backed financing, investment banks raise cash for companies in exchange for:

- Future income
- Future asset appreciation
- Sale or pledge of company assets

In one sense, asset financing is as old as the history of civilization. A property mortgage, in the strictest sense, is an asset-backed financing, and mortgages are as ancient as Rome. The modern history of asset-backed securities begins in the mid-1980s. It was the bundling of individual consumer and corporate asset-backed financings into securities that contributed enormously to the explosive financial growth of the 1990s. The significance of these transactions to Wall Street cannot be understated. The Board of Governors for the Federal Reserve reported a nearly 500 percent increase in these instruments (from $285 billion in 1990 to $1.4 *trillion* in 1998).[2] This is a 22 percent per year growth rate. Is the economy growing its tangible asset base fast enough to keep pace? Definitely not, and this is precisely why IP asset financing is so intriguing.

The general mechanics of an asset financing are illustrated in Exhibit 21-1. For a fee, the investment bank functions as an intermediary to channel investor capital into companies in exchange for financial obligations collateralized by the asset of interest. The obligations can take various forms, although most asset-backed deals are either a debt or equity instrument. Organizing the IP asset process in

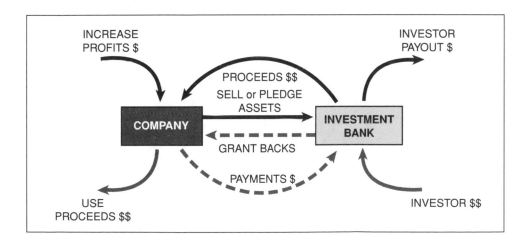

Exhibit 21-1   Asset-backed financing flowchart.
Source: © 2000 T^{EQ} Development

parallel with these investment banking conventions can be helpful. A problem peculiar to most internally generated IP is the complete absence of a book value for these assets. While this absence is the consequence of a beneficial tax treatment, the void is a vexing problem to investment bankers—how should they price the IP asset? There are two related methods for pricing an asset-backed financing. The first method arranges the cash flows associated with the deal on a time line and calculates an internal rate of return (IRR) which is expressed as percentage/year. The second method takes the same cash flows but divides each value by a discount rate which is an interest rate or "cost of capital" value compounded over time. The sum of these discounted cash flows is the net present value, or NPV (expressed in cash), of the transaction. The diagrammatic form of asset-backed transactions is illustrated in Exhibit 21-2. The IRR is the discount rate which makes the NPV equal to zero.

These are not new concepts to licensing executives. Most spreadsheet software offers calculations for IRR and NPV, so the use of these techniques is straightforward. Net present value calculations can be used to calculate a lump-sum out-license royalty payment in lieu of time installment payouts. The IRR calculation can indicate whether in-licensing an existing intellectual property involves a lower cost of capital than funding internal research and development (R&D). What makes for a good IRR or good NPV depends on your point of view. In out-licensing IP, the IRR might have to be a multiple of the out-licensee's internal investment returns to mitigate the risk of introducing a new competitor into an established marketplace. But to maximize the NPV of a lump-sum royalty, a risk-free discount rate (e.g., treasury bill interest rates) is preferable because it conserves more of the future royalty stream in the proposed current payment. In each case, competing

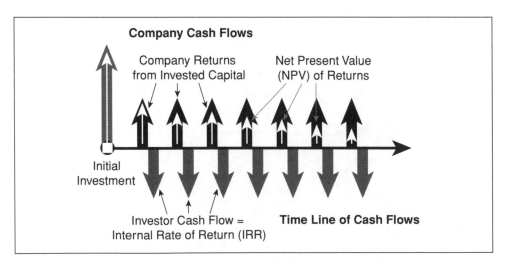

Exhibit 21-2 Asset-backed financing flowchart.
Source: © 2000 T^{EQ} Development

business interests push and pull the analysis so that neither side (assuming each is represented by equally competent licensing professionals) gains an unfair advantage in the resulting deal.

Investment bankers have no "dog in the fight" in the sorts of licensing deals just discussed. Their interests commence when cash changes hands. Underlying transactions may then be material in assigning risks to financing these ventures. On the investor side, the mechanics of most investment banking deals looks a lot like a lump-sum royalty purchase to which an annuity is attached. This is also illustrated in Exhibit 21-2. By and large, the investment banker is an agent for other investors' capital. The capital marketplace broadly divides into two segments—investors seeking income (e.g., a debt financing) and investors seeking appreciation (e.g., an equity offering). Devising a suitable investment instrument is a function of the market segment being wooed. It is also a function of "asset inventory" —the volume and quality of "like-kind" assets for future transactions.

Examples can be instructive. Currently there are nearly $120 billion per year in IP royalties (2000 estimates), which consist mostly of "business-to-business" out-licenses or cross-licenses.[3] If we visualize those cash flows (net of expenses) as 10-year annuities, their face value as income securities would fall somewhere between $550 to $650 billion. If we visualize them as an equity asset and use a NPV discount factor consistent with a price-earnings (P/E) ratio of 15, then a current market capitalization of $800 billion is reasonable. These examples assume future licensing royalties will at least equal current royalties. By all measures of recent licensing activities, this is a conservative position. Therefore, the IP asset values we compute from the preceding revenue forecast are the realistic floor values for assessing their suitability as financial derivatives.

Exchanging cash for property rights is a securitization. Securitizing existing license agreements is not appreciably different from equipment leasing or mortgage-backed securities. Certainly there is plenty of IP inventory that is collecting royalties. So why have we securitized less than 1 percent of these royalty streams to date? That is the $640 billion question. Different perceptions of risk may be an answer. When negotiating licenses for even proven intellectual properties, it's not unusual to discount future expectations with risk capital hurdles that are typical of basic R&D. If a typical R&D risk hurdle rate of 50 percent/year is applied to the licenses now in existence (and grossing $120 billion per year), the NPV of a presumed 10-year royalty life is $180 billion, or about 18 months' worth of current royalty revenue. This is hardly worth the time and effort of an asset-backed financing. So who is right?

The "asset gap" between an investment banking appraisal versus a licensing negotiation stems from different assumptions about risk. The risk capital perspective severely discounts the value of any long-term license revenues. Negotiating the risk out of a prospective license is an entirely different proposition compared to managing a portfolio of existing licenses. Existing licenses have had the risk wrung out of them by the licensing process, but criteria appropriate for negotiating prospective licenses are not apropos to a portfolio of existing of licenses. After negotiation, licenses can and should be viewed as financing properties—more like mortgages than venture capital. Failure to adjust the risk hurdle hides a wealth of IP assets from financial markets, about $640 billion worth by my calculation. Furthermore, transacting these assets multiplies the wealth effect of IP because cash is the most flexible instrument for accessing new opportunities.

In truth, most businesses don't develop IP to do out-licensing. They develop IP to strengthen the competitive positions of their core businesses. The best IP is usually retained for the exclusive use of the inventing business. What does this behavior say about the financing value of internal IP assets? Unfortunately, nothing. Value has to be imputed, indirectly, to the earnings performance of the underlying business. Given the misadventures of financial markets to successfully interpolate IP value and stock price, this prospect is not completely reassuring. Short term, there is an enormous opportunity to exploit the inventory of existing interbusiness licenses. But if IP were fish, we're only talking about minnows. Longerterm licensing needs to furnish a set of blueprints for exploiting the internal IP of global corporations. That's where the whales are.

INVESTMENT BANKING: MECHANICS FOR INTELLECTUAL PROPERTY ASSETS

Clearly many companies profit handsomely from their licensing activities. Why then should licensing departments upset the status quo by entering the unproved world of IP asset financing? The business responsibility of most licensing organizations is maximizing out-license revenues and minimizing in-licensing costs. Financially speaking, these activities never stray far from the profit and loss (P&L) statements. More often than not, IP assets are unvalued anywhere else on the financial sheets. This one-dimensional representation of the licensing business is a misnomer. It robs senior management, particularly the CFO and CEO, of the opportunity to extract maximum financial advantage from the IP portfolio. In other words, it denies management access to a significant resource for raising cash. Turning intellectual property into cash serves many useful purposes, including:

- Improving corporate cash flow
- Financing new R&D
- Increasing short-term profits
- Funding acquisitions
- Increasing shareholder assets
- Supporting and increasing share price

Cash won't change hands for nothing so securitized assets—including IP—must have a defensible fair market value. Appraisers traditionally rely on three methods to assign fair market value—cost, market, or income. Determining which methods are appropriate for particular IP securitizations depends on the transaction of interest. There are four which we will explore later:

- Technology IP sale
- Royalty trust
- IP debt leveraging
- Synthetic license monetization: sale and back-license

A defensible basis for pricing a financial instrument must use the best available data for measuring value and risk. Because there is no trading market for IP asset derivatives, valuation must, of necessity, focus on cost and income methods. In thinking about either cost or income valuations, the concept of portfolio is vital. By portfolio, I mean the collection of properties that results from the R&D process. Were this not so, the volatility of data on the cost and efficacy of individual R&D projects would turn IP pricing analysis into a fool's errand. Fortunately, this may be the one case where inventing at a loss can actually be made up by volume.

Cost Method Valuation

The book value of IP is zero. Since this is inconsistent with the business rationale for creating IP, a better explanation is required. Recapitalizing IP assets needs to reconcile the reason for their conspicuous absence from the financial sheets, tax policy. The U.S. tax code in IRC Sec. 174 gives taxpayers an election to expense research and experimental expenses. Similar deductions are permitted for sales and marketing expenditures, which promote and enhance the value of a taxpayer's trademarks and copyrights. The tax deduction is justified by the "at-risk" character of endeavors that have no assurance of a particular outcome.

A better reason is that by taking a short-term deduction, every dollar spent on R&D produces around 40 cents in tax savings at current U.S. tax rates. If the "at-risk" presumption was literally true, it would be impossible to justify the nearly $250 billion spent on U.S. R&D (2000 estimates), tax savings notwithstanding. R&D budgets fund hundreds of thousands of research projects. At a portfolio level, there is great certainty that enough R&D succeeds to more than offset its total cost. If the immediate tax benefit is factored in, $10 million in R&D need only produce $6 million in IP assets to achieve break-even. Because accounting prohibits "double counts," an expense can never be an asset, at least on the financial sheets. Therefore the economic benefit of these IP assets is "ghosted" in the enhanced returns on equity (ROE) for other business assets.

If it were otherwise, the R&D function would become extinct and rightly so. Studies of economist Baruch Lev[4] analyze the relationship between R&D and the knowledge capital of corporations. In general, increasing R&D elevates corporate financial performance. Unfortunately, R&D is only a forward-looking activity because there is no accounting residue for successful past research. There is something unsettling about this notion. The work product of R&D is IP, and "intellectual property" is property. If we tracked IP by its "acquisition cost"—that is, capitalized R&D expenses—it would represent a greater annual property investment in the United States than commercial building outlays and nearly half the value of business inventories (see Exhibit 21-3). Property and inventory financing are staples of commercial finance. Leaving "knowledge property" on the sidelines is sort of like telling a coach to pay millions for an all-star quarterback to sit on the bench for his entire career. Like quarterbacks, IP assets—patents, copyrights, trademarks, and the like—have finite performance lives. For investment banking, this defines the absolute time frame for an IP derivative. As a practical matter, technology obsolescence can further discount the economic life of IP to a portion of its legal life. Licensing is already familiar with the practical effects of economic life on IP and uses it regularly to negotiate royalty revenues or technology transfer prices.

A cost method for IP should integrate portfolio production costs with economic life. The effect is a recurring investment cost, less amortization (e.g., the depreciation of an intangible asset), spread over the IP portfolio life. As an example, consider the U.S. history of private R&D expenditures. In 1998, around $150 billion was spent in the U.S. private sector. One way to delineate the portfolio is to measure the assets created by R&D against the average legal life of a patent, 17 years. Patents issued before 1981 would have expired by 1998 and have no proprietary value to their owners. This becomes a useful temporal benchmark. We can reasonably assume this would be as true of any IP created by R&D, patented or otherwise. Intellectual property created in 1982 would have one year or 6 percent of its useful value left while 1983 IP would have two years or 12 percent left and so on. If placed side by side in chronological order, these fractional values build an asset triangle, the area of which represents the replacement cost of all proprietary IP produced in the private sector.

There are two additional considerations in arriving at the IP replacement cost: summing the unamortized IP acquisition costs, or triangulating with current IP acquisition costs ($1/2 \times$ IP cost x IP life). In the first case, the unamortized IP equals $1.08 trillion compared to $1.3 trillion using 1998 R&D costs to calculate IP replacement assets (see Exhibit 21-4). We prefer the latter cost method because it more

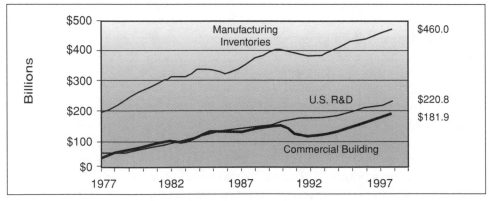

Exhibit 21-3   U.S. business asset markets.
Source: © 2000 T^{EQ} Development

accurately models the investment required to obtain "like-kind" IP assets at current replacement costs.

The process can be scaled to an individual company which benchmarks corporate IP replacement costs. It can be thought of as a salvage value that competitors would likely pay to obtain the IP franchises of a company that exits its core businesses. It also represents the most likely R&D investment required for a competitor to create IP equal in value to the company's existing IP portfolio. In an asset-backed financing, IP replacement cost calculations represent a hedge value to investors in the event of a default. It is also a doorway to the internal IP assets of a company because cost methods measure IP creation and are not preoccupied with indications of use.

The legitimacy of cost-based valuation rests on two assumptions—generating the IP is the result of rational business processes, and a portfolio of IP properties is less risky than a single IP asset. The "rational businessman hypothesis" can be tested by observing the financial performance of the company over the economic life of the IP. If the measures of financial performance (ROE, profit margin, cash flow, etc.) increase or improve, then odds are good that the investment in R&D was justified. The second assumption, that IP portfolio risk decreases with increasing IP properties, is intuitively obvious but difficult to reconcile to current licensing practices, which concentrate on single assets.

The benefits of use in IP are highly personal to the holder. That investors would purchase an income interest in IP for a cash flow return based on the use

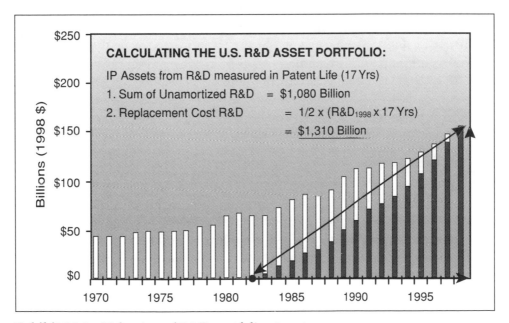

Exhibit 21-4 Valuation of R&D portfolio at cost.
Source: 2000 Statistical Abstract of the United States

of IP by others is a fundamental paradigm shift. The incentive for IP owners to consider such strategies becomes more obvious when IP valuation is based on income.

Income Method Valuation

If cost methods are historians, income methods are futurists. Income methods consider only what future economic value is added by IP in use; the cost to acquire IP is incidental. This point of view is extremely familiar to the licensing executive because it is the premise under which most licenses are drawn. As pointed out earlier, where an existing out-license is considered, the royalty payment stream less costs is the income value of the IP. Applying IRR or NPV analysis makes conversion of these sorts of properties into financial instruments a very straightforward affair. However, it does not provide much insight to the value of interior IP that supports a business because self-licensing is still not a modus operandi for most companies entering the twenty-first century.

Recently, formation of technology holding companies (THC) has gained popularity as a method to maximize the tax benefits of domestic and global R&D activities. A THC is typically a wholly owned subsidiary situated in a jurisdiction favorable to R&D tax treatments into which IP is transferred and R&D expenditures are routed. It can also be a convenient foil for creation of a "synthetic license," which benchmarks the royalty stream of interior IP. A synthetic license is the agreement that would exist between a THC and its parent corporation that reflects the fair market value of the technology if acquired from an independent third party. Computing a use royalty consistent with the value of the technology lets a company use the already familiar IRR and NPV techniques to compute the underlying IP asset value. Income valuation can also be performed on an IP portfolio level as well as for individual properties.

IP is useful if it does one of three things:

1. Creates a product or service for sale
2. Reduces the cost of making a product or service
3. Lets a company stay in business by complying with applicable regulations

Internal IP income-based value turns on that fraction of profits (less necessary expenses) that would not exist but for the existence of the IP itself. The various conventions for deducing IP contributions to profit center income are too numerous to discuss here. Needless to say, a method actually used to out-license a company's technology would be an excellent candidate for valuing a synthetic license of the same company's interior IP.

Traditionally, technology obsolescence defines the economic life of IP. There is a subtle difference in economic life for an out-license versus interior IP and it is worth some discussion here. A licensing manager is very mindful of competing technology alternatives when out-licensing IP because, in an ideal marketplace, a licensee will have equal access to license any technology. Obsolescence can materially affect a royalty stream because future sales or profits denominate the royalty payment. A licensee whose IP is eclipsed by better art is unlikely to have the profitability in future sales to support a meaningful royalty stream.

A company already ensconced in a profit center is unlikely to abandon the business solely on account of a competitor's improved IP position. A change in market share discounts, but rarely eliminates, business value expectations. The economic life for in-place IP should be timed against the expectation of an independent third party (and not a licensee to any existing IP, yours or your competitors') acquiring the IP necessary to gain market entry. This is an investment banking point of view of asset transactions. Value assessed to an IP asset is more likely to be viewed as collateral supporting a term license payment. Unless there a dramatic shift in market players, the ability to fulfill an IP asset-backed payment will depend more on the credit-worthiness of the issuing company than the competitive position of the technology itself. Among other benefits, licensing managers have infinitely better access to business data when examining the interior IP assets, and investment banking views risk as inversely proportional to knowledge.

The cost and income methods provide two ways to consider the portfolio value of IP assets, and neither produces an insignificant sum. Exhibit 21-5 provides an IP portfolio sketch of several Dow Industrials companies using these methods in connection with their 1998 financial statements. Not surprisingly (but not always), income methods deduce higher IP portfolio values. A less direct measure of IP asset value is found in the determination of a company's intellectual capital. Intellectual capital is sometimes defined as the difference between the book value of the company's tangible assets and its share price. The argument is an interesting one, although it subjects the corporate IQ, financially speaking, to the whims of markets not renowned for picking accurate asset values. There is also a macroeconomic perspective, proposed by Dr. Lev, that the intellectual capital of a company is based on the residue of profits not accounted for by the static returns of tangible assets. This is a more satisfying explanation of hidden value, but it does not identify specific assets of value that can participate in a financial transaction. This is the role that an IP portfolio serves. It defines a class of property within legal boundaries that are discrete from other corporate assets. The discreteness makes clear what IP is being transferred, what rights it possesses, and what attributes define its value.

So why can't we just talk about individual properties? We can. Cost and value methods are completely scaleable, even down to single IP properties. But markets abhor a vacuum and individual IP deals are still too rare today to define a marketplace. A portfolio is a collection of IP and collections look more like markets. Legally, a portfolio can take the form of a trust, a special purpose vehicle, or a holding company. In this form, company owners of IP can consider securitizing

Company	Company Tangible Book (MM $)	R&D Cost Valuation (MM $)	IP Income Valuation (MM $)
General Motors	$ 4,762	$ 48,028	$ 64,532
IBM	$ 19,433	$ 45,414	$ 31,156
Hewlett-Packard	$ 16,919	$ 30,195	$ 24,365
Microsoft	$ 28,438	$ 26,730	$ 183,545
Intel	$ 23,377	$ 22,581	$ 62,778
Pfizer	$ 7,997	$ 20,511	$ 18,349
Johnson & Johnson	$ 6,381	$ 20,421	$ 10,994
AT&T	$ 17,574	$ 19,639	$ 16,765
Boeing	$ 10,004	$ 17,055	$ 19,456
Merck & Co.	$ 4,515	$ 16,390	$ 41,491
Eli Lilly & Co.	$ 2,912	$ 15,624	$ 15,005
American Home Products	$ 1,684	$ 14,893	$ 11,851
Procter & Gamble	$ 5,236	$ 12,003	$ 5,722
United Technologies	$ 5,214	$ 11,835	$ 8,154
DuPont de Nemours	$ 11,388	$ 11,772	$ 12,851
3M Co.	$ 5,936	$ 9,463	$ 8,647
Exxon Mobil	$ 62,030	$ 8,346	$ 6,774
Eastman Kodak	$ 2,756	$ 7,920	$ 4,770
Warner Lambert	$ 1,885	$ 7,895	$ 4,033
Dow Chemical	$ 5,788	$ 7,263	$ 6,433
Honeywell International	$ 2,298	$ 7,216	$ 8,054
Caterpillar	$ 3,890	$ 5,787	$ 6,692
International Paper	$ 6,277	$ 1,759	$ 262
Union Carbide	$ 2,449	$ 1,287	$ 6,292
Alcoa Inc.	$ 4,515	$ 1,156	$ 9,283
TOTALS	$ 263,656	$ 391,189	$ 588,245

Exhibit 21-5 1998 Dow Industrials Survey of R&D Assets.
Note: Income Method based on Products or Services only.
Source: ©2000 T^{EQ} DEVELOPMENT

either a portion or the entirety of the IP portfolio. This addresses a great unvoiced concern of industry—how to reap value from IP without losing control of the asset.

CEOs and CFOs generally succeed to leadership because they:

- Develop consistent track records in making decisions on matters they understand
- Delegate to others with proven track records to make decisions on things they do not understand
- Effectively manage the change process

Until very recently, the idea of transferring any rights in IP other than by conventional licensing methods was not even on the radar screen of most board rooms. Yet the fact remains that new asset pools are continuously drawn into commerce to give companies the financial resources to implement change. Management will require education or delegations and who better than the licensing executive to direct the nuances of IP asset financing? The notion that the process is divisible and not "all or none" should assuage the fear reflex. Building knowledge of the financial methods for IP value management will be essential to the education of senior management.

TECHNOLOGY IP SALES

Selling off technology is not a new concept within IP management. Using technology sales to benchmark an IP asset portfolio is new. To understand the significance of this distinction, it is useful to review how licensing today is charged to perform its duties. Exhibit 21-6 lays out, albeit simplistically, the current art for managing technically useful IP. R&D is the basic power plant in most corporations for IP. There are two outcomes that matter in R&D: First, R&D must produce useful and protected IP for deployment within core businesses. In a distant second position, R&D that fails to produce useful internal assets must create assets that produce out-licensing royalties. Everything else is unrecoverable expense (except for tax deductions). For the CFO, this is a cost-centered strategy for R&D. Because R&D is viewed as a cost, R&D outlays compete directly with profits. From this perspective, technology sales seem more like salvage auctions than profit center activities. The driving consideration is to offset expenses.

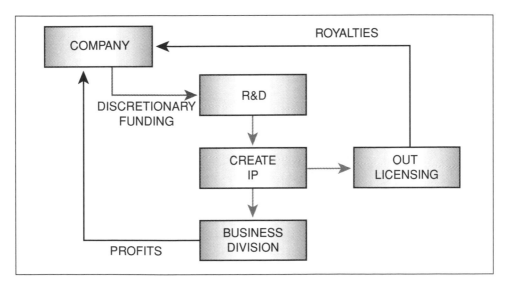

Exhibit 21-6 Current management practices for technology-based IP.
Source: © 2000 T^{EQ} Development

In a cost-driven universe, IP belongs to those who pay for it. In some cases, corporate policies dictate that business units control the technologies when they pay the R&D. Unlike the current R&D process, profit centers are measured by profits. A license royalty, even if unrelated to the core business, is mostly profit. Not surprisingly, business general managers are loath to sell off profit-generating activities (even unrelated ones) because management's success in business is measured by continuing profits—not one-time capital gains.

Where does this place the licensing function? All too often, it winds up attempting to play the role of therapist in a dysfunctional business strategy. Even when the sale of technology IP can dramatically improve cash resources, profit center factions will object if the sale removes royalty revenues from future earnings. The objection is understandable when profit centers are the payers for R&D. Regrettably, licensing is rarely a true profit center in its own right. Licensing can offer a better model when it incorporates investment banking strategies into current practices.

Two kinds of IP asset sales—sale of technology property and sale of royalty income—are illustrated in Exhibit 21-7 together with their impact on company cash flow. The technology sale supposes that a licensee exists (or will exist) for the IP and the buyer only wants a financial interest in the form of a royalty stream. This is different from a direct sale of IP to a new user. In the latter case, the universe of potential users is extremely limited. A "scarce user" environment tends to lower

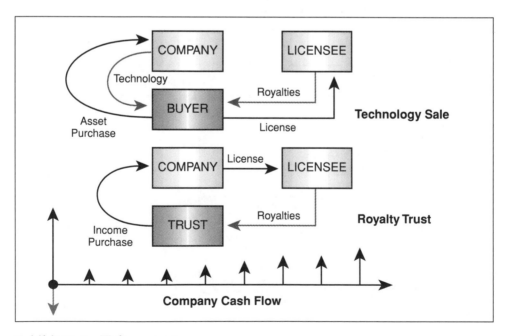

Exhibit 21-7   IP financings.
Source: © 2000 T^{EQ} Development

purchase price or make payment conditional on the future business success of the new holder. In contrast, there is an inventory of capital investors that (in general) greatly exceeds the population of IP users. When more buyers are inserted into the process, it is possible to negotiate a higher price and to lower the cost of capital on the transaction. If needed, the selling company and/or the prospective licensees can convey additional assurances to the investor-purchaser in the form of minimum royalties or additional security interests.

From the licensee perspective, the front-loading risk of the investment is assumed by the cash investor in exchange for defined future payments. The licensee accounting effect is similar to an "off balance" sheet financing because royalty obligations are not generally recorded until payments are actually made. Concurrently, the IP seller has an opportunity to exchange a noncore IP asset for a larger lump-sum of cash that can be employed to make greater returns than the IRR of future royalties. Lastly, the investor-purchaser obtains a perfected security interest in assets not otherwise available to the financial markets. Unlike the sale of a business, an investor-purchaser is a recurring client for IP asset sales. A recurring client can also be thought of as a customer, and where there are customers, there can be markets.

The customer concept is a useful way to reconcile business profit centers to the notion that IP sales can be a recurring business since R&D is a recurring activity. R&D, by its very nature, cannot guarantee the creation of internally useful IP assets. Intellectual property customers make licensing executives look more like sales managers. Because the function of sales manager is well understood by the corporate chain of command, positioning IP assets within a sales modality portrays licensing as a bona fide profit center.

Still, the picture is incomplete without a prospect list of IP purchaser-investors. This is where the CFO plays a vital role. A core mission of the CFO is to make sure that his or her company does not run out of the cash needed to pay its bills. In fulfilling this mission, CFOs develop relationships with financiers and investment bankers who swap cash now for cash flows later. These swaps for cash flows are the contracts that define a large swath of the financial marketplace. This is also where asset investors are found. An asset-backed technology sale, in addition to being a sale, is also a swap. Since sales and licenses are contracts for money, the licensing executive now has an opportunity to fulfill a role for the CFO as a cash flow underwriter. The CFO becomes a willing sales agent for the licensing executive who is judiciously converting unrecorded, noncore assets into cash flow. While a technology asset sale is tactical in nature, a successful implementation has the effect of reinventing corporate cash strategy.

IP sales are a useful benchmark against which other IP asset-backed conveyances can be studied. Likewise, the role of licensing in bundling IP for an asset-backed transaction is the same when considering alternate transaction strategies. Outright IP sales make sense when there is no continuing nexus between the technologies conveyed and their foreseeable utility to current or future core businesses. Selling IP assets frees the licensing and legal functions of further maintenance expenses and, more important, frees up personnel to pursue better opportunities. Still, there are other options within IP asset financing to which we now turn our attention.

ROYALTY TRUST

The royalty trust is the concept at the core of a "Bowie Bond." A royalty trust can also be the intention of an intermediate sale of IP to a special purpose entity whose sole purpose is to collect royalties, maintain the IP estate, and distribute proceeds. It is also useful with technical IP where outright sale of the underlying assets is impractical. As shown in Exhibit 21-7, the structural dynamics of a royalty trust are nearly identical to an IP sale. For a price, the IP owner sells off all or part of the income to be derived from an existing license.

The legal holder of the IP is typically required to maintain filings and registrations and to perform licenser obligations under the license. The asset transferred in this case is not the IP itself but the right to income from the IP. The purchaser-investor holds an unperfected security interest in an IP instrument. This may require either a higher pay-out or additional collateral to mitigate the purchaser's risk of loss. The increased benefits to the IP owner in a royalty trust are inversely mirrored in the diminution of the purchaser's rights. Simply put, the seller has not put his or her technology up for grabs.

Except for pricing considerations, the cash flow effects to the conveying company in a royalty trust are nearly identical to an IP technology sale. There are two noteworthy differences. First, the sale of a future royalty stream, to the extent that it is taxable, is taxed as ordinary income, rather than at capital gains rates as is the case in a technology sale. Second, the IP holder has continuing maintenance, defense, and support costs for the IP, and this can lower the future free cash flow of the transaction. For some companies, the sale of an income stream rather than the asset can overcome change in ownership concerns, especially when companies have continuing interests in the use and development of the IP. Royalty trusts overcome restrictive covenant issues for certain enterprises like universities or research institutes which impose prohibitions on sales of inventions or other creations. In the areas of university drug research, genomics, and biotechnology, the royalty trust is gaining credence because selling income rather than the IP itself does not breach restrictive covenants imposed on not-for-profit organizations.

There are two further distinctions between a royalty trust and technology sale. A provable income stream is essential to crafting a royalty trust, preferably one with a certifiable history of royalty payments. This explains in part the concentration of past deals involving trademarks and copyrights. A second requirement is the continued viability of the IP holder at least for the economic life of the asset. Otherwise continuing good title of the IP can end up in jeopardy. The trust instrument itself can provide effective safeguards for the conveying company, particularly those instruments that prevent the untimely transfer of IP rights to competitors. Because the trust only transfers a right to income, a competitor can obtain no more advantage in IP controlled by a royalty trust than any other arm's-length financial investor.

IP DEBT LEVERAGING

IP debt leveraging is a further iteration of asset financing methods that securitize existing royalties. In debt leveraging, an IP holder borrows the net present value of his or her royalty stream using the royalty stream as the collateral for loan payments. Many of the so-called Bowie Bonds are in fact IP debt instruments. Intellectual property debt leveraging behaves much like a line of credit where a "lockbox" arrangement for royalties assures the lender of repayment. By segregating the collateral interest to the royalty payments only, the IP holder may keep this borrowing "off balance sheet."

In many respects, this is the best of all possible worlds for IP holders, because the company gets to keep absolute control of its IP. By borrowing against its assets instead of selling them, the company avoids taxes and gains full use of the transaction proceeds. Since the IP carries no leverage, the effect is like an unsecured borrowing with a downside restricted to total a payout of the royalty stream. The company IRR includes both the royalty stream and cash flow returns of the invested borrowings net of loan repayments. A company can afford to pay a higher interest rate because of the downside stopper.

But there are two possible complications. Commercial banks fund many of the short-term borrowing needs of corporations. To minimize default by a corporation on these borrowings, lenders require that company debts not exceed its equity by a specified ratio (in general significantly less than 1.0). A borrower can go into technical default by exceeding the debt-to-equity ratio. This can trigger a "call" on the outstanding loan balances which pays down either the entire debt balance or enough debt to bring the borrower back into compliance. Needless to say, CEOs can become very agitated with CFOs who fail to keep the company within loan compliance. A debt leveraging of IP that increases the debt-to-equity ratio then becomes a "zero sum" game, only with higher interest rates.

It may be possible to escape an on balance sheet recording of the borrowing, if loan repayment occurs only when royalties are actually received. But this raises a second risk—treatment of the transaction as either a sale of future IP income or sale of the IP asset, either of which is a taxable event. The degree of restriction on the royalty stream between the issuing company and the lender is a critical factor in determining tax, credit, and accounting treatments.

Discussion of IP debt leveraging provides a convenient excursion into the relationship of IP assets to the credit and debt processes of companies. Commercial borrowing contracts—also known as secured transactions—give lenders rights to file security interests against all foreseeable property interests of a company. Selling or disposing of secured assets requires permission of the borrower to remove the lien. Intellectual property is intangible property, and the law does not recognize secured transactions in intangible property. Instead, borrowers rely on loan covenants to restrict the transfer of IP and other intangibles. The point of all this is that while traditional lenders do not lend against IP for value, they can restrict its conveyance. All the methods discussed here will invariably require lenders to give permission for IP asset financing. Doing so is an opportunity to educate credit markets on the overlooked benefits of IP. They may even relax debt-to-equity ratios.

IP sales, royalty trusts, and IP debt leveraging work best in the IP arena containing the current universe of "business-to-business" license agreements. The $120 billion per year they generate in license revenues provides an immense inventory of deals in waiting. Although the former royalties involve just a fraction of the IP assets now in existence, the techniques employed with existing licenses provide a window of opportunity into the greater marketplace of internal, unlicensed IP.

SYNTHETIC LICENSE MONETIZATIONS

Synthetic licenses are vehicles that compute IP asset value, no matter how it is used by corporations. Monetization of synthetic licenses is the most ambitious approach to IP asset financing because, theoretically, it includes everything in the IP portfolio. The trade-off is a degree of complexity greater than other IP asset financing methods. A synthetic license is the license a company would enter into to forgo its R&D expense and still obtain the fair value use of the resulting IP. The NPV of the fair value use defines the selling price of the IP asset portfolio. It can also be thought of as the divestiture price of a company's IP portfolio.

A synthetic license is realized once a customer is found to purchase and back-license a company's IP. This is a variation on the theme of the technology holding company (THC). The difference is that the THC actually acquires external funds that purchase an interest in the conveyed IP. In the case of technical IP, we call this enterprise a Patent Investment Entity or PIE™. The conveying company receives back the use rights in the IP from the PIE™ in the form of a license for which it pays royalties. If the entire interest in the IP is sold, the purchase price should include a consideration for the uses not back-licensed. Additional out-licensing income becomes a property right of the PIE™. Most likely some support of the IP is required; the PIE™ and conveying company are well advised to enter into a service support contract for out-licensing. A hypothetical synthetic license monetization is illustrated in Exhibit 21-8.

Once formed, a PIE™ can be a closed-end vehicle, or it can be used for successive conveyances of IP from the original company or independent third parties. The PIE™ adopts many of the legal tenets of a royalty trust. This is equally crucial in addressing IP control issues for both conveying companies and investors. The PIE™ functions as a financial rather than economic customer for IP. A PIE™ can hold a very diverse range of IP provided it operates through a common set of

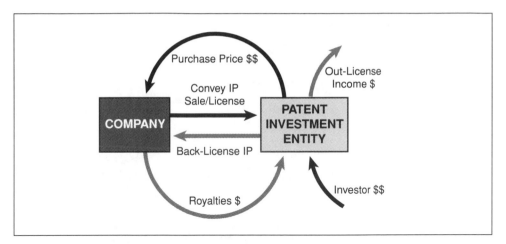

Exhibit 21-8 Synthetic license monetization*
Source: © 2000 T^{EQ} Development
*U.S. Patent Pending

financial mechanics. While highly speculative PIE™s can be built around emerging technologies, the appetite for such deals is limited to risk capital entrepreneurs. Far larger pools of capital are interested in steady cash flow returns of proven, risk-averse IP applications. In this regard, a PIE™ can closely parallel the operation of a real estate investment trust (REIT).

About 25 years ago, the investment community recognized that bundling the lease income of commercial properties with the deeds to the property created a financial security that paid a handsome yield and was backed by an appreciating asset. The REIT was born, and its scorecard is an impressive one. In 1980, REIT securities had a total value of $8 billion. By 1998, REIT securities had increased 2,500 percent to $206 billion. A 20 percent/year growth rate for 20 years is a stellar track record. REITs have been equally adept vehicles for corporations to sell off real estate and lease it back. Such a sale lets the company take advantage of long-term appreciation in real estate values. Interestingly, for the last 10 years, annual U.S. R&D expenditures have consistently outpaced commercial building activity by more than 20 percent. Using the PIE™ model for synthetic IP licenses implies a staggering inventory of potential deals is waiting for Wall Street.

A PIE™ is a method which converts the R&D function from a cost to profit center. It builds on the technology sale concept because a back-license makes even interior IP accessible to asset financing (see Exhibit 21-9). PIE™ also reconciles IP control issues by restricting it with operating covenants, exclusive back-licenses, and "income-only" financial instrument issues. A PIE™-like entity can also be formed by a company through the pledge of a stock voting trust, creating a security interest for lenders while debt leveraging the back-license royalties. Likewise, a partial sale of equity in such an enterprise can provide an equity investment

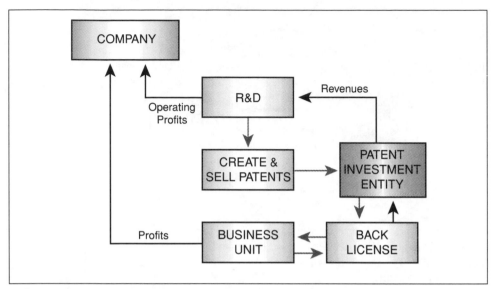

Exhibit 21-9 Future IP management practices using PIEs.*
*U.S. Patent Pending
Source: © 2000 T^{EQ} Development

backed by an undivided interest in the IP. The unsold equity provides the inventing company with sufficient control to avoid competitor access to IP assets or license rights.

In other words, the form of a synthetic license monetization can utilize a
myriad of legal constructs that still fall within the basic business method. It is sufficiently unique and scaleable that business method patents are pending on its
novel uses. The selection of options can also tailor these IP transactions to produce
events on or off the financial sheet. Likewise, the synthetic license method can
obtain various tax treatments (or none at all), which is an additional benefit to CFOs
in plotting financial strategies. Posttransaction control of the IP assets and income
streams is critical to determining the tax treatment and accounting requirements.

IP FINANCING STRATEGIES: PROS AND CONS

Financing IP is not an absolute requirement for business success. Attempting to
leverage trade secrets and unregistered know-how would be a naïve and unwise
use of IP asset financing techniques. Neither should a company securitize its IP for
the sake of securitization when it has no other compelling use for the cash it generates. Intellectual property financing strategies serve two constituencies—profit
center management and the CFO. Both must be served well for an IP asset financing to be a business success. Fortunately the dual market characteristic of IP financing is more often a synergy than an antagonism of opportunity. For the CEO, IP
financing can be another venue for growing shareholder value.

Each method for IP asset financing has pros and cons. The threshold question is whether and how IP assets should influence corporate strategy. As we tell our clients, use your cheapest sources of capital first. While IP financing is well below venture capital risk horizons, it is likely to be fractionally more costly than bonds. Nondeferred taxable IP asset financing has additional cost of capital burdens that a company should factor into its decision-making process.

Needless to say, there are enough tax and accounting nuances to an IP financing to fill a book all by itself. In IP financing methods, the transaction can employ a vast array of licenses, transfer contracts, and enterprise law to craft relationships. But the exercise is meaningless until the benefits are clearly understood. It will require patience and skill to walk diverse corporate functions through the process to recognize the benefits within. Knowledge of intellectual property is the fundamental constant. Whether IP asset financing succeeds or fails will ultimately rest on the shoulders of licensing professionals. The question remains: Are licensing executives ready to become the investment bankers of the twenty-first century?

NOTES

1. R. Binns, et al., "Using IPR to Raise Debt Capital." *Les Nouvelles*, June 1999.
2. U.S. Bureau, No. 797, "Flow of Funds Accounts—Financial Assets of Financial and Nonfinancial Institutions, by Holder Sector: 1980–1998." *Statistical Abstract of the United States: 1999.*
3. K. Rivette, D. Kline, "Discovering New Value in Intellectual Property," *Harvard Business Review*, January 2000.
4. S. L. Mintz, "A Better Approach to Estimating Knowledge Capital," *CFO Magazine*, February 1999.

ABOUT THE AUTHOR

Douglas R. Elliott is a venture capitalist and CEO for technology-driven enterprises. Since 1987, he has managed the turnaround, development, sale, and public financing of several technologically diverse companies. In 1998, Elliott cofounded TEQ Development, LLC to address the unmet financial needs and opportunities in intellectual property management. Mr. Elliot began his career as a research engineer and, later, venture capital associate for a Fortune 500 company. He is an inventor of several issued and pending patents ranging from heat transfer processes to financial derivatives. Mr. Elliott is a frequent contributor to periodicals and lecturer on the topics of venture capital, technology enterprise, and intellectual property financing. Presently, he is a Director of the Missouri Venture Forum and a member of Missouri Governor's Roundtable for Venture Capital. He holds degrees in Biology and Chemistry from Case Western Reserve University, a Masters in Chemical Engineering, and a JD of Law from Cleveland State University.

TEQ Development, LLC is a financial technologies company that provides tools and expertise to convert existing intellectual properties into financial derivatives. Because of accounting practices and tax regulations, these intellectual assets are frequently unvalued and unrecorded on financial statements. Formed in 1998, TEQ Development developed proprietary software, management practices, and business method patents that are used to value, monetize, and create investment vehicles for patents.

CHAPTER TWENTY-TWO

New Patent Issue: BioPharma Royalty Trust

by Bernhard H. Fischer

PERSPECTIVES

The first time pharmaceutical patent royalties were turned into a marketable security occurred quietly in August 2000. The credit, BioPharma Royalty Trust (BRT), totaled $115 million. It included $57.15 million in senior debt, $22.0 million in mezzanine debt, and $22.16 million in equity. Standard & Poor's (S&P) in an October 2000 report (which follows) rated the senior debt single A, largely on the basis of the strength of the pledged revenues, creditworthiness of the institutions involved, Bristol-Myers Squibb Co., the licensee responsible for paying the royalties, and the assignee on the patent, Yale University.

What is most special about the BioPharma Royalty Trust is that it was completed. If successful for those who bought the debt, as it appears it will be, the transaction could lay the groundwork for future patent royalty securitizations. Royalties as an asset class have shown significant growth over the last decade. In 1992, they were $417 million; in 1994, $757 million; in 1996, $996 million; and for 2000E, $2.6 billion. Compound annual growth from 1992 to 2000 was 24 percent. While there have been more than a dozen copyright-and-brand related securitizations over the past decade (see "Known Completed IP Securitizations" in the Data Bank section of this book), patent royalties are by nature more difficult to predict. With an estimated trillion dollars in patent asset value and almost 200,000 patents being issued annually in the United States alone, the potential has been established for a new asset class. While patent royalty-based securities are not likely to rival the mortgage-backed market, they will give business executives, investment bankers, and different investors new opportunities to extract more value from their IP assets.

The BioPharma Trust royalties involved licenses on a patent covering Bristol-Myers Squibb's HIV-AIDS medication Zerit®. Like other drugs in its class, Zerit is expensive. According to an article in *The New York Times* (April 24, 2001), the annual wholesale cost of Zerit in the United States is $3,432. The company's discount price in Africa is $55. The foreign generic cost of the active ingredients on an annual basis (dfT or stavudine) is $23. Organizations, even not-for-profits like universities, need to be compensated for the successful products they develop so research on other drugs can be properly funded. Standard and Poor's was aware of the potential pressure to discount Zerit in Africa, where there had been little or no market for the drug. Its credit analysis, says S&P analyst Bern Fischer, reflected pricing models in markets where sales had already been established. Other threats to the seven-year term of cash flow also were accounted for in S&P's credit analysis, including the remote possibility of finding the patent invalid as a result of litigation, and the drug being rendered obsolete by rapid advances in HIV-AIDS pharmacology.

Zerit sales in 1997, 1998, and 1999 were $398 million, $551 million, and $605 million, respectively. This represents an average annual growth rate of 26 percent. The average of street analyst forecasts project sales of $699 million in 2000 followed by 10 percent growth in 2001, slowing thereafter and remaining very stable. The underwriter or issuer of the BioPharma Royalty Trust was Royalty Pharma AG and the senior holder was Westdeutsche Landesbank Girozentrale in London. To date, Royalty Pharma AG has investments in a total of seven healthcare-related royalty interests.

RATIONALE (OCTOBER 25, 2000)

The rating on BioPharma Royalty Trust's (BRT) $57.15 million senior notes due quarterly beginning September 6, 2000, through June 6, 2006, is based on:

- The strong legal structure that segregates the revenue stream supporting the notes
- The credit support provided by subordinate debt and equity investors
- The strength of the historical and projected performance of Zerit patent royalty revenues, which support the timely payment of principal and interest on the senior notes
- The AAA credit rating of Bristol-Myers Squibb Co. (BMS)

In addition, the rating benefits from the strong cash flows that, even under severe stress assumptions, are sufficient to make timely payments of interest and principal on the senior notes. The senior notes will not and have not been registered under U.S. Securities Act of 1933, and are represented by a permanent global certificate without interest coupons. Although this transaction has been privately placed and is to be sold outside the United States, S&P has received written authorization from all parties to publish this analysis.

This transaction is the first pharmaceutical patent royalty securitization rated by Standard & Poor's. Standard & Poor's has rated other royalty securitizations, including film receivables and natural resources (oil, timber, precious metals). Standard & Poor's applied structured finance future flow criteria that analyzed the level of cash flows expected to be generated under this transaction. The cash flow in this transaction must be generated by BMS through the sale of Zerit in the worldwide HIV/AIDS marketplace. The rating analysis includes corporate and structured analysis focusing on industry and business fundamentals, growth prospects, vulnerabilities, projected cash flows, and legal framework. A key transactional risk is insufficient cash flow to service debt due to competing and new products, slower or declining sales, and product obsolescence. Standard & Poor's has received and reviewed several legal opinions issued in connection with this transaction, including the true sale of the royalty receivables by an academic institution to BRT and the BRT's grant of a first perfected security interest in the receivables and other collateral to a collateral trustee.

TRANSACTION OVERVIEW—BIOPHARMA ROYALTY TRUST

A major research-based academic institution rated AAA by Standard & Poor's owns 100 percent of the asset (patent and licensing agreement). The royalty is divided among several parties: 30 percent to two inventors, 70 percent to the institution. Under a conveyance agreement, the academic institution has irrevocably sold to BRT, a bankruptcy-remote, special-purpose entity established as a Delaware business trust, its 70 percent of the royalties payable under a licensing agreement dated December 23, 1987, between the academic institution and BMS for just over $100 million. BioPharma Royalty Trust funded the purchase of the institution's royalty interest through the issuance of these senior notes and subordinate mezzanine notes and equity investments.

The licensing agreement includes U.S. patent applications 911,200 (September 24, 1986) and 942,686 (December 17, 1986), the last of which currently expires June 24, 2008, and several other nonU.S. patents, the last of which currently expires in 2011. Under the licensing agreement, BMS pays royalties based on worldwide sales of Zerit. Zerit sales in 1999 totaled $605 million with average annual sales growth of 26 percent since 1997. Market estimates forecast Zerit sales of $699 million for 2000, followed by 10 percent growth in 2001 and remaining stable thereafter. Patent royalty revenues are based on the sales volume of Zerit, an antiretroviral HIV/AIDS medicine produced, distributed, and marketed by BMS. The patent and licensing agreement has generated royalty payments of $26.2 million in 1997, $37.5 million in 1998, and $41.6 million in 1999. Payments for the first half of 2000 totaled $20.4 million, with $24.4 million forecasted for the second half, for a total of $44.8 million.

Historical and issuer projected quarterly royalty revenues cover maximum required debt service on senior notes in excess of 200 percent. Standard & Poor's stress scenarios reflect the transactions' ability to pay timely principal and interest on the senior notes over the term of the transaction. Standard & Poor's stress scenarios incorporated Zerit user population variability, market share vulnerability, and price declines. Additional analytical considerations include the recent Africa AIDS conference, the presentation of several AIDS/HIV vaccines into the marketplace, the recent presentation of three new classes of AIDS drugs, and Glaxo Smith Kline's recent release of Trizivir.

Based on transaction structure, underlying asset analysis, and the transactions' ability to survive severe stress cases, the A senior note ratings are supported. The ratings are based on a number of forecasts and assumptions that are subject to change over time. The current ratings reflect the increased predictability of these factors over the short term. Standard & Poor's will adjust its forecast as the situation warrants. The ratings on the senior notes will be subject to Standard & Poor's surveillance process and therefore are subject to change.

STRUCTURE—THE ROLE OF THE COLLATERAL TRUSTEE

The transaction structure is highlighted by the academic institution's irrevocable assignment of rights outlined in a patent licensing agreement to a bankruptcy-remote trust, BRT under a conveyance agreement, combined with an executed estoppel agreement by BMS. BioPharma Royalty Trust has pledged the quarterly cash flows to a collateral trustee, Bankers Trust Co., under a collateral trust and intercreditor agreement that created various operating accounts and authorizes the collateral trustee to collect and distribute funds. One hundred percent of the license receivables are paid by BMS directly to the collateral trustee and deposited into a collection account.

The collateral trustee distributes the not-pledged 30 percent of the deposited monies to the account of the academic institution and the pledged 70 percent to a distribution account for distribution to various parties including senior noteholders. Quarterly distributions first cover collateral trustee and other parties' service expenses (subject to a cap); then senior noteholder interest; senior noteholder principal, repurchase, or redemption of senior notes subject to a senior note ratio test; and then to mezzanine holders, other expenses, escrow accounts, and finally to the owner trustee (equity holders). Furthermore, transactional events of default include failure to meet the senior coverage ratio test for three consecutive payment dates.

The fiscal agency agreement includes an important senior coverage ratio test covenant. The ratio is expressed as a percentage of 70 percent of the amount of royalties payable by BMS under the licensing agreement, assuming net sales were equal to four times net sales in a quarterly report, divided by the amounts required in the cash flow distribution through, and including, principal on the senior notes. In the event that the senior coverage ratio test is not met at any payment date, it will result in the repurchase or redemption of all or any part of senior notes, then outstanding in an amount equal to the amount available.

ASSET ANALYSIS—HIV/AIDS MEDICINES

Standard & Poor's analyzed historical product sales, marketing, market share, and patent royalties, and modeled projected patent royalty revenues to be generated over the life of this transaction. Modeling included analysis of the product's historical, current, and future worldwide market, position, competition, and pricing. Keys to this analysis include BMS's continuing position as one of the world's largest pharmaceutical firms, its diverse and growing revenue base, and its solid financial position. BMS's pharmaceutical franchise leads the company's operations, accounting for more than 60 percent of total sales. Zerit and Videx are BMS's two antiretroviral HIV/AIDS medicines. Currently, Zerit is the most commonly prescribed thymadine nucleoside reverse transcriptase inhibitor in HIV therapy in the United States. In 1999, Zerit and Videx received regulatory approval for use as first-line components of a combination antiretroviral therapy regimen for HIV-infected patients.

RATINGS DETAIL PROFILE

Transaction Summary

New Rating	**A**
Closing date:	August 16, 2000
Lead Arranger:	Westdeutsche Landesbank Girozentrale
Originator:	Pharmaceutical Royalties LLC
Issuer:	BioPharma Royalty Trust
Trustee:	Bankers Trust Company

This report was reproduced from Standard & Poor's RatingsDirect, the premier source of real-time, web-based credit ratings and research from an organization that has been a leader in objective credit analysis for more than 140 years. To preview this dynamic online product, visit our RatingsDirect web site at www.standardandpoors.com/ratingsdirect. Standard & Poor's.

Published by Standard & Poor's, a Division of The McGraw-Hill Companies, Inc. Executive offices: 1221 Avenue of the Americas, New York, NY 10020. Editorial offices: 55 Water Street, New York, NY 10041. Subscriber services: (1) 212-438-

BIOPHARMA ROYALTY TRUST—FACT SHEET FOR A PATENT SECURITIZATION

Originator:	Pharmaceutical Royalties LLC, a Delaware limited liability company
Servicer and Trustee:	Wilmington Trust Company
Seller:	"Major U.S." University (AAA S&P rating)
Issuer:	BioPharma Royalty Trust, a Delaware business trust, Owner trustee

Securities issued:

$57.15 million senior loan
$22.0 million mezzanine loan

$79.15 million total debt

$21.16 million equity

$115 million purchase price ($123 net of 12/99 receipts)

Class	Maturity	Quarterly Amount
Senior notes	9/6/00–6/6/06 Qtly	$3.045 million
Mezzanine notes	9/6/00–6/6/06 Qtly	$1.33–1.2 million

Principal and interest payment dates:

Quarterly P&I through due June 2006.
Will match P&I payment dates with royalty payment dates with minimum six-day cushion.

Royalty is due 90 days after quarter closes.

BMS pays typically 60th day.

Licensing agreement and transaction documents (Conveyance Agreement requires payments not later than 60 days after the end of the calendar quarter.)

Collateral:
70 percent percent royalty interest in the patent and licensing agreement between University and Bristol-Myers Squibb Company (AAA rating) pertaining to the anti-retroviral use of 2′, 3′-dideoxy, 2′, 3′-didehydrocytidine, and 2′, 3′-didehydrothymidine and compositions described in the U.S. Patent applications serial numbers 911,200 (9/24/86) and 942,686 (12/17/86). (Zerit = BMS brand name.)

Legal structure:
Irrevocable sale by University to the SPV trust of 70 percent of the royalties payable under the licensing agreement dated 12/23/87 between University and BMS.

Asset coupon:
LIBOR (London Interbank Offering Rate)—Hedge Agreement, swap to fixed rates with West LB rated (AA+/Neg/A-1+)

Maturity:
June 6, 2006; Interest period commences September 6, 2000

Quarterly P&I   March, June, September, December 6th

Ratings:
"A" rating for senior debt

Confidential rating on mezzanine debt

Credit support:
Overcollateralization
(from mezzanine notes and equity for senior notes)

Senior representative holders:
Westdeutsche Landesbank Girozentrale, London Branch

Underwriter:
Royalty Pharma AG

Underwriter/Issuer Counsel:
Clifford Chance

West LB counsel:
Shearman & Sterling

KEY TRANSACTION DETAILS AND FEATURES

- Represents the first pharmaceutical patent royalty rated by S&P
- S&P has rated other royalty deals: film (Sony), natural resources (oil, precious metals)
- Analysis and criteria follows future flow methodology (tobacco, timber, music)
- *Royalty Pharma AG* (Underwriter), 675 Third Avenue, New York, NY 10017
  - Experienced management team from biotechnology and financial industries

- Acquire royalty interests in leading pharmaceutical and biotechnology products and related medical technologies; create a diversified portfolio of income-producing assets; accelerate growth through IPO and exchange listing
- Approximately $80 million invested in seven royalty interests ($120 million in capital commitment)
- Royalty income 1999E = $23.7 million; 2002E = $34.1 million
- Four managing members; seven-member advisory board
- Business strategy
  - Target academic/research institutions, individual inventors, and biotech and pharma companies; acquire products approved by the FDA; selective acquisition of early-stage products
  - Finance the commercial launch or late-stage clinical development of products
  - Acquire companies rich in intellectual property during market downturns
- Management strategy—"Royalty streams have unique and desirable financial characteristics"
- Holders of existing royalties include:
  - Institution/Inventor owned—academic and research institutes that receive royalties in exchange for licensing their technology to biotech and pharmaceutical companies
  - Company owned—Royalty interests on products or technology licensed to pharma or biotech companies for commercialization
  - R&D Partnerships—placed with individual investors to finance clinical development of drugs or devices
- Royalties as an asset class have shown growth over the last decade: 1992 = $417 million; 1994 = $757 million; 1996 = $996 million; 2000E = $2.6 billion (1992–2000 CAGR = 24 percent)
- Pharmaceutical company credit ratings are generally very strong (AA and AAA) and stable over the past decade

Yale University—AAA/Stable/A-1+ (August 2000)

Rating reflects an overwhelming financial cushion afforded by the Yale University's $7.1 billion endowment, highly competitive student demand for all programs, and strong board and administrative management.

Yale University School of Medicine, founded in 1810, educates leaders in research, medical education, and patient care. The Yale University School of Medicine is one of the nation's premier research institutions. Research at the Medical Center covers a broad spectrum, from clinical studies implementing cutting-edge techniques for improving the diagnosis and treatment of human diseases to fundamental studies exploring new areas of biology, biotechnology, biomedical engineering, and informatics. The 1,230 full-time faculty members and 2,009 part-time and voluntary faculty members of the School of Medicine contribute to the research programs of the Institution as well as to the Medical Center's educational, patient care, and service missions.

Yale Medical Center owns several pharmaceutical patents. Most of these patent licensing agreements generate little royalty income (most well under $500,000 per year). Zerit is by far the largest revenue-producing patent the university currently has. The university has never sold a patent or royalty stream. The university approached the capital markets proposing to sell the Zerit royalty stream, from which proceeds would fund the construction of an approximately $100 million research facility at the Medical Center.

Yale owns 100 percent of the asset (patent). The royalty is divided among several parties—30 percent to two inventors, 70 percent to the university. Of the 70 percent to the university, half goes to the Medical Center and half to the university. The university will assign rights to 70 percent of the royalty stream to the SPE in exchange for $123 million (subject to adjustment). The 30 percent share of the asset payable to the inventors was left out of the sale for simplicity.

The patent and licensing agreement has generated royalty payments of $26.2 million (1997), $37.5 million (1998), and $41.6 million (1999).

Bristol-Myers Squibb Co. AAA/Stable/A-1+ (August 2000)

This rating reflects the company's continuing position as one of the world's largest pharmaceutical firms, its diverse and growing revenue base, and its solid financial position. Bristol-Myers' pharmaceutical franchise leads the company's operations, accounting for more than 60 percent of total sales.

Zerit and Videx are BMS's two antiretroviral HIV/AIDS medicines. In 1999, Zerit and Videx sales increased 10 percent to $605 million and 27 percent to $205 million respectively. First-quarter 2000 sales remained at prior-year levels of $151 million for Zerit and $45 million of Videx. Zerit sales in 1997, 1998, and 1999 were $398 million, $551 million, and $605 million respectively. This represents an average annual growth rate of 26 percent. The average of street analyst forecasts project sales of $699 million in 2000 followed by 10 percent growth in 2001 slowing thereafter and remaining very stable.

Currently, Zerit is the most commonly prescribed thymadine nucleoside reverse trascriptase inhibitor in HIV therapy in the United States. In 1999 Zerit and Videx received regulatory approval for use as first-line components of a combination antiretroviral therapy regimen for HIV-infected patients.

Transactional features include:

- University's irrevocable assignment of certain rights under the license agreement to the SPE under the "Conveyance of Patent Royalties Agreement"

- Bankruptcy remote SPE, BioPharma Royalty Trust, a Delaware business trust
- Executed Estoppel Agreement by BMS
- Nonrecourse of noteholders to university or BMS
- An irrevocable interest in the royalty stream
- Quarterly deposit of 70 percent of actual collections to trustee/SPE

- Cash Flow Coverage
  - Projected senior D/S coverage of between 2.54–3.29 times from September 2000 to June 6
  - Stressed (A Rtg) Senior D/S coverage of greater than 1.38 times from September 2000 to June 06

Rating Analysis:

- S&P corporate ratings analysis, model, and projections for Zerit Royalties for the period 2000 through 2007
- Analysis included: historical sales, competition, competitive advantage, market share, pricing, HIV/AIDS population (United States and worldwide), expected trends in population, market share and pricing, product obsolescence risk, patent challenges, generic risks, and currency/foreign exchange risks
- Zerit sales analysis conclusions include:
  1. Population—U.S. HIV/AIDS population growth +30,000 per year
  2. Penetration—Zerit market share maintained constant at 1997 level (lower than 1998 and 1999)
  3. Pricing—Maintain price flat for a period then decline
  4. Population times penetration times pricing = U.S. Sales
  5. Western Europe sales are calculated at 65 percent of U.S. sales
  6. Other worldwide (Asia, Canada, Australia) sales = 26 percent of U.S. sales
  7. United States + Western Europe + Other = Total worldwide sales
- Total worldwide sales times Royalty percentage = Projected royalty payments due
- Royalty payments due times 70 percent (to trust) = Projected cash flow to trust (Base Case Stress)
- Applied stresses to each rating category up to A to projected cash flows

Transaction Documents include:

- Conveyance agreement
- Collateral trust and intercreditor agreement
- Trust agreement (Pharmaceutical Royalties LLC & Wilmington Trust)
- Administration agreement

- Account control agreement
- Fiscal agency agreement
- Senior note purchase agreement
- Mezzanine note purchase agreement
- Insurance and indemnity agreement
- Form of senior surety bond
- Form of mezzanine surety bond

ABOUT THE AUTHOR

Bernhard H. Fischer is a Director in the Structured Finance Ratings Group at Standard & Poor's Corporation, focusing on unique credits including intellectual property, municipal revenues, stranded costs, franchise loans, tobacco settlements, structured settlements, and charged-off credit cards. Mr. Fischer has been with Standard and Poor's since 1991, when he joined the Public Finance Ratings Group as a rating analyst. He received his Bachelors of Science degree in Accounting from the University of St. John's, New York, and Masters degrees in Finance and Economics at New York University, New York. He is also a Certified Public Accountant within the state of New York, and has worked as an auditor for a major public accounting firm, where he worked closely with financial institutions.

The New Assets Group of Standard & Poor's Structured Finance Ratings was formed in 1995 to meet the challenge of reviewing unique asset classes and evaluating the risks they present. The goal of the New Assets Group has been to set precedents and benchmarks in risk and credit analysis for the industry. Through these efforts, Standard & Poor's assists the investor community, issuers, and investment bankers with innovative structuring techniques by offering its guidance and expertise. New Assets Group analysts and Standard & Poor's legal department regularly publish articles to provide insight into Standard & Poor's criteria and rating process. By publishing criteria, Standard & Poor's hopes to expand the understanding and acceptance of these new asset types in the asset-backed securities market. Standard & Poor's, a division of The McGraw-Hill Companies (NYSE: MHP), provides independent financial information, analytical services, and credit ratings to the world's financial markets. Among the company's many products are the S&P Global 1200, the premier global equity performance benchmark, the S&P 500, the premier U.S. portfolio index, and credit ratings on more than 220,000 securities and funds worldwide. The company has more than 5,000 employees located in 21 countries.

CHAPTER TWENTY-THREE

The Relevance of IP Analysis in Technology-Driven M&A Transactions

By R. Russ O'Haver

PERSPECTIVES

Transactions involving company mergers and acquisitions (M&A) have grown in frequency and size. So have the volume and value of intellectual property rights associated with them. Transactions involving M&A grew approximately four-fold between 1992 and mid-1999. The size of deals and the amount and value of IP owned by purchasers and sellers have grown, as well. No longer is a cursory IP "audit" sufficient to reveal hidden value. "Companies that fail to secure a solid grasp of their IP assets and competitive position put themselves at a severe disadvantage," says R. Russ O'Haver, who advises companies on IP-related transactions.

Better analysis of IP attributes at key points during the M&A process should, says Mr. O'Haver, "enhance the likelihood of more successful technology-driven deals." He cites recently developed mapping, assessment, and valuation tools that can assist in the IP due diligence process: IBM's Delphion software, IP Capital, M-CAM, CHI Research's citation analysis, and The Patent & Licensing Exchange (in which Ernst & Young is an equity partner). These products are among the cutting-edge products designed to help assess and rank the quality of a company's patent portfolio. Using these tools effectively can be difficult. However, without them, as Mr. O'Haver illustrates in the following chapter, predicting the potential returns on M&A transactions would be an even more daunting task.

INTRODUCTION

Intangible (or intellectual) property is generating a high level of attention from a variety of perspectives, including increased opportunities for companies to extend and monetize their patents and brands, the need for greater innovation given shortening technology cycles, increased IP litigation, and significant growth in business process patents. IP is also front and center for another significant trend in the business world, M&A activity, both as a motivating force and as something to be proactively analyzed and managed to raise the likelihood of successful deals.

Understanding the relative importance of patents, trademarks, and other proprietary rights in driving, protecting, and monetizing a company's innovation has become an integral part of successful M&A strategies. Companies that fail to secure a solid grasp of their IP assets and competitive position put themselves at a severe disadvantage.

M&A TRENDS AND IMPLICATIONS

For U.S. public companies, data over the past year indicate that intangibles contribute on the order of 70 to 80 percent of market value (and even higher in many prominent cases) making it difficult to ignore IP as in M&A transactions.[1]

Exhibits 23-1 and 23-2 profile the trend activity (as reported by Mergerstat[2]) of the total numbers and deal values of M&A activity over the past 20 years.

Strong Growth

From the two exhibits, it is readily apparent that in recent years there was explosive growth in terms of the number and value of deals. Total transaction volume

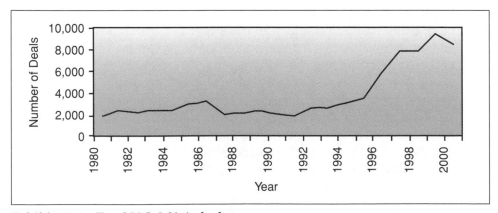

Exhibit 23-1   Total U.S. M&A deals.

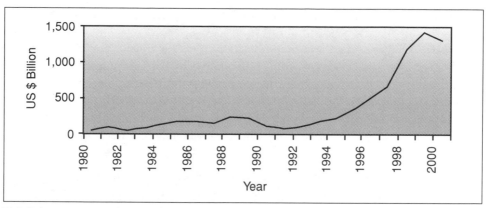

Exhibit 23-2 Total U.S. deal value.

continued at a significant pace over the past five years, while transaction values also continued to climb even more dramatically as stock market values rose. Different strategic drivers were behind these trends, including

- Industry roll-up and scale strategies
- Globalization
- The effects of favorable accounting treatment from pooling transactions on boosting returns on invested capital performance
- The need to accelerate innovation (in periods of dynamic technology change, interindustry technology transfer opportunities, and shortening technology cycles) and fill product gaps through technology-driven transactions

This chapter is particularly concerned with the last item above, or how IP tools and processes, particularly those germane to patents and technology, can be used throughout the M&A process to identify and facilitate successful deals. This is important as numerous studies find that a significant number of M&A transactions have not been successful in increasing shareholder value. In part, this is caused by a poor assessment of the synergistic fit of the parties, an incomplete assessment of the risks and opportunities associated with the intangible assets to be acquired, and/or failed postmerger integration. Better analysis, at various points during the M&A process, of the IP attributes should enhance the likelihood of more successful technology-driven deals.

Tech Focus

For the year 2000 (through early November), relative to overall industry M&A activity, technology-intensive industries were prominent. Of the top 15 industries (ranked by transaction value), almost half were technology-intensive industries (e.g., software, electronics, communications, aerospace, drugs, and medical equipment). The leisure and entertainment industry was the industry leader, an industry that is certainly intellectual property-intensive. With emerging digital technologies, this is an industry where technology and patents will play an increasingly important role. Indeed the Time Warner merger with AOL (with a total deal value exceeding $165 billion in market capitalization) was the largest and indicative of the vertical impact of "new economy" technology and channel opportunities.

CASE EXAMPLE 1

On one of the large transactions (a $17 billion transaction involving JDS Uniphase E-Tek Dynamics and SDL), Exhibit 23-3 provides an illustration of the degree of overlap in the relative patent portfolio of the merged entities. As one can see, there is a high degree of overlap for selected technology areas (as delineated by international patent code classifications), indicating potentially good technology synergy in the deal. More specifically, upon inspection of the underlying detail (using IP mapping tools known as Delphion and CoBrain[3]), E-Tek has a technology focus in light guides and other optical elements such as couplings, class "G02B" on the exhibit) while JDS and SDL have significant emphasis in laser technology (particularly patents on devices for generation amplification, modulation, class "H01S"). Hence, the complementary nature of these technology sets drive the fit of the portfolios. As discussed later, IP tools can be used to make these types of assessments, particularly in greater detail within each patent class.

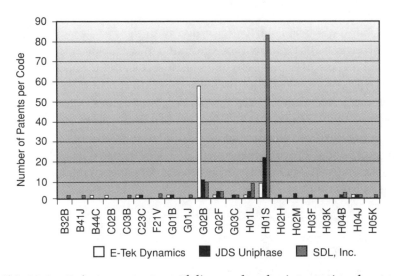

Exhibit 23-3   Relative patent portfolio overlap, by international patent code class.

Financial Services

The banking, finance, and brokerage industries were also prominent in the deal rankings. Traditionally, these industries have not been patent-intensive but are certainly industries with significant intangibles, which span brand, technical know-how and systems, relationship capital, networks, and other types. With the *State Street* legal case,[4] however, companies in these industries are increasingly looking to business process patent opportunities as a way to formally protect and profit from their technical and knowledge capital. This is occurring both in traditional banking spaces (e.g., asset management) as well as in new spaces pertinent to e-commerce applications. As patents provide a strong form of durable competitive advantage, this becomes increasingly relevant to strategic merger activity. Hence, the tools and processes relevant to patent analysis are becoming more relevant to a wider range of industries.

IDENTIFYING AND EXECUTING THE TRANSACTION

IP tools and processes have a great deal of relevance for the following areas of the M&A process:

- Identifying targets for technology-driven deals
- Due diligence on the quality/risk of the IP portfolio to be acquired
- Postmerger assessment as to the optimal use of all the newly acquired IP

The Front End: Lead Advisory and Identifying Targets

On technology-driven deals, the catalyst (as illustrated with the previous E-Tek example) is typically to fill a gap relative to the acquirer's own technology and/or brand portfolio relative to expectations of potential demand for certain parts of an existing or emerging product space.

Additional motivations include the desire to acquire greater R&D expertise (e.g., specifying deal value multiples per engineer is one way of looking at value), enlarge the patent arsenal to enhance the ability to cross-license and therefore enlarge a company's number of strategic options, and also to leverage significant brand intangibles across more product categories. There are two major IP analytical considerations here at the very front end. The first involves an identification of the strategic technology gaps in the acquirer's portfolio relative to expected demand. The second involves a strategic assessment of the relative advantages of acquisition versus in-licensing, self-funded R&D investment, alliance, or related strategy.

Gap Analysis

More in-depth evaluations involve the R&D specialists and strategists of the firm. In the R&D area, there should be an ongoing assessment process of so-called fuzzy front-end opportunities devoted to identifying emerging technologies and the strategic implications therein. In addition, marketing personnel should be involved in monitoring customer's needs and/or wants to keep R&D informed of the market forces. IP advisors and lawyers often work in this field using IP tools that help map out existing and emerging technology landscapes for particular product spaces. For example, IBM's Delphion software facilitates easy searches of any companies' patent filings in global jurisdictions. This is a well-used tool that has the obvious benefit of determining the breadth and legal status of the target's patent portfolio and how it might fit with that of the acquiring company.

The previous example of the E-Tek and JDS deal provided a high-level view of how the respective patents portfolio might fit. Other tools are being developed to extend the researcher's ability even further. For example, IP Capital,[5] NERAC,[6] M-CAM,[7] and other companies have and/or are working on software to link patents to products so that a more complete assessment can be made of which patents are in use commercially and in what products. CHI Research[8] provides tools that assess and rank the quality of a company's patent portfolio based upon each patent's frequency of citation by other companies and the extent of linkage to cutting-edge scientific research (helpful for assessing "fuzzy" front-end conditions). Another method to assess the product/technology gap issue is to use periodic focus groups, with specialized equity analysts, that may be of value relative to a high-level assessment depending on the industry (e.g., in biotech, the analyst community will be much more involved with the technology direction and competitive positioning of the incumbent companies). This will enable an "outside-in" perspective.

Some of these tools help determine and depict the existing patent landscape, which parts of the landscape are experiencing the most level of activity (in terms of actual patents and in some cases patent applications), and by which competitors. This, combined with an assessment of the breadth of the underlying claims (legal assistance is particularly valuable here) to relevant patents as well as the effect of protective walls built around core patents, helps frame the strategic strength of the target company's patent portfolio. Overlaying this on a global basis with other tools that identify research (and, to a limited extent, funding activity), and early-stage licensing activities and trends generates insights into prepatent areas of focused research. This can help identify areas of emerging innovation for a product space. Legal analysis of cross-licensing opportunities and constraints is also relevant at this juncture. Finally, overlaying this landscape further with an assessment of potential market demand (growth patterns, new competitive entry, profitability) can help narrow the list as to which open research areas are particularly attractive from both demand and potential return perspective. Financial modeling tools (using advances on traditional discounted cash flow techniques such as Monte Carlo and real option applications) are often used at this point to assess the value proposition. Similar processes and tools can be used for the brand asset side of IP.

Acquisition versus In-Licensing versus Other Alternatives

Relative to the choice of action (e.g., acquisition, in-licensing, or joint venture) for moving into an open technology space deemed desirable, there are a number of important strategic variables. These include:

- Identification of the potential players relative to each scenario, and the associated competitive position and bargaining strengths associated with each action
- Risk and investment preferences of the acquirer
- Size of the market opportunity and timing dimensions
- Extent of market change and uncertainty, among other variables

The business development function of most large companies will often lead this analysis with a formal set of financial modeling tools, which again may include a "real options" framework[9] for strategic decision making.

In this time of short technology cycles, globalization, and disruptive technologies, having a process in place can facilitate consistent, ongoing, and timely (quick response) evaluation of opportunities. This is important and a derivative feature of a good IP management program. Involvement in M&A activities is a good function for a centralized IP management group within a company: increasingly, companies such as Dow, DuPont, Xerox, Lucent, Ford, and others have such groups, often with a profit and loss focus. Intellectual property mapping tools assist these groups in monitoring the technology cycles in the following ways:

- Trending patent activity by technology space identifies the players and their relative strengths, as shown in the JDS/E-Tek case.
- Trending the acquirer's IP portfolio is a method to gauge its R&D investment preferences, which can be valuable in negotiating licenses or joint ventures.
- Trending the patent activity (issued and in some cases applications) is a good indicator of the technology life cycle as well as the innovation cycles.

Due Diligence/Strategic Valuation

Once a company identifies its targets, develops its strategic approach, and generates interest, the focus shifts to more formal valuation, due diligence, tax structuring, accounting, and related issues.

Valuation is obviously of significant importance, particularly in a technology-driven deal. Existing approaches include the "relief from royalty" method, which involves looking at comparable licensing deals for particular technologies and applying the associated royalty rate to the expected sales stream related to the technology being valued and then discounting back (risk adjusted) to a lump-sum value. Various forms of discounted cash flow analysis (projecting the anticipated cash flow stream—again with Monte Carlo or real option enhancements to adjust for uncertainty and the notion of embedded options relative to the deployment of the technology in the future—and discounting back to a lump-sum value) are also used for valuation purposes. "Cost to recreate" can also be used as a floor valuation level in certain situations. Trademark and brand valuations employ similar approaches with enhancements for relative brand strength and other attributes.

New valuation applications include both real options and enhancing the relief from royalty method combined with patent mapping features. A real option is a technique that treats technology, particularly partially developed technologies, as a call option. Analogous to a financial call option, partially developed technology has an underlying derivative asset (instead of stock shares, the asset is the revenue stream expected to accrue to the technology), from which volatility can be measured with comparables and/or simulated and a strike price (or the remaining investment needed to commercialize the technology). Using a financial option pricing methodology (e.g., Black-Scholes formula), the option premium or value of the technology in the current state can be estimated. Innovations have made the use of the "real options" approach much more practical. The Patent License Exchange (Pl-x) has been particularly successful in gaining attention for its TRUU metrics method[10] of using real-option methodology to value technologies in development. When combined with traditional valuation methods, more robust technology valuation results can be generated.

New (as yet unpublished) research by Professor F.M. Scherer of Harvard University depicts how patent-mapping analysis, which includes an identification of the number of times a patent is cited (known as both backward and forward citations), as well as the number of countries where the patent is legally protected, can provide indications of value. Other researchers are exploring how patent mapping techniques can determine the relative strategic strength of a patent as an additional variable to use with the more traditional relief-from-royalty approaches.

For the due diligence process, these valuation tools not only help with formal valuations but can be important in helping to screen a target's patent portfolio to make a top-level assessment of which patents may be of value. This process is often combined with a factual assessment of the patent portfolio (e.g., the relative age of the patents is important to being able to reap future value) and the level of invention activity. Patent-mapping techniques enable one to determine the breadth, in terms of numbers of key R&D personnel, of invention activity, which has implications for future patent generation and hence value. Relative to the key inventors, determining the extent of such innovation activity within the target company and whether such resources are in some way "locked in" to continued innovation is important.

Analysis of the patent portfolio, and benchmarking against comparable or competitive companies, will also provide:

- Information on the rate of innovation of the target company
- The remaining useful lives on the core patents, ownership issues, and/ or constraints associated with the patent estate (e.g., previous joint venture restrictions)
- The degree to which the target's patent estate overlaps and/or complements that of the acquirer

Patent mapping and other research tools will shed light on both companies' patent quality (e.g., extent of citations by competitors, degree of scientific linkages) and the extent to which changes in technology cycles may impact the value of core patents going forward. Legal analysis is also highly relevant. A review of valuable unpatented technologies is also important.

A particularly important source of value that may be overlooked in the deal is the opportunity to monetize the noncore patents that may belong to the acquired company (discussed in more detail in the following section of this chapter).

Finally, tax planning strategies and opportunities relative to intangibles should be evaluated at some level relative to additional opportunities to boost the return from the potential deal.

Postmerger Integration

Once the deal is consummated, the next crucial step is successful and expedient integration of the newly acquired assets. This step, often referred to as postmerger integration, is a critical success factor for any merger or acquisition, and particularly relevant for technology and brand deals. Many companies have the right M&A strategy, but fail to successfully evaluate and integrate the new assets.

For technology-driven deals, from a buy-side perspective, there is first a need to identify all the relevant patented and unpatented technologies that have been acquired and then to pool or map the assets according to the acquirer's existing classifications. In general, this will be most easily accomplished for patents, as companies will have formally organized their patent portfolio to monitor the registration process and maintenance fees. Companies that have good IP management programs will also have not just a listing of patents (inclusive of such information as remaining patent life and geographical registration), but also a taxonomy of how the patents are grouped by technology and/or product area (ideally including identification of which patents are actually used in current or planned products/ services). Further, such companies may also overlay or include unpatented technologies, significant trade secrets or know-how, and possibly emerging areas of R&D focus.

This process of identification, filtering, assessment, and categorization helps separate the "wheat from the chaff" in the sense of identifying the strategically relevant or core IP from the noncore assets acquired in the transaction. The core assets are then to be deployed and harmonized relative to the strategy identified as part of the "front end" effort or part of the deal. Where value is often lost or overlooked is in evaluating and executing effective monetization efforts for the noncore patents and unpatented technologies.

CASE EXAMPLE 2

As an example, an American Stock Exchange company was acquired by a company in an unrelated industry. The acquirer wanted to determine if there was any way to leverage the value of the patent acquired in the transaction either by seeking licensing partners, looking for potential infringing opportunities, or donating patents. Using extensive patent mapping, coupled with market and technical research on each patent cluster, helped identify the relevance of each patent cluster to current technology cycles to help determine market interest in these bundles. The patent mapping, coupled with an in-depth claims analysis (to identify how the claim set of a particular patent may overlap with other patents and/or unpatented technologies in the market), identified other companies where there may be interest and licensing opportunities for the subject patents. For patents that were not sufficiently developed to warrant licensing interest, research tools were used to identify universities having active research platforms relevant to the subject patents (valuation analysis was then used to identify the potential benefit from donation). The result of the analysis was definitive recommendations as to which patents should be pursued for licensing opportunities with a smaller subset of the subject patents directed toward patent donation.

It was also found that a portion of the patents had been overlooked in terms of technology cycles and were found to have little or no value. Hence, abandonment (to save ongoing registration costs) was the recommendation. The specific tool used in this case was patent-mapping software developed by a company known as M-CAM. This software analyzes not only direct citation linkages (the citations of prior art or preexisting patents in the same space), but also the indirect. The indirect linkages citations are also known as "cousins," using a family tree analogy as to how patents evolve over time in a particular space. In this case, the M-CAM software identified companies that had indirect citations to the acquired patents. These companies also had an extensive history of infringement litigation which may have raised the cost of the acquired company in seeking new licenses on these technologies and consequently, as a result of a cost/benefit analysis, shifted the recommendation for specific patents from licensing to donation.

A general depiction of the process noting that the use of tools such as patent mapping are embedded in such processes of identifying and assessing the core versus noncore nature of the technologies (a similar process exists for brand intangibles) as well as evaluating monetization alternatives is shown in Exhibit 23-4. The alternatives include:

- *Licensing.* Evaluating opportunities for technologies to be outlicensed to others either in the same industry or increasingly, with the availability of new IP marketplaces (e.g., the Patent License Exchange), licensing plays in other industries where different applications may exist for the technology. IP advisors also undertake an active role by identifying, in a proactive manner, such licensing opportunities and/or quantifying the potential licensing benefits (through the use of large databases that track licensing deals and the returns generated). Various analytical tools, such as patent mapping (a representative site is *www.m-cam.com*), can facilitate identifying such opportunities. Also, various tools can be used to evaluate whether there may be potential situations where other companies may be (advertently or inadvertently) infringing on one or more of the newly acquired patents. These situations can lead to royalty opportunities from so-called stick licenses. The potential cash flow opportunities should not be underestimated. Patent licensing revenues in the United States were reported to have totaled more that $100 billion.[11] There are a number of high-profile public examples of what companies have done in this regard, led by IBM with patent-related royalties on the order of $1.6 billion a year.

- *Spin-outs.* It may be more appropriate to bundle some of the noncore technologies into a spin-out vehicle. This happens when such bundles may have particular value, but may not be suitably aligned with the strategic direction of acquiring company. Technology venture funds (e.g., the

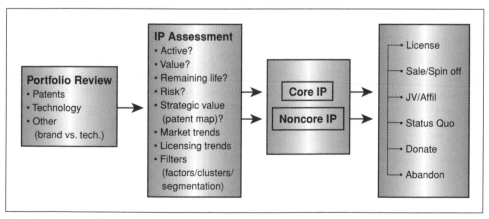

Exhibit 23-4 IP monetization focus: "decision tree" analysis.

technology group at Spencer Trask led by one of the former leaders of IBM's highly successful IP management team) are particularly active in this area. Another example was the 3Com spin-out of Palm, Inc.

- *Patent Donations.* The tax laws allow charitable contributions of technologies to qualified institutions (typically research universities) whereby the donating company is able to generate a benefit of the fair market value of the technology multiplied by their effective tax rate. There have been a number of large company examples of these transactions over the past two years. Such activity requires tax, valuation, and technical analysis to identify candidates within the relevant technology research field as well as to identify appropriate universities where relevant research fields exist. Again, notable public examples exist including Eaton Corporation[12] and DuPont[13] as companies that donated patent bundles valued at $17 million (57 patents) and $64 million, respectively.

- *Other alternatives* include tax free swaps, joint ventures/alliances with other companies, a "hold" strategy (effectively treating the noncore technology as a call option relative to potential market changes in the future), and abandonment (again, some of the patents may be of no, or low, current or future value; removing these patents from the portfolio may be cost-effective given the registration expense of maintaining patents).

These processes represent a brief overview of the focus of leading companies in the IP management field relative to the full evaluation of newly acquired patents. The potential returns generated from the noncore patents can represent hidden or overlooked value relative to the overall return on the deal.

Accounting and tax considerations are also important in all three of the above phases as intangibles represent one of the most significant levers for state and international tax planning for U.S. corporations.

In the reporting arena, current deliberations by the Financial Accounting Standards Board (FASB) will likely lead to changes in how companies account for mergers (relative to purchase versus pooling methods and goodwill treatment), which could have implications for intangibles' valuation and related amortization costs that could impact financial earnings. In the competition policy area, there are an estimated 80 antitrust regimes globally, which can review potential mergers for undue concentrations of market power. As patents are one of the few forms of sustainable market power, reviews of patent strength from a merger becomes very important in these deliberations.

CONCLUSION

While it is readily acknowledged by most M&A practitioners that IP is very important in M&A transactions, frequently the IP-related front-end due diligence and postmerger integration processes (specific to IP in technology-driven deals) may be conducted only at a high level, which could result in lost financial and strategic opportunities. By increasing (either through more in-depth training in these tools by participants frequently involved in M&A transactions within a company and/or through the use of outside service providers) the skilled use of new IP tools such as the mapping, assessment, and valuation tools described from M-CAM, IP Capital, CHI Research, The Patent & License Exchange, and other companies, as well as related processes, potential returns can be enhanced and risks reduced.

NOTES

1. D. Steinberg, "Money from Nothing," *Smart Business*, April 2001.
2. 2000 Mergerstat (*www.mergerstat.com*).
3. *www.Delphion.com, www.cobrain.com.*
4. *State Street Bank & Trust Co. v. Signature Financial Group, 149F, 3d1368* (Federal Circuit 1998).
5. *www.IPcapital.com.*
6. *www.nerac.com.*
7. *www.m-cam.com.*
8. *www.CHI.com.*
9. M. Amram, and N. Kulatilaka, *Real Options: Managing Strategic Investment in an Uncertain World* (Boston: Harvard Business School Press, 1999).
10. *www.pl-x.com.*
11. J. Wild, "Riding the Intellectual Property Boom," *The Times* (London), September 9, 1999, p. 33.
12. "Eaton Sends Wealth Out of State," *Crains Cleveland Business*, May 3, 1999.
13. "DuPont Donates $64 Million in Intellectual Property to Three Universities," API EnCompass News, February 8, 1999

ABOUT THE AUTHOR

R. Russ O'Haver leads the Intangible Property Practice in Corporate Finance at Ernst & Young (New York). He is responsible for the content development and execution of IP services relating to client shareholder value strategies, IP creation and development (R&D tools), IP protection services, IP commercialization analysis (out-licensing and other processes for underutilized technology), and IP management and measurement issues. In over 14 years with Ernst & Young, Mr. O'Haver has been involved in more than 150 projects involving IP identification, valuation, strategy, transfer pricing, and/or litigation or other controversy defense. He is skilled in advanced quantitative techniques and has delivered more than 30 speeches and published over a dozen articles on these topics. He has a PhD in Economics.

CHAPTER TWENTY-FOUR

Patents on Wall Street
Investment Banking Meets Intellectual Property

by Christopher R. Fine and Donald C. Palmer

PERSPECTIVES

Wall Street may finally be getting with the program. According to Christopher Fine and Donald Palmer, investment bankers with Goldman, Sachs & Co. who look at IP from a finance perspective in the following chapter, Wall Street is becoming more aggressive about understanding and deploying patents and other IP assets. Bankers, unlike other IP investors, focus on value, provide advice, and rely on their experience and contacts to facilitate transactions. Their awareness and perspective of IP may differ from those of equity analysts, investors, and other financial professionals. "The history of finance," say Mr. Fine and Mr. Palmer, "while riddled with boom and bust cycles of speculation and its aftermath, shows one consistency: assets or strategies that can have value eventually are valued . . . [The mystery is] why hasn't there been consistent thinking about IP asset value?"

IP has become more recognized as a strategic asset class. Investment advisors have been forced to pay greater attention, not only from the standpoint of liability and exposure, but as an opportunity to uncover value, enhance the banking franchise, and, ultimately, provide the best service to clients through innovative transactions and reliable advice. In this chapter, the authors look at four transaction elements that affect IP: strategic advice, negotiation, due diligence, and valuation.

The ideas and opinions expressed in "Patents on Wall Street: Investment Banking Meets Intellectual Property" are those of the authors and do not necessarily reflect those of Goldman, Sachs & Co. or any other party.

"It is no longer acceptable for the banker to remain at arm's length, trusting IP attorneys, accountants, and other experts to catalog IP assets and identify encumbrances or other limitations of the assets," say the Goldman Sachs technology advisors. "The banker must take a proactive role to identify and evaluate the IP assets . . . The IP assessment phase is often a fascinating window into the seller's corporate character and culture. The results of the assessment can speak volumes about the seller's care, honesty, and diligence in the conduct of their business. An incomplete or ill-maintained IP asset portfolio can point to trouble elsewhere in the company—perhaps weak financial management or lack of strategic leadership. This type of information can be very useful to the buyer's decision-making and valuation process."

Wall Street itself is showing signs of "waking up" to the value of IP within its own walls. A number of major banks have set up internal groups or IP departments to identify and secure their own patent-worthy IP. In addition to Goldman, players include Citigroup (with the most patents issued to date), Morgan Stanley, JPMorgan Chase, and Merrill Lynch. However, not every invention or process that Wall Street recognizes as valuable IP will be patented. The last thing an investment bank wants is public disclosure through an issued patent (or filed patent within 18 months) of a lucrative financial technique or product. Financial institutions are no doubt relying upon a combination of trade secrets, patents, copyrights, licenses, and perhaps even trademarks, to protect and monetize their own IP assets. Like many of their clients, they are fast becoming acquainted with the need to accurately identify and nurture IP.

Fine and Palmer's work provides insight into some of the ways in which IP awareness can enhance the role of the investment banker and increase his or her value-added. They believe that bankers "can and must become more conversant with the world of IP, as IP becomes more and more important to their clients."

INTRODUCTION

As in many areas of human endeavor, the world of intellectual property is filled with aggressiveness, innovative thinking, and success, counterbalanced by complacency and neglect. The exact composition of this mixture tends to vary with time, industry, and perspective. In recent years, many enterprises and individual inventors have become more proactive with respect to patents and other IP, but what about the financial community, AKA "Wall Street"?

Some experts in the area of IP believe, and quote, the maxim that "there are no patents on Wall Street,"[1] arguing that the financial community clearly falls upon the "complacency and neglect" side of the balance. Wall Street's tendency to ignore patents and other IP assets is discussed in detail by Kevin Rivette and others in two well-known books about IP, *Hidden Value: Profiting from the Intellectual Property Economy*[2] and *Rembrandts in the Attic*,[3] both of which present well-argued cases documenting both the importance of IP to corporate finance and strategy and the tendency of analysts and investors to overlook or discount the value and importance of IP.

This chapter discusses the importance of IP from the perspective of the investment banking profession. The state of investment bankers' awareness of IP may be dissimilar to the perspectives and levels of sophistication shown by equity analysts, investors, and other financial professionals. In fact, we believe it is quite important to differentiate these various constituencies within the overall Wall Street financial industry.

A CEO, CFO, or other manager who works with investment bankers may find this chapter useful as a shopping list. If your company values its IP and considers IP to be an important part of corporate strategy, then it pays to be sure that your investment bankers are aware of, focused on, and familiar with IP issues as well.

Investment bankers are advisors to corporations, assisting in the strategies and processes related to capital raising, capital structuring, and mergers and acquisitions (M&A). Investment bankers are paid advisory fees, typically calculated as a percentage of the value of a transaction.

In certain instances, rather than serving as advisors in situations already resolved or in progress, investment bankers are a driving force behind the creation of new industries and corporate entities. For example, in the 1980s, investment bankers helped to create the high yield bond market and, using the proceeds from bond financings, sparked a takeover boom. "Junk" bonds and other financial innovations enhanced the tremendous growth of such industries as gaming, media, and transportation. Investment bankers also participated in the invention of mortgage-backed securities, which led to a revolution in the housing loan industry and to a shift of power in the commercial banking industry. In earlier times, investment bankers helped to build the railroad, steel, and auto industries through innovative financing activity and consolidation of companies.

Some investment bankers are becoming increasingly focused on IP as a key element of both financing and M&A transactions. In our view, as IP becomes a more strategically important and widely recognized asset class, investment bankers *must* pay attention, not only from a liability and exposure standpoint, but also as an opportunity to uncover value, to enhance the banking franchise, and, ultimately, to provide the best service to clients through innovative transactions and accurate advice.

This chapter explores IP as it relates to several aspects of an investment banker's role. We define these components as follows:

- *Strategic advice.* The investment banker participates in ongoing dialogues with corporate managers and investors about corporate strategy, M&A

opportunities, and financing options. Bankers also consult with governments on their financial strategies.

- *Negotiation.* The investment banker represents a corporate client during the process of reaching an agreement with a potential partner (in most cases, another company, which will be the buyer or the seller in an M&A transaction).

- *Due diligence.* The investment banker and a team of experts attempt to verify the true state of a company's assets, operations, and other claims, as part of a financing or M&A transaction process. Due diligence includes the effort to uncover hidden value as well as hidden concerns in the overall picture of a company, its industry, its suppliers, its customers, its partners, and its competitors.

- *Valuation.* In the context of an M&A or financing transaction, the investment banker provides an opinion and analysis of the value of a corporation's assets and/or operations.

- The only key role of an investment banker we have chosen not to examine here is *deal structuring.* Deal structuring has previously been covered by other sources in detail. Examples of IP-related structures include:
  - Royalty-backed securitizations such as the recently issued Bowie Bonds[4]
  - Patent-backed securitizations such as the BioPharma Royalty Trust[5]
  - A company's sale of solely its IP assets while in bankruptcy, as in the case of boo.com's IP asset sale to Bright Station PLC[6]
  - A company's termination of product R&D and agreement to transfer this R&D over to a competitor, as in the case of IBM's "switches and routers" deal with Cisco[7]

We believe IP can and should play an important role in all these functions, and will discuss ways to maximize IP value in each of them.

WHY SOME BANKERS UNDERVALUE IP

In conversations with junior and senior investment bankers, we found a wide range of attitudes with respect to IP. Comments ranged from "any patent can be circumvented" to "[IP] has crossed over [from legal due diligence] into the realm of business due diligence." The latter comment is a powerful statement; *business due diligence* is the verification and evaluation of vital and strategic aspects of the business, while legal due diligence is more of a "checkbox item," partially entrusted to attorneys, with banker oversight. One senior banker went on to state specifically that "IP has moved beyond a checkbox item and into the mainstream."

There was also a wide range of views in between these two extremes, which we believe are correlated to each particular banker's experience in transactions specifically involving IP. Comments generally supported the notion that IP awareness is not normally part of an investment banker's training, but is instead gained through experience. In some cases, a banker may have been trained in IP issues as part of his or her background prior to entering the banking profession. However, in the normal course of a business school education, and via experience accumulated as a junior banker (the most important two elements of banker training), IP awareness and knowledge are gained purely "as encountered" per the situation.

Once a banker has been involved in an IP-related transaction, he or she tends to realize the importance of IP—often to his or her surprise! From then on, IP awareness becomes an ongoing part of his or her value as a banker. We believe the general level of IP awareness and knowledge will increase as the issue is encountered during increased exposure to "live" situations. This level of awareness could and should be accelerated by more specific focus on IP during banker training.

The range of responses, on one level at least, is puzzling. Why wouldn't all investment bankers be cognizant of the importance and strategic value of IP? Certainly, IP continues to play a prominent role in the media. For example, a Dow Jones News search on "patent" or "intellectual property" yields 27,612 stories.[8] The battle over Napster and its treatment of copyrighted material garnered numerous headlines since Napster's debut in 1999, with high-profile international law enforcement programs and treaty negotiations attempting to reduce the impact of audio and video piracy. What, then, has driven the average banker's thinking—or lack thereof—with regard to IP?

Some of the thinking reflects certain enduring characteristics of the financial community, including conservatism and the tendency to stick with conventional thinking until disruptive innovation creates a new standard. The history of finance, while riddled with boom and bust cycles of speculation and their aftermaths, clearly illustrates one consistency: assets or strategies that can have value eventually are valued.[9] Why hasn't there been consistent thinking about IP asset value? The answer to this question has a long history.

After several decades of intense patent and other IP activity beginning in the nineteenth century, the 1930s saw the beginning of a decline in the focus on IP. Antitrust policy and popular sentiment at the time caused government to take the view that patents were anticompetitive. Even after the federal antitrust policy became more liberal, the "eclipse" persisted, due perhaps to an inherent mistrust of government and legal mechanisms by the opinion-makers of Silicon Valley and elsewhere during the 1960s and 1970s. Another factor may have been the relatively low visibility and commercialization rate of patents, many of which originated in pure R&D labs and were often funded by the government.

IP has only started moving back onto the CEO's agenda. According to the authors of *Rembrandts in the Attic*:

> Until very recently, in fact, few CEOs ever used the words *patents* and *strategy* in the same sentence. Patents were seen merely as legal instruments, to be filed away in the corporate counsel's office and forgotten.

Strategy, on the other hand, was that opaque and slippery stuff that the people in the executive suite were supposed to hammer into shape. What did one have to do with the other?[10]

Bankers, as advisors, tend to follow their clients' lead in terms of priorities, so did not focus on IP.

Prior to the patent court reform legislation of the 1980s, and before the debut of softwarespecific and business process patents, it was costly and difficult to win a patent infringement lawsuit—if indeed the product or method could be patented in the first place. There were no such things as business process patents. To cite a well-known case, Microsoft came to dominate the world of PC software with a graphical user interface—Windows—derived partly from the work of Xerox PARC, as appropriated and enhanced by Apple Computer.[11] There was a view at the time that Microsoft came to its power through business acumen, aggressiveness, and clever marketing, not by erecting a wall of patent protection. In recent years, Microsoft seems to have reversed its point of view on intellectual property. Bill Gates and his team are now looking to build "one of the all-time great research organizations—an R&D dynasty that people will mention in the same breath with such legendary empires as Bell Laboratories, IBM's Thomas J. Watson Laboratory, and Xerox's Palo Alto Research Center (PARC)."[12] It may also be that several near misses with potential claims for patent infringement have helped to wake up Microsoft. Microsoft is emblematic of many companies that have increased their focus on IP. Where the corporate clients go, bankers will inevitably follow.

Bankers sometimes view a patent as a "negative right," as opposed to an intangible asset. Bankers distinguish a "right," or the ability to gain or protect access to an asset, from an actual asset. The legal term "negative right" means that a patent does not grant rights to its owner, but, instead excludes others from the right to create or reproduce a certain product or process for a period of time. Bankers recognize and understand monetary value, whether it is in the form of explicit cash flow, the market value of an asset, or an option on an asset (i.e., a "positive right" to the asset). In cases where patents explicitly generate royalties—such as when licensing arrangements are in place—bankers are in familiar territory. It is a relatively straightforward exercise to value and model these cash flows. Patents and other IP, however, often fall into the broad category of intangible assets, which are usually treated as a whole rather than individually. These assets are often unmonetized and their future value is uncertain. In some cases, a negative right has option value, but only recently have techniques been developed to value these options in a consistent manner.[13]

Patent grants and litigation are slow processes, but the technology industry runs at "Internet speed." Bankers and technology executives have tended to believe that the speed of innovation in the technology industry is too rapid to rely upon patents and other IP protection. By the time a patent is granted, so the thinking goes, the battle is long over, with a given company having either won or lost the market opportunity. This point of view was widely held during the Internet boom.

Some highly-publicized IP value-extraction efforts have had mixed results. While there are some notable success stories of when IP assets have translated directly to revenue—IBM and Qualcomm come to mind—there have been far more examples, particularly in recent decades, of companies failing to capitalize on IP. Bankers are inherently skeptical people. For a banker, an unmonetized asset has little positive presence; it is a legal construct rather than something that can be added to the balance sheet. Similarly, patent royalty revenue that is not explicitly separated from other revenue may become lost in the noise unless the amount is large compared with other sources of revenue. Recent, precipitous declines in the values of companies like Xerox, Dell Computer, and Priceline, all of which had much-touted IP assets,[14] have not diminished banker skepticism.

There have been many instances of company-sponsored innovation, often protected by patents, which ultimately ended up benefiting other companies that built upon the basic patents and filed subsequent patents to cover all the relevant aspects of production and manufacturing necessary to commercialize the product. Examples include color television, VCR technology, dot matrix printing, laser printing, and linear stepper motors. In some cases, the patents were licensed or sold from the United States or Europe to Asian companies at reduced rates when businesses exited a particular product area. The investment banker always tries to determine whether the inventing company will ultimately be the beneficiary of patents and other IP. How can the banker tell whether the body of patents held by the original inventor is sufficient to enable and protect commercialization? And does the inventor even know how to commercialize the patents? Whom should the banker or investor bet on?

These are not trivial issues. There are elements of truths in, and historical support for, each argument. Nevertheless, we believe that the investment banker who clings to these shibboleths for comfort will suffer from missed opportunities and will be subsumed by more IP-savvy competitors, as IP assumes an increasingly meaningful role as a strategic asset.

THE REEMERGING POWER OF IP AS A CORPORATE ASSET AND STRATEGIC WEAPON

We believe that several forces are dramatically adding to the importance of IP, not only as a strategic asset but also as a weapon for successful competition. Market dynamics, competition, and the pace of innovation are the primary driving forces.

In traditional, mature industries, bankers could evaluate the worth and prospects of companies by looking at indicators of growth and success such as customers, tangible assets, market share, revenues, and profits. For example, underwriters would rarely take an unprofitable company public in a traditional industry—the normal requirement would be 9 to 12 months of ongoing profitability prior to IPO. However, during the Internet bubble these metrics were often discarded as "old fashioned" in the case of start-up technology companies. The results have shown that this was a highly risky approach—some companies have succeeded, but many have failed.

Although there has been a significant move away from the "Internet-speed" approach to company-building and management since the first half of 2000, the fact remains that companies, particularly technology companies, must be prepared to innovate and grow at an accelerated pace. Technology breakthroughs are constantly occurring, and, as a result, company life cycles are shortened. We may have moved away from the age of what *Wired* Magazine called "disposable companies"—companies as experiments, subject to failure, but designed to quickly cash out through IPO or merger—but as the pace of venture funding resumes, the pendulum may well swing back.[15] It is an enduring truth that a smaller company must be more nimble than a bigger company in order to survive. The big company has more resources (generally speaking), better sales channels, more brand recognition, and many other advantages. The new competitor's chief advantage is superior intellectual property. In the world of technology, IP really does matter.

One way of looking at an IP-centric approach is to consider that mature-company measurements such as customers, profits, and so on, are the outputs of a company's operations, whose inputs are IP, capital, raw materials, and successful management. The outputs take some time to generate after the company's inception; in their absence, one must look at the inputs in order to assess value. Traditionally, investment bankers did not enter the picture during the inputs-only phase of company growth; that was the province of venture capitalists, angel investors, and other early-stage investment professionals. However, the successful banker today focuses on earlier-stage companies for several reasons, including the need to build and maintain a strong relationship with a potential client, the opportunity to evaluate the quality and potential of the company, the ancillary opportunity to gain increased industry knowledge from the relationship, and the need to stave off banking competition if the company is a strong candidate for IPO or other transactions.

Even during the negative aftermath of a boom, or during the technology industry's normal pattern of growth, IP-specific M&A can take place. Exuberant acquisitions, such as Lucent's June 2000 acquisition of Chromatis Networks for $4.6 billion, may not happen again for some time,[16] but IP-centric acquisitions such as Texas Instrument's acquisition of Amati may continue, particularly given the lower prices at which such deals may be done.[17] (In the case of Amati, TI actually discontinued the company's operations, but the Amati IP enabled TI to dominate the market for certain types of DSL-related integrated circuits.) It is our view that, going forward, IP-centric M&A will continue at a healthy pace. Given rational pricing, the approach remains a powerful way for buyers to acquire rights and assets that can pay off handsomely over a long period of time.

If companies move quickly, what are the earliest assets to materialize—the earliest components of value? The answer is obvious: people, processes, accumulated expertise, and patent filings—IP! These examples, and many others, also illustrate the growing trend toward IP-centric acquisitions. Even with the return of more traditional measures of value, the banker who most accurately assesses company value early on stands the best chance of winning as the situation plays out. The banker may also realize that a key component of acquisition rationale is the reduced time to market obtained via the purchase of outsourced R&D.

Another important force is competition. Business is no longer a gentleman's game, if indeed it ever was. Today, a company must successfully use offensive and defensive strategies and tactics when competing; IP can play a decisive role in both areas. The traditional use of competitive IP is to obtain patents that protect market position and restrict potential competitors. From pharmaceutical companies to technology to manufacturers of packaged consumer goods, this method is commonly used. Today, a company looks to protect as much as it can with patents and other IP. The company that does not aggressively protect itself is left vulnerable to its competition, which is often more mature, better funded, and equipped with a more experienced legal staff.

General Electric is an example of a company that has often demonstrated its willingness to pursue an aggressive patent strategy. In a recent case, GE was involved in a patent battle lasting over three years as a result of litigation brought by Whirlpool and Inglis.[18] Despite losing in multiple rulings, GE persisted. The case went all the way through Canadian courts to the Supreme Court of Canada, only to have the Court reaffirm lower court rulings against GE. A process such as this can be a very long and difficult one for companies with limited funding or that are involved in extremely high-paced industries and cannot afford to be distracted by protracted court battles. Although GE ultimately lost in this instance, the company has shown time and again that it is willing to fight an expensive and lengthy battle to enforce or defend its IP.

Another example of IP's use as a competitive weapon is the use of litigation to create costs for and, ideally, to restrict another business that has already entered the market as a competitor. Some might contend that an example of this type of patent strategy was GE's lawsuit against Nintendo in 1995. Ultimately, GE's suit was dismissed by the Federal Court of Appeals in June of 1999. GE had sued Nintendo for $50 million, claiming the company had violated patents that GE had acquired from RCA in the early 1980s for television circuitry.[19] A more recent example of this approach involves Proxim, which launched two suits in March 2001, in which it accused over 10 companies of infringing on its intellectual property patents in wireless networking.[20] One defendant describes the claims as "without merit."[21]

Finally, there is the fundamental force of innovation. From new business methods, such as Priceline's "name your own price," to breakthroughs in optics, to new digital signal processing (DSP) algorithms, to the constant progress in networked storage, data switching, and other infrastructure technologies—not to mention genetic engineering and other areas of biotechnology that promise to revolutionize our basic understanding of the life process—the fruits of research are bursting forth. History has shown that such cyclical conditions lead to a greatly intensified focus on IP. Examples include the late nineteenth century of Thomas Edison and Alexander Graham Bell, the period after World War II, and the 1960s. By properly recognizing and capitalizing upon IP-related opportunities, bankers can help to generate great wealth for their clients. For example, in the early twentieth century, David Sarnoff and his bankers worked together to create and build RCA, the Radio Corporation of America. RCA was a great stock market success for an extended period of time, due in large part to its ownership of fundamental patents in all areas of radio, electronics, television, and sound recording. RCA's stable of inventors included Edwin Armstrong, the creator of FM[22]; Vladimir Zworykin, developer of one of the first commercial TV camera tubes; and the team that invented the color TV standard eventually adopted in the United States. The company went on to further success in areas such as defense electronics, satellite technology, and semiconductors.

Though damaged by the crash of 1929, RCA enjoyed many decades of success before its sale to GE in 1986 for $6.4 billion, the largest nonoil merger up until that time.[23] General Electric today, of course, is stronger and bigger than ever before, and continues to hold sway over an impressive arsenal of patents and other IP in many areas, including IP purchased from RCA. GE has licensed and sold RCA-related IP to other companies, including Thomson and Bertelsmann.

We believe that the forces described above will persist, despite some adjustment in the wake of the recent technology stock decline. Why? First, these forces are not new, but, as described above, have been dormant for the last few business cycles—the same forces have surfaced many times in history during periods of innovation and rapid growth. Second, there is an increasing amount of sophistication in the techniques used to harness these forces, and successful exploitation of basic forces is a powerful way to add value in any situation.

It is arguable that, without the contribution of bankers and other financial professionals, IP by itself may have limited value in the marketplace. Successful and ambitious innovators realize this truth and capitalize on it. Many more inventors do not realize the limited value of IP without capital, and end up with nothing.

The most successful examples of corporate IP strategy blend IP into the operating business model from the beginning, rather than attempt to trap it in the lab. The ideal mixture of ingredients for creating an explosion of value and a dominant, lasting franchise is the combination of innovative scientific and engineering talent, savvy management, and proper financial and strategic advice, all successfully acted upon.

IP AND THE ROLE OF THE STRATEGIC ADVISOR

It is vital for an investment banker to have an ongoing strategic dialogue with his or her clients. In the best banker-client relationships, there is powerful synergy. The banker maintains a wide range of contacts within the industry and in financial markets, constantly develops his or her expertise in the industry or with products in which he or she specializes, and is thoroughly familiar with the management, structure, history, and financial requirements of the client's organization. The client brings new opportunities, to which the banker may add value. As the company grows, the banker assists with both financing and M&A, and often brings ideas and opportunities to the client, including information about companies which may be targets for the client to acquire and analyses of the ways in which the client can raise capital.

This section describes how IP can play a role in the banker's strategic advice. The list of situations described here is by no means complete; the intent is to convey how important IP can be in a wide range of circumstances.

Companies today often perform IP audits that may reveal patents for which royalties can be charged or for which infringement may be claimed. Assuming that the company is successful in its efforts to extract and enforce royalty payments from others, a stream of cash begins to flow into the company's coffers. What is the best use of this cash flow? An investment banker may advise on options such as securitization, in which the future cash flows are converted into current cash assets. The banker may also advise the client to use either the securitization proceeds or cash flows, without securitization, to acquire companies or assets. An alternative option is the creation of a licensing structure that is tax-advantaged in some way. The proceeds could then be used to pay down debt or for other corporate finance purposes.

In another instance, a company may be considering a move into new areas of technology that require the purchase and/or creation of intellectual property. The investment banker can help to identify external sources of the required intellectual property and the conditions under which the IP might become available. For example, the banker may know of another company with patents in a particular area available for sale or licensing. The banker can also help craft the rationale for expansion into the new area and can execute the transaction on the client's behalf.

As another example, imagine an investment banking team working to convince a reluctant management team to make an acquisition based on the fact that the target holds important IP related to integrated circuits. The management's reluctance to acquire the target might be based on the desire to avoid buying the capital assets involved with physical fabrication of intellectual capital, but the bankers' point of view might be that such capital assets could be avoided through the purchase of a Silicon Intellectual Property (SIP) or "fabless"[24] company. The banking team might make a presentation to the company's Board of Directors, advising on the purchase or licensing of external IP and surveying the industry landscape.

In some cases, the key patents or other IP in an M&A situation might be totally outside the familiar industry players, or might be held by a diversified industrial company. The latter case has often occurred in technology acquisitions when patents are held by defense and aerospace companies. The banker can help identify these embedded IP assets based on knowledge of a broad range of companies.

By leveraging his or her contacts within other companies, the banker can advise a client on the true nature of the assets of a potential seller. This assessment can have a direct effect on price negotiations and can yield higher returns for the buyer. There is relatively low probability of another accidental windfall like Tandy's GRiD laptop patent discovery that yielded a considerable bounty sometime after Tandy's acquisition of GRiD.[25] However, the probability of hidden jewels, and the ability to arrive at an understanding of their value, can be greatly increased by proper advice and analysis. The banker can work with the client to set up an approach to the acquisition that helps avoid accentuating the existence of the hidden IP assets. Tools such as patent mapping software can assist in this type of advisory situation.

In other cases, the banking team can, through its analytical efforts, help determine the client's maximum purchase price and the proper structure to ensure that all relevant assets are fully valued and are retained as intended. This type of advice is particularly valuable during early-stage technology acquisitions, during which the seller may not have any tangible assets, customers, or ongoing operations.

As a sample exercise in strategic thinking, consider how a strategist/banker might categorize the IP assets of a particular company. Once the assets have been categorized by strategic importance based on an audit, the banking and company teams can approximate the valuation, plan negotiating strategy, or determine whether a particular target company or line of business is worth pursuing at all. The company's IP assets might be divided into distinct categories, such as:

- *Gating/Must have.* These are the crown jewels of the organization—the assets that allow industry participation, propel success in a business, or inhibit competitors in a meaningful way. Fundamental patents and closely guarded trade secrets are often key elements of this category. A classic example of just such an asset is the formula for Coca-Cola. More recently, acquirors like Corning have purchased fundamental patents related to optoelectronics that have opened up entirely new and protected businesses.
- *Enabling/Facilitating.* This category comprises key know-how or patents that enhance a company's position in a business but that are not absolutely necessary for the company to enter or to remain in the business. An example would be a proprietary manufacturing process that significantly reduces costs for a business that is already operating, but that does not reduce costs enough to drive everyone else out of the business.
- *Augmenting.* This category represents assets that provide new business opportunities not directly related to the core business or area of expertise covered by the company's other IP assets. This is a rich area for hidden jewels, and should be explored and reviewed carefully. For example, an optical systems company might buy a company with component-related IP because the buyer needs the IP in order to create and sell a super-fast interconnection system. The IP might include other core patents for a new type of component technology that the systems company can license to other manufacturers or use as the basis for a new business unit.

- *Defensive*. Sometimes patents are valuable principally for the exclusion of others, even if the owner does not plan to commercialize them. For example, a company might be the leader in an industry in which a weaker competitor has invented a much better technology that might one day be commercialized. The larger, older company could buy the weaker competitor even if the larger company were not planning to commercialize the innovations in the short or medium term. This is a type of "freeze the market" approach that large companies often use for competitive advantage. Of course, the buyer may need to defend its strategy later on, as shareholders may be curious why the technology was bought and set aside.
- *Not relevant/Cash value*. These are IP assets that probably will be sold or put aside. They may be relevant to a business the company does not wish to pursue, or might be patents for which collecting royalties would not be worth the trouble.

Once the IP has been analyzed in this way, the company has a strategic map that can prove far more valuable than a simple list of IP assets. The investment banker can add value by helping to define the proper categorization scheme, by applying valuation analysis to the assets in each category, by obtaining financing to buy or develop the most valuable assets, by negotiating to obtain the most desired assets, and, finally, by finding creative ways to maximize the proceeds of asset disposition.

In some cases, bankers can add value by identifying licensing or sale opportunities which are outside a client's industry but which are nonetheless of considerable value to the client. An example of this is a laundry detergent manufacturer that licenses the intellectual property surrounding an enzyme within its laundry detergent in order to enable a noncompetitor, such as a contact lens solution manufacturer, to improve its cleaning solution.[26] Investment bankers possessing multiple-industry awareness and a broad set of contacts can add considerable value to both client and seller in these types of situations, thereby exposing value that might have previously been unknown to either buyer or seller. Given all the ways that a banker's strategic advice on IP can be vital, it is easy to see why bankers who do not add value in this area risk being unseated by more IP-savvy rivals. Investment banking is a constant, shifting quest to add value in client situations—ideally, more value than the competition's bankers. Just as overlooking a key area of innovation can prove disastrous to a business, overlooking an area of interest and importance to a client, such as IP, can be similarly disastrous to a banking franchise.

IP AND DUE DILIGENCE

In such increasingly common situations as those in which a seller's assets consist almost entirely of IP and other intangibles, the investment banking team representing the buyer must take responsibility for, and properly oversee, the process of verifying the assets to be acquired. This is the vital and somewhat arcane process of due diligence. It is no longer acceptable for the banker to remain at arm's length, trusting IP attorneys, accountants, and other experts to catalog IP assets and to identify encumbrances or other limitations of the assets. The banker must take a proactive role to identify and evaluate the IP assets. Only through a thorough understanding of the IP assets can an accurate transaction valuation be achieved.

In M&A transactions, a banker may work either for the buyer or for the seller. We will first examine the case in which the banker works for the buyer.

Buy-Side Due Diligence

When the banker is working on the buyer's behalf, the first step in IP due diligence is to thoroughly catalog the IP assets to be purchased. This is done by examining documentation, by speaking to employees, by collecting input from the seller's corporate counsel, by looking up federal patent records, by conducting Web searches, and by other investigative means. Without a reasonably complete catalog, the rest of the due diligence process will be impaired.

With the asset catalog in hand, the banker then works with outside counsel and subject matter experts to assess the strength, retainability, and defensibility of each IP asset. For example, there are probably vital employees at the selling company. Who are they? What are their unique skills and what is the magnitude and value of these skills? How can they be induced or required to stay on after the company is acquired?[27] What role will the key employees have in the combined companies?

This stage of due diligence is the time to determine the strength of the seller's patent portfolio. At this point, the banker must rely heavily on outside counsel and industry experts, as well as on his or her own judgment and on the input of the buyer's management team. The objective is to find out how comprehensive the patent portfolio is, how broad the claims are in each patent, the age of each patent, how complete the company's rights to the patents are, and whether the company owns the entire set of IP necessary to protect its discoveries, processes, products, brands, and expertise. The strength or weakness of the IP portfolio will affect both the buyer's judgment of the seller's attractiveness and the ultimate price. This due diligence step can also help to identify such dangers as patent lawsuits by or against the seller, potential (but not yet litigated) infringements involving the seller, imminent expiration of an important patent, or incomplete registration of IP, any of which might leave the door open to unrestricted duplication of IP by others. Another useful exercise is to compare the seller's IP portfolio against the buyer's portfolio. Are there overlaps? Where are the synergies and/or potential conflicts?

The IP assessment phase is often a fascinating window into the seller's corporate character and culture. The results of the assessment can speak volumes about the seller's care, honesty, and diligence in the conduct of the business. An incomplete or ill-maintained IP asset portfolio can point to trouble elsewhere in the company—perhaps weak financial management or lack of strategic leadership. This type of information can be very useful to the buyer's decision-making and valuation process.

An important aspect of an assessment process on the buyer's behalf is the search for patents held by entities other than the seller. For example, in one recent case, a major communications technology manufacturer sought to acquire a rich IP portfolio in a particular area. In this particular example, a major due diligence issue concerned the patents held by a third major player in the industry. This third party, a competitor of both the buyer and the seller, held many patents in the subject area. Conversely, the seller had more of a niche patent position. Thus, the proposed valuation was vitally affected by the limited extent of the seller's patent position. An IP assessment should not be limited to patents granted. The due diligence team must also assess pending applications and records of invention to fully comprehend what innovations or patents are in the pipeline. This type of pending IP can also have a significant affect on valuation.

Finally, the bankers should work with experts to ensure that all the appropriate IP assets and rights are actually purchased by the buyer. This is an issue of particular importance in cases in which the purchase involves the separation of just one business unit from the seller as opposed to the sale of all of the seller's assets— for instance, if the buyer is purchasing a division from a diversified company. There is at least one well-known case in which a key piece of intellectual property was overlooked and the buyer ended up paying royalties on assets that were left out of the deal.[28]

This issue of overlooked IP applies even in cases in which the seller is not formally part of another organization.[29] In each case, the buyer's due diligence team must determine whether any cross-company arrangements exist and whether these arrangements will survive a change of control. Many cross-licensing agreements include change-of-control termination provisions that help prevent a competitor from gaining access to the IP indirectly via purchase of a licensee.

Cataloging and assessment practices will lead the banking team toward a set of conclusions that the bankers deliver to the client's management team. In some cases, the IP due diligence can become part of a formal opinion delivered to the Board of Directors.

Sell-Side Due Diligence

Due diligence is no less important if the banker represents the seller. The basic two steps are the same—cataloging and assessment. The seller's banking team may or may not have complete access to the buyer's asset catalog but should, in any event, make every attempt to discover as much as possible about the buyer's assets. The seller should also make an honest assessment of its own IP strength, including identification of any potential issues that might arise during negotiations. This is no less important than the financial and accounting due diligence performed by the banking team and by outside counsel on the seller's behalf.

Consider a case in which the buyer has infringed upon a patent and litigation is pending. The effect on the value of the buyer's business, if judgment goes against the buyer, will impact the seller as well. Even in the case of a cash acquisition, an IP lawsuit during the time between definitive agreement and closing can prevent the acquisition from transpiring.

The seller's bankers, along with other appropriate experts, may seek to verify the buyer's claims that it has IP that is synergistic with the seller's IP. Due diligence can also help to determine whether the buyer is in a position to adequately exploit the IP it intends to purchase. This is important if the seller expects the buyer to add value to the seller's IP by deploying the IP in a product line or in some other strategic use. Lack of synergies, presence of overlap, incompetence, or conflicts between buyer and seller's IP can lead to the waste of IP created with brilliance, love, money, and toil over an extended period of time. Wasted IP can diminish the ultimate wealth and happiness of the seller after the transaction, or may reduce the gain to the buyer from the transaction. Many individual inventors and entrepreneurs can attest to the unfortunate consequences of this scenario.

The seller's bankers must also make sure the seller's IP assets are exactly as represented, as they do for the buyer's assets. This IP audit should be done before the sale process commences. The bankers and company management can thereby maximize the strength of their negotiating position.

Intellectual property due diligence can be a tedious and lengthy process, but it is a vital one nevertheless. At the very least, the banker must utilize a legal team to determine whether there is meaningful IP involved and, if so, whether it is unencumbered. However, the banker who does not think beyond the checkbox may be missing an enormous opportunity for his or her client. Intellectual property due diligence offers an opportunity for the banking team and company management to be creative and proactive in discovering and exploiting new sources of value and in planning their negotiating strategy.

IP IN NEGOTIATIONS

Intellectual property can play an important role in the process of negotiating the terms of an M&A or financing transaction. In most M&A situations, the negotiation takes place after the initial approach has been made, after the parties have both expressed interest, and after some preliminary due diligence has been completed. Negotiations typically end either with the signing of a definitive agreement or with the termination of the deal. In a financing transaction, the potential value or realized cash flow from IP can play an important part in determining the cost of capital, the share price, the amount to be raised, the appropriate target group of investors, and any other terms of the deal.

The character and content of negotiating processes vary widely. Negotiations may be rapid or prolonged, friendly or adversarial, continuous or sporadic, with endless shades of gray in between. Negotiations lead to success or failure for many different reasons, as likely to be related to the individual personalities involved as to the actual terms being discussed.

We will consider the role of IP in negotiations from two perspectives—that of the buyer and that of the seller. Investment bankers may represent, or serve as agents for, either or both sides in an M&A or financing transaction. A single bank rarely serves on both sides of a transaction.[30]

In today's technology industry, negotiations often center on the valuation and treatment of intangible assets for the simple reason that many technology companies have few tangible assets. Since the art of valuing intangible assets is inherently less concrete than traditional methods used to value tangible assets (see below), it becomes even more important for the negotiator to be able to argue his or her case clearly during the negotiation process.

One important concept in IP negotiations is that rights can be broadly defined. Unlike tangible assets, where in many cases ownership is the primary right being negotiated, rights to IP assets may be owned, licensed, lent, borrowed, or optioned. Of course, the exact treatment depends on the terms of the IP ownership. The broad definition of IP rights presents both a challenge and an opportunity to the negotiating team.

First, we will consider the role of the negotiator who represents the seller. The goal of the negotiations is to obtain maximally favorable terms for the seller, which include such general considerations as:

- *Highest price.* This is not as simple as it sounds if the transaction is paid for with stock rather than cash. If stock is to be paid, the seller and its bankers must consider the value of the currency, which requires significantly more due diligence to evaluate the true worth of the buyer's enterprise and the strength of its operations.
- *Short-term liquidity for the seller's shareholders.* In most cases in which a company is purchased for stock, the seller shareholders are "locked up" for some period of time, and they cannot sell their buyer's shares.
- *Freedom of choice, as quickly as possible, for the principal employees of the seller.* The buyer will seek to retain key people for as long as possible under employment contracts, vesting schedules, or the equivalent. The buyer may also insist that the key people sign noncompete agreements, which enjoin them from entering the same industry for some period of time. The negotiator for the seller seeks to minimize or eliminate such provisions wherever possible. If the key people are going to stay on as employees of the buyer, the negotiator works to ensure that they obtain agreeable and lucrative jobs with the buyer. The negotiator may, on the seller's behalf, mandate the buyer to provide jobs or severance packages for the seller's employees.

When the seller's assets comprise significant IP, the seller's negotiator must also focus on several additional objectives, including:

- *Obtaining maximum value for the IP assets, individually and collectively.* Having already cataloged and assessed the seller's IP assets, the banking team should also craft an IP-related positioning and strategy in advance of the negotiating phase. During negotiations, the banking team's representative should clearly and forcefully articulate the nature, extent, and strength of the seller's IP as well as the methods used to value it. In the case of a patent portfolio, the negotiator should describe—with expert support—the combined strength of the portfolio as well as the merits and claims of individual patents. The role of the negotiator here is to translate the "legalese" into a story that the buyer's management team and board of directors will understand. For example, lawyers can describe the copyright and trademark positions of a set of brand names, but it is the banker's responsibility to show how valuable and strategic these brand names are, through analysis of the business's revenues and profits as well as via comparison to other comparable businesses.
- *Retention of certain IP rights.* The seller or its principals may wish to retain certain IP rights for use in future endeavors. For example, the inventors of a fundamental technology may wish to retain the rights to certain applications of the technology that are under license or that are unrestricted. Without these preagreed conditions, the buyer may be able to enforce broad claims and prevent competition from former employees of the seller. Another example is a so-called rights reversion, wherein the original inventors may regain claim to IP if the buyer does not commercialize it or meet other stipulated conditions within a given period of time. This type of arrangement may be attractive in cases in which the seller has a broad range of IP above and beyond the particular and immediate interest or capability of the buyer.
- *Preservation of the core team, if necessary.* In certain instances, the eventual value of an acquisition can be seriously compromised if key team members do not remain after the transaction is complete. With this in mind, the seller should be focused on arriving at agreeable terms for both the mission-critical operating team and other shareholders. Shortsighted investors or team members who desire immediate returns can sometimes inhibit this process. Bankers work with management to create terms that maximize long-term value for all participants.

The buyer's banking team sees a mirror image of the same issues. Their objectives include:

- *Completing the deal for a minimum price.* The buyer's negotiating team tries to minimize the price paid in the transaction. Therefore, the team may do an extensive IP audit and other due diligence in advance to measure whether the seller's assets and operations are exactly as stated, with no encumbrance. Examples of encumbrances related to IP assets include incomplete patent portfolios; patents with weak or challengeable claims (as verified by experts retained by the buyer); licenses from third-party patent holders that may be canceled if there is a change of control; "golden parachute" severance agreements for key individuals; noncancelable cross-licenses to third parties who compete with the buyer; and outstanding patent litigation. Any of these conditions can be used to negotiate a lower price.

- *Complete and unencumbered control of the seller's IP.* The buyer's negotiator will resist any attempt by the seller to maintain rights under any condition. Even if part of the seller's IP belongs to the "cash value" category defined above, the buyer will seek to make this IP part of the transaction. There are several reasons why the buyer seeks this:
  - The assets may prove to be more valuable than initial analysis indicates; for example, the technology may be commercializable later, when other technologies are perfected.
  - The assets may be related or immediately relevant to other assets, in which case a lack of control may prove expensive if not disastrous.
  - The buyer may feel pressured to act on IP prematurely if the rights can revert to the sellers after a period of time.
- *Preservation of the core team.* Here, the buyer and seller may be in harmony if the core team wants to stay rather than sell out and move on. The difference in perspective usually involves the conditions imposed to keep the core team in place. Often, this is a negotiation over price alone, but it may be more complex. As described above, the buyer may seek to put vesting schedules or earn-outs in place for key team members—"not all the money up front." Sometimes, the earn-outs are tied to product performance. These types of arrangements are powerful insurance for the buyer and, in many cases, are quite negotiable. We would also observe that these negotiations tend to be more fruitful in tougher economic times.

These points by no means cover the entire spectrum of circumstances a negotiator may encounter. Even taken by themselves, however, these should illustrate that IP awareness is vital in negotiations any time IP is involved. Positions taken on these issues can powerfully affect the price and viability of a transaction. Intellectual property can be a gold mine, a toxic swamp, or perhaps a bit of both, for the buyer and the seller. The trick is to know the terrain.

VALUING IP FOR M&A AND OTHER TRANSACTIONS

In the past, intellectual property was typically valued as a portion of goodwill, defined as "expenditures to acquire other companies in excess of the book value of their net assets."[31] However, today's economy requires a much more thorough approach to accurately value IP assets in order to ensure that both companies and investors arrive at a more accurate approximation of IP asset value.

Unfortunately, it is often extremely difficult to measure the value of intangible assets. In time, and through further study, the sophistication of the methodologies will likely improve. Recent proposals from the Financial Accounting Standards Board (FASB) on accounting for goodwill in business combinations alone will assure that more scrutiny is placed on this topic.

In valuing IP assets, it is important to avoid common pitfalls. These include failure to recognize encumbrance of the asset; inability to recognize each of the individual IP assets within the company; and, when these assets are identified, failure to accurately value them either by understating their worth or by underestimating postmerger integration risk. These pitfalls can be avoided by ensuring that each IP asset is assessed individually, early on in the transaction process.

Some common valuation methodologies that can be applied to intellectual property assets are:

- Fair value measurements
- Present value of expected future cash flows
- Option pricing models
- Conjoint and relative utility analysis
- Cost of development
- Cost of replacement
- Expected cost of infringement
- Price minus book value

The key benefit that experts in valuation offer is the ability to choose the best combination of approaches. The use of multiple approaches allows the expert to triangulate on a value, which can increase the accuracy of the valuation.

FAIR VALUE MEASUREMENTS

The fair value measurement approach measures what a third party would be willing to pay for an intellectual property asset. Typically, this is based on stated amounts or derived from precedents observed in the marketplace. Examples of these types of comparables have included:

- Price per engineer or programmer
- Price per patent
- Price per copyright
- Price per line of code
- Price per customer
- Licensing fee per brand recognition rate
- Value of similar infringement settlements and their consequences (e.g.,

> Eastman Kodak's $924 million payment to Polaroid and Kodak's forced exit from the instant photography business)
- Price per unit of revenue generated from IP assets

Today, with the emergence of online IP marketplaces such as yet2.com and pl-x.com, and with the growing trend for corporations with large R&D departments (such as Procter & Gamble) to generate revenue through IP licensing, evaluation of fair value for intellectual property is a much simpler process. Even so, it is still likely that comparable analysis will yield too few data points to be sufficiently accurate for valuation.

PRESENT VALUE OF EXPECTED FUTURE CASH FLOWS

This approach is simply a discounted cash flow model of the anticipated value of the intellectual property, as produced by an analysis of the discounted free cash flow that the asset is expected to generate. In the inflows section of the analysis, all cash inflows that could reasonably be expected from the intellectual property are listed. These inflows might include product sales, licensing fees, royalties, cost avoidance from IP ownership, and so on. In the outflows section, all costs associated with obtaining the inflows are listed. These costs might include the cost of maintaining or updating the intellectual property, defending the intellectual property through patent fees or court costs, or retaining key employees. Once inflows and outflows are listed, the free cash flows are discounted at a rate equal to the market's expected rate of return on an intellectual property asset of similar risk. The sum of the discounted cash flows represents the present value of the asset.

In many cases, the cash inflows and outflows will be difficult to predict. There may be considerable uncertainty with regard to development and adoption rates for the intellectual property asset being evaluated. In these cases, complex simulation models such as Monte Carlo simulations can be effectively employed to produce a range of scenarios with different probabilities.

In other instances, the value of cash flows is measurable. A good illustration of this is provided by the comparison of branded drugs and generic drugs, wherein the economic returns of the two products are differentiated by nothing more than branding. An analysis of the incremental free cash flow generated by the branded drug versus that produced by the generic drug will yield an estimate of the value of the drug manufacturer's brand name. This analysis should include not only the increased revenue that results from the brand name, but also the decreased cost resulting from efficiencies created by the brand in distribution channels, manufacturing operations, and other processes.

OPTION PRICING MODELS

Option pricing techniques can be employed to value both the expected benefits of new R&D and the actual value of existing intellectual property. The most common of these is the Black-Scholes model, wherein patents and other forms of intellectual property are effectively treated as options. Patents may be viewed as call options on future technology. The Patent & License Exchange, Inc., for example, uses the Black-Scholes formula to value the IP assets of its clients by replacing variables for call options on stock with variables applicable to intellectual property in a process they refer to as Technology Risk/Reward Unit (TRRU) Metrics[32]:

Black-Scholes variables for call options on stock	Variables for IP asset analysis
Strike price	Remaining development cost
Time in which the option must be specified	Remaining length of development
Market price of underlying stock	Market value of underlying product
Variance of stock price return	Variance of product value return
Risk-free rate	Risk-free rate
Output: Call option present value	Output: Estimate of IP asset value

The Patent & License Exchange, Inc. calculates the market value of the underlying product by comparing the market-inferred value of a similar asset of small "pure play" companies whose products are similar in nature to the intellectual property asset being evaluated. The "variance of product value return" is calculated as the variance in the market-inferred value of similar assets at "pure play" companies.

Option-pricing methodology is relatively new to the IP industry, but is growing in popularity as an evaluation technique.

CONJOINT AND RELATIVE UTILITY ANALYSIS

In a conjoint analysis, product attributes are evaluated through a standard questionnaire given to many customers in an effort to appraise the value these customers place on different product attributes. For example, the average consumer of word processing software might be willing to pay five dollars extra for a word processing package offering an effective Norwegian grammar scanner, but only one dollar extra for a Norwegian spell check. If a company wanted to know whether it was worthwhile to add the product functionality for a Norwegian grammar scanner, it would perform the following calculation:

$$\text{Value of Norwegian grammar scanner} = \frac{\begin{array}{c}(\$5 \times \text{\# of new product sales}) + (\text{Product price} - \$5) \times \text{\# of sales} \\ \text{that would not have happened without Norwegian} \\ \text{grammar scanner}) - (\text{Cash cost of Norwegian} \\ \text{grammar scanner development})\end{array}}{\begin{array}{c}\text{Market's expected discount rate of return for intangible} \\ \text{assets of a similar risk profile}\end{array}}$$

If the equation's result is positive then, all other things being equal, the company would generate incremental value by investing in the Norwegian grammar scanner.

Should the company choose not to do a full conjoint analysis, a process that can take several weeks, it could also value the Norwegian grammar scanner based on a relative utility analysis. By plotting different product features available in word processing software that are currently marketed by three separate companies in the marketplace, the company would be able to produce a rough estimate of the value of the Norwegian grammar scanner by placing it in between the known market capitalization and the utility levels of other products (see Exhibit 24-1).

In this case, the simple relative utility chart seems to indicate that the value of the Norwegian grammar scanner would be between $175 million and $190 million in market capitalization. This approach can provide a quick assessment of the value of an IP asset to the market. In cases where there are no "pure play" companies in the market with which to compare functionalities, the retail price of selected products can be assessed to determine the price a company might reasonably expect to charge for a newly developed product. This anticipated retail value could then be used to determine the actual value of the intellectual property.

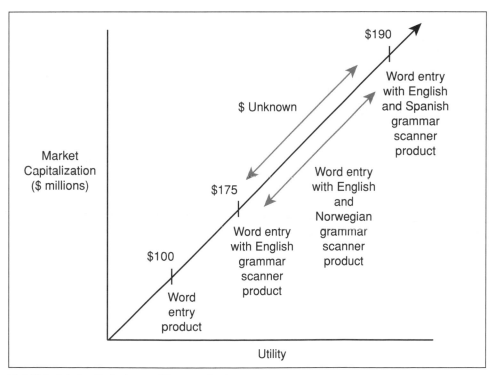

Exhibit 24-1   Relative utility analysis.

COST OF DEVELOPMENT

This approach is best used by companies that have already developed an intellectual property asset and that now wish to assess its value through a historical analysis of what it cost to develop that asset. However, companies can also use this approach to value their competitors' intellectual property assets, provided enough information is available. Based on the economic principle of substitution, the cost approach can assess the value of intellectual property by determining what it might cost a competitor to produce comparable intellectual property. This approach is useful in many cases. However, its limitations are that it cannot be used when the intellectual property is unique, is not fully understood, or is nonreplicable, and it does not necessarily represent the value that someone would be willing to pay for the asset.

COST OF REPLACEMENT

If a company chooses to sell one of its intellectual property assets currently in use, losing that asset will have a cost to the company. For example, in the case of a well-known brand, the owner of the brand would incur costs on three broad levels if it were to sell the brand name to a competitor:

- Infrastructure costs
- Marketing costs
- Revenue decline

Infrastructure costs are incurred during the conversion of all corporate assets—factory names, printing presses, and so on—that contain the brand name. Marketing costs include the necessary changes to all existing marketing materials such as television and magazine ads, along with costs associated with the buildup of a new brand to the recognition and prestige level of its former brand. Finally, as the new brand is being built, there will likely be a substantial decline in revenue while the company works to transition consumers to the new brand.

EXPECTED COST OF INFRINGEMENT

In many cases, IP assets are protected by such measures as patents, copyrights, or other legal instruments. The somewhat ambiguous nature of these defenses opens the door to infringement attempts by other parties. The expected cost of infringement can be evaluated to determine the potential cost to a party considering any potential infringement. The best method by which to calculate this cost is via an expected-value analysis based on various probabilities of outcomes and their associated costs and benefits. Inputs to this analysis can be derived from advanced quantitative analysis or from lawyers, accountants, industry experts, and other professionals. To provide a basic example of this approach, we will assume that when mobile phones were first invented, Mobile Phone Company (MPC) sought and was issued a 17-year patent on mobile phone technology. Plastic Corporation is evaluating whether it should begin producing mobile phones without a license, or whether it should purchase an $80 million license from MPC to produce mobile phones (see Exhibit 24-2).

In this case, it makes more sense for Plastic Corporation to pay the $80 million licensing fee to Mobile Phone Company, assuming that Plastic Corporation's additional economic analysis of discounted free cash flow from mobile phone sales is positive. However, it is important to note that the outcome of the expected cost of infringement analysis is highly dependent upon the probabilities and estimated values at each stage of the analysis. That is why having the most informed opinions as input for this analysis is critical. Insofar as the Plastic Corporation case is concerned, if the probability of winning the lawsuit jumps from 10 percent to 20 percent, the outcome of the entire analysis will change.

PRICE MINUS BOOK VALUE

The least sophisticated of all methods, price minus book value is probably the method most commonly used to value IP assets. This approach simply takes the market value of a company and subtracts the book value to arrive at the value of intangibles. There are, however, four inaccurate assumptions underlying this approach that may severely limit its effectiveness.

1. The price minus book value approach assumes that as a company's market value varies—as in the case of stock price fluctuation—the value of the company's underlying IP assets varies proportionately.
2. The value of tangible assets is assumed to be exactly equal to their reported value on the balance sheet.
3. The value of the IP assets does not necessarily fluctuate with the entity's effectiveness at leveraging these assets to generate incremental revenue from new product innovation, third-party licensing, third-party patent sales, and so on.
4. The price of the company's stock may be affected by numerous factors, only one of which is the perceived value of the intangibles.

CONCLUSION

This chapter provides some examples of the ways in which IP awareness can enhance the role of the investment banker and increase the banker's value-added to his or her client. We believe that bankers can and must become more conversant with the world of IP as such assets become more and more important to clients.

We have described the importance of IP to bankers' clients but, in addition,

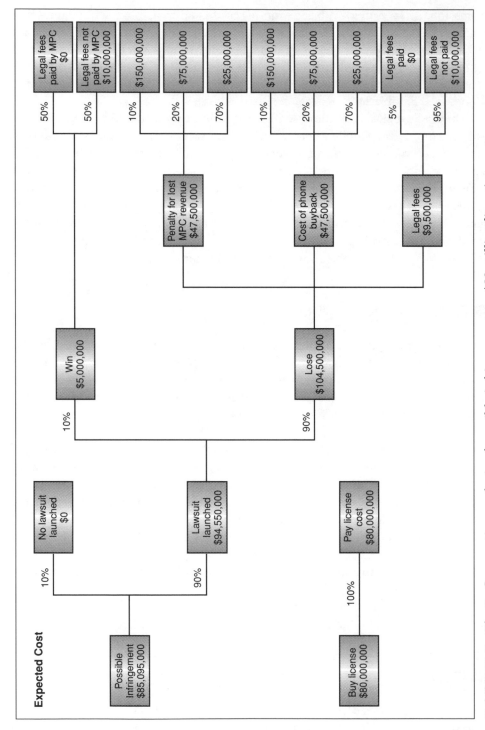

Exhibit 24-2 Plastic Corporation analysis of possible infringement vs. $80 million licensing cost.

bankers themselves are starting to show signs of waking up to the importance and potential value of IP to their own organizations. Many major banks have set up internal groups to search for patent-worthy IP. These groups are in the process of unearthing a trove of innovations, ideas, and know-how. The Merrill Lynch and State Street process patents[33] were just the beginning of what promises to be a wave of financial-engineering, trade-processing, and other Wall Street patents. Other Wall Street IP will not be patented, but will be cataloged, filed, and recognized by senior management; after all, the last thing that an investment bank wants is public disclosure (an issued patent or published application) of all its financial techniques. There will indeed be patents not only in the heart of Wall Street, but in its consciousness as well. There is no longer any excuse for neglect. The opportunities are enormous.

NOTES

1. Kevin Rivette, "Wall Street's Untapped Patent Opportunities," in Bruce Berman, ed., *Hidden Value: Profiting from the Intellectual Property Economy* (United Kingdom: Euromoney-Institutional Investor, 1999), p. 127.
2. Ibid.
3. Kevin Rivette and David Kline, *Rembrandts in the Attic: Unlocking the Hidden Value of Patent* (Boston: Harvard Business School Press, 2000)
4. Berman, ed., *Hidden Value*, Chap. 12: "Taking David Bowie to Market."
5. Frank Musero, "Biotech nters securitization jungle." *Asset Sales Report*, January 22, 2001.
6. James Fallon, "Boo.com Technology Assets Sold for $400,000," *DNR*, Vol. 30, No. 64 (May 31, 2000), p 11.
7. Loring Wirbel, "IBM Passes Switches, Routers to Cisco; MMC Takes Hit," *Electronic Engineering Times* (September 6, 1999), p. 26.
8. Dow Jones Interactive database as of March 17, 2001.
9. In fact, the recognition and full utilization of previously underutilized or illiquid assets is one of the most important and common ways to derive value in a financial situation. For example, the sale-leaseback structure allowed the liberation of value from previously untapped real estate assets. Pension fund assets were massively restructured in the 1980s with the creation of ESOPs (Employee Stock Option Plan), 401Ks, and other vehicles. Factoring—the practice of borrowing on inventory—is another example. Finally, the everyday home equity loan is a major source of interest and fee revenue for banks that was rarely seen until recently. Today, very few assets are "frozen" on the balance sheet without being put to work in some fashion.
10. Rivette and Kline, *Rembrandts in the Attic*, p. 37.
11. Apple ultimately settled a widely publicized "look and feel" case against Microsoft.
12. Randal Stross, "USA: Microsoft Research—Mr. Gates Builds his Brain Trust." *Fortune Magazine* (December 8, 1997).
13. Example: The Technology Risk/Reward Units (TRRU) Metrics IP valuation approach of The Patent and License Exchange, Inc., which is based on the Nobel Prize-winning Black-Scholes Options Pricing Model.
14. In Dell's case, a patent for its online ordering business method; in Priceline's case, a business method patent for "name your own price." Rivette and Kline, *Rembrandts in the Attic* discusses both these cases.

15. "Giga Trends." *Wired Magazine* (April, 2001), p. 183.

16. Source: Securities Data Corporation.

17. Berman, ed., *Hidden Value*, p.132

18. "Inglis and Whirlpool Vindicated in Patent Battle Against General Electric, Camco and Maytag," *Canada Newswire* (December 15, 2000).

19. "Nintendo defeats General Electric in Game Patent Suit," *KYODO News* (June 8, 1999).

20. "Proxim Broadens Effort to Protect Wireless Networking Patents," *Business Wire* (March 9, 2001).

21. "IntersilCorp Says Proxim Patent Suit 'Without Merit.'" *Dow Jones News Service* (March 16, 2001).

22. Armstrong's relationship with Sarnoff and RCA was tempestuous and, ultimately, tragic. The two partners made millions from Armstrong's invention of regenerative feedback and the superheterodyne AM receiver (the basis of all AM receivers, even today). However, in later years, Sarnoff and Armstrong disagreed over the development of FM. FM promised to make AM technology obsolete, threatening both RCA itself (a major producer of AM technology) and the AM broadcasters who were important RCA customers. After profiting handsomely from FM in military equipment manufactured during World War II, RCA tried to shelve the technology after the war. Armstrong won the right to pursue FM independently after a protracted legal battle, and promptly started to build a network of commercial FM stations. When the new medium gained popularity, Sarnoff led a lobbying group that prevailed upon the FCC to move the frequencies assigned to the FM broadcast band—immediately silencing Armstrong's network and rendering useless the thousands of Armstrong FM receivers in circulation. Bankrupt and despondent, Armstrong committed suicide by leaping from his landmark FM broadcasting tower in Alpine, New Jersey. For further information about this fascinating story, the authors recommend Tom Lewis's *Empire of the Air: The Men Who Made Radio* (New York: HarperCollins, 1992).

23. "GE Finishes Its Takeover Of RCA Corp.," *Associated Press* (June 10, 1986), as reported in *Newsday*.

24. *Fabless* means that the company does not have any semiconductor manufacturing facilities, or "fabrication lines" of its own.

25. "Tandy Unit, Toshiba In Patent Pact On Laptop Computers," *Dow Jones News Service* (September 28, 1989).

26. Julia King, "Corporate Secrets Up for Grabs at New Exchanges," *Computerworld*, Vol. 34, No. 46 (November 13, 2000), p. 8.

27. One type of inducement, sometimes called an "earn out" or "vesting schedule," is an arrangement whereby the employee is unable to access certain proceeds from transaction for an extended period of time, or may earn additional compensation if certain milestones are achieved after the transaction is completed.

28. For an excellent example of "AWEE" Inc., *see* Terji Gudmestad, "Protecting Intellectual Pproperty During Divestitures and Acquisitions," *Research-Technology Management*, Vol. 41, No. 5 (September 1998), pp. 36–39.

29. For example, there are extensive cross-licensing agreements and other IP-related arrangements among the present and former components of AT&T.

30. The exception is an occasional "prewired" transaction where the banking team is merely facilitating the details of a set of terms previously agreed upon and assisting the process to completion. Otherwise, if terms are not yet fully negotiated and agreed upon, a single bank would likely have a conflict of interest serving on both sides.

31. Tom Copeland, *Valuation: Measuring and Managing the Value of Companies,* 2nd ed. (McKinsey & Company, Inc., 1996), p. 176.

32. Cited with permission from the Patent and License Exchange, Inc.

33. Berman, ed., *Hidden Value*, p. 127.

ABOUT THE AUTHORS

Christopher R. Fine is a Vice President in the High Technology Investment Banking Group at Goldman, Sachs & Co., based in New York City. He is involved in corporate finance, M&A, and strategic advisory assignments, with particular focus on communications technology and software. Trained as an engineer, he is often asked to participate in transactions and financings involving complex technology and significant intellectual property. Mr. Fine received an Electrical Engineering and Computer Science Degree from Princeton University and a MBA from New York University. He began his career as a hardware and software engineer designing data communications systems. This was followed by a period of time as an information technology professional in the commercial real estate industry where he designed and created applications software for investment analysis and property management. Mr. Fine then spent several years as a senior IT manager in the investment banking industry, specializing in telecommunications and IT infrastructure. Mr. Fine's interest in patents dates back to a childhood fascination with his father's patented innovations in sound and video technology.

Donald C. Palmer started his business career with the Procter & Gamble Company in brand management, where he developed and helped implement a successful strategic plan for the Tide brand. After P&G, he joined the consulting profession as a management consultant with McKinsey & Company. While at McKinsey, Mr. Palmer worked at offices in Asia, Europe, and North America, where he helped solve problems on issues ranging from launching and operating e-businesses for international financial institutions to effective deployment of cash reserves for a major private equity organization. Today, he is a member of the Investment Banking Division's High Technology Group at Goldman, Sachs & Co., with a primary focus on mergers and acquisitions. Prior to joining the business world, Mr. Palmer served as a Lieutenant in the Canadian Infantry and attended the Richard Ivey School of Business, where he received his degree in business administration.

Goldman Sachs is a leading global investment banking and securities firm, providing a full range of investing, advisory, and financing services worldwide to a substantial and diversified client base, which includes corporations, financial institutions, governments, and high net worth individuals. Founded in 1869, it is one of the oldest and largest investment banking firms. The firm is headquartered in New York and maintains offices in London, Frankfurt, Tokyo, Hong Kong, and other major financial centers around the world.

CHAPTER TWENTY-FIVE

Creating Tomorrow
IP and the Future of Business

by Ian Harvey

PERSPECTIVES

Companies are just starting to understand that Intellectual Property can play an integral role in their success. A generation ago, approximately 70 percent of the patents litigated in U.S. courts were held to be invalid. Today, the reverse is true. Ian Harvey, CEO of BTG, a company that finds, develops, and commercializes technologies, believes that patents are destined to become the center of corporate strategy. He believes that in the coming few years international investors will assess companies' patent policies in ways they have never before and that managers and organizations that understand the dynamics of patents as the building blocks of business will be at a premium.

"CEOs who fail to understand the difference between cash flow and profit are extremely rare," he writes. "In the same way, we should soon be unable to find a chief executive who does not understand the difference between patentability and freedom to use (a simple question which tests the very basic knowledge of what a patent can, and cannot, do for you). The appearance of what we might call 'patent literacy' is going to be driven by investors who ask the difficult questions and focus their attention on companies where they can see clearly that management understands and uses IP effectively."

Mr. Harvey believes that to survive in an increasingly competitive world, businesses need to pay much greater attention to identifying, nurturing, and deriving value from their IP. "Knowing that some companies have failed to manage their IP assets effectively, investors should be asking fundamental questions of the companies they are thinking of investing in. How much do they know about IP? Is IP part of their corporate strategy? If it is, does their IP strategy make

sense?" IP is about unlocking the value of knowledge, asserts Mr.
Harvey. "Whatever else happens, the next decade is going to mean
many people have to become 'patent literate.' And this time, it isn't
going to be just the lawyers."

Mr. Harvey's provocative and visionary perspective is something
from which business executives, lawyers, and investors alike can
benefit.

INTRODUCTION

Intellectual property is about creating the future. In the past, IP has been central
in providing a platform on which investments to develop and market new products was based. A myriad of IP-based products has changed our lives, from new
antibiotics to the latest silicon chips. Today, the role of IP is growing fast and it will
increasingly underpin much of the innovation that will make us both healthier and
wealthier in the decades ahead. This is important both to us as individuals and to
the companies that will depend on IP for their future.

Standing back, first of all, and looking at the big picture, there is little doubt
today that technology and, thus, IP have a central role in global economic growth.
There are three primary drivers of economic growth: the growth in the input of
labor; the growth in the input of capital; and what the economist Robert Solow
called "Total Factor Productivity." What he meant by that is the efficiency with
which inputs are turned into outputs, and that means almost solely through the
impact of technology.

If you look at growth in the 10 largest world economies from 1970 to 1990,
the Organization for Economic Cooperation and Development (OECD) has recently
found that of the average global growth rate of 2.9 percent per annum, the biggest
single element of that growth (about 42 percent) was Solow's Total Factor Productivity—the impact of technology. This is a critical finding, because it shows very
clearly just how technology has become *the* major driver of world growth (see
Exhibit 25-1).

If you look at the impact of investment in technology in the United States over
the past five years, we have seen a combination of high growth, low unemploy-
ment, and low inflation. Many economists now claim that this golden combination—whether or not it manages to survive the current turbulence—was driven by
the heavy investment in technology from the early to late 1990s, which was much
higher than Europe's investment.

It is still not easy to prove a definitive causal relationship between IP and
technological development or investment, but most governments now believe that
some form of protection needs to be given to inventors and companies to encourage investment in developing the inventions, turning them into products, and
bringing them to market.

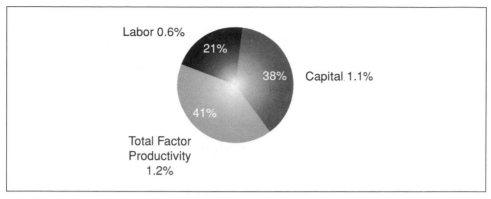

Exhibit 25-1 Impact of technology on GDP growth, 1970–1990, average 2.9%. *Source:* "21st Century Technologies"—OECD 1998

Even if this link is hard to prove definitively, the reality is that governments all over the world continue to strengthen their IP laws. This is also true in the developing world where, once a country has passed a certain development threshold, it begins to see that IP protection helps (rather than hinders) its companies to develop and compete. For example, India—which was leading the opposition to IP 20 years ago—is coming into the IP fold, just as Japan, Taiwan, and Korea did in the 1960s, 1970s, and 1980s, and as China is doing today. It is likely that the politics of pharmaceuticals in South Africa (the "access to medicines" issue) will have an effect in the other direction, but the overall IP trend remains the same.

In practice, governments know that IP laws are vital to creating technology and capitalizing on innovations in their countries. Intellectual property underpins one of the strongest drivers of growth, which we all need for our well being, and that includes the developing world as well as Wall Street and the City of London. The growing recognition of the importance of IP is a key trend for the future. This new central role is intricately bound up with other trends in the rapidly changing world marketplace. This is, after all, a market where competition is intense, where returns are being driven down in an increasingly frictionless market, pushed in turn by IT, communications, and the Internet and trade agreements like GATT/WTO (General Agreement on Trade and Tariffs/World Trade Organization), all of which are breaking down the barriers to world trade.

As many companies in the United Kingdom have been finding out, that means a whole new environment for manufacturing. Manufacturers relying solely on the competitiveness of their prices will have a miserable time competing with low-cost, high-quality manufacturers from East Asia. Instead, manufacturers have to try to compete based on brand, by being first to market and by continuous evolution.

None of these can give companies a sustainable edge selling a product that might have developed over decades. The one thing that can really give companies a sustainable competitive advantage—which might encourage them to develop this new product in the first place—is IP. With strong patents, they can go to court and they can stop other people from manufacturing or selling their patented product.

This is the basic underlying story that is driving the development of IP across the world, but it implies much more than that. The increasing importance of IP, in many areas from investment to political debate, is driving a range of related IP trends. This chapter focuses on the companies poised to be at the top.

IP FUTURES #1: PATENTS AT THE CENTER OF CORPORATE STRATEGY

Some of the most successful and forward-thinking companies are putting patents at the heart of their plans—for research focus, for new product development, for new markets, for mergers and acquisitions (M&A), and thus for corporate strategy as a whole. The need to include IP in the strategic mix is compelling.

When Texas Instruments (TI) defined Digital Subscriber Line (DSL), a high speed Internet access, as a critical technology, they bought Amati's patent portfolio. In the same way, when Microsoft decided that they wanted to play a key role in Internet broadcasting, they bought WebTV Networks, then a minor Internet start-up. At the time, analysts were unable to understand why Microsoft was paying $425 million for something so small. The reason was that WebTV owned 35 key patents that covered Internet content over television.

Microsoft has been playing a leading role in this particular IP trend, and they have been ahead of the game. Historically, Microsoft relied mainly on IP in the form of copyright; competitors are prevented from copying what Microsoft has created. But if someone independently creates a product that provides a similar result, there is little Microsoft can do. Patents are different; they can stop a competitor from operating in your patented area. So Microsoft has changed its strategy to include patents as well as copyright.

Five years ago, Microsoft owned around 30 patents. Now they have around 300, with another 3,000 in application. They appear to be looking ahead to where the market will be in 5 to 10 years' time and what technology will be needed to make that happen. They have then been either acquiring patents or filing their own patents in those areas. By doing so, they have been creating a patent road in front of them, where they will be free to walk, but they can choose who else walks on that road with them.

This is a fundamental strategic change in the way Microsoft is creating a competitive position for itself. In the future, they can stop competitors encroaching on Microsoft's strategic areas; assuming, of course, their judgment about the future is correct.

But there is a virtuous circle about that too. Owning the patents means that Microsoft is able to invest heavily in innovations in this area, which means that they are more likely to be able to create the future themselves. But at the heart of their strategy is IP and being able to protect their innovations, now and in the future.

IP FUTURES #2: INTERNATIONAL INVESTORS INCREASINGLY WILL ASSESS COMPANIES' PATENT POLICIES

Despite the unquestionable importance of patents, there is an extraordinary lack of interest and sometimes sheer ignorance about them among some of the world's largest companies. At least one significant British company files few patents outside the United Kingdom, even though 80 percent of its product revenues come from abroad. Another large U.S. pharmaceuticals company, which took advantage of the 12-month grace period for filing patents in the United States for a major new product, lost 60 percent of a potential $400-million-per-year market by doing so.

IBM, for example, developed high-temperature superconductors in the late 1980s, published their findings, but did not file a patent for 10 months. Not only had they completely lost out on patent protection outside the United States, but competitors had been able to replicate their work with time to file patents covering their own developments. It was a painful learning experience for IBM—but they have clearly learned.

Things are different at IBM now. Over the last 10 years they have increased their IP-based annual license income from $30 million to $1 billion and are expected to lift that by another $500 million in the next year.

It is clear that to survive in this increasingly competitive world, companies need to pay much greater attention to their IP. A few—but still only a few—have begun to include IP at the heart of their corporate strategies. In the meantime, there are important implications for the behavior of investors. Knowing that some companies have failed to manage their IP assets effectively, investors should be asking fundamental questions of the companies they are thinking of investing in. How much do they know about IP? Is IP part of their corporate strategy? If it is, does their IP strategy make sense?

We are at a moment in corporate history when the ability of companies to compete worldwide in an increasingly crowded and competitive marketplace is becoming increasingly tough. The ability of IP to sustain a commercial advantage is one of the few lifelines that companies can look to for regaining competitive advantage. Taken together, these trends add up to a situation in which a company that fails to think very hard and seriously about IP as a critical part of its corporate strategy is much less likely to succeed in the future.

Of course, IP alone will not save a poor strategy or a badly managed company. It also needs extraordinary marketing and brilliant sales. But those alone will not save a company which has failed to protect its products through good use of IP—nor will investors buy their shares. It also seems likely that managements that fail to protect their IP assets adequately, or lose value by inadequate geographic coverage, may find themselves faced with shareholder suits for loss of value of the companies' assets.

CEOs who fail to understand the difference between cash flow and profit are extremely rare. In the same way, we should soon be unable to find a chief executive who does not understand the difference between patentability and freedom to use (a simple question which tests the very basic knowledge of what a patent can and cannot do for you).

The appearance of what we might call "patent literacy" is going to be driven by investors who ask the difficult questions and focus their attention on companies where they can see clearly that management understands and uses IP effectively.

IP FUTURES #3: PEOPLE WHO UNDERSTAND PATENTS WILL BE AT A PREMIUM—AND SO WILL PATENT INTERMEDIARIES

Any patent professional knows the difference between patentability and freedom to use. She knows that patents only give you the right to stop someone else using without your permission the technology you have patented. They do *not* give you the right to sell your patented product, because it could still infringe someone else's patent. The more sophisticated companies know this very well, but it is still surprising how many of their competitors have yet to grasp this fundamental fact.

The failure of some of the biggest companies in the world to manage the differences between patent law on different continents—not to mention their failure to patent their developments in the first place—can often cost them a substantial proportion of the income they might have expected from a new product. It is also astonishing how many companies fail to use effectively the patents which they have painfully, and expensively, created.

Most companies seem to build patent portfolios without serious thought as to why they have them in the first place. Is it to keep competitors out of their space, or is it to license competitors and take revenues from the whole marketplace? For too many companies, filing a patent is a knee-jerk reaction to making an invention. What they should ask themselves is "What will this patent do for us and how do we intend to use it?" This is because a patent on a single invention may be written in several different ways, depending on the use to which it will be put and the existence of other patents inside or outside the company. It is vital to know the context in which a patent will be used before it written or finalized. The combination of this ignorance and the growing importance of patents in corporate strategy implies another important trend in the short to medium term—a serious shortage of patent know-how.

According to the management guru Arie de Geus, capital is no longer a scarce factor of production. There is plenty of capital out there, searching for new places to invest and driving down its cost. The major shortage is of ideas and products— it is knowledge that is in short supply.

The first implication is that investors are having to accept higher risks and longer-term investments, which equates to lower average returns. That's what happens when capital is plentiful but ideas and products are not. Second, the people who create these ideas will be in demand. Third, people with an understanding of the strategic value of patents are going to be in high demand too.

Investors are beginning to understand better how patents can give these ideas an enforceable advantage, to provide investors with a higher and sustainable return on their capital. More than ever before, patents give business the space to create products. That makes patents all the more important, given the following shifts in the reality for business. There is going to be a serious scarcity of people who understand the linkages between IP, technology, and the marketplace. That creates opportunities for both individuals with the right skills and for businesses, like BTG, that have a track record and IP skill base.

There is probably a bottleneck emerging: Companies will want to embody an intelligent understanding of patents as part of their forward strategy, and will find there are not nearly enough patent professionals or patent intermediaries to go around. In the longer term, the business schools may close this gap, but judging by their current attitude to IP, that may take some time. In the meantime, IP know-how is going to be at a premium.

IP FUTURES #4: SMALL RESEARCH COMPANIES

One of the implications of the trend is that access to inventive skills, of the kind that can produce commercial and patentable ideas, is going to be one of the key—if not *the* key—critical success factors for companies in the immediate future. The trouble is that, however large an R&D department may be, it is still very hard to predict which of these killer ideas are going to emerge as the winners.

If you look at historical trends in scientific literature, you will find that research often becomes increasingly tightly focused. Suddenly, there will be a completely unexpected area that opens up—the unpredictable *paradigm shift* (the phrase coined by Thomas Kuhn of MIT)—which sets scientific thinking on a new course. Companies can no longer risk relying solely on their own researchers to make that leap. Any company today has to be connected to a network of other sources of research to be able to identify key technology changes early and then capitalize on them.

This has probably always been the case, but it is an unpredictability that will be far more important as competition gets more fierce, which means we are going into uncharted R&D territory. Interconnections are also all the more important given the lessons of history about where the real breakthrough technologies tend to come from, which often tend to be at the interstices between existing areas.

At the moment, for example, there is a very creative area at the interface between the life sciences and the physical sciences. The knowledge being created by the sequencing of the human genome is just part of the explosion of knowledge in the life sciences. In the physical sciences, the combination of electronics, with the ability to handle huge amounts of data (coming from astrophysics and particle physics), together with nanotechnology (the ability to build molecular-size machines), creates huge opportunities. It is not just the potential to build biochips, but also the immense diagnostic and therapeutic potential of both understanding and then treating disease at the cellular level. Many interesting technologies are expected to emerge from this convergence.

Any company wanting to capitalize on future innovations needs to be able to both draw on a wide network of researchers in different fields and to find ways of getting the different disciplines to rub up against each other to make the ideas happen. The old model of big research departments, divided into disciplinary teams, is unlikely to help achieve either of those objectives.

This new unpredictability has its own effects. It means, for example, that instead of separate blocks of corporate researchers, there are likely to be increasing relationships between networks of companies in the research field. This seems likely to turn some small research outfits into highly valuable companies in their own right.

There are many scenarios here, of course, but it will accelerate the trend to have strategic alliances between companies that specialize in different parts of the process from creating a new product to bringing it to market. Corporations can, and do, buy in the research expertise, the patent expertise, and the global marketing from a range of different companies and knit them together into a single product strategy. Networks are the future but they are still in their infancy, and effective ones remain in short supply.

IP FUTURES #5: COUNTRIES THAT ARE GOOD AT INNOVATION

As the investors seek out innovation, the spotlight falls on those countries that create and encourage new ideas better than others (see Exhibit 25-2). As well as the United States, that means Canada and Europe—especially the UK, Switzerland, the Netherlands, and Sweden, which are at the head of the world creativity league. It probably does not mean Japan, which comes about tenth in the world in the citation indices. The number of patents in Japan is also misleadingly high because of the still-prevailing culture of filing large numbers of patent applications covering quite small new developments. The result is a list of patent applications that looks large, but is actually rather thinner than appears at first sight. The underlying culture of Japan is driven by an education system which is excellent in many respects but encourages conformity—the enemy of innovation and creativity.

The investors' search is also likely to take in some of the less obvious places too, nations that buck the regional trend by successfully encouraging creativity and innovation. For example, that probably means Taiwan as a country to watch and invest in.

Taiwan has an American-style education system, which encourages people to ask questions and to challenge the accepted way of doing things, which are vital parts of the ingredients for innovation. The government supports failing companies, as they do in so much of the rest of the region, which is another key ingredient: innovation is unlikely to thrive if there is no incentive to solve problems or to face up to the consequences of failure.

Share of Papers	%	Share of Citations	%	Relative Citations	
USA	35	USA	49	USA	1.4
UK	8	UK	9	Switzerland	1.4
Japan	7	Germany	6	Sweden	1.2
Germany	7	Japan	4	Denmark	1.2
France	5	France	4	UK	1.1
Canada	4	Canada	4	Netherlands	1.1
Italy	3	Italy	2	Canada	1.0

Exhibit 25-2   Research rankings.
Source: Reprinted with permission from BM May, Science 275, 793 (1997). Copyright 1997 American Association for the Advancement of Science.

Taiwan also benefits from its proximity to China: as many as 200,000 Taiwanese businesspeople are now running factories in China, and 80 percent of the population of Taiwan is a cross-section of mainland Chinese people whose families came to the island with Chiang Kai-Shek after the Second World War. Access through Taiwan gives access to all of China, quite different from Hong Kong, whose relations are primarily with the local coastal littoral.

Some way behind, but coming up fast, is Korea. It still has a bloated business system that endlessly seems to prop up failing and poorly focused corporations, but Korea also has an education system that is similar to the United States. Koreans will challenge accepted wisdom—and when they do that, innovation should follow. There are student riots in Korea, which you never see in Japan. Although that might seem inconvenient if you are caught up in them at the time, this unwillingness to accept the status quo is a subtle indicator of future creativity.

Look out for increasing innovation from Taiwan and Korea, as well as increasing investment. In the meantime, one of the other countries targeted by BTG is Canada, which ranks sixth in the world in terms of its share of scientific papers and its share of citations, which is way ahead of its position in terms of population. In relative strength, it ranks seventh. This helped BTG conclude that Canadian technology was abundant, high quality, and as yet undercommercialized.

That's why we have set up a Canadian joint venture (Primaxis) where we have provided the IP, technology, and market know-how, and the Royal Bank of Canada provides the initial money for a seed capital fund. Expect more similar ventures like these around the world in the future.

IP FUTURES #6: WATCH OUT FOR A WHOLE RANGE OF NEW KINDS OF BUSINESS PARTNERSHIP

The traditional patent strategy was about sole ownership of an invention, but the sheer unpredictability of innovation has meant the emergence of a complex range of other ways and relationships in creating value from IP. BTG, the company I have headed since 1985, plays a leading role in this (see Exhibit 25-3).

BTG brings together an understanding of the IP needed to protect a new technology, calibrating how an emerging technology will fit into a future marketplace and products, and finding the right partners who can bring it to market. The inventions that BTG commercializes were not created by the company, but by clients, sometimes companies, sometimes research institutes, sometimes universities. BTG commercializes these inventions and the patents covering them by several different and flexible routes.

A traditional route that inventions take to market is through straightforward licensing. Where a technology is likely to become a single product, then licensing to an existing company often is the fastest and most effective route to market. What is also clear from BTG's experience is that a *paradigm shift* technology is often the least welcome by an existing major player because it is so disruptive to their existing business and product lines. In these cases, the licensee may often be a small player or one that is not yet a player in that market but wants to be. Sometimes the new product is so different from existing products that companies choose not to follow significant opportunities and the best route is then a start-up.

One such start-up is Provensis, which is developing a radical, new and better outpatient treatment for varicose veins. This technology was developed by a vascular surgeon in Spain and has already been used to treat 7,000 patients successfully. It is an active microfoam injected into the varicose vein, causing it to collapse and then disappear. When BTG spoke with the medical industry, their reaction was "it's not a simple pharmaceutical" (from the pharmaceutical compa-

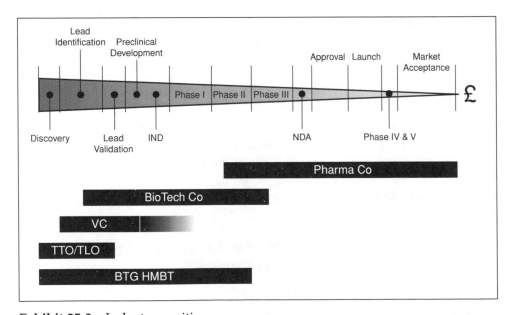

Exhibit 25-3   Industry position.

nies), or "it's not just a medical device" (from the medical device companies). Each of these is true; it is a combination of active pharmaceutical, device, and procedure. But it also has blockbuster market potential, so in this case BTG created a company to take it through full clinical trials, after which it will choose the marketing partners best suited to each of the global markets in which it will be used.

Where a technology is likely to become a platform technology (providing the basis for a number of different products in different areas), a start-up company often makes sense to take the development to the point where a number of partners can each start to create their own particular product.

The result is that the range of players is considerably increased. The complex interrelationships between different organizations also mean you can create a strategy that is tailored to each new innovation, with partnerships built around specific patents and IP. Increasingly, companies will look at the range of different markets available to them and realize that there may be different methods of getting to those different markets. Those methods may not involve selling into those markets yourself.

JVC, for example, licensed other companies around the world to use VHS and made its technology ubiquitous by so doing. Their competitor, Sony, decided not to license other companies with its (better) Betamax technology, but kept it solely for its own products. In practice, VHS became the industry standard by letting it go, under license, so that everyone started using it. Similarly, GlaxoSmithKline chose to sell its second-into-the-market ulcer drug Zantac through the U.S. sales organization Roche Pharmaceuticals, demonstrating to the pharmaceutical industry that partnerships can create real value by drawing on the strengths of each partner.

Another great example of this was glassmaker Pilkington, after they developed their flat-glass process. They decided to market the idea by licensing their competitors, a decision that earned them $750 million in royalties (in today's money). They then used the proceeds to buy up many of their licensees to become the world's largest manufacturer of flat glass.

This strategy may involve licensing companies with which you also compete. That is exactly what IBM has done, by licensing their erstwhile Taiwanese competitors to manufacture IBM's state-of-the-art liquid crystal displays. This kind of partnership would have been unthinkable under a traditional approach, but it means IBM gets early, guaranteed, and low-cost production, and, of course, they get revenue from the whole industry.

IBM will still have to stay ahead of the market by inventing, or acquiring rights to, the next generation of liquid crystal displays, but they have decided the best way to capitalize on their research investment is to license their competitors rather than to manufacture the technology and keep it to their own products. That is a fundamental shift in corporate strategy and a key trend.

The result of this kind of thinking will be the growth of companies that no longer integrate all their functions vertically, but which specialize in different aspects of the business of bringing products to market. There will be invention companies, development companies, and marketing and sales companies, all coming together in a range of fluid partnerships to turn inventions into products (see Exhibit 25-4).

Take GlaxoSmithKline, for example. The world's biggest pharmaceutical company has been reported to be suffering from a pipeline shortfall, which means an acute shortage of late-stage products. That in turn led to media reports that they were scouring the world trying to find late Phase III products by Easter 2001, when their quarterly report to shareholders was due.

In practice, that means creating instant partnerships with a range of organizations that have the technology and the patents. Since most breakthrough innovation comes from small research groups, universities, and biotech firms, the pattern of future business is becoming clearer—networks of partnerships built around strong IP.

IP FUTURES #7: PATENTS AT THE HEART OF CORPORATE VALUATIONS

There is considerable debate these days about the valuation of companies and how it is possible to calculate value—much of it difficult to justify. There are academics and accountancy standard-setters all over the world now struggling to understand and calculate in some definitive way the value of intellectual assets, many of which are as intangible as the word suggests.

Undoubtedly intellectual assets are a key driver of value—but to try to ascribe accounting value to them is a misconception of what company accounts should be about. The value of a company should be reflected though market value rather than balance sheet value. This is not the place to discuss the theory of knowledge man-

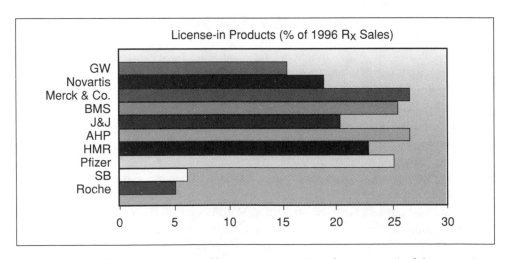

Exhibit 25-4 The importance of licensing to major pharmaceutical (companies 1–10).
Source: IMS Health Inc., 1997

agement, and a company clearly needs to understand that its intangible assets have value, but to try to value those intangible assets on the balance sheet confuses something that was designed to reconstruct the *historic costs* of a company with the *market value* of a company (which can and probably should change from day to day). Market value will continuously change, but there is no reason why a balance sheet should go up and down in line with market value (see Exhibit 25-5).

When companies have more tangible intellectual assets like patents, companies like BTG can help them understand what kind of value might be locked up in them and help them understand how best to communicate that potential value to shareholders, but that does not belong on the balance sheet. At BTG, we keep our patents on our books but we keep them at cost, not at some guessed value. We also communicate their estimated future value at each of the 200 presentations we make each year to our shareholders, as well as in lengthy discussions with analysts.

Patents are going to be playing an increasing role in determining the market value of the company that owns them. Putting them to work to generate revenue (and estimating what that revenue might be) is always going to be an art, not an exact numerical science, feeding into the perception of the value of the company as a whole.

Does the company hold patents that may control strategic areas of the future market? Has the company been able to protect critical "choke points" in the processes they are using in manufacturing or service? Do they have the necessary expertise to make those patents work for them imaginatively across the world? And, of course, the fundamental question: does the management really understand what patents are about? Those are the key questions investors will be asking—and they will increasingly determine the value of your shares.

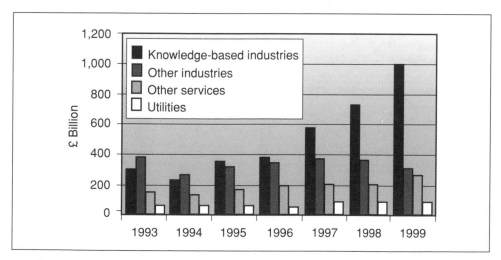

Exhibit 25-5   Market value (equity-ordinary shares) UK public listed companies.

The future is going to be as much about IP-based value as it is on projected product sales, because IP is going to increasingly determine the future sales of a product or process. Intellectual property is going to be at the heart of the valuation of companies in the future.

It is becoming widely accepted that this will be the case in manufacturing, but it may also involve service companies too. Although service companies tend to grow or die based on quality of their services, there are often ways that they can create something patentable about the service that defends it and allows companies to invest more in it.

British Airways, for example, has put fully reclining sleeper beds into the first-class sections of their planes with a clever seating layout to give greater privacy and space utilization. They have also recently introduced a fully reclining business-class seat, which also has a unique staggered layout. They have patented both the design of the seats and the layouts. By doing so, they have made it much more difficult for their competitors to emulate the service level British Airways now provides. But it also helps justify the heavy investment to develop the new seats, which their competitors cannot simply replicate in their own aircraft. They may be a service company, but in both cases they are much more likely to defend their new quality of service by stopping other airlines from doing what they did or by creating revenues by licensing them.

So whether they are for products or services, patents and IP will increasingly underpin the value of companies.

IP FUTURES #8: PATENT LAW WILL SLOWLY COALESCE ACROSS THE WORLD

There are different patent laws in Europe and the United States, but they are not as different as they used to be. The GATT trade agreement included an agreement on Trade-Related Aspects of Intellectual Property, known as TRIPS. President Clinton signed the agreement for the United States in December 1994, and it has meant major changes in U.S. patent law, bringing it more into line with the rest of the world.

But there remains a fundamental difference. The "first to file" a patent wins the race in most countries. But, for the time being, the United States still has a system where the race is won by the first to *invent*. That means that where two or more people claim to have created an identical invention, the U.S. Patent and Trademark Office declares an "interference" and sets out to find out who invented it first. There are difficulties with that approach, not least because the cost of deciding an interference can be prohibitive to all but the best-heeled inventors and can create uncertainty for many years.

U.S. patent law also means that patent officials allow a grace period for 12 months after you publish research, but before you need to file a patent. Any publication within that grace period does not count as prior art, which is the term used to describe proof that the invention had already been published.

In practice, though, any U.S. company or university that makes use of this grace period before filing for a patent will have destroyed its patent position in every country outside the United States where there is (so far) no such thing as a grace period. It is amazing how many companies in the United States do not realize this and how many major U.S. corporations (not to mention U.S. universities) have destroyed a hefty percentage of their potential revenue stream by this omission.

These patent law differences are inconveniences for companies and a source of confusion in the new interlinked world. If they become any more than inconvenient, then we can expect moves to reduce the tension between the two models of patent law.

That is why there will be a long-term trend that brings these two patent systems more into line. The position on patenting business methods in Europe is currently unclear, and it is unlikely that the current law would allow patenting to the same extent as in the United States. There is, however, an active debate in progress, and it is possible there may be some alignment.

Amazon's Jeff Bezos has suggested there may be other forms of patent protection that would give companies a protectable advantage if they were going to invest in Internet-based businesses. We look set to have a debate in the near future about what kind of protection this might be. Intellectual property professionals watched the investment flooding into the dot.coms in astonishment because it seemed pretty clear to many of us that they had no sustainable competitive advantage. Amazon has survived not just by having a good business model and delivering to customer expectations, but they have good processes and they filed patents on those processes. Their successful patent suit against barnesandnoble.com for infringing Amazon's "one-click shopping" underscored the impact that effective patenting can have in the business methods arena. It seems likely that the coming debate on protecting Internet innovation will bring Europe and the United States closer together. Whether they will ever fully align their patent philosophies is another question.

One unexpected and worrying implication of the Internet is the creation of deep-running torpedoes, which could undermine key patent positions in future. Imagine that a researcher has tried an idea in her laboratory, and put the results onto her home page. Once that home page was updated, there would be no accessible record of it. Yet if somebody, somewhere, has taken a copy off the Internet, then many years later, those published results could pop up suddenly and destroy a patent position. It would constitute prior art for which, currently, you cannot search.

IP FUTURES #9: PATENT LIFE WILL COME UNDER SCRUTINY

As IP grows in importance, particularly in the healthcare market, there will be debate about whether the patent term of life is long enough to do the job properly. Patent professionals are going to be asking increasingly whether a single patent life suits every kind of innovation. After all, it has to provide the time to recoup research costs for a minor technical innovation as well as the years of research and trials for a drug designed to tackle an intractable disease like Alzheimer's. The bottom line is whether a company is prepared to make a huge investment over a long period for something that can make a real difference to modern life and yet have a very short earning period under its remaining patent protection.

This debate comes at a time when governments are taking patent protection increasingly seriously. And it is not just governments, it is the courts too—especially in the United States. A generation ago, 70 percent of patents litigated in the U.S. courts were held to be invalid. Now the reverse is true, and many American lawyers are saying that IP is already the fastest-growing area of law.

The courts have also been increasingly energetic in their awards. The record damages awarded in the Polaroid versus Kodak case reached an exceptional $437 million, and awards are now consistently up to 10 times the value of the original infringement in the first place, which is certainly punitive.

When legislators and lawyers start discussing whether patent protection lasts long enough, then change is in the air. In the United States, patent protection used to be 17 years from the date your patent was granted. It is now 20 years from the date of filing. That change closes the loophole that some companies relied on, delaying the patent grant to keep the starting gun for the 17-year life as late as possible. But that has refocused the spotlight back onto patent life: Some think it is too short and others too long.

The key diseases in the sights of the biggest pharmaceutical companies are becoming more difficult to treat. You can test a new antibiotic relatively quickly; you can see very quickly whether it kills bacteria or not. Developing anything to tackle something like Alzheimer's disease, or for cardiovascular protection, or to prevent osteoporosis or breast cancer, requires a much longer process—if only because you have to wait so much longer to see whether they work. In pharmaceuticals, that means longer time to market and longer-term investment, pushing increasingly hard against a patent deadline that—thanks to patent harmonization—has recently got much shorter in the world's key market, the United States.

In electronics and computing, there is much less concern about patent life (perhaps that it is *too* long), but a parallel concern that the patent system is too slow to be effective in the rapidly moving industry. Something may have to give.

IP FUTURES #10: IP PROFESSIONALS MUST BE DRAWN INTO WIDER POLITICAL DEBATE

It is sometimes frustrating for IP professionals, used to the abstruse language of the patent world, but many of the central issues of the age seem to relate in one way or another to IP. Yet the IP professionals often seem to exclude themselves from taking part. There are debates on genetic engineering and the human genome, and extensions to that debate relating to health and food. There is a debate on the

International Exhaustion of Rights, and others about the access of developing countries to patented technology—or the iniquity of the developed world patenting the third world's birthright, depending on where you live or how you see it. There are debates about copyright in the digital age. And there are others, some less worth discussing. But throughout them all runs a common theme of IP and its benefits.

Often IP professionals seem to feel above the debate, sometimes they feel excluded from it, and sometimes they feel it has little to do with them. That is going to change: the IP industry is going to be forced to take part, and to do so in a language that everybody and anybody can understand.

The problem is that the ignorance of most people about the most basic principles of IP is simply not compatible with its growing importance. When someone as senior as the former EU trade commissioner Leon Brittain can say, "Patents are a restraint on free trade," you know there is a problem.

Yet when you communicate the basic arguments about IP—that the only way you will get corporations to invest in expensive development is if they can have a patent position to defend their revenues when (and if) their products reach market—people can shift their positions very quickly. The only alternative, in genetics research, for example, is that the government will have to fund it, and we all know that governments have a pretty poor track record in investment. The point is simply that to get new products, you must have patents to create the platform for investment.

This is a complex debate partly because it is also seen to be a moral issue. Society is said to be morally obliged to create new treatments if it is able, so it follows that the moral high ground is taken by creating patents on which the research and development of new products will be based. But it is not enough for IP professionals simply to assert this view: we have to take part in the debate in order to convince people.

That means tackling some of the myths about IP head on. Many people say, for example, that patents keep research secret. The reality is that they make it public. The whole purpose of the patent system is to force inventors and corporations to publish the details of an invention so that other people can experiment on it. Patents are designed to *encourage* publication and hence innovation.

Many people say that patents confer ownership on what has been patented. The reality is the opposite: they stop someone else from selling it; there is no element of ownership whatsoever. A patent doesn't give you the right to do or own anything, except the right to stop other people using your invention commercially.

None of this implies that IP is uncontroversial. The first biotech patents were controversial in the 1970s, just as the first software patents were when BTG was involved in filing them a decade or so later. Now people just accept them. The company was one of the first to file patents on gene sequences (for the Factor IX gene). Had it not done so there would be no life-saving treatment for hemophiliacs today—yet some still say that properly granted patents on genes are somehow wrong. How wrong *they* are!

These debates will and should carry on, just as everyone from economists and social scientists to politicians and activists are all examining why we need IP in the first place. Intellectual property professionals must stop hiding behind their arcane language and must get involved. It is right to debate these issues, but it is the responsibility of the patent professionals to make sure that these debates take place in full knowledge of what patents are, and are not, so that the debates are properly informed.

CONCLUSION

There are different scenarios for the future of IP, of course. It is difficult to know in practice the extent to which U.S. and European patent law will move closer together. It is even harder to know whether the remaining peculiarities of European patent law are going to be sorted out, though—if a common European Union patent law means translating many pages of complex scientific text into all the national EU languages—we can expect some resistance to remain. The same goes for the suggestion that there should be a common single language for patents. Areas where the trends overlap will create change and patent law convergence.

The patent system is founded on the belief that people will invest more in R&D if they are given a limited monopoly over their inventions, just the same way that copyright encourages artists to invest the time they need to create their works. This case is increasingly accepted not just in the developed countries but around the world. It is increasingly clear that IP strategy is going to be the beating heart of corporate strategy. That in turn implies that IP portfolios, IP strategy, and the external perceptions of IP will underpin the value of companies in the future.

Knowledge is at the heart of the new business world at the start of the twenty-first century. IP is about unlocking the value in that knowledge. Whatever else happens, the next decade is going to mean many people having to become "patent literate." And this time, it isn't going to be just the lawyers.

ABOUT THE AUTHOR

Ian Harvey is the CEO of BTG Plc, one of the leading organizations for acquiring, developing, and licensing intellectual property rights. He was with Vickers and then Laporte Industries for 10 years, and served for seven years at the World Bank, operating in Asia and in Africa. He joined BTG in 1985 as CEO. Between 1988 and 1993, he was a member of the UK Prime Minister's Advisory Council on Science and Technology. Mr. Harvey is a Fellow of Nottingham University (1994), and since 1989 he has been a member of the Advisory Panel for SPRU (Science and Technology Policy Research Unit of Sussex University). He became a Director of the Intellectual Property Institute in 1998 and Chairman in 1999. Mr. Harvey serves on the Board of Primaxis Technology Ventures, Inc. and on the European Advisory Council of Air Products and Chemicals, Inc. He is also a director of other BTG companies. He has an MA in Mechanical Sciences from Cambridge University and an MBA from Harvard University.

BTG's business is finding, developing, and commercializing technologies that will shape the markets of tomorrow. BTG creates value by investing in further technical development and enhancing the scope of the intellectual property. The company captures value by either licensing the rights to the technology or by developing new business ventures, and returning significant value to its sources of technology, business partners, and shareholders. With its headquarters in London and offices in Philadelphia and Tokyo, BTG capitalizes on a global network of contacts in companies, universities, and research institutions to identify and commercialize the most promising technologies. Since its founding in 1949, BTG has help to bring to market such major innovations as magnetic resonance imaging (MRI), Interferon, and wide-spectrum cephalosporin antibiotics. BTG (*www.btgplc.com*) is quoted on the London Stock Exchange under the symbol "BGC."

IP Glossary

Abandonment—The forfeiture (real or implied) of a potential patent right as a result of an action or failure to act within a certain time frame.

Abstract—A concise (50–150 word) introductory technical summary that outlines the technical problem faced, solution offered, and principal uses of the invention as contained in the description, the claims, and any drawings.

Alternate Dispute Resolution (ADR)—A process that permits conflict resolution without a lawsuit. A certified arbiter or mediator assists the parties involved in arriving at a mutually agreeable solution to their dispute. Arbitration is usually legally binding while mediation is not.

Amendment—An applicant's modification to a patent application to be resubmitted after the original application is denied by the U.S. Patent and Trademark Office (USPTO).

Anticipation—Demonstrated knowledge of an innovation, before the claimed invention date, that is nearly identical in the form of a prior art patent, publication, or use of the innovation, thus negating the novelty aspect of a claim.

Anti-Dilution—The body of legal doctrines and statutory provisions which protects a familiar trademark against a reduction of its value through unauthorized use in a sphere outside of its traditional product area.

Applicant—The person or corporate body who files a patent application with a patent office, intends to manufacture or license the technology, and must be the inventor, except in extraordinary circumstances.

Application—A patent request given to a patent office, which includes petition, specification, oath or declaration, claims, drawings (required when they are necessary for the understanding of the invention), and appropriate filing fees.

Arbitration—A mini-trial conducted by a person or a panel of people who are not judges. It may be agreed to by the parties, may be required by a provision in a contract for settling disputes, or may be provided for under statute.

Art—see Prior Art.

Assignment—The legal transfer of all or limited rights to an intellectual property.

Assignment in Gross—A trademark assignment rendered invalid because it lacks the assignment of the associated goodwill.

Assignor Estoppel—A standard that prohibits the assignor of an intellectual property from later denying the validity of that assigned property.

Auslegeschrift—An examined German patent application (second publication) now eliminated. See also Offenlegungsschrift and Patentschrift.

Automatic Rights—Copyrightable material is protected from the moment of creation without any formal registration.

Basic Patent (or Pioneer Patent)—The first patent granted in a specific area. It is composed of broad claims.

Berne Convention—An international treaty allowing reciprocity of copyright registration between countries.

Best Endeavors—The British, and more stringent, equivalent of Best Efforts.

Best Efforts (or Reasonable Diligence)—An American legal term that varies with the specific court, but typically means a reasonable level of effort.

Blocking Patent (or Essential Patent)—A patent on a product that details infringements on its claims that will necessarily occur.

Broad Claim—Within a patent, a statement of invention that covers an extensive field of invention variations without using a different method of presentation.

"But For" License—A provision within a patent license grant or royalty payment obligation, in which the product or process in question would infringe on other patents, but for the payment agreement.

CAFC (Court of Appeals for the Federal Circuit)—In 1981 replaced the CCPA as the court that hears all patent cases and acts as the final authority in patent law, for practical purposes. The Supreme Court may overturn CAFC rulings but rarely takes patent cases.

Carrot Mining—Mining a portfolio for valuable technologies that can be combined with related patents to generate revenue.

Carrot-and-Stick Mining—Mining an intellectual asset portfolio to reveal both carrots (valuable technologies that can be combined with related patents to generate revenue) and sticks (patents that are being infringed upon and as a result have value to be licensed or sold to the infringers).

CCPA (Court of Custom and Patent Appeals)—Until 1981 served as the appellate court that heard patent office decisions, has since been replaced by the CAFC.

Citations—A list of references, made by the examiner or author, that are believed to be relevant prior art and which may have contributed to the "narrowing" of the original application. The examiner can also cite references from technical journals, textbooks, handbooks, and sources.

Circuit Layout Rights—Rights that protect original layout designs for integrated circuits and computer chips.

Claim Chart—A tool used when looking for agreement between the words of a claim and the features of another product or process that allegedly infringes that claim.

Claim Differentiation—Given that one claim has a limitation that another claim does not have, the limitation will not be read into the second claim when examining either validity or infringement.

Claims—Numbered paragraphs at the end of a patent application that define what the patent-seeker considers the invention to be and therefore the monopoly rights the applicant seeks. The claims define the legal scope of that patent and an exclusionary right is granted within the claim definition.

Clayton Antitrust Act—Legislation enacted in 1914 to prohibit certain, then common, monopolistic practices in finance, industry, and trade. The act was adopted as an amendment to the Sherman Antitrust Act, and was designed to deal with new monopolistic practices, including provisions covering corporate activities, remedies for reform, and labor disputes. Unfavorable court interpretations weakened the act, however, and additional legislation was required finally to carry out its aims. As it pertains to the IP arena, the act specifically makes unlawful any asset combination or acquisition which significantly harms commerce and competition.

Click Wrap License—An online license created when the potential licensee views a screen detailing the license terms and then must use the cursor to click agreement to these terms.

Cluster—See Patent Cluster.

Cluster Analysis—Research and computer analysis of a group of patents to reveal any opportunities for licensing and overall revenue generation.

Cluster Ranking—The listing of various clusters or affinity groups in a portfolio according to their revenue potential.

Clustering—This procedure sorts a patent portfolio into various affinity groups or clusters.

Codified Asset—See Codified Knowledge.

Codified Knowledge—Knowledge that has been committed to some form of communication medium. It might be a handwritten document, a computer program, a blueprint, or a cartoon.

Collective Intelligence—A situation in which each member of an organization can access all of that organization's relevant knowledge instantly.

Common Law—The traditional unwritten law of England, based on custom and usage that has passed into U.S. federal and state laws.

Complete Specification—See Specification.

Complementary Business Assets—The string of business assets through which innovations must be processed to reach the customer.

Conception—The initial, mental formulation of the idea upon which a patent is based.

Constructive Notice—An act that achieves the same legal result as giving actual notice. Publication of a summons is constructive notice while handing it to someone is actual notice. Placement of a patent number on a product is considered constructive notice.

Continuation—A patent application subsequently filed while the original parent application is pending to preserve the filing date of the original application, even though no new material has been added.

Continuation-in-Part (CIP)—A continuation that has had new material added; it may claim the same or a different invention from the original parent application and receives the original filing date benefit to the extent that the two applications have common subject matter.

Continuing Applications—There are three types of continuing applications: division, continuation, and continuation-in-part.

Contributory Infringement—Assistance to an infringer by selling a nonstaple article that is a portion of an article or is used in a process that infringes a patent, copyright, or trademark. A nonstaple article has no primary use that does not infringe.

Copyright—The exclusive right to make authorized copies of an original expression of ideas in literary, dramatic, musical, artistic, or electronic form, such as an article, photograph, book, software, or other authored work.

Covenant Not to Sue—A promise not to sue a third party for a tort or contract breach. The courts sometimes consider a nonexclusive license a covenant not to sue by the licensor and therefore deem the license not transferable. If a patent owner grants a covenant not to sue, the recipient cannot transfer patent infringement immunity to his or her customers unless expressly permitted by the agreement.

Date of Application—The date signifying when the U.S. Patent and Trademark Office receives properly completed application papers.

Date of Patent—The date of the printing of notice for the patent grant as well as the effective date of patent in the Official Gazette of the U.S. Patent and Trademark Office.

Declaration—The statement in a patent application specifying that the invention described by the patent applicant was made by that individual.

Defensive Publication—A disclosure and publication to the public of a pending patent application.

Defensive Suspension—A condition of either a license agreement or a standards-based undertaking to license a blocking patent; the license is suspended should the license holder sue the owner of the patent, the licensee claiming patent infringement or a declaration of invalidity.

Dependent Claim—A claim that refers to and includes all of the features of another claim; it will also include all of the limitations of the claim it depends on, and should state the additional features claimed.

Description—See Disclosure.

Design Patent—A type of patent covering the shape characteristics, or aesthetics, of an object. In contrast, a utility patent protects the process or functionality of the product.

Direct Infringement—Infringement in total of all features of a claim.

Disclosure (Description)—A statement within the patent application that provides the necessary information for an individual skilled in that field to carry out the invention. The term "disclosure" may also refer to details of the invention that are deliberately revealed outside the patent system to the public to make the invention unpatentable.

Disposal—When an application has been resolved, either by being withdrawn, rejected, or granted. It may also connote rejection only.

Division—Should the patent office determine that the application covers more than one invention, then the application is split into one or more divisional applications.

Divisional Application—The application for the remaining invention(s) from a division; it has the same specification as the "parent" but claims a different invention.

Doctrine of Double Patenting—Designed to prevent the extension of patent exclusivity beyond the life of a patent. Double patenting occurs when the right to exclude granted by a first patent is then wrongfully granted to a later issued patent. The public has the freedom to use an invention from an expired patent or modifications to that patent. Constructed to provide the inventor with the ability to assert a patent when the invention would be obvious to those in that subject area.

Doctrine of Equivalents—Differences between the inventor's and an infringer's product are not significant. The doctrine states that although a patent claim may not literally read on a potentially infringing device, it can be more broadly read if it does not read on the prior art.

Doctrine of Exhaustion (First Sale Doctrine)—A doctrine denoting that the initial sale of a patented, copyrighted, or trademarked item by the owner or licensee exhausts the right to the intellectual property.

Domain Name—A domain name represents the unique name corresponding with an Internet Protocol address. For example, the domain name of Ventius is *www.ventius.com*.

Drawing—One or more specially prepared figures filed as a part of a patent application to explain and describe the invention, typically found with inventions for mechanical or electrical devices. In general, chemical patents will include use formulas in the description of the invention and/or in the examples rather than drawings. At the time of filing, drawings are either informal (do not meet standardized specifications) or formal (have been approved by a draftsperson).

Duty of Disclosure—A patent office demand that everyone involved within the patenting process disclose any information (such as patents, articles, laboratory data, and research) to the patent examiner that may affect the decision to grant a patent.

Electronic Commerce—The exchange of business utilizing computer networks, including the transfer of products and services between buyers and sellers through the medium of the Internet.

Enhancement—A revised computer program that incorporates additional or refined areas of functionality.

Entire Market Value Rule—If a product includes a patented component, then any infringement damages on the component may be calculated from the market value of the entire unit, not just the component.

Essential Patent—See Blocking Patent.

European Patent Convention—A patent application filed under this convention of 19 European countries will, when granted, typically be effective in each of the member countries that the applicant elects.

European Patent Office (EPO)—The European agency responsible for examining and issuing patents.

Examination—The process of analyzing a patent application in the U.S. Patent and Trademark Office to ascertain whether it is in proper form (preliminary examination) and of such a nature that the invention described therein can be given a patent (substantive examination).

Examiner—An official of the U.S. Patent and Trademark Office with the responsibility of appraising the patentability of patent applications.

Exclusionary Right—The legal right granted by a patent, wherein the patent owner may prevent an infringer of one or more claims from creating, having created, trying to sell, selling, using, or importing any infringing product or process, for a specified and finite period of time. Having a patent on a particular invention does not provide authority for the patent owner to create, use, sell, etc., the invention if the manufacturing, usage, or selling of the patented invention infringes another individual's patent.

Exclusive License—An assignment of intellectual property rights where the licensor may not make subsequent grants of the same property to others.

Expiry Date—The end of the life of a patent, and thus the protection granted by that patent.

Field of Use License—A license granting rights to an intellectual property that is restricted to a specific or predetermined use.

File Wrapper Estoppel—When the USPTO rejects a claim as unpatentable over prior art, often the applicant will then limit the claim. File Wrapper Estoppel prevents this restricted claim from being understood more broadly than the new restriction would allow.

Filing Date—The date when the application reaches the patent office in complete form.

First Sale Doctrine—See Doctrine of Exhaustion.

First to File—The European patent system which awards the first person to file an application for a patent the rights to that invention over all others.

First to Invent—The United States patent system which awards the person who first makes an invention the rights to obtain a patent on that invention, regardless of the date on which the patent is filed.

Force Majeure Clause—"Greater force"—A contract clause that excuses a party from a liability in the case that an unforeseen event, outside the party's control, takes place and prevents it from performing its obligations. This sort of clause usually covers natural disasters, wars, and third-party failures.

Forfeited Application—An application on which the issue or maintenance fee has not been paid within the designated period.

Forward Citation Analysis—The analysis of a particular patent in conjunction with any later patents that cite it.

Foundry Right—A patent license giving the licensee the right to manufacture licensed products for a nonlicensee that designed the products.

GAAP—Generally accepted accounting principles.

Georgia Pacific Factors—A list of 15 factors often used to determine reasonable patent license royalties in patent infringement lawsuits.

Goodwill—An intangible asset that puts a value on the good reputation associated with a trademark or servicemark.

Grant—A temporary right given by a patent office to an applicant that prevents others from using the technology claimed in the application for a designated period of time.

Grant-back—A license of IP improvement rights granted by a patent licensee to the licensor.

Have Made Right—The right for a patent license holder to sell a third party manufactured licensed product.

Human Capital—The collective amount of creativity, skills, and productivity of an organization's employees. One of the two major elements comprising intellectual capital, the other of which is intellectual assets.

In re Pardo—A legal precedent affirming the legitimacy of an algorithm as the point of novelty for a patent.

Industrial Design—The look of a manufactured product that goes beyond mere functionality to encompass artistic considerations. An original ornamentation, shape, configuration, or pattern is protected if registered with the appropriate governmental agency.

Industrial Property—The subcategory of intellectual property with industrial applications, specifically patents, trademarks, trade secrets, servicemarks, designs, circuit layout rights, and plant breeder's rights.

Infringement—Use of an intellectual property without the legal consent of the property owner.

Inoperativeness—The failure of an invention to work due to either mechanical or methodical imperfections or due to an inaccurate description of the invention in the disclosure.

Intangible Assets—Confer legal rights and economic benefits upon their owner but are not physical, or tangible, objects. Examples include patents and copyrights.

Integration Clause—A contract clause to bar parol evidence that might alter the contract, it encompasses ". . . the entire agreement between the parties."

Intellectual Asset Management—Increasing the flow of innovations that can be considered for patenting and for commercialization, whether legally protected or not.

Intellectual Assets—The codified, tangible, or physical descriptions of specific knowledge to which an organization may assert ownership rights. Intellectual assets are one of the two major elements comprising intellectual capital, the other of which is human capital.

Intellectual Capital—Knowledge that can be converted into profit. This capital comprises two major elements: human capital and intellectual assets. Also known as knowledge capital.

Intellectual Property—A legal term describing intellectual assets for which legal protection has been obtained. Two main subcategories of IP are industrial property and copyright.

Intellectual Property Management—Developing a portfolio of defined intellectual properties, then devising the broadest number of avenues for commercializing the properties in the portfolio.

Interference—A USPTO *inter partes* (between two or more parties) proceeding to determine the legally recognized inventor of a specific invention. Occurs when the same invention is described in multiple patents or patent applications, or both a patent and patent applications. Typically, about 0.1 percent of patents are involved in an interference suit.

International Application—A patent application that secures protection from participating countries in the Patent Cooperation Treaty (PCT), it contains a request, a description, one or more claims, an abstract, and one or more drawings (where required).

International Bureau (IB)—Maintains the master file of all international applications and acts as the publisher and central coordinating body under the PCT. The World Intellectual Property Organization performs this function.

International Filing Date—The date an international application is received and complete; serves as the date for determining novelty of the invention.

International Searching Authority (ISA)—Looks for prior art, unity of invention, and inventive step of inventions claimed in international applications. At the option of the applicant, either the USPTO or the EPO will act as an ISA for international applications filed in the United States.

Invention—An original idea that allows for the solution of a specific problem in a technology field. To qualify for legal protection in most countries, the invention must be novel, nonobvious (or involve an inventive step), and capable of industrial application (industrial manufacture or use).

Inventive Step—An international counterpart to unobviousness, usually means that the invention would not have occurred to a specialist in the technological field of the invention.

IP—See Intellectual Property.

IPR Hygiene—Intellectual Property Rights Hygiene, ensuring that each sponsor of research that ends in IP protection and licensing receives credit and/or compensation.

Issue Date—The date on which a patent actually issues, as distinguished from the filing date (the date the USPTO physically receives the application).

Joint Inventor—An inventor who is part of a group and contributes to an invention. Joint inventors can still file jointly even though they may not have worked together or during the same period of time, or did not contribute equally in type of work or amount, or did not make a contribution to the subject matter for all of the claims in the patent.

Joint Venture—A term used to describe a range of multiparty relationships. Most often, each party owns an equal share (not to exceed 50 percent ownership between two partners, 33.33 between three partners, etc.) in a joint venture corporation.

Kinds—The letter, often with a number after it, that indicates the level of publication of a patent.

Know-How—Unpatented technical information that is useful and important.

Knowledge Capital—The sum of human capital, customer capital (customer attachment to/involvement in a business), and structural capital.

Knowledge Companies—Companies that make their profits by converting knowledge into value. Those companies whose profits come predominantly from commercializing innovations through value creation and value extraction. Examples include Microsoft, 3M, and Netscape.

Knowledge Management—Developing and following a system to extract value from information.

Kokai—An unexamined Japanese patent application.

Kokoku—An examined and allowed Japanese patent application.

Lapse—The date when a patent is no longer valid in a country or system due to failure to pay maintenance fees. A provision often allows reinstatement of the patent within a limited period.

Last Antecedent Doctrine—A doctrine of contract interpretation that a succeeding modifier of more than one noun applies to the last noun in a clause only, unless the context clearly dictates otherwise.

License—The privilege granted to a licensee to use an invention; it does not constitute an assignment. It can be either exclusive or nonexclusive and does not give the licensee the legal title to the patent.

License Monitoring—Ensuring that the licensee is in full compliance with the terms of the license agreement.

Licensee Estoppel—The principle that prevents a licensee from denying the validity of the rights licensed.

Life of a Patent—The maximum number of years that the monopoly rights conferred by the grant of a patent will last. In the United States, a patent lasts 20 years from the filing date.

Maintenance—Paying the scheduled fees necessary to keep an issued patent valid.

Manner of Manufacture—Legal terminology used to differentiate patentable inventions from those that are not. Artistic creations, mathematical methods, plans, schemes, or other purely mental processes cannot typically be patented.

Marks—Trademarks and servicemarks used to differentiate goods or services from other goods and services; they do not prohibit others from offering similar goods and services under a different mark.

Markman Determination—A court proceeding in which a judge interprets patent claims. This interpretation is for use by juries in patent infringement trails.

Markush—The practice when a single claim defines similar alternatives that offer the same technical features. Used almost exclusively for chemical patent applications, where the compound is defined as a basic structure with a variable list of possible substituents.

Means Plus Statement of Function Claim (Means Plus Function Claim)—A claim which describes a claim element's capabilities (e.g., "means for writing") as opposed to what it actually is (e.g., "a pencil").

Mediation—The use of a neutral third party to help parties in conflict find points of agreement and a mutually agreeable resolution to the dispute.

Metes and Bounds—The legal description of the precise property protected by a patent.

Misuse—An equitable defense to an infringement charge based on a violation of the letter or spirit of antitrust laws.

Most Favored Licensee Clause—See Most Favored Nations Clause.

Most Favored Nations Clause—Guarantees the right of a licensee to the most favorable terms granted to succeeding licensees.

Mutatis Mutandis—Meaning "appropriate (obvious) changes," a Latin term used to indicate that a clause is identical to a previous clauses, save obvious differences between the two.

Names Used in Trade—A nonproprietary name that workers in a subject area use to refer to an article or product. The name describes a single article or product independent of any one producer and may or may not be known to the public.

Net Sales—The difference between gross sales of a licensed product and designated deductions.

Nominated Person—The person(s) or corporate body that owns an invention.

Nonexclusive License—The grant under a patent that allows the licensor to grant license rights to more than one person.

Nonobvious—Criteria that must be met before a patent is granted. The claimed invention must be nonobvious to a person of ordinary skill in the art.

NonConvention Equivalents—An application filed in a second, or subsequent, country that does not claim a priority application in another country. Typically filed after the one-year Paris Convention application deadline expires.

Notice of Allowance—Announces that a patent application has met the statutory requirements for the U.S. Patent and Trademark Office to issue a patent. The notice verifies that the patent will "issue" at a future date.

Novelty—Criteria that must be met before a patent is granted. In order for an invention to be "novel," it must have not been known or used by others.

OEM—Original Equipment Manufacturer. Frequently, one company will buy a product from an OEM with the intention of selling it under their own trademark.

Offenlegungsschrift—A published unexamined German patent document.

Office Action—A formal patent office letter informing an applicant of the rejection of their application including the reason for their decision.

Omnibus claim—A distinct claim that refers to the invention description and drawings and indicates the preferred form for an invention.

Opposition—The time period allowed for an interested party to post oppositions to the grant of a patent. For European patents, opposition lasts nine months.

Option—In the IP arena, a contractual right to obtain ownership or license of an IP right by a certain future date at a particular exercise price.

Paid-up License—A license to which additional royalty cannot be paid; it is said to have vested.

Paris Convention—An international patent treaty with most industrial countries as members. Allows applicants one year from first filing their patent application (usually in their own country) in which to make further applications in member countries and claim the original priority date.

Patent—A monopoly dispensed by a government office or agency for a limited time (usually 20 years from the application date) for a new, useful, and nonobvious invention. A patent provides the exclusive right to practice, manufacture, sell, license, or use that invention. A patent consists of drawings of the invention, a specification explaining it, and claims that define the scope of exclusivity.

Patent and Trademark Office (PTO)—The office of the Department of Commerce that is responsible for examining and issuing patents, also commonly referred to as the USPTO.

Patent Assertion Insurance—Insurance on patents which will pay legal fees and expenses in the event of patent infringement litigation.

Patent Cluster—Patents linked by the similarity of the technology protected by these patents.

Patent Co-operation Treaty (PCT)—An international treaty that allows inventors to file an international patent application (for acceptance in as many countries as the applicant designates). The treaty also facilitates international patent application prosecution through the designated International Bureau (currently the World Intellectual Property Organization) and International Search Agency.

Patent Examiner—See Examiner.

Patent Family—A geographically diverse group of applications claiming a single invention.

Patent Infringement—See Infringement.

Patent Office—The government agency responsible for examining and granting patents. The Patent Office in the United States is officially known as the Patent and Trademark Office, PTO, or USPTO. The EPO is the European Patent Office.

Patent Prosecution—Describes the events following legal action taken by the Patent Office against a patent applicant (usually represented by an attorney) when a patent application is seen as unpatentable.

Patentability—A determination of whether or not an invention should receive a patent, determined by its novelty, unobviousness, and utility, and also based on a review of the U.S. Patent and Trademark Office's publications and patents.

Patentability Search—A search of existing patents and publications to determine whether or not an invention fills the criteria necessary to be patentable.

Patentschrift—A granted German patent application.

Pending—The period in which the patent office has not yet made a decision on a patent application, and it has not yet been withdrawn.

Permanent Injunction—A court order permanently prohibiting a defendant in a lawsuit from performing a specified act or specified acts.

Pioneer Patent—See Broad Claim.

Plant Patent—A patent granted to inventors or discoverers of new and unique, asexually propagated plants.

Plant Breeder's Rights—Certain rights granting exclusive commercial rights to breeders so that they may protect new plant varieties.

Portfolio Analysis—Examining a portfolio to detect valuable, revenue-generating IP.

Portfolio Maintenance Analysis—An analysis that involves sorting through a patent portfolio and examining the fees associated with each group of patents to identify patents which should be discontinued (by failure to maintain them) due to low revenue potential.

Portfolio Mining—Performing a portfolio analysis which leads to portfolio development and revenue generation.

Portfolio Paring—Selling or discontinuing fee payment for patents of low revenue potential.

Portfolio Valuation by Sampling—A statistical technique used to value a sample group of patents in a portfolio. The value of the statistical sample is extrapolated to determine the approximate value of the portfolio as a whole.

Preliminary Examination—The beginning stage in application processing at the patent office in which an official ensures that the specification is completed correctly and drafts initial search reports.

Preliminary Injunction—A court order given after an evidentiary hearing that prohibits a defendant from performing a certain action until a complete trial on merits occurs.

Presumption of Validity—Entitles every issued U.S. patent to fall under the statutory presumption that it is valid.

Principle of Territoriality—States that an IP right granted by a sovereign nation is only valid within the territory of that nation.

Prior Art—Previously used, published, or patented technology which was available before a patent application and may support the rejection or limiting of a claim due to lack of novelty.

Priority Date—A date set when an inventor first files a patent application. The priority date is used to determine novelty. In the United States, specifically, the date refers to the date the invention was first conceived and reduced to practice.

Prosecution—The process a patent attorney goes through before the U.S. Patent and Trademark Office.

Provisional Specification—Used to establish a priority date for an invention. Its does not offer patent protection or replace a complete application. It is rendered invalid if it is not accompanied by a complete application within 12 months.

PTO—Abbreviation for United States Patent and Trademark Office. Also in common use is USPTO.

Publication—A disclosure in any form that is readily accessible or publicly distributed.

Read On—A claim reads on something, if every aspect of the claim occurs in that which it reads on. If a claim reads on prior art, then the claim is not valid. For infringement to take place, a claim has to read on an accused device.

Reasonable Diligence—See Best Efforts.

Reduction to Practice—The first practical execution of an invention, it can be in the form of a model.

Reinstatement—The restoration of a patent to protected status after it has apparently lapsed by error or been revoked.

Rejection—A refusal of a claim of an awaiting patent application that is given by the patent office to the applicant or representing attorney.

Renewal fees—Scheduled payments that must be made by the applicant to the patent office in order to keep the patent active and prevent it from lapsing. These are known as maintenance fees in the United States.

Repair v. Reconstruction Doctrine—A licensed, patented article may be repaired, but its reconstruction would be an infringement.

Research Disclosure—Defensive publications which are published, often anonymously, to give companies and inventors "freedom of use" rather than legal protection. Once research disclosures are published, the invention ceases to be patentable.

Restraining Order—See Temporary Restraining Order.

Revocation—Termination of the protection given to a patent on one or more grounds.

Right of First Negotiation—The contractual right which is granted by an owner of something, as in a patent or other IP right within the context of IP, to deal solely or exclusively with the grantee of the right for a designated amount of time following the owner's decision to sell that right. The Right of First Negotiation differs from a Right of First Refusal, because the grantee is given no certainty besides an advantage of time.

Right of First Refusal—The contractual right which is granted by an owner of something, as in a patent or other IP right within the context of IP, to give to the grantee any third-party offer to sell the right that the owner is preparing to accept. The owner must first receive a finalized proposal to purchase the right from a third party and, before selling to the third party, must offer to sell to the grantee on the exact same terms as the offer. This can hamper the freedom of the owner to receive third-party offers, because the third party may be less willing to take the time and effort to determine whether to buy and then negotiate the deal and be preempted by the grantee. A method to appeal more to the third party would be to extend a compensation fee, or break-up fee, to compensate the third party for its time and effort should the right be sold to the grantee.

Right of Publicity—An inherent right of every individual to retain control over the commercial usage of his or her identity and likeness that is recognized in most states (either via common law or statutes).

Royalty—Payment for the use of licensed intellectual property, usually a stated percentage of sales.

Royalty Base—The volume of units to which a percentage royalty is applicable.

Royalty Rate—The percentage that is multiplied by a royalty base to calculate a royalty payment.

Royalty Stacking—Multiple royalties due to several patent owners for a product which infringes upon more than one patent.

Search—A study of information (both patent and nonpatent literature) in order to determine if any prior discovery makes a potential invention unpatentable due to novelty concerns or, if patentable, to determine if it infringes upon an already issued patent.

Search Report—A list of published items checked by the patent examiners in determining novelty and possible infringement of other patents.

Secondary Considerations—A list of objective considerations that may be used by the judge or jury to assist in the subjective determination of whether or not an invention is nonobvious.

Securitization—When an owner grants a stake in an intellectual property to a lender.

Security Interest—The use of intellectual property as collateral for a debt or liability.

Semiconductor Mask Works—The design of a semiconductor chip which has a special category of protection under U.S. intellectual property law.

Servicemark—A word, symbol, or other mark that is used to designate the identity and source of a service, a type of industrial property.

Set-off—A legal term for the demand a defendant makes to subtract the amount of a cross debt, or counterclaim, from the amount of money owed to the plaintiff.

Shrink Wrap License—An unsigned, nonexclusive software license that comes with the software package. Use of the software indicates acceptance of the license terms.

Small Entity—A patent statutes classification for companies that have less than 500 employees, nonprofit organizations, and academic institutions, that allows them to pay about half the fees a large entity would pay for a similar service.

Source Code—The version of a computer program that humans can read (e.g., HTML).

Specification—The written description of an invention that includes enough detail to ensure that another person skilled in that field could re-create it.

Standards Licensing—An obligation that the owner of an essential patent must license it to all companies for a reasonable royalty without discriminatory behavior.

Status—The legal standing of a patent or patent application (e.g., lapsed, pending, standing, revoked).

Statutory Bar—Prior art that is available more than one year before the filing date of a patent application, and therefore invalidates that application for lack of novelty.

Statutory Law—Laws crafted by individual legislatures, as distinguished from common law.

Statutory Subject Matter—The types of patentable inventions, including process, machine, (article of) manufacture, or composition of matter, or any new and useful improvement thereof.

Stick Mining—Examining an intellectual property portfolio to find any patents that are currently infringed with a plan to sell or license those patents to infringers.

Structural Capital—The physical support and infrastructure firms provide for their human capital. It includes both direct and indirect support.

Substantive Examination—The full examination of the substance or content of a patent application by a patent office examiner to determine whether it merits a patent.

Support—The network of services that assist users with a computer program.

Tacit Knowledge—The knowledge and know-how residing in an employee's mind, also known as human capital.

Technology Transfer—The methods employed to license patentable intellectual property and make it marketable.

Temporary Restraining Order (TRO)—A short-term court order to maintain a certain condition until an evidentiary hearing can be conducted. Can be used to keep a defendant from infringing on another's intellectual property.

Term of Patent—See Life of a Patent.

Tort—A civil wrong, either intentional or accidental, in which injury occurs to another person. Results in more civil litigation than any other major area of law, including contract, real property, and criminal law. Patent infringement is considered a tort.

Trade Secret—An intellectual asset that is confidential, valuable in nature, and not to be shared with anyone without prior approval. Proprietary and significant business information (e.g., technical, financial, and marketing know-how) which can be legally protected.

Trade-Related Aspects of Intellectual Property (TRIPs)—An international set of guidelines created in 1995 concerning intellectual property issues, including copyright, marks, geographical indications, industrial designs, patents, circuit layout rights, and trade secrets. It establishes common standards, enforcement procedures, and methods of dispute settlement.

Trademark—The right to use a particular word, phrase, or artwork to distinguish the goods and services of the trademark owner from those of competitors. A trademark is legally protected and can be in many forms. Examples are letters, phrases, words, symbols, and logos.

Tying—Placing the sale of one good or service dependent on the sale of another.

Unfair Competition—Activities or practices which take place during business or trade that restrain fair competition and are not in congruence with honest practices, including:

    a. acts leading to confusion with the products or services, or the industrial or commercial transactions, of a business;

    b. discrediting products or services, or the industrial or commercial transactions, of a business by making false allegations;

    c. allegations or suggestions which may deceive the public, especially as to the manufacturing procedures for a product or as to the integrity, amount, or other aspects of products and services;

    d. unlawful possession, divulgence, or usage of trade secrets;

    e. acting so as to dilute or harm the distinctive power of another business's mark or taking unfair advantage of the goodwill or name of another business.

Unobviousness—See Nonobvious.

Unpatentable—Used to describe an invention that does not significantly depart from what was previously known in the area or that does not relate to the proper subject matter for the patent for any other reason.

University Research—All research done within the term of an inventor's employment by the university including, but not limited to, the performance of a grant, contract, or award made to the university by an extramural agency or with the usage of university resources. However, the usage of office space and/or library facilities does not constitute working with university resources.

Update—An enhancement of a computer program to meet current specifications. An example would be adjusting the team rosters of a football game to reflect real-life changes made for the new season.

USPTO—United States Patent and Trademark Office, the Department of Commerce office responsible for examining and issuing patents. Also referred to as the PTO.

Unity of Invention—Any international application must relate to one invention only or to a group of inventions that form a single general inventive concept.

Utility—Suitability for some desirable practical or commercial purpose.

Utility Model—A type of patent available in some countries that involves a simpler inventive step than is necessary in a traditional patent. These patents usually have a shorter life than traditional patents.

Utility Patent—A patent that protects a process or the functional aspects, rather than the aesthetic aspects, of a product. A utility patent relates to what the process or function is or what it does; a design patent protects the aesthetic elements.

Valid—A valid patent is an issued patent that is not invalid for one of several reasons, the most common reason is that one or more of its claims read on prior art that was not considered by the patent office during patent prosecution.

Validity—Whether a patent claim meets the patent office requirements of statutory subject matter, novelty, utility, and nonobviousness.

Value Added—The value of a firm's product to its customers.

Value Creation—The generation of new knowledge and its conversion into innovations with commercial value.

Value Extraction—Harvesting the level and degree of value from an intellectual asset portfolio that is required to achieve the strategic vision and long-term objectives of a firm.

Vested License—See Paid-up License.

Work-for-Hire—The work product of an individual hired specifically to complete a task, therefore owned by the individual or organization that paid for the work.

World Intellectual Property Organization (WIPO)—Located in Geneva, Switzerland, it is the central coordinating body of intellectual property and acts as the International Bureau defined by the PCT.

Data Bank

301 Top Patentees, 2000

Rank	Organization	Patents
1	International Business Machines Corp.	2886
2	NEC Corp.	2021
3	Canon K.K.	1890
4	Samsung Electronics Co., Ltd.	1441
5	Lucent Technologies Inc.	1411
6	Sony Corp.	1385
7	Micron Technology, Inc.	1304
8	Toshiba Corp.	1232
9	Motorola, Inc.	1196
10	Fujitsu Ltd.	1147
11	Matsushita Electric Industrial Co., Ltd.	1137
12	Advanced Micro Devices, Inc.	1053
13	Hitachi, Ltd.	1036
14	Mitsubishi Denki K.K.	1010
15	Siemens A.G.	912
16	Hewlett-Packard Co.	901
17	Eastman Kodak Co.	875
18	Intel Corp.	795
19	General Electric Co.	787
20	U.S. Philips Corp.	693
21	Texas Instruments, Inc.	686
22	BASF Group	589
23	Sharp Corp.	586
24	Xerox Corp.	569
25	Robert Bosch GmbH	546
26	Fuji Photo Film Co., Ltd.	542
27	3M Co.	483
28	Procter & Gamble Co.	465
29	Sun Microsystems	465
30	Honda Motor Co., Ltd.	463
31	Telefonaktiebolaget LM Ericsson	463
32	E.I. DuPont de Nemours & Co.	450
33	University of California	434
34	United Microelectronics Corp.	430
35	Ricoh Co., Ltd.	416

(continued)

Rank	Organization	Patents
36	Hon Hai Precision Ind. Co., Ltd.	397
37	Seiko Epson Corp.	396
38	Nortel Networks Corp.	392
39	Applied Materials, Inc.	386
40	Taiwan Semiconductor Manufacturing Co., Ltd.	385
41	Denso Corp.	369
42	Ford Motor Co.	355
43	U.S. Navy	351
44	Microsoft Corp.	344
45	Toyota Jidosha K.K.	341
46	Caterpillar, Inc.	334
47	Minolta Camera Co., Ltd.	333
48	LSI Logic Corp.	325
49	Daimler Chrysler A.G.	322
50	Compaq Computer Corp., Inc.	315
51	Ericcson, Inc.	312
52	Bayer A.G.	304
53	Yazaki Corp.	304
54	Murata Manufacturing Co., Ltd.	302
55	Daimler Chrysler Corp.	295
56	AT&T Corp.	294
57	Hyundai Electronics Industries Co., Ltd..	294
58	Olympus Optical Co., Ltd.	281
59	Nikon Corp.	278
60	TRW Inc.	275
61	Exxon Mobil Corp.	271
62	Whitaker Corp.	257
63	LG Semicon Co., Ltd.	255
64	General Motor Corp.	254
65	Nissan Motor Co., Ltd.	251
66	Sanyo Electric Co., Ltd.	251
67	Alcatel Thomson Faisceaux Hertziens	248
68	Seagate Technology, Inc.	235
69	Asahi Kogaku Kogyo K.K.	233
70	Medtronic Inc.	231
71	L'Oreal S.A.	227
72	Brother Kogyo K.K.	224
73	Kimberly-Clark Worldwide, Inc.	224
74	Oki Electric Industry Co., Ltd.	223
75	LG Electronics Inc.	220
76	Raytheon Co.	205
77	Industrial Technology Research Institute, Taiwan	198
78	Eaton Corp.	194
79	Alps Electric Co., Ltd.	193
80	Smithkline Beecham Corp.	193
81	Fuji Xerox Co., Ltd.	192
82	National Semiconductor Corp.	187
83	Allied-Signal, Inc.	183
84	Hughes Electronics Corp.	183
85	Merck & Co., Inc.	182

Rank	Organization	Patents
86	Tokyo Electron Ltd.	179
87	Lockheed Martin Corp.	175
88	AGFA-Gevaert N.V.	174
89	Nokia Mobile Phones Ltd.	169
90	ITT Manufacturing Enterprises, Inc.	166
91	Eli Lilly & Co.	161
92	Institut Francais du Petrole	160
93	TDK Corp.	160
94	CIBA Specialty Chemicals Corp.	158
95	3Com Corp.	155
96	Semiconductor Energy Laboratory Co., Ltd.	155
97	Sumitomo Wiring Systems, Ltd.	154
98	Pfizer Inc.	153
99	Konica Corp.	152
100	Micron Electronics, Inc.	152
101	Mitsubishi Heavy Industries Co., Ltd.	149
102	Sumitomo Chemical Co., Ltd.	149
103	Incyte Pharmaceuticals, Inc.	147
104	Sci-Med Life Systems, Inc.	147
105	STMicroelectronics S.R.L.	144
106	Philips Electronics North America Corp.	142
107	U.S. Army	142
108	Yamaha Corp.	141
109	Halliburton Energy Services	140
110	Novo Nordisk A/S.	140
111	Illinois Tool Works Inc.	138
112	NCR Corp.	138
113	Boeing Co.	136
114	Sumitomo Electric Industries Co., Ltd.	136
115	VLSI Technology, Inc.	134
116	Baker Hughes Inc.	133
117	Dow Chemical Co.	133
118	Shell Oil Co.	132
119	Vanguard International Semiconductor Corp.	131
120	Northrop Grumman Corp.	130
121	Pioneer Electronic Corp.	130
122	Abbott Laboratories	128
123	Bayer Corp.	126
124	Electronics & Telecommunications Research Institute	124
125	Henkel Corp.	124
126	Agilent Technologies, Inc.	122
127	Heidelberger Druckmaschinen A.G.	122
128	Schlumberger Technology Corp.	122
129	Daewoo Electronics Co., Ltd.	120
130	Lexmark International, Inc.	118
131	United Technologies Corp.	118
132	Eastman Chemical Co.	117
133	Rohm Co., Ltd.	116

(continued)

Rank	Organization	Patents
134	NGK Insulators, Ltd.	115
135	Winbond Electronics Corp.	115
136	Xilinx, Inc.	115
137	Fuji Photo Optical Co. Ltd.	114
138	Isis Pharmaceuticals, Inc.	114
139	Nokia Telecommunications OY	114
140	Cypress Semiconductor Corp.	113
141	Massachusetts Institute of Technology	113
142	Phillips Petroleum Co.	113
143	Corning Inc.	111
144	Shin Etsu Chemical Co., Ltd.	111
145	STMicroelectronics, Inc.	111
146	Aisin Seiki K.K.	110
147	Bristol-Meyers Squibb Co.	110
148	Toyoda Jidoshokki Seisakusho K.K.	110
149	Molex Inc.	107
150	Bridgestone Corp.	106
151	Dai Nippon Printing Co., Ltd.	105
152	Air Products & Chemicals, Inc.	104
153	UOP	104
154	Yamaha Motor Co., Ltd.	104
155	California Institute of Technology	103
156	Stanford University	103
157	Cisco Technology, Inc.	102
158	Dana Corp.	102
159	Goodyear Tire & Rubber Co.	101
160	Honeywell Inc.	101
161	Cirrus Logic, Inc.	100
162	Qualcomm, Inc.	100
163	Carrier Corp.	99
164	Zeneca Ltd.	99
165	Akzo Nobel NV	98
166	Mitsui Chemicals, Inc.	98
167	Becton, Dickinson, & Co.	97
168	Unisys Corp.	97
169	Altera Corp.	96
170	PPG Industries Ohio Inc.	96
171	U.S. Department of Health & Human Services	96
172	U.S. National Aeronautics & Space Administration	96
173	Novartis A.G.	95
174	Seiko Instruments Inc.	95
175	Delphi Technologies, Inc.	94
176	Dell USA, L.P.	93
177	Digital Equipment Corp.	92
178	Colgate-Palmolive Co.	91
179	Matsushita Electronics Corp.	90
180	University of Texas	89
181	Mannesmann Sachs A.G.	87
182	Intermec IP Corp.	86
183	Mitsubishi Chemical Co.	86

Rank	Organization	Patents
184	Apple Computer, Inc.	85
185	Casio Computer Co. Ltd.	85
186	Trimble Navigation, Ltd.	85
187	SGS-Thomson Microelectronics S.A.	84
188	Warner-Lambert Co.	84
189	Lear Automotive Dearborn, Inc.	83
190	Sanshin Kogyo K.K.	83
191	Hoechst A.G.	82
192	Kao Corp.	82
193	Sarnoff Corp. & Co., Ltd.	80
194	Shimano Inc.	80
195	Chartered Semiconductor Manufacturing PTE Ltd.	79
196	Victor Company of Japan, Ltd.	79
197	Case Corp.	78
198	Genentech, Inc.	78
199	Lam Research Corp.	78
200	Rohm & Haas Co.	78
201	Baxter International Inc.	77
202	Citizen Watch Co., Ltd.	77
203	McDonnell Douglas Corp.	77
204	Monsanto Co., Inc.	77
205	Oracle Corp.	77
206	STMicroelectronics S.A.	77
207	EMC Corp.	76
208	Pitney-Bowes, Inc.	76
209	Sandia Corp.	76
210	U.S. Air Force	76
211	Dow Corning Corp.	75
212	Ebara Corp., Nikkiso Co., Ltd.	75
213	Ethicon, Inc.	75
214	Southpac Trust International, Inc.	75
215	Tetra Laval Holdings & Finance S.A.	75
216	L'Air Liquide	74
217	Merck Patent Gesellschaft Mit Beschrankter Haftung	74
218	Smithkline Beecham PLC.	74
219	Black & Decker Inc.	73
220	FMC Corp.	73
221	MCI Communications Corp.	73
222	Fuji Electric Co., Ltd.	72
223	Litton Systems Inc.	72
224	Nestec, S.A.	72
225	Sumitomo Rubber Industries, Ltd.	71
226	Advantest Corp.	70
227	Agency of Industrial Science & Technology	70
228	British Telecommunication, PLC.	70
229	DSM N.V.	70
230	Johns Hopkins University	70
231	Nippon Shokubai Co., Ltd.	70

(continued)

Rank	Organization	Patents
232	Northern Telecom Limited	70
233	NSK Limited	70
234	Takeda Chemicals Industries Ltd.	70
235	Toray Industries Inc.	70
236	Asahi Kasei Kogya K.K.	69
237	Clariant GmbH	69
238	Deere & Co.	69
239	Komatsu Ltd.	69
240	SGS-Thomson Microelectronics S.R.L.	69
241	SMS Schloemann-Siemag A.G.	69
242	University of Michigan	69
243	Conexant Systems, Inc.	68
244	Mannesmann A.G.	68
245	Silicon Graphics, Inc.	68
246	United Semiconductor Corp.	68
247	Nippon Telegraph & Telephone Corp.	67
248	Samsung Display Devices Co., Ltd.	67
249	Alcatel USA Sourcing, L.P.	66
250	American Cyanamid Co.	66
251	Mosel Vitelic, Inc.	66
252	Breed Automotive Technology, Inc.	65
253	Elf Atochem S.A.	65
254	Emerson Electric Co.	65
255	National Science Council	65
256	Sandvik Aktiebolag	65
257	Aktiebolaget Astra	64
258	Berg Technology, Inc.	64
259	Chiron Corp.	64
260	Fraunhofer-Gesellschaft E.V.	64
261	Wisconsin Alumni Research Foundation	64
262	Asea Brown Boveri A.G.	63
263	Harris Corp.	63
264	Mazda Motor Corp.	63
265	Unisia Jecs Corp.	63
266	Voith Sulzer Papiermaschinen GmbH	63
267	Cardiac Pacemakers, Inc.	62
268	Commissariat A L'Energie Atomique	62
269	Avery Dennison Corp.	61
270	Cummins Engine Co., Inc.	62
271	G.D. Searle & Co.	61
272	Hoffman-La Roche Inc.	61
273	Koito Manufacturing Co. Ltd.	61
274	Schering A.G.	61
275	Worldwide Semiconductor Manufacturing Corp.	61
276	Daikin Industries Ltd.	60
277	Hilti A.G.	60
278	Hyundai Motor Co., Ltd.	60
279	Kawasaki Steel Corp.	60
280	Matsushita Electric Works, Ltd.	60
281	Hubbell Inc.	59

Rank	Organization	Patents
282	Seagate Technology, LLC	59
283	Adaptec, Inc.	58
284	Degussa-Huels A.G.	58
285	Lear Corp.	58
286	Tektronix Inc.	58
287	Texas Instruments - Acer Inc.	58
288	University of Washington	58
289	Acuson Corp.	57
290	General Hospital Corp.	57
291	Honeywell International Inc.	57
292	Toyoda Gosei K.K.	57
293	Westinghouse Air Brake Co.	57
294	Brunswick Corp.	56
295	Nippon Steel Co.	56
296	Nitto Denko Corp.	56
297	Praxair Technology, Inc.	56
298	U.S. Department of Energy	56
299	Iomega Corp.	55
300	Storage Technology Corp.	55
301	U.S. Department of Agriculture	55

Source: Intellectual Property Owners

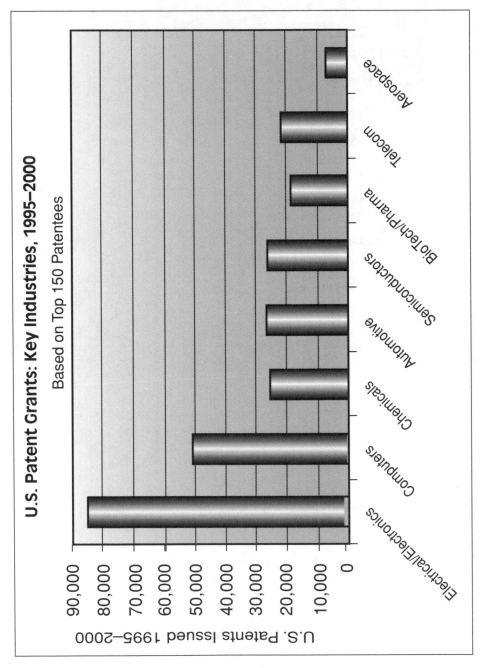

Source: MIT Technology Review.

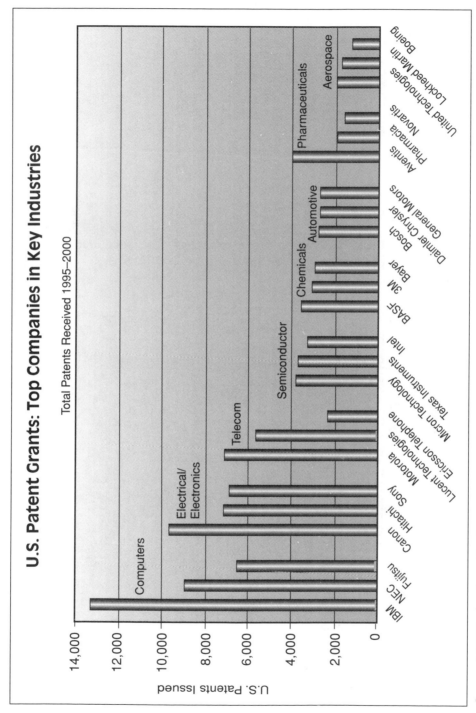

U.S. Patent Grants: Top Companies in Key Industries

Total Patents Received 1995–2000

Source: MIT Technology Review.

Top IP Damages Awards, Licenses, and Transactions (1980–2001)

Note: P= Patents, C= Copyright

Amount	Year	Parties	Legal Action	Technology
	2001			
$400,000,000	2001	Pitney Bowes <— Hewlett-Packard*	P. Settlement	Electronics
$340,000,000	2001	Winnie-The-Pooh estate <— Walt Disney	C. Buyout	Story characters
$187,000,000	2001	OSI Pharmaceuticals <— Genentech, Roche	P. License	Drugs
$78,000,000	2001	Southern Clay Products <— Sued-Chemie	P. Lawsuit	Chemicals
$46,580,000	2001	Honeywell <— Hamilton Sundstrand	P. Lawsuit	Mechanical
$35,000,000	2001	Crystal Semiconductor <— Tritech Microelectronics	P. Lawsuit	Electronic
$19,000,000	2001	Brian Webster <— 20th Century Fox	C. Lawsuit	Movie Script
$18,000,000	2001	BioTime <— Akzo Nobel	P. License	Pharmaceutical
$15,800,000	2001	Ricoh <— Nashua Corp.	P. Settlement	Mechanical
$8,700,000	2001	William Riles <— Shell Exploration	P. Lawsuit	Mechanical
$4,000,000	2001	20th Century Fox <- Fox Broadcasting	Copyright	Movie
$1,500,000	2001	Acres Gaming <— Mikohn Gaming	P. Lawsuit	Software
$1,000,000	2001	Great Lakes Chemical <— Archimica	P. Lawsuit	Pharmaceutical
$480,000	2001	BSA <— ThoughtWorks	C. Piracy	Software
	2000			
$1,000,000,000	2000	SnapTrack <— Qualcomm	Buyout	Electronics
$324,000,000	2000	Cordis/Johnson & Johnson <— Boston Scientific	P. Lawsuit	Medical
$275,000,000	2000	Caldera <— Microsoft	Settlement	Software
$270,000,000	2000	Cordis/Johnson & Johnson <— Medtronic	P. Lawsuit	Medical
$200,000,000	2000	Exelixis Pharmaceuticals <— Bayer	R&D Pact	Drugs
$200,000,000	2000	Gemstar <— Motorola	P. Settlement	Electronics
$170,000,000	2000	Kinetix Pharmaceuticals <— Amgen	Buyout	Drugs
$112,000,000	2000	3Dfx <— Nvidia	Buyout	Electronics

Amount	Year	Parties	Type	Industry
$100,000,000+	2000	Chiron <— Hoffman-LaRoche	P. License	Biotech
$100,000,000	2000	Pioneer HiBred <— Cargill	Trade Secrets	Biotech
$100,000,000	2000	Abbott <— Cephalon	P. License	Drugs
$80,000,000+	2000	ETRI <— Qualcomm	P. Royalties	Electronics
$80,000,000	2000	Avery Denison <— Four Pillars	Trade Secret	Chemicals
$77,000,000	2000	Abgenix <— ImmGenics	Buyout	Biotech
$68,750,000	2000	General Technology Apps. <— Conoco Liquid Power	P. Lawsuit	Chemicals
$55,000,000	2000	David Bowie <— Prudential Insurance	Copyright	Music
$53,000,000	2000	Universal Music <— MP3	C. License	Music
$52,600,000	2000	Caliper Technologies <— Aclara Biosciences	P. Lawsuit	Electronics
$50,000,000	2000	P.O. Market <— Wal-Mart	Trade Secrets	Software
$45,000,000	2000	Rodime <— Seagate Technology	Settlement	Computers
$45,000,000	2000	Barr Laboratories <— DuPont	Settlement	Drugs
$41,000,000	2000	Alexion Pharm. <— Prolifaron	Buyout	Biotech
$35,000,000	2000	Caliper Technologies <— Aclara Biosciences	Trade Secrets	Chemical
$26,000,000	2000	Simon Property Group <— MySimon.com	Trademark	
$25,000,000	2000	Lubrizol <— Imperial	P. Settlement	Chemical
$25,000,000	2000	Bausch & Lomb <— Alcon Laboratories	P. Settlement	Chemical
$20,000,000	2000	Tyson Foods <— ConAgra Foods	Trade Secrets	Chemical
$18,000,000	2000	Edmark Industries <— S. Asia Intn'l	P. Lawsuit	Mechanical
$18,000,000	2000	SIBIA <— Cadus Pharmaceuticals	P. Lawsuit	Pharmaceutical
$16,350,000	2000	Integra Lifesciences <— Merck KgaA	P. Lawsuit	Biotech
$16,000,000	2000	Eastern Michigan Univ. <— ExxonMobil	Patent Donation	Chemicals
$15,000,000	2000	BroadVision <— Art Technology Group	Settlement	Software
$14,400,000	2000	Coley Pharm. <— Isis Pharm.	Buyout	Biotech
$13,000,000	2000	C.R. Bard <— Boston Scientific	P. Lawsuit	Medical
$13,200,000	2000	Frank Calabrese <— Square D	P. Lawsuit	Software
$12,000,000	2000	Caliper Technologies <— Flehr Hohbach	Trade Secret	Electronics
$11,000,000	2000	Smith Engineering <— Eisenmann Corp.	P. Lawsuit	Mechanical
$10,200,000	2000	Trident Microsystems <— Via Technologies	Settlement	Electronics
$10,000,000	2000	ID Biomedical <— Third Wave Tech.	Settlement	Biotech

(continued)

587

Amount	Year	Parties	Legal Action	Technology
$10,000,000	2000	Nycomed Imaging <— Mallinckrodt Medical	Settlement	Medical
$9,000,000	2000	Angeion <— Medtronic	License	Medical
$8,500,000	2000	Celltech Group <— Cistron Biotechnology	Buyout	Biotech
$8,000,000	2000	SanDisk < Lexar	P. Settlement	Electronics
$2,000,000	2000	Lexar < SanDisk	P. Settlement	Electronics
$7,700,000	2000	Truck Stop Operator <— Truck Stop Operator	Copyright	Floorplan
$7,000,000	2000	GE Harris <— Wabtec	Settlement	Electronics
$6,500,000	2000	Enzia Inc. <— Accord Video Telecom	Settlement	Software
$5,700,000	2000	Bose <— Harman Inter.	P. Lawsuit	Mechanical
$5,000,000	2000	R.G. Barry Corp <— Domino's Pizza	Settlement	Mechanical
$4,250,000	2000	Serta <— Simmons	P. Settlement	Mechanical
$4,200,000	2000	Quickturn Design <— Aptiz	P. Lawsuit	Legal fees
$4,000,000+	2000	Baxter Intern. <— Spectranetics	Settlement	Medical
$2,218,000	2000	Tate Access Floors <— Maxcess Technologies	P. Lawsuit	Mechanical
$2,000,000	2000	Novell <— Myung Je	Copyright	Software
$1,000,000	2000	National Instruments <— PPT Vision	Settlement	Software
$650,000+	2000	CoolSavings <— e-centives	Settlement	Software

1999

Amount	Year	Parties	Legal Action	Technology
$200,000,000	1999	Univ. California <— Genentech	P. Settlement	Drugs
$165,000,000	1999	Viskase Corp. <— American National Can	P. Lawsuit	Chemicals
$100,000,000	1999	Inprise(Borland) <— Microsoft	License	Software
$60,000,000+	1999	Ranbaxy Labs <— Bayer AG	License	Drugs
$47,900,000	1999	AcroMed <— Sofamor Danek	P. Lawsuit	Medical
$40,000,000	1999	AccuScan <— Xerox	P. Lawsuit	Electronics
$35,000,000	1999	Angeion <— Guidant	License	Medical
$32,300,000	1999	Power Integration <— Motorola	P. Lawsuit	Electronics
$31,700,000	1999	Columbia Pictures <— Krypton Broadcasting	C. Lawsuit	Television
$29,000,000	1999	Int. Game Tech. <— WMS Gaming	P. Lawsuit	Electronics

Amount	Year	Case	Type	Category
$25,200,000	1999	Tec Air <— Denso Manufacturing	P. Lawsuit	Chemical
$20,000,000	1999	Crystal Semiconductor <— Opti Inc.	P. Lawsuit	Electronics
$13,700,000	1999	RIAA <— Global Arts Production	C. Lawsuit	Music
$12,900,000	1999	General Surgical <— Guidant	P. Lawsuit	Medical
$12,500,000	1999	Intermatic <— Lamson & Sessions	P. Lawsuit	Mechanical
$9,500,000	1999	Lucent <— Newbridge Networks	P. Lawsuit	Electronics
< $9,500,000	1999	Syquest <— Iomega	Buyout	Electronics
$5,400,000	1999	Guidant <— Medtronic	P. Lawsuit	Medical
$5,000,000	1999	Lucent Technologies <— Ascend Communications	License	Electronics
$3,500,000	1999	Varian Medical <— David Kern	Trade Secrets	Electronics
$3,100,000	1999	CFM Technologies <— Steag Electronics	P. Lawsuit	Electronic
$3,000,000	1999	Quickturn <— Mentor Graphics	Settlement	Software
$2,700,000	1999	SunTiger <— Scientific Research Facility	P. Lawsuit	Optics
$2,000,000+	1999	Lonnie Johnson <— Laramie Ltd.	Royalties	Mechanical
$1,450,000	1999	Freeman <— First Years	Settlement	Mechanical
$1,000,000	1999	Interactive Pictures <— Infinite Pictures	P. Lawsuit	Software

1998

Amount	Year	Case	Type	Category
$170,000,000	1998	Exxon Chemical <— Mobil Chemical	P. Lawsuit	Chemical
$90,000,000	1998	Sepracor <— Eli Lilly	P. License	Drugs
$70,000,000	1998	Odetics <— Storage Technology	P. Lawsuit	Electronics
$64,000,000	1998	Bourns <— Raychem	Antitrust	Electronics
$36,000,000	1998	Interactive Tech. <— Pittway/Ademco	P. Lawsuit	Electronics
$30,000,000	1998	Real 3D <— Silicon Graphics	License	Software
$13,000,000	1998	Variable Parameter Fixture <— Morpheus Lights	P. Lawsuit	Electronic
$12,500,000	1998	Interactive Networks <— TCI	P. Lawsuit	Software
$1,250,000	1998	Eaton <— Meritor Automotive	P. Lawsuit	Mechanical
$1,230,000	1998	Samuel Zervitz <— Hollywood Pictures	C. Lawsuit	Movie Script

Amount	Year	Parties	Legal Action	Technology
		1997		
$700,000,000	1997	Digital <— Intel	P. Lawsuit	Computer
$150,000,000	1997	Apple Computer <— Microsoft	License	Software
$102,000,000	1997	Viskase <— American National Can	P. Lawsuit	Mechanical
$98,000,000	1997	Fonar Corp. <— General Electric	P. Lawsuit	Electronics
$68,000,000	1997	Unocal <— Six oil companies	P. Lawsuit	Chemical
$57,000,000	1997	Celeritas Tech. <— Rockwell	P. Lawsuit	Electronics
$18,000,000	1997	Comark Communications <— Harris Corp.	P. Lawsuit	Electronics
$13,000,000	1997	Escom/Commodore <— Gateway	P.Buyout	Electronic
$13,000,000	1997	Applied Medical Resources <— US Surgical	P. Lawsuit	Medical
		1996		
$211,000,000	1996	Haworth <— Steelcase	P. Lawsuit	Mechanical
		1995		
$90,000,000	1995	Wang <— Microsoft	License	Software
$64,000,000	1995	Schneider/BCSI <— Scimed	P. Lawsuit	Medical
$44,000,000	1995	Haworth <— Herman Miller	P. Lawsuit	Mechanical
$6,000,000	1995	Celeritas Tech. <— ATT	P. Lawsuit	Electronics
		1994		
$129,000,000	1994	Exxon Chemical <— Lubrizol	P. Lawsuit	Chemical
$83,000,000	1994	Stac Electronics <— Microsoft	P. License	Software
$82,500,000	1994	Novell <— Sun Microsystems	Copyright	Software
$50,000,000	1994	Atari <— Sega	License	Software

Amount	Year	Parties	Type	Field
$1,200,000,000	1993	Litton Industries <— Honeywell	P. Lawsuit	Electronics
$301,000,000	1993	Motown <— Polygram	Copyright	Buyout
$48,000,000	1993	Eli Lilly <— SciMed	P. License	Medical
$21,000,000	1993	Barr Laboratories <— ICI	License	Chemical
$14,000,000	1993	Amgen <— Genetics Institute	P. License	Biotech
$7,500,000	1993	Sepracor <— Marion Merrell Dow	Exclusive Rights	Chemicals

1992

Amount	Year	Parties	Type	Field
$127,000,000	1992	Honeywell <— Minolta Camera	License	Electronic
$107,000,000	1992	3M <— Johnson & Johnson	P. Lawsuit	Medical
$3,500,000	1992	Hilton Davis <— Warner Jenkinson	P. Lawsuit	Chemical

1991

Amount	Year	Parties	Type	Field
$873,000,000	1991	Polaroid <— Eastman Kodak	P. Lawsuit	Chemical

1990

Amount	Year	Parties	Type	Field
$125,000,000	1990	Procter & Gamble <—	P. Lawsuit	Chemical
$17,000,000	1990	Modine Manufacturing <— Allen Group	P. Lawsuit	Mechanical

1986

Amount	Year	Parties	Type	Field
$205,000,000	1986	Hughes Tool <— Smith International	P. Lawsuit	Mechanical

(continued)

Amount	Year	Parties	Legal Action	Technology
		1980		
$5,000,000	1980	Willemijn Holdings <— IBM	License	Software
$1,300,000	1980	Laurie Visual <— Chesebrough-Pond	P. Lawsuit	Mechanical

Annual Damage Awards

Amount	Year	Parties	Legal Action	Technology
$500,000,000	1999	Semiconductor IP	Royalties	Electronics
$50,000,000	1990s	SanDisk Corp.	Royalties	Electronics
$5–10,000,000	1990s	Advanced RISC Machines	Royalties	Electronics
$5,000,000	1990s	Univ. Penn. <— Genovo	Excl. Rights	Biotech

*Information supplemented
Source: Internet Patent News Service

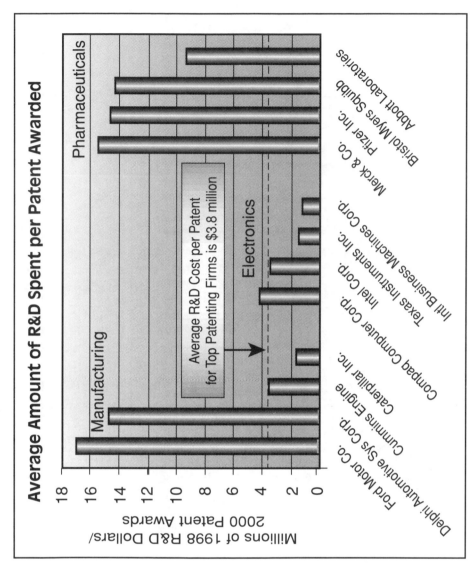

Source: Brody Berman Associates, Deloitte & Touche LLP, IFI CLAIMS.

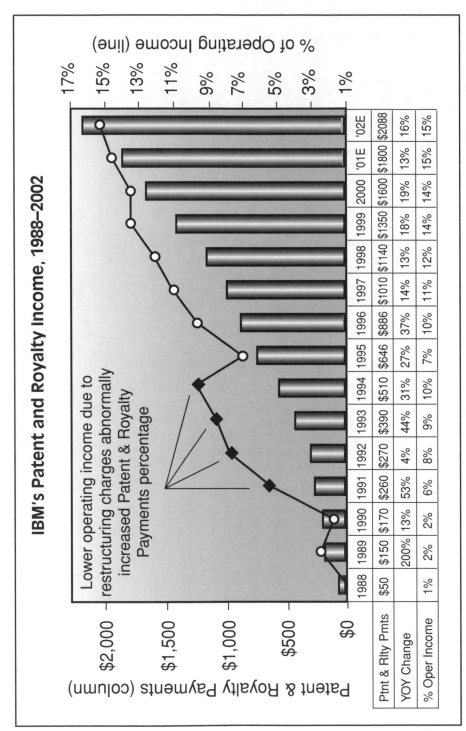

IBM's Patent and Royalty Income, 1988–2002

	1988	1989	1990	1991	1992	1993	1994	1995	1996	1997	1998	1999	2000	'01E	'02E
Ptnt & Rlty Pmts	$50	$150	$170	$260	$270	$390	$510	$646	$886	$1010	$1140	$1350	$1600	$1800	$2088
YOY Change		200%	13%	53%	4%	44%	31%	27%	37%	14%	13%	18%	19%	13%	16%
% Oper Income	1%	2%	2%	6%	8%	9%	10%	7%	10%	11%	12%	14%	14%	15%	15%

Lower operating income due to restructuring charges abnormally increased Patent & Royalty Payments percentage

Source: Salomon Smith Barney

Licensing Revenue: Universities & Research Institutions

Top 20 University Licensing Income
Fiscal, 1999

Institution	Adjusted Gross License Income Received	Invention Disclosures Received	Total U.S. Patent Applications Filed	Licenses & Options Executed	Total Sponsored Research Expenditures	Licenses & Options Yielding Income	U.S. Patents Issued
1 Columbia University*	$89,159,556.00	182	109	98	$279,275,674.00	212	77
2 Univ. of California System	$74,133,000.00	818	670	219	$1,864,901,000.00	715	281
3 Florida State University	$57,313,014.00	23	15	8	$132,664,855.00	14	5
4 Yale University	$40,695,606.00	70	110	23	$315,953,000.00	28	37
5 University of Washington/ Washington Research Foundation	$27,878,900.00	226	114	115	$479,654,994.00	185	36
6 Stanford University	$27,699,355.00	236	237	147	$417,037,000.00	339	90
7 Michigan State University	$23,711,867.00	85	82	33	$207,912,000.00	48	63
8 University of Florida	$21,649,577.00	136	127	10	$280,408,217.00	45	58
9 W.A.R.F./University of Wisconsin-Madison	$18,011,400.00	278	162	106	$421,600,000.00	191	79
10 Massachusetts Institute of Technology	$16,131,334.00	381	341	95	$725,600,000.00	346	154
11 Emory University	$15,257,565.00	89	50	13	$205,600,000.00	35	44
12 SUNY Research Foundation	$13,538,619.00	201	123	46	$405,238,284.00	149	53
13 Baylor College of Medicine	$12,280,879.00	89	39	35	$239,000,000.00	110	25
14 New York University	$10,700,000.00	50	NA	NA	$149,000,000.00	18	30
15 John Hopkins University	$10,353,453.00	250	256	106	$1,010,088,334.00	137	111
16 Harvard University	$9,886,404.00	109	186	48	$401,849,500.00	166	72
17 Washington University	$6,999,971.00	104	78	114	$333,196,000.00	107	39
18 California Institute of Technology	$6,500,000.00	143	212	21	$150,000,000.00	35	62
19 Cornell Research Foundation	$6,070,000.00	172	147	150	$376,784,000.00	199	70
20 Carnegie Mellon University	$5,892,284.00	104	36	23	$167,675,342.00	51	30

Top 5 Hospital/Research Licensing Income
Fiscal Year 1999

Institution	Adjusted Gross License Income Received	Invention Disclosures Received	Total U.S. Patent Applications Filed	Licenses & Options Executed	Total Sponsored Research Expenditures	Licenses & Options Yielding Income	U.S. Patents Issued
1 Sloan Kettering Institute for Cancer Research	$43,065,502.00	36	24	22	$100,982,132.00	44	7
2 New York Blood Center	$35,000,000.00	9	NA	6	$14,000,000.00	30	14
3 City of Hope National Medical Center	$23,752,074.00	40	31	0	$65,890,000.00	24	10
4 Health Research, Inc.	$6,996,742.00	19	7	7	$75,800,000.00	35	14
5 Massachusetts General Hospital	$6,603,343.00	174	170	40	$247,034,000.00	60	85

* CU's adjusted gross revenue from patent royalties for 2000 was $143.6M. Other universities have not yet reported.
Source: Association of University Technology Managers (AUTM)

Comparing the Company Patent Profiles
of Merck and Pfizer

CHI's Company Patent Profiles provide insights into the quality and direction of companies' technological innovations. They also allow investors to compare the relative strength of competing companies' patent portfolios, which are often the driving force behind their future successes.

The two companies profiled here are Merck and Pfizer. In comparing the two companies, the first matter of note is that, while Merck has increased its patenting steadily over the past decade, Pfizer was granted the same number of patents in 2000 as it was in 1991. Also, Merck's Current Impact Index (CII) has been higher than Pfizer's in recent years, showing that Merck's recent patents have had a greater impact on technological developments than those of Pfizer. Merck's patents are particularly strong in core technologies—Pharmaceuticals and Chemicals—compared to Pfizer. This is shown in the lower table in the profile, which details patent indicators by technology area. Merck's CII is more than double that of Pfizer in Pharmaceuticals and 50 percent higher than Pfizer in Chemicals. Meanwhile, Pfizer has a very high CII in noncore areas such as Medical Equipment and Medical Electronics, which may show that it is diversifying into new technologies.

Two other technology indicators also reveal differences between the patents of Merck and Pfizer. Merck's Technology Cycle Time is around $6^1/_2$ years, compared to 9 years for Pfizer. Merck's patents are thus citing patents whose median age is $2^1/_2$ years lower than the patents cited by Pfizer. This shows that Merck is building on more recent technology and is thus innovating more rapidly than Pfizer. Merck's Science Linkage is also higher than Pfizer's. On average, each Merck patent cites over 10 scientific papers, whereas Pfizer's patents cite an average of around six papers. This suggests that Merck's scientists are working more closely with cutting-edge scientific research, which is important in science-intensive industries such as pharmaceuticals.

Editor's note: Patent totals for both Pfizer and Merck are not definitive and may not represent subsidiary, division, or holding company assets.

Patent Profile: Merck & Co. Inc.

Company Name: **Merck & Co Inc**
Tech-Line Industry Group: Pharmaceuticals
Primary SIC: 2834
Country: United States
Ticker/Exchange: MRK/NYSE
Description: An international drug and pharmaceutical research and development leader. Co. produces pharmaceuticals for humans and animals, and water treatment, also food processing and paper manufacturing chemicals.

Ultimate Parent in T-L: Merck & Co Inc
Subsidiary(s) in Tech-Line: Banyu Pharmaceutical Co. Ltd.
Sister Co(s). In Tech-Lines: none

Technology Indicators based on all U.S. utility patents of company/organization:

		No. of Patents	Patent Growth %	Curr. Impact Index	Technol. Strength	Cites/ Patent	Technol. Cycle Time	Science Linkage	Science Strength
Patents Granted in:									
5 Years Ending	1995	1,037	36	0.95	985	#N/A	6.3	4.5	4,689
5 Years Ending	2000	1,211	17	0.81	981	#N/A	6.5	10.3	12,509
Year-by-Year 10 Years									
	1991	178	7	0.79	141	7.0	8.0	3.0	533
	1992	195	10	1.03	201	6.2	6.2	4.5	878
	1993	270	38	1.15	311	5.2	5.9	3.3	885
	1994	210	-22	0.99	208	4.4	5.7	5.1	1,076
	1995	184	-12	0.78	144	4.0	6.3	7.2	1,317
	1996	184	0	0.90	166	3.4	7.2	7.7	1,424
	1997	239	30	1.01	241	1.6	6.5	8.6	2,064
	1998	247	3	0.76	188	1.3	6.3	12.9	3,193
	1999	276	12	0.78	215	0.3	6.2	11.3	3,117
	2000	265	-4	0.64	170	0.0	6.5	10.2	2,711
Year-to-date:*									
0.25 Years Ending	2001	55	-17	0.85	47	0.0	8.9	8.9	490

*Year-to-date data is only provided at the end of the first, second, and third quarters

Technology Indicators by Technology Area, based on patents granted in 5 years ending 2000

Technology area:	No. of Patents	Patent Growth %	% of Pats in Area	Curr. Impact Strength	Technol. Patent	Technol. Cycle Time	Science Linkage	Science Strength
01- Agriculture	36	29	3.0	0.27	10	6.0	7.1	254
02- Oil & Gas, Mining	0	-100	0.0	2.39	0	0.0	0.0	0
03- Power Generation & Distribution	0	0	0.0	0.00	0	0.0	0.0	0
04- Food & Tobacco	4	-56	0.3	0.75	3	10.5	3.3	13
05- Textiles & Apparel	0	-100	0.0	0.76	0	0.0	0.0	0
06- Wood & Paper	0	-100	0.0	1.70	0	0.0	0.0	0
07- Chemicals	386	-4	31.9	0.69	266	6.3	10.2	3,927
08- Pharmaceuticals	614	44	50.7	1.04	639	6.3	7.2	4,395
09- Biotechnology	129	14	10.7	0.44	57	6.5	28.7	3,701
10- Medical Equipment	5	-64	0.4	0.97	5	6.6	7.2	36
11- Medical Electronics	1	0	0.1	0.00	0	5.5	6.0	6
12- Plastics, Polymers & Rubber	3	-40	0.3	1.15	3	17.5	3.3	10
13- Glass, Clay & Cement	0	0	0.0	0.00	0	0.0	0.0	0
14- Primary Metals	2	infinity	0.2	2.11	4	7.4	4.0	8
15- Fabricated Metals	0	-100	0.0	0.00	0	0.0	0.0	0
16- Industrial Machinery & Tools	2	100	0.2	0.93	2	8.5	1.0	2
17- Industrial Process Equipment	7	75	0.6	#N/A	#N/A	19.0	1.3	9
18- Office Equipment & Cameras	1	0	0.1	0.00	0	3.5	3.0	3
19- Heating, Ventilation, Refrigeration	0	0	0.0	0.00	0	0.0	0.0	0
20- Misc. Machinery	10	-44	0.8	0.91	9	12.5	0.0	0
21- Computers & Peripherals	1	infinity	0.1	0.00	0	2.8	0.0	0
22- Telecommunications	0	0	0.0	0.00	0	0.0	0.0	0
23- Semiconductors & Electronics	0	0	0.0	0.00	0	0.0	0.0	0
24- Measurement & Control Equipment	0	-100	0.0	0.68	0	0.0	0.0	0
25- Electrical Appliances & Components	0	0	0.0	0.00	0	0.0	0.0	0
26- Motor Vehicles & Parts	0	0	0.0	0.00	0	0.0	0.0	0
27- Aerospace & Parts	0	0	0.0	0.00	0	0.0	0.0	0
28- Other Transport	0	0	0.0	0.00	0	0.0	0.0	0
29- Misc. Manufacturing	0	-100	0.0	0.00	0	0.0	0.0	0
30- Other	10	25	0.0	1.14	0	7.2	14.5	145
All Patents	1,211	17	100.0	0.81	981	6.5	10.3	12,509

Source: Copyright 2001, CHI Research, Inc.

Patent Profile: Pfizer Inc.

Company Name: **Pfizer Inc**
Tech-Line Industry Group: Pharmaceuticals
Primary SIC: 3826
Country: United States
Ticker/Exchange: PFE/NYSE
Description: Major drug company, engaged in health care pharmaceuticals and medical equipment, consumer products including over-the-counter drugs, animal health, chemicals and specialty minerals.

Ultimate Parent in T-L: Pfizer Inc
Subsidiary(s) in Tech-Line: Warner-Lambert Co
Sister Co(s). In Tech-Lines: none

Technology Indicators based on all U.S. utility patents of company/organization:

	No. of Patents	Patent Growth %	Curr. Impact Index	Technol. Strength	Cites/ Patent	Technol. Cycle Time	Science Linkage	Science Strength
Patents Granted in:								
5 Years Ending 1995	1,014	-7	1.06	1,075	#N/A	8.2	2.0	1,986
5 Years Ending 2000	1,080	7	0.73	788	#N/A	9.4	6.2	6,660
Year-by-Year 10 Years								
1991	257	21	1.18	303	8.3	8.1	1.3	331
1992	213	-17	1.14	243	8.1	8.6	1.2	253
1993	194	-9	0.93	180	5.5	8.6	2.3	441
1994	178	-8	1.09	194	3.9	7.6	2.0	358
1995	172	-3	0.95	163	3.7	8.7	3.5	603
1996	165	-4	0.83	137	2.5	9.2	5.2	866
1997	217	32	0.81	176	2.0	10.1	7.3	1,582
1998	217	0	0.67	145	0.9	8.6	5.4	1,173
1999	222	2	0.66	147	0.4	9.5	7.0	1,546
2000	259	17	0.65	168	0.0	9.4	5.8	1,493
Year-to-date:*								
0.25 Years Ending 2001	64	-1	0.74	47	0.0	9.5	7.0	448

* Year-to-date data is only provided at the end of the first, second, and third quarters

Technology Indicators by Technology Area, based on patents granted in 5 years ending 2000

Technology area:	No. of Patents	Patent Growth %	% of Pats in Area	Curr. Impact Strength	Technol. Patent	Technol. Cycle Time	Science Linkage	Science Strength
01- Agriculture	50	178	4.6	0.54	27	9.1	9.5	476
02- Oil & Gas, Mining	0	-100	0.0	0.00	0	0.0	0.0	0
03- Power Generation & Distribution	0	0	0.0	0.00	0	0.0	0.0	0
04- Food & Tobacco	12	-71	1.1	1.21	15	9.4	0.1	1
05- Textiles & Apparel	0	0	0.0	0.00	0	0.0	0.0	0
06- Wood & Paper	2	100	0.2	2.43	5	9.8	0.0	0
07- Chemicals	304	-16	28.2	0.42	128	8.5	6.0	1,838
08- Pharmaceuticals	565	65	52.3	0.47	266	9.2	6.8	3,834
09- Biotechnology	39	105	3.6	0.16	6	14.1	9.2	359
10- Medical Equipment	37	-58	3.4	3.34	124	9.5	0.4	14
11- Medical Electronics	10	43	0.9	4.23	42	9.9	4.6	46
12- Plastics, Polymers & Rubber	5	-67	0.5	2.98	15	9.8	0.4	2
13- Glass, Clay & Cement	1	-50	0.1	0.40	0	0.0	0.0	0
14- Primary Metals	0	-100	0.0	0.21	0	0.0	0.0	0
15- Fabricated Metals	1	-67	0.1	0.36	0	15.5	1.0	1
16- Industrial Machinery & Tools	28	-50	2.6	0.69	19	14.4	0.9	25
17- Industrial Process Equipment	3	-40	0.3	#N/A	#N/A	7.3	2.3	7
18- Office Equipment & Cameras	0	-100	0.0	0.23	0	0.0	0.0	0
19- Heating, Ventilation, Refrigeration	0	0	0.0	0.00	0	0.0	0.0	0
20- Misc. Machinery	6	-71	0.6	0.70	4	11.0	0.0	0
21- Computers & Peripherals	0	-100	0.0	#N/A	#N/A	0.0	0.0	0
22- Telecommunications	0	-100	0.0	1.14	0	0.0	0.0	0
23- Semiconductors & Electronics	0	0	0.0	0.00	0	0.0	0.0	0
24- Measurement & Control Equipment	3	50	0.3	0.55	2	13.5	6.7	20
25- Electrical Appliances & Components	0	-100	0.0	0.34	0	0.0	0.0	0
26- Motor Vehicles & Parts	0	0	0.0	0.00	0	0.0	0.0	0
27- Aerospace & Parts	0	0	0.0	0.00	0	0.0	0.0	0
28- Other Transport	1	0	0.1	0.61	1	8.5	0.0	0
29- Misc. Manufacturing	5	-17	0.5	0.69	3	10.3	0.4	2
30- Other	8	-33	0.7	0.52	4	9.8	4.4	35
All Patents	1,080	7	100.0	0.73	788	9.4	6.2	6,660

Source: Copyright 2001, CHI Research, Inc.

NOTES ON CHI COMANY PATENT PROFILES

1. Coverage through First Quarter 2001.
2. Company profiles updated quarterly.
3. Only Type 1 (utility) patents are counted.
4. Company names are unified, i.e., rigorously standardized and assigned to current corporate parents, and so may differ from tabulation of corporate assignee patent counts from other sources.
5. Major patenting subsidiaries may be available as separate Tech-Line profiles as well as having their patents incorporated within parent company profile statistics.
6. Technology areas are based on a proprietary mapping of International Patent Classifications (IPCs).

Technology Indicators:

1. Number of patents (Type 1 utility patents only)
2. Percentage growth in patenting (from previous time period)
3. Percent of patents in area (Technology area table only)
4. Current impact index (CII)—normalized measure of citations received from other patents; e.g., CII of 1.2 indicates this company's patents are cited 20% more than average, shows the impact of a company's patents on technological developments in its industry
5. Technological strength—CII × number of patents, shows the overall impact of a company's patent portfolio
6. Cites received per patent (year-by-year table only)—average number of cites received (from later patents) by company patents issued in a given year, a basic indicator of the impact of company patents
7. Technology cycle time—median age of cited patents, shows the speed at which a company is innovating
8. Science linkage—average number of cites to scientific papers by patents, shows the texent to which a company's patents are building on cutting-edge scientific research
9. Science strength (Science Linkage × number of patents)—total cites to science by company patents, shows the overall strength of the link between company patents and scientific research

Detailed explanations and discussions of CHI Research's technology indicators included in the profiles and patent citation analysis in general are available at *www.chiresearch.com/techline/tlbp4.htm.*

CHI Research, Inc. (CHI) is providing this data for academic research and for internal company use. The data are not to be resold, repackaged, or redistributed without the express written consent of CHI. Further, the commercial use of the data in a financial model, mutual fund, hedge fund, or similar financial instrument may infringe upon one of CHI's granted or pending patents, and therefore the data are not to be used in that manner without the express written consent of and license from CHI.

Intellectual Property Value Trends (1Q and 2Q 2001)

Summary of IAM Index

1. The IAM Index® is a tool for tracking value, in the same manner as other indices such as the Dow 30, the S&P 500 or Nasdaq Composite. Whereas the 103-year-old Dow Jones Average tracks changes in value in the industrial economy and the Nasdaq Composite index tracks changes in value of technology companies, the IAM tracks changes in intangible value in the knowledge economy.

2. The index allows for quantitative risk measurement of unique IP assets through the calculation of IP Sector Beta.

3. The index may be a leading indicator for stock price movements in technology-rich large companies.

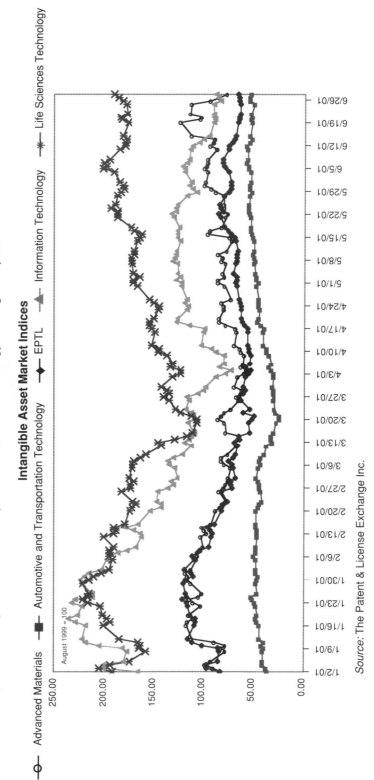

Source: The Patent & License Exchange Inc.

603

IP Sector Beta

IP Sector Beta measures the sensitivity of a technology sector's return relative to movements in the S&P 500. A Beta of greater than one indicates that sector's return risk is greater than the S&P 500. A Beta of less than one indicates that the sector's return is less risky than the S&P 500. Beta is often used to measure the sensitivity of a stock's return relative to an underlying index and also in calculating the cost of capital.

Sectors	Most Recent 90 Days	Previous 90 Days	YTD
Advanced Materials	1.34	1.01	1.71
Automotive and Transportation	1.17	0.19	0.58
EPTL Technology	1.44	0.34	1.04
Information Technology	2.03	0.47	1.34
Life Sciences Technology	1.49	0.25	0.81

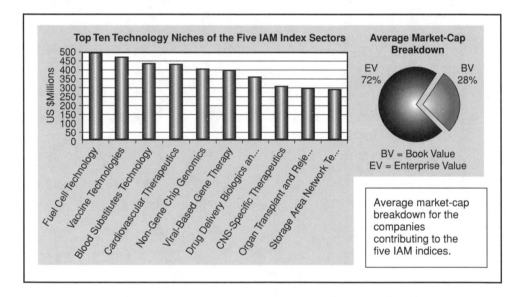

Top Ten Technology Niches of the Five IAM Index Sectors

Average Market-Cap Breakdown

EV 72%   BV 28%

BV = Book Value
EV = Enterprise Value

Average market-cap breakdown for the companies contributing to the five IAM indices.

Intellectual property asset values determined by markets:
Enterprise value (market capitalization less book value) of large companies is determined by a large number of factors. The enterprise value of a small, early-stage, technology niche-specific company, however, is a nearly pure proxy for intellectual property value in a given niche. When divided by the number of products each small company is developing, it becomes a live, market-driven product valuation. Approximately 1,500 microcap "pure play" companies with approximately 6,500 products from around the world contribute enterprise value data to 411 technology niche categories tracked by the Patent & Licensee Exchange Inc. (*www.pl-x.com*), a provider of financially-oriented IP management, valuation, and marketing products.

Source: The Patent & License Exchange Inc.

Known Completed IP Securitizations

Closing	Borrower	Type	Industry	Placement Agents	Amount ($ mil)
Feb-97	David Bowie	Royalty Income	music	The Pullman Group	$55
Nov-97	DreamWorks I	Royalty Income	film	Bear Stearns	$325
Jun-98	Motown Bonds	Royalty Income	music	The Pullman Group	$30
Nov-98	Ashford & Simpson Bonds	Royalty Income	music	The Pullman Group	$25
Jan-99	Corinthian Group	Master Recording & Publishing Income	music	CAK Universal Credit Corp.	$4
Feb-99	TVT Records	Master Recording & Publishing Income	music	CAK Universal Credit Corp.	$24
Apr-99	Sesac Inc.	Licensing Revenues	music	CAK Universal Credit Corp.	$29
Apr-99	L.A. Arena Funding	Naming Rights	sports	Bear Stearns	$315
May-99	Curtis Mayfield	Royalty Income	music	CAK Universal Credit Corp.	$6
Jun-99	Barret Strong	Royalty Income	music	CAK Universal Credit Corp.	$4
Jun-99	James Brown	Royalty Income	music	The Pullman Group	$30
Jun-99	Iron Maiden	Royalty Income	music	Global Entertainment Finance	$30
Aug-99	A.B. Quintantilla III	Royalty Income	music	CAK Universal Credit Corp.	$2
Oct-99	Bill Blass	Licensing Revenues	apparel	CAK Universal Credit Corp.	$24
Jan-00	DreamWorks II	Royalty Income	film	Bear Stearns, Chase Securities	$540
Jun-00	Isley Brothers	Royalty Income	music	The Pullman Group	$20
Aug-00	BioPharma	Patent Rights	pharmaceutical	West LB	$100
Sep-00	Marvin Gaye*	Royalty Income	music	The Pullman Group	$100

*Information supplemented
Source: Thomson Financial

The World's Most Valuable Brands[+]

2001 Rank	Brand	2001 Brand Value ($MM)	% change (2001 vs 2000)	% change (2000 vs 1999)	1999 Brand Value ($MM)	Market Cap (Jan 1999)	Brand Leverage (2001)*	Total Patents Granted 1990–1999	Design Patents
1	Coca-Cola	68,945	-5%	-13%	83,845	142,164	4.18	369	119
2	Microsoft	65,068	-7%	24%	56,654	271,854	3.16	1,120	40
3	IBM	52,752	-1%	21%	43,781	158,384	0.67	15,463	444
4	GE	42,396	11%	14%	33,502	327,996	0.38	8,207	81
5	Nokia	35,035	-9%	86%	20,694	46,926	1.37	648	140
6	Intel	34,665	-11%	30%	30,021	144,060	1.15	3,082	19
7	Disney	32,591	-3%	4%	32,275	52,552	1.91	110	22
8	Ford	30,092	-17%	10%	33,197	57,387	0.27	2,504	26
9	McDonald's	25,289	-9%	6%	26,231	0.75	1	1	1
10	AT&T	22,828	-11%	6%	24,181	102,480	0.39	1,841	40
11	Marlboro	22,053	0%	5%	21,048	112,437	2.28	**	**
12	Mercedes	21,728	3%	19%	17,781	48,326	0.59	936	72
13	Citibank	19,005	1%	N/A	N/A	42,030	0.86	29	-
14	Toyota	18,578	-1%	53%	12,310	85,911	0.23	2,445	48
15	Hewlett-Packard	17,983	-13%	20%	17,132	54,902	0.41	4,985	161
16	Cisco Systems	17,209	-14%	N/A	N/A	N/A	1.01	63	-
17	American Express	16,919	5%	28%	12,550	35,459	0.80	**	**
18	Gillette	15,298	-12%	9%	15,894	42,951	3.89	391	130
19	Merrill Lynch	15,015	N/A	N/A	N/A	N/A	0.63	12	-
20	Sony	15,005	-9%	15%	14,231	28,933	0.29	8,295	852
21	Honda	14,638	-4%	37%	11,101	30,050	0.31	3,333	177
22	BMW	13,858	7%	15%	11,281	14,662	0.54	265	81
23	Nescafe	13,250	-3%	N/A	N/A	N/A	2.72	**	**
24	Compaq	12,354	-15%	N/A	N/A	N/A	0.33	1,155	98
25	Oracle	12,224	N/A	N/A	N/A	N/A	1.35	162	1
26	Budweiser	10,838	1%	26%	8,510	26,036	1.70	**	**
27	Kodak	10,801	-9%	-20%	14,830	24,754	0.86	8,859	136
28	Merck	9,672	N/A	N/A	N/A	N/A	0.26	1,656	9
29	Nintendo	9,460	N/A	N/A	N/A	N/A	2.11	150	61

30	Pfizer	8,951	N/A	N/A	N/A	N/A	0.57	901	14
31	Gap	8,746	-6%	18%	7,909	20,481	1.32	**	**
32	Dell	8,269	-13%	5%	9,043	97,327	0.37	19	-
33	Goldman Sachs	7,862	N/A	N/A	N/A	N/A	0.27	**	**
34	Nike	7,589	-5%	-2%	8,155	10,565	0.99	1,037	970
35	Volkswagen	7,338	-6%	19%	6,603	22,071	0.20	188	6
36	Ericsson	7,069	-9%	-47%	14,766	45,739	0.27	610	8
37	Heinz	7,062	N/A	N/A	N/A	18,555	2.54	4	-
38	Louis Vuitton	7,053	2%	69%	4,076	11,935	2.77	10	9
39	Kellogg's	7,005	-5%	4%	7,052	13,445	1.16	31	7
40	MTV	6,599	3%	N/A	N/A	N/A	2.55	**	**
41	Canon	6,580	N/A	N/A	N/A	N/A	0.30	13,453	742
42	Samsung	6,374	22%	N/A	N/A	N/A	0.23	5,640	70
43	SAP	6,307	3%	N/A	N/A	N/A	1.19	**	**
44	Pepsi	6,214	-6%	12%	5,932	43,450	0.88	63	12
45	Xerox	6,019	-38%	-14%	11,225	27,816	0.36	5,589	22
46	IKEA	6,005	0%	N/A	N/A	N/A	0.79	3	3
47	Pizza Hut	5,978	N/A	N/A	N/A	N/A	0.87	11	2
48	Harley Davidson	5,532	N/A	N/A	N/A	N/A	2.17	111	73
49	Apple	5,464	-17%	54%	4,283	5,574	0.76	1,225	129
50	Gucci	5,363	4%	4%	N/A	4,141	4.00	**	**
51	KFC	5,261	N/A	N/A	N/A	N/A	0.87	8	1
52	Reuters	5,236	7%	N/A	N/A	N/A	1.40	17	5
53	Sun Microsystems	5,149	N/A	N/A	N/A	N/A	0.37	1,617	71
54	Kleenex	5,085	-1%	12%	4,602	N/A	2.08	**	**
55	Philips	4,900	-11%	N/A	N/A	N/A	0.15	344	24
56	Colgate	4,572	3%	24%	3,568	20,330	2.00	954	217
57	Wrigley's	4,530	5%	-2%	4,404	8,809	2.36	191	6
58	AOL	4,495	-1%	5%	4,329	23,979	0.65	10	-
59	Yahoo!	4,378	-31%	258%	1,761	12,673	4.42	2	-
60	Avon	4,369	N/A	N/A	N/A	N/A	0.86	48	2
61	Chanel	4,265	3%	32%	3,143	N/A	2.03	18	7
62	Duracell	4,140	-30%	N/A	N/A	N/A	1.79	93	2
63	Boeing	4,060	N/A	N/A	N/A	N/A	0.09	1,377	8

(continued)

2001 Rank	Brand	2001 Brand Value ($MM)	% change (2001 vs 2000)	% change (2000 vs 1999)	1999 Brand Value ($MM)	Market Cap (Jan 1999)	Brand Leverage (2001)*	Total Patents Granted 1990–1999	Design Patents
64	Texas Instruments	4,041	N/A	N/A	N/A	N/A	0.38	4,885	9
65	Kraft	4,032	N/A	N/A	N/A	N/A	1.05	703	408
66	Motorola	3,761	-15%	22%	3,643	24,394	0.11	9,823	797
67	Levi's	3,747	N/A	N/A	N/A	N/A	1.17	16	-
68	Time	3,724	N/A	N/A	N/A	N/A	0.89	3	2
69	Rolex	3,701	4%	47%	2,423	N/A	2.76	32	32
70	Adidas	3,650	-4%	5%	3,596	2,158	0.94	91	5
71	Hertz	3,617	5%	-3%	3,527	4,691	0.79	**	**
72	Panasonic	3,490	-7%	N/A	N/A	N/A	0.08	86	2
73	Tiffany & Co.	3,483	N/A	N/A	N/A	N/A	2.33	2	-
74	BP	3,247	6%	3%	2,985	88,619	0.04	265	-
75	Bacardi	3,204	1%	10%	2,895	N/A	2.90	**	**
76	Amazon.com	3,130	-31%	233%	1,361	18,510	1.26	7	1
77	Shell	2,844	2%	4%	2,681	164,157	0.02	2,013	**
78	Smirnoff	2,594	6%	6%	2,313	N/A	2.75	**	**
79	Moet & Chandon	2,470	-12%	0%	2,804	N/A	2.29	11	9
80	Burger King	2,426	-10%	-4%	2,806	N/A	0.24	2	-
81	Mobil	2,415	N/A	N/A	N/A	N/A	0.04	2,225	22
82	Heineken	2,266	2%	2%	2,184	14,886	1.27	30	10
83	Wall Street Journal	2,184	0%	N/A	N/A	N/A	1.60	**	**
84	Barbie	2,037	-12%	N/A	N/A	8,196	1.74	170	18
85	Polo Ralph Lauren	1,910	4%	11%	1,648	N/A	1.14	9	8
86	Fedex	1,885	N/A	N/A	N/A	N/A	0.12	9	5
87	Nivea	1,782	N/A	N/A	N/A	N/A	1.06	**	**
88	Starbucks	1,757	32%	N/A	N/A	N/A	0.90	15	13
89	Johnnie Walker	1,649	7%	-6%	1,634	N/A	2.36	**	**
90	Jack Daniels	1,583	7%	N/A	N/A	N/A	1.91	**	**
91	Armani	1,490	2%	N/A	N/A	N/A	1.36	**	**
92	Pampers	1,410	1%	-2%	1,422	N/A	1.71	**	**
93	Absolut	1,378	N/A	N/A	N/A	N/A	4.57	**	**
94	Guinness	1,357	11%	-3%	1,262	N/A	0.48	19	-

95	Financial Times	1,310	14%	N/A	N/A	1.72	**	**
96	Hilton	3,333	-17%	1,319	N/A	1.33	**	**
97	Carlsberg	1,075	N/A	N/A	N/A	0.51	7	2
98	Siemens	1,029	N/A	N/A	N/A	0.02	4,857	47
99	Swatch	1,004	N/A	N/A	N/A	1.57	44	42
100	Benetton	1,002	-1%	N/A	N/A	0.95	18	13

Big Brand Groups++

P1	Johnson & Johnson	68,208	N/A	N/A	N/A	2.61	702	74
P2	P&G	45,435	-6%	49,193	95126.9	1.27	3056	251
P3	Nestle	41,688	4%	38,769	77489.9	0.92	654	19
P4	Unilever	37,847	2%	33,929	67214.5	0.94	265	18
P5	L'Oreal	17,798	N/A	N/A	N/A	1.66	1238	54
P6	Diageo	15,004	3%	13,704	33810	1.41	**	**
P7	Colgate-Palmolive	14,361	5%	11,333	20329.9	1.71	954	217
P8	Danone	13,583	N/A	N/A	N/A	1.13	6	2

*Brand Leverage reflects Brand Value in relation to the previous year's Branded Sales. The higher the leverage, the more value is being generated from each $ of sales.

**Indicates that firm did not appear on Intellectual Property Owners top 300 patent awards list for 2000.

+The table identifies the top 100 global brands with a value greater than $1 Billion. Selections were based on three criteria: (1) the brand must be global, generating significant earnings in the main global markets, (2) the brand must be a leader in one of the 25 mainstream industries and (3) the brand must have marketing and financial data publicly available for preparing a reasonable valuation. Privately owned and non-profit brands were not included. The brand valuation process examines three areas: the future economic earnings the branded business is expected to generate, the role of the brand in generating those earnings, and the risk profile of the brand's expected earnings.

++The table includes separate valuations of leading brand portfolios that recognize that some companies create significant brand value, not from the management of a single brand, but the management of a portfolio of brands.

Source: Interbrand and IFI CLAIMS

Highest Market Capitalizations + Patent Awards

Company Name	Market Capitalization December 31, 2000 (in millions)	Total Patents granted 1990–1999	Design patents 1990–1999
GENERAL ELECTRIC CO	$475,003	8207	81
EXXON MOBIL CORP	302,211	-	-
PFIZER INC	290,216	901	14
CISCO SYSTEMS INC	268,662	63	0
WAL-MART STORES	237,274	-	-
MICROSOFT CORP	231,290	1120	40
CITIGROUP INC	229,368	29	0
AMERICAN INTERNATIONAL GROUP	228,227	-	-
MERCK & CO	215,908	1656	9
INTEL CORP	202,321	3082	19
ORACLE CORP	162,676	162	1
SBC COMMUNICATIONS INC	161,632	-	-
COCA-COLA CO	151,112	369	119
INTL BUSINESS MACHINES CORP	149,122	15463	444
JOHNSON & JOHNSON	146,072	702	74
EMC CORP/MA	144,995	199	8
BRISTOL MYERS SQUIBB	144,574	741	19
VERIZON COMMUNICATIONS	135,292	-	-
BERKSHIRE HATHAWAY—CL A	108,253	-	-
HOME DEPOT INC	106,053	-	-
LILLY (ELI) & CO	105,114	1363	6
PROCTER & GAMBLE CO	102,265	3056	251
NORTEL NETWORKS CORP	98,312	1213	60
PHILIP MORRIS COS INC	97,835	344	24
TYCO INTERNATIONAL LTD	97,050	-	-
WELLS FARGO & CO	95,181	-	-
SUN MICROSYSTEMS INC	89,712	1617	71
MORGAN STANLEY DEAN WITTER	89,697	-	-
FANNIE MAE	88,433	1	0
AMERICAN HOME PRODUCTS CORP	83,285	565	8
SCHERING-PLOUGH	82,971	81	37
TEXAS INSTRUMENTS INC	82,040	4885	9
AOL TIME WARNER INC	80,879		
PHARMACIA CORP	78,629	521	16
BELLSOUTH CORP	76,408	92	1
BANK OF AMERICA CORP	75,359	-	-
ABBOTT LABORATORIES	74,866	1434	82
AMERICAN EXPRESS	73,066	11	0
MEDTRONIC INC	72,425	1027	13
UBS AG	72,369	-	-
PEPSICO INC	71,522	63	12
VIACOM INC—CL B	71,000	4	0
QWEST COMMUNICATION INTL INC	67,886	1	0
AMGEN INC	65,722	169	2
AT&T WIRELESS GROUP	64,981	64	3
AT&T CORP	64,764	1841	40
HEWLETT-PACKARD CO	62,431	4985	161
QUALCOMM INC	61,512	366	18
ENRON CORP	61,422	3	0
DISNEY (WALT) COMPANY	60,323	110	22
J P MORGAN CHASE & CO	59,194	-	-
BOEING CO	58,638	1377	8
INTERNET ARCHITECTURE HLDRS	57,563	-	-
CHEVRON CORP	55,110	660	3

Sources: Compustat and IFI CLAIMS

Notes on U.S. Patent Issues for 1990–1999 for Market Cap and Brand Value Charts

ExxonMobil has no patents in this period since the company was recently formed. For various Exxon subsidiaries, total is 2,416, one of which is a design patent. For Mobil Oil Corp, total is 2,225, with 22 designs. Mergers and acquisitions create a constantly changing ownership dynamic, as in the case of ExxonMobil.

No patents are assigned to SBC.
Two large subsidiaries: Southwestern Bell and Ameritech Corp hold 51 total, 2 designs.

Tyco International has one utility patent.
Other Tyco names and totals:
    Tyco Group SARL, 11 total, 2 designs
    Tyco Ind Inc, 21 total, 12 designs
    Tyco Submarine Systems Ltd, 11 total, no designs

AOL Time Warner—0
AOL—10 total, no design
Time Warner—50 total, five of which are design patents

Marlboro is a Philip Morris brand.
Philip Morris has 344 patents, 24 designs.

Budweiser is an Anheuser-Busch brand.
Anheuser—total 14, 4 designs

Gucci—two companies:
    GUCCI TIMEPIECES S A CH—7 total, 7 designs
    GUCCIO GUCCI SPA IT—5 total, 5 designs

Kleenex is a Kimberly Clark brand.
Kimberly Clark—667 total, 34 designs

The totals for Nortel recognize the name change from Northern Telecom.

Subsidiaries for some companies have been combined where they were easily identified by name (e.g., some of the Johnson & Johnson companies that were so named), but this was not done for all companies. In many cases it is difficult to determine if companies with similar names are actually related. In general, we did not attempt to find other subsidiaries with dissimilar names unless we were already aware of them, as with SBC.

The U.S. patent system does not combine assignee subsidiaries with parent companies, nor does the U.S. Patent Office. In many cases, parent companies acquire relatively few patents, while their subsidiaries may hold significant patent portfolios.

Further Reading

Berman, Bruce (Editor). *Hidden Value: Profiting from the Intellectual Property Economy*. Euromoney-Institutional Investor, 1999.

Blair, Margaret M. and Wallman, Steven M.H. *Unseen Wealth: Report of the Brookings Task Force on Intangibles*. Brookings Institution Press, 2000.

Buderi, Robert. *Engines of Tomorrow: How the World's Best Companies Are Using Their Research Labs to Win the Future*. Simon & Schuster, 2000.

Davis, Julie L. and Harrison, Suzanne S. *Edison in the Boardroom, How the Leading Companies Realize Value from Their Intellectual Assets*. Wiley/Andersen Intellectual Capital Series, 2001.

Glazier, Stephen C. *Patent Strategies for Business*. Law & Business Institute, 1997.

Knight, Jackson H. *Patent Strategy*. John Wiley & Sons, 1996 (revised 2001).

Lev, Baruch. *Intangibles: Management, Measurement, and Reporting*. Brookings Institution Press, 2001.

Parr, Russell L. *Intellectual Property Infringement Damages: A Litigation Support Handbook*. John Wiley & Sons, 1999.

Parr, Russell L., and Sullivan, Patrick H. (Editors). *Technology Licensing: Corporate Strategies for Maximizing Value*. John Wiley & Sons, 1997.

Pooley, James H.A. *Trade Secrets*, American Marketing Association, 1989.

Rivette, Kevin G., and Kline, David. *Rembrandts in the Attic: Unlocking the Hidden Value of Patent*. Harvard Business School Press, 2000.

Shulman, Seth. *Owning the Future*. Houghton Mifflin, 1999.

Smith, Douglas K. and Alexander, Robert C. *Fumbling the Future: How Xerox Invented, Then Ignored, the First Personal Computer*. W. Morrow, 1988. Currently available from iUniverse.com.

Smith, Gordon V. and Parr, Russell L. *Valuation of Intellectual Property and Intungible Assets*, 3rd Edition. John Wiley & Sons, 2000.

Stewart, Thomas A. *Intellectual Capital: The New Wealth of Organizations*. Doubleday, 1997.

Sullivan, Patrick H. *Value-Driven Intellectual Capital: How to Convert Intangible Corporate Assets Into Market Value*. John Wiley & Sons, 2000.

Warshofsky, Fred. *The Patent Wars: The Battle to Own the World's Technology*. John Wiley & Sons, 1994. Currently available as an E-book from amazon.com.

IP Web Sites and Links (Annotated)

The Internet provides a growing if occasionally confusing body of IP information that can be useful to investors, managers, and others. Some of the web sites that target IP professionals are worth visiting. For your linking convenience, the following sites and URLs, as well as the previous glossary of IP terms, can be found at *www.brodyberman.com*. E-mail me, *bberman@brodyberman. com*, if you have additions or changes worth sharing with other readers. We shall try our best to keep the list timely.

GENERAL IP INFORMATION

www.autm.net—AUTM (Association of University Technology Managers) represents the growing and increasingly entrepreneurial world of technology transfer. This site includes a summary of AUTM's annual survey of university and research institution licensing income.

www.bl.uk/services/stb/etalmenu.html#key—The British Library Science Technology and Business. Several hundred links to associations and resources. Some sections need updating.

www.btgplc.com/what_btg_does/frequent_questions.html#notes—Patent basics, good for attorneys to give to their clients, as well as for those who want to know more. BTG is a publicly held IP management company traded on the London Stock Exchange.

www.bustpatents.com—Where you can find a regular news summaries form the Internet Patent News Service, an often-controversial e-newsletter that provides news, commentary, and gossip. Edited by prior art consultant Greg Aharonian.

www.epo.org—European Patent Office site includes a searchable database and access to *The Gazette*, which publishes notice of patents which are still in the application process.

www.intelproplaw.com—This general information site from a Canadian law firm features a proprietary "News Grid" for monitoring the news of the day found on several key search engines: *www.intelproplaw.com/NewsSrch.shtml*

www.ipcapitalgroup.com—*Short* glossary under FAQ is useful for basic IP concepts. ipCapital, Inc. focuses on M&A and reengineering.

www.ipmall.fplc.edu—Well-researched, well-maintained, and useful portal from Franklin Pierce Law Center, a law school which focuses on IP.

www.ipo.org —Intellectual Property Owners' members are primarily large companies. Site lists top U.S. patent recipients for past several years, including those that are not based in the United States.

www.ipr-helpdesk.org—Excellent source for European patent information and databases.

www.jpo.go.jp/homee.htm—Japan Patent Office Homepage. Pleasant and user-friendly introduction to system (in English).

www.kuesterlaw.com—Still one of the best-researched and linked IP portals.

www.law.com—Accessible IP-related law news and legal developments. Useful for nonlawyers as well as lawyers.

www.les-usa.org—The Licensing Executives Society (LES) is the key organization for anyone seriously interested in IP. Site is useful for staying up to date on LES's fine conferences and committees. Chapters meet locally in most major metro areas. (Can be used to reach LES International.)

www.loc.gov/copyright/—U.S. Copyright Office and The Library of Congress. A good general overview of copyright basics and some links.

www.patentcafe.com—Lively IP portal which targets diverse audiences, including inventors, owners, and licensees. Partially owned by Gray Carey law firm.

www.patents.com—Excellent basic information from Colorado law firm Oppedahl & Larson includes filing costs. However, parts of this site are woefully out of date.

www.piug.org—Patent Information Users Group meets regularly for conferences focusing on patent data and trends.

www.uspto.gov—U.S. Patent and Trademark Office site. Good and getting better. Site is useful for general information, as well as for the more serious researcher.

www.wipo.org—Simplified summary of IP basics is worth reviewing. World Intellectual Property Organization, a United Nations agency based in Geneva, Switzerland, administers 21 international IP treaties.

IP AVAILABLE/WANTED—LICENSING TRANSACTIONS

www.btgplc.com—Publicly held British Technology Group is a sort of merchant bank for IP assets. They represent, manage, develop, trade, and finance patent rights. U.S. operations in Pennsylvania.

www.cc.columbia.edu/cu/cie/index.html—Columbia University's Innovation Enterprise home page. Provides a window into top tech transfer organization. Shows patent royalty and joint venture equity performance, as well as listings of inventions available for license.

www.gpci.com—General Patent Corporation owns, manages, and, when necessary, asserts proprietary rights on behalf of its clients. Site provides information about available technologies and links.

www.inventorsdigest.com—Associated with a thoughtful monthly (print) magazine for independent inventors. Offers tips about commercialization, financing, and enforcement.

www.ipnetwork.com—Posts primarily brand and trademark assets available for license.

www.patentcafe.com—Portal (see above) also provides posting of technologies and other IP properties for license.

www.patex.com—Licensing site from publicly held IP data company Corporate Intelligence.

www.pl-x.com—Patent & Licensing Exchange focuses on patented inventions that are available for license or that are desired. Site provides pl-x's TRUU® valuation index.

www.uventures.com—Postings from primarily universities and research institutions. Other information includes recent IP books.

www.yet2.com—Listing of available technologies. A number of large companies are subscribers.

IP ANALYSIS AND MANAGEMENT TOOLS

www.aurigin.com—Aurigin Systems provides patent visualization tools and data integration software. Site explains what it takes for innovation to become assets. Free *Harvard Business Journal* article (click on home page) underscores IP's strategic importance.

www.chiresearch.com—Analyzes patent strength based on key indicators, such as citations by other patents and papers. CHI also has a stock market index based on patent indicators.

www.computerpackages.com—CPi provides software and services to help manage IP and to monitor incoming and outgoing annuity payments worldwide.

www.cpana.com—Computer Patent Annuities monitors trademark and patent payments.

www.delphion.com—Provides online patent searches and analysis. Site is partially owned by IBM.

www.derwent.com—Provides worldwide patent and science information. Part of Thomson Scientific. Can be accessed through other information providers, including Delphion, Dialogue, and WESTLAW.

www.getthepatent.com—Quick, downloadable access to U.S. patents.

www.ifiplenum.com—Provides detailed patent issuance and classification data unavailable from the PTO and useful in licensing and financial transactions.

www.ip.com—IP disclosures and information online. Owned in part by Rochester, New York, money management firm Manning & Napier.

www.micropatent.com—Internet-delivered patent and trademark information.

www.thomson-thomson.com—T&T delivers trademark, copyright, and script research services worldwide.

Index